KOSOVO

*Contending Voices
on Balkan Interventions*

KOSOVO

*Contending Voices
on Balkan Interventions*

Edited by

WILLIAM JOSEPH BUCKLEY

WILLIAM B. EERDMANS PUBLISHING COMPANY
GRAND RAPIDS, MICHIGAN / CAMBRIDGE, U.K.

© 2000 Wm. B. Eerdmans Publishing Co.
255 Jefferson Ave. S.E., Grand Rapids, Michigan 49503 /
P.O. Box 163, Cambridge CB3 9PU U.K.

Printed in the United States of America

05 04 03 02 01 00   7 6 5 4 3 2 1

Library of Congress Cataloging-in-Publication Data

Kosovo: contending voices on Balkan interventions /
edited by William Joseph Buckley.
p.   cm.
Includes index.
ISBN 0-8028-3889-8 (cloth: alk. paper)
1. Kosovo (Serbia) — History — Civil War, 1998-
2. Kosovo (Serbia) — Politics and government.
I. Buckley, William Joseph.

DR2087.C75 2000
949.71 — dc21   99-059275

Contents

CONTENTS

II. VOICES FROM THE BALKAN PAST
What Is the Historical and Cultural Context?

III. VOICES OF TODAY'S BALKAN PEOPLE
What Do People from the Region Think?

ALBANIANS

SERBS

CONTENTS

IV. VOICES OF WORLD LEADERS
What Do Authorities Say?

Contents

V. VOICES OF POLITICAL COMMENTATORS
How Is the Intervention Debated?

VI. ETHICAL AND RELIGIOUS VOICES
How Is the Crisis Ethically and Religiously Evaluated?

CONTENTS

VII. VOICES FOR THE FUTURE

What Issues Must Be Faced?

Contents

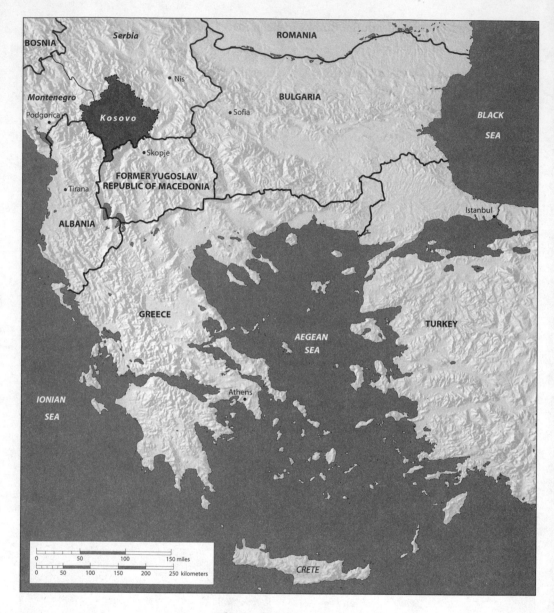

The Balkan Region

The Former Yugoslavia

NOTE: City names in Kosovo on these maps are given in the English forms of Serbian names in Latin letters (e.g., Pristina). For a list of the English forms of their corresponding Albanian names (e.g., *Prishtina*), see p. 472 below (in the Appendix "Balkan Spellings and Pronunciations").

Kosovo

NOTE: City names in Kosovo on these maps are given in the English forms of Serbian names in Latin letters (e.g., Pristina). For a list of the English forms of their corresponding Albanian names (e.g., *Prishtina*), see p. 472 below (in the Appendix "Balkan Spellings and Pronunciations").

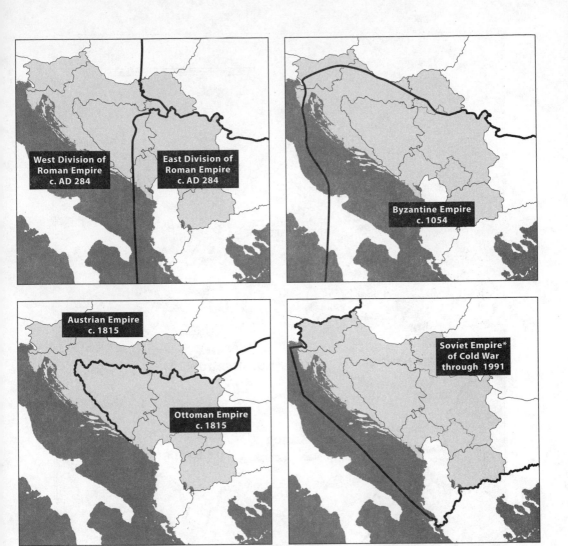

Imperial Control over the Balkans AD 284 to 1991

(After F. W. Carter and H. T. Harris, *The Changing Shape of the Balkans*,
Boulder, Colorado: Westview Press, 1996)

* Yugoslavia and Albania epitomized the inaccuracies of cold war stereotypes and the fluid situation of Soviet relations. Neither nation was an absolute Soviet satellite. Yugoslavia was a Soviet ally from 1945 until 1948, during which time Albania was under the Yugoslav shadow. Albania was a Soviet ally until 1961. Overemphasizing similarities among the political communisms and economic socialisms of these nations risks overlooking important differences in economic reforms, culture, and foreign policies, as well as the complex histories of Yugoslavian and Albanian (frequently conflictual) relations with the Soviet Union.

KFOR Peacekeeping Sectors in Kosovo

NOTE: City names in Kosovo on these maps are given in the English forms of Serbian names in Latin letters (e.g., Pristina). For a list of the English forms of their corresponding Albanian names (e.g., *Prishtina*), see p. 472 below (in the Appendix "Balkan Spellings and Pronunciations").

Acknowledgments

Begun during the conflict, this work emerged from the combined efforts of many. An editor accumulates more than travel and phone debts; this book would not have been possible without the work of many others who deserve thanks. My colleagues at Georgetown University, and especially the Center for Clinical Bioethics, have offered a wonderfully supportive atmosphere for cross-disciplinary research. Thanks go to Edmund Pellegrino, Carol Taylor, Roberto Dell'Oro, Dan Davis, John Harvey, Marty Patchell, and David Miller — as well as John Esposito. The University of Chicago nurtured and disciplined my interest in social conflict and ethnicity that had arisen during my early experiences working with a nongovernmental organization (NGO) in Northern Ireland from 1976 to 1979. These wonderful scholars and teachers will always have my appreciation: James Gustafson, David Tracy, William Schweiker, Robin Lovin, Anne Carr, Stephen Toulmin, Langdon Gilkey, Martin Marty, Chris Gamwell, Jon Levenson, Don Browning, Bruce Lincoln, Stewart Herman, and William French.

Eerdmans Publishing Company deserves tremendous credit for its farsightedness, patience, and enthusiastic encouragement. William B. Eerdmans Jr. saw the need for such a work and graciously supported the project from its earliest days. Reinder Van Til deserves extensive editorial credit; his acute skills shaped a chaotic vision into a coherent whole. Jennifer Hoffman was graciously patient.

I am indebted not only to those whose timely contributions appear herein, but especially to those three dozen contributors whose essays regrettably could not appear due to space limitations. Most contributions were submitted under conditions that interrupted other commitments — for which I am grateful. I sought interviews with virtually every major political leader, including numerous figures in the U.S. State Department, who are listed in the notes to Morton Halperin's essay. Baton Haxhiu provided invaluable assistance in helping me contact Kosovar contributors; Alexandar Jokic and Jovan Babic graciously did the same with Serbians. Special thanks to Dusan Batakovic, Jokic, and Babic for their assistance in helping me contact Bishop Artemije and Fr. Janjic. I also wish to thank Dr. Rexhep Boja, president of the Islamic Community of Kosovo; Prof. Qemal Morina, Dr. Mustafa Ceric (Reis of Sarajevo); and especially Rabbi Arthur Schneier of the Appeal of Conscience Foundation (New York).

These Balkan essays are especially noteworthy because they were written under the most difficult circumstances, in which authors literally wrote while refugees (Haxhiu, Maliqi, Aferdita Kelmendi, Flora Kelmendi, Shala), in hiding in Prishtina (Surroi), or under NATO bombing (Babic, Papic, Samardzic, Stojanovic, Cosic). The multicultural accomplishments of this cell phone and internet anthology are due in no small part to their courage and generosity. It is also a tribute to their intellectual honesty that none objected to my efforts to solicit opinions from all sides.

Kate McCann was an invaluable research assistant; without her hard work and superb editorial assistance, the book would be vastly inferior. For their translation assistance, thanks to Lindita Imami (Albanian), Gordon Bardos (Serbian), Catherine Bodin (French), John Torpey, Thomas McCarthy, and John J. Buckley Jr. (German), Václav Havel's office (Czech), Sally VanderHoof and Roberto Severino (Italian). For their special advice and assistance, thanks to David Buckley, James Buckley, Mark Danner, Fokko De Vries (and Barbara Kancelbaum with Médicins Sans Frontières), Irinej Dobrijevic, Dmitri Djordjevic, Gabriel Fackre, Jürgen Habermas, Michael Ignatieff, Mark Juergensmeyer, Hans Küng, Dennis McManus, Julie Mertus, Richard Miller, Patricia Morrisroe, Jasna Samic, Stephen Toulmin, and Alexander Webster. Jane Curry generously responded to an early version of the manuscript with helpful suggestions about the need to assess foreign policy assistance as a tool of prevention. In addition, my gratitude goes to all whose special advice and writings have been very helpful to me: Fouad Ajami, John Allen Jr., Justice Louise Arbour (Payam Achavam), Lyn Back (Alan Jones and Erik Torch of the Balkan Peace Team), Frederick Bonkovsky, Bojan Bugarcic, Pam Campbell, Thomas Croak, Jack Cunnihan, Metropolitan Christopher, Maj. Gen. Arthur Clark, Lt. Col. Conrad Crane, Alexander Dragnich, Misha Glenny, David Goodhart, Vigen Guroian, Stanley Hauerwas, Celia Hawkesworth, Stewart Herman, Anna Husarska, Sava Janjic, John Kavanaugh, John Kelsay, George Kennan, Veselin Kesich, Vesna Kesic, Indira Kajosevic, Steven Larrabee, William Lawbaugh, Bernard Lewis, Arthur Liolin, Marta Mauras (and Louise Frechette), George Mitchell, Paul Mojzes, Noel Malcolm, Radmila Nakarada, Aryeh Neier, H. T. Norris, Aleksandar Pavkovic, Rick Ryscavage, Daniel Serwer, Pedrag Simic, Laura Silber, Chris Spirou, Ken Thompson, Desmond Tutu, Katarina Vanden Heuvel, Miroslav Volf, Stevan Weine, Elie Wiesel, Paul Williams, Susan Woodward, Rebecca Young, Stephen Zunes and the offices of UNHCR, and various persons at the State Department and the National Security Council who have requested to remain unnamed. For any I have overlooked, my apologies.

I have tried to be scrupulously fair in letting many sides air their views. Such wide-ranging inclusion (1) does not imply that I regard each author's contribution as equally convincing; (2) nor does it mean that I am neutral with respect to the human suffering we have witnessed. Where appropriate, I have inserted editorial footnotes. In two places, I use "discourse analysis" to closely examine arguments made by authors (Halperin, Clark) so as to sharpen public conversations that continue. Most of the following sixty-five essays rightly claim that something momentous has happened; as editor I am not alone in believing that public discussion in the spring of 1999 of the issues involved was woefully inadequate. Knowing how many contributors to this book themselves have books in progress, I hope for further and broader discussions.

Special thanks are due for the love and support I receive from my beloved friend and wife, Mary Elizabeth Kaslick, and our daughter, Grace.

*   *   *

This book is dedicated to the memory of all who died in — and to the living who continue to suffer from — the past decade of Yugoslavia's civil wars. And it is dedicated to my parents, John Joseph Buckley and Esther Marie (Morrisroe) Buckley, whose religious faith and human love in over five decades of work with the marginalized continues to nourish my commitment to justice in a better world.

Introduction

WILLIAM JOSEPH BUCKLEY

*. . . On 25 March [1999], [Yugoslav/Serbian] police ques-
tioned her husband regarding the OSCE/KVM and why
OSCE-KVM personnel had been allowed to live in his house
[in Suva Reka/Suhareke, Kosovo], and then proceeded to
beat him unconscious. Around midday on 26 March the police again called at the house where the witness was staying.
A policeman whom she knew called her brother-in-law's son
outside and shot him dead. The police "screamed" at them
and when the families ran outside they found their house
"under siege" from police, and Serb and "Gypsy" (Maxhupi)
civilians. She witnessed as some of her family were shot dead
immediately. She and others were chased to another location,
apprehended and pushed into a café. The police shot every
person in the room of the café with machine guns and rifles.
The witness had her four children, two girls aged 16 and 14
and two sons aged 10 and 2 years old, gathered around her.
They were all killed. She was trying to protect her two-year-
old son with her legs. She was also hit in the abdomen with a
bullet that passed through her eldest son. She urged him to
pretend he was dead. As they took the bodies outside they saw
that her eldest son was still breathing and shot him again.*

I have profited immensely from discussions with numerous colleagues and the critical responses
to separate contributions I was privileged to make at the following conferences: the U.N. Independent International Commission on Kosovo, New York University Seminar, 3-5 December
1999; the International Law and Ethics Conference Series, "Secession, Transitional Justice, and
Reconciliation," 29-31 October 1999, at the University of San Francisco; the panel discussion on
"Ethnic Violence in the Balkan States for the Task Force on Eastern, Central Europe and Newly
Independent States," 7-10 October 1999, at the Fulbright Annual Meetings, Washington, DC;
and the "Capitol Hill Panel on the Kosovo Crisis," 9 June 1999, hosted by the National Clergy
Council.

She heard him cry out. At least 12 children under 17 were killed and 10 adults including a pregnant woman. The witness pretended to be dead as the police removed all valuables from their bodies. She saw them cutting off fingers from dead bodies to remove rings. She was placed in a truck on top of other bodies including the children. During the journey towards Prizren she jumped from the truck and was found by people who took her to UCK [Kosovo Liberation Army]—held territory where her wounds were treated.[1]

On 11th October [1999] an international staff member of UNMIK [United Nations Mission in Kosovo] who had only arrived in Kosovo/Kosova earlier that day was killed on the street in the centre of Pristina/Prishtine. He was asked the time by a passer-by. When he answered in Serbo-Croat, he was separated from his colleagues, and was beaten and shot dead allegedly by Kosovo Albanians who seem to have identified him as a Serb.[2]

"In today's Serbia one-third of the inhabitants are not Serbs. In an ethnic sense, Serbia is the United States of the Balkans. Therefore, I am convinced that if they were alive today, both George Washington and Abraham Lincoln would be on Serbia's side." — Vuk Draskovic[3]

This book is about listening to such voices, conversations, and arguments. Contributors speak to you and to one another, and they argue contending positions about events in Kosovo, Serbia, and the surrounding region. Distilled to sixty-five brief essays in English from six languages and more than one hundred contribu-

---

1. "Kosovo/Kosova As Seen, As Told," *The Human Rights Findings of the Kosovo Verification Commission*, Part III, Chapter 5. OSCE-KVM refers to the Organization for Security and Cooperation in Europe's Kosovo Verification Mission.

2. Ibid., Part II, June-October 1999, "Annex II: Human Rights Violations by Category: Right to Life."

3. Vuk Draskovic, president of the "leading pro-European party in Serbia" prior to the 1999 NATO intervention, regarding meetings among Ibrahim Rugova's negotiating team, the EU, OSCE, the Contact Group, and the U.N. It is important to note that Draskovic's presentation is a criticism of Milosevic's way of handling the Kosovo situation. In the process of proposing alternatives that he argues can protect the interests of all sides, Draskovic has estimated the percentage of Serbs by including Kosovars as part of Serbia.

2

tions, this is the first book in any language on the Kosovo conflict to bring together opposing viewpoints from internationally know and regionally renowned Western and Balkan authors.[4] Two of every three authors have contributed new essays that are exclusive to this volume. The names of many contributors are recognizable around the world; but contributors with less familiar Balkan names appear together here for the first time in English. As the bookshelf of literature about Kosovo and the region grows, the question of who is heard becomes acute. Voices in this volume engage in an ongoing public conversation that has reached a new stage: international figures who have refused to be in the same room with one another are featured within the covers of this single volume.

We outsiders to the decade-long civil wars of the former Yugoslavia must ask ourselves, How can we understand the *scale* of what has happened in Kosovo?

Force most of the 1.5 million people of Philadelphia from their homes, taking away drivers' licenses and other documentation and property, as part of a planned street-by-street effort to eradicate alleged criminals, drug-dealing terrorists, and their sympathizers who control some territory and are said to seek secession with support from outsiders, who see these people as part of a repressed minority. Offer freedom and arms to several thousand federal prisoners if they will serve as the first wave of gangs to empty the territory by using systematic and random atrocities. Send special police to execute designated leaders. Order army units to protect the 10 percent of the population who have marked their own doors, are judged to be "safe and law-abiding," and have been encouraged to remain. Ignore threats that you are about to be bombed by the largest military alliance in the world. Protect your human and material assets by studying the first ten days of bombing targets that a friendly alliance member has secretly given you.[5] Let alliance bombing be the trigger for your plan.

Encircle the 1.5 million of Philadelphia's population in a giant horseshoe, forcing most out toward the southwest. Frighten half a million people into camping outside near Philadelphia in the hills of eastern Pennsylvania (Kosovo). Compel another half million to caravan and walk between twenty and fifty miles to Maryland to live for ten weeks in camps, with families and outdoors (Albania). Coerce another quarter of a million from Philadelphia to walk to camps and community centers in the sourthern tip of New Jersey (Macedonia). Pressure some ninety thousand to travel by foot further west into Pennsylvania (Montenegro).

4. I am using the term "the Balkans" in a geographic and cultural sense to refer to territories in and around the former Yugoslavia. See note 39 below for Maria Todorova's comments on uses of this term. As explained further in the appendix of Balkan Spellings and Pronunciations, we have usually used the Anglicized form of the Serbian term *Kosovo* rather than the Albanian *Kosova* merely because this is the form that most (Western) news media have adopted.

5. European and American military sources confirm the truth of Belgrade reports that some source secretly gave the Serbs, in advance, NATO's plans for its first ten days of bombing targets.

Intimidate thirty-two thousand into traveling on their own into New York City and southern New York State (Bosnia-Herzegovina). Watch the opposing alliance evacuate another ninety thousand (at least temporarily) to areas west of the Mississippi River. Combine the populations of the two largest American cities, New York and Los Angeles (about 11 million), to get the population of Serbia, and give them the rest of the territory of Pennsylvania in which to live. Add the population of the city of San Francisco (750K) to their numbers over the next eight years. Of those displaced people who are returning to Philadelphia, ask more than half of them to live for the winter in single-room dwellings with plastic canvas ceilings while they are rebuilding their homes (Kosovo); tell them they must respect the rights of those who were not expelled from their homes.

Witness mass reprisals, revenge killings, and the effective cleansing of the territory of those who remained, some of whom collaborated with the original expulsion. Add the 11,000 Kosovars and 6,500 Serbs who have been killed to the total in the Balkans over the past decade, a group conservatively estimated to be about the size of the city of Newark, New Jersey (260,000) — or only 27,000 fewer than all American battle deaths in World War II.[6] Don't forget that these massive upheavals have happened to one of the most economically depressed areas in Europe. Is the picture becoming clearer? As insightfully described by the leader of one refugee NGO, the needs of refugees are signs of deeper problems. We must not only take notice *that* such huge numbers of people have been killed and displaced, but *why*.[7]

6. Estimates vary and numbers blur, but the United Nations High Commission for Refugees reports that approximately one million refugees left Kosovo, and another 300,000 to 500,000 remained as internally displaced persons (IDPs) within Kosovo. Of the one million who left, about one of ten had been previous asylum-seekers in Europe; one of ten stayed in eight tented camps and two collection centers in Macedonia; another 140,000 stayed with host families there. About 300,000 stayed in forty-nine tented camps in Albania and 100 community centers (schools, etc.); another 144,000 stayed with host families in Albania. Some 90,000 went to Montenegro, and 32,000 went to Bosnia, while approximately 96,000 went to third countries under the Humanitarian Evacuation Program (by October that number was at 41,000). Since June, some 200,000 non-Albanian IDPs from Kosovo (Serbs and Roma) have gone to Yugoslavia, which already has 550,000 refugees from previous Yugoslavian civil wars. In September, 4,000 Serbs from Bosnia and Croatia living in refugee camps in Yugoslavia came to the U.S. via Romania. As UNHCR Special Envoy Dennis McNamara says, "Yugoslavia has the largest number of refugees and displaced persons in Europe." These figures are drawn from my personal conversations with staff at the UNHCR. Numerical comparisons are drawn from *The 1999 World Almanac* (Mahwah, NJ: Premedia, 1999), pp. 209, 382ff.; demographic data are drawn from some foreign embassy materials and from the 1999 CIA *World Factbook*, available online at www.cia.gov. Kosovo casualty figures are extrapolations from conversations with NGO and Inter-Governmental Organization (IGO) field-workers who have examined and documented about one fourth of the graves in Kosovo. Estimated mortalities from Serbia are from the *East European Constitutional Review*'s staff and affiliates as listed in *EECR* 8, no. 3 (Summer 1999): 38.

7. Rick Ryscavage has insightfully noted: "Refugees tend to be viewed as secondary symptoms of a broader political crisis or war. But increasingly in modern life, creating refu-

But what do we hear after a decade of Yugoslavian civil wars and the recent NATO intervention? We hear dying wishes from more than a quarter million people who have perished in the killing fields of Split, Krajina, Vukovar, Sarajevo, Gorazde, Mostar, Srebrenica, Racak, Pristina, and cities in Serbia. Mortal gasps from 2,400 documented by the International Criminal Tribunal who are buried in 295 mass graves around Kosovo. Muffled death rattles from at least four times that number of people still missing. Anguished pleas from past captives and the remaining two to five thousand who are known to be captives still. Wrenching despair from 6 million who were once displaced or still are displaced in the former Yugoslavia. Vindictive outrage from them or their relatives now living among Croatia's population of 4.6 million, Slovenia's 2 million, Bosnia-Herzegovina's 3.4 million, or Serbia and Montenegro's 11.2 million (including Kosovo's 1.5 million). Cynical exasperation that effective outside help was not offered sooner. Infuriated indignation that "outsiders" have interfered in the internal matters of a sovereign state and unjustly sympathized with terrorist secessionists. Intricate planning by the political and military leaders who designed and executed Croatia's "Operation Storm" against Krajina Serbs in 1995; Serbia's "Operation Horseshoe" against Kosovo Albanians in 1999; NATO's "Operation Allied Force." Exhausted diplomats or sonorous academic leaders from capital cities of Zagreb, Ljubljana, Sarajevo, Pristina, Belgrade. Distressed religious leaders from Islam, Orthodox Christianity, Catholicism, assorted forms of Christianity, Judaism, and other traditions. Concerned outside governments, impassioned nongovernmental and intergovernmental organizations (NGO/IGOs), troubled Western academics, and astonished journalists. One thing is clear: the question is not who is speaking, but to whom shall we listen?

---

gees is precisely the point of going to war. . . . [T]he NATO bombing campaign served as a cover for realizing the Serbian political goals of emptying Kosovo of Albanians. But refugees, once generated, shift the political dynamics of a situation. They can bolster arguments for intervention by the international community, and they can put a human face on a complicated political scene. Refugees can become both threats and opportunities for the host country's economy. Although seen as victims, refugees often make critical decisions — where to go, when to return — that leave the international community breathlessly trying to catch up to them. . . . In general, one can say that humanitarian practices in refugee crises are anchored in very little authoritative data or research. . . . [R]ather than lunging from one refugee disaster to another, those involved in the international humanitarian world, including governments, should take the time and make the resources available to reflect critically on what was a vast movement of human beings in search of protection." Ryscavage has served as the National Director of the Jesuit Refugee Service/USA and also as Secretary for Social and International Ministries at the Jesuit Conference in Washington, DC.

I

We listen first as those who have suffered the ravages of war, individuals chased and bombed in Kosovo and Serbia, tell their dramatic stories ("Voices Under the Bombs"). Any account of refugees is complicated by the fact that there were already internally displaced persons (IDPs) in the region from prior Yugoslavian civil wars. In addition, many refugee camps were simply bilateral arrangements made between one government and another government, as well as with NGO's. Although most displaced persons did not live in refugee camps, the stories of those who did live in them make compelling reading.

II

But compelling first-person narratives don't tell the whole tale. Today's Kosovar and Serb voices echo those of their ancestors, many of whom lived together for centuries. Please examine the maps included on pp. xii-xvi of this volume. Along this regional faultline of East and West have existed oases of multicultural richness, next to periodic slaughterhouses of history. An assortment of empires, peoples, kingdoms, states, and nations have staked claims on this contested terrain, frequently using local populations as "buffers" in military outposts. Thus the people of this area have lived on the edge of dramatic face-offs between contending empires for nearly two millennia: the Eastern and Western Roman empire split here in 284 C.E.; the Byzantine and Western empire from 1054; the Ottoman empire and their Habsburg challengers from the fourteenth century until almost the First World War; various nationalist expansions and contractions until 1945; the Soviet empire until 1991; the "Western empire" of the Atlantic Alliance is here now.[8] The past century began with a World War here, endured a second, and now has concluded with a third "Little World War" here. Given such a volatile history, cynics might regard the past decade as merely another chapter in the huge population movements that have always accompanied war, especially in this region.[9] Others argue that certain native historical voices should receive a privileged hearing — the Kingdom of Serbia until 1355 under Dusan, the Kingdom of Yugoslavia

---

8. For example, see F. W. Carter and H. T. Norris, eds., *The Changing Shape of the Balkans* (Boulder: Westview, 1996); Hugh Poulton and Suha Taji-Farouki, eds., *Muslim Identity and the Balkan State* (New York: New York University Press, 1997), and the historical works of Judah, Malcolm, and others discussed below.

9. Although Paul Magocsi argues that as many as 800,000 people from Yugoslavia and northern Greece were displaced to surrounding regions after World War II from 1944-1949, Tim Judah contests his account and finds those figures vastly inflated (in a personal communication to the editor). See Paul Robert Magocsi, *Historical Atlas of East Central Europe*, vol. 1: *History of East Central Europe* (Seattle and London: University of Washington Press, 1993), p. 48.

in 1918, a "Greater" Croatia, Serbia, or Albania. Still others would urge us to heed the words of heroic resistance to oppression by assorted occupations — Ottomans, Bulgarians, the Axis powers of 1941 to 1945. Some would have us listen instead to members of minority traditions, such as Yugoslavian Jews, whose cultural identities have undergone tremendous changes — or to the darker voices of Balkan anti-Semitism.[10]

But war and conflict have been the exception, not the rule, in this region. Contrary to the widespread and mistaken assumption that this is a region of intractible (and religiously based) fratricidal hostilities, many have lived ordinary lives in the midst of remarkable cultural diversity. The second section ("Voices from the Balkan Past") features succinct essays by world-renowned Western and Balkan contributors who detail the historical and cultural context of the region. Short essays narrate the history of Serbia, Kosovo, Albania, the KLA, Eastern Christianity, Islam, and the diasporas of Serbs and Albanians in the United States. Historians, journalists, and regional scholars offer fresh insights for hearing anew these past voices. These authors present a "thick description" of the cultural landscape of a region overrun by numerous civilizations that have left distinctive footprints. One legacy of such a mixed history is that in certain locales differing traditions have combined, much like other places throughout the world. As revealed in fascinating studies based on his fieldwork examining ethnically and religiously mixed pilgrimages in Kosovo, anthropologist Ger Duijzings has found local areas where differing identities blend in surprising ways based on shared religious practices.[11]

---

10. Paul Bejamin Gordiejew, *Voices of Yugoslav Jewry* (New York: SUNY, 1999); Lucy S. Dawidowicz, *The Golden Tradition: Jewish Life and Thought in Eastern Europe* (Syracuse, 1996); and Philip Cohen, *Serbia's Secret War: Propaganda and the Deceit of History* (College Station, Tex.: Texas A & M University, 1996).

11. According to Duijzings, "At present this seems almost unthinkable, but until recently Muslims and Christians of different ethnic backgrounds visited one another's sanctuaries, worshipping the same saints. Muslim and Christian forms of pilgrimage and saint veneration have amalgamated and formal religious divisions have become blurred. At certain shrines Muslims and Christians have found each other in their devotion for a certain saint, regardless of his or her religious 'identity.' Their motives as pilgrims were the same and are probably universal: health, well-being and happiness for their close relatives and themselves. To mention only one example, the Serbian Orthodox monastery of Gracanica (south of Prishtina), although serving as an important rallying point for Serbian nationalists in recent years, has traditionally attracted numerous pilgrims in the more traditional sense as well. Every year in August, on Assumption Day, the shrine is visited by numerous Muslims (particularly Gypsies)." (Duijzings to the editor.) In his 1992 fieldwork in a Croat and Catholic enclave at the border with Macedonia (called Letnica), Duijzings witnessed a shift from blending to conflict as the war raged around it. See his fascinating book, *Religion and the Politics of Identity in the Balkans* (London: C. Hurst, forthcoming).

III

In our third section, "Voices of Today's Balkan People," Kosovar and Serbian intellectuals and politicians argue passionately about the NATO intervention by appealing to historical and current political ambitions. The former president of Yugoslavia, Dobrica Cosic, calls for President Milosevic to resign; KLA leader Hashim Thaqi calls for international recognition of the Kosovar Albanians' political will for freedom and independence. Almost everyone believes that the will of the majority should now be heard. But a majority of what and according to whom? Not only has a decade of deportations, mass population movements, and ethnic cleansings dramatically changed the demography and internal boundaries of the former Yugoslavia (not to mention other factors, such as high birthrates among Albanian Kosovars); but differing populations have political ambitions now distributed among nearly 200 political parties. To help us make sense of this wide array of voices, this third section presents a dozen short contributions from some of the most prestigious contemporary figures in Kosovo/Albania and Serbia — literary and political figures, journalists, activists, and academics. They demonstrate the variety of internal political sentiments and visions for Kosovo and Serbia. It is helpful for readers to know that certain essays, such as those by Haxhiu and Maliqi, were written basically in response to essays by Cosic, Samardzic, and Stojanovic, while later articles such as that of Veton Surroi were written in response to Strobe Talbott. These are passionately written accounts that address difficult questions about violence, ethnic cleansing, secession, justice, political legitimacy, oppression, and repression in ways guaranteed to provoke further conversation — even if agreement remains elusive.

Why listen to Balkan natives argue about their contentious political identities and ambitions? Because we are pledged to help them listen — at some point — to one another, it is important for us to be instructed by them. If horizons are ever to be brought closer by conversation and negotiation, they must first be seen together. But ethnic, political, and even religious fragmentation is hardly conducive to coherent conversation. Despite common clustering, there is no exact correlation among political affiliations, ethnic background, and religious identity in the various regions of the former Yugoslavia. While it was not the same as multiculturalism, complete ethnic integration in pre–civil-war village and town life was not widespread. Yet several hundred political parties have arisen at the same time that territories in each of the regions of the former Yugoslavia have become *more* ethnically homogeneous. Political parties face the need to build coalitions precisely at the same time that popular sentiments can be manipulated to oppose compromises. Ethnic and religious constituencies have been gerrymandered by ethnic cleansing and peace treaties. Today almost ten of ten Kosovars are ethnic Albanians; nine of ten Slovenians live in Slovenia, eight of ten Croatians inhabit Croatia. Officially, Bosnia-Herzegovina in its entirety currently includes 40 percent Serbs, 40 percent "Muslims," and 20 percent Croatians; but estimates are that

51 percent of its territory (the Muslim/Croat Federation) contains perhaps 95 percent of its own groups, and the remaining territory (Republika Srpska) is perhaps 95 percent Serbian.[12] Kosovo itself had a prewar population that was 90 percent ethnic Albanian and 10 percent Serbian (compared to 1948, when Albanians represented 63.7 percent of the population, and 1981, when they were 77.4 percent). This is part of what Belgrade sociologist Mirjana Vasovic has called the "ethnification of consciousness."[13] The postwar period has witnessed, paradoxically, the burgeoning of Kosovo's political parties and the cleansing of its population of some 250,000 non-Albanian IDPs (Serbs and Gypsies or "Roma"), who now live as refugees in Serbia.[14] Emigration from Kosovo has sent over one-third

12. Categories are rightly contested and numbers can only be estimated, but consider the following example: with 82 political parties that participated in the September 1997 municipal elections (30 of which were national in 1999), Bosnia-Herzegovina currently has three major ethnic groups (Serb 40%, Muslim 38%, Croat 22%) and five categories of religious traditions (Muslim 40%, Orthodox 31%, Catholic 15%, Protestant 4%, other 10%). Although significant changes have occurred in Croatia since its 1995 recapture of the Krajina region and the expulsion of Serbs — including the emergence of no fewer than sixteen political parties — its prewar ethnic composition in the last reliable count of the 1991 census included six ethnic groups (Croat 78%, Serb 12%, Muslim 0.9%, Hungarian 0.5%, Slovenian 0.5%, others 8.1%) and five religious traditions (Catholic 76.5%, Orthodox 11.1%, Muslim 1.2%, Protestant 0.4%, others and unknown 10.8%). The influx of 750,000 refugees from previous wars into Serbia has also made accurate numbers tenuous, but in addition to six major and more than 100 minor political parties, one 1999 estimate lists five ethnic categories (Serbs 63%, Albanians 14%, Montenegrins 6%, Hungarians 4%, other 13%) and five religions (Orthodox 65%, Muslim 19%, Roman Catholic 4%, Protestant 1%, other 11%). By this same 1999 estimate, Slovenia has seven political parties and five ethnic groups (Slovene 91%, Croat 3%, Serb 2%, Muslim 1%, other 3%) as well as five religious traditions (Roman Catholic 70.8% [including 2% Uniate], Lutheran 1%, Muslim 1%, atheist 4.3%, other 22.9%). Most of these data, with all their limitations, were drawn from the latest analyses and estimates contained in the 1999 on-line version of the CIA *World Factbook*. It illustrates how territories (sometimes demographically redrawn) with prewar ethnic and religious majorities have seen their enlargement in the postwar period. Other data have come from Republic of Croatia, Central Bureau of Statistics, *Statistical Information*, 1998, and the Embassy of the Republic of Croatia, *Croatia and USA: Toward the New Millennium*, n.d.

13. I have learned a great deal from Mirjana Vasovic's important manuscript, based on nearly three decades of empirical research, entitled "Why Serbian Hatred Is a Propaganda Myth."

14. There are contending perceptions of Kosovar Albanian population growth. The OSCE Report states: "However, as Noel Malcolm has written, while the birthrate is among the highest in Europe, this reflects the traditional nature of the society rather than 'a deliberate and politically motivated policy,' since among working Kosovar Albanian women in urban areas, where other factors such as economic security and access to reproductive healthcare are much more in evidence, the birthrate is much lower." OSCE Report (*Kosovo: A Short History*, 2nd ed. [London: Macmillan, 1998], ch. 17, pp. 331-32). One of the most detailed and up-to-date accounts of contemporary Kosovo political parties and figures can be found on the web site of the International Crisis Group, cited in the appendix entitled "Further Resources for On-line Inquiry."

of its population abroad in the past decade and perhaps half that number of university-trained students out of Serbia and Montenegro.[15] Not since the Second World War has such a fracturing conflict demolished so many and so much so quickly in Yugoslavia. Rarely, if ever, has its entire population been so violently segregated into ethnic groups. If these people do not deserve our attention, who does?

IV

What do world leaders have to say about what has happened in Kosovo? Because they brought us to the Kosovo intervention, I solicited and received contributions from many, some of whom responded to their counterparts among the other essayists. United Nations Secretary-General Kofi Annan responds to NATO Secretary-General Javier Solana's justification for the Kosovo intervention, as well as to the essays by Zbigniew Brzezinski and Henry Kissinger (contained in section V). Using Madeleine Albright's ideas articulated in her speeches during and after the intervention, Morton Halperin of the U.S. State Department responds to these and other essays. Here the Clinton Administration, for the first time, offers a public-policy rationale for humanitarian intervention that can be linked to what is enshrined in just-war reasoning about when and how armed conflict may be fought. As editor, I analyze the State Department statement and link it to the contributions of others. Other world leaders state their views: Czech President Václav Havel, the Vatican's Archbishop Jean-Louis Tauran, Yugoslav President Slobodan Milosevic, and KLA leader Hashim Thaqi. NATO's supreme military commander, General Wesley Clark, offers his account of the "success" of the NATO intervention, and several authors respond to his claims.[16] These voices and conversations reflect vital arguments about questions that remain crucial for public discussion. How are claims about intervention a terrible sign of the failures of negotiation and

15. Comparisons are notoriously invidious, but Northern Ireland, a territory that is geographically and demographically the same size as Kosovo, has achieved a fragile peace after no fewer than eight major failed efforts at political and constitutional reform since 1969, with an ethnic minority of 42% and majority of 54%. Despite only a third as many deaths in thirty-five years (3,500) as Kosovo had in eight weeks, as well as intense government efforts at the national level to de-urbanize populations, outlaw house-swapping and social attitudes favoring residential mixing (79% majority favor; 60% minority favor), so-called "voluntary" segregation remains high. Thus two-thirds of the people of Northern Ireland live in communities that feature 80% or more of one ethnic tradition (50% of areas feature 90% or greater of one tradition). See John Darby, *Scorpions in a Bottle: Conflicting Cultures in Northern Ireland* (London: Minority Rights Group, 1997), p. 66; and Paul W. Geddis, ed., *Focus on Northern Ireland: A Statistical Profile* (Belfast: NI Statistics and Research Agency, 1997), p. 45.

16. Additional insightful military assessments by Richard O'Lear, Col. Conrad Crane, and Arthur Clark helped me appreciate the complexities involved in assessing NATO's intervention.

prevention? Can a legal case for NATO's intervention be made, or was it legally un-founded but morally compelling?[17] What are the possibilities and limits of using military intervention for humanitarian purposes? How should the United Nations Security Council be reformed?

V

But world leaders do not always make compelling arguments. Because significant questions require deeper scrutiny, we turn in the fifth section to the voices of nine distinguished political and philosophical commentators who argue for and against the NATO intervention. These essayists raise practical and theoretical is-sues that lie behind the intervention, such as its wider diplomatic implications. For example, the debate continues about why Milosevic decided to end the con-flict so abruptly. Also, many are dissatisfied (for a variety of reasons) with the lim-its of *Realpolitik* (as it is variously understood to be a theory of international rela-tions relying on notions of state interests) and seek to promote various forms of "systems analysis."[18] Proponents and opponents of the intervention raise cautions about it as a precedent. "But who is guarding the guards themselves?" is the pithy rhetorical question of the first-century Roman satirist and poet Juvenal.[19] Further public discussions about the global responsibilities of being a superpower are re-quired in order for us effectively to assess the "humanitarian" nature of the Ameri-can foreign policies known as "aggressive multi-lateralism," "blending diplomacy and force," and "coercive diplomacy." Competing interests must be addressed and tensions balanced: for example, a crucial interest in protecting populations from abusive leaders, widespread injustice, and intolerable suffering; the principles of national sovereignty and highly stipulative international intervention; the risks that "regional interventions" might return us to a hazardous "spheres of influ-ence" system.[20] In the preceding section, U.N. Secretary-General Annan has called for a "more widely conceived definition of national interest in the next century."

17. For example, see Paul Williams and Michael P. Scharf, "NATO Intervention on Trial: The Legal Case That Was Never Made," *Human Rights Review* (2000): 184-88.

18. In various writings, Elliot Abrams has relied upon some of these *Realpolitik* assump-tions, despite his trenchant criticisms of the contradictions between the American Administra-tion's appeals for intervention in the name of humanitarian idealism yet aversion to military risks.

19. Decimus Junius Juvenalis (60 C.E.?–140 C.E.?), *Satires* #1, line 347.

20. In his writings and at several conferences, Princeton's Richard Falk has drawn atten-tion to these tensions, even suggesting that a reformulated view of self-determination might construe state criminality as resulting in a conditional loss of sovereignty, especially if victims belong to a distinct community.

VI

After political and foreign policy analyses come ethical and religious voices, those scholars and thinkers who scrutinize deeper justifications behind interventions and sanctions. Has NATO's manner of intervention undercut its own rationale for intervention to protect human rights? Could an early and credible threat of a ground war have averted the air war? Might a ground war really have had lesser loss of life in the long run? Should we focus attention on abysmal violations of human rights prior to and throughout the former Yugoslavia's civil wars or target Belgrade's key roles in them? Does the manifest incivility of civil wars disclose why a key assumption of just war theory — that war can be a rule-governed activity — is a fiction? Were all nonviolent means of resolving the conflict exhausted?[21] Are sanctions defensible — or has their ineffectiveness merely criminalized day-to-day life in Serbia?[22] Does genocide remain a compelling exception to religious presumptions against war?[23] Some speculate whether local religious traditions have become so thoroughly secularized with nominal practitioners as to have marginal

21. In conversations and writings, Stephen Zunes has very cogently argued that the actual cost of military peacekeeping forces (not to mention intervention) far exceeds less expensive methods of locally based nonviolent initiatives and economic development that could have prevented the conflict.

22. Based on a moral analysis (that does not appeal to the unjust consequences of sanctions for Yugoslavians), which is contained in the February 2000 issue of *The Fletcher Forum*, Aleksander Jokic and Jovan Babic argue that there can be no principled justification of sanctions.

23. This seems to be how Pope John Paul II interprets Catholic tradition. Was Kosovo a case of genocide? As demonstrated, e.g., by North American Catholic debates about the justifiability of the Kosovo intervention, opinions abound. For a sample, see the contributions of various authors in this volume (notes on the Vatican position), as well as Bruce Russett, "Is NATO's War Just? Questions about Kosovo," *Commonweal* 126, no. 10 (May 21, 1999): 13-15; Drew Christiansen, "Peacemaking and the Use of Force: Behind the Pope's Stringent Just-War Teaching," *America* (May 12, 1999): 13-18; Drew Christiansen, "What We Must Learn from Kosovo: Military Intervention and Humanitarian Aid," *America* 181, no. 5 (August 28, 1999): 7-10; John Kavanaugh, "Outcasts and the In Crowd," *America* (May 8, 1999): 20; Editorial, "Introducing Peace to Kosovo," *America* (July 3, 1999): 3; and Margaret O'Brien Steinfels, "Intervention: When and How?" *Commonweal* 126, no. 18 (October 22, 1999): 5-6. As noted, American Catholic Church leaders have also disagreed: Cardinal John Mahoney speculated in an April interview about the conditions under which the intervention could be justified; Cardinal John O'Connor eventually argued that the means of intervention were not justifiable (*Catholic New York*, 4/29/99); Bishop Thomas Gumbleton maintained that both the reasons and means of armed intervention were inadequate. For a sample of views opposing the bombing see Richard John Neuhaus's views in "The Clinton Era — At Home and Abroad," *First Things* 93 (May 1999): 77-95; "Dropping Bombs into Tangled History," *First Things* 95 (August/Sept. 1999): 80-99; as well as subsequent "Correspondence" and essays in *First Things* in vols. 96 (Oct.); 98 (Dec.). Also see the discussion between Neuhaus and William F. Buckley (no relation to the editor) entitled "Kosovo: What Do We Do Now?" on the 5/2/99 show "Firing Line."

influence. Others wonder whether such religious traditions have so aligned themselves with pernicious nationalisms as to become complicit in atrocities. Still others wonder whether their local revivals are retrograde or "fundamentalistic" (despite the inadequacies of that vague Western category). It remains an open question whether these religious traditions can nourish particular identities and engage as public communities willing to work with one another. Some speculate that deep local suspicions based on five decades living under the "imposed internationalism" of Tito's Yugoslavian communism of "brotherhood and unity" have so poisoned the waters that widespread acceptance of the "imposed multiculturalism" of the Western Alliance is unlikely. Others argue that democracy makes new beginnings for civil society possible. Larger issues are also at stake: What role should localized communal (even "national") identity have in our "globalized" and multicultural world?

Such local and communal identities need not be hostile forms of nationalism; nor are religious traditions inevitably complicit in narrow collectivisms. However, two regrettably pervasive Western sentiments make it difficult to enter empathetically into these deeper levels of communal and religious meaning. One is illustrated by the findings of psychiatrist Stevan Weine, who has done seminal work with refugees and torture victims from Bosnia-Herzegovina and Kosovo. These victims are persons who remain in shock over what neighbors did to them and who think of themselves in terms of their families, not as individuals first. Hence, widely held Western convictions about individual human rights have not been translated into ideas that are persuasive to us about our *common* human interests based upon our connectedness to one another. Put another way, our ("Western") public moral language has shifted from notions of honor and shame to "human dignity"; but that human dignity is still construed in relatively individualistic ways.[24] The following quote illustrates the importance of kinship for interpreting the trauma of Kosovars:

> "Nobody believed that in this time human beings could do something like that."
>
> A child sits next to his father, and when the father speaks of the moment when the child was threatened at gunpoint, the child has a heavy expression, shaking hand, and tears. A woman sits between her husband, who says "Go ahead, it's okay, tell them more details," and her sister-in-law, who says, "Do not fear, you can trust them."[25]

24. See Charles Taylor, "The Politics of Recognition," in *Multiculturalism*, ed. David Theo Goldberg (Cambridge, MA: Blackwell, 1995), pp. 75-106, as well as Taylor's *Sources of the Self: The Making of the Modern Identity* (Cambridge, MA: Harvard University Press, 1992).

25. From personal testimonies collected from Kosovar refugees by Weine. Weine's *When History Is a Nightmare: Lives and Memories of Ethnic Cleansing in Bosnia-Herzegovina* (New Brunswick: Rutgers University Press, 1999) "uses survivors' stories to investigate how collective memory has shaped history and lives in Bosnia-Herzegovina, and how the mishandling of mem-

Related to but distinct from these philosophical discussions of such Western individualism are sociological debates about "privatization." Even the eloquent portrayal of religion as a human right risks reducing religion to the sphere of personal choice and private meaning. For some, "freedom for self-determination" is narrowed to "freedom from restraint," which is further reduced to "freedom from any influence other than personal preference." This final reduction to "choosing what we want" can begin to serve as a litmus test for what we find most meaningful and that to which we want to be ultimately loyal. Hence, when they are not dismissed as outdated and oppressive myths (forms they have at times assumed everywhere, including in Kosovo and Serbia), cultural traditions that aim to persuade, form character, or nourish communal identity are easily seen as threatening collectivisms that interfere with such private meaning and personal choice.[26] But ethics and religion are matters that involve more than personal choice and speak to wider human interests — interests about which few people are seriously neutral.[27] These wider interests can be distorted or expressed in complicated ways. In fact, the public culture and political discourse of the former Yugoslavia are so saturated with secularized versions of religious symbols and images that one cannot adequately comprehend them without a nuanced appreciation of their religious eggshells. Crude dismissals of religious traditions as mere expressions of nationalism completely ignore the differing

---

ories of traumatization actually made ethnic cleansing possible. . . . The scholarly discourse on testimony has focused far more on individuals and has left the family out, as do both the refugee and trauma mental health literatures in general. These Kosovar testimonies remind us of the necessity of putting the family back in." Weine's work on the links between truth-telling, performance, and memory are the most interpretively rich accounts available. He is co-director of the Project on Genocide, Psychiatry and Witnessing and Associate Professor of Psychiatry at the University of Illinois at Chicago.

26. In a theological reflection on some of Michael Ignatieff's work, Stanley Hauerwas observes that much Western braying over "nationalism" and "historical hatreds" comes from those who live in an individualistic culture of late consumer capitalism that discourages people from having memories of connectedness. "Why Time Cannot and Should Not Heal the Wounds of History But Time Has Been and Can Be Redeemed," *Scottish Journal of Theology* 53 (2000). For a criticism of the way neo-liberal political theories have refined rules governing the relations of states to individuals, rather than focusing on the alleviation of collective suffering, see William F. Felice, *Taking Suffering Seriously: The Importance of Collective Human Rights* (New York: SUNY, 1996).

27. See Paul Mojzes's invaluable discussion in "Religious Human Rights in Post-Communist Balkan Countries," in *Religious Human Rights in Global Perspective: Legal Perspectives,* ed. Johan D. van der Vyver and John Witte, Jr. (Boston/London/The Hague: Martinus Nijhoff, 1996), pp. 263-84. Other essays in this and its companion volume *(Religious Perspectives)* are also informative. Paul Mojzes's other works demonstrate why a nonreductive understanding of religion is crucial for adequately understanding conflicts in the former Yugoslavia; see his *Yugoslavian Inferno: Ethnoreligious Warfare in the Balkans* (New York: Continuum, 1994) and a collection he edited entitled *Religion and the War in Bosnia* (Atlanta: Scholars Press, 1998).

finely grained types of nationalisms that abound — as well as the various religiously based narratives that undergird them.[28] Human rights talk is neither inherently individualist nor privatistic — but these and other cautions addressed below deserve close attention. To summarize: (1) Communal attachments can nourish social responsibility in multicultural societies without exclusive reliance on individualistic understandings of human rights. (2) Adequate understanding of these cultures requires a nuanced appreciation of their religious traditions and not simplistic dismissals by our own postmodern assumptions that such traditions are merely disguised forms of intolerant nationalisms, even when elements within them have been complicit with bigoted nationalistic regimes. Whether or not religious traditions will influence future civic life constructively

28. A call for better understanding of such religious roots is hardly a disguised request that they (or their political aspirations) be endorsed. Quite the contrary; only when they are made public and their claims to truth carefully examined can one hope to disentangle the chaotic and decentralized expressions of quasi-religious myths pervasive in the allegedly "secular" Serbian culture. Hence, the widespread belief among Serbs that they are victims destined to suffer at the hands of others, decisively influences their political claims about justice. Thus, a common response to some of our Serbian authors is that they complain too much. Confronted by a Serbian lacrimose theory of history and fatalism about being the recurrent victims of other powers, one senses a chronic avoidance of issues of collective responsibility and agency. However, as Tim Judah, Miranda Vickers, Michael Sells, Alexander Webster, and others have shown, deeper analysis reveals that this genre of lament is deeply inscribed by a combination of certain religious symbols and a selective reading of their own past history. Without our careful examination of the interactions among these religious symbols, interpretations of history, and cultural identity, any Serbian political discourse about Golgotha, Kosovo, and self-sacrifice can sound like the ideologically driven rantings of madmen. In addition, many (but not all) religious leaders in these traditions have stood alone and together in opposing oppression, defending the "human rights" of minorities, and opposing ethnic cleansing and cultural destruction. Even among cultural traditions immersed in historical hostilities, religious traditions elsewhere have demonstrated a capacity to legitimate, delegitimate, or reframe collective identities in nonantagonistic ways (e.g., Northern Ireland). For appeals for justice based on the history of Albanian nationalism, see the essays by Lubonja, Shala, and Kadare in this volume. In addition, I have found the following works helpful: Sabrina Ramet, *Balkan Babel* (Boulder: Westview Press, 1996), and *Nihil Obstat: Religion, Politics, and Social Change in East-Central Europe and Russia* (Durham: Duke, 1998); Ivo Banac with Katherine Verdery, *National Character and National Ideology in Interwar Eastern Europe* (New Haven: Yale, 1995); Misha Glenny, *The Balkans 1804-1999: Nationalism, War and the Great Powers* (London: Granta, 1999); and Tim Judah, *The Serbs* (New Haven: Yale, 1997). Among the more finely grained analyses of nationalism from a Serbian perspective is Alexsandar Pavkovic's *The Fragmentation of Yugoslavia: Nationalism in a Multinational State* (New York: St. Martin's Press, 1997); see also "Anticipating the Disintegration: Nationalisms in Former Yugoslavia, 1980-1990," *Nationalities Papers* 25, no. 3 (1997): 427-40; "From Yugoslavism to Serbism: The Serb National Idea 1986-1996," *Nations and Nationalism* 4, no. 4 (1998): 511-28. Another interesting perspective from one of the distinguished members of the Praxis group (and contributor to this volume) is Svetozar Stojanovic's *The Fall of Yugoslavia: Why Communism Failed* (New York: Prometheus, 1997).

remains an open question. No one seriously recommends that religious traditions alone can remedy all injustices, especially given their association with the intertwined tentacles of unjust nationalism in a decade of Yugoslavian civil wars.[29]

VII

Yet conversation, arguments, and analyses are not enough. This is not the "end of history" for the region. What practical issues remain to be faced? Nine essays in our concluding section look ahead. Contributors speculate about whether or not the "Kosovo Protectorate" is a "mission impossible" as well as what will happen to Montenegro. Two Balkan authors offer heated opposing viewpoints about whether Kosovo should remain a part of Serbia — or now must be independent. Several contributors probe resources that religious traditions offer for future cooperation. Others explore the possibilities for building democracy from below. Each author acknowledges the problems and points the way toward further discussion of important issues: Can the international protectorate successfully evolve into a functioning civil society? On what terms should Serbia be brought back into the international community? What will come of the war crimes prosecutions in the rebuilding of civic society? Without denying its important benefits, is the International Criminal Tribunal for the former Yugoslavia (ICTY) legally ungrounded and hypocritical (Rubin), a necessary but regrettable victor's justice (Falk), or the important beginning of a long task (Minow)?[30] How should we assess the fact that the indictments against Milosevic were handed down in March 1999 to foreclose the possibility of clemency and immunity as part of a settlement

29. Conversations with Michael Ignatieff, Stanley Hauerwas, and Jean Bethke Elshtain helped me sort out some of these issues, but the formulation is my own, and none can be said to agree with all of these points. Lurking behind my views are some of the ideas expressed by Douglas Johnston and Cynthia Sampson in *Religion: The Missing Dimension of Statecraft* (Oxford: Oxford University Press, 1994), as well as the larger debates in social theory between so-called communitarians and liberals (Michael Sandel, Alasdair MacIntyre, Charles Taylor, Michael Walzer, John Rawls, Ronald Dworkin, Richard Rorty).

30. The International Court of Justice (ICJ) is distinct from the International Criminal Tribunal for the former Yugoslavia (ICTY). As distinct from its predecessor, the Permanent Court of International Justice (1922-1946), the ICJ was established in 1945 and is the primary judicial organ for the United Nations; only states can bring cases against other states. The ICTY was established by the U.N. Security Council in May of 1993. It is mandated to prosecute persons responsible for serious violations of international humanitarian law committed within the territory of the former Yugoslavia since 1991; these include grave breaches of the 1949 Geneva Conventions (Article 2); violations of the laws or customs of war (Article 3); genocide (Article 4); crimes against humanity (Article 5). In contrast to the ICJ, the ICTY can prosecute only individual persons.

under discussion by Finnish President Martti Ahitisaari and former Russian envoy to Belgrade Victor Chernomyrdin (and the U.S. State Department)? Did this strategy have unforeseen postwar consequences in strengthening intransigence to domestic Serbian political change? Might the West have become involved earlier and in different ways?

*   *   *

Many have concrete expectations about responsibility for the future. For example, without equating their scale but echoing the language of human rights and sentiments of outrage at the reverse ethnic cleansing of Kosovo's Serbs (articulated in the November 6, 1999, OSCE report), Serbian Orthodox Bishop Artemije, who had earlier spoken out against the oppression of Kosovar Albanians, demanded (on July 15, 1999) that KFOR protect the interests of Serbs:

> Now the Albanians are oppressing Serbs and are committing the same crimes against Serbs and other non-Albanian communities that were committed against the Kosovo Albanians in the time of Milosevic's regime. But these recent crimes occur in the time of peace and with the presence of KFOR, very often right in front of their eyes!
>
> Undoubtedly, the wartime acts of kidnapping, rape, murder, and the massacre of innocent people and the burning of their homes and their religious sites (just because they belong to the people of another religion) are horrendous crimes. But in our opinion it is a much greater crime to commit and allow similar criminal acts after the peace has been established. That is exactly what the Serbian population is suffering at the moment. At the same time, besides the exodus of the Orthodox Serbian people and numerous crimes and atrocities (forceful expulsions from flats and houses, robberies, rapes, kidnappings, murders, massacres of innocent people), there is a process of systematic eradication of the Serbian spiritual heritage. So far there have been several serious attacks on our churches and monasteries. The churches are being looted, burned, demolished, and vandalized.[31]

In addition to the loss of life, the economic impact of the war has been devastating locally and regionally. Though financial figures become outdated rather quickly in certain respects, three important initial assessments by experts not included in this volume contain valuable information later confirmed by the more comprehensive assessments of the World Bank, the OSCE, and the Economic Sta-

31. For the OSCE Reports, see the OSCE website listed in the appendix, "On-line Resources for Further Inquiry." Similar sentiments have also been echoed by Rev. Saba Janjic. For Artemije's letter to the U.N., see the website for the Decani monastery (www.decani.yunet.com).

bilization Agreement.[32] Thus Prof. Muhamet Mustafa, of the University of Pristina, estimates Kosovo damages just for households and their economies at about $6 billion, or approximately eight years' worth of Kosovo's gross domestic product (GDP) in 1997 ($4,000 per person in a culture where the prewar annual average income was $300). Dr. Bosko Mijatovic, of Belgrade's Economics Institute, estimates war damages in Serbia to be between $30 and $60 billion, somewhere between $3,000 and $6,000 per person (in a country which in 1998 had a GDP per person of $2,300). To put it in another perspective, this damage represents between one-sixth and one-third of the total amount that American Christmas holiday shoppers spent in 1999 (about $660 per person).[33] Yves Thibault de Silguy, who was acting European Monetary Affairs Commissioner and Coordinator of Kosovo Reconstruction, properly set the issue of damages in a wider regional context. By comparison, the cost of the war to the West was between $3 and $5 billion, most of which was paid for by the United States. This amounts to about $15 per person in America — about the price of two tickets to a movie theater or one-sixth of what the average teenager in North America spends each week ($89).[34] The cost of rectifying injustice has been high, when purchased exclusively by military means, for the people of the Balkans — but not for us.

*　　　*　　　*

Our essayists discuss many, but not all, of the issues raised by the conflict in Kosovo. The fact that no one can adjudicate all of these contending claims does not mean that they should be denied a fair hearing. Longer and broader views of the Yugoslavian civil wars are emerging — even though these wars have already generated a vast and informative literature in many languages. Listening to refugees, workers from the camps, and forensic experts as well as reading several decades of human rights reports about this region (especially Kosovo) are distressing. The institutionalization of human rights as codified in fifty years of international agreements signed by Yugoslavia is remarkable for how consistently they have been violated (*Human Rights Watch*, U.N. Missions, OSCE Reports, Helsinki Reports, reports by various religious groups, etc.). Kosovars and Serbs in this book (and elsewhere) agree: a failure to develop local civic society rooted in democracy, human rights, and the rule of law has been one key factor in the conflict. In the face of such widespread abuse by collective powers *over* individuals (or ethnic groups), no one disputes the need for more "human rights" to demarcate basic

32. These institutional and related resources are available on-line from websites and their links listed in the appendix, "On-line Resources for Further Inquiry."

33. According to the National Retail Federation, U.S. Department of Commerce, available at Mercurycenter.com.

34. Data determined by a July 1999 U.S. population estimate of 272,639,608, from the CIA *World Factbook* on-line (www.cia.gov).

protections from political society that everyone deserves. However, some continue to raise astute questions about whether the language of human rights adequately addresses all that is needed to rebuild civic society *from below* in federated networks of communal identity built on shared responsibility.[35] Of course, a failure to be implemented does not mean we should jettison human rights. Indeed, given what has happened to them, who will begrudge the appeals of Kosovars in this book to the liberal tradition of human rights as the basis for their European citizenship if not their own independence? The language of human rights is now used almost everywhere throughout the world; in our time, it has become a kind of *lingua franca*. For some, this signals international recognition of the rule of law and reason.[36]

Others wonder whether the "rationality" of this rule of law and human rights really will bring about greater justice.[37] Those of us who work for human rights at home and abroad should not allow our practical endeavors for *institutional* change to be undermined by the value we see in important *critical* questions posed by contemporaries to this language of human rights. In addition, there are those who question whether the "reasonableness" of this human rights language masks yet other forms of cultural oppression. Some so-called postmodern and poststructuralist thinkers criticize the all-powerful influence of Western economic and political institutions, of naive assumptions about a "common humanity" that ignore valuable cultural differences, of the universal salvation promised by consumer capitalism, of the threats that the implementation of our own alleged idealism poses to foreign cultures, of how terrifying our multiethnic sermonizing in

---

35. This formulation is my own, but I have learned much from Jean Bethke Elshtain's discussions of sovereignty and nationalism in *New Wine and Old Bottles: International Politics and Ethical Discourse* (Notre Dame: University of Notre Dame Press, 1998).

36. In a hopeful sign of change, some leaders of respective religious traditions there have used the language of human rights in reference to both communities; one hopes to see further development of the language of shared civic responsibility.

37. In the face of widespread human suffering and atrocities, precise distinctions about human rights seem offensively irrelevant. Yet the language we use to describe our outrage at what is abhorrent has assumptions worth examining. The uses of rights language are complex and cannot merely be dismissed due to so-called "philosophical ambiguities." (Are human rights considered to be powers, liberties, entitlements, claims, or immunities?) The narrative and advocacy settings of NGOs and IGOs differ from the institutional contexts of legal documents (the U.S. Bill of Rights) or the critically reflective analyses of others. These more theoretical analyses do not always distinguish issues of social context, historical development, legal implications, and philosophical groundings. Hence skeptics such as Rorty and critics such as Glendon talk past proponents such as Perry. See Richard Rorty, "Human Rights, Rationality, and Sentimentality," in *On Human Rights: The Oxford Amnesty Lectures 1993*, ed. Stephen Shute and Susan Hurley (1993); Michael Perry, *The Idea of Human Rights: Four Inquiries* (Oxford: Oxford University Press, 1998); Mary Ann Glendon, *Rights Talk: The Impoverishment of Political Discourse* (New York: Free Press, 1991), p. x.

foreign policy can be to those who have recurrently been subject to external powers. In other words, healthy "suspicions" about shallow defenses of "freedom, democracy, and human rights" can serve as valuable antidotes to the assumption that everyone in the world is a disguised American or "Westerner" (surely an unstable category).[38]

Observations about the limits of rights language must not paralyze us in the face of injustice and should not make us isolated or apathetic. Claims about what is reasonable or just are influenced by distorted arrangements of social power. Alerting ourselves to the intricate connections between language and social power can help us listen to one another more appreciatively and act decisively yet appropriately. Thus, postmodern thought offers important tools for understanding the simultaneously "fascistic and anti-colonial aspirations of emergent nationalisms and ethnic antagonisms." The absence of a perfect common life together need not prevent us from mutual cooperation to responsibly improve the common lives we have.[39] In that regard, is the West's insistence on a civic life of democratic institutions culturally appropriate to the Balkans? Or is it too much too soon for a region that continues to make the transition from outmoded archaic structures of (even enlightened) *nomenklatura* to the factionalism of opportunistic nationalisms?[40] Is such "gradualism" itself culturally paternalistic? As Michael Ignatieff has shrewdly observed, "The Balkans are not a pipe organ — and the pipes don't always blend."[41] Few contributors are neutral about such questions. The plurality of styles

38. We should be alert to how groups and territories are categorized. Describing oneself or accusing another as being part of "the West" is not only imprecise; it is frequently part of a persuasive effort to justify or criticize some action or policy. For example, some of our essayists equate "the West" with NATO as an actor in "the Balkans" — as a kind of extension of legitimate national interests (Halperin, U.S. State Department). Others link "the West" more closely to "Europe" and its interests in "Southeastern Europe" (NATO's Solana). Some of our Balkan essayists use the term "Western" approvingly to align themselves as Europeans (e.g., Shala); others reduce "Western" and "NATO" to "American" and presumably imperialist (e.g., Stojanovic). Similar remarks can be made about other relevant categories (e.g., "the Balkans").

39. Mark Wallace, William Schweiker, and Slavoj Zizek continue to help me appreciate the value of these discussions. For an interesting indictment of naive postmodernist thought with respect to the Gulf War, see Christopher Norris, *Uncritical Theory: Postmodernism, Intellectuals, and the Gulf War* (Amherst: University of Massachusetts Press, 1992).

40. Harry L. Humphries, "National Sovereignty and Ethnic Violence in the Balkan Region: The End of Our Familiar Understanding of the World" (unpublished paper for Fulbright panel discussion, 1999).

41. Ignatieff's observations were made at the aforementioned meeting of the International Independent Commission on Kosovo. It is particularly from my conversations with and study of the work of Maria Todorova that I have learned about the devastatingly pejorative and typically Eurocentric view of the Balkans as negative and retrograde: "As in the case of the Orient, the Balkans have served as a repository of negative characteristics against which a positive and self-congratulatory image of the 'European' and the 'West' has been constructed. With the reemergence of the East and orientalism as independent semantic values, the Balkans are left in

of writing in this volume merely sample the variety of genres that continue to emerge: testimonials, eyewitness accounts, historical and social analyses, appeals to rules, prophetic indictments, and so forth.[42] Deeper cultural analyses continue.

Many questions remain unanswered, and the difficulties of interpreting Kosovo's crisis and NATO's intervention (and the wider Yugoslavian wars) will persist. What do we say to others about what has happened? How will we in "the West" and our Balkan colleagues explain it to each other and to our children? Was the NATO intervention the West's last crusade of the millennium, mounted ironically on behalf of ethnic "Muslims" (many of whom are secularized) in the name of the secular international "religion of human rights"?[43] Is it the continuation or the betrayal of Western modernity's great epochal event, the French Revolution?[44] Was "the West" faced with one of the last gasps of nationalism or a feared forerunner of future ethnic fragmentation within nations? What shall we say about the causes, events, symbols, movements, rituals, and persons of this most recent in a decade of conflicts that continues to affect us all? If we are to understand ourselves and all the peoples of the former Yugoslavia to be now linked as never before in a future common history, then surely we must interpret

---

Europe's thrall, anticivilization, alter ego, the dark side within" (Todorova, *Imagining the Balkans* [New York: Oxford University Press, 1997], p. 188).

42. I am thinking of the narratives and analyses of many of Julie Mertus's writings, most recently her *Kosovo: How Myths and Truths Started a War* (Berkeley: University of California Press, 1999); the indictments of Noam Chomsky in his periodical writings and *The New Military Humanism: Lessons from Kosovo* (Monroe, ME: Common Courage, 1999); the questions raised by David Fromkin about American idealism in *Kosovo Crossing: American Ideals Meet Reality on the Balkan Battlefields* (New York: Free Press, 1999); the historical and political works of Vickers, Malcolm, Judah, Glenny, Holbrooke, Mojzes, Gordy, Wachtel, Zimmerman, Ramet, Owen, Woodward, Jelavich, Sells, Campbell, Anzulovic, Bennet, Gordiejew, Hall, Denitch, Clark, Scharf, Webster, Udovicki, Ridgeway, plus others in this volume, as well as works by Judah (*Kosovo: War and Revenge* [New Haven: Yale University Press, 2000]), Silber (on Milosevic), Ignatieff (*The Virtual War: Kosovo and Beyond* [Holt]), Hawkesworth (*Religious Quest and National Identity in the Balkans*), Mark Danner, *The Saddest Story: America, the Balkans and the Post–Cold War World* (Pantheon: forthcoming).

43. John Kelsay has pointed very astutely to the "ironic" elements in how Muslims around the world have viewed the "Western intervention" in Kosovo, with its use of the Serbian term "Kosovo" rather than the Albanian term "Kosova"; invoking national sovereignty yet blocking Kosovar self-determination; hesitating to protect Kosovars, then eventually demanding that they disarm themselves; a bombing campaign with many innocent victims that shifted Serbian strategy from discrimination and persecution to wholesale ethnic cleansing — all perhaps in the service of various national European agendas designed to avoid a strong Muslim presence in Europe.

44. This formulation has been decisively influenced by my conversations with David Tracy. He eloquent states the dilemmas of interpreting such significant events (called "classics") as social conflict. See his *Plurality and Ambiguity: Hermeneutics, Religion, Hope* (San Francisco: Harper and Row, 1987), pp. 3-8.

this "classic" event. Was the breakup of Yugoslavia its deplorable disintegration or its long-denied liberation?

What internal and external *causes and events* were crucial to Yugoslavia's collapse and the Kosovo intervention? Consider a few of the many factors involved: the West's recognition of Tito and the consolidation of Yugoslavia after World War II; the 1974 constitution granting Kosovo autonomy; the emergence of various nationalisms (which Ivo Banac persuasively argues remained active in various forms under the veneer of Tito's "brotherhood and unity" communism); Milosevic's incendiary 1989 Kosovo speech to Kosovo Serbs; the end of the Cold War and the collapse of various proposals for Yugoslavian unity as a federation, confederation, refederation, or alliance of republics; declarations of independence following referendums in Slovenia and Croatia in 1991 as well as resistance to secession and boycotts of votes; the fragmentation of the federal Yugoslav army; a similar breakup leading to war in Bosnia-Herzegovina in 1992-1994; failed conferences, peace plans, and efforts to resolve differences by "outsiders" (the CSCE/OSCE, the U.N., and NATO); hollow international threats to belligerents; foreign acceptance of the Yugoslavian regime's construal of Kosovar Albanians as a "nationality" (with another homeland in Albania) and — unlike the Croats and Slovenes — not a nation, hence without the right to secede and form an independent nation; the failure of pacifist movements; the ascendance of armed secessionists (the KLA); the plans of some Serbs for a "Greater Serbia" (or the ambitions of others for a "Greater Croatia" or "Greater Albania"); the massacre at Racak.

What *texts* are crucial — predecessor texts (the 1986 Serbian Academy Memorandum, the 1995 Dayton Accords), anticipatory texts (Rambouillet), contemporary texts (peace proposals), or subsequent texts (the G-8 talks accepted by Belgrade on May 31, 1999; the language and terms accepted by Belgrade on June 3; the Military-Technical Agreement signed on June 9; and U.N. Security Council Resolution 1244 on June 10)?

Who will adjudicate contending interpretations of these issues and texts and their commentators? How shall we analyze the *symbols, pictures, and rituals* of the Kosovo intervention? They include refugees and refugee camps; the feared knock on the door" in Kosovo or the air-raid sirens of Belgrade; men, women, and children executed in their homes; raped women dumped in wells; the "Bomb Here" bull's-eyes; "downed USAF bomber"; mass graves; Belgrade rock concerts; satellite photos of population movements; videos of exploding targets; the three-fingered sign of the Trinity; bombed hospitals in Belgrade; bomb-laden schools in Kosovo; the dead being removed from bombed-out buildings and family wells; the "accidentally" bombed Chinese embassy; the release of American prisoners following Rev. Jesse Jackson's visit. New symbols, rituals, and texts are emerging: KFOR, UNMIK, "reverse ethnic cleansing," the Economic Stabilization Agreement. There are various "individuals whom no novelist could invent and no biographer exhaust" (Tracy): Milosevic, Thaqi, Rugova, Draskovic, Djindjic, Clinton, Albright,

Clark, Blair, Ahtisaari, Yeltsin, and Chernomyrdin. The effects of the conflict continue — in Kosovo, Serbia, and around the world. Who are we, in the words of David Tracy, as the "uneasy postmodern heirs of this [ongoing] pluralistic and ambiguous heritage"? The crisis of Kosovo is at once theirs and our own.

Despite the limits of viewing ourselves as a singular "West" and Westerners, we and the non-West international community now have a role, but not the only role, in the Balkan future as never before. One can only hope that our work with them — not for them — serves their interests well. In the face of future similar conflicts elsewhere, perhaps conversations in this book can teach us something useful, so we are never compelled to agree with Alexis de Tocqueville's famous claim about the French Revolution: "Never was any such event so inevitable yet so completely unforeseen."

I. VOICES UNDER THE BOMBS

What Have Persons Experienced Firsthand?

A Tale from Prishtina

FLORA KELMENDI

All of a sudden you are in the middle of a muddy field, out in the open and you are supposed to feel happy, because you were the lucky one to get out alive. . . .

I was living in Prishtina with two of my sisters and my brother. We were all studying. I had two more exams left to finish my studies in English language and literature. My parents, together with my grandfather and two other sisters and one brother, were living in Peja (Pec), about an hour's drive from Prishtina — that is if you were not stopped on the way by the Serbian police, in which case it took much longer.

At first sight, life in Prishtina seemed normal, just more policemen in the streets. Compared to the other towns in Kosovo and the countryside, where villages were set on fire, Prishtina was indeed relatively safe. But almost everyone in Kosovo was already an IDP (internally displaced person) or a refugee. While studying, I was working as a translator for an Albanian NGO that worked closely with the British relief organization Oxfam. They distributed food and clothes to the displaced.

When the peace talks in France were taking place last February, everybody was hoping that some agreement would be reached and that life would be a bit normal again. But nothing happened, and all the foreigners — embassy staff and journalists — started to pull out. The last ones, on March 19, were the OSCE-observers. They were the only ones in whom we saw some security safeguard, and when they left it created real panic among the Albanians. People got very scared; whoever was able to get out left for Macedonia or elsewhere.

Life in Kosovo was already bad, but now it became a real hell. If you were Albanian, you became a kind of outlaw. Anything could happen to you. You could be shot in the middle of the street just because you were Albanian. The streets in Prishtina were dead. The only time you could see some Albanians on the streets was between 11:00 a.m. and 3:00 p.m.; otherwise the streets were full of Serbian soldiers, police, and armed civilians. My nineteen-year-old brother could not go out because he would jeopardize his life if he did. Only my older sister, Nora, and I went out in the street to buy bread. The curtains of our apartment had been closed for days now. Only one small window was open. Our Serbian neighbors, who were walking around with guns, knew that we were there; we were just careful not to remind them of our presence.

We wanted to go to Peja (Pec) to join our parents, but all the roads were blocked. We phoned them every day to find out if they were still all right. Then the NATO bombardments started on Wednesday, March 24. We were very grateful for that support, but it did not stop the ethnic cleansing. During the bombardments we felt safe, but as soon as they stopped, we waited in fear that the Serbs would come. It was not long before we heard Serbian tanks and jeeps rolling up and down the streets chasing and rounding up Albanians.

On the third day of the bombings we tried in vain to get our parents on the phone. Nobody answered. Finally we got in touch with our parents' neighbors; they told us that our grandfather had been killed by the Serbian police and that our parents and the other children had moved to safer areas. What were they talking about? Safer areas did not exist in Kosovo. As to the death of my grandfather, I did not dare to ask how he had been killed. I just felt something breaking inside me. He was 90 years old and had always lived with us. That night we were sitting in the dark: electricity was always cut off after 6:00 p.m. We were waiting for the sky to become red from the NATO bombs and the sound of them falling somewhere. We were all quiet except for Lena, my younger sister, who simply could not stop crying.

Life was getting worse. Every day we saw lines of Albanians heading to the train station to leave for Macedonia or Albania. From our appartment we could see Serbs demolishing and looting Albanian property — shops, cafes, cars. Every day there were fewer Albanians in the line for bread.

One night our Serbian neighbors in Prishtina were gathered in the yard and we heard them counting the Albanians who were still left in the apartment building. One of them was saying, "There are only the four students at Enver's apartment" — meaning us. We were terrified. They could come in whenever they wanted and do whatever they wanted. Nothing could stop them.

The next day our uncle and his family were thrown out of their home, and we decided to join them. We walked to the station and got on the last train that left Prishtina. The train was packed — people were even stuffing themselves inside the train through the windows — and nobody knew where we were going. I remembered films I had seen of World War II with trains full of Jews being deported. Our train stopped some kilometers before the border of Macedonia. Everybody had to get out, and we were told not to walk on the sides of the railways because they were mined. Each time someone accidentally stepped outside the line, my heart was bumping.

That day — it was the 3rd of April — we got to Blace, the place in no-man's-land where one had to get registered. It was a huge, muddy field with thousands of Albanians and improvised tents. There were no toilets, no water, and no food. Later that day we got a piece of plastic sheeting and some blankets; we put them on the ground, covered ourselves, and tried to get some rest. But it started raining. So we had to get up, take the plastic sheet and put it over our heads, and stand on foot. It was a freezing night — my sister Lena's 21st birthday.

It took us four days of surviving to get "processed," after which we were taken by buses to the NATO camp at Brasda. It was another big field, but this time it was surrounded by a fence outside of which were unfriendly Macedonian guards, who made sure that no Kosovar could get out of there. Inside the camp the NATO troops were putting up tents as fast as they could, but the flood of people was so great that it was impossible to shelter them all during the day. We were again out in the open waiting our turn to get a tent, and we needed a phone. Maybe our niece in Germany had some news about our parents and brothers and sisters. But there were no phones inside Brasda; only journalists and people working with NGO's had phones. The only way was to ask them.

It took Nora and me the whole afternoon to get a phone from a NATO soldier, but still there was no news of our family. I felt like I had a big hole in my stomach — I was so utterly desperate, empty, and powerless. I thought I would go crazy from all the wild guesses that came to my mind about the fate of my family. I needed to do something to get my mind off it. Translators were needed everywhere, so I started with that — first translating for a NATO major and then for the international medical relief organization Médecins sans Frontières (MSF). I was occupied with the problems of others, and for some hours I forgot about my own problems. At least I tried to forget.

Brasda was getting more crowded every day. Refugees were being evacuated to foreign countries, but many more of them were coming in. Everything was getting more and more difficult. We spent most of the day waiting for things: finding a phone, getting food, and even going to the toilet meant waiting in the line for hours. Every new group of refugees had worse news to tell about Kosovo. There seemed to be no end to the killing and the "cleansing" of the Kosovars. There was still no news of our parents, and I felt exhausted from everything. We all were exhausted, so we decided to put our names on the lists to be evacuated to a foreign country. It did not matter which one, just to get out of Brasda, which had become almost like a prison. At least we would be able to move freely if we could go abroad. It is horrific how your life can be completely destroyed and how you are still able to make a decision about your future. Kosovars were now being dispersed all over the world, and God knows when or if they would ever get back to their homes.

I kept busy as a translator for MSF, and my sisters and brother made sure that one of us was near the IOM tent (International Organization for Migration) every night when the lists were put up, hoping to see our names on one of them. And every time we did not see our names there was another disappointment. It meant another cold night sleeping on the ground in a camp surrounded by hostile Macedonian guards.

Finally, our names were on the list on Sunday, the 25th of April. The next day at 6:00 p.m., buses were to come to take us to the NATO base, where a plane was waiting to fly us out to The Netherlands. It was a country I did not know more about than that they had windmills and tulips. I was not happy. I felt that the further I went away, the longer it was going to take me to get back. I phoned our niece in Germany one more time just to see if she had some news. I had almost lost hope, but then I heard my niece say: "Your parents are alive and safe in Albania, together with the other children."

They were alive! I could not believe my ears. The walk back to my tent, to my brother and sisters, seemed to never end. The next day I got my parents on the phone. My father was overcome with emotion and started crying when he heard my voice; nor could I say a word. It was my brother who had to continue the conversation. We discussed with our parents our possible evacuation to Holland. It was a huge dilemma we were facing: take a one-time chance to get out of Brasda, this prison-like camp, or wait for God knows how long to join our parents in Albania. We decided in favor of the first option.

We got on the plane and arrived in the Netherlands, where we were put up in a tent camp in the middle of the country, a camp especially assembled for the Kosovars. New country, new people, new surroundings — and a lot of energy needed to find our way around. Here we were not sleeping on the ground anymore; we had beds, we had showers, food three times a day, and a phone cabin within reach. But I was still feeling empty and more remote from my family than ever.

Now after all the agreements and all the NATO troops are inside Kosovo, everyone says that the future is bright for the Kosovars. The suffering has ended and we can all go back. I hope they are right. For some reason, however, I just cannot stop thinking of my grandfather. Whenever I go home, he will not be there anymore, and nobody can tell me why.

Belgrade Sisters under Siege:
Excerpts from the War Diary of Ivanka Besevic

IVANKA AND OLGA BESEVIC

I am Ivanka Besevic, a 74-year-old retired journalist from Belgrade. My daughter, Silvia Miller, who lives in San Francisco, asked me to write to her daily about my life with my sister Olga and our survival during the NATO bombing of Belgrade. She published my e-mail letters and phone calls on the Internet daily while Yugoslavia was under attack.[1] This diary, "Keep Faith," was never intended to be an impartial record. It would be impossible for me to do so while my own country is getting blown to pieces and my friends are getting older and sicker under neverending sirens. From the letters sent to me by some who have viewed the website, I know that a few letter writers are angry at me because I don't write more about the Kosovo coverage, or Albanian refugees, and show a side of the war they don't have a chance to see on CNN. It's my family's personal decision to publish my thoughts: to keep us all busy and give us a sense of purpose in this insanity; to keep a loving record in the case of something bad happening; to process the terror and forget for a moment our fears for each other.

I tell about the things I see, feel, and experience, and the things that happen to my family and friends. If I were living in Kosovo, I'd be writing about it, and my experiences there. The refugees I meet on my doorsteps, however, are only the ones that arrive here. They are of all nationalities (there are quite a few Albanian and Roma [Gypsy] refugees in Belgrade too), but they have never stayed in a refugee camp in Albania and don't know about life in it. Knowing that there are so many interested in more knowledge about our disaster is a very hopeful sign for all of us here.

---

1. The Besevic family website is at www.keepfaith.com.

Sample Postings to "Keep Faith"

March 24

Ivanka: We found out that the nearest shelter is fifteen minutes away. There was no way that we could get to it — the defense says that we have only nine seconds to get somewhere when the sirens start. Besides, Olga refused to leave Timmy, and they don't allow pets in the shelters, it's too crowded. I can't say that I blamed her. . . . Olga and I worked on cleaning up the basement of my apartment building and converting it into a shelter for us and the neighborhood children. It's scary and dark in there, as there is only one entrance and no windows. . . .

Olga: I am worried. You never know when the air-raid is going to start. . . . The worst of all is the terrible speed with which everything happens. I hear detonations, start running home to the basement, the sirens start wailing, and everything is happening in slow motion — except for the bombs coming fast, very fast. The whole war is almost surreal, a video game. Half the time we pretend that nothing's happening; city transportation is running better than ever, driven by volunteer drivers, and concert halls and theaters are giving free performances to all who want to see them. Other times, we are running to turn off all the lights and sit in the dark, underground, waiting to die.

April 7

Ivanka: I sleep well, but Olga rarely shuts her eyes before dawn. Hearing the growl of the bombs in the dark is still better than the silence — at least we know that they are far away; the anticipation of waking up in the fires of a man-made hell is much worse. We cope. During the day, everyone goes to work, the stores are open, doctors heal, artists create beauty. Then, as the night approaches, we scatter to our darkened holes, usually in groups. This will teach us a hard lesson in humanity. We watched the massacres in other parts of the world, always thinking, "We are a civilized country; a thing like that could never happen here — the homeless, the hungry, sicknesses this continent hasn't seen since the holding pens of German occupation." Now people die in concentration camps, not in Yugoslavia, but in the cannibal alliance trying to devour it. All the atrocities that the nationalist Serbs have committed, and all the horrors that the terrorist KLA have wrought pale by comparison. Are they trying to show us what *real* atrocities are, so we would hang our heads in shame for our petty terrorism and all get along, dead or alive?

May 1

Ivanka: We were spared last night, but had no rest nevertheless. There was such a storm that we were not able to tell the thunder and lightning from the bombs. At this point we are so jumpy that we leap into the air at any sudden noise — both from the lack of sleep and the realization that the gloves are off and NATO really wants us dead, all of us. It was a strange storm that started with the first sirens (the entire day was sunny and quite warm), blasted through the night, and died out with the morning and the end of the air danger. We are spread so widely around our poor violated country that there is always an eyewitness account to anything that happens. The downside is that, wherever the Bombing du Jour happens, we have to fear for our loved ones. I don't care for myself: I am old and had a full, wonderfully fulfilled life. I am angry because of the children screaming in nightmares of bombing, because of a generation sentenced to grow up in poisons (fishing in the Danube is now banned — the water is deadly), sentenced to starve because their parents' workplaces are now bomb craters. Sentenced to live in shame of their nationality being linked to the worst crimes, with no proof. I am angry because of having money taken from my every paycheck, my entire working life of forty years, to fund the development of Kosovo, just to see NATO bomb all that we built into dust — so that no one, not Serbs or Albanians, will ever have any use of it.

May 16

Olga: It's really hard to figure out where to be safe. The people living near the most obvious targets stay with family or friends in the more innocuous areas, just as Ivanka does, living with me now. There are a several "legitimate targets" up and down the street from my apartment, but at least we are not next to Yugoslavia's biggest newspaper, where Ivanka's home is. My friend Danka, who lives on the second floor nearby, says that as soon as the sirens start, she goes to one room of her apartment that has no apartment over it on the third floor — just the roof. She's terrified of being buried and crashed by concrete from the floors above her, and afraid of having to live mutilated or as an amputee, so she counts on a quick death by exposing herself to a direct hit, if there is one. Even the children are trying to process what goes on in their own way. I heard a new version of the Red Riding Hood story told by a little girl, in which Red Riding Hood's parents warn her not to talk to strangers in the forest, as well as to run and hide if she hears the sirens start. One of my violin students said that they call a feared biology teacher "Madame Albright."

June 1

Ivanka: Ah, we are starting another month of war, with bigger and better bombs, and more carpet bombing than ever. In the last three days, they hit point blank a bridge full of people during a major religious holiday, Pentecost, and Sunday market crowds (casualties included a priest and many others who came in to help after the first wave); also hit were a hospital, an old folks home, a convoy of foreign journalists, and now the apartment building in Novi Pazar. Dozens and dozens of dead — the old, the sick, and children. The bombers have been returning after the first hits to bomb the relief workers and good Samaritans, too. Surdulica, where the hospital and old folks home were hit, has only 12,000 people living in it. By the time everyone is killed, they'd have spent a bomb for each person dying in there. What really chills me is the thought that the bombing really *is* a success, as they are stating — that they are doing exactly what they intended when destroying the cities and people and children like this. I believe this is correct. All of us who are being bombed here — who can smell the air rushing from the bomb hits and see the dead bodies — think the same. We are here, and we see it with our own eyes: every civilian target, our neighbors' homes. They are still counting the bodies. . . .

June 12-16

Olga: I am sleeping a bit better, but still have some troubles. It's so quiet — with no bombs and no Ivanka.[2]

I despise nationalism of all kinds, and this atmosphere is more and more conducive to it. During all these years of sanctions and the breakup of the country, it was natural, but not excusable, that some would turn to nationalism — usually the loudest ones. What to expect now, after the country has been bombed into the Middle Ages, but the strengthening of the medieval attitudes. Even the most moderate factions are turning strongly to the religious right of some kind; and what is going to happen now, if there *is* an election? The ruling party is not the most nationalistic party, not by far. War never has brought moderation. Many of the Serbs who had no grudge against the Albanians are now — now that they have lost their own homes and children to bombing — hateful of them. Kosovo is a terrible, terrible mess! Serbs, Gypsies, and other ethnicities, as well as the Albanians who were against secession — people are now running in thousands (from 15,000 to 30,000, according to different sources) in the three days we have had peace. The KLA is burning and pillaging Serb houses, and it has not been demilitarized at all, as NATO was supposed to

---

2. Ivanka Besevic is with her daughter, Silvia, in San Francisco at this point. [Ed.]

insist on according to the signed peace accord. I can only suppose that there's a lot of burning being done the other way around too (not much of that in papers here) — by the retreating paramilitary and people. I heard reports of Serbs burning their own houses and those of their neighbors in order to leave nothing to the advancing enemy. . . . It doesn't matter anymore. We are all so tired. Nobody won, except for the bomb-makers.

July 5

Olga: I spoke again with [our friend] Zivka, and she said it's still war in Kosovo. Her family was forced out. Their cows are loose and dying without people to take care of them, and they lost all they ever had. It's chaos down there. There are gangs all over the place. What the papers are saying — that the province is getting more peaceful — is plain untruth. . . . Another one of my friends, an army electric repairman who recently returned from Kosovo, was very, very serious when he told me that it's not over, that it's complete destruction and chaos in the south, and that he would not be surprised if our whole country goes up in flames. Everyone expects the continuation of war in August. I haven't removed the protective tape from my windows. No one else is pretending that the war is over either. It's true only for the safe countries that have the luxury to select soldiers, not civilians, to be sent to die. War is all around us here, in power struggles, rubble, and guns.

"My Father Was Burned Alive": Testimonies from Kosovo Refugees

EDITED BY SEVDIJE AHMETI

My Father Was Burned Alive

15 October 1998

On July 28, 1998, at 12:00 sharp, the village of Terpeze e Ulet was shelled from a distance of 1,000 meters. During the 30-minute break, the Serb forces came out of their tanks and armored vehicles and stood on the street. They started to sing. While singing, they ordered all the barns, with the animals and all the animal food inside, to be burned down. It was during these moments of fire that the UCK resistance began. Suddenly, and without warning, the Serb paramilitary, walking in front of the tanks and armored vehicles like the infantry, entered the village houses. They started to fire butane pistols at the Albanian houses, which caught fire and were completely destroyed. Those houses cannot be lived in anymore. Six other village houses were shelled from afar.

When the Serb forces were at a distance of 20 meters from our house, I heard their voices and their singing. I begged my father to run away with me since the other villagers had already left at least two hours earlier. My father, Jashar (53), was very adamant about not wanting to leave the house. He said to me, "Leave me here, I want to die in my own house and not run away to the mountains. I want to remain near my house, which I built with a lot of hard labor." Even though the situation was very difficult, with bullets showering us from all sides, I filled a glass with water and gave it to my father; I also left him some food. I wanted to leave with my father and had no heart to be parted from him. But at that time my father was very determined and emotional. He got even more emotional and begged me, "My daughter, go, run away so you don't fall into their hands."

I wasn't even 20 meters away when my home was set ablaze. It was this fire that took my father. I understood that this meant war, but I was feeling restless and wanted to go back to see what exactly had happened to my father and my home.

But I was unable to penetrate the lines, since the Serb infantry was also in the mountains. I had to crawl on the ground for the next two hours.

By the time I managed to reach my family, who had fled earlier, I saw 57 children in one cave, which we call "Lluga e Shales." Among those children were my brother's five children, who were crying and asking for bread. I had two loaves of bread with me. We divided those two bread loaves into 57 pieces and handed them out to the hungry children.

We spent that night in the woods. The next day we left for the mountains of Novoselle. It was impossible to remain in those mountains; the children were at risk of infection, and therefore we had to continue our trip on foot to the village of Nekovc. We remained in Nekovc for ten days, but it also came under attack, again making our stay there impossible. We were forced to move again, and we started out for the village of Lladrovc. Here again we were in danger, and after four days we ran toward the mountain village of Pagarushe. My family had consisted of eleven members before my father was burned alive. Now we were ten people.

My father was burned alive only because he did not want to leave his home. He was an elementary school teacher who had spent twenty-nine years in education. He was decorated five years in a row as the best school teacher in Malisheve.

"I Had to Run with Pains, My Baby Died While Delivering"

1 March, 1999

Hani i Elezit (Deneral Jankovic in Serbian) has, with its five villages together, some 9,000 inhabitants. Its mountainous villages were attacked by Serb forces — at first by Serb paramilitary forces. All the residents fled for their lives to where they thought it would be best — they were heading for Macedonia. Serb authorities did not allow the 3,000 IDPs [internally displaced persons] to cross the border. With machine guns pointed at them, the IDPs were forced after some six hours to return to Hani i Elezit, where they are now finding refuge. On the way to this small town, VJ [Serbian] army forces were patrolling the highway, and some of them were positioned just beyond the exit of the first tunnel, where the mined bridge is situated, aiming at the mountain on the right side.

Accounts of IDP Women

Bedrije Shiti (40), mother of five, from Dimce village:

"I was having pains to deliver my baby when we were forced to leave the village. We heard the severe shooting, and we saw tanks and army members running straight to the village. We fled as we were. I was with pains, but I had to run; I had to save the lives of my children. We decided to go to Macedonia, to a safer area. My pains started at 2:30 in the morning, and at that stage we were forced to flee through the night. I could not walk, but I had to. Who could carry me? At the border, as I started to deliver my baby, we had guns pointed at our heads. I gave birth to a dead baby girl. She died because I was so scared and faced such a hard time. She had been alive when the pains started — I could feel her.

We decided to come back to the village. I am so afraid for my other children. Look at the army moving around. Look at them! What are we going to say now? 'They see you. They are watching you. They will ask us what we told you.' My God, how scared I am! Only 100 meters away from our home we have had mines planted for one year already. Look at the tanks. . . ."

"We Are Tired from Fleeing for Our Lives"

Domanek, Kosova
16 March 1999

Domanek village of Malisheve municipality in Kosova has become a key gathering village of IDPs from the attacked areas of Kline municipality. According to the data gathered today, some 4,800 fresh internally displaced persons were refugees in this village. By the time we were trying to meet the IDPs and especially to see how women and children were, another flow of 200 people from Dush village came, some on foot, some being driven by tractors. Altogether, the number of IDPs in Domanek village reached 5,000 people, all facing catastrophe — hungry, ill, frozen, intimidated, and traumatized. They were fleeing for the seventh time from their villages of Sferke, Perceve, Dush, Cupeve, Volljake, etc.

Most of these people needing to find a safe shelter are children, women, and elderly. They have left behind everything they had — their ruined houses, their plastic roofs, their much-needed flour brought by the humanitarian organizations, and their clothes donated from people abroad. They have nothing else to be counted as their property or private possession. They have lost their rest as well.

"We are tired from fleeing for our lives. Maybe we should get killed. God knows how — but it is some energy that pulls us running anywhere for safety," says a tearful Erfete Gashi (47) from Sferke village of Kline. "We came to Domanek village the day before yesterday. We are hungry; we had nothing to eat these two days. Look at my son: while fleeing for his life he was wounded. I asked for some jam to take away the bitterness I have in my mouth. This bitterness actually comes from my heart. But the people here don't have any — they are poor themselves. They themselves were IDPs somewhere else when they were forced to flee, and of course their houses were looted as ours were."

"We were forced to run through the rain of bullets and grenades on us," begins the account of Myvedete Januz Gashi (17), also from Sferke village. "Is there any chance of peace in Paris?" asked Myrvete, and none of us was able to give an answer. All we could say to her was that the Kosovar delegation was going to sign the agreement, but it was not sufficient for her. "The OSCE KVM came close to the village and they tried to persuade the Serb forces to go away, not to attack us, but the answer was, 'We are ordered to attack.' We are endangered. One month ago, on Saturday, February 17, when we were attacked and forced to flee for our lives right out in the open, we were forced to leave my dead four-year-old niece Valmire in the middle of the room. She died from the hard conditions we are facing. We had no roof and no home because it was burned during the summer offensive. We went back home but lived inside plastics, which let in no air; the damp was killing us. Besides having no food and no security, we could not even send Valmire somewhere to be treated. So she died of the harsh living conditions, and we were forced to leave her corpse like that in order to flee for our lives. When the shelling stopped and it had become dark, we came back home in hiding. The plastic roof was burned again, but our dear dead Valmire was still there resting in peace amidst the severe attacks. We buried her somewhere in the mountains.

We are twenty-seven people altogether, counting my uncles and cousins, and we are homeless. My brother, Ramiz Januz Gashi (27), was killed at the border with Albania when he was trying to come to visit us. It seems as though our fate is to deal with graves. We still do not know where my brother's grave is."

Close to Domanek village, there is Cupeve village of Malisheve. When the attacks on the Kline villages started and were reported to continue, this village was shelled too. Due to the sudden attack and the fear they had experienced before, people fled for their lives immediately. Two people were wounded during the flight. Two women delivered their babies on the way. Because the villagers could not carry the disabled with them, they were forced to leave them behind. The next day, when they went to collect the two disabled people, 26 bullet shells were laid as a "design" around the old disabled Mr. Gashi, but he was not killed.

Huge [Serbian] Offensive Has Started in Kosova

19 March 1999

Right after the exodus of the OSCE KVM to Macedonia, Serbs have started an offensive against the numerous sites in Kosova.

Podujeve: Today at about 08:00 CET, Serb forces concentrated for quite a time along the Kosova-Serbia border, at the place called Prepelac. They were backed up with tanks and other vehicles as they entered Kosova and stationed them-

39

selves at the village Dumnice e Eperme. The population has started to flee in panic from Dumnice e Eperme, Dumnice e Poshtme, Llaushe, and Perpellac. The villages of Penuh, Godishnjak, and Sallabaje are being shelled fiercely. The Podujeve-Prishtine highway is blocked.

Prishtine: Serb forces concentrated at Besi and Lebane villages have started to shoot on the villages of Barileve, Besi, Prugovc, Rimanishte, and Vranidol of Prishtine municipality. The population is fleeing for their lives in panic and are being blocked by the combat machinery. The Serb infantry has entered the village of Drenovc, where a big number of residents is blocked and did not manage to flee. This is the first time that these villages (5 kilometers away from Prishtine) are being attacked. Police arrested Selim Berisha (50) together with his son Agron (18) in the village of Drenoc.

Drenice: Over 300 tanks have entered the village of Korretice e Eperme of Gllogovc. The villages of Vasileve and Gllobar are burning. The Residents, together with IDPs, have fled to Gllogovc. The situation in Gllogovc is very tense. The villages of Gllanaselle, Dobroshec, and Gllobar are being shelled. The population is also fleeing for their lives toward the villages of Baice and Obri. A segment of the population is blocked close to the village of Cikatove e Vjeter, close to the Ferrou Nickel.

Mitrovice: The Mitrovice-Skenderaj roadway has been blocked since 6:00 a.m. Serb forces have become concentrated, starting from Skenderaj to Ternavc village. Infantry has entered the village of Kline e Eperme, at the hamlet Tahiraj. The crossroad of Skenderaj is blocked by 3 APCs. Infantry is heading toward the villages of Prekaz i Poshtem and Polac. One convoy of 50 armored vehicles has headed from Mitrovice toward Skenderaj. At 6:30 a.m., Serb forces started to shell the villages of Oshlan, Pantine, Galice, and Liqej of Vushtrri, and the villages of Lubovec, Mikushnice, and Prekaz of Skenderaj. Mitrovice town roads are full of police forces and armed Serb civilians.

NATO Missiles and Kosova

25 March 1999

Last night at around 8:00 p.m., NATO threats came true. Missiles started to fall like rain on Prishtina. Some five of them were seen and they were furtive. They looked like flames and falling stars. One of them, perhaps one hour later, before the start of the NATO air strike, was so furtive that those watching from the windows felt the rush of the windblow on their noses and chests. Some few moments later, a big smoke and fire was observed on the Western side of Prishtine. Right at the start of the strike, Prishtine was out of electricity; the outage came at about 8:25 p.m. on the 25th of March.

So far there is no report from the field, except for one very confidential and fearful report from Gjakove, where the old part of the town was set ablaze. Gjakove is a town from the Middle Ages, with its old conserved part that serves as a picture of beauty and history and culture. Over 98 percent of the population is Albanian. Last year, during the Serb offensive, this town, west of Prishtine and bordering on Albania, was sealed off. It faced a long-time isolation and had at least 60,000 IDPs from the villages affected by war, which are now empty and have become like ghost towns, especially in the Reka e Keqe region.

At about 2:00 a.m., only two hours after midnight, local sources say they heard some vehicles going through side roads, and then running steps and the setting of fire to all the shops of the famous Carshia e Madhe, the very picturesque part of the old town. Meanwhile, they heard the screams around some houses. Serb paramilitaries entered the home of Dr. Izet Hima, famous, respected, and elderly — and they killed him. Then they entered the two homes of the Zherka family and killed three people.

Just as we had feared retaliation, it happened. Now we anxiously wait for other reports. There is a need to report also that Gjakove town had electricity all the time. People were watching the CNN reports of the attacks. Many arrests have happened. No one knows how many.

Center for the Protection of Women and Children
Report on Damages and Rape

7 July 1999

Qirez: The Qirez community of the municipality of Skenderaj is a compound of six villages: Qirez, Baks, Kozhice, Krasmirovc, Krasaliq, and Prellovc. The population of the Qirez community no longer exists. Over 50 percent of the animals have been killed. Food has either been looted or set ablaze by the Serb forces. The needs of the population are very grave. Almost all of the villages are scorched. They need shelter, food, clothing, and medication. All of the returnees are traumatized by war. Drinking water is missing. The only water for drinking comes from waterfalls. Over 70 percent of the water wells are contaminated (often by dead bodies that were thrown into them).

Before the NATO air strikes, the community was known for sheltering over 20,000 IDPs. During the NATO air strikes, the majority of IDPs and the local population were used by Serbian forces as human shields. According to the accounts of local people who are now returnees, rape was one of the war weapons used against women and young girls. Many men are still missing, and no one knows their whereabouts. One woman from the village of Kozhice was killed in front of her children. Three people have been burned alive in the village of Prellovc and two others as IDPs in the village of Qirez.

Kozhice: Before the war, Kozhice village had 572 inhabitants living in 57 compound families. Out of 77 houses, only 3 of them are intact; the others are completely burnt. This village has 20 people killed (among them 1 child and 6 young women who have been raped before being killed and thrown into water wells); 3 people are missing, and 8 others are wounded. Over 60 percent of the animals have been killed.

When Serb forces entered the village of Kozhice on 17 April 1999, they kidnapped six young women (they call them girls since they were single) and another young IDP woman from the village of Dubovc. According to the accounts of the witnesses that were present and escaped from the kidnapping, these young women were raped by Serb forces, later killed, and then thrown into the water wells of the village. There are rumors that some raped women were thrown into the wells alive. Their hair was in a mess. The throwing of women into wells was age-selective, and it certifies that the crime against them was on purpose and well planned. So far, the corpses of the raped women who have been found have been identified as:

— Lumnije Zymeri (age 20), Bukurije Dibrani (age 20), Mirishahe Dibrani (age 27), and Antigona Dibrani (age 16) — thrown into the water well of Mr. Hilmi Aliu, resident of the village of Kozhice.

— Miradije Dibrani (age 50), Fahrije Ademi (age 53), and Tahire Shalaku (age 60, IDP from the village of Dubovc) — thrown into the water well of Mr. Asllan Xhemajli, resident of the village of Kozhice.

— Zahiide Xhema (age 21) — thrown into the well of Mr. Azem Rexhepi, resident of the village of Kozhice.

The corpses of the rape victims were removed by the Hague Tribunal Team (ICTY), without any residents being present, on July 2, 1999. Not even family members of the victims were allowed to be present.

Besarta Seferi (age 12) died immediately on the day of the attack on the village of Kozhice, at the moment when the Serb forces took the women by force and raped them. She died because her heart broke out of fear that she might be taken, too.

Diary of a Refugee Camp Doctor

FOKKO DE VRIES

Wednesday, 7 April

We depart from Rotterdam Airport in a Russian freight plane chartered from a Romanian airline. We are Médicins sans Frontières (MSF) — Doctors without Borders — a mixed company of doctors, nurses, logisticians, and press people. We try to conceal our fear of flying with jokes about drafty windows, rusted-up wings, and loose bolts. The cargo is made up of all sorts of aid supplies, presenting us with a view of several hundred squatting plates. These are mobile squat toilets, consisting of a piece of plastic with a hole and two footprints; they make me think of the footprints of Gavrillo Princip, the assassin of the Habsburg crown prince Frans Ferdinand, in the pavement of Sarajevo. They were preserved at the exact spot where he fired the fatal shots that led to World War I. They have since been removed, hacked out of the pavement since the last war in Bosnia, because Princip was a Serb.

The flight is breathtakingly beautiful, with a detour via Italy because the airspace is partially closed as a result of the tomahawk diplomacy being waged below. On our arrival at the Skopje airport, a uniformed individual gratuitously snarls at us that it's all Clinton's fault. In the corner of the airport a group of refugees waits for a flight to an unknown destination in a "third country." Turkey? Norway? There are rumors about Cuba — why not? There are even Bosnians who have landed in Bangladesh. Of their own free will, of course. After all, people who have been driven out of their homes, separated from their families, and are utterly exhausted are perfectly able to make decisions. At least that's what the host countries would have us believe.

Thursday, 8 April

Visit the refugee camp at Stenkovac, between Skopje and the Kosovar border. Stenkovac is a former airfield that still has a hangar and two old propeller planes. There is a large NATO presence in both camps. Soldiers are working day and night

43

at setting up tents, distributing food and blankets, setting up water facilities, building latrines, and carrying away refuse. Stenkovac accommodates some 20,000 people, a number that is constantly changing with the continued arrival of new refugees and the evacuation of the ad hoc camp at Blace. The presence of so much armed green comes as a shock to the MSF veterans, something without precedent. A humanitarian mission is difficult to square with a military mission. The initial confusion gives way to a purposeful approach: the building up of an MSF presence and the planning for a seamless handover with the military.

Around the Stenkovac camp stand armed Macedonian police and soldiers. There is no freedom of movement. This is against international law, which says that refugees are free to move around after being registered. But we now know that many international treaties — with a nod to Bismarck — are not worth the paper they are written on.

Friday, 9 April

I carry out a reconnaissance mission to check out the situation on the Yugoslav/ Macedonian border. Driving through the part of Macedonia mainly populated by Albanians, we hear on the radio a travestied version of the former Eagles hit "Welcome to hotel Macedonia." Our driver, of mixed Albanian, Macedonian, and Turkish descent — a typical specimen of *Homo balkanus* — shakes his head pityingly.

The Macedonian border is closed. On a pretext, I manage to cross the hundred-meter-wide no-man's land. A stethoscope around the neck works wonders! Some 250 people have been camping in the strip since yesterday evening. The Serbian border police had (mis)informed them that they would be allowed into Macedonia if they left their cars behind. And would they be so kind as to hand over the car keys?

Much more serious is the report that some 300 cars — number of people unknown, but including the people already in no-man's-land — were sent back to Yugoslavia in a joint action by the Serbian and Macedonian police. There are stories that they are to be used as human shields. It can't be verified in the present circumstances, but nothing can be excluded either.

A long queue of people stands waiting at the closed Serbian border. A human chain of misery stretching out toward the border from every little village in Kosovo, facing an uncertain future. A chain of hundreds of thousands of innocent citizens. Nobody dares to cross the mountains along this part of the Serbian border. The rumor of landmines alone is enough to stop people, whether true or not. A busload of people is carried off under police escort to the Neprostance refugee camp, which is run by German NATO troops.

Saturday, 10 April

This morning, visit the mobile hospital set up by the Israeli army in Stenkovac refugee camp. They have an operating theater, laboratory, X-ray equipment, and even a blood bank. The way they work and speak is extraordinarily professional. But there again, they already have more than fifty years of war experience. I then hold a clinic myself. MSF has set up a number of polyclinics, a dressing station, and a dispensary. All rather improvised at first. It's not exactly easy listening to heart and lung murmurs through the noise of the generators powering the high-tech mortuary set up by the Norwegians.

Most of the medical problems are chronic conditions: people with high blood pressure, diabetes, epilepsy, and asthma who no longer have any medicine, since most of the refugees have nothing more than the clothes they stand up in. Other problems are typical camp complaints: diarrhea, colds, mange, and lice. Finally, there are the mental problems. People present vague complaints, but as soon as they feel somewhat reassured, we give them an opportunity to let it all out, to tell their stories.

There is a constant pattern in the stories, which are now generally familiar. Everybody speaks of masked paramilitaries, looting, threats, the midnight knock on the door, the bodies lying here and there. Some people recognized the voice of their neighbors behind the masks. The people are mostly still anesthetized — in a phase of denial and disbelief. In the coming weeks this will crystallize into more specific psychiatric problems of unrestrained aggression, nightmares, and depressions. A growing number of women are no longer able to breastfeed as a result of the tension.

My colleague, a pediatrician who has his tent close by, tells his personal story to the refugees. How he as a twelve-year-old child was driven out of Hungary by the Russians. He tries to convey the message that it doesn't have to represent the end of someone's life, and that it means a lot for him personally to be able to help other people now.

A girl of fifteen has a panic attack. I try to calm her, and we chat about the Spice Girls and Brad Pitt. But she's a Back Street Boys fan, which puts me in a different generation. Members of our team share our feelings of rage and powerlessness with the refugees. In the evening we chat over a glass of the local ouzo. A clear sky above us, blossoming trees in front of us. In the distance is a white streak above and below the mountains. Snow is lying above, and the tents are standing below. It's cold in Stenkovac.

Sunday, 11 April

Today — Easter Sunday according to the Orthodox calendar — the medical care in the Stenkovac camp is formally handed over by NATO to the aid organizations.

This is an historic event, something that has never happened before. British, German, Dutch, Italian, and Norwegian soldiers stand in a semicircle. A priest in army uniform gives a speech full of Bible quotes about good and evil. Many blink away a tear, and they sing some psalms. A Kosovar boy has pushed to the front. His shoes are three sizes too large. The serene silence is broken now and then by low-flying helicopters or a mobile phone with the tones of Big Ben. But the most startling is the British colonel who, with an eye to the watching cameras, finishes with "See you all in Prishtina!"

We hold a clinic for the rest of the day. We're having more and more trouble with journalists. I have mixed feelings about them. The American press in particular gives me the feeling of wanting to soften up public resistance to a possible ground war. A number of journalists in search of steamy stories ask specifically for women who have been raped. I break off a number of interviews because of their attempts to make me come out with explicit political statements concerning NATO and Doctors without Borders (MSF).

I continue my clinic. A patient tells me that he was tortured by the Serbian police one and a half years ago. He was struck repeatedly on the neck until he lost control of the right side of his body. Then they let a tear-gas grenade explode in his hand and cut off the remains of his fingers with a pair of scissors. I can do no more than report the facts. He needs plastic surgery, but above all he needs pyschosocial therapy. He is alone in the camp. There is no news of his family.

The whole conflict consists of numbers. So many refugees here, so many people killed there. But in the end it is a summation of individual suffering. Each person has his or her individual story. The stories are of expulsion, flight, waiting at the border, the conditions in the camp, the loss of all future perspective, but above all the uncertainty as to the fate of loved ones and the absolute certainty as to the fate of loved ones who have already been murdered.

I suggest to this young man that he should have psycho-social counseling and some psychiatric medication. He dismisses this on the grounds that he is not worth it. An extremely low self-valuation is another expression of trauma. However, he does agree to have his story written down by human rights experts; perhaps in this way the guilty parties may one day be brought to justice — though he believes they never will.

In addition to its medical mission, Doctors without Borders (MSF) also has a clear advocacy mission, and we are very well aware of our special responsibility in this respect. Apart from medical secrecy, it is unethical to get traumatized people to tell their story without providing for aftercare. MSF will therefore survey the need for a psychological trauma treatment program, based on know-how previously acquired in Sarajevo. This is especially desirable for people being cared for by private individuals at home. It is also a preventive activity, to avoid having people end up in psychiatry.

Monday, 12 April

This morning I examine a patient who is eight months pregnant. I let her hear the baby's heart beating. She begins to cry. She has waited ten years for the pregnancy. And then this. What sort of life will her child have? In the afternoon it is the turn of the Italian medical troops, our neighbors in the camp, to leave. How different from the British ceremony! An officer blows up a plastic glove, draws a face on it, calls it Pinocchio, and gives it to us as a mascot. Ciao bambini! We will miss them.

Afterwards I see the patient who has been tortured once again. He has become unreachable and is experiencing hallucinations about cetniks pursuing him in the camp. Alas, I have to give him an injection to calm him down, but he deserves better treatment. As I walk through the camp for a "house call," I'm assailed from all sides by people asking whether I have a telephone. Just as in Africa you constantly hear "mzungu, mzungu" (white person) all around you, and in Amsterdam "hashish? hashish?" — here you constantly hear "telephone? telephone?" Information from the home front is terribly important for the refugees. In this postmodern age there could well be a place for a humanitarian organization that distributes mobile telephones, for example, TSF: "Télécommunication sans Frontières." The few times that we lend someone a mobile phone are particularly emotional. What conclusion should you draw if nobody answers at home? Or if the line is busy? Sometimes a stranger picks up the phone.

That evening there is an internal discussion at MSF about whether or not we should go into Kosovo. We share our concern about the situation there. The refugees that we are caring for now — however bad their situation may be — are at least safe for the time being. The majority of the Kosovars are still in Kosovo, for the moment at least. We can only guess at their fate. The discussion brings up all sorts of aspects that touch on individual consciences and fears. But the feeling of powerlessness predominates.

I drive back home with a Kosovar cardiologist who has started today with MSF. His name is Lullie. He tells me that as a refugee he was taken in by total strangers, ethnic Albanians. I can't see my Dutch countrymen doing that. When I ask whether Macedonians have also taken in Kosovars, he simply laughs. He then tells me of rumors that Yugoslavia wants to become a member of the Russian Federation.

Tuesday, 13 April

The taxi driver who drives me to the office holds forth in a monologue in broken German, French, and English — the lingua franca of all taxi drivers — about Greater Albania, Clinton, Lewinski, and the usual. He has worked for three years in Iraq. Yugoslavia built the military airfields there, which, of course, have now also been destroyed by American bombs. We drive past the wrecked station building where the clock on the front wall has remained stopped at the moment when the earthquake struck Skopje in 1963. I then leave for the Radusa refugee camp near the Yugoslav border. Or is it the Serbian border? Or soon just the Kosovar border? Time will tell.

The trip is breathtaking — through an empty, innocent landscape. There is a rusted railway line, a relic from the time when the iron mines were still being worked. Since then there has been an economic slump. Birds of prey circle above our heads. Suddenly we see the camp, a large number of tents set up without intervening spaces on the side of a mountain. Some 1,200 people are living on this patch of mud, far from the inhabited world. The camp is organized by the Macedonian government; it is guarded by police on all sides, and patients are not allowed to leave. We hold a clinic in a tent. There is a pregnant woman, a man with cancer, a boy with a bad knee who suffers from hemophilia, and a three-month-old baby with a scrotal hernia — all patients who should be taken away from here. But in fact everyone should be moved from here. The living conditions are unacceptable.

I make a short visit to the health post for the local people. There are hardly any facilities. No telephone, no ambulance, and hardly a laboratory. In the empty room that once housed the X-ray equipment hangs a portrait of Tito. Nothing now remains of his heritage: the workers' self-management, the movement of nonaligned countries, and the socialist Federal Republic of Yugoslavia. Shortly afterwards a gleaming Mercedes drives up. The Bulgarian ambassador comes to visit and makes all sorts of promises for medical facilities. Even Taiwan has already promised twenty-six doctors for the village, which will surely become the healthiest place in the world.

Afterwards I hold a clinic in Stenkovac. Some youths are burning a few pallets; somebody has a radio, and there is dancing. For a few moments they are back in Kosovo.

Wednesday, 14 April

Out in the sun and in the waterproof waiting room of the Out Patient Department, children are invited to make drawings. It only takes a few hours to have the whole wall covered with colorful pieces of art. A more detailed observation reveals destroyed houses, tanks, airplanes, and uniformed men with guns. Some children have included dead bodies. . . .

In the evening, seven buses packed with people arrive in the already overcrowded camp of Radusa. This is organized deportation at the end of the twentieth century in Europe — somewhere between Athens and Vienna. It is ethnic cleansing, and it is done because one has the wrong family name, religion, or language. Or just because of nothing. We try to perform some sort of triage. It is so unreal; it feels like we are on a film set surrounded by actors. If this were only the case. Using a satellite phone — the refugees are back in the stone age, but we have the latest sophisticated technology — we order 500 blankets and baby food, and within an hour they are brought to us by MSF logisticians from Skopje. Among the new refugees are three hemodialysis patients. Just across the border, Serbs have cleansed the nephrology department of a hospital. This is a de facto death sentence because, without medical care, they will die within a few days. And yet this is nothing unusual for the perpetrators, who without doubt will justify their terror by referring to it as an act of self-defense. They have also cleansed mental institutions, homes for elderly people, and institutions for the handicapped. The dialysis patients had to surrender all their documents; nothing but the shunt on their arms (for dialysis) can prove that they are indeed dialysis patients. It takes a lot of time to convince the camp police to let them go. Radusa is, after all, a prison — with no freedom of movement. The first thing the Macedonian doctors do, after we bring the patients to a hospital in Skopje, is to phone the police, rather than treating them directly. Not even seven years ago these patients were fellow countrymen; now they are treated like criminals.

Thursday, 15 April

There is an increase in stress-related pathology. Women stop breastfeeding and having their periods. Children start bedwetting again — though it is somewhat inappropriate to put it like that, since the children have no decent beds in the tents. There is a first suicide attempt. Another phenomenon is the process of hospitalization: people become disoriented to space and time. It is essential that daily activities are introduced and that the refugees cook for themselves, though this is logistically infeasible. It is important in a situation where one has lost so much to regain some minimum control over life.

In the evening I pick up a wounded child in Blace, the notorious piece of no-man's-land between Macedonia and Kosovo. Blace is a synonym for hell for most of the refugees. They all spent several nights there in the open among people who were dying. The Serbian border looks unreal because of the total silence. War never looks like you expect it to be. Ten years ago I visited this region as a tourist on my way to Austria; now I have to cross at least three new borders to get there. I never expected to return here under these conditions.

Back in Stenkovac another surprise is waiting for us. Angry Macedonian farmers, who oppose the camp, have diverted a nearby brook, and part of the camp is under the threat of inundation. Volunteers with sandbags have managed to turn the tide for the moment in a joint counterattack. One wonders if there is a limit to what people can do to each other — especially to vulnerable people who have already lost everything they had in life.

In front of the OPD a family with two young children is sitting in the cold. It is more and more difficult to accommodate newcomers. Already people are sleeping under plastic sheeting. The family crossed the border illegally on foot. The father tells me that his brother was killed in front of his eyes. Will it ever stop? No, it won't — not for the months to come.

Friday, 16 April

Should I bother the reader with today's patient? He is a survivor of the Racak massacre. His nose has been cut with a knife, his arms are covered with cigarette burns, and he was severely beaten on his testicles. I feel that there is so little I can do for him. One comforting point, however, is the integrated approach of MSF. Apart from doctors, there are mental health counselors, human rights specialists, and press officers. Each of these specialists is very much needed for such a patient.

The rest of the day we spend waiting for more buses. Our dedicated local staff, who work as translators, tell their own stories. They are in their twenties and about to graduate from the self-managed Kosovo University; they were denied access to the official Serbian University. This was equally true of the Serbian hospitals. This system of apartheid and parallel structures has been in place for more than ten years. It hardly received the world's attention.

The last patient of the day is a young mother who spent twelve days in the mountains. She kept her twin babies alive by breastfeeding. I think she deserves the Nobel Peace Price and all the medals in the world.

In the evening I write up this diary at the office. An icon hangs on the wall in front of me. To the right I look over the town of Skopje, rebuilt after the 1963 earthquake; to the left hangs a recent map of Europe. How will it look in ten years?

Blackbirds: Experiences of a Refugee Camp Worker

DAVID HOLDRIDGE

It is really something to see. The invasion of blackbirds over Pristina at dusk. They come in fast, thousands of them, and cause a great riot over the people going home. And then, just as fast, with last light, they disappear. Not far from the city is a vast field where they alight. On a rise in the field there has been for some time an inn, hammered together without much care. The inn has, typically, various heads and skins of game tacked to the boards, and the inn people will put big plates of mixed grill before you. Nick, our manager, brought me there last February, by which time he was feeding 400,000 displaced Kosovars. Catholic Relief Services (CRS) trucks pushed daily through two-thirds of the province. Steady Nick, a young man from Virginia, already with bags under his eyes, has taken to smoking and too much Turkish coffee. His office back in Pristina on Dragodan Hill, filled with smoke and the aroma of brewing coffee, is a war room. Maps cover the walls, and at the security briefings each morning wide-eyed expatriates and nationals sense the last act. It's dark when we leave. He takes me over to a chicken-wire pen, where a thin wolf paces. An attraction. Nearby is the monument to the Serb resistance against the Ottomans 600 years ago. In disrepair, with some paper blowing

---

This essay is an account of certain moments in the overall response of Catholic Relief Services to the crisis in Kosovo. It begins in February at the famous "Field of Blackbirds," which was the ancient battlefield where President Milosevic declared the end to Kosovar autonomy in 1989 — an event that, by February, had caused massive internal conflict in Kosovo and the displacement of Kosovars. It moves on to Blace, on the border of Macedonia, where thousands of Kosovar refugees were held back by the Macedonian government before it finally succumbed to Western pressure and allowed them into refugee camps within Macedonia. By June, camp life had somewhat stabilized, thanks primarily to the large open camp constructed in Cegrane and managed by CARE and to the more cooperative behavior of the Macedonian government. The last three episodes in the narrative recount the intimations of trouble ahead as we witness the Kosovars themselves involved in crimes against humanity; the rush of the return to Kosovo in mid-June as Milosevic capitulates, and to Prizren in particular, the CRS area of operations; and, finally, the return to Belgrade, where the uncertainty and despair continue today.

around it. Blackbirds sing and Nick smiles, a good Southern boy. Blackbird singing in the dead of night.

Six weeks later, toward the end of March, I am in the Belgrade archbishopric with Francis Xavier. In a back room with dark drapes and a thick rug we stand in a tight circle around a kerosene heater, still in our overcoats. Close by is an end table with a radio on it. The Archbishop and I are having a Perkovac, which burns slowly, right down to the belly. His own concoction, he tells us. He laughs again at that old joke as he moves his large hands over the heater and the radio and talks to us about how, as an old bishop, he is now welcoming heaven. But my boss and I think there is too much life in his eyes for that. Then the news starts and the three of us lean in. The Philadelphia Irishman and the Hartford Yankee hang on the news from the lips of Archbishop Perko. Red faced, we wait. Finally, at the end, Perko opens those great hands, palms up, and tells us that Holbrooke has failed.

Two weeks later, in early April, in the drizzle and the mud of Blace, there is the mess and waste of fifty thousand huddled at the Macedonian border under the flaps of plastic sheeting. And just across the line, the great klieg lights illuminating the fate of these poor souls for Western civilization. Faster than you can snap your fingers, from the trickle of rainwater through the tear in the plastic and onto the child — through the camera's eye to the living room in Philadelphia and Hartford. Nick is there, trying to ply through the chaos with provisions, his eyes now like red dots under the kliegs. The tractors from the Tetova farms are allowed through; they push into the mess with the CRS trailers behind. From inside, Jessica Pearl is talking to Nick, telling him that their batteries are gone. All around her are the long arms of supplicants: they need her phone. From Blace, in the muck of the early morning, they need to talk to their diaspora — a half million strong in Switzerland and Germany. There it is: the misery of this tribe locked at the border, amidst the babies' fevers and the diesel fumes, can be seen in the hundreds of huddled men around the phones that are not yet dead and the constant, tentative reach toward brown-eyed Jessica for a minute of her phone.

By the beginning of June, as Nick would say, the CRS camp in Macedonia was starting to fire on all eight. Then he'd stop himself, look over the mishmash of tents, and chuckle a bit. Well, how about on all seven? We had as many as 30,000 at Stankovec 1, a closed camp in refugee parlance. All that despair fenced in, on the edge of western Europe. And it was just too much to resist for those good hearts in the West: they would offer to fly in, on their own nickel, just to touch it. CNN had a permanent booth at the entrance; other networks roamed the inside of the perimeter. There were three choices of milk — whole, skim, and chocolate. Refugees put on weight. A free cell-phone service was established. Tony Blair came; Clinton came, and so did Hillary. Our press person, Nancy, created more electronic minutes on and for CRS than it had had during the previous fifty years of its existence. Yet, despite a general end in the intervening months to the mud and drizzle and the mad rush to put enough plastic over the victims of Milosevic — still, stewing in the dust on hot June days as the West came to touch you was no salve for what ached.

The mood shifted. "UCK" (US), in a scribble, began to proliferate across the tents. There was thanks for clear skies — because it meant good bombing. And finally, the anger would out. It would out after dark, when a dark rumor spread through the tents about a Roma refugee who had been seen with the necklace of a murdered Kosovar. They ran down the Roma family, ran them through the tents and the cook fires. The hundreds of shadows of the mob after the family of five. It produced heroes. For a while, the CRS managers Chris Hennemeyer, Ed Joseph, and Drew Hanson stood between the mob and the CRS Op center, where the family had fled. Then the the mob broke through — first through the gate, then smashing the front door down, and then down the hall to the latrine, where the Roma were hiding. Ed told me that they were trying to take the eleven-year-old's arm off when Hill arrived. Hill is special — and at that time and in that place, sacred — for what he is and what he represented to those ruined people. He talked the mob back and then away from the op center. The U.S. ambassador promised that America would get them home. He talked until the managers had got the Roma family beyond the fence and in a car to the hospital.

Think of it as an exodus, our resident priest told me afterward. A million driven out, scattered — so close they can sense, on the wind, their land. That was about a week before the return, but I didn't know it at the time and was in my drinks about the great divide between those who were in this soup and those who were on the periphery. The old complaints of the front. "Dave," said Father Bill, "this is biblical. Employees of CRS have to see it that way. They have to see it in terms of the Old Testament. They have to understand it as a deeper and more abiding story. If they are not seeing it as Exodus, then they are not understanding it. Nor their role in it."

A week later, in mid-June, it broke — so fast it left heads spinning. A million, in NATO's wake, on the road home. The tractors had never left Kukes (a mining town in northeastern Albania where hundreds of thousands of Kosovars had fled from the region around Prizren and Jacova and Pec in western Kosovo). The plastic from their shelters got wrapped around the belongings on the trailers. The family and the dozens of wild-eyed children with fingers in a V on top of the pile. Ignition. They were rolling down the Kukes-to-Prizren road, miles of them. From the wasteland of Kukes to the valley below.

For our man Phil in Albania and me it was a race to Sopi, the great humanist lodged in his Prizren residence with his wonderful sisters, the bishop of Catholic Albanians who never thought to leave. For Phil, the running fool, who had kept himself together during the dark days of Sarajevo by racing 10K's around the old Olympic track in the early morning hours, before the snipers on the surrounding mountains had slept off their booze — for him it was off the food lines at Kukes and into the 4-by-4 and onto the handsets that connected the fully loaded

Bedfords he was bringing down. And for the other return team from Macedonia, it was the early-morning wait at the border for NATO to give the go-ahead to push our food pipeline farther — from the port of Thessaloniki on the Adriatic to Prizren. It was sunlit. KFOR crowding the roads with their great trains of armor and ordnance. Young Serbian troops passing on the way north, who were also, strangely, waving to us: young men, undoubtedly, under a different impression. Fields yet to yellow, and everywhere the children, always with their fingers in a V.

The race to Bishop Sopi was not won that day. Phil was stuck in the tractors going down the mountain; and the Macedonia team was sitting in the capital, Pristina, waiting for an onward escort to the West. And Prizren was itself at the moment in turmoil. The Serb military was packing up, and the local Serb people were now enduring what they had long fought against: refugees themselves, cars packed overnight, the peddle down, they headed north in flight. The hunt for Serbs had begun. The next day, in the courtyard before the nineteenth-century church, cracked down the middle now, Phil and I met. But the bishop was absent. The man who had been in our hearts over the three months of bombing had gone out to his parishes. Phil and I waited under the locust tree, he looking askance at the renewal of my smoking, and I thinking that this guy could have been a general if he had gone the way of the military. Just before nightfall, the great man pulled in. He stepped from his car and saw us under the locust and raised his arms to the sky. We walked toward each other and our greeting was consummated in his great bearhug.

By August we were still saying that the last chapter would be in Belgrade; and for me and Richard, our expat manager in exile, it was. We finally had our entry visas for Yugoslavia, and now we were going back to CRS/Belgrade — to Jasmina and Velko and Jelko and Snezana, who had carried on our work in Belgrade during the hiatus. Serbs working for an American Catholic agency that delivered U.S. government foodstuffs to social cases all during the worst of it. "So put that in your pipe," I said to Richard from my seat on the roadside curb as he paced, peering into the guardroom every few minutes to see whether he could divine why they were so troubled with our visas. I was thinking about Sartre's fly in the soup. I mean, here we have been bombing them for almost three months, and now two eminent representatives of the West show up and profess kindness. And there was Velko, about a hundred meters down the road, waving like hell. With patience it was sorted out, and soon enough we were talking a mile a minute with Velko as we raced down an empty road to Belgrade. They were back in the arms of CRS, and Richard was out of exile.

To my sad eyes, the bombing was surely precise. As we traveled down the main streets in Belgrade, one fine block after another moved past. It's complete: the windows are in place; the utilities are hooked up; the stoop is swept. But then there is this slice — an empty space with rubble at the bottom. A slice between two whole buildings. Not to be profane, but like Santa, right down the chimney from fifteen thousand feet and off the map. No more folks or furniture at that address. And no casualties in the sky. It's the uncanny mix of the crushed skull and squashed body under the rubble and the electronic wizardry from above. Yes, so this is a thinly disguised purgative. It is trying to get the event out of the system or rather into the system. It is also a tribute to some Americans, mostly Catholic, who worked alongside a dozen nationalities in a visible and heartfelt rebuff to the current "by-bread-alone" attitudes of much of the American public.

Kosovo is a defining moment. Later it will be studied as such. Think of the issues that were being played out. The most obvious and talked about, of course, were the sovereignty/self-determination argument; the emerging U.S. foreign relations in the context of unchallenged American military supremacy; the future of the NATO and the global intrusion of Western values. But there were additional signs that the times are changing, more significant indicators of what's afoot. The klieg lights illuminating Blace; the cell phones connecting the refugees to their diaspora; the smart bombs illiminating addresses — signs of the greatest technological upheaval known to mankind thus far. Yet these lay over stories as old as the field of blackbirds and the hunt for the Roma. "Biblical," as Father Bill would say.

Endgame in Kosovo: Ethnic Cleansing and American Amnesia

MARK DANNER

1

Across this near-exhausted century, imagery recurs. The knock at the door, the mass evacuation, the forced march — expressions now impossible to hear without their attendant echoes:

> PRISTINA: The Albanian districts of the city have been pretty much emptied of their residents by now. Almost every home has been broken into, not even looted but simply destroyed.
>
> The streets are filled with the sound of heavy gunfire both day and night. . . . Everyone seems to be shooting. . . .
>
> I just interviewed the doctors who saw the body of the slain human-rights lawyer Bayram Klimendi. They said they could not confirm how many times he'd been shot because his body showed "bad and deep signs of maltreatment" — torture. . . .
>
> My friends in the outside world call and tell me to leave. God, I do want to get out of here. I can't stand it anymore. . . .
>
> But now it seems we have no choice. The knock on the door we had long feared has finally come. My family and I have been ordered to leave.
>
> There is no time to finish this report. We have to leave NOW. I don't know where. It seems I am about to join the ranks of the refugees I was writing about only a few days ago.
>
> Pray for me. Goodbye.[1]

---

1. See "The Knock on the Door: Letter from Pristina," by an anonymous correspondent. Global Beat Syndicate, New York University Center for War, Peace, and the News Media: www.nyu.edu/globalbeat/syndicate, April 1, 1998.

This article appeared in *The New York Review of Books* on April 7, 1999, two weeks into the Kosovo war.

One can envision the scene even as these words were hastily written: looming in the doorway heavily armed Interior Ministry troops — automatic weapons, long knives, red berets, woolen masks covering their faces. Even as the correspondent and his family drag their suitcases out the door, the men prod them with the muzzles of their rifles, hustling them as they stumble out into the packed street, there to join a great river of frightened people trudging in silence toward the railway station. They arrive to find scenes of unmitigated chaos: jammed coaches, mobbed platforms, vast crowds waiting for hours in fields around the building. Babies cry, the old and the sick moan. Each family's story is much the same:

> Then they were herded into passenger cars and livestock cars. Their money and their documents were stolen. . . .
>
> Before the trains departed . . . , Serbian troops joked bitterly that refugees were being given free train trips to Macedonia in exchange for their homes and belongings. . . .
>
> Enver Vrajolli, 25, an economics student, said he saw what happened to a neighbor in his sixties who refused to leave his house. He was shot.
>
> "We had only one choice: to leave or be killed. We chose to go," said Vrajolli. . . . "As we were leaving, [the city] was empty. There were only military forces and police left."
>
> "It was very horrible," Gjylizare Babatinca, 32, said as she described how her family was forced out of a house Wednesday by masked Serbs with automatic rifles. . . . "We were forced into the train cars they use for animals. We were packed tightly together. . . . It was completely dark, and we did not know where we were going."[2]

The historical echoes could not be stronger, of course, and indeed perhaps the main difference is that here the victims themselves could hear them: "You can't imagine what kind of silence there was as we walked through the streets of Pristina," one young woman said. "I thought Hitler's time was coming back, and we were going to some kind of Auschwitz."[3]

Such drawing of half-century parallels, of *the* parallel, derives in fact from a failure of memory. How much more comfortable to invoke Europe in the 1940s than Croatia and Bosnia in the 1990s, a mere few years ago. It is no accident that Serb forces — regular army soldiers, Interior Ministry specialists, and paramilitary marauders — were able to "cleanse" hundreds of thousands from Kosovo in a matter of days. For nearly a decade now, while Presidents George Bush and Bill Clinton and other Western leaders watched — while we watched — Slobodan

---

2. See John Daniszewski and Elizabeth Shogren, "With Refugees from Kosovo, Tales of Terror," *Los Angeles Times*, April 2, 1999, p. A5.

3. See Daniszewski and Shogren, "With Refugees from Kosovo, Tales of Terror."

Milosevic of Serbia, his Bosnian Serb henchman Dr. Radovan Karadzic, General Ratko Mladic, and various army and paramilitary commanders have been developing these techniques, refining them, perfecting them. From the well-documented stories of a great many cities and towns and villages, dating back to the cleansing of the Krajina of Croats during 1991 and 1992, one can extract a rough standard operating procedure:

1. *Concentration:* Surround the area to be cleansed and after warning the resident Serbs — urging them to leave or at least to mark their houses with white flags — intimidate the target population with artillery fire and arbitrary executions and then bring them out into the streets.
2. *Decapitation:* Execute political leaders and those capable of taking their places — lawyers, judges, public officials, writers, professors.
3. *Separation:* Divide women, children, and old men from men of "fighting age" — sixteen years to sixty years old.
4. *Evacuation:* Transport women, children, and old men to the border, expelling them into a neighboring territory or country.
5. *Liquidation:* Execute "fighting age" men, dispose of bodies.[4]

Too highly schematic to do justice to the Serbs' minute planning — for each town, each village, each situation is different — these five steps nonetheless comprise the elements of the program that worked for the Serbs from 1991 to 1995, the main years of the Yugoslav wars. Serb troops, both regular army and security forces, working closely with their savage paramilitary protégés, managed to "cleanse" more than 70 percent of Bosnian territory during a mere six weeks in the spring of 1992.

Percentages of Bosnians actually killed varied widely, partly according to the strategic value of the target. In Brcko, for example, which commands the critical and vulnerable "Posavina Corridor" linking the two wings of Bosnian Serb territory, Serb troops herded perhaps three thousand Bosnians into an abandoned warehouse, tortured them, and put them to death. At least some U.S. intelligence officials must have strong memories of Brcko:

> They have photographs of trucks going into Brcko with bodies standing upright, and pictures of trucks coming out of Brcko carrying bodies lying horizontally, stacked like cordwood. . . .[5]

4. For a description of the techniques of ethnic cleansing, see my earlier articles in *The New York Review of Books,* among them "America and the Bosnian Genocide," December 4, 1997; "Clinton, the UN, and the Bosnian Disaster," December 18, 1997; and "The Killing Fields of Bosnia," September 24, 1998, all three of which form part of a ten-part series.

5. Though "photographs of the bloodbath in Brcko remain unpublished to this day," this description comes from "an investigator working outside the U.S. government who has seen the pictures. . . ." See Charles Lane and Thom Shanker, "Bosnia: What the CIA Didn't Tell Us," *The New York Review of Books,* May 9, 1996, p. 10.

Similarly, pilots of American U-2 spy planes took photographs of the monumental "cleansing" operation General Ratko Mladic unleashed in and around Srebrenica during July 1995. An angry Madeleine Albright, then the U.S. representative to the United Nations, released the photographs to her colleagues — doing so long after anything could have been done for the men of Srebrenica but at a time when "the international community" had begun to show sympathy for the Krajina Serbs, whom the Croats were then expelling en masse from their homes.[6] Thus we are able now to gaze upon photographs of Bosnian men gathered in a field, guarded by Serb soldiers; then of the same field days later, its grass now disrupted by what appear to be newly dug and refilled mass graves.

Together with a videotape showing another group of Bosnian men sitting terrified at the feet of their Serb captors, and a relatively large number of survivors' accounts, we can now piece together the intricately planned and flawlessly executed minuet that allowed Gen. Mladic and his Serbs, in less than a week, to expel nearly twenty-five thousand women, children, and old people from Srebrenica and to murder and bury perhaps seven thousand "fighting age" men there.[7]

What cannot be overemphasized, both in Bosnia and now in Kosovo, is the planned rationality of this project, the mark of brutality routinized. Though many people were "indiscriminately" killed, tortured, beaten, and threatened, the process was anything but random. The first objective was to force the Muslim populations to flee their hometowns and create an ethnically pure Serb territory. A certain amount of immediate "demonstrative atrocity" was therefore deemed necessary. The more random and indiscriminate the terror and violence, the easier this goal would be achieved.

Imposition of terror, the more "indiscriminate" the better, breeds fear; fear breeds flight. Some there were, however, who would not be encouraged to flee:

> The second objective was to minimize possible future Muslim resistance. To the Yugoslav military, steeped in the Titoist tradition of territorial defense and people's war, every man was a potential fighter. Thus, men of military age were singled out for particularly brutal treatment. In Visegrad, one observer witnessed a paramilitary gunman announcing, "The women and children will be left alone. . . ." As for the Muslim men, he ran his finger across his throat.[8]

6. In August 1995, with Srebrenica's Muslims buried, Franjo Tudjman's Croats launched a lightning attack to retake the Krajina region and succeeded in "cleansing" the territory of perhaps 200,000 Serbs, most of whom belonged to families that had lived in the territory for centuries. It was, until recent weeks, the largest single act of ethnic cleansing of the war.

7. For an account of the Srebrenica operation, see my article "The Killing Fields of Bosnia," *The New York Review,* September 24, 1998, pp. 63-77.

8. See Jan Willem Honig and Norbert Both, *Srebrenica: Record of a War Crime* (New York: Penguin, 1996), pp. 75-76.

Today, as this plot is reinterpreted in the stories of refugees interviewed hard upon the Albanian and Macedonian borders — reinterpreted, that is, as *news* — we must struggle to remember that by now the stories could not be more familiar, and hence more predictable.[9]

Consider Selim Popei, for example, from the village of Bela Krusa, who on April 3 paused not far from the Albanian border to speak into the microphones and tell the world's television viewers how, at eight o'clock on March 25, the morning after the NATO planes started bombing, the Serb army tanks came and surrounded his village; how the Serb special police caught two hundred of the fleeing villagers; how from those they separated out forty-six men. For his part, Selim was sent over with the women: an old man, he had now become a witness:

> They killed five of my children. The youngest was thirteen, the oldest was forty-five. The others were thirty-two, twenty-two and eighteen. They killed my brother's sons too. I was about twenty steps away when I saw it with my own eyes. We all saw it, the women too.

And then Mehmet Krashnishi, who comes from Krusa Evolva, a tiny village next door. He appears younger than the others, even with the burns on his face and his hands heavily wrapped in white bandages. Early on the morning after NATO warplanes dropped their first bombs, he said, Serb troops came to his village.

> They rounded up all the villagers. They separated men from women. To the women they said, "You may go to the border," and they put us men in two big rooms. They said, "Now NATO can save you," and then they started to shoot. And when they finished shooting us they covered us with straw and corn and set it on fire. We were one hundred and twelve people. I survived with one other man.

Mehmet, reenacting a narrative familiar from the massacres at Srebrenica, collapsed and played dead as soon as the Serbs began shooting. He was burned in the fire, he said, but when the Serbs left to fetch more fuel to finish burning the bodies he managed to flee.[10]

Why, then, look to Auschwitz when Prijedor and Srebrenica and Brcko lie so much closer to hand? The answer is not far to seek.

9. At this writing it appears that the Serbs have so far limited their massacres of military-age men to villages and towns, while in Pristina and other cities they have been more selective, murdering politicians, human rights lawyers, and other members of the intelligentsia. In some cases they have detained large numbers of men in police stations and military barracks.

10. These stories are drawn from Christiane Amanpour's report, "Strike on Yugoslavia," broadcast on Cable News Network, April 3, 1999.

2

Endgame: we have finally stumbled into it, the confrontation the West has labored so long and so hard to avoid, the consequences of a politics of gesture. All the hesitations, hypocrisy, half-solutions, compromises, and wishful thinking on which Western, and above all American, policy have rested for nearly a decade — all stand revealed for what they are in the reality of those hundreds of thousands of people massed along the Macedonian and Albanian borders, deposited there with such efficiency by Slobodan Milosevic, the great peacemaker of Dayton.

Under the pressure of such events, memories of high officials flicker, grow dim. Consider Lawrence Eagleburger, George Bush's former secretary of state and perhaps the dominant American official during the first months of Yugoslavia's implosion, who wrote, on Day Ten of the bombing:

> When the Yugoslav Federation began to break up . . . and the first signs of ethnic strife became apparent, the Bush Administration took a relatively hard look at what to do. We had no illusions about the fact that to have an effect would mean involving several hundred thousand ground troops, and for better or worse we decided that it was a swamp into which we did not want to walk. NATO may no longer feel it has that choice; if so, it is vital that those who make the decisions take as realistic a view as we did as to what intervention would entail.[11]

It is almost impossible not to admire the artistry here, the rhetorical subterfuges so densely interwoven and blithely deployed — from preventative shilly-shallying ("a relatively hard look," "for better or worse") to dubious and self-justifying opinion masked as inarguable conclusion ("would mean involving several hundred thousand ground troops") to illogical severing of present difficulties from past mistakes ("NATO may no longer feel it has that choice") — as if Mr. Eagleburger had nothing to do with the "realistic view" that "those who [now] make the decisions" found themselves forced to take.

Of the half-dozen or so opportunities that "the international community" had to avert and then to halt the violence in the former Yugoslavia, at least two — and those with the lowest potential cost — came during the administration of Mr. Eagleburger's former boss, the "foreign policy president," George Bush. At least from September 1990, when the CIA issued a "National Intelligence Estimate" predicting that "the Yugoslav experiment has failed, that the country will break up" and that "this is likely to be accomplished by ethnic violence and unrest which could lead to civil war,"[12] Eagleburger and others knew the war was coming, and

11. See Lawrence S. Eagleburger, "NATO, in a Corner," *The New York Times*, April 2, 1999, section 4, p. 11.

12. See David Binder, "Yugoslavia Seen Breaking Up Soon," *The New York Times*, November 28, 1990, p. A7.

for a number of reasons — including the victory in the Gulf War and a strong reluctance to endanger the political benefits it brought — they undertook no serious
diplomatic effort to prevent it.

When, on the very eve of Yugoslavia's breakup, in late June 1991, Secretary of
State James A. Baker III's one-day "flying visit" failed to solve the problem — the
use of force had already been taken explicitly, and quite unnecessarily, off the table
— Baker returned to Washington, licked his wounds, and uttered the now-famous
dictum: "We've got no dog in this fight." The wisdom of this homely judgment is
now clear for all to judge. President Bush unceremoniously handed off the Yugoslav problem to the Europeans, who, pleased to be granted such an important task,
declared (in the words of Luxembourg's foreign minister) that "this is the hour of
Europe." "Europe," unfortunately, discovered it had no military — America's retreat from the field had removed the NATO alliance as a factor — and thus was
forced to negotiate while lacking any powers of coercion.

By the fall of 1991, as the Serbs prosecuted bloody artillery sieges on the
Croatian cities of Vukovar and Dubrovnik, the Europeans' diplomatic effort had
clearly failed. President Franjo Tudjman of Croatia begged the Americans to send
the Sixth Fleet on a "sail-by" of Dubrovnik which might, he thought, warn the
Serbs off. General John Galvin, the Supreme Allied Commander in Europe, prepared plans, which could have included "clearing the Serb gunboats off the water,"
but Washington declined to go forward, unsure what the Serbs' response would be.
Said Eagleburger:

> They "might" have gotten the message. They might also not have gotten the mes-
> sage and then we would be faced with the question of what to do next.

This is a rather puzzling attitude, as Wayne Bert writes in *The Reluctant Superpower:*

> Eagleburger seemingly had no misgivings about the value of American credibil-
> ity unless some overt threat was made for which there was no follow-through.
> Complete inaction, in his view, did not compromise U.S. credibility.[13]

And complete inaction, of course, did not pose the terrible risks that action
did; for if in the case of any forceful action, even a warning, the United States could
have no guarantee the Serbs would be deterred, and since, if they were not, the administration would be obliged to take another action to see that they were (for to
do less would be to destroy American credibility) — well then, by definition, to act

---

13. Wayne Bert, *The Reluctant Superpower: United States Policy 1991-95* (New York: St.
Martin's, 1997), p. 19; see my "The US and the Yugoslav Catastrophe," *The New York Review,* November 20, 1996, pp. 56-64, for a full treatment of this period.

at all risked losing all control of American policy. Under this odd logic, even the slightest warning, or the refusal to take the use of force "off the table," virtually equals a slide down a "slippery slope" to the use of Eagleburger's "several hundred thousand ground troops."

Missing from this calculus, of course — leaving aside the highly questionable assumption that only ground troops might have halted the war at this point, before fighting broke out in Bosnia — is any notion that the war in Yugoslavia should be prevented or stopped, that the prosecution of a brutal war in post–Cold War Europe might somehow be harmful to American interests: that inaction, in a word, might hold its own severe risks. On this point Secretary Eagleburger, a former ambassador in Belgrade who had known Slobodan Milosevic there, was quite emphatic:

> I have said this 38,000 times and I have to say this to the people of this country as well. This tragedy is not something that can be settled from outside and it's about damn well time that everybody understood that. Until the Bosnians, Serbs, and Croats decide to stop killing each other, there is nothing the outside world can do about it.[14]

Eagleburger believed that the war could be — indeed must be — left to "burn itself out." The war's continuance posed a risk, apparently, only to the people "killing each other" — itself a remarkably misleading and harmful characterization coming from a high American official, since by then no one could doubt that, though all sides had committed atrocities, the Serbs, who were using "ethnic cleansing" as their main technique of war, had committed the overwhelming number. Rape, massacre, deportation — these were not regrettable by-products of the fighting but actions intrinsic to achieving the Serbs' territorial objectives.

3

The war did not burn itself out. Indeed, it was in implicit recognition that it might not that Lawrence Eagleburger, by then secretary of state for a lame-duck George Bush, chose in late 1992 to send Slobodan Milosevic and his military commander the so-called "Christmas Warning," advising that "in the event of conflict in Kosovo caused by Serbian action, the United States will be prepared to employ military force against the Serbs in Kosovo and in Serbia proper." Croatia and Bosnia could burn and smolder for years, and did; Kosovo, bordered by Macedonia and Albania, was deemed to be the geopolitical limit, the "red line," as a

---

14. Quoted in "Method to the Madness," *Decision Brief* (Center for Security Policy, Washington, DC), October 2, 1992, p. 3.

Clinton official later called it. If Eagleburger or other Bush officials even suspected that their refusal to commit resources of any sort, political or military, to stop Milosevic in Croatia or Bosnia might lead him to doubt their determination to prevent him taking what action he pleased in Kosovo — which, after all, remained Yugoslav territory — they showed no sign of it.[15]

For Governor Bill Clinton, campaigning against the "foreign policy president," Bosnia and the atrocities being committed there had served as a superb issue; for President Bill Clinton, struggling to enact a tax bill and other controversial domestic programs, Bosnia represented a black hole that threatened to swallow his administration. As a candidate he had uttered bold words threatening the Serbs with bombing; as president he limited his boldness to scuttling the "Vance-Owen plan," the peace proposal then on the table, which he criticized as not "going far enough" in reversing the Serb war gains, and then blamed his failure to attack the Serbs from the air on the recalcitrance of the European allies, whose troops were on the ground in Bosnia escorting food convoys to besieged civilians.

And so, beneath the great welter of diplomatic activity, the matter essentially rested until the summer of 1995, when the Serbs seized Srebrenica, which had been designated, in a policy strongly advocated by then U.N. Representative Albright, a U.N.-protected "safe area." The Americans, however, had been unwilling to commit troops; the bedraggled city was defended only by a few hundred Dutch "blue helmets." In their concern for the safety of those peacekeepers, the Europeans blocked air attacks, the only way possible to save the city. Shortly before Srebrenica was overrun, a Bosnian Muslim soldier showed a Dutch U.N. "blue helmet" a simple formula he had written on a sheet of paper meant to show the true value the "international community" placed on human life: "30 UN = 30,000 Bosnians."[16]

In Srebrenica, no U.N. soldier died at the hands of the Serbs; seven thousand Bosnian men did. The savagery and humiliation of Srebrenica, together with the pressures of the coming U.S. presidential election and Clinton's belated realization that if the Europeans decided to withdraw their troops from Bosnia, as they now threatened to do, he would be obliged, because of his own pledge, to commit U.S. troops to help extract them — all of these, in late August 1995, led NATO to send its warplanes at last to bomb the Serbs.

Three months later, Slobodan Milosevic sat at the peace table at Wright-

15. See David Binder, "Bush Warns Serbs Not to Widen War," *The New York Times*, December 28, 1992. Mr. Eagleburger's recent statement that "NATO may no longer feel it has [the] choice" to avoid intervening in Kosovo seems further evidence that the "Christmas Warning," however uncompromising its language, had hardly been a firm commitment to "employ military force."

16. See David Rhode, *Endgame: The Betrayal and Fall of Srebrenica, Europe's Worst Massacre since World War II* (New York: Farrar, Straus and Giroux, 1997), p. 68.

Patterson Air Force Base in Dayton, Ohio. He had come, many American officials believed, because "the bombing had worked." He had come because the tide had turned against his Bosnian Serb protégés; because Franjo Tudjman's American-supported Croatian army had driven the Serbs out of Krajina, whch they had occupied during the war's first days; because under the umbrella of their new NATO air force the Croats and Bosnians had fought and begun to win on the ground — and Milosevic had come, finally, because he knew the time had arrived to make a deal and to reap all the international prestige as "peacemaker" that would come with it.

4

As had the Yugoslav wars, the Dayton peace sprang from the forehead of Slobodan Milosevic, the architect of Greater Serbia, the man who had built his power by inciting and exploiting Serb nationalism. Milosevic would now be the "acceptable" representative of Dr. Radovan Karadzic and his Bosnian Serb associates; he "brought them along," guaranteed their compliance. When the foreign troops arrived in Bosnia to enforce the agreement, his intelligence agencies provided information about the movements and intentions of Muslim and Serb "terrorists" — an indispensable service for the American military especially, whose first priority, because of the lack of political support for the mission at home, was to avoid casualties.

As Milosevic could not have failed to see, this priority would make of Dayton a "cold peace," an agreement that would put an end to the fighting but would show little success in reversing ethnic cleansing or in punishing its most notorious practitioners. Clinton, in one of the more eloquent speeches of his presidency, had explained to Americans why he must send their sons or daughters to Bosnia. Still, approval ratings stayed low; his audience remained unconvinced. Given such inescapable realities, American officials sadly concluded, as they had in Haiti the year before, that the loss of even one soldier might threaten the mission. (Who could forget Mogadishu or the perils of "mission creep"?) Certainly they did not intend to risk American troops to capture Karadzic or Mladic or to escort refugees back to their homes.

And so it was left. The peace of Dayton was a half-peace. The Bosnian people were left with half a country, a quasi-protectorate. Though at the start of each of the first two years that American troops were stationed in Bosnia, President Clinton had twice promised they would be home in twelve months, he did not keep his promises, nor has he renewed them; for Clinton well knows that if American soldiers go home, so will Europeans, and that without either, Dayton — fragile as it remains — will surely collapse.

Milosevic, meantime, saw the men he had created, Karadzic and Mladic, marginalized and named as criminals while he attained an importance to the West none could have imagined even months before. At home, however, he confronted an economy destroyed by sanctions and war and a political world that seemed to be closing tightly around him. Having bid a humiliating goodbye to Slovenia when it declared its independence in 1991; having fought a bloody war over the Croatian land of Krajina and then watched Franjo Tudjman's tanks, three years later, sweep through and cleanse it of its two hundred thousand Serb residents; having seen the Dayton Accords make of the Republika Srpska an unworkable parastate built of stolen land and mass graves; having watched his last republican allies, the Montenegrins, vote into office an unsympathetically liberal government — having watched all this from his darkened Belgrade palace now become the heart of a shrunken, imploding Yugoslavia, was it not perfectly natural that Slobodan Milosevic would return to the scene of his greatest triumph, the Serb holy land of Kosovo?

5

How appropriate, then, that Kosovo should be the scene of the endgame, the confrontation that Slobodan Milosevic himself helped the West to escape in Bosnia. For Kosovo was not only the Serb leader's political birthplace, where he had traveled in 1987 to declare to resentful Serbs (who by then comprised scarcely one in ten Kosovo residents) that the Kosovar Albanians "shall no longer dare to beat you!" — Kosovo was also where George Bush had drawn the "red line" on Christmas Day 1992, recognizing implicitly that however many people "killed each other" in Bosnia and Croatia, only "conflict in Kosovo" — beyond the red line — would so severely threaten American interests as to demand that the U.S. "employ military force." Four months later, Clinton's secretary of state, Warren Christopher, was rather more explicit:

> We fear that if the Serbian influence extends into [Kosovo or Macedonia], it will bring into the fray other countries in the region — Albania, Greece, Turkey. . . . So the stakes for the United States are to prevent the broadening of that conflict to bring in our NATO allies, and to bring in vast sections of Europe, and perhaps, as happened before, broadening into a world war.[17]

One might have expected a matter of such magnitude to have occupied a central place on the peace table at Dayton, and yet, though the Americans, according to Richard Holbrooke, "repeatedly emphasized to Milosevic the need to re-

17. See Stephen Engelberg, "Weighing Strikes in Bosnia, US Warns of Wider War," *The New York Times,* April 25, 1993.

store the rights of Kosovo's Albanian Muslims, which he had revoked [in 1989],"
the accords ignored Kosovo. The Americans were in a hurry: they needed a Bosnia
agreement, only Milosevic could deliver it to them, and he knew it; and he would
brook no diplomatic meddling in what was unquestionably "Serb land."

To say that at Dayton "the long-feared crisis in Kosovo was postponed, not
avoided,"[18] as Holbrooke does, does not go far enough; for the fact that the peacemakers, in "solving" Bosnia, ignored Kosovo dealt a severe blow to the prestige of
Dr. Ibrahim Rugova, then the nonviolent "leader" of the Albanian "shadow republic" in Kosovo. Rugova, writes Noel Malcolm,

> had spent four years telling his people, in effect, that they must be patient until
> the international community imposed a final settlement on ex-Yugoslavia, in
> which their interests would also be respected. But that settlement . . . left the Al-
> banians of Kosovo exactly where they were.[19]

Very quickly Rugova would find his political primacy challenged by the leaders of the Kosovo Liberation Army [. . .] an organization American officials described publicly, and until very recently, as "terrorist."

Scarcely a year ago, Milosevic began responding, as was his custom, by sending his security forces and policemen to storm those villages where the guerrilla
presence seemed strongest — and to massacre anyone they found. [. . .] It seemed,
however, that the red line had begun to fade; Clinton officials now spoke not of
warplanes and tanks but of "using every appropriate tool we have at our command" and making "the Serb economy . . . head further South."[20]

In May, Richard Holbrooke managed to persuade Milosevic for the first time
to meet with Rugova; then the Clinton Administration brought the pacificist
leader to Washington to "increase his international prestige." It was a significant
achievement — or would have been, had not American diplomacy already been
overtaken by the reality on the ground, as Milosevic's men went on murdering civilians, sending tens of thousands fleeing into the mountains. Under these conditions the "terrorist" KLA had decisively seized the political initiative.

Throughout the summer of 1998, the Americans and their Western allies
struggled to negotiate a Kosovo agreement but were confounded both by
Milosevic's intransigence and by the Russians' insistence that the matter should be
handled under the auspices of the United Nations (where the Russians, increasingly concerned about the West's exclusion of them from Balkan diplomacy, could
have made use of their veto to protect their Serb allies). Only in October would

18. See Richard Holbrooke, *To End a War* (New York: Random House, 1998), p. 357.
19. See *Kosovo: A Short History* (New York: New York University Press, 1998), p. 353.
20. See "US Warns of 'Serious Action' against Belgrade on Kosovo," *Agence France-Presse,*
March 4, 1998, and "U.S. State Department Press Briefing," March 5, 1998.

Richard Holbrooke manage to negotiate a "unilateral" deal with Milosevic in which the Serb leader recognized Kosovo as a legitimate "international" issue; agreed to permit an "air reconnaissance regime" over the territory; and pledged to admit to Kosovo two thousand "unarmed observers."

Perhaps it would have worked had they been armed peacekeepers, but this Holbrooke had not even proposed. Milosevic would, of course, have resisted an armed force, whatever it was called; more important, President Clinton, who would have had to contribute American troops to any such mission, felt himself too weakened by the impeachment scandal even to contemplate asking Congress or the public to approve it. Still, Holbrooke's October agreement saved many lives: for a time Milosevic's forces withdrew, and tens of thousands of civilians were brought down from the mountains.

But as Milosevic's forces moved out, in many areas KLA fighters moved in. And on January 15, Serb interior ministry troops stormed the village of Racak. Even as the operation unfolded, a Serb deputy prime minister was ordering the Kosovo police commander to "go in heavy."[21] Arriving in Racak the following day, Kosovo Verification Mission investigators would find:

> 1 adult male shot in the groin. He appeared to have been shot while running away.
> 3 adult males shot in various parts of their body including their backs. . . .
> 1 adult male killed outside his house. The top of his head had been removed and was found approximately 15 feet away from his place of death. The wound appeared to have been caused by an axe. . . .
> 5 adult males shot through the head.
> 1 adult male shot outside his house with his head missing. . . .
> 1 adult male shot in the head and decapitated. All the flesh was missing from the skull.
> 1 adult female shot in back. . . .[22]

And so on. The Serbs had "gone in heavy." Forty-five were dead.

6

From the bloody village of Racak to the elegant castle of Rambouillet: here the French held a farcical gathering complete with all the trappings of a grand diplomatic conference — Secretary of State Albright and her staff, her Western counter-

21. See Julius Strauss, "Massacre Evidence Mounts Against Milosevic," *Sunday Telegraph,* January 31, 1999.
22. See "Massacre of Civilians in Racak," Kosovo Verification Mission, January 17, 1999.

parts, various guerrilla leaders of the KLA. The two most important seats, however, were empty. No high-ranking NATO military leader attended, and neither did Slobodan Milosevic. Western leaders made their demands: Milosevic must withdraw most of his troops from Kosovo; must accept 28,000 armed peacekeepers (4,000 of them American); and must agree to a three-year transition to Kosovo's autonomy. If he did not accept these conditions by the end of the conference, the West would bomb Serbia. President Clinton vowed not to let the deadline pass, then did. Western leaders again threatened bombing, then seemed surprised that Milosovec didn't give in. Finally, caught in their own ultimatum, they were forced to send their warplanes, and this time without Croatian tanks or Bosnian infantry to fight for them on the ground.

All the while, it is now clear, Slobodan Milosevic was preparing his vast operation in Kosovo. In a long career, this would be his masterpiece, cleansing the Serb homeland of its Albanian interlopers in a matter of weeks. This should, again, have come as no surprise: as late as February, George Tenet, the director of Central Intelligence, had predicted in public testimony that Milosevic would do precisely this.[23]

As I write, the refugees keep coming, the bombs go on falling, in Washington the talk grows of dispatching ground troops. Though Milosevic may be trying to overthrow the Montenegrin government, though Macedonia is dangerously swollen with refugees, we hear less now of the "red line" or of the geostrategic importance of Kosovo. Matters, at last, have come to appear simpler than that: American officials, if they wish to consider themselves "leaders" in the "most successful military alliance in history," are obliged to accept the reality of Bosnia and now of Kosovo — that in a country bordering a NATO member, soldiers shelled cities packed with defenseless civilians; paramilitary troops raped, tortured, mutilated, murdered; troops took away many young men who have not reappeared. All of this happened under the eyes of American leaders; all of it was quite well known at the time, or very shortly afterward. And it happened, and is happening, in Europe, America's strategic "backyard."

That these events were allowed to unfold, and so soon after Germans tore down the Berlin Wall, says something about America. Not only is the world's great liberal power, with all its might, unwilling, as we are so often told, to serve as "the policeman of the world" — even on territory where every precept of *Realpolitik* would suggest it should — but the idealist values that were proudly assumed to be a vital part of America's vision of itself as a democratic power in the world, and that American leaders so often hailed during the Cold War, appear suddenly dessicated and pale. Whatever happens in the coming weeks — whether Western leaders order their troops to fight in the Balkans, or Slobodan Milosevic holds

23. See Craig R. Whitney (with Eric Schmitt), "NATO Had Signs Its Strategy Would Fail Kosovars," *The New York Times*, April 1, 1999, p. A1.

onto Kosovo and a reluctant West accepts the Kosovars — the ugly history that led up to this bloody impasse has not been confronted. Will Americans recognize this? What conclusions will they draw? These are the questions posed by Kosovo's future, and our own.

The Milosevic Generation

BLAINE HARDEN

In the cafe at Tennis Club Max, not far from where American cruise missiles shredded Slobodan Milosevic's house, a law student explained the secrets of being certifiably crazy in Serbia. "My final diagnosis from the army, the one they stamped on my passport, says I am a paranoid depressive," he said proudly.

As Serbs with racquets thwacked away a humid Balkan afternoon on clay courts in front of our table, the law student told me how his finest moment of make-believe madness, what he called "my extraordinary performance," had helped him to escape the war in Kosovo.

Unlike Serbia's previous lost wars in the former Yugoslav republics of Slovenia, Croatia, and Bosnia, which the law student saw coming months in advance, the Kosovo conflict broke out too quickly for him to make his usual preparations. In the past, he had left his shoulder-length hair unwashed for weeks. In a well-chosen uniform of rubber gardening boots, worn-out pants, and ragged sweaters, he muttered obscenities, spoke of suicide, and cried uncontrollably. The Yugoslav Army psychiatrists were impressed: on six separate occasions, they exempted him from service.

In the spring, when NATO began bombing and Yugoslav Army recruiters came sniffing after conscripts again, the law student had no time to grow a convincing head of nut-case hair. Working with his parents, the law student, who is 26 years old and not nearly crazy enough to allow his name to appear in this magazine, came up with Plan B. His mother called for an ambulance from Lazar Lazarevic Psychiatric Hospital (where the chairman, insanely enough, is Milosevic's wife, Mirjana Markovic). She said her son was once again acting odd. Meanwhile, in his bedroom in the house where he still lives with his parents, the law student sprawled out on the floor beneath a window, and his father smashed it to pieces. While the family waited for the ambulance, both parents sprinkled shards of glass on their son's head. He was whisked off to the hospital, where — refusing to speak to doctors or nurses — he spent the Kosovo war taking antidepressant pills, hiding them under his tongue, and spitting them out in the bathroom.

While the law student whispered his story to me, a prominent surgeon, from a Serbian family that has produced doctors for generations, sat down at the table next to us. He had come to Tennis Club Max to watch his seven-year-old daughter take lessons. The surgeon had time on his hands. Taking advantage of United Nations sanctions imposed during the Bosnian war, he had put down his scalpel six years ago and become a gasoline smuggler. It was an excellent move. The government pays doctors about $140 a month; gasoline smugglers with government connections make many thousands of dollars a month. The surgeon has made so much money that he no longer smuggles. He plays tennis instead.

A bit later in the afternoon, after the law student had left, Radovan (Rade) Markovic sat down in the same chair to wait for his regular doubles match. He arrived with ten thick-necked, skinheaded young men carrying automatic weapons. They staked out the perimeter of the tennis club, whispered into radios, hid behind trees. Markovic, a short, beefy man with a steel-gray crewcut, is the head of state security and a protégé of Milosevic's wife (but no relation to her). Besides being the country's top spy master, Markovic commands state paramilitary forces that helped lead the campaign of murder, theft, and house-burning in Kosovo that war crimes investigators say killed at least 11,000 Kosovar Albanians. American officials say he is likely to be indicted by the War Crimes Tribunal in the Hague, but Markovic has not allowed this unpleasantness to rattle his tennis game. Throughout the three-month Kosovo war and on into this summer, he played at Tennis Club Max as much as weather permitted. The weather, however, has been rough.

All summer, the rain punished Belgrade. Thunderstorms rolled over the city night after night, flooding homes, washing away cars, and ruining the clay courts at Tennis Club Max. The booming storms kept Serbs awake, making them feel as helpless and hunted as on those spring nights when American missiles were picking apart government buildings. By midsummer, with the storms still pounding the city, it was widely rumored that the American Government was orchestrating the rain.

I found Tennis Club Max through Helena Zdravkovic, whose father owns the place and plays doubles regularly with Markovic, the state security boss. Helena drives a Mercury Capri convertible with expired Florida plates, but the police let her get away with it. They seem to know whom her father plays tennis with. Belgrade is that kind of town. Welcome to the capital of Serbia, where bureaucrats with bodyguards and blood on their hands have become private-club swells, where middle-class professionals have been forced to choose between penury or criminality, where feigned lunacy is a sane way to stay safe.

Four lost wars, international isolation, and gangster economics have combined to make Belgrade especially cruel to the young people who have come of age during the twelve-year reign of Milosevic. The city has descended into its own sad, slacker category among major European capitals. It's a metropolis where hard work, professional excellence, and saving for the future are wastes of time.

This is the Milosevic generation. Unemployed or stuck in jobs that usually pay less than $100 a month, young Serbs between the ages of 18 and 30 typically live with their parents, spend nearly all their money on night life, postpone marriage, avoid parenthood, and put off plans for the future — except to get out of the country. Estimates of the number of university-trained young people who have fled the city since 1990 range from 100,000 to 300,000. That's a catastrophic drain of talent and skills from a nation where in 1991 just 622,000 people in a population of 10 million had more than a high-school education. This summer even the option of running away has run out. The war in Kosovo forced most Western countries to close their embassies in Belgrade, making obtaining visas far more difficult.

"Delayed gratification is what the whole civilized world is based on, but in Belgrade, it makes no sense," says Svetlana Logar-Djuric, a prominent psychologist at the University of Belgrade and the mother of an 18-year-old son. She has spent several years researching, among other things, the lives of Belgrade's smart set — those whose professional parents had, as late at the mid-1980's, constituted the only well-paid, widely traveled middle class in the Communist bloc.

"For young people here, it makes sense to be depressed," she says. "Many go to bed at 4 o'clock in the morning and sleep all day. They don't see a point in growing up to become responsible adults. The city teaches them to be helpless." Her own son, Jovan, scolds her for having wasted her time working long hours to earn a Ph.D. He has a point. Her university job pays approximately $100 a month, and the money always arrives several months late.

"If you are a criminal, you are, like, cool," Jovan said one afternoon as we sat with his mother and four of his high-school friends in their Belgrade apartment so choked with cigarette smoke that it was difficult to see across the cramped living room. (Jovan and his friends were all chain-smokers.) "You can't blame anyone for being a criminal. I have respect for those who have the will to do what they want. Life in the fast lane — how can that not be attractive?" His friends' heads bobbed in agreement.

Burglary, for instance, is one of the few promising career paths for savvy young Serbs. Home is where the money is — about $2.5 billion, according to the Yugoslav Association of Banks. In the Milosevic era, it's much less risky to hide money in a mattress than to deposit it in a bank. The regime has seized the hard-currency savings accounts of most private depositors — about $4.1 billion in the last decade. The regime also tacitly encourages the young to consider careers in car theft. The streets of Belgrade are filled with gleaming late-model cars that have no license plates. They are driven by mean-looking young men and are often ignored by the police. For the past two years, the Government has offered a month-long amnesty to car thieves, allowing them to register any car, even one that is obviously hot, in order to raise money from licensing fees. Many of the vehicles have been swiped by gangsters and paramilitary thugs from other republics in the former Yugoslavia, as well as from Western Europe.

73

As much as Jovan and his friends were mesmerized by life in Belgrade's fast lane, they saw dark motives behind the West's bombing of their city. They told me that the reasons for the war were: American fear of a united Europe, the desire of the military-industrial complex to use up its old Bombs, and multinational corporate hunger for Serbia's mineral wealth. As for war crimes, Jovan and his friends told me to get real.

"It was war," Jovan said. "As much as Serbs did something bad, so did the Albanians."

Besides the streets flooded by unrelenting rains, the conspiracy theories, the stolen cars and the 20-somethings who were morbidly depressed, Belgrade was drowning in denial. Some of it was merely the posturing of a defeated demagogue, as state-controlled television insisted in late June that Serbia had won the war. At a time when about 35,000 NATO troops had occupied Kosovo and when Kosovar Albanians, bent on revenge, were harassing, ripping off, and murdering Kosovar Serbs, Milosevic's minions were announcing what every sentient Serb knew to be a lie: "Our country's territorial integrity and sovereignty have been defended," Momir Bulatovic, the Yugoslav Prime Minister, said in parliament.

More fundamental and more pernicious was the denial that bubbled up in conversation this summer with well-educated young people in Belgrade. Almost without exception, they could not bring themselves to admit that atrocities had been committed in their name. Even as war-crimes investigators were digging up mass graves in Kosovo, they refused to concede what was obvious to the rest of the world: Serb forces had committed crimes against humanity on a scale and with an organized savagery that was grossly disproportionate to the threat posed by ethnic Albanians.

The people of Belgrade, about a fifth of Serbia's 10 million people and 40 percent of its college-educated population, were far less upset at the bestial way in which the war was fought than by the fact that Milosevic had compounded their poverty and isolation by losing it.

I first started coming to Belgrade as a reporter in 1990, as Yugoslavia was beginning to come apart. On the first day I set foot in the country, I had the dubious privilege of spending several hours sitting next to Milosevic, listening to a windy lecture about wronged Serbian greatness, unable to get a question in edgewise and trying not to stare at his exceptionally big ears. He struck me then not as a nationalist zealot, but as an opportunist, scrambling to save himself from the fate of other Communist thugs from across the former East bloc. In 1989, most of them had been tossed out of office, jailed, or, in the case of Romanian dictator Nicolae Ceausescu and his Stalinist and much-hated wife, Elena, lined up against a wall and machine-gunned to death. Milosevic, incidentally, also has a Stalinist, much-hated wife.

The Serbian leader dodged this bullet by hiding behind nationalism and exploiting his republic's fear of foreign domination. The splintering of Yugoslavia in the early 1990s, which left about two million Serbs outside of Serbia, gave

Milosevic an excuse for using violence to change borders and protect his people. Then a swaggering nationalist regime in Croatia bullied Serbs and handed him an even better rationale for war. When there were no facts to justify Serbian paranoia, Milosevic used state television to manufacture them. He showcased a grisly procession of mutilated corpses. They were introduced to viewers as the bodies of innocent Serbs slaughtered by Croats or Bosnian Muslims or Kosovar Albanians. It worked. After the evening news, calls often flooded into spouse-abuse hot lines in Belgrade, as wives screamed that their husbands were beating them up.

Milosevic used nationalism as a kind of Orwellian Victory Gin. It intoxicated the masses and blurred their vision as everyone around Milosevic — his son, his ministers, and his paramilitary henchmen — got rich off smuggling and war profiteering.

The final pillar of Milosevic's nationalism was murder — of civilians whose sole crime was not being Serbian. I stayed in Sarajevo during the worst of the Serbian siege of the Bosnian capital. It was a barbaric exercise in which Serbs in the surrounding hills used artillery and sniper fire to randomly murder tens of thousands of people, most of them unarmed civilians. I remember being bounced out of bed by shells that struck apartment buildings near the pension where I was trying to sleep. The silence after an explosion was often broken by the screams of people discovering that their children or their parents had been blown to pieces. I visited these shattered apartments and once, after leaving, found a bit of human flesh sticking gumlike to my shoe.

But it never occurred to me in the early part of this decade that the Serbs of Belgrade were collectively responsible for these and other horrors perpetrated by the Milosevic regime. Far from it, Belgrade was for me an intellectual and cultural oasis in the ruins of Yugoslavia. Tito's brand of Communism had allowed Belgrade's middle class to become far more affluent and Westernized — from foreign travel and foreign investment, from a hybrid economy that mixed socialism with private enterprise, from a flood of foreign movies, books, and music — than residents of any other capital in eastern Europe.

Until the war in Bosnia began in 1992, Belgrade had been the destination city in the East bloc for young Poles, Czechs, and Hungarians seeking to be cool. It teemed with outspoken politicians, well-informed journalists, and insightful academics — not to mention beautiful women, smart nightclubs, and excellent restaurants.

Milosevic was a curiously tolerant dictator. As long as he controlled television, he allowed the intelligentsia to fuss and fume against his regime in their low-circulation magazines. That tolerance dried up after mass demonstrations in the winter of 1996-1997 nearly brought down his regime. Milosevic imposed draconian laws that all but silenced criticism. During the Kosovo war, one of the few journalists who continued to denounce the regime was shot dead in the streets of Belgrade.

Atrocities in Kosovo this year have blackened the name of Serbia as never before. Outside the country, the very word "Serb" took on the sinister resonance of "Nazi." Even if they were not the ones doing the fighting, an argument grew that Serbian civilians should be held morally responsible for crimes committed in their name. In Belgrade this summer, though, people didn't feel responsible. Nor did they tolerate politicians who suggested that they were. At the huge opposition rally last week in Belgrade, as during earlier rallies outside the capital this summer, speakers who said that Serbia had been "shamed" in the eyes of the world were careful to blame Milosevic and a few maniacs in his regime — and to distance the people of Serbia from any accountability for the conduct of the war.

I had asked Helena Zdravkovic, who is 21 and speaks perfect American-accented English, to take me around Belgrade. Having spent her teen-age years hanging out at Tennis Club Max, she was familiar with the lifestyles of the rich and criminal. She went to an elite public high school in Belgrade, and many of her closest friends were the children of middle-class professional parents who in the past ten years have slid into poverty. She was both a player in the city's social scene and a skeptic, having studied journalism for the past two academic years at Florida International University, in Miami, and the American University in Paris. She plans to attend Emerson College, in Boston, next year.

Helena also happened to be blond, attractive, and fitted out in fetching summer dresses, which does not hurt in Belgrade. Her father, Dejan Zdravkovic, opened Tennis Club Max nine years ago after retiring at the age of 40. He had made what he told me was a substantial amount of money in Italy selling machine tools to governments around the world. Most of the equipment was for making cannons and artillery pieces. He came home to Belgrade and opened the club in the exclusive residential diplomats' neighborhood of Dedinje. He did it, he told me, because he wanted to spend more time with his wife and two children and play lots of tennis with his friends. The club has just thirty-five members, many of them businessmen who have grown rich under the United Nations sanctions imposed this decade on the Milosevic regime.

"Sanctions are paradise," Dejan said as we sat beneath "Just Do It!" sun umbrellas in the cafe of his club. "Normally, you import and you pay duties and then taxes. But under sanctions, if you know the right people, you pay no duties and no taxes, and you have the excuse of charging more. Sanctions are what cemented Milosevic's power."

Dejan, who drives a bright red Porsche with four-digit license plates that signal to police his connections to the regime, said repeatedly that he hates what Milosevic has done to Serbia. But he told me that he is a pragmatist.

"Tell me who surrenders money and power voluntarily?" he asked. "I'll tell you. Nobody."

Although Dejan and his wife, Ivana, play tennis, do business, and socialize with well-connected people in the regime, they are nervous about the future. They are sending both their children to college in the United States. Ivana, a former professional translator who operates a travel agency exclusively for tennis club members, prefers that the children stay on in the States after college. Their son, Pedja, 19, won a four-year tennis scholarship to the University of Hartford and starts there in the fall. Helena plans to return after college; she doesn't want to live anywhere but Belgrade. Her boyfriend, a tennis coach and concert clarinetist, is here. So are her friends and the comfortable accouterments of her upper-middle-class life. On a hot July morning, Helena treated me to one of those accouterments — an apartment-turned-boutique in central Belgrade that admits only customers known to the owner. The shop, which has no name, sells designer clothing and fashion accessories shoplifted from Italy and smuggled into Serbia.

The owner, a Montenegrin with a shaved head, gold chains, and leather vest, kissed Helena (and glared at me) before we climbed the stairs to his third-floor boutique. He is a regular at Tennis Club Max, where he comes with the latest issues of *Vogue* and *Marie Claire* to sit with well-heeled women. They point to clothes that tickle their fancy. His men in Italy then try to steal them. During the owner's brief conversation with Helena, he told her that one of his men in Italy had "fallen," meaning that he was arrested trying to break into a warehouse full of merchandise.

There were video cameras on the stairs leading up to the shop and a monitor inside that gave clerks a chance to scrutinize visitors before letting them enter. Helena, of course, was more than welcome. The place was piled high with panties and sunglasses, handbags and evening gowns. I saw pink-and-gray stiletto-heeled Versace shoes in the living room, Fendi white leather skirts in one bedroom, and a handsome charcoal-gray Kenzo business suit in the second bedroom. Most of the clothes bore stickers from the stores where they had been stolen. The prices were about one-third retail. Helena was not impressed.

"It is nothing like it was last year," she said. "I mean I could find really nice clothes for myself, and I am really picky."

The shopkeeper explained to Helena that the springtime war in Kosovo had constricted his supply line for summer fashion. But with the war over, he was expecting new shipments.

Then we were off in Helena's convertible, her six-month-old, purebred English bulldog, Boobi, drooling in the back seat, for a look at what American cruise missiles have done to Belgrade. Like ice-pick punctures in the neck, the chilling quality of the strikes was not their size but their placement. We stopped at an intersection in the heart of the city. At each corner of the intersection, but only at each corner, there were ruins. The Serbian government center, the foreign ministry, and two defense ministry buildings had been reduced to rubble or were fire-gutted shells. The precision of the destruction suggested a war with an invisible, all-seeing enemy and of a city helpless to protect itself.

Eerily, all around the destruction, traffic flowed, shops were open, and apartments were being lived in. Except for long lines for rationed gasoline, the surface of everyday life in Belgrade seemed remarkably placid. The summer's rain and heat had produced bumper crops, and fresh vegetables and meat were plentiful. But the surface was deceptive. The war in Kosovo had plunged the Serbian economy into free fall, incomes were collapsing, and the United Nations World Food Program was warning of massive wintertime shortages of food, electricity, and fuel.

We were invited to a late lunch in the private restaurant of a friend of Helena's father, a former gangster turned prominent businessman. We met in his office at a gleaming car dealership in the city center and were served espresso by a team of leggy, young female attendants whose skirts were short and T-shirts tight. Besides automobiles, the businessman imports blue jeans, designer sportswear, gasoline, and engine lubricants. He told me, rather vaguely and under the condition that I not use his name, that he enjoys profitable connections with the Milosevic government. But as a precaution against Milosevic's possible ouster, he said, his wife and children live in Athens.

In the weeks before we met, the opposition movement in Belgrade had been holding demonstrations around Serbia, demanding that Milosevic resign. The businessman said he did not approve, not because of any affection for Milosevic, but because it would probably be bad for profits. According to him and according to American government officials, opposition parties in Serbia often demand kickbacks and bribes from businessmen, just like the ruling Socialist party that Milosevic controls.

"I think it is more expensive to deal with opposition politicians than with the Socialists," the businessman told me. "The new parties are very hungry for bribes. I am afraid that any political change may be worse."

The businessman got his start in Belgrade's gangster economy in the early 1990s, using money acquired from several years of working in Germany as a thief, according to a longtime friend. Asked how someone gets ahead in Milosevic's world, the businessman, with a straight face, said, "Everybody who is smart, who is willing to spend 16-hour days in the office like I do, can work and do well."

Being smart and hard-working has nothing to do with getting rich in Serbia, says Robert S. Gelbard, who until this summer was the United States special envoy to the Balkans. Gelbard, who spent the past two and a half years watching the Milosevic regime, estimates that only a few thousand people have profited from the crony capitalism of what he calls "Serbia Inc."

"This is a kleptocracy," he says. "People who are senior members of the party structure or of the government have been sucking the country dry, although the terrain has become pretty arid."

A few of the kleptocrats are notoriously well connected to the regime.

Milosevic's only son, Marko, made a fortune smuggling gasoline and cigarettes. The paramilitary warlord Zeljko Raznatovic, better known as Arkan and indicted in 1997 for war crimes in Croatia and Bosnia, amassed a fortune of his own in gasoline smuggling and money laundering in the early 1990s before turning to politics, marrying Serbia's hottest pop star in a ceremony broadcast on state-run television, and buying a Belgrade soccer team. (Apparently nervous about the future in Belgrade, Arkan sounded out officials in Belgium about moving there; he was told that he would be arrested.)

Private businessmen have also made fortunes by paying off the regime to secure import licenses that give them monopolies inside Serbia on consumer goods. The real players in Serbia Inc., though, are government ministers who typically regulate and award contracts to firms that they also control. Dejan Kovacevic, for example, is the Serbian minister of construction, as well as chairman of Mastrogradnje, a major construction company that wins large government contracts from his own ministry.

The Serb businessman who attributed his wealth to intelligence and hard work took Helena and me to lunch at his private restaurant, which he bought this summer and where the only diners are his friends and business associates. With a Puccini opera playing softly in the background, we were served caviar pasta and an elegant pinot noir in the restored dining room of a nineteenth-century townhouse. The conversation turned, as did nearly every conversation I had this summer with Serbs in Belgrade, to Kosovo.

Describing the Kosovar Albanians as "the most criminal people in the world," the businessman said Americans should have known what the Serbian reaction would be to the NATO bombing.

"When you put your bombs on Belgrade, we had to make ethnic cleansing in Kosovo," he said. "This is normal. Everybody in Serbia knows it, even little children."

The downwardly mobile in Belgrade do not mind being quoted by name. Helena took me one evening to meet her friend Darko Susnjar, who grew up in Belgrade's upper middle class, but who has since been skidding into the ranks of the working poor. He worked this summer as a ticket taker on a private bus, making about $5.50 for a twelve-hour day. With a ring in his left ear, day-old stubble, and long brown hair tied in a ponytail, Susnjar, 26, bears a passing resemblance to a young version of the comedian George Carlin.

We met at a pizza place beside the Danube River in Zemun, a Belgrade suburb of newish but dismal apartment buildings. Darko was late because thieves, for the third time in a month, had tried to steal his 1983 Opel Cadet. The car's door and trunk locks had all been broken, and he had just learned that it would cost $125 to fix them. That was about a month's pay.

"My car is sixteen years old and falling apart. I can't understand the mentality of people who want to steal that kind of junk," he said.

Darko was depressed, and not just about the car. An only child, he lives with his parents and admits to being a desultory student at the University of Belgrade. Like many students there, he sees no point in graduating. He studies ethnology, a field that he acknowledges is a waste of time, given the circumstances in Serbia.

"If someone had told me 10 years ago that I would be working on a bus, I would have had to fight him," Darko said, after a beer.

He grew up expecting more. His parents were supervisors at two major hotels in Belgrade, he said, making a combined salary of more than $70,000 a year until the early 1990s. Foreign investors have since pulled out of the Intercontinental Hotel, where his mother worked. His father worked at the Hotel Yugoslavia, which on May 7 was hit by three American cruise missiles. The Americans were apparently trying to take out the hotel's casino, which was partly owned by Arkan, but missed by a few feet and gutted a wing of rooms in the hotel. Darko and his family live near that hotel, and he happened to be out that Friday night in May getting a hamburger at a fast-food kiosk. He paid for his burger a few minutes before midnight, just as the missiles ruined his father's livelihood.

"I stood there for a minute and watched the hotel burn," Darko said. "What to do? I walked home and ate my hamburger. Now, from day to day, we sink lower. You ask yourself, 'How much more?'" He said his parents now live on a sort of severance pay that totals about $45 a month.

"Until this country went to hell, my mother and father and I had really great lives," he said. "They took me all over the world. We lived like normal people in Europe. We went to the sea. We went skiing. We had normal new clothes and normal new cars, not junk like now. We used to fly to Rome to go shopping. My father once called me long-distance from CBGB in New York, where he was on a business trip, just to say that he was in the place where the Ramones got their start. These are the reasons why I can't picture myself as a ticket taker on a bus."

Darko has a plan to escape. It depresses him, but still it's a plan. He calls it the "Green Card" option, a reference to the 1990 movie in which Gerard Depardieu marries Andie MacDowell to win legal residency in the United States. Darko's Andie MacDowell will be his girlfriend's sister, who lives in Lucerne, Switzerland.

"She doesn't like it, but she will do it," he told me.

I asked Darko about politics, mentioning that I had been attending opposition rallies and heard a couple of speakers who dared to mention Serbian atrocities in Kosovo. Darko, who listened to Radio Free Europe throughout the war, had also heard about atrocities. He did not argue that they were justified by Albanian treachery. He simply did not care to talk about the subject. To avoid thinking about war and to salve depression brought on by the summer of endless rain, Darko said he was reading nineteenth-century novels and listening to sunny Cuban music.

"Politics here is a kind of sickness, and I'm not interested," he said. "Democratic change will take many years. In the meantime, the Serbs will hibernate, like bears. At this time, Thanatos is much stronger than Eros. It is dark here now. That is our reality."

The morning after we drank beer with Darko, thugs attacked young people from the opposition Democratic Party who were asking residents in the suburb of New Belgrade to sign a petition calling for Milosevic's resignation. Three opposition party workers were injured, and one was hospitalized with head and internal injures. As usual in Belgrade, no arrests were made. The incident was not reported on state television.

While the opposition activists were getting their heads kicked in, Helena and I were just two blocks away in a newly built shopping center that was leaking in the summer rain. Shoe-shop clerks took advantage of a clear morning to set hundreds of pairs of soaked sneakers out on a sidewalk to dry in the sun. We went to a bar in the shopping center to have coffee with a young woman who, until that morning, had worked as a news writer at a television station in Belgrade.

BK Television is a private station owned by the five Karic brothers, among the richest businessmen in Serbia. The station has sleek broadcast studios, attractive anchor people, and a jazzy news format. But it slavishly toes the government line. When it mildly challenged the regime in 1997, Milosevic threatened to take away the station's broadcast license. Ivana Konstantinovic, 22, a diminutive woman with large brown eyes, has worked for BK Television for nearly three years. Mostly, she repackaged news from state-controlled television, trying to make it into a more zippy product. She cut out words like "hegemony" and "international organs." But still, as she conceded over coffee and nearly a pack of cigarettes, her final product was usually distorted and misleading.

"We tried to tell the truth, but it was a matter of luck whether we succeeded," said Ivana, also a student at the University of Belgrade studying international relations. "Sometimes, by being clever, we could tell things the government didn't want known. During the rallies against Milosevic in 1996, we were not allowed to say how large the crowds were. So we said buses were having trouble getting through the city."

In the wake of the Kosovo war, state television this summer demonized Serbian opposition leaders, often calling them traitors and spies in the pay of the CIA. Ivana dutifully rewrote these accusations, although she said she did not believe them. She could mention opposition rallies only after they had been denounced by government officials.

Ivana wants to get out of Serbia with her boyfriend, Bojan Dragicevic, a technician at BK Television. Her three best friends have already fled to Botswana, France, and Holland. That was before the war in Kosovo and before the visa situation tightened. She now lives at home with her parents, both of whom are engineers. One designs plastic bags, the other works in a tractor factory. Ivana gets paid about $110 a month, which is roughly a tenth of what she would have been paid for the same job a decade ago.

"In this situation," she said, "that is quite good money for me."

On the morning we spoke, Ivana had been promoted. She had started a new job as an early-morning on-air personality, reading traffic reports and community-service bulletins.

"I was very depressed writing lies," she said. "Now on the morning program, at least, I can honestly look into the camera and say: 'There is no electricity this morning.'"

For young women in Belgrade, career choices tend to lie somewhere on a continuum between honest-impoverishing and criminal-lucrative. In the dispiriting middle lies the temp work done by "sponsor girls" — middle-class high-school girls who tart themselves up and trade their bodies to gangsters in return for designer clothes, cell phones, and fancy dinners. *The European,* a Belgrade magazine banned by the regime at the beginning of the year, described a sponsor girl as "a symbol of the absolute commercialization of sexuality, the newest manifestation of the subjugation of women. She is the target of malicious gossip and the dark subject of her fellow teen-agers' dreams, the reason for her parents' distress."

I had dinner with two buxom, bejeweled, and elaborately made-up young women, one of whom used to date Helena's brother. We met around midnight in the Fortress, an elegant new outdoor restaurant built amid Roman and medieval ruins on a hilltop at the confluence of the Danube and Sava Rivers. It's an expensive place where gangsters gather late at night to show off new cars, gold chains, and teen-age babes in designer duds. The heavy night air smelled of grilled beef and American cigarettes and French perfume. Serbian rock music washed across the terrace from a nightclub next door.

The young women agreed to meet me only to discuss the phenomenon of sponsor girls, not to talk about themselves. But after about a half-hour of conversation, they both began to slip in and out of the first person while explaining the costs and benefits of hanging out with older men with guns, shaved heads, and deep pockets.

"If you are with a guy who makes his living that way, you can be the center of attention," said Olja Karleusa, 18, who was dressed in a powder-blue satin jacket over a tight tank top. Her dyed blond hair was teased Tina Turner style, and her milky white lipstick matched her nails.

"Gangsters are a normal element of life," Olja said. "The girls don't think they are doing anything wrong. The possibility of earning money is very small. Everyone here does illegal stuff, so it seems so normal."

Her friend, Milena Markovic, 19, who wore glitter makeup on her cheeks and whose breasts were bursting out of a low-cut T-shirt that said "Power Girl," told me that every high-school girl in Belgrade is tempted by the life gangsters can offer.

"It feeds your ego if you are with a guy like that," she said.

Helena had told me that Olja's boyfriend is a Belgrade criminal whose best friend was shot this summer in a cafe. Olja did not want to talk about it. She and Milena did want to talk about the short shelf life and poor marital prospects of a sponsor girl after she turns twenty-four.

"The guys go from one girl to another, and there is a very small chance of him falling in love," said Olja. "There are so many girls that he can always find another younger one."

"The guys are aware of the situation and that they have all the power," added Milena.

"They realize what scum the girls are and they use them," Olja said.

The more they talked, the angrier they became and the more "they" became "we."

"We are furious because without a gangster friend, you can't really enjoy Belgrade," said Olja. "Girls have no possibility to do what they want with their lives unless they are from rich families."

Both the girls had graduated from high school and said they were planning on enrolling this fall in the law faculty at the University of Belgrade. It didn't make sense to become a lawyer in a country without laws, they said, but they didn't know what else to do.

I asked them about Kosovo, about the bodies of Albanians that were being dug up there from mass graves and if they were aware that, outside Serbia, many people had the impression that Serbian forces had committed genocide. It was as if I had belched or insulted their makeup. The conversation paused awkwardly. Both girls seemed offended.

"I don't know what happened in Kosovo," Olja said, dismissively. "I didn't hear that we did any more atrocities than what the Albanians did to us."

They wanted to talk about the weather. Both Olja and Milena said the summer's thunderstorms reminded them of the spring months when Americans bombed Belgrade. They said they'd been having trouble sleeping and that they'd heard the Americans were causing the rainstorms. I said I did not think that was very likely. They left for another nightclub.

It was about 1 a.m., but the restaurant was still crowded. Sullen men were knocking back whiskey and being adored by young women who looked like Olja and Milena. A friend of Helena's spotted us and invited us for a drink. He was eager to talk about Kosovo. In fact, Vukoje Dobric, a Serb who was born and raised in Kosovo, found it difficult to talk of anything else. He chain-smoked cigarettes and drank beer after beer, and his left leg twitched incessantly. A medical student, he looked much older than his twenty years. His nerves seemed shot.

Vukoje lives in a Belgrade apartment next door to what used to be the headquarters of the Federal Interior Ministry. The massive building was demolished this spring by American cruise-missile strikes. They came at night, as Vukoje, just a few yards from the blazing building, lay terrified in his bed. His parents fled their home in the Kosovo town of Klina two weeks after Milosevic signed the June peace deal that pulled Serbian forces out and let NATO in. They left behind two houses, two pharmacies, several cars, and more than forty acres of land that had been in the family since the mid-nineteenthth century. On the night I talked to Vukoje, his parents and four other relatives were sleeping in the two-bedroom Belgrade apartment he had been sharing with his sister.

"My parents just sit in the apartment all day long," Vukoje told me. "They don't do anything. I am afraid they are going to go crazy. I blame the Americans for not protecting the Serbs from the Albanians. I blame Milosevic for losing in Kosovo. I blame my parents for not selling out and leaving sooner. They left everything we own behind."

Before I could ask about the Serbian war crimes, Vukoje acknowledged that Serbs had done "a lot of bad things."

"You have maniacs and war is like that," he said. "But someday the Americans are going to discover who the Serbs are and who the Albanians are. The Albanians want to take over. They will live fifty in a house."

Vukoje said Serbs will wait until NATO loses interest and then will take Kosovo back by force. It did not matter to him that Albanians outnumber Serbs in Kosovo by more than 9 to 1.

"I know that what is mine is mine, whether I live to see it or not," he said. "No one can take it away from me. The Turks took our land for five hundred years, and we took it back."

The next day I visited Vukoje's apartment and spoke to his father, Rados, who is a pharmacist. As recently as last year, Rados said, he could have sold his houses and land to Albanian buyers for about a half million dollars. He held on until June, when, panicked by what returning Albanian refugees might do to his family, he gave his keys to an Albanian neighbor and fled.

"I had a new Mitsubishi Pajero, and I told my neighbor he could keep it if he protected my house," said Rados, who did not know if his property had been protected or burned. I asked him about the future. He looked at his medical-student son and shook his head in disgust.

"I don't see any future for him," Rados said. "I made him study to be a doctor. But when I see that a doctor in Belgrade makes 250 German marks a month [about $140] and does not get paid on time, I don't know what to tell him."

Rados said he had always expected war in Kosovo. His father had been shot by Albanians in 1945. He bought an apartment in Belgrade fifteen years ago as a precaution — a place away from Albanians who he suspected might one day kidnap his son and rape his daughter. I asked Rados if he felt the Serbs had done anything wrong in Kosovo and mentioned the mass graves being dug up by war-crimes investigators.

"I am not a politician, how should I know?" he said. "NATO bombing was the biggest crime. No one wants to be our friend. We have been betrayed by everyone."

Rados was proud that he had refused to sell his land in Kosovo. Like his son, he believed Serbs would one day fight to get it back. If he did not get the land back before he died, well, there were more important things than death: "Something inside told me I would be guilty and sinful toward the graves of my ancestors if I sold."

At Tennis Club Max on the afternoon before I left Belgrade, Helena and I spent an afternoon with her next-door neighbor, a 19-year-old who seemed to know precisely what Serbia needed before it could embrace democracy. Vlada Pejovic, who has a long, sad face and large brown eyes, graduated this summer as the valedictorian of the Nikola Tesla High School for Engineering. Since he was 15, he has been tutoring high-school seniors (including Helena) on how to take the S.A.T. so they can get into an American college.

"People here think all the world is against us," Vlada told me. "But I don't think the world has interest in us. There is a mass hypnosis here. The government wants to stay in power so it suffocates free thought."

Before democracy can gain a foothold, Vlada said, the first thing Serbs have to do is be honest with themselves and come to grips with what happened in Kosovo, as well as in Bosnia and Croatia.

"Until that happens, they are going to blame the world, rather than their own leaders," he said.

Vlada, though, had no idea who would teach Serbs the truth. He was planning to travel to Budapest to take the college boards. During the bombing of Belgrade he had made up his mind. He was getting out.

The night before coming into Belgrade, I had dinner with Milka Tadic, a prominent Yugoslav journalist. During an evening in which she grew increasingly combative and angry, she warned me not to be taken in by Serbs who claim that they do not know about the atrocities committed in their name in Kosovo.

"The silence in Belgrade about what went on makes me really sick," she said. Tadic is the managing editor of *Monitor,* a weekly political magazine published in Montenegro.

"Serbs don't want to know, but most of them know," she went on. "They have satellite dishes and short-wave radios. They know, but they don't care. All they care about is themselves. For them, Albanians are not really human beings. The Serbs believe they are the chosen people. It is racism. I hate to say it, but it is like what the Germans did."

As our dinner ended, Tadic told me a jarring story about the huge winter demonstrations that nearly toppled Milosevic two years ago. She remembered a chant — "Go to Kosovo! Go to Kosovo!" — that University of Belgrade students shouted when the police confronted them with clubs. Tadic said the students objected to police brutality only because it inconvenienced them. "These are the nice young liberals of Belgrade," she said.

I argued with Milka that night. I said it was unfair to tar an entire people for the depravity of their leaders. But after a month in Belgrade, after listening to intelligent and cultured people dismiss the savagery in Kosovo as "no worse than what they did to us," I came to share Milka's rage.

II. VOICES FROM THE BALKAN PAST

What Is the Historical and Cultural Context?

A Brief History of Serbia

TIM JUDAH

Serbs always say that Kosovo is the Serbian heartland. If so, retort Kosovo Albanians, then the Serbian heart beats inside a foreign body. Rhetorical and emotional arguments aside, what is clear is that Kosovo, both in and of itself and as a metaphysical notion, has played a key role in determining the Serbian fate and Serbian history.[1]

Kosovo lay at the heart of the Serbian medieval kingdoms. To this day the monasteries and churches that were built by the Serbian kings attest to this fact. They also suggest (although Albanian historians dispute this) that the majority of medieval Kosovo was either Serb or at least Orthodox Christian on the way to developing a national identity as Serb. Population and churches apart, there is another reason why Kosovo lay at the heart of medieval Serbia: the gold and silver mines of Novo Brdo, close to Gracanica, were then a major asset and, of course, a major source of income for the Serbian kings.

Today potted histories of Serbia and Kosovo often start with Prince Lazar and his fabled defeat before the Turks at the Field of Blackbirds (Kosovo Polje) on June 28, 1389. Vitally important though Lazar was, a real understanding of Serbian history needs to look somewhat further back. By the time Lazar came to prominence, the medieval Serbian state, which had been fashioned during two hundred years of rule by the Nemanjic dynasty, had fallen apart. Serbia was now run by feuding dukes and princes, Lazar Hrebeljanovic being the most powerful of them all at this particular moment. Although the death of Emperor Stefan Dusan in 1355 saw the effective end of Nemanjic rule, the legacy of that dynasty endures to this day. Not only did it give future generations of Serbs a glorious and prosperous kingdom — and a short-lived empire — to look back on, especially during the centuries of Ottoman rule; it also gave the Serbs the wherewithal to survive as the

---

1. For texts in English on Serbian history, see Thomas Emmert, *Serbian Golgatha: Kosovo, 1389* (New York, 1990); Barbara Jelavich, *History of the Balkans,* 2 vols. (Cambridge, 1989-1993); Michael Boro Petrovich, *A History of Modern Serbia, 1808-1918* (New York and London, 1976); Stevan K. Pavlowitch, *The Improbable Survivor: Yugoslavia and Its Problems, 1918-1988* (London, 1988); Laura Silber and Allan Little, *The Death of Yugoslavia* (London, 1995). [For additional texts in many languages, consult the bibliography in Judah's *The Serbs.* Ed.]

nation they are today. The reason for this was that, under the Nemanjics, a Serbian Orthodox autocephalous (i.e., national) church was founded by Rastko, the son of King Stefan Nemanja, in 1219. Rastko was canonized as St. Sava, and so, indeed, were most of the Nemanjic monarchs.

These facts are key. What they meant was that, following the final demise of Serbia and its subjugation to the Turks, the Serbs retained, in the church, a powerful national institution. Its survival meant that it was then able to propagate the notion that, just as Christ had been resurrected, so would Serbia. In the meantime, though, the churchgoing Serbian peasant could pray for salvation under the watchful eyes of the Serbian saints — many, of course, the kings of Serbia's glorious past whose images were preserved for eternity in church frescoes. In this way, and through the tradition of Serbian epic ballads, the past was kept alive while still retaining the promise of the future.

It is in the same light that we should interpret the myths that grew up following the Battle of Kosovo in 1389. The Serbian kingdom of the Nemanjics had, as we have noted, already fallen apart. By now the Ottomans were moving up rapidly through southeastern Europe. Their tactic was, where possible, to co-opt local rulers as vassals rather than fight them. The vassals retained their power, at least for the foreseeable future, but they were bound to fight alongside the Sultan when summoned. In this way some Serbs were aligned alongside the Turks when they faced Lazar and the coalition that he had assembled when he decided not to submit to vassal status. They included troops from Bosnia and probably Albanians too. The legend has it that Lazar chose "to die in battle rather than live in shame" and that he chose the kingdom of heaven — that is, the kingdom of truth — rather than one of earthly riches. In fact, the origins of this story lie in the propaganda spun by the church and Lazar's widow in the aftermath of the battle. They related to her need to build up Lazar's young son in the face of claims from rival Serbian nobles.

The battle, so often painted as a great defeat, was in fact much more of a draw. Lazar died, but then so did the Ottoman sultan. Serbia was not immediately conquered by the Turks, but it is true that it was fatally weakened. It finally fell in 1459.

The centuries of Ottoman domination were to have a seismic effect. Above all, they produced major demographic shifts, the effects of which we are still living with today. At various points, Serbs migrated to what are now Croatia, Bosnia, and Hungary (many to what is now Vojvodina), and, of course, to what is now Serbia proper. In the main, their place was taken by Albanians, who had mostly — but not all — converted to Islam.

Although there were long periods of peace under the Ottomans, there were also periods of extraordinary turbulence and war, especially with the Habsburg monarchy. Thus part of what is now central Serbia became, between 1718 and 1739, the Austrian-controlled Kingdom of Serbia. Between 1788 and 1791 the

Austrians also organized units of Serbian Freikorps to fight deep inside Turkish territory. Although this war-cum-rebellion collapsed, it gave the Serbs valuable military experience. When a new insurrection began in 1804, it was led by a former Freikorps soldier, a pig merchant known as Black George (Karadjordje). Karadjordje, who proclaimed that his aim was "throwing off the yoke that the Serb has borne since Kosovo," was initially incredibly successful. However, by 1813 the international situation had changed, and a new Turkish onslaught saw the collapse of Karadjordje's Serbia. In 1815, however, Milos Obrenovic began a new revolt. He soon struck a deal with the Ottomans, and Serbia — or rather a small part of it centered on Belgrade — became an autonomous entity within the empire. Obrenovic was a shrewd leader. He constantly sought increased concessions from the Turks while he gradually undermined their residual power in Serbia. In 1817, as Karadjordje sought to slip home, Obrenovic had him murdered and had his skinned head stuffed and sent to the sultan. In 1830 the sultan recognized Obrenovic's claim to found a hereditary princeship.

By 1878 the Serbian principality had expanded southward to the borders of Kosovo, Sandzak, and Macedonia, and in the same year it was also formally recognized as a fully independent state. Internally it was subject to occasional turmoil as, until 1903, the monarchy alternated between rival houses, those stemming from Karadjordje and Milos Obrenovic respectively. In Belgrade a small middle class had begun to prosper, and Muslims, Turks, and Albanians who had, under the Turks, been the country's main urban dwellers had either emigrated, fled, or — to use today's terminology — been ethnically cleansed.

The development of an educated Serbian middle class was crucial because, in an age that saw the rise of nationalism across Europe, Serbia was no exception. Educated people demanded books, plays, and . . . national myths. Thus "Kosovo," the idea of Serbia's Christlike resurrection and the development of an ideology that demanded the liberation of the Serbs still under Ottoman rule, began to mature. One of the key figures in this was Ilija Garasanin, a Serbian politician who set forth his ideas in his text "Nacertanije" (or "draft plan"), which foresaw the creation of a Greater Serbia. It is important, however, to view this document in the context of that time and not through modern eyes. Garasanin foresaw the end of the Ottoman Empire and wanted to make sure that when it did collapse, Serbia would be well placed to emerge as the predominant Balkan power. In this way he wanted to head off any possible territorial carve-up between the Austrians and Russians or the creation of several small and weak Balkan statelets that would be vulnerable to domination by outside interests. Ironically, some 150 years later, the second of Garasanin's fears appears to have come true.

As it happened, the Ottoman Empire lingered on until the first Balkan war of 1912. At this point Serbia reconquered Kosovo. The emotion of a Serbian army returning to the heartland was such that the Serbs failed to notice that they were no longer in a majority here. While for the Kosovo Serbs, perhaps now no more than 40 percent of Kosovo's population, the return of the Serbian Army was nothing less than a liberation, for Kosovo's Albanians it was a conquest by a foreign, Slavic power, which meant that Kosovo could not unite with the emerging independent state of Albania. Albanians who opposed the return of the Serbs were met with fire and brutality; but they did not have to wait long to take their revenge. In 1915, after the Serbs had at first heroically repelled Austro-Hungarian attacks, the whole of Serbia was overrun by the Austro-Hungarians, Germans, and Bulgarians. The entire Serbian government and army then began an extraordinary trek, some of it across Kosovo itself; huge columns trudged out to the coast of Albania, where the French and British rescued the men who made it. But many, especially stragglers, were picked off by vengeful Kosovo Albanians. Those Serbs who did make it, first to Corfu, were then sent to Salonika, where they fought alongside the Allies on the Salonika Front.

The end of the war saw the creation of the first Yugoslavia, which was very much dominated by Serbia and its institutions. Apart from Montenegro, no other part of the former Ottoman or Austro-Hungarian empires had any experience of independence in modern times; but still the Serb notion that Yugoslavia was really just another name for Greater Serbia was to arouse antipathy among the smaller nations of the kingdom. This was true, of course, for the Albanians of Kosovo, who were not even Slavs. But in terms of political opposition, it was of far greater consequence among the educated and sophisticated Croats, who resented Serbian dominance more than anyone else. Although the political origins of Yugoslavism lay in Croatia, many Croatians now felt deceived, believing that they had simply exchanged the tyranny of Vienna for that of second-rate, backward, and Orthodox Belgrade.

Attempts to reach a compromise between Serbs and Croats came too late. In 1941, when Hitler's troops, alongside those of Mussolini, began their invasion of Yugoslavia, they met with little resistance. The country was divided up. German-occupied central Serbia was run by a quisling government, while Kosovo was initially divided between the Germans, the Italians, and the Bulgarians. While the Germans made sure that they took the all-important Trepca mines in the north, the lion's share of Kosovo was joined to what was now an Italian-run Greater Albania.

Although Josip Broz Tito was half-Slovene and half-Croat, the initial resistance to Nazi rule came from Serbia. Tito's communist Partisans were eventually to be forced out of Serbia, but it is important to understand that, in Serbia as well as in other parts of occupied Yugoslavia, two wars were taking place simultaneously. In Serbia — or rather among the Serbs — there was, apart from resistance to the Nazis, a civil war. On the one side were the Partisans (originally Serbian dominated), and on the other were the so-called Chetniks, forces led by the Yugoslav Army officer Draza Mihailovic, who foresaw the restoration of the old Serb-dominated royal Yugoslavia. Suffice it to say here that the Chetniks were doomed when the Allies made the decision in the spring of 1944 to switch support from them to Tito. Mihailovic was executed after the war. The other important point that should be made here is that hundreds of thousands of Serbs perished at the hands of the Croatian Ustashas in Croatia and Bosnia, and that more were either killed in Kosovo or expelled from it. Of course, Serbs retaliated wherever they could, especially in Bosnia. But in the new communist Yugoslavia that arose from the ashes of war, to talk of such national or ethnic conflict was strictly prohibited. This meant that grievances lay festering for almost half a century.

Tito's new federal Yugoslavia sought to end the conflict between the country's various nations and the requirements of the state. Federalism sought to create a balance between the demand for home rule and recreating the Yugoslav state at the same time. While Tito was alive, and the final arbiter of any quarrels, the system worked. As for Serbia itself, another compromise was made: although it incorporated Kosovo and Vojvodina, these provinces were also given autonomy. But in the case of Kosovo, this meant little until the 1960s. While this constitutional arrangement sought to make sure that Serbia, by far the biggest and most populous republic, could not dominate the rest of the country, it also created a new grievance. Serbs thought — or were later encouraged to think — that Serbia had been cut down to size in order to keep it weak for the sake of "a strong Yugoslavia."

The fact that Kosovo's autonomy meant little, at least until the 1960s, is directly attributable to the war years. In effect, Kosovo's Albanians were paying for their pact with the devil. That is to say, the vast majority preferred an Italian-run Greater Albania to a return to any form of Slav-dominated Yugoslavia. For that reason it was difficult, at first, to find any willing recruits to the ranks of the Partisans. Later, those who joined the fighting did so with the belief that, after the war, Kosovo would be given the option of remaining united with Albania. In the end this promise turned out to be an empty one, and Kosovo was forcibly reunited with Yugoslavia, remaining under military rule for some years. However, the lack of significant numbers of pro-Yugoslav communist Kosovo Albanians meant that, in the absence of anyone else, the province had to be run mainly by Serbs.

After the demonstrations in 1968, though, things began to change, and by 1974 Kosovo was a Yugoslav republic in all but name. By now a full-scale Albanianization was underway, and Pristina University was churning out large numbers of educated Kosovo Albanians for the first time. Kosovo could not, of course, become a republic since that would have caused too much of a backlash among the Serbs, and because republics had the theoretical right to secede. With the death of Tito in 1980, two things happened: first, in 1981 there were renewed demonstrations calling for republican status; second, the church began to complain that Serbs were being persecuted and were leaving the province. There is little doubt that Serbs were leaving and that many did feel persecuted. But that is not the whole story. Many were also leaving for economic reasons, gravitating, for example, to the industrial cities of central Serbia. Many also believed that in an Albanian-run Kosovo there was little prospect of advancement, either for themselves or their children. Still, as communist power — or rather the fear of it — began to dis- sipate, the "Serbian Question," the fate of the Serbs of Kosovo, began to figure in political debate.

Leading that debate was Dobrica Cosic, a famous Serbian novelist who, at times, had played an important role in Serbian politics. Indeed, as far back as 1968, he had fallen afoul of the authorities after warning that Kosovo Albanian and Vojvodina Hungarian leaders were "separatists" and that promoting Bosnia's Mus- lims to the status of a Yugoslav "nation" was senseless. Despite his problems, Cosic was a respected figure and a member of the Serbian Academy of Sciences and Arts. In 1985 a group of sixteen academicians began work on a document that became known as the *Memorandum*.[2] Its aim was to examine the state of contemporary Serbia and the situation of the Serbs in general. Although Cosic was not one of the academics, it is clear that he was its inspiration. Leaked to the press in 1986, this document was to light the fuse that would lead to the destruction of Yugoslavia. Most of the *Memorandum* was rather dull; however, when it came to discuss the Serbs of Kosovo and of Croatia (then 12 percent of its population), its language suddenly took on a tone of shrill hysteria.

The *Memorandum* asserted that, over the last twenty years, 200,000 Serbs had already been "forced to leave Kosovo." It said: "It is not just that the last rem- nants of the Serbian nation are leaving their homes at an unabated rate, but ac- cording to all evidence, faced with a physical, moral and psychological reign of ter- ror, they seem to be preparing for their final exodus." And then, in its most extreme, grotesque, and inflammatory paragraph it added: "The physical, politi- cal, legal and cultural genocide of the Serbian population in Kosovo . . . is a worse historical defeat than any experienced in the liberation wars waged by Serbia from the First Serbian Uprising in 1804 to the uprising of 1941."

One source of particular anger was Kosovo's constitutional situation. Serbs ar- gued that it was unfair that Kosovo had a say in the running of Serbia in general but that Serbia had no say in the running of Kosovo. In other words, Kosovo could and generally did vote against Serbia on the federal presidency; but Serbia itself was pow- erless to remedy the hazardous situation of the Serbs in Kosovo. Of course, none of this was anything that politicians of goodwill could not have sorted out. Instead, Slobodan Milosevic, hitherto a grey communist apparatchik, emerged on the scene. He was the head of the Serbian Communist party's central committee but had al- ways lived in the political shadow of his friend and mentor Ivan Stambolic, then the President of Serbia. Stambolic understood the sensitivities involved in Kosovo, so he asked Milosevic to go to Pristina to see what he could sort out.

2. As Professors Djordjevic, Dragnich and Babic have pointed out, interpretations vary concerning the role and consequences of the *Memorandum* for subsequent events in Yugoslavia. [Ed.]

Milosevic went south and returned a different man. He went to Kosovo and saw the future — his future. Seizing the emotive issue of the Kosovo Serbs, he began his transition from communist to nationalist, from second-fiddle politician to the leader of a Serbia reborn. This would be a resurrected Serbia, which would now take care of its own and, as the *Memorandum* had exhorted, would no longer be weak for the sake of a strong Yugoslavia. In fact, Milosevic was not interested in the Serbs of Kosovo, just as later he was not interested in the Serbs of Croatia or Bosnia. They were simply useful tools in his bid to gain power and then to keep it.

Milosevic now betrayed Stambolic, took his job, and moved to abolish Kosovo's autonomy. In Kosovo itself this was fiercely resisted by the Albanians, but the Serbs were euphoric. At one of the giant rallies "of truth" that Milosevic held at the time, he said: "We shall win the battle for Kosovo regardless of the obstacles facing us inside and outside the country. We shall win despite the fact that Serbia's enemies outside the country are plotting against it, along with those in the country. We tell them that we enter every battle . . . with the aim of winning it."

On February 20, 1989, Albanian miners in Kosovo staged a last-ditch attempt to stall the reimposition of Serbian rule in Kosovo. They refused to come to the surface. Their strike failed, but in the midst of the Serbian euphoria came a shot across the bow. Although Slovenes and Serbs had been wrangling over the future of Yugoslavia, they liked each other and had no historic quarrels. So when Slovene president Milan Kucan declared that Yugoslavia was being "defended" by the Albanian miners, his statement shocked the Serbs. For the first time they realized that Yugoslav politicians really meant what they said and were not just talking, as politicians are wont to do.

It did them no good though. For most Serbs, the Slovenes were now insolent, the Croats were fascists, and the Albanians treacherous separatists. Since Serbia was "rising," everyone else could just shut up or get out. This was, of course, exactly what everyone else in Yugoslavia now decided to do. Milosevic's reimposition of Serbian power in Kosovo sparked a cycle of competitive nationalisms that by 1991 was to lead not only to the demise of the old Yugoslavia but to war as well.

The rest of the story is well known. So what about the future? As Dobrica Cosic argues in another essay in this volume (originally a speech delivered to the Academy of Sciences and Arts in July 1999): "We lost Kosovo. . . ." But after more than a thousand years, can that really be the end of the story? Citing Stendhal, Aleksa Djilas, the Serbian historian and political commentator, says: "The possibility of revenge increases the desire." So, while today Albanians wreak their revenge on the province's Serbs, the day may yet come when Serbs can wreak theirs. The way the Serbs have lost Kosovo means that tomorrow the Serbs will have no chance to get it back. How could they while it is controlled by 55,000 NATO and other troops? But what will happen in ten or twenty years? Just over a decade ago no one could have predicted the shape of the world as it is today. So what if, in twenty or thirty years, America is locked in isolationism, Russia is rearmed and strong, and Europe is weak and divided? He says that the spirit of revanchism may grow. "Of course," he adds, "I would not support such a thing, but Serbs are not exactly a 'forgive and forget' nation. If they have remembered the 1389 defeat for 610 years, why not this one?"

Kosovo, the Illusive State

MIRANDA VICKERS

The Kosovo region of southern Serbia has not only proved to be historically an illusive state entity for the majority ethnic Albanian inhabitants; it has also become an equally illusory homeland for the minority Serb population.

The Albanian writers Arshi Pipa and Sami Repishti describe the term Kosovo as a metaphor used by both Serbs and Albanians for the "suffering and injustices" inflicted upon both nations throughout their turbulent history. They explain that relations between Serbs and Albanians in Kosovo have not, however, always been confrontational. The history of the Balkans in modern times has been a sequence of battles and wars, instigated by immoderate ambitions for domination and fanned by nationalism and outright chauvinism. Differences of language and religious traditions and customs have invariably been overemphasized in order to allow social groups and classes to use nationalism as a smokescreen for satisfying their desire for power. The victims thereof have invariably been the Balkan peoples, be they Slavs, Greeks, Albanians, or Turks.[1]

Nowadays, Albanian and Serbian scientists — most of whom are nationalist in orientation — have totally opposing theories about the ethnic development of Kosovo, a fact that has proved to be an important issue in the background to the present conflict. The Serbs are convinced that, prior to their arrival in the region during the sixth and seventh centuries, Kosovo was virtually uninhabited, and that Albanians only arrived in the region in the fifteenth century together with the conquering Turks, and again in the seventeenth century following the exodus of a great number of Serbs. The Albanians, however, consider theirs to be the stronger historical claim to Kosovo since their ancestors, the Illyrians, are known to have inhabited parts of what is now Kosovo for several centuries before the arrival of the Slavs.

At the time of the arrival of the Ottoman Turks in Kosovo — at the end of the fourteenth century — the formal adoption of Catholicism by northern Albanians drew a clear line of demarcation between Albanians and the Eastern Orthodox Serbs in Kosovo. Nevertheless, despite this fact, there was little animosity between the two peoples, who shared a common layer of culture derived from

---

1. A. Pipa and S. Repishti, *Studies on Kosova* (New York, 1994), p. 250.

various historical circumstances. Following the Russo-Turkish wars of the eighteenth century, however, the previous Ottoman policy of religious tolerance began to decline. Uncertain of the loyalty of their Christian subjects, the Ottomans encouraged Islamization in sensitive regions. Of all the Balkan subject peoples, the Albanians were the most willing to convert to Islam and thereby gain a number of privileges denied to Christians. Muslims had a far better chance in courts, paid fewer taxes, and possessed a recognized superior status. In contrast, the restrictions on the Christian population were many.[2]

All Ottoman subjects were divided into national groups, or millets, not according to their ethnic origin or language but according to their religion. Thus, because of their Muslim faith, most Albanians were classified as Turks, thereby straining relations between the Christian Serbs and their Albanian neighbors. After World War I, following the collapse of the Ottoman Empire, almost half a million Albanians were included by force and against their will within the borders of the newly created kingdom of Serbs, Croats, and Slovenes.

Serbian-Albanian relations in Kosovo, since the creation of the Yugoslav state, have gone through several stages. Throughout the first stage, 1918-1941, the Albanian minority had no specifically guaranteed minority rights and lived under virtual Serbian domination. The elite structure of pre–World War II Kosovo resembled a system of internal colonialism with an imported Slav peasantry together with an intelligentsia that ruled the region's majority Albanian population. In the second stage, during World War II, a large part of Kosovo was united with Albania under Italian rule, and thus the situation was reversed: Serbs and Montenegrins found themselves in a vulnerable and inferior environment when many Albanians openly collaborated with the occupying German and Italian administration in subduing the predominantly Slav resistance forces, causing the emigration of a large number of Serbs and Montenegrins.

The third stage, 1945-1966, was a period of oscillations in these relations, ranging from armed conflict to attempts at a political resolution of disputes, including administrative restrictions of the rights of Albanians and the authorities' refusal to allow the return to Kosovo of those Slavs who were forced to flee the region during the war. The fourth stage, 1961-1981, was the so-called post-Brioni period, characterized by the acknowledgment and assurance of the minority rights of the Albanians. During this period the national emancipation and affirmation of Kosovo's Albanian population was encouraged, which, in the aftermath of the controversial 1974 Constitution, developed into a powerful Albanian national movement. This in turn served to further alienate the region's dwindling Serb and Montenegrin population, who felt threatened by the new mood of Albanian self-assertiveness.

2. For a detailed discussion of the status of Christians in Ottoman Kosovo, see Miranda Vickers, *The Albanians: A Modern History* (London, New York: I. B. Tauris, 1997, 2nd edition, 1999).

The fifth stage, 1981-1992, was marked by the disintegration of Yugoslavia and the strengthening of all nationalist movements, which led to open conflicts and civil war in the territories of the former Yugoslavia. During this period the Kosovo crisis became acute: Serbia reestablished its control over Kosovo by abolishing the province's autonomous status in 1989; in response, the Albanians sought to create their independent republic. All areas of life in Kosovo subsequently remained divided into two parallel worlds, one belonging to the legal Serbian system of government, the other to an Albanian illegal system for organizing all other aspects of life. Intolerance and open hostility between these two worlds steadily increased, and with it the inevitability of open conflict.[3]

Following the 1995 Dayton Peace Accords, international diplomatic recognition of the new political map that took shape in the former Yugoslavia left the Albanian population of Kosovo deeply unsatisfied. The overwhelming majority of Albanians believed that outright independence from Serbia was the only way of guaranteeing their national rights. The Dayton Accords clarified that the international community would not sanction any change of borders in Yugoslavia. This stance was viewed as sheer hypocrisy by the Kosovar Albanians, who argued that Dayton allowed the Bosnian Serbs to retain their separate Republika Srpska, and even offered them prospects of confederal links with Serbia. Why, then, could the Albanians not have their Republika Kosova within the framework of Yugoslavia? The Albanians felt that they should not be put at a disadvantage because they had, until then, refused to back up their demands with violence.

Despite countless statements from human rights organizations about serious human rights abuses, the international community continued to ignore the issue of Kosovo's self-determination, insisting that the Kosovo problem was an internal Yugoslav issue. Consequently, the ethnic Albanians were forced to reevaluate their political stance. Aware that their passive policy throughout the Yugoslav war had denied them an invitation to the peace talks, many Kosovars were now determined to prevent any compromise solution to fit in with the timing and wishes of the international community rather than that of the Albanians themselves. They had learned from Dayton that value was accorded to the armed struggle of the Bosnian Serbs — by the recognition, even if only partially, of the Serb Republic of Bosnia. This convinced many Albanians that the international community understood only the language of armed conflict, not that of nonviolence. In re-

---

3. Today Serb churches and monasteries dot the Kosovo landscape as a living testimony to their medieval Slav state; but the fact that Albanians have become demographically far stronger than the Serbs in Kosovo has contributed to the two nations' hostility toward each other over the past two centuries. Kosovo has always been the most densely populated region of Yugoslavia, with the country's (and Europe's) highest natural population growth rate. Kosovo's economy was persistently unable to absorb such a high birthrate, and this has greatly contributed to the constant depression of Kosovo's standard of living and forced thousands of young Albanians to leave the region in search of employment.

sponse, therefore, a hitherto unknown ethnic Albanian guerilla group, the Kosovo Liberation Army (KLA), launched a series of attacks on Serb targets in the spring of 1996.[4]

Swift and harsh Serb reprisals to the KLA assaults forced thousands of Albanian families to flee their homes. On March 4, 1998, perhaps as a provoked reprisal for the killings of Serb policemen, Serb military police raided the village of Prekaz in the KLA heartland of central Kosovo, home to KLA strongman Adem Jashari. The police killed virtually the entire Jashari clan — 58 people in all, including women and children. This reprisal resulted in an enormous groundswell in the KLA in Kosovo and the Diaspora, thus making it possible for the KLA to conduct operations over a much wider territory. Sympathetic media reporting of their struggle, and of the plight of their displaced families, gave the KLA an exaggerated impression that the West would soon intervene on their behalf. Confidence subsequently grew among the KLA's command structure. From being an illusive, shadowy, and ill-defined entity, the KLA suddenly opened up and began granting interviews to the world's media. Off came the balaclavas, and names were put to hitherto masked faces.

The ultimate goal of the KLA's "liberation" struggle was an independent and sovereign Kosovo. The United States and the European Union (EU), however, categorically stated that political autonomy with guaranteed minority rights was the only internationally acceptable solution for the status of Kosovo. The dilemma facing the international community, therefore, was to attempt to ensure territorial integrity for Yugoslavia, together with self-determination for the ethnic Albanians, by asking both Serbs and Albanians to find a middle way. However, this was a difficult task, since the starting point for such a compromise was that Kosovo be treated as a constituent part of Serbia.

In the aftermath of the recent bloody conflict, however, virtually all Kosovo Albanians now believe that they can never again live within the borders of Serbia. And Kosovo's beleaguered Serbian population now fears that the Albanian call for independence, if enacted, would emasculate the Serb minority completely. Hence the anxiety pervading the Serb population and their dilemma about whether to stay or leave.

---

4. The KLA had its origins in an initiative adopted in 1993 by an exiled Kosovar political group, the People's Movement for the Liberation of Kosovo (LPK), which had been active in Switzerland and Germany since the early 1980s. During the winter of 1993, as the war in Bosnia raged and tension and human rights violations increased in Kosovo, the LPK created a military wing funded by donations from the Kosovar diaspora. Thus was born the KLA.

Reinventing Skenderbeg:
Albanian Nationalism and NATO Neocolonialism

FATOS LUBONJA

In the center of Tirana stands a monument to the Albanian national hero. Skenderbeg is at the center of the Albanian collective awareness. He was the son of an Albanian prince. He was taken away by the Ottomans as a child and brought up and trained by them to become a powerful Ottoman general. However, according to the myth as it is always retold, he did not forget his origins, and when he grew up he turned against the Turks and liberated his fatherland in 1443. He fought for its freedom for twenty-five years — until his death. Skenderbeg represents a climax in the Albanian historical memory, just as the battle of Kosova in 1389, in which Prince Milos killed the Turkish sultan, is considered one of the most important myths in the Serbian collective awareness. Despite centuries of repetition, both these myths increasingly "forget" two historical truths: that the mother of Skenderbeg (Vojsava) was a Slav; and that Albanians, too, fought alongside the Serbs against the Ottomans at the Battle of Kosova under the flag of Christianity. After six centuries, this historical "oversight" has also produced its own anticlimax: Albanians and Serbs are now killing each other. They hate each other as never before in their history, convinced not only that they are fighting for the sake of the injustices perpetrated against them, but that they are settling the accounts of their forebears.

History Shorn of Myths

Writing in the nineteenth century about nationalism, Engels made a distinction between "historical" and "nonhistorical" peoples. According to him, the first, among whom he counts the larger states of western and central Europe, have been able to construct viable states. The second, among whom Engels counts the southern Slavs (without even mentioning the Albanians), lack the necessary ability and energy. Hence, on Engels' view, these nonhistorical peoples were to be banished from the stage of history in order to facilitate the development of the historical peoples. This reflects one of the concepts of Hegel, who wrote that annexation is a crime against which one has a right to revolt only if the annexed people equally represents as large, fertile, and viable an *idea* as the *idea* personified by the occupier. There are nations that represent no *idea* and have lost their reason for existence; these nations are doomed ultimately to disappear. Yet, since that time, history has shown that the nations which, in Engels' view, were to disappear as peoples "without a history" have survived. During this time, some of these nations have liberated themselves and have made their own history (to a greater or lesser extent, earlier or later in time). It appears that "history-making" has been the main factor in forming these nations. However, the Serbs and the Albanians have pursued different paths of forming nations, and these different paths have created a widening gulf between them.

Serbs and Albanians both split from the body of the Ottoman Empire about a century ago. Yet Albanian nationalism began later than Serbian nationalism. At the beginning of the nineteenth century, when Greeks began to aspire for political freedom, nationalism was seen as the harbinger of a movement of humankind toward a better and fairer world. These views impelled Byron to fight for Greek independence. A similar movement had taken place in Serbia: guerilla wars and uprisings by Serbs brought them limited autonomy in 1815. Meanwhile, the Albanian nationalist movement was as yet unborn. The largely Islamicized Albanians still felt themselves to be part of the Ottoman Empire, which secured high offices and privileges for their leaders.

It is very important to realize that Albanian nationalism took root later, and in a different historical context. It appeared at the close of the Russian-Turkish war (1878) and subsequently, in the course of the Ottoman Empire's rapid decay, in response to the need to preserve Albanian territories from the Slavs and Greeks. Note the contrast: on the one hand, the nationalism of the Albanians' neighbors began as part of the need to achieve liberation from Ottoman rule by those with a shared Christian religious identity; on the other hand, Albanian nationalism, at this time largely Muslim, started first in response to the need to be free from the dangers posed by the Albanians' neighbors, who were Christians. Turkish support was an important factor in this. However, those who are today known as the leaders of the Albanian national rebirth, who conceived the spirit of romantic nationalism, have felt the need for separation from Turkey, and began to appeal to history and legends evoking the pre-Ottoman period. It was in this way that they came across and retrieved the national hero of Skenderbeg, who had fought against the Turks. This dualism in Albanian history is reflected in the very name of this hero. He has two names, and it is hard for Albanians to say which is the most important: Gjergj Kastrioti, which is his Christian name, or Skenderbeg, which is his Turkish title.

The historical hatred of Serbs for Albanians is rooted in the latter's links to the Turks. For Serbs, Albanians conquered their lands by means of Turkish expansion. Albanian hatred for Serbs concerns the fact that after the Russian-Turkish war and later — after the Balkan wars (1912) — the better organized and more powerfully allied Slavs of the south ("Yugoslavs") took the land where Albanians had lived for centuries. According to their own myths, Albanians claim themselves as descendants of the Illyrians, who lived in the north of Greece since the times of antiquity; hence, in their view, Albanians had inhabited this land for centuries prior to the Serbs. Kosova is the biggest part of that land.

Why Have There Been Recurrent Ethnic Cleansings of Albanians?

Contending Albanian and Serbian nationalisms have been territorially hungry for a long time. Since 1878, and throughout the twentieth century, Albanian nationalism has been fed by a desire to defend inhabited territories and aspirations for a union of separated lands. Meanwhile Serbian nationalism, which never really regarded the consolidation of their own nation-state as complete, has been nourished by a recurrent yearning to ethnically cleanse their own territories inhabited by the Albanians, as well as by ravenous racism toward Albanians. Throughout these conflicts, Serbs have been almost always in the position of the strongest and of the aggressor, while Albanians were typically victims who often tried unsuccessfully to defend themselves. These territorial longings became more and more complex as each group gradually became more regionally dispersed (especially the Serbs).

The first ethnic cleansing of the Albanians happened in 1878 (after the Russian-Turkish war), when Serbs had their independent state and took a part of the Ottoman Empire inhabited by Albanians. "The more Albanians you kick out of our land the more patriotic you are" was the slogan of Serbian King Obrenovic. It was successful. More than 100,000 Albanians were removed at that time from the area surrounding the city of Nish to other parts of the Ottoman Empire.[1] The second ethnic cleansing dates from the year 1913, just after the Balkan wars, when the Serbs took Kosova and the part of the Ottoman Empire that is now Macedonia. This second wave of cleansing was stopped by the explosion of World War I.

In the 1920s, agricultural reform gave the Serbs another pretext by which to expel more Albanians — by claiming that the land was given to them unjustly by the Turks. In the 1930s, Serbia made an agreement with Turkey to accept Albanians. During this time many Albanians left for Turkey. In 1937 a Serbian academic named Vaso Cubrilovic presented a memorandum to the Serbian fascist prime minister Stojadinovic entitled "For the Ethnic Cleansing of the Albanians." It is a long document consisting of several chapters. After one historical chapter, a second describes the Serbian need for more vital space; this is followed by chapters

---

1. The city of Nish is in current eastern Serbia. [Ed.]

that describe how the Albanians needed to be removed and were; then the document portrays how the colonization of this area with Serbs needed to be organized.[2] The project never materialized because, one year later, the troubles of World War II began. (During Tito's time, Cubrilovic became first a Serbian then a Yugoslavian academic and a member of the Yugoslavian Communist League.)

During World War II, Albanians thought that their moment of revenge had finally arrived, when the Italians and then the Germans created a "greater Albania." The Kosova Albanians even created a military division named "Skenderbeg," which fought alongside the Germans against the Serbs. But that moment would be short-lived. Even during Tito's time, in the 1950s, when an effort to disarm the population was made, many Kosova Albanians found it easier to go to Turkey (as permitted by the prewar treaty) than to relinquish their weapons or remain undefended. Nevertheless, generally speaking, we can say that communism somehow stopped the ethnic cleansing of Albanians from Kosova. In order to remain at the center of power in a multiethnic Yugoslavia with careening ethnic tensions, Tito was forced to juggle ethnic balances with the internationalism of the communist ideology. That is why he gave autonomy to Kosova in 1974. Another factor that has helped the Albanians survive ethnic cleansing has been their demographic explosion, which the Serbs have always regarded as very threatening.

The Disintegration of Yugoslavia

Often it has been simplistically remarked that fifty years of communism were like a long sound sleep that froze the memory of a people who, after waking up, found themselves back in the precommunist period. But the memory of the communist period is much more complex, like history itself. A half-century of communism in Tito's Yugoslavia revealed that different ethnic groups can live together without hate. This is only part of that history, yet it is precisely this aspect that manipulators of history want us to forget. Another part of that history disclosed a strong nationalist substratum under the communist ideology; this substratum started to appear more and more with the failure of communism as an economic system and as a hope for a better future. Even worse, the communist regime did not allow the development of some of the key elements of civil society, such as the pluralism of parties and values, as well as the acceptance of diversity. Thus new struggles for

---

2. Vaso Cubrilovic was one of the Bosnians who participated in the plot to kill Archduke Franz Ferdinand. The language of "vital space" echoes wartime Nazi language of *Lebensraum* ("living space") that was used as a pretext for expansion and aggression. According to Tim Judah, in 1937 Cubrilovic invoked the examples of German expulsions of Jews and forced population movements by Russians; during and after the war, Cubrilovic again suggested (then to communist authorities) that Albanians (and others) be expelled from Yugoslavia. See Judah, *The Serbs* (New Haven: Yale University Press, 1997), pp. 149-50. [Ed.]

power (which in the Balkans means the manipulation of crowds without individuals) were grounded in nothing other than a nationalist substratum.

If there was a crucial moment for the outbreak of evil, that was the year 1989, when Slobodan Milosevic, realizing the end of the magic power of communist symbols as instruments of power, turned to nationalist symbols and promised the Serbs that he would repair all the injustices done to them during Tito's time. That promise was made in Kosovo Polje during the 600th aniversary of the lost battle against the Turks. The first concrete action to emerge from his promise was the removal of the autonomy of Kosova. That event marked the beginning of the disintegration of Yugoslavia. There were prophets who, at that time, predicted that the process of disintegration would come full circle to return to where it started — in Kosova.

In the Yugoslavia of that time, a crack began to deepen and widen — a crack that had remained invisible and silent under the ice and iron of the Cold War and the communist principles of internationalism. That was the stress fracture caused by the crushing opposition between the principle of self-determination on the one hand and that of unchangeable borders on the other. One ideal way for resolving such powerfully opposing forces was shown by the experience of western Europe. But the problem was: Were the people of the Balkans mature enough to follow that example or not? The disintegration of Yugoslavia showed that they were not. The solution of that widening split in Yugoslavia offered three models: a clean separation, such as the separation of Slovenia, Croatia, and Macedonia; an imposition of connivance by the international community, as in Bosnia; and, what the Serbs had applied until the beginning of the war in Kosova, the domination of the stronger over the weaker, combined with a gradual ethnical cleansing.

During that period the Albanians of Kosova fooled themselves. By comparing themselves to Slovenia, which had achieved independence with only one million inhabitants, these Albanians naively pretended that, because they were two million in number, they had twice as much of a right to live separately from the Serbs as did the Slovenians. To this fantasy the Albanians of Kosova even added the argument that they should be independent because they were quite different from the Slavs; indeed, they maintained, they were not members of the Slavic family of peoples (such as Serbians, Croatians, Slovenes, Russians, Ukrainians, Bulgarians, Belorussians, Czechs, and Poles). They would reassure themselves that Albanians spoke quite a different language and had a different religion. Or again, these Albanians of Kosova would remind themselves that they had started their movement for independence as a peaceful movement. Their leader, Ibrahim Rugova, in keeping with the times, was increasingly referred to as the Gandhi of Kosova.

Meanwhile, the growth of Serb repression created a new and more frustrated generation. Most young Kosova Albanians had no chance to be well educated so that they might support a peaceful movement that respected new Western myths such as human rights, and so forth. Especially after the Dayton Accords of 1995, during which the Kosova issue was taken completely off the agenda, the Albanians of Kosova became convinced that their issue would be considered by the international community only if they would start fighting with arms for their cause. It goes without saying that the Albanians started their rebellion knowing their military inferiority but having in mind that the main protagonists of the division of borders in the Balkans — those who had made the Congress of Berlin in 1878 and that of London in 1913 — today have different relationships with each other and another vision for the world. These Albanians of Kosova were convinced that the powers that be would not let the Serbs carry out their ongoing ethnic cleansing. They were right, at least partially.

Controversy of the War

In Kosova there have been simultaneously two wars and three protagonists: the protagonists have been the Western world, the Serbs, and the Albanians; the two wars have been the nationalist war between Serbs and Albanians and the war of the Western world against the Serbs in the name of human rights and multiethnicity. In fact, Serbs and Albanians have been and still are in an anachronistic situation toward modernity. The mainstream of their politics, based on ethnic nationalism, goes against the actual Western mainstream, which supports peace rather than war, democracy rather than dictatorship, multiethnicity rather than ethnic nationalism, and integration rather than separatism. This mismatch between the times and the spirits of the peoples who live in them was especially evident in the old medieval castle of Rambouillet during the failed negotiations in February 1999. The Albanian and Serb representatives remained in separate halls while the three negotiators, the American Hill, the Austrian Petrish, and the Russian Majorski were running from one team's hall to the other team's in order to convince them to sign the agreement. The failure of Rambouillet because of the signature of only the Albanian representatives was essentially an expression of the conflict between these two spirits of time.

Despite interpretations claiming that the declared goals of the war of NATO against Serbia were not its true goals, and despite the fact that the Albanians were forced to sign that agreement because they needed Western help, Serbs bear great responsibility for opposing the aspirations of humanity for more peace, integration, and human rights. It is true that neither Serbs nor Albanians were fighting for multiethnicity in Kosova. "Nonhistorical peoples" fight for different myths. As has been the case several times in this century, these myths and their battles change the history of the so-called "historical peoples." Yet now is the time when Albanians have the opportunity to embrace the better myths of universal human rights than the earlier myths of nationalism and communism.

To paraphrase the Prussian Karl von Clausewitz's definition of war as "a continuation of politics by other means," bombardments were the continuity by military means of what the West tried to realize peacefully in Rambouillet. Now there exists an especially intractable situation. Historical events have created a horrible memory for these so-called nonhistorical peoples. Albanians and Serbs are forced to live together at a time when they hate each other more than ever in their history. There is no sign that Serbs feel guilty for the atrocities they committed toward Albanians. On their side, Albanians have never been less ready to forgive the Serbs. The West has to impose its civilization through its army. It is a new form of colonialism that has its good and bad sides.[3] We are being called to a wider and deeper history, but exactly what will come next is very difficult to predict.

Perhaps some future Albanian savant will rediscover Skenderbeg's heterogeneous origins and shifting allegiances (such as his father's conversion from Orthodoxy to Catholicism) as prototypically Western and worthy of emulation; hence Skenderbeg can be retrieved as a champion of a multiethnic Albania/Kosova. Anything is possible, but don't hold your breath. One of the essential things the recent conflict has taught us is that we nonhistorical peoples have historical memories and myths, not just changeable allegiances and preferences. But therein also lies our hope. Today Albania remains a fascinating illustration of the kind of existential questions about the necessity and harm that myths bring to the creation of a community and its transition toward a civil society — a society in which some of the most important values are the acceptance of diversity, a critical spirit, and consciousness that to err is an essential part of being human.[4]

3. As the author clarified for the editor, he favors a presence of the West, in the name of the myths of human rights, as long as it is a "wise presence." The author has further developed these themes in an article entitled "Neocolonialism and Responsibility." [Ed.]

4. This concluding sentence paraphrases a similar claim in another essay by the author, entitled "Between the Glory of a Virtual World and the Misery of a Real World," on the myth of the West as a sort of continuity of the national-communist myths in Albania. The editor would like to thank the author for his clarification of this issue based on our discussions about how the postmodern West has developed many criticisms of its own human rights discourse and its own alleged universalism. [Ed.]

A History of the Kosovo Liberation Army

TIM JUDAH

It is hardly an exaggeration to say that the Kosovo Liberation Army (KLA) must rank as the most successful guerrilla organization in modern history.[1] In the nineteen months following its first public appearance it had all but fulfilled its aims — having managed to subcontract the world's most powerful military alliance to do most of its fighting for it. After all, it hardly matters how the Serbs were ejected from Kosovo; what matters is that they have been — and had it not been for the existence of the KLA, they would still be there.

The roots of the KLA can be traced to Kosovo's years of political upheaval in the early 1980s, which centered on Pristina University. These were, of course, the years of substantial Albanian political autonomy in Kosovo, but there were those who demanded more. Specifically they wanted republican status for the province because, at least in theory, republics — as opposed to Serbia's two autonomous provinces — had the right to secede, as happened with Croatia and Slovenia. Among the agitators were so-called Marxist-Leninist groups, known as Enverists. Their name derived from Enver Hoxha, the then Stalinist dictator of neighboring Albania who ruled the country until his death in 1985.

Daut Dauti, the London correspondent for the Pristina magazine *Zeri*, sums up the Enverists succinctly: "The Marxist-Leninists were for an armed uprising in the 1980s. They had no idea what Enverism was — they just wanted to get rid of the Serbs." Many of them went to jail and, when they came out, many of them then went abroad. Bardhyl Mahmuti, who was jailed for seven years for telling Macedonian television that he wanted a Kosovo Republic and subsequently went into exile in Switzerland, says of Enverism: "It was not a question of ideology, rather Leninist theory on clandestine organizations." Not to mention the fact that making the right revolutionary noises secured at least a little help and money from Tirana.

Most Kosovars sympathized with calls for a republic, but during the 1980s the idea of an armed uprising seemed ridiculous, especially because the Serbs were

---

1. Aside from recent brief essays in assorted periodicals, as yet there is no book-length study of the KLA. This essay is the result of more than two years of interviews and research in Kosovo and elsewhere. I have also just written *Kosovo: War and Revenge*.

not even running autonomous Kosovo. Still, the Yugoslav secret services were taking no chances. On January 17, 1982, three Kosovars, militant activists abroad, were assassinated in Germany. They were the brothers Jusuf and Bardhosh Gervalla and the journalist Kadri Zeka. For the tiny group who espoused the armed uprising, and who assumed that the killings were the work of the Yugoslav secret services, it was the defining moment of their lives. Blood had been spilled. War had been declared. Later in the year these radicals founded their own party, in fact, a splinter from an existing group. It was called the Popular Movement for the Republic of Kosovo (LPRK). In Kosovo it operated by means of a secret cell structure, with members being called on to help produce and distribute radical leaflets.

Throughout the 1980s, though, the LPRK remained a marginal, extremist, and underground organization. In terms of the history of the KLA, however, a turning point came in 1989, when Slobodan Milosevic, the president of Serbia, using the sensitive issue of the Kosovo Serbs, abolished the province's autonomy. Demonstrations again shook Kosovo; and just as 1981 had been the formative moment for one generation, this renewed unrest forged the political outlook of a new crop of young activists, including the then nineteen-year-old Hashim Thaqi.[2]

But despite the unrest, the LPRK and its calls for a violent uprising against Serbia and the Yugoslav state continued to be regarded as ridiculous by the majority of Albanian Kosovars. This continued to be the case when, following the end of communist one-party rule in Serbia in 1989, Kosovo's political vacuum was filled by the new Democratic League of Kosovo (LDK). It was led by Ibrahim Rugova, an academic who preached nonviolence and wore a trademark silk scarf. Believing that the tide of history was turning their way, many members of the LPRK and other underground groups loosely known as the "the movement" left their secret organizations to join Rugova. So only the hardest of the hard remained, men who said it was beneath their dignity to be members of a party that was legal in the eyes of the Serbian state.

As Yugoslavia was crumbling, Rugova restrained his people. War would bring disaster, he argued in 1992: "We would have no chance of successfully resisting the army. . . . In fact, the Serbs only wait for a pretext to attack the Albanian population and wipe it out. We believe it is better to do nothing and stay alive than be massacred." The Kosovars had declared their independence in 1990, but under the circumstances it remained mostly a declaration of intent rather than a statement of fact. Mostly, that is, because some institutions were set up. Parallel education and health systems were formed. A government in exile headed by Bujar Bukoshi, a former surgeon, was also dispatched to live abroad, in a kind of roving regime that eventually settled near Bonn. These acts seemed to hold the promise that one day soon independence really would come.

Kosovo Albanians were now told to contribute 3 percent of their income to

---

2. See Hashim Thaqi's essay in this volume.

Mr. Rugova's republican coffers. Even more importantly, though, the *gastarbeiters* (foreign workers) in Germany, Switzerland, Sweden, and elsewhere gave money as well. The tax was not compulsory, but in this close-knit society anyone who did not contribute risked being ostracized; even worse, there were vague threats about who would be "called to account" once independence became a reality.

Horrified by the wars in Croatia and Bosnia, most Kosovars thought that Rugova, now "president" of a phantom republic, had got things right. Independence could wait a few years, especially if that meant avoiding the horrors of ethnic cleansing. Not everyone agreed. In the Albanian clubs of Stuttgart, Zurich, and Malmo (Sweden), members of the LPRK denounced Rugova as a Serbian agent. They argued that the Serbs only understood the language of force and that the quicker the Albanians realized this, the quicker they would achieve their liberation. Independence needed sacrifices, they argued, and they said that, during the time that most LDK leaders had been members of the old Communist party, they had been in prison.

As Yugoslavia slid ever further into war, most Kosovars continued to regard the LPRK as a fringe organization that did not deserve to be taken seriously. However, what was taking place on this fringe of Kosovar politics was eventually to transform the southern Balkans. In exile, people like Bardhyl Mahmuti and Jashar Salihu, another Swiss-based Kosovar, began to solicit money for their campaign among the *gastarbeiters* and to prepare for war. They also began to link up with the next generation of radicals inside Kosovo, people such as Hashim Thaqi. A series of secret meetings were held in 1993. These had two results. The LPRK split into two, one of its successors being the Popular Movement for Kosovo (LPK). In turn the LPK set up a four-man group to begin work on recruiting a guerrilla army, which they were to call the KLA. One of those men was Hashim Thaqi.

In Kosovo itself, organizing the KLA consisted of recruiting a network of "sleepers," secret sympathizers ready to fight and take command of their village or town when the time came. Arms were an enormous problem, for two reasons: first, the Serbian police, bolstered by a network of informers, were constantly raiding houses and surrounding villages in search of weapons; second, because Kosovo is landlocked, there was no way to import significant quantities of guns into the province.

From 1993 to 1995, the odd policeman was being shot down, and the KLA was claiming responsibility. But no one knew who they were; besides, Rugova was telling anyone who would listen that not only did they not exist but that these attacks were in fact being mounted by the Serbian secret police in a bid to discredit his campaign of peaceful resistance. By November 1996, though, it was clear that local Serb officials did not share this view. They had begun to take fright. Then, in January 1997, the KLA took its first casualties: three KLA members were gunned down by the police. Showing its own more ruthless side, the KLA also now took to killing Albanians whom it deemed to be "collaborators," even though many of them held the humblest of positions, such as foresters within the state forestry service.

By now the war in Bosnia was over. In November 1995, following a NATO bombing campaign against the Bosnian Serbs, they had caved in and signed up to a peace agreement at a U.S. Air Force base in Dayton, Ohio. In Kosovo, though, despite the slowly increasing numbers of KLA attacks, what was not yet clear to outsiders was that Kosovar society, both at home and abroad, had gone into deep shock. Dayton had dealt with Bosnia, and the great powers had stated unequivocally that, since Kosovo had not been a Yugoslav republic but a mere province, it had to remain part of Serbia, or at least part of Yugoslavia. And worse was to come. The EU states recognized the rump Yugoslavia of Serbia and Montenegro — and of course Kosovo, too — as an integral part of Serbia. Rugova's passive resistance had come to nothing.

In Kosovo, some Albanian politicians now began to argue that Rugova should step up the pressure, call for demonstrations, do something — anything — to get the attention of the world. But he did nothing. He appeared to have gone into a form of political paralysis. He drove around Pristina in his presidential Audi and simply did nothing.

At last, after all those years in the wilderness, the LPK sensed that things were going its way. Jashar Salihu, his friend Bardhyl Mahmuti, and the rest of the exiles, the men who had passed through Serbia's jails, could tour the clubs and meetings of Kosovar *gastarbeiters* and asylum-seekers and say, "We told you so." Still, there was no way around the fundamental problem: how to import large quantities of arms and ammunition into Kosovo. The answer to the arms question would come in the most bizarre way imaginable. In the spring of 1997, out of the blue, Albania, as state and country, simply imploded. Hundreds of thousands of people had invested their savings in fraudulent pyramid banking schemes, which the government failed to stop. Inevitably, they collapsed. Outraged, Albanians took to the streets and rose in anger against their president, Sali Berisha. As the rioters broke into arms depots, the army dissolved and the police ran away. Suddenly, Albania was awash with hundreds of thousands of Kalashnikovs. The significance of this could hardly be lost on the Kosovars: a million guns going for $10 each, and no more central government in Albania.

Abroad, the LPK began stepping up its campaign. Slowly but surely, money began flowing into the Homeland Calling fund, which was managed by Jashar Salihu, and Kosovars began buying up guns from their impoverished Albanian brothers. Disillusionment with Rugova and the notion that the armed struggle was, for the first time, a real possibility meant that recruitment at home and abroad proceeded apace. At the end of November 1997, the whole of Kosovo was electrified when masked KLA men turned up at a funeral. Still, even at this point, the number of active KLA members on the ground is reckoned to have been small, perhaps no more than a couple hundred.

By January 1998 things were proceeding well for the KLA. In the Drenica region, famous for its *kacak*, or brigand-cum-freedom fighter uprisings, the most recent having been against the Serbs in 1918 and 1944, they began ambushing police cars and shooting so-called collaborators to death. Abroad, they were making contacts with Kosovo Albanian former Yugoslav Army officers in a bid to get them to join the KLA. All that was needed now was the spark to light the fire. The KLA men thought they had things under control, but the first lesson of the Balkans is to expect the unexpected. Foreigners always forget this. This time even the Kosovars were taken by surprise.

By February the police had been forced to withdraw from much of Drenica. In one village, Prekaz, lived a local tough named Adem Jashari. Several years earlier, he had killed a Serbian policeman and was convicted, but the Serbs were afraid to pick him up because he would shoot at them from his house. They had tried in January but were forced to retreat. Jashari was a maverick. He hated the Serbs; but, though he was one of the KLA's early, and important, recruits, he was no ideological guerrilla. In the words of one source: "He liked to get drunk and go out and shoot Serbs." In this sense he was a true, dyed-in-the-wool Drenica *kacak*. Maverick though he was — and associated with the KLA — the police decided they had had enough. Foreign journalists had been hunting for him, but policemen were still being killed. On February 28, 1998, after a firefight with the KLA, they took their revenge on some other Drenica families who, they believed, were connected to it, killing twenty-six people. Then, on March 4th, they moved on the Jashari compound. Jashari resisted fiercely, so they shelled his house and other family houses, killing fifty-eight people, mostly members of his extended family.

Kosovars were now seething, and so the KLA began to move. They began to dispatch arms and uniforms rapidly over the Albanian border into Kosovo. The sleepers "awoke," village militias began to form, and clan elders, especially those in Drenica, decreed that now was the time to fight the Serbs. Whether they were KLA or not, they soon began to call themselves KLA. In this way a small guerrilla movement that was making preparations for war suddenly found itself welded to a far older tradition of Kosovar *kacak* uprisings.

The KLA made a series of lightning advances. They punched through a supply corridor from the Albanian border, close to Tropoja, in northern Albania. They were shocked by how easy everything seemed. The Serbs hardly fought back; so the Albanians proclaimed more and more "liberated territory." Milosevic seemed uncertain what to do, and the uprising, which had begun in Drenica, spread like a brushfire. But the KLA were hardly prepared. Things were moving too fast for them: their military structures were not complete, and they had not laid in stocks of anything other than Kalashnikovs, grenades, and other light weaponry. They were, in fact, winning territory, but only because the Serbs were barely fighting back.

Hearing that the KLA had set up rear bases around Tropoja, young Kosovar men began to trek across the countryside, up over the mountains, and into Albania to collect arms. It was chaotic. Some had to buy their own guns, while others were given supplies for their villages. By July 1998, though, Milosevic's period of indecision was over. Orders went out to the Serbian police to roll up the rebellion. The police swept through Drenica and other areas held by the KLA, burning the villages as they went. But, chaotic as its command structures were, the KLA made the eminently sensible decision not to fight; and the Serbs fell into a trap. The KLA's fighters withdrew to the hills, ready to fight another day, while the Serb offensive created some 200,000 displaced people. Their plight, played out nightly on television across the world, galvanized the "international community" into action.

In October, Richard Holbrooke, the architect of the Dayton Agreement and the one man deemed up to doing business with Milosevic, was drafted back into the diplomatic frame. In a deal that averted threatened NATO air strikes, Milosevic agreed to the pullback of his forces and the deployment of "verifiers" from the Organization for Security and Cooperation in Europe. As the Serbs pulled back, though, the KLA simply reoccupied territory — while both sides talked openly about a spring offensive.

The presence of the OSCE monitors helped calm the situation, but it was not enough. The KLA stood accused of kidnapping and killing Serb civilians, while the Serbs stood accused of massacres themselves, the most notorious being of some forty-five civilians from the village of Racak on January 15, 1999. This spurred the diplomats to renewed action. For months Chris Hill, the U.S. ambassador to Macedonia, had spearheaded a diplomatic shuttle mission between Kosovo and Belgrade in a bid to find some middle ground. On the KLA side, Hill had problems identifying exactly whom to speak to and who was in charge. What this proved, above all, was that, although there was a theoretical high command, much of the KLA's organization came, in fact, from the grass roots. That is to say, it was local and hence loath to take orders from unknown superiors. For example, catastrophic local initiatives by two KLA groups were the backdrop to the Serb decision to launch a counteroffensive in July 1998.

Another complication arose with the formation of the Armed Forces of the Republic of Kosovo, or FARK. These were units established under the aegis of Bujar Bukoshi, who was anxious that the government in exile not be marginalized. However, on September 21, 1998, Colonel Ahmet Krasniqi, Bukoshi's Minister of Defense, was gunned down in Tirana. Three days earlier, the KLA had issued a communiqué accusing an FARK commander of treachery. It said: "One day these kinds of people will pay for the damage they have caused to our nation." After that, FARK units stopped operating under their own name but, confusingly, began operating as the KLA, though their chain of command remained unclear: they cooperated with other KLA units on the ground but still had their own minister of defense.

Following the Racak massacre, the Western powers and the Russians, working together in the Contact Group for the former Yugoslavia, decided that the situation had become so critical that the parties should be forced to accept a compromise based on the work done by Chris Hill. Discreet threats were issued to the KLA in a bid to make sure they sent representatives to Rambouillet, a chateau outside Paris, which was chosen for the meetings that began on February 6, 1999. The Kosovar Albanian delegation included Rugova and Bukoshi; but, significantly, it was led by Hashim Thaqi, who was by now the head of the KLA's twelve-man political (as opposed to military) directorate. This signified two things: first, that Rugova's power and influence had definitively been eclipsed; and second, that the internal wing of the KLA, as opposed to the émigré LPK-dominated wing, was in the ascendant.

Thaqi dithered at Rambouillet, uncertain what to do. The deal offered was an interim proposal for the next three years; and though it did not include a promise of a referendum on independence at the end of that period, it did not rule out independence either. Neither the Serbs nor the Albanians signed. Thaqi and the others returned to Kosovo, where they discovered that the overwhelming majority of the Albanian people were in favor of the deal. Thaqi then agreed to sign.

Milosevic, for reasons still unclear, now decided to reject the deal. Although his negotiators had been upbeat toward the end of Rambouillet, convinced that a way could be found to bridge various differences, Milosevic made clear that he was not going to accept an agreement that involved the deployment of foreign troops on Serbian soil. When a second round of talks convened in Paris on March 15, the Serbs obstructed any progress, and the talks collapsed. In a bid to prod the Serbs, Western countries threatened air strikes; and when the Serbs still refused to deal, those air strikes began on March 24, 1999.

The NATO bombing campaign lasted seventy-eight days. During the first few weeks of that period, the KLA came close to being eliminated by a massive Serbian offensive. But the situation then stabilized. This was not due to the KLA's own strength but rather to the debilitating effects of the NATO raids, which helped pin down the Serbs by restricting their movements. In the interior of the province bands of KLA men roamed the countryside, and in larger concentrations they held patches of territory, some filled with refugees. Along the Albanian border the KLA held a foothold; but despite what amounted to aerial support from the U.S., if not NATO as a whole, they were unable to punch through a corridor to resupply troops in the interior. During this period the KLA was also reinforced by thousands of volunteers from the Kosovar diaspora, who flowed into the training camps of northern Albania, including a small contingent (perhaps 170 men) from the United States, known as the Atlantic Brigade. Estimates are impossible to verify, but at its peak KLA ranks may have reached 17,000 under arms.

Just before the bombing campaign the KLA appointed General Agim Ceku to be its chief of staff. Ceku was a former Yugoslav Army officer who defected to the embryonic Croatian Army in 1991. He was involved in Operation Storm in

August 1995, which saw the elimination of the self-proclaimed Republic of Serbian Krajina from the map of Croatia — and the effective cleansing of its population of 200,000.

In the aftermath of war, several things happened. Serb forces pulled out of Kosovo as the NATO-led Kosovo Force or KFOR entered on June 12. Serbian administrative structures instantly collapsed across most, but not all of the province. The KLA now moved to fill the power vacuum, not only installing its people in town halls but also setting up a provisional government led by Hashim Thaqi. At the same time tens of thousands of Serbs and others fled, fearing the vengeance of returning Kosovo Albanian refugees and of the KLA. Many KLA men, including some commanders, have been involved in acts of revenge against Kosovo Serbs. Some have talked openly of their "zero tolerance" policy, which means that they will allow no Serbs to remain in their areas.

At first the U.N. administration in Kosovo, known as UNMIK, coexisted uneasily with both the KLA and the KLA-dominated provisional government and its other so-called parallel structures. However, by the end of 1999 UNMIK and KFOR succeeded in securing a formal dissolution of both the provisional government and the KLA itself.

In what amounted to a compromise deal, much of the military high command of the KLA transferred to the Kosovo Protection Corps (KPC), which was supposed to be a purely civil emergency force absorbing some 3,000 ex-fighters. Thousands of weapons were also handed in. Although the KPC was supposed to shovel snow and help out in the aftermath of things like earthquakes, it was clear that most Kosovo Albanians regarded it as the nucleus of their future army, and it was an open secret that it still possessed large quantities of arms.

On the civilian front the U.N. secured the formal dissolution of the provisional government and the agreement of Thaqi and other leading figures to help set up a joint administration with the U.N. Parallel structures lingered on, however. Thaqi and others formed a successor political party to the KLA, although there were others that also emerged from the former guerrilla movement.

In the absence of institutions of law and order, many former KLA commanders used their influence to seize property and businesses. This led to a significant diminution in the popularity of the former KLA, as did the growing reputation of many former members of having close links to organized crime.

Although Kosovo is not (yet) independent, and thousands have died since the KLA made its first public appearance in November 1997, there is little doubt that, as far as the organization is concerned, its strategy led to complete triumph. Few believe that Serbian power will ever return to Kosovo — which means that, starting out as an organization of perhaps two hundred men in November 1997, the KLA managed to achieve what can only be regarded as an extraordinary political feat.

What Is Eastern Christianity?
The Christian East: Unity and Diversity

KALLISTOS WARE

The Christian East: Unity in Diversity

In most parts of the world, and certainly throughout the Balkans, there is a powerful interconnection between faith and nationalism, between religious allegiance and ethnic identity. We shall not begin to understand the conflicts in the former Yugoslavia without taking into account the complex religious history of the region; and this means in particular that we need to appreciate the history and the distinctive outlook of Eastern Orthodox Christians. Unfortunately for all too many observers in the West, even for those who claim to be experts, Orthodoxy remains a closed book, a strange and enigmatic world.

What do we mean by "the Orthodox Church"? Eastern Christendom in its present form constitutes a complex unity-in-diversity. The divisions that have brought about the present fragmentation of the Christian world occurred in three main stages,at intervals of approximately five hundred years. The first stage in the separation came in the fifth and sixth centuries, when what are known today as the Oriental Orthodox Churches became divided from the main body of Christians. The second stage, conventionally dated to the year 1054 — but in reality the schism developed very gradually over a lengthy period of time — resulted in the division between the Roman Catholic or Latin Church in the West, under the Pope, and the Greek Orthodox Church in the East, headed by the Patriarch of Constantinople. The third stage, in the sixteenth century, resulted in the division within Western Christendom between Catholics and Protestants. This last division did not directly affect the Christian East, although in the nineteenth century Protestant missions were established in many areas that had traditionally been associated with the Eastern churches.

At present the Christian East is subdivided into three main bodies, unequal in size:

1. By far the largest of the three is the Eastern Orthodox Church, which forms the direct continuation of the Church of the East Roman or Byzantine Em-

pire. Limited on the eastern side by the separation of the Oriental Orthodox Churches, and then on the western side by the split with the papacy, Eastern Orthodoxy expanded northward into the Slav world. Today it has perhaps 100 to 150 million baptized members.

2. Second in size are the Oriental Orthodox Churches, which exist in two groups: (a) the Church of the East, sometimes called the "Assyrian" or (less correctly) the "Nestorian" Church, with perhaps 250,000 adherents, mainly in Iran, Iraq, and Syria (also in the West); and (b) the five Non-Chalcedonian Churches (so called because they reject the Council of Chalcedon, held in 451; sometimes they are termed "Monophysite"): the Syrian Church of Antioch (the so-called "Jacobite" Church), the Syrian Church in India, the Coptic Church in Egypt, the Ethiopian Church, and the Armenian Church, altogether numbering about 30 million.

3. Smallest of all, and numbering perhaps between 5 and 10 million, are the Eastern Catholic Churches, often called "Uniate." These are groups of Eastern Christians who on different occasions since the twelfth century have entered into communion with Rome, while still retaining their different languages and liturgical practices. They are most numerous in the Ukraine but can be found in almost all the countries where the Eastern Orthodox or the Oriental Orthodox Churches are established.

Let us concentrate our attention on the first of these three groups, the Eastern Orthodox Church. This is the second largest church in the contemporary Christian world, next to — but much smaller than — the Roman Catholic Church. Its main centers today are in Greece, Serbia, Bulgaria, Romania, and Russia. It is a family of some fifteen sister churches, all of them agreed in faith, all using the same forms of worship (but in different languages), and all united with the others in sacramental communion. Each of the fifteen, however, is administratively independent. Orthodoxy is in this way decentralized in its outward structure; for, though all fifteen acknowledge the honorary primacy of the Ecumenical Patriarch at Constantinople (Istanbul), he does not lay claim to a supremacy of universal jurisdiction such as is ascribed to the Pope in Roman Catholicism. His position is more similar to that of the Archbishop of Canterbury in the worldwide Anglican communion.

These fifteen sister churches vary widely in size. At one extreme is the Russian Church, with over 100 million members before the 1917 revolution (today there are no exact statistics). In the middle range are Romania (23 million), Greece (9 million), Serbia (8 million), and Bulgaria (8 million). (These are the numbers usually claimed by these churches; but the figures, especially as regards Bulgaria and Serbia, seem greatly inflated, and in any case they represent nominal rather than active membership.) Other churches are considerably smaller: the Orthodox Church of Albania has at most about 100,000 members; and the Patriarchate of Jerusalem and the Church of the Czech Republic with Slovakia each have no more than 60,000 faithful. Emigration during the twentieth century has formed large Orthodox communities in the West, especially in North America, where there are about 3 to 5 million persons of Orthodox origin.

Certain outstanding features distinguish the Orthodox Church, although care should be taken not to exaggerate the contrasts between the Christian East and Christian West. In Orthodoxy the heart of church life is to be found in the divine liturgy — the Eucharist or service of Holy Communion. This is frequently described by the Orthodox as "heaven on earth"; for in all Eastern Christian worship there is a strong sense of the unity between the earthly church and the communion of saints. During the dark period of Turkish domination, from the fifteenth to the nineteenth centuries — in some areas for considerably longer — it was the celebration of the liturgy, more than any other single factor, that kept alive the Christian faith among the Greeks, Serbs, and Bulgarians, and that also preserved a sense of national identity.

In the annual cycle of fasts and feasts that make up the church year, a central place belongs to the festival of Easter (but at the same time Christ's resurrection is never separated from his crucifixion). Western Christians who have spent Easter in an Orthodox country will not easily forget the Paschal midnight celebration. In the words of the Romanian theologian Dumitru Staniloae, "The deepest foundation of the hope and joy which characterize Orthodoxy and which penetrate all its worship is the Resurrection. Easter, the center of Orthodox worship, is an explosion of joy, the same joy which the disciples felt when they saw the risen Saviour. It is the explosion of cosmic joy at the triumph of life, after the overwhelming sorrow of the death of the Lord." Although Orthodoxy has often been a persecuted and suffering Church — not least in the twentieth century — at its best, when it is true to itself, it has never lost this sense of Resurrection joy.

A feeling of joy is conveyed more particularly through the presence of holy icons in Orthodox churches and homes. For Orthodox Christians, an icon is not merely a piece of decoration but part of an act of prayer and worship. By the same token, they cannot envisage any act of liturgical worship that does not involve the use of icons.

Orthodoxy is strongly traditional; indeed, we Orthodox often like to describe ourselves as "the Church of Holy Tradition." All too easily in Orthodox history this devotion to tradition has degenerated into a rigid and formalized conservatism. But, properly understood, tradition is not only a protective, conservative principle but primarily a principle of growth and regeneration. It signifies not simply a slavish copying of the fast but an openness to the action of the Holy Spirit in the present. The Russian religious thinker Vladimir Lossky rightly calls tradition "the *life* of the Holy Spirit in the Church," and even "the critical spirit of the Church," while Dumitru Staniloae says that tradition is "not a sum of propositions learnt by heart but a *lived experience*."

Another feature of Orthodoxy that is bound to strike a Western observer is the close link that exists, in the religious consciousness of Orthodox Christians, between church and nation. Most — though not all — of the sister Orthodox churches are national churches. Alexander Solzhenitsyn was expressing a characteristically Orthodox standpoint when he affirmed in his Nobel Prize speech: "Nations are the wealth of humankind, its collective personalities; the very least of them wears its own special colors and bears within itself a special facet of divine intention." But at the same time Orthodox are aware of the dangers of an exaggerated nationalism such as seeks to exploit the Christian faith for selfish ethnic ends. The Orthodox Church condemns as a heresy what it terms "phyletism," that is to say, the subordination of church life to narrowly nationalist ambitions. Nationhood is indeed a gift from God, yet it must not be allowed to eclipse the universality of the Christian message. Patriotism is a precious quality that deepens and enables human personhood; but patriotism must also undergo a profound *metanoia,* a genuine repentance or "change of mind."

Patriarch Pavle of Serbia showed that he was well aware of the need for such *metanoia* when from 1992 onward he publicly dissociated himself from the excesses of the Milosevic regime. Unfortunately, his witness, and that of other Serbian hierarchs such as Bishop Artemije of the Raska-Prizren diocese, were largely ignored by the West during the Kosovo crisis. This is nothing less than tragic.

Muslim Identity and Ethnicity in the Balkans

HUGH POULTON

This paper will look briefly at the close entwining of religion and ethnicity in the Balkans, especially in those areas where Ottoman control lasted for centuries. Following the Ottoman invasion, sizable groups of indigenous inhabitants converted to the religion of their new rulers. These included the majority of the Albanians, the Pomaks (Islamicized Slavs) of the Rhodope mountains, the Serbo-Croat–speaking Slavs in Bosnia-Herzegovina and the Sandzak, and many of the Roma. Ottoman rule in the Balkans was essentially nonassimilative and "multi-national" in spirit, and as a result the peoples of the Balkans were able to retain their separate identities and cultures. Nationalism penetrating the Balkans from western and central Europe in the course of the nineteenth century was essentially a secular ideology. However, the close correlation between religion and identity in the Balkan context — a legacy of the Ottoman millet system — issued in an entwining of national and religious identities.

The Millet System

The Ottoman Empire was ruled, ostensibly at least, by Islamic precepts for most of its existence, precepts that divided its populations not along ethno-linguistic lines but by religious affiliation — the millet system. This system remained in place until changes that began with the Tanzimat reforms from the mid-nineteenth century. In accordance with traditional Islamic beliefs that uphold these as "People of the Book," the Christian and Jewish populations were readily accepted, albeit as second-class citizens.

Leaders of the various millets enjoyed wide jurisdiction over their members, who were bound by their own regulations rather than Islamic law. The Ottoman state treated the millets like corporate bodies, encouraging the perpetuation of their internal structures and hierarchies by dealing exclusively with their leaders as opposed to the individual members. These structures included educational systems specific to each religious community. The millet became established as the prime focus of identity outside of family and locality, bequeathing a modern legacy of a confusion of concepts of citizenship, religion, and ethnicity. Furthermore, as the millet system placed control of education and much of their internal affairs beyond official state control, it proved ideally suited to the transmission of the new ideology of nationalism intruding from the West in spite of the frequent tension between the traditional millet leaders and the new nationalist radicals.

The Greek patriarchate in Istanbul controlled the millet into which the Orthodox Balkan populations were organized. Until the nineteenth century, when the Bulgarian Exarchate Church was finally established, only the Serbs escaped Greek spiritual tutelage for the majority of the period under Ottoman rule due to the granting of the autocephalous patriarchate in Pec in 1557. Following the Ottoman invasion, the separate Bulgarian church and its corresponding educational system were placed under the control of the Greek Orthodox Church and the Greek patriarch in Istanbul. It can thus be argued that Orthodox Bulgarians, prior to the Bulgarian national revival in the nineteenth century, faced assimilation from the Greeks, who controlled religious services and education, both of which were held in Greek. The illiterate peasants in the countryside spoke the Slav vernacular, while the urban educated became Hellenized and spoke Greek.

While certain Christian populations faced a threat of ethnic assimilation arising out of the nature of the millet system itself, Muslim populations in the Ottoman Empire clearly faced a parallel threat of Turkification. It is important to note, however, that the modern notion of being a "Turk" was until the end of the nineteenth century alien to the Ottoman elites, who regarded themselves as Ottomans. In fact, the term "Turk" had the connotation of being an uneducated peasant. Ottoman Turkish, the language of the state, was not the vernacular of the mass of the Turkish-speaking population, and, along with being a Muslim, knowledge of Ottoman Turkish was a requirement of high office in the Ottoman state. Ethnicity was not a factor in this respect, and many Grand Vezirs and high officials were originally from Albanian, Muslim Slav, or other Ottoman Muslim populations. In spite of this, however, vernacular Turkish became widespread as the mother tongue among the Muslim populations (and even the Christian populations) of Anatolia, although this process was much less pronounced in the Balkans. What is always important to note is that, while peoples like "Turks" or "Greeks" or "Serbs" obviously predate the advent of modern nationalism, it is very dangerous to backdate modern notions of identity that have been formed and cemented under the influence of nationalist ideologies. In the Balkans "ethnic" identities have often been in a state of flux; for example, in Kosovo peoples became Serbs or Albanians over generations due in no small part to the millet system and the religion to which they adhered.[1]

In many ways the legacy of the Ottoman millet system has endured, as reli-

---

1. See Noel Malcolm, *Kosovo: A Short History* (London: Macmillan, 1998), pp. 55-56, 113-14, 131-32.

gion continues to be an important differentiating factor among people. Minorities who shared the Orthodox religion of the new Orthodox Christian national states arising from the Ottoman Empire — Bulgaria, Greece, Montenegro, and Serbia (though after the First World War the latter two became incorporated into the multinational, multireligious Yugoslav state) — have tended to be more easily assimilated into the mass of the new nation. This was especially true of "non-territorial" minorities, that is, those without an ethnic "kin state" to provide support. In some cases, even if a kin state did exist, assimilation of Orthodox minorities took place on a large scale. This is illustrated by the Orthodox Albanians in Greece, the kin state in this case (Albania) being especially weak. In contrast, it was much more difficult for the Orthodox majorities to assimilate Muslim minorities. There was, however, a tendency for smaller Muslim groups to be assimilated by the dominant Muslim minority within a particular country. This phenomenon was clearly assisted by the legacy of the millet system, as well as the concept of Islam as a transnational community of believers. While Arabic is the language of the Koran, the regional language used by hodzhas and in mosque schools has no doubt facilitated this process.

In the Balkans, the three "dominant" Muslim groups since the decline of the Ottoman Empire can be seen as the Turkish one concentrated in the East, which is in two parts: one in Western Thrace and over the border in southern Bulgaria, and the other in northeastern Bulgaria centered on Razgrad; the Albanian mass of Albania, Kosovo, and western Macedonia; and the Serbo-Croat–speaking Muslims in Bosnia-Herzegovina and also in the Sandzak.[2] For the purposes of this book, I will look at the Albanian case, which of course has direct relevance. The Turkish case has less relevance, and I will not examine it, although in some places in Kosovo, especially in Prizren and to a lesser extent in Tetovo and Gostivar in Macedonia, there remains a continuance of old elite ethnic Albanian families speaking Turkish rather than Albanian as a sign of status. (However, the growth of Albanian nationalism since the 1960s has seen something of a change in this, and it appears that this use of Turkish by Albanian families is on the decline.) I will also look at the case of the third group, Serbo-Croat–speaking Muslim Slavs, since it illustrates the central point of Islam and ethnicity in the area, as well as the problems of the identity of Muslim Slavs in the area.

---

2. Of course, this is something of a simplification: in areas like Macedonia where there is a sizeable and influential Turkish Muslim minority as well as the larger Albanian one, smaller groups of Muslims such as the Macedonian-speaking Torbesi or Gorans face potential and actual assimilation by both groups. See H. Poulton, "Changing Notions of National Identity among Muslims in Thrace and Macedonia: Turks, Pomaks and Roma," in *Muslim Identity and the Balkan State*, ed. Hugh Poulton and Suha Taji-Farouki (London: C. Hurst/New York: Hurst/New York University Press, 1997).

The Albanian Case

Albania's "late arrival" in the nineteenth-century race for territory of the ailing Ottoman Empire resulted from the fact that the majority of the population shared their faith with that of the Ottoman rulers and hence were initially less receptive to the new ideology of nationalism, as well to outside Western, Christian benefactors. Indeed, it can be argued that the impetus for the Albanian national awakening, which significantly was initially led by Christian Albanians, arose out of a realization that unless the Albanians claimed their own state, there was a danger of being swallowed up by Greece from the south and Serbia and Montenegro from the north.

The picture here is complicated by the prevalence of Bektashism among Albanians. The Bektashi Sufi sect became a major factor in southern Albania and the Albanian-inhabited areas of western Macedonia. The Bektashis are a Sufi order (named after the founder, Haci Bektash) that was widespread in the Balkans during Ottoman rule. Sufi organizations tended to absorb popular movements, and the Shiites within the Sunni Ottoman empire in particular were forced to seek asylum within them. The heterodox Bektashi order gave this phenomenon its fullest expression. This situation also applied in relation to Christian communities in the Balkans who adopted Islam. Indeed, the Sufi orders or *tarikats* facilitated the conversion of non-Islamic peoples by allowing a certain symbiosis between Islamic and other religious beliefs and practices: the wandering dervishes who accompanied or followed in the wake of the conquering Ottoman troops were thus a crucial component in this conversion of large sections of the Christian Anatolian and Balkan populations. In the Albanian case, the presence and influence of local power boss Ali Pasha of Janinna, who was a Bektashi himself, seemed to have been a major factor in spreading the sect in the areas under his control and those adjacent. Indeed, by the end of the nineteenth century, Albania had become the second Bektashi area after Anatolia. This process was no doubt also aided by the similarity between many Bektashi rites and Christian rites. Bektashism tolerated Christian saints and rites, and many Bektashi saints were deliberately ambiguous; Christian pilgrimages were allowed and stimulated by the Bektashis.[3] Some see the rise of Bektashism in this period as an expression of an "Albanian" Islam in protest to the progressive "Turkish" Sunni Islam of the Ottoman state, and the Bektashis as something akin to an Albanian national church playing a role similar to other Balkan national churches. The tolerance of Bektashism is, in this view, seen as a delib-

---

3. In addition, the elite praetorian guard of the Ottoman empire — the Janissaries — had been a stronghold of Bektashism for centuries up to their violent dissolution by Mahmud II in 1826. The Janissaries were initially formed from those Christian youths taken by the *devsirme* system to Istanbul, circumcised, and brought up as the Muslim "slave elite," and the tolerance and similarities in Bektashism of many Christian rites must surely have been a factor in the strength of Bektashism in the Janissaries.

erate policy to try to bridge the Albanians' religious differences and unite them all in one "Albanian" belief. The works of the Frasheri family, and especially Naim Frasheri, are used to support this argument.

However, I believe we should treat this theory with some caution. The theory seems to backdate concepts of nation and nationalism among the Ottoman Muslims, and it is somewhat "Albano-centric" in its view of the Bektashis of this period. The Ottoman empire was not a "Turkish" one in the parlance of modern nationalism until the Young Turks — at the very earliest.[4] Sultan Abdülhamid II, who ruled through the last quarter of the nineteenth century up to the Young Turks' revolution of 1908, was an arch-centralizer who used Islam and pan-Islam as a means of combating fissiparous tendencies among the empire's Muslim subjects.[5] Additionally, the Sufi tarikats of the empire tended to be strongly unifying rather than divisive. While there has been a symbiosis of tarikats with nationalist movements in some places,[6] this combination of Sufism and incipient nationalism — or at least the preserving of a group identity — appears to have been confined to the Caucasus. As such it can perhaps be seen as a local defense mechanism of predominately mountainous, and thus compartmentalized, Islamic communities against attack from an outside non-Muslim enemy. Elsewhere, the Sufi movements tended to be, like orthodox Islam itself, transethnic and transnational. Indeed, Sufism encouraged direct contact between Bosnia, Albania, Kosovo, parts of

4. Early harbingers of an ethnic Turkish nationalism, often émigrés from Russia and other countries where Muslim Turks found themselves minorities faced with aggressive Christian nationalism, such as Yusuf Akcura, tended to be definite outsiders in this period. Akcura's seminal work *Uç Tarz-i Siyaset* (Three Kinds of Politics) was published in Cairo in 1904 and was mostly ignored by the Ottoman elite, which still saw itself as part of the universal Muslim community. Even the Young Turk period saw outright Turkism hidden at first, and it was not until a few years after the Young Turk takeover that Albanian uprisings became a major factor. See H. Poulton, *Top Hat, Grey Wolf and Crescent: Turkish Nationalism and the Turkish Republic* (London: C. Hurst, 1997), ch. 3.

5. Poulton, *Top Hat,* ch. 3. See especially his use of Islam and pan-Islam to combat incipient Arab nationalism in the Egyptian crisis of 1881-82, and the rise of the Mahdi in Sudan. See S. Deringel, "The Ottoman Response to the Egyptian Crisis of 1881-1882," *Middle Eastern Studies* 24 (1988); Serif Mardin, *Religion and Social Change in Modern Turkey: The Case of Bediüzzaman Said Nursi* (Syracuse: State University of New York, 1989), p. 127; and F. A. K. Yasamee, "The Ottoman Empire, the Sudan and the Red Sea Coast, 1883-1889," in *Studies in Ottoman Diplomatic History,* ed. S. Deringel and S. Kuneralp (Istanbul: Isis, 1990); see also his use of Abdulhuda and the prorogation of the Rifai Sufi order in Syria to combat nationalism there; see Mardin, *Religion and Social Change in Modern Turkey,* p. 127.

6. This is especially evident in the resistance of Muslim minorities in Russia and even more so in the USSR. Faced with acute hostility from the atheist communist state, Sufism proved to be a powerful method of resistance. See Alexandre Benningsen and S. Enders Wimbush, *Mystics and Commissars: Sufism in the Soviet Union* (London: C. Hurst, 1985), *passim,* and Marie Benningsen Broxup et al., *The North Caucasus Barrier: The Russian Advance towards the Muslim World* (London: C. Hurst, 1992), *passim.*

Bulgaria and Thrace, the Arab World, Iran, and Central Asia.[7] Thus the very universality of the various Sufi movements helped bring about contacts between the widely geographically and ethnically divergent parts of the Muslim community. It helped to promote and strengthen unity in the "imagined" Islamic community (in Benedict Anderson's usage).[8]

Finally, the Bektashis, despite their popularity in southern Albania and western Macedonia, were not seen at this time as primarily an Albanian phenomenon. The population of modern Turkey is estimated to be between 10 and 20 percent Bektashi/Alevi, which (taking 15 percent as the mean) translates into a figure of between 8 and 9 million — far in excess of the total current Albanian population. Given the high birthrate of ethnic Albanians and the Sunni nature of the Ottoman and modern Turkish state, as well as Atatürk's ban on all Sufi tarikats, including the Bektashis in 1925[9] (which in theory is still in operation, though it is not enforced), there is no reason to doubt that at the turn of the century there were considerably more Turkish Bektashis than Albanian ones. This somewhat undermines the claim that Bektashism was an Albanian national religion at that time. On the contrary, Bektashis were, in Anatolia, later to be held up by the Atatürk regime as the true "Turks" since their language had not been infiltrated by Arabic infusions through Sunnism.[10]

Thus it seems likely that while some intellectual leaders such as Naim Frasheri did try to use Bektashism as a vehicle for Albanian nationalism, it was very much an elite attempt and one that at the time did not become a mass movement. Indeed, it is relevant to note that far from becoming an Albanian national church, Bektashism, despite its popularity among Albanians and its elite backing, remained a minority sect within the Albanian Muslim community.[11]

7. Harry T. Norris, *Islam in the Balkans: Religion and Society between Europe and the Arab World* (London: C. Hurst, 1993), *passim*.

8. See his *Imagined Communities: Reflections on the Origin and Spread of Nationalism* (London: Verso, rev. ed. 1991), *passim*.

9. In 1925 the World Bektashi Community headquarters was transferred to Tirana after the suppression of the Sufi Tarikats by Atatürk. See J. K. Birge, *The Bektashi Order of Dervishes* (London, 1937), pp. 84-85. This has, I suspect, aided the Bektashis as an Albanian national church by overemphasizing the Albanianism of Bektashism at the expense of the more numerous Turkish (and smaller numbers of Kurdish) Bektashis in Anatolia.

10. See Poulton, *Top Hat*, pp. 125-27.

11. The above by no means detracts from those, like Ger Duijzings, who see the rise in influence of Sufi tarikats in Kosovo as a vehicle for Albanian nationalism and Albanian identity vis-à-vis the official Sunni hierarchy of Yugoslavia dominated by Sarajevan Slav Muslims. In this much later period, Albanian nationalism was undoubtedly a mass phenomenon unlike what it was in the late nineteenth century.

The Bosniaks

The historic indeterminacy of national identity of the Muslim Slavs in the region is highlighted by the development of the largest Muslim Slav group in the region — the "Muslims" (now called Bosniaks) of Bosnia-Herzegovina and the Sandzak. Historically, this community has been claimed by both the Serbs and Croats. In order to overcome this rivalry, Tito's Yugoslavia progressively saw the Muslim Slavs as a separate people. The change can be seen in succeeding census terminology: in 1948 they were classified as "indeterminate Muslims"; in 1953 as "indeterminate Yugoslavs"; in 1961 as "Muslims in the ethnic sense"; in 1971 as "Muslims in the sense of nationality"; and finally in 1981 as a separate "nation" of Yugoslavia. This clarification as one of the "Nations of Yugoslavia" can be seen, similarly with the Macedonians and Montenegrins, as at least in part propagated by the state.[12]

It should be noted that religious observance as measured in an opinion poll in 1985 was low — only 17 percent[13] — and thus their identity rested more on customs and culture and the millet legacy than on religious observance. However, the Islamic religious community (IZ) was, for most of former Yugoslavia's life, dominated and controlled by the Sarajevo Muslim Slavs, and the prevalence among Yugoslavia's Muslim Albanians of Sufi sects like the Rufai of Prizren, as opposed to the orthodox Sunnism of the IZ, can be seen on one level as expressions of ethno-national differences within Yugoslav Islam.[14] By the late 1980s, the IZ began to change and attempted to become less Bosnian-dominated, culminating in the unanimous election of Jakup Selimovski, a Macedonian and the first ever non-Bosnian, as Reis-ul-Ulema in November 1989. The new line, while condemning Albanian irredentism, showed solidarity with the Kosovo Muslims and gave an increasing emphasis to a supranational Islamic identity that would unite Yugoslav and east European Muslims, but supported individual national identities. In line with this latter point, the IZ joined the Party of Democratic Action (SDA), the main Muslim political grouping, in calling on Bosnian Muslims to give their mother tongue as "Bosnian" rather than Serbo-Croat in the 1991 census.[15]

While the concept of a "Muslim" or "Bosniak" national identity was perhaps

12. See Poulton, *The Balkans: Minorities and States in Conflict* (London: Minority Rights Group, 1993), ch. 4, *Muslim Identity and the Balkan State* (New York: New York University Press, 1997), ch. 4, and *Who Are the Macedonians?* (Bloomington: Indiana University Press, 1995).

13. This was lower than Kosovo (44%), Croatia (33%), Slovenia (26%), and Macedonia (19%), but higher than Serbia (11%) and Vojvodina and Montenegro (both 10%) [Interview, Belgrade, 28 March 1986].

14. See Ger Duijzings, *Religion and the Politics of Identity in the Balkans* (London: C. Hurst, forthcoming), though Duijzings warns that this is somewhat simplistic and is careful not to fall into the trap of ethno-reductionism.

15. Cornelia Sorabji, "Islam and Bosnia's Muslim Nation," in *The Changing Shape of the Balkans,* ed. Frank Carter and Harry Norris (London: UCL, 1996), pp. 57-58.

weak within the life span of former Yugoslavia, it has become cemented by war and bloodshed. Here I should note that both the Serbs and the Croats viewed them as "different," as competitors for territory, and pursued policies of "ethnic cleansing" against them — this despite historically claiming them for their own particular group. Increasingly, the SDA has adopted Islamic insignia and symbols, and there has been a steady drift toward Islam as a basic source of identity in place of the more citizen-orientated multiethnic and multidenominational approach represented by Haris Silajdzic and others.[16]

Conclusion

In conclusion we can note that identity in the Balkans is intimately entwined with religion. The successor states to the Ottoman Empire that pursued policies of assimilating and homogenizing the diverse populations within their territories tended to view Muslims as "alien" and essentially nonassimilatory. The exception here is Albania, where Muslims made up a majority (and to a lesser extent Bulgaria, where the Pomaks have periodically been subjected to assimilatory policies seeking to make them "true Bulgarians").[17] While this caused no problems of identity for Turks or Albanians, it did for Muslim Slavs, who shared their mother tongue with the Orthodox majorities but were separated from them by religion and religious customs and the millet heritage. The concentrations of Muslim Slavs in Bosnia-Herzegovina and the Sandzak, which were comprised of both village communities and, perhaps more importantly, urban elites, have slowly evolved their own "Bosniak" identity, while other smaller groups of predominantly village Muslim communities have faced assimilatory pressures from the "dominant" Muslim groups in the Balkans.

16. Examples of this are Reis-ul-Ulema Mustapha Ceric's remarks in late 1994 criticizing mixed marriages. Furthermore, renowned journalists who were considered to be unsupportive of the new line were removed from the state television, TV BiH, by SDA executive member Amila Omersoftic. Omersoftic has also led attacks on Silajdzic. See Milica Pesic and Aim Sarajevo, "Battle for Bosnia's Soul," in *Balkan War Report: Bulletin of the Institute for War and Peace Reporting* (London, February 1995, no. 310), p. 7. Another example appeared at an SDA rally near Sarajevo on September 10, 1996, when speakers stressed the three elements of "Bosniak" identity with Islam and faith as the first pillar, followed by Bosnian land and unity of the Bosnian people (Radio Bosnia-Herzegovina, Sarajevo, September 10, 1996).

17. See Hugh Poulton, *Minorities in Southeastern Europe: Inclusion and Exclusion* (London: MRG 97/6, 1998).

Serbs and Muslims in the
Distorted Mirror of the Yugoslav Crisis

DARKO TANASKOVIC

In the analyses and attempts to interpret and understand the contemporary Yugoslav crisis, which deepened at the beginning of this decade, one of the factors that has been given special attention has been the "Serbian-Muslim conflict." And indeed, when viewed superficially, Serbs and Muslims entered into a phase of mistrust, mutual suspicion, political friction — and even engaged in armed conflict — practically everywhere they lived together or next to each other in the territory of the former Yugoslav federation (in Bosnia-Herzegovina, in Kosovo-Metohija, in the Raska district, i.e., the Sandzak in Serbia). Considering the fact that this conflictual situation was created between Serbs and the two largest Muslim communities in Yugoslavia — the Muslims of the Serbo-Croatian/"Bosniac" language in Bosnia-Herzegovina and the Albanians in Kosovo-Metohija — a notion has arisen about a Serbian conflict with Islam, that is, with Muslims as Islamic believers.

That notion, however, along with many others connected to the Yugoslav crisis, does not fully reflect reality. There has not been any disagreement between, for instance, the Serbs and members of the ethnic Turkish national minority in Kosovo or the Islamized Roma (Gypsies). This, of course, does not mean that a renewed, traditional matrix of the Orthodox-Muslim conflict has not been ideologically, motivationally, propagandistically, and emotionally activated and made effective in the complex meeting of politics and nations on the territory of the former Yugoslavia.

Produced by two decisive factors in world politics from the early 1990s, namely, the global redistribution of power and the process of Yugoslavia's internal disintegration, the Yugoslav crisis has been the focus of much international attention; hence it is understandable that the trend toward tendentiousness in reporting, analyzing, and explaining could not be avoided in Yugoslavia. In fact, the greatest amount of the voluminous literature dedicated to this challenging topic, or some of its aspects, is decisively marked by uncritical biases.

This essay was translated from the Serbian by Gordon Bardos.

Depending on whose goals they are supposed to serve, the lines of tendentiousness in the approach to the Yugoslav crisis and its explanation are, naturally, different and even contradictory. It is necessary to point out the unfounded basis of the judgments concerning the predominantly fundamentalist character of the new system of political values among the Muslims in Bosnia-Herzegovina, but also to reveal the phenomenon of politicized Islam in one part of the social spectrum in this republic. Science must reject the anachronistic thesis about the "original sin" of those accepting Islam, used as a hypothesis that is supposed to serve as a political handicap for their contemporary Yugoslav descendants.[1]

The connections between Islamic organization and Albanian separatism/irredentism must be followed and analyzed carefully through history, and not included, as some Serbian or Greek theoreticians do, in the ideologization of a threatened "green transversal."[2]

On the other hand, the strengthening of the Islamic element, for the first time since the Ottoman Empire's withdrawal from these regions, cannot be denied in some strategically strained parts of the Balkans; this not only concerns Serbs and Greeks, but Macedonians, Bulgarians, and others as well.

The dynamics of the ebb and flow, which through the centuries have been characteristic of the migrations of Christians from the Muslim advance and of the Muslims from the Christian "reconquests" in the Balkans, along with the customary suffering of the civilian population, should be examined objectively. But all too often the ebb is overlooked in silence while the flow is criminalized, and vice versa. Because of that, it is most urgent to critically scrutinize the globally dominant tendency of analyzing and explaining the Yugoslav crisis as a "Serb-Muslim conflict." The global dominant tendency in the presentation of the Yugoslav crisis, including the "Serbian-Muslim conflict" and the tragedy in Kosovo, has been expressly anti-Serbian. That makes it scientifically unacceptable, not because of the systematic guilt placed on the Serbs but because it is a simplified and distorted picture projected on the complex reality — not only to contemporaries but to future generations as well.

In this short review I will limit myself to formulating a few methodological designations, especially necessary when confronting the works of "experts" on the Yugoslav crisis, such as Noel Malcolm, Jacques Juillard, Branka Magas, and even so well-known a person as Paul Garde. . . .[3]

1. This refers to criticisms sometimes leveled against Muslims from Bosnia-Herzegovina, whose orthodox Christian ancestors converted to Islam. [Ed.]

2. The "green transversal" mentioned here is sometimes used by political observers to refer to an "Islamic belt" of territory stretching across the Balkans from Istanbul through Muslim-populated areas of Bulgaria and Macedonia, and into Albania. [Ed.]

3. Among his other works, Noel Malcolm is author of *Bosnia: A Short History* (New York: New York University Press, 1994) and *Kosovo: A Short History* (New York: New York University Press, 1998); Branka Magas is author of *The Destruction of Yugoslavia: Tracking the Break-Up 1980-92* (London: Verso, 1983). [Ed.]

I am convinced that my antitheses will stand the test of time and the demands of a truly scientific approach to the Yugoslav crisis. Over the following years, with adequate argumentation and the development of the corrective I present here, I hope that a necessary interpretive counterweight to the dominant representation of the "Serbian-Muslim conflict" will appear. Given the limited space, I have had to be extremely selective in naming these methodological antitheses:

1. "Ethnic cleansing" is an innovative term brought into the discourse on the Yugoslav crisis/"Serbian-Muslim conflict" to give the impression of some new phenomenon that characterizes Serb politics and political culture. What this suggestive neologism refers to is not, unfortunately, anything new in the Balkans — or even in Europe; and it is incorrect and unscientific to tie it exclusively or primarily to the contemporary phase of the "Serbian-Muslim conflict," the Yugoslav crisis in general, or just one nation. "Ethnic cleansing, throughout the whole history of Europe, was not an exception, but the rule."[4]

2. The Muslim communities in southeastern Europe in the post-Ottoman period and their relations with the majority non-Muslim communities in the newly created independent states (except in Albania) have still not been researched to a satisfying degree. There are many reasons for this, of which one is essential: the pronounced "ideologization of conflict" approach to this difficult theme, especially in Balkan national historiographies.[5]

3. Because of this, a high degree of caution is necessary in making sweeping judgments and evaluations of the whole or individual aspects of this problematic. Methodologically, it is unsound to choose just those sources and works that correspond to the original thesis.

4. A primarily negative representation of Islam, and especially of Muslims, is not unique to the Serbs but is in fact part of the historical consciousness and the collective psychological stereotypes of all Christian nations of southeastern Europe, which during parts of the past were in conflict with Islamic believers or under their rule. Innumerable proofs of this exist in practically all spheres of spiritual life and culture, as well as a voluminous literature. It seems to me that some contemporary "experts" find it difficult to believe that Serbs overcame their hostility to their recent Muslim rulers even more quickly than did other Balkan peoples.[6]

4. See G. Bocchi and M. Ceruti, "Solidarieta e barbarie. L'Europa delle diversita contro la pulizia etnica" (Milan, 1994), p. 1.

5. See A. Popovic, "Les musulmans du Sud-Est Europeen dans la periode post-Ottomane. Problemes d'approche," *Journal Asiatique* 263 (1975): 317-60.

6. See D. Tanaskovic, "Les themes et les traditions ottomans dans la litterature bosniaque," in *Die Staaten Sudosteuropas und die Osmanen* (Munich, 1989), pp. 299-307.

5. In the conflict with Muslims during the disintegration of the Yugoslav feder-
    ation, Serbs were not, as is sometimes portrayed, motivated primarily by
    mythical, historical, and hereditary reasons, but by quite real and existential
    contemporary reasons, as were their Muslim opponents. The "Kosovo
    myth," on which some contemporary "experts" insist, was activated only
    secondarily, as was, for instance, the thesis of a "new crusade" on the Mus-
    lim side. The sources of the conflict were political, territorial, economic, and
    existential — far from a mythic consciousness or some kind of endemic
    mytho-mania obsessed with the past. The myth spoke only when life be-
    came unbearable, and injustice inexplicable and incomprehensible, about
    the order of things in the contemporary world, for which it was (naively)
    believed to be based on at least a few stable international axioms.

6. From 1945 to the outbreak of the Yugoslav crisis in the Socialist Federal Re-
    public of Yugoslavia (SFRY), Muslims were in no sense an oppressed social,
    ethnic, or religious group, as some "experts" wish to portray it. In fact, it can
    be said that the Slavic Muslims in Bosnia-Herzegovina during this specific
    period were the favorites of Tito's regime.[7]

7. The same can basically be said of the Albanians, with the exception, of
    course, of those who were especially oriented toward separatism. The limits
    for Muslims in some areas of spiritual and cultural life were a consequence
    of the ideological and political dogmas of the regime, and they affected all
    ideological nonconformists — without distinction between Orthodox or
    Muslims. The Catholic church, all in all, managed its way the best.

8. As soon as the breakup and destruction of Yugoslavia began — and in con-
    trast to the other Yugoslav peoples (the Slovenes, Croats, and to a lesser ex-
    tent the Macedonians) and the Albanian national minority — Serbs and
    Muslims/"Bosniacs" in Bosnia-Herzegovina were the only ones who did not
    have at their disposal articulated, nationalist, state-forming projects and de-
    veloped separatist plans of action that were orchestrated by the interna-
    tional situation. They were not ready for the impatiently dictated requests
    of the so-called "international community." Both existentially tied their
    statehood and national identity to the six-member Yugoslav federation,
    which was destroyed in a planned manner. Serbs and Muslims were dragged
    into a tragic conflict against their own real vital interests because they were
    left in a kind of ideological and political vacuum, and not, as it is "politically
    correct" to interpret things today, because of the effort to realize the idea of
    a Greater Serbia (on the Serbian side), or even the fundamentalist utopia of
    a theocratic state (on the Muslim side). Serbian nationalism was objectively
    reactive, and to some extent grotesquely artificial, and because of that,

---

7. See A. Popovic, *Les musulmans yougoslaves, 1945-1989: Mediateurs et Metaphores*
(Lausanne, 1990).

deeply inauthentic and politically unproductive. It was not *projective*. Neither did the majority of Muslims/"Bosniacs" in Bosnia-Herzegovina feel much better in the attire of the newly composed "Bosniac-hood" or in imported fundamentalist Islam. Yugoslavia suited both ethnic groups the most.

9. The infamous project of "Greater Serbia" never really became politically, militarily, or governmentally operational, despite being characterized as the key destructive factor in the negative dynamics of the Yugoslav crisis. On the contrary, from the initial conservative desire to continue life in a common Yugoslav state, the Serbian state and ethnic territory during the Yugoslav crisis always became smaller; the same can be said of the Croatian and the Albanian state and ethnic territory as well — especially for the latter. The idea of the "greater states" is characteristic of all of the political traditions of the relatively small Balkan states, and is in no way simply unique to the Serbs.[8]

10. As things now stand, only the "Greater Albania" concept has any explicit chances of being partially realized, due to the support of the so-called international community. The chances for a "Greater Croatia" are somewhat poorer, even though in Zagreb they still do not have reason to reject all hope. A "Greater Serbia" is too funny even to discuss; the "experts" are now full of anti–Greater Serbian rhetoric as the key to proclaiming the regime in Belgrade — and Serbs in general — the black sheep of the Balkans in transition.

11. The conflict in Kosovo contains a dimension of a religious, that is, Orthodox-Muslim conflict; but it is not primarily religiously motivated. The human or minority rights of Albanians in Kosovo are not endangered, as widely portrayed in the world. Rather, the issue is a contemporary phase in the struggle for the territory of the region, to which, using different expansions, both Serbs and Albanians lay claim. With changing fortunes for both sides, that battle has lasted through the last several centuries. At this moment it looks as though contradictions that are difficult to reconcile among the principles of international relations, the inviolability of state borders, and the right of peoples to self-determination (in the case of Kosovo) are beginning to be resolved in favor of the Albanian minority in Serbia. Why? Because, thanks to the will of the main centers of power in the world, after the military intervention against the sovereign state of the FRY, preconditions are being created for violent self-determination, along with the implementation of a planned ethnic cleansing, of which Serbs had earlier been accused.

8. See, e.g., S. Bianchini, *Sarajevo-le radici dell' odio* (Rome, 1993), p. 21.

Vuk's Knife: Kosovo, the Serbian Golgotha, and the Radicalization of Serbian Society

MICHAEL A. SELLS

Critics of the NATO air war over Kosovo argued that NATO's use of force strengthened Yugoslav President Slobodan Milosevic and silenced the vigorous dissent that had existed in Serbia. The more determined critics called for an immediate end to the NATO air campaign and worked fervently to achieve such a halt. The stakes of these debates were high. A sudden abandonment of the bombing, after Serb forces had launched a savage assault on Kosovar civilians, would have left Kosovar Albanians hostage to the goodwill of the Serbian military, paramilitaries, and police — who would have been able to act with impunity.

Earlier in Bosnia, in 1995, U.N. military commander General Bertrand Janvier abandoned the air-strike option and turned the thousands of unarmed captives from the "safe haven" of Srebrenica over to the Serb army. Some 8,000 boys and young men were separated out (some in front of U.N. troops) and led away for extermination, despite Serb General Ratko Mladic's assurances that the unarmed captives would not be mistreated. Had the air campaign been halted before an enforceable peace agreement, Kosovo risked suffering the fate of Srebrenica on a much grander scale.

Among the factors ignored by those who opposed the use of force against the Milosevic regime is the radicalization of Serbian society over the last fifteen years. Most demonstrators on the streets in 1996 were not, as the NATO critics have maintained, protesting the Serbian regime's policy of "ethnic cleansing" or demanding civic democracy. Of the three leaders of the demonstrations, only Vesna Pesic opposed Belgrade's policies of ethnic and religious conflict. The two leaders with larger followings, Zoran Djindjic and Vuk Draskovic, have been proponents of ethnic and religious confrontation. When Milosevic left the Serbian presidency (constitutionally limited to two terms) to become president of Yugoslavia, his candidates for president of Serbia were defeated by Vojislav Seselj, the most extreme proponent of ethnic cleansing, and Milosevic was forced to use fraud to keep his party in power. Meanwhile, the indicted war criminal Arkan had become a major celebrity and popular hero in Serbia. With the exception of

Bishop Artemije and Father Sava Janjic, the leaders of the Serbian Orthodox Church, while critical of Milosevic for losing wars and leaving behind hundreds of thousands of Serbian refugees, have been among the most ardent proponents of religious nationalism. Any responsible attempt to respond to conflicts or to work for long-range reconstruction must acknowledge how religious nationalism has damaged the region and, in particular, the social fabric of Serbia. Though connected to the past, this virulent nationalism is neither "age-old" nor inevitable, but rather a product of the past two decades.

Kosovo is at the center of Serbian national mythology and has now become the arena of its most intractable violence. Attached to Kosovo is a symbolic complex, a set of symbols each of which links into the others and compounds their power. For the sake of clarity and brevity I will present these elements one by one.[1]

1. Mythic Time

Ritual and symbol work to create a collapse of mythic time into the present. In a passion play, the actors who kill the martyr (e.g., Jesus or Imam Hussein) exit the stage quickly to avoid being pummeled by the audience. When rushing the stage, the crowd is no longer an audience watching a reenactment of an ancient event; they now experience themselves within the primordial moment.

Prince Lazar, the hero of the famous battle of 1389 against the Ottoman forces, is an explicit Christ figure. His death is referred to as the "Serbian Golgotha." In the modern period he has been depicted at a last supper surrounded by twelve disciples, one of whom is a traitor, and ministered to by a Mary Magdalene figure known as the Maiden of Kosovo.

The collapse of time was clearly evident at the momentous 600th anniversary commemoration of the death of Lazar that occurred on June 28, 1989. The relics of Lazar were transported around Serbia and through Kosovo and arrived at the monastery nearest the battle site on the feast day of Lazar (Vidovdan), where they were ceremonially unveiled for the first time in history. References to the battle of Kosovo dominated Serbian society in the period leading up to the commemoration. A huge throng of more than a million Serbs turned out to hear Milosevic's bellicose speech as they waved images of Lazar next to photos of Milosevic, the proclaimed new or resurrected Lazar. Rage was directed against

1. For a full presentation of this symbolic matrix, see Michael Sells, *The Bridge Betrayed: Religion and Genocide in Bosnia* (Berkeley: University of California Press, 1996). The 1998 printing of *The Bridge Betrayed* includes a preface, written on June 28, 1998, discussing the impending war in Kosovo and the violence that would be unleashed within it, as well as systematic documentation of each of the statements made below. I have also been constructing, in connection with the book, a Balkans human rights and war-crimes web page: http://www.haverford.edu/relg/sells/reports.html.

all Muslims. Intellectuals and academics in Belgrade wrote openly that the Muslims of today have the blood of the Serbian martyrs and the Christ-prince Lazar on their hands. In view of the known effects of similar charges against Jews, this was libel of the most ominous nature.

Western commentators tend to dismiss as bizarre the Serb veneration of a defeated hero and commemoration of a defeat. In fact, the veneration of fallen martyrs is common to most nations and cultures, and the particular mode of the veneration of Lazar is an extension of the Christian commemoration of Christ's passion, with all the power that story entails. What was not bizarre, but tragic, was the way this deep paradigm was tied to an ideology of genocide.

2. Sacred Place

The historian of religions Mircea Eliade popularized the notion that cultures return periodically or cyclically, through their rituals and symbols, to a sacred time and sacred place that imbue life with meaning and contrast to the linear world of purely historical time. The sacred time of the battle of Kosovo is tied to Kosovo as sacred place: Kosovo's sacrality resides both on Kosovo Polje, "the field of the blackbirds," the spatial manifestation of the Serbian Golgotha, and in the artistically magnificent medieval monasteries of Kosovo, epitomized by Gracanica, which represent the golden age and, more mythically, the time of paradise.

3. Christoslavism and Mythic Versions of Classical History

No people can be expected to appreciate their colonizer. But the contemporary nationalist reaction to Serb history is dominated by a mythification of Ottomans, Turks, and Muslims as pure evil. The most important work of nineteenth-century Serb nationalism was *The Mountain Wreath,* a verse drama published in 1857 by the Montenegrin Orthodox bishop known as Njegoš. *The Mountain Wreath* opens as Serb bishops and knights decide to "cleanse" Montenegro of non-Christians. The Vlad (Prince-Bishop) summons the Slavic Muslims and offers them a last chance to convert. The Muslims reply that Orthodox and Muslim are one people, and they request a "godfather" *(Kum)* ceremony through which blood feuds were healed. When Serb elders reply that the ceremony requires baptism, the Muslims suggest baptism for the Christian child and ritual tonsure for the Muslim child. The Orthodox reject the interreligious *Kum* ceremony and drive the Muslims away as "Turkifiers" and "spitters on the cross." The play ends with a celebration of the Christmas extermination of the Muslims, the annihilation of all traces of their existence, and a ceremonial communion (without the confession obligatory after all killings) for the Serb knights. *The Mountain Wreath* was reprinted, disseminated, and celebrated as a major part of the preparations for the 1989 commemoration. And as Serb forces "cleansed" villages in Bosnia, Serb nationalists posted on the Internet verses that depicted the most graphic images from *The Mountain Wreath* celebrating the annihilation of the "Turkifiers."[2]

The concept of "Turkifier" in *The Mountain Wreath* reflects Christoslavism, the belief that Slavs are Christian by nature, that any conversion from Christianity can only be done out of cowardice or greed, and that conversion transforms the convert into a non-Slav. Specifically, a Slav who converts from Christianity is transformed ethnically into a Turk. Twentieth-century writers (both Catholic and Orthodox) combined this ideology of Christoslavism with racialist ideas. Conversion was simultaneously a race-betrayal and race-transformation that left one perpetually outside the "people" and placed one alongside those with the blood of the Christ-prince Lazar on their hands. The novels and non-fiction of Ivo Andric were particularly important in popularizing the vision of Slavic Muslims as race-betrayers and Turks.

Christoslavic assumptions about conversion were linked to the portrayal of Ottoman and Islamic rule as one of unremitting savagery. Serb nationalists claimed that the Ottomans: (1) refused to allow the building of Serb churches and monuments (though in fact they authorized hundreds and supported the Serbian Orthodox Patriarchate); (2) took vast numbers of Serbs as Janissaries in a "blood tribute" that drained Serbia of its life and manhood (though in fact the number of Janissaries, both Christian and Muslim Slavs, was far less than the genocidal proportions claimed); and (3) destroyed the existing Serbian churches and monasteries. Ironically, the last claim is commonly elaborated from within the very Orthodox monasteries in Kosovo that have survived both Ottoman rule and Albanian neighbors, and derives an ironic symbolic power from the artistically and religiously potent site of that claim.[3]

---

2. Bishop Petar Petrovic II (Njegos), *The Mountain Wreath*, translated by Vasa Mihailovich (1986).

3. This claim and its essentialist view of Islam has been adopted by polemicists such as Jacques Ellul and Bat Ye'or. Thus Bat Ye'or, who relies on Serbian nationalist writers such as Jovan Cvijic, declares as an essentialist truth that 'The umma claims a monopoly of culture: the dhimmis' languages are banned, relegated to the liturgy, their monuments, testimony to their civilizations' greatness, are destroyed or Islamized.' Bat Ye'or, *The Decline of Eastern Christianity under Islam* (Madison: Farleigh Dickinson University Press, 1996), p. 239. In 1994, Bat Ye'or testified in U.S. congressional hearings as an expert on Islam and is cited as an expert on Islam in writings of extreme Serbian nationalists in the U.S. and their political supporters in Congress.

4. Recent Historical Memory

After the death of Marshall Tito, the deep wounds of World War II, in which hundreds of thousands of Serbs had lost their lives through Ustashe and Nazi genocide, resurfaced. Tito had forbidden the discussion of World War II grievances; thus when they resurfaced after his death, they did so with the power of the return of the repressed. Tragically, Serbian intellectuals, frequently making use of Serbian Orthodox publications, turned the pain of World War II toward their own dehumanizing of Croats, Bosnian Muslims, and Albanians. Rather than focusing blame on the individuals and groups responsible for the World War II grievances, Serb intellectuals presented all Croats, Bosnians, and Albanians as inherently genocidal. They also offered a revisionist history of World War II that ignored or denied the participation of significant numbers of non-Serbs in the Partisan resistance, as well as the organized atrocities carried out by the Serbian royalists known as Chetniks against non-Serbs.

At the same time that Lazar's relics were transported around Serbia and Kosovo, the remains of Serb victims of World War II atrocities were being disinterred. The disinterment of the remains of family members of those still living was done at emotional ceremonies dominated by nationalist portrayals of non-Serbs in Yugoslavia as genocidal by nature and eager to carry out a new genocide against Serbs; the ceremonies combined with the transport of the relics of Lazar and its mytho-historical time to create a potent mixture.

5. False Claims of Contemporary Genocide

In 1982, as tensions between Albanians and Serbs grew, Serbian Orthodox clergy published claims that Albanians were attacking and destroying Serb monasteries and their cultural heritage, committing genocide, and reinstituting a centuries-old Albanian plot to exterminate Serbs and carry out another Serbian Golgotha. These claims, along with charges that Albanians were committing organized rape against Serb women, dominated the media and were presented as fact. They were repeated by numerous intellectuals in articles written for volumes commemorating the 600th anniversary of the death of Lazar. The genocide charge was central to the infamous *1987 Memorandum of the Serbian Academy of Sciences and Arts* (SANU). The *Memorandum* was a vehement attack on other Serb republics, based on the charge that Albanians were engaged in genocide against Serbs and that other republics were their accomplices.[4]

---

4. The *Memorandum* was never published, but rather leaked to the media. A new document of SANU defending the *Memorandum* is even more extreme in its charge that Croats and Muslims are inherently genocidal and that Serbs cannot live with them. See Kosta Mihailovic

Tragically, those Serb intellectuals, such as Dobrica Cosic, who had the power to present valid Serb grievances in Kosovo in a more accurate manner and to resist the hazardous use of false charges of genocide, instead joined in the instigation of fear and rage. While Serbs suffered from a variety of factors in Kosovo, the charges of mass rape, systematic annihilation of Serb sacral heritage, and genocide were pure fabrications and were proven to be so by human rights workers and Serbian dissident journalists. But by being tied into the other four elements of the Kosovo mythology and presented by the church, state, and media as facts, they became impervious to factual refutation. The myths became too powerful not to be believed.

These charges led to a chilling reversal, a counterlanguage. The very program that the Serbian Orthodox Church and authors of the *Memorandum* falsely attributed to Kosovar Albanians became in fact a code for Serb military, police, and paramilitary action. In Bosnia, claims broadcast on Serb nationalist radio that Muslims were destroying Serb churches, engaging in mass rape of Serb women or kidnapping Serb women for their "harems," and engaging in mass killing became signals to Serb militias to begin such activities against Muslims.

The Kosovo monasteries were still standing, intact after centuries of Ottoman and Albanian rule in the area; but within three years Serbian militias had destroyed every Islamic monument in the areas of Bosnia they controlled. More than a thousand mosques and shrines, including major masterworks dating back to the sixteenth century, such as the Ferhadiya in Banja Luka and the Colored Mosque of Foca, were annihilated. In Sarajevo, the Serb army burned the National Library (more than a million volumes and 100,000 rare books) and the Oriental Institute (over 5,000 manuscripts in Arabic, Persian, Turkish, Slavic, and Aljamiado). Their goal was to establish as fact the myth that Muslims and Christians never were and never could be "one people" and were doomed to "age-old antagonisms," and they sought to accomplish it by effacing 500 years of evidence of shared civilization.[5] During and after the NATO air campaign, the Serbian Orthodox Church continued its abuse of the Serbian sacral heritage with a website containing a page entitled "The Bombing of Serbian Shrines." The site included, along with claims that NATO was bombing the shrines, a map with icons of bomb blasts over each shrine, as if NATO's bombs were falling directly on them. Like the earlier charges in the 1980s, these charges turned out to be false; but they continued to stoke the flames of fear and hatred in Serbia.[6]

---

and Vasilija Kvestic, *Memorandum of the Serbian Academy of Sciences and Arts: Answers to Criticisms* (Belgrade: SANU, 1995), available at the SANU website at http://www.beograd.com/sanu/.

5. See Andras Riedlmayer, "Bosnia's Cultural Heritage and Its Destruction" (Philadelphia, 1994), videocassette, as well as the photo essays on the Community of Bosnia Web page: http://www.students.haverford.edu/vfilipov.

6. The site existed at http://spc.org.yu/index03.html until July of 1999.

Each of the elements discussed above contains the others within it, in a highly intertwined set of relations. Thus Vuk Draskovic's novel about World War II, *The Knife,* now being revived in Serbia in a popular movie, demonizes all Croats and Muslims as subhuman sadists. It portrays Muslims as race-betraying Serbs, treats Nazi occupation as a return to Muslim rule, and links the Muslim sub-humanity to the crucifixion of Christ in a way that would evoke for its audience the Serbian Golgotha, thus making eternal and unchangeable the depravity of Muslims. One scene from the movie version has been described as follows:

> The gruesome images on the screen include blood dripping on the face of Christ as liturgical music pumps out of the sound system. Father Nikifor, the Orthodox priest, cries out as he is burned alive in his church: "God sees everything. We will get justice."
>
> His Muslim killers grin and chuckle as the flames engulf him. And justice, if justice means revenge, becomes the theme of the film.[7]

The Kosovo mythology did not act of its own agency. Media propaganda and se-cret-police terror were needed to provoke the violence. But to persuade someone to kill his lifelong neighbor or friend requires a robust rationale. The mythology of Kosovo was integrated into the "ethnic cleansing" operations down to the most lo-cal level. Serb paramilitaries wore shoulder patches depicting the battle of Kosovo, sang songs of the Kosovo battles, forced their captives to sing such songs, and dec-orated themselves with medals named after Milos Obilic, who assassinated the Sultan Murat in order to avenge the fallen Lazar.

Bosnian Serb leader Biljana Plavsic, a biological geneticist and former head of the Academy of Natural Sciences in Sarajevo, announced in 1994:

> [I]t was genetically deformed material that embraced Islam. And now, of course, with each successive generation this gene simply becomes concentrated. It gets worse and worse. It simply expresses itself and dictates their style of thinking and behaving, which is rooted in their genes.[8]

7. Chris Hedges, "Movie Sets Serbs' Emotions on Edge," *New York Times,* 20 July 1999. Cf. Vuk Draskovic, *Noz* (Knife) (Belgrade: Zapis, 1982). For a superb analysis of the original book, other hate literature by Draskovic and other nationalists, and the role of Serbian Orthodox Church journals in disseminating it, see Norman Cigar, *Genocide in Bosnia* (College Station: Texas A&M University Press, 1995).

8. Biljana Plavsic, *Svet,* Novi Sad, September 1993, cited and translated by Slobodan Inic, "Biljana Plavsic: Geneticist in the Service of a Great Crime," *Bosnia Report: Newsletter of the Alli-ance to Defend Bosnia-Herzegovina* 19 (June-August 1997), translated from *Helsinska povelja* (Helsinki Charter), Belgrade, November 1996.

As the cases of Plavsic and her many formerly secularist and communist colleagues show, the effectiveness of the Kosovo nexus of religious and historical mythologies is not dependent on personal piety, self-conscious beliefs, or sincerity. For leaders such as Plavsic and their followers, it provides an alternative system of logic that makes plausible their sudden conversions and their willingness to engage in acts they normally would never have contemplated. It is impossible to understand how Plavsic could have made such a claim plausible to herself or her audience without understanding the ideology of Christoslavism and the way in which it transforms religious difference into ethnic and racial betrayal and deformation.

No mythology can act on its own, and this set of powerful symbols did not come together and become instrumentalized by any kind of historical inevitability. The symbols were woven together over a period of years by the concentrated efforts of Serb intellectual, political, and religious leaders. They were instrumentalized, again over a period of years, through media saturation, secret-police repression, government support of paramilitaries, and the provocation of atrocities and insecurity. But to ignore their role in the radicalization of Serbian society is to forfeit any possibility of constructively working toward peaceful and democratic Balkans.

To speak of religious mythology or simply of religion as a major factor in this tragedy is to encounter some immediate objections. It is true that neither Slobodan Milosevic nor most of his military, police, and paramilitary commanders are religious in the sense of having a committed sense of theological beliefs and a faithful religious practice based on them. It is also true that the vast majority of Yugoslavs in 1989 were largely secular and many of them are still committed atheists. Indeed, a common theme among Bosnian genocide survivors is the shock of realizing that they were in fact Muslims, a realization imposed on them by Serb paramilitary leaders rounding them up based on their name or the name of their parents. However, the power and role of religious symbols and structure extend far beyond the domain of personal piety.

No conflict has a single cause. The religious nationalist symbols discussed here are one key factor among several. The question is not whether the organized atrocities in Bosnia and Kosovo were a "religious war," whatever such a vague phrase might mean. At issue is the role of symbols in a conflict where church leaders, church publications, and religious symbols are central to the motivation and justification of mass fear and rage, and where the victims, particularly in Bosnia, were selected, in large part, on the basis of an ethnoreligious identity and history constructed for them.

The complex symbol or symbolic nexus that was invoked in 1989 on the occasion of the 600th anniversary of the death of Lazar was invoked in a manner that turned it — as any powerful symbol can be turned — into a destructive force. Such abuse of the Kosovo heritage was a desecration of Serbian culture and religion that deserves better, a desecration far greater than any of the acts of vandalism that have occurred against monasteries. Whether Serbia will retrieve a constructive version of its symbols and its past remains to be seen.[9]

9. The militant use of Kosovo mythology is succinctly expressed in the famous curse of Kosovo that was popularized in the nineteenth century and revived during the preparations for the 600th anniversary commemoration. See Milorad Ekmecic, "The Emergence of St. Vitus Day," in *Kosovo: Legacy of a Medieval Battle*, ed. Wayne Vucinich and Thomas Emmert (Minneapolis: University of Minnesota Press, 1991), p. 335:

> Whoever is a Serb of Serbian blood
> Whoever shares with me this heritage,
> And he comes not to fight at Kosovo,
> May he never have the progeny
> His heart desires, neither son nor daughter;
> Beneath his hand let nothing decent grow,
> Neither purple grapes nor wholesome wheat;
> Let him rust away like dripping iron
> Until his name be extinguished.

Kosovo's Parallel Society:
The Successes and Failures of Nonviolence

DENISA KOSTOVICOVA

Power changed hands many times in Kosovo's troubled past, but it always followed the pattern of one ethnic group's domination over the other.[1] Caught between competing Serbian and Albanian claims for sovereignty ever since the age of nationalism arrived in the Balkans, Kosovo became a prime example of the shared land that divided its occupants. As the issue of irreversible control over Kosovo remained pending, the two ethnic groups in Kosovo sought security in the proximity of their ethnic kin as mixed areas of Kosovo became "unmixed," initially through a process of voluntary withdrawal into ethnically homogenous areas, and later as a consequence of Serbia's revocation of Kosovo autonomy in 1989.

In examining the relationship between segregation and violence in Kosovo, I will argue that ethnic segregation explains both why the conflict in Kosovo escaped a violent resolution in the early 1990s, defying all expectations, and why Kosovo was plunged into an orgy of violence once both Serbs and Albanians adopted force to attain their mutually exclusive national goals over Kosovo.

As Boal notes, "spatial concentration allows ethnics a better defensive position through which they can more easily protect themselves emotionally and politically against outside groups."[2] But, as Pringle points out, separation not only allows for the protection of ethnic identity; it is also conducive to the development and perpetuation of erroneous myths about the other ethnic group, which in turn

1. Nebojsa Popov, "Srpski populizam: Od marginalne do dominantne pojave." Special supplement to *Vreme*, 24 May 1993.

2. F. W. Boal, "Ethnic Residential Segregation," in *Social Areas in Cities: Processes, Patterns and Problems,* ed. D. Herbert and R. J. Johnston (Chichester: John Wiley and Sons, 1978), quoted in David Kaplan, "Nationalism at a Micro-Scale: Educational Segregation in Montreal," *Political Geography* 11, no. 3 (May 1992): 259-82, especially p. 261. Cf. David Sibley, "Outsiders in Society and Space," in *Inventing Places: Studies in Cultural Geography,* ed. Kay Anderson and Fay Gale (Melbourne: Longman Cheshire, 1992), p. 129.

feed ethnic fears and may eventually result in violence.[3] These two contradictory sides of segregation, as I will show, made their mark on the Serbian-Albanian conflict in Kosovo in the 1990s.

The Communist period in post–World War II Kosovo was marked by a gradual upgrading of Kosovo's autonomy and the empowerment of Albanians in the province, the process that peaked in 1974 with the adoption of a new federal constitution. No amount of constitutional engineering and efforts to achieve equality of nations and nationalities in the Socialist Federal Republic of Yugoslavia (SFRY), one of the tenets of Yugoslav Communism, helped ease the legacy of ethnic tensions in the province. Defined as a nationality, Albanians could only enjoy a provincial autonomy, not a republic.[4] But Albanians thought of themselves as a nation and believed that they too were entitled to a republic in Kosovo. Serbs had their own grievances as well. The constitutional assertion of Kosovo within Serbia was seen as directly weakening the Serbian state.[5]

Due to their numerical preponderance in Kosovo, Albanians emerged as chief beneficiaries of the new federal constitution.[6] Their empowerment in Kosovo spawned Serbian complaints about the Albanianization of the province that left the Serbian minority disenfranchised. Two parallel processes unfolding in Kosovo during Communism are illustrative. The official policy in all spheres of political, economic, and social life provided a structural incentive for ethnic mixing, while the introduction of the so-called "national key" system ensured that the ethnic makeup of the province was reflected in the distribution of public offices.[7] Yet in the background a process of voluntary ethnic segregation proceeded quietly apace. Serbian and Albanian Communists held offices next to each other in the provincial political institutions; Serbian and Albanian workers worked next to each other; and many Serbs and Albanians still lived next to each other — especially in apartment blocks and flats distributed and owned by the state.

Most notable efforts at bringing the two communities together were undertaken in Kosovo's educational system, as Albanians obtained the right to secular

3. Dennis Pringle, "Separation and Integration: The Case of Ireland," in *Shared Space: Divided Space,* ed. Michael Chisholm and David M. Smith (London: Unwin Hyman, 1990), pp. 168-70.

4. Ivan Kristan, "The Constitutional and Legal Status of the Autonomous Provinces in the Socialist Federal Republic of Yugoslavia," *Review of International Affairs: Relationship between Yugoslavia and Albania* (1984): 135-69, especially p. 158.

5. Svetozar Stojanovic, "Jugoslovenska kriza: Sukob 'etnosa' i 'demosa,'" in *Srpsko pitanje,* ed. Aleksa Djilas (Politika: Beograd, 1991), p. 126.

6. Branka Magas, *The Destruction of Yugoslavia: Tracking the Break-up* (London and New York: Verso, 1993), p. 35.

7. Dusan Janjic, "National Identity, Movement and Nationalism of Serbs and Albanians," in *Conflict or Dialogue: Serbian-Albanian Relations and Integration of the Balkans,* ed. Dusan Janjic and Shkelzen Maliqi (Subotica: Open University, 1994), p. 128.

education in their mother tongue for the first time ever.[8] But education's aim was to give rise to "Yugoslav socialist patriotism."[9] The identity of respective nations and nationalities was to be anchored in the common revolutionary struggle during World War II, which in turn would legitimate the existence of multi-ethnic Yugoslavia in the future.

Serbian and Albanian pupils studied in mixed schools,[10] while Prishtina University, founded in 1970 primarily to cater to the educational needs of Albanians in Kosovo as the only university in SFRY to provide instruction in the Albanian language, also offered equal opportunities to Serbs. Hence the university emerged as a bilingual institution: the student body, academic staff, and management were both Albanian and Serbian, while courses, libraries, administration, and publishing were provided in Albanian and Serbian.[11]

Education represented the most important social field for interaction across ethnic lines in Kosovo. By the early 1980s, some 52 percent of the population in Kosovo was younger than twenty, and every third inhabitant was being educated. There were 300 university students to every 10,000 inhabitants in Kosovo, and the provincial university was the third largest in Yugoslavia, after those in Belgrade and Zagreb.[12]

However, a glance at the ethnic makeup of settlements (communities where people actually live) indicates that the trend in Kosovo was that of voluntary ethnic separation rather than of ethnic mingling. Research has shown that Kosovo's villages and towns, as well as suburbs of bigger cities, were gradually becoming homogenized along ethnic lines. In the period between 1961 and 1981, 1,154 of 1,445 settlements in Kosovo became ethnically uniform, with the population of one ethnic group often reaching 100 percent. The number of Albanian settlements in this period grew by 250; the number of Serbian and mixed settlements dropped by 61 and 78 respectively.[13] One's ethnic kin was one's favored neighbor.

While the ratio between the ethnic groups in Kosovo was relatively constant in the period between 1931 and 1961, standing at 60-67 percent Albanians to 27

8. *Politika*, 19 May 1981. For a review of the development of education in Kosovo, see Dennison Rusinow, "The Other Albania: Kosovo 1979," Part I: Problems and Prospects, American Universities Field Staff Reports, Europe, no. 5 (1980): 1-17, especially pp. 4-9.

9. Cf. Pedro Ramet, "Kosovo and the Limits of Yugoslav Socialist Patriotism," *Canadian Review of Studies in Nationalism* 16, nos. 1-2 (1989): 227-50, especially pp. 237-38. Niksa Nikola Soljan, "The Saga of Higher Education in Yugoslavia: Beyond the Myths of a Self-Management Socialist Society," *Comparative Education Review* 35, no. 1 (February 1991): 131-53.

10. Jens Reuter, "Educational Policy in Kosova," in *Studies on Kosova,* ed. Arshi Pipa and Sami Repishti, East European Monographs no. 155 (New York: Columbia University Press, 1984), pp. 259-60.

11. Author's interview with a high communist official in Pristina at the time, Spring 1998.

12. *Politika*, 10 June 1981.

13. Branko Krstic, *Kosovo: Izmedju istorijskog i etnickog prava* (Kuca Vid: Beograd, 1994), pp. 129-84.

percent Serbs/Montenegrins, it dramatically shifted in the post-1961 period: Albanians reached 82 percent and Serbs/Montenegrins 11 percent in 1991. The shrinking of the Serb/Montenegrin presence in Kosovo accompanied the Albanians' acquisition of power in Kosovo.[14]

The private initiative of people to live and stay apart from the other ethnic group was offset by the problems that came with officially endorsed ethnic mixing. Pupils and students in Kosovo, for example, did share the same buildings but not the same classrooms. The language barrier ensured that they remained firmly knitted into the ethnic worlds of their own group. Hence Prishtina University was often described as "two universities [Albanian and Serbian] in miniature." Also, Serbian and Albanian pupils reportedly found it easier to communicate in English than in either language of the two ethnic groups in the late 1980s.

The adult world created its own set of problems. Serbs complained that they were marginalized at work, where they alleged they were regularly outvoiced by the Albanian majority. They also complained that they were at a disadvantage in the employment policy since preference was given to Albanians in a Communist-era Kosovo that was practically run by the Albanians.[15] Nor did the fact that the majority of Kosovo Serbs spoke no Albanian help their job quest.

The outbreak of the Albanian demonstrations in 1981 and their violent suppression by the Yugoslav security forces shattered the myth of Communist-style "brotherhood and unity" in Kosovo. Albanian demonstrators' most prominent demand was for a "Kosovo Republic." To Serbs — and to Communists throughout Yugoslavia — it amounted to the call for secession from Yugoslavia, even unification with Albania, and as such it was considered an utmost threat to the fickle structure of the entire Yugoslav federation. Prishtina University, where the protests started, subsequently spreading throughout the province, no longer was a showcase of brotherhood and unity in practice. It was labeled a "fortress of nationalism."[16] What began as a Communist-led activity aimed at suppressing Albanian nationalism in education eventually grew into the Serbian campaign aimed at abolishing Kosovo's autonomy in 1989.[17]

The Yugoslav Serbs did not stop at suppressing the political institutions of Kosovo's autonomy and at the province's constitutional integration into a now

---

14. Ibid. Cf. Srdjan Bogosavljevic, "A Statistical Picture of Serbian-Albanian Relations," in *Conflict or Dialogue: Serbian-Albanian Relations and Integration of the Balkans*, ed. Dusan Janjic and Shkelzen Maliqi (Subotica: Open University, 1994).

15. Some figures seem to indicate that actually the reverse was the case — that Albanians suffered the proportional disadvantage in employment in Kosovo. Cf. Ramet, "Kosovo," pp. 238-39.

16. *Politika*, 14 May 1981.

17. Kjell Magnusson, "The Serbian Reaction: Kosovo and Ethnic Mobilization among the Serbs," *Nordic Journal of Soviet and East European Studies* 4, no. 3 (1987): 3-31.

"unified" Serbia. In the period between June 26, 1990, and August 8, 1992, the Serbian parliament passed an average of eighteen laws a month that ended Kosovo's autonomy from Serbia in all spheres of life.[18] The endorsement of the so-called temporary measures by the Serbian parliament paved the way for a tide of dismissals of Albanians from their jobs in Kosovo's economy, education, health-care, culture, sports, and media, and their replacement by non-Albanians, primarily Serbs and Montenegrins, but also Turks and Muslims.

The subjugation of Kosovo's primary and secondary schools, as well as its university, as sites of primary symbolic importance for the reproduction of nationhood was deemed to be as necessary as Serbia's territorial unification. The beginning of the school year in the autumn of 1991 found Albanian students on "extended holiday." The Albanians' refusal to accept the nationalized curricula tailored to promote the Serbian national identity led to the barring of Albanian students from Kosovo's schools. The imposed curricula, Albanians protested, were aimed at suppressing their national identity. The price of protecting that identity implied that Albanian students would stay out of schools.

The segregation in Kosovo cut through all spheres of life. The Serbs and Albanians in Kosovo closed their national ranks, and their uneasy coexistence in Kosovo turned into open confrontation. With tensions running high, the province appeared on the verge of an all-out war. But bloodshed was averted when Albanians embraced nonviolent resistance as a means of achieving independence in Kosovo, inspired by a 55-kilometer peaceful march and a hunger strike by Albanian miners in defense of Kosovo's autonomy.

Disenfranchised and forced to marginal spaces, Albanians focused their energies on building a shadow state and society in Kosovo. The effort was spearheaded by the building of institutions of a proclaimed independent "Republic of Kosovo," which was overwhelmingly endorsed in a referendum, and the holding of parliamentary and presidential elections in 1991 and 1992 respectively.[19] Indeed, the Serbian assault on Kosovo's autonomy created, albeit unwittingly, an Albanian parallel state in Kosovo. The state-building effort was accompanied by the resurrection of the Albanian educational and health-care systems, as well as cultural and sports activities. Privately owned Albanian houses became schools and health clinics; arts exhibitions moved to Albanian cafes and restaurants; a meadow was turned into a field for the Albanian soccer match. Serbs took over jobs in the state-supported public sector, while their former Albanian colleagues became entrepreneurs in the Albanian-dominated private sector.[20]

18. *Vreme*, 7 September 1992. Cf. Negibe Kelmendi, *Discriminatory and Unconstitutional Laws and Other Judicial Acts on Kosova Passed by the Assembly of Serbia* (Prishtina: Qendra per Informim e Kosoves, 1994).

19. Cf. *Albanian Democratic Movement in Former Yugoslavia — Documents: 1990-1993* (Prishtina: Kosova Information Centre, 1993).

20. *Vreme*, 7 March 1994.

Even those spaces that Serbs and Albanians were forced to share reinforced their respective sense of nationhood. The main street in Kosovo's capital Prishtina was no longer named after Marshall Tito, the founder of socialist Yugoslavia. The Serbs renamed it St. Vitus Day Street, commemorating the day on which the infamous Kosovo Battle was fought in 1389. But the Albanians called it Mother Theresa's Street after the world-famous charity worker of Albanian origin. Reminders of a common past were erased.

The two communities in Kosovo went about their daily lives in utter ignorance of the other community. "We used to dip bread in the same goulash, and now we don't know each other," an Albanian said of the Serbian colleague with whom he worked in an electrical plant. In those apartment blocks that remained mixed, Serbian and Albanian neighbors no longer greeted each other.

The Serbs held the reins of power in Kosovo. And yet, paradoxically, within the conditions that Albanians referred to as "Serbian occupation" they attained an unprecedented degree of freedom from the Serbs to decide on a wide range of political, economic, and social issues. The ability to organize and maintain the shadow state and society in Kosovo uplifted the Albanians' morale and emerged as a source of pride; but it was also what Albanians considered a proof of their political maturity and ability to run their own state in Kosovo once they would achieve independence.

Following their exclusion from school and university buildings, Albanian students flocked to makeshift classrooms in private houses, garages, and attics. There Albanian educators applied their own curricula, which they first rid of old communist content and then amended to give full expression to the Albanian national identity. Indeed, the independent Republic of Kosovo was already a reality in Albanian students' textbooks. The poems they wrote in literature courses sang of blood, sacrifice, and freedom. Their Serb counterparts in state schools also learned about their national duty and the ultimate sacrifice necessary to hold onto Kosovo, the cradle of the Serbian nation.

The Serbian authorities largely tolerated Albanians in primary school buildings because, the official explanation went, primary education up to eighth grade was obligatory according to the law. Still, Serbian and Albanian students had no contact: they were either separated by walls built in school corridors or by being organized into "ethnic shifts," whereby Albanian and Serbian students used the same classrooms at different times of the day. Secondary school and university students were consigned to private houses, the only exception being a limited number of secondary school buildings made available to Albanians as a result of the "human exchange of students," in which two mixed schools became one all-Albanian and one all-Serbian.

It was arguably the existence of ethnically compact Albanian areas in Kosovo that allowed for the flourishing of the Albanian "parallel" society. Yet it is precisely in those areas that the Albanians felt the presence of the Serbian state most acutely because of harassment by the Serbian police. Albanian students were often mistreated by the police, especially for possessing school certificates and university ID's with the stamp of "Kosovo Republic." This, as Maliqi argues, turned Albanian education into a singular "life school of resistance."[21]

But no matter how successful the parallel education may have been, it also took its toll. The number of primary-school students dropped by 12 percent, from 304,836 in 1989-90 to 268,543 in 1995-96,[22] while the number of secondary-school pupils dropped from 71,257 in the 1990-91 school year to 56,187 in 1995-96, or by 21.4 percent.[23] A rapid decline in the student enrollment was also recorded at the university level, from 25,260 Albanian students in 1989-90 to 13,763 in 1995-96.[24]

The first to say no to Serb-Albanian segregation were Albanian university students. In the autumn of 1997 they staged a series of peaceful protests demanding the "liberation of the occupied [university] buildings."[25] The students proved that resistance to Serb rule could be active and still peaceful, and thus they also challenged the entire philosophy of Albanians' passive resistance in Kosovo. But it was the first public emergence of the Kosovo Liberation Army (KLA), roughly coinciding with the student protests, that henceforth defined the activism of the Albanian national movement in Kosovo. The KLA vowed to fight for Kosovo's independence; and unlike the students, the KLA made an impact on the Serbs. If fear was heretofore reserved only for the Albanians, now fear spread among Kosovo's Serbian community as well.

The violent showdown on the eve of spring 1998 in the hamlets of Drenica, the region northwest of the provincial capital, set the deadly dynamics of the conflict in Kosovo. Defenseless Albanian civilians were bound to be the prime victims of a clash between the KLA and Serbian security forces in Kosovo. The province's notorious history of human rights violations was only to be compounded by a grisly list of war crimes and crimes against humanity.

The walls of separation between the two ethnic communities in Kosovo were torn down not by an agreement but by shell and arson attacks. Now, as the formerly uneasy ethnic neighbors looked at each other, they faced the enemy, and it was an enmity made more bitter for all the years they had lived together but divided in Kosovo. Ethnically homogeneous settlements provided a clear target for the attackers, whose belief in the righteousness of their own claim over Kosovo had in the meantime become only more entrenched.

21. Shkelzen Maliqi, "The School of Resistance" in *Kosova: Separate Worlds* (Peja: MM Society & Dukagjini, 1998), pp. 113-17.

22. Halim Hyseni dhe Bajram Shatri, "Studim: Gjendja dhe pozita e arsimit shqip ne Kosove ne periudhen 1990-95 dhe mundesit e zhvillimit te metejme," Instituti ekonomik, Prishtine, Janar 1996, pp. 38-39.

23. Ibid., p. 66.

24. Hajrullah Koliqi, *The Survival of the University of Prishtina 1991-1996* (Prishtina: The University of Prishtina Press, 1997), p. 61.

25. See subheading "Students," in *Kosovo Spring*, International Crisis Group Report 20 (March 1991), Pristina-Sarajevo.

Balkan Diaspora I:
The Albanian-American Community

FRON NAZI

The March 1998 Serb massacre of the Kosovars in Drenica was the turning point for the Albanian-American community. Overnight, they went from supporting the pacifist movement of the Democratic League of Kosova to supporting the more militant Kosova Liberation Army (KLA).

According to unofficial estimates, there are between 250,000 and 500,000 Albanian-Americans. Much like the early émigrés, the Albanians are hard-working, have held onto their traditions and language, and are much more nationalistic than their kin back home. For the past fifty years the enemy for Albanian-Americans has been defined as: Communism, the occupier of Albania; Serbia, the occupier of Kosova; Greece, the occupier of the Cameria (the northern region of Greece); and, most recently, Macedonia and its treatment of its ethnic Albanians as second-class citizens. The Albanian-American political movements can be broken down into three stages: national self-identification, anticommunism, and Kosova liberation. Each of these movements stems from the arrival of new émigrés. Some of the newcomers influenced existing Albanian-American organizations; others established their own interest groups. Like the émigrés before them, the Albanian community found "sanctuary in the U.S., where they could launch their criticism against their country, or occupier," notes American historian Jim Shenton of Columbia University. However, like most scholars, Dr. Shenton quickly makes the point that "even today there is an absence of knowledge regarding Albania and the Albanians. They are present but not identifiable." (In this paper I refer to Albanians from Albania proper as Albanians, and Albanians from Kosova as Kosovars.)

Albanians have come to the U.S. in three major waves — and each has had its own economic and political agenda: 1906-1930 (an economic migration); the 1950s (anticommunist); and the 1970s (anti-Yugoslavian). The first émigrés from Albania proper arrived in Boston at the turn of the century. Today the largest ethnic Albanian communities in the U.S. are in Boston, Chicago, Detroit, and New York City. Adopting the idea to travel to the U.S. from their Greek neighbors, the first Albanians to arrive were from the southern village of Korce: 90 percent of the arrivals were young males who came in search of work and hoped to return home with their hard-earned savings. In 1907, the death of a young man from Korce in Boston brought the issue of national self-identification to the surface. By turning down a Greek Orthodox burial service, the Albanians began the long process of national self-identification in the U.S. The period between 1906 and 1930 was followed by the founding of numerous Albanian-American newspapers, including *Kombi* (Nation), *Morning Star, Republica,* and *Dielli* (Sun), the longest-surviving Albanian-American newspaper. At the same time, such nationalistic organizations as Vatra (Hearth) in Boston were founded. During World War II and thereafter, Vatra and the Albanian Orthodox Church served as the political hub for Albanian émigrés. Since little if any information regarding the political developments of their homeland reached the émigrés, these organizations were content with leader Enver Hoxha (1908-1985) and his Communist party because they saw them as liberators of Albania from Fascist Italian and Nazi German occupation.

With the beginning of the Cold War in the 1950s, a large wave of Albanian émigrés arrived in the U.S. These new Albanian émigrés brought with them strong anticommunist feelings and quickly infiltrated the already established newspapers and organizations, especially Vatra. At the same time, the U.S. State Department began its anticommunist campaign by establishing the Free European Committee for its newly arrived, educated Eastern European bloc émigrés. The new émigrés joined a group funded by the U.S. State Department called The Albania Free Committee. The committee brought to light the atrocities that were taking place in Albania and slowly introduced the Kosova issue. Vatra took a back seat to the committee and concentrated its efforts on cultural programs. By the mid-1950s and early 1960s, the main anticommunist political party representatives of Legality (the Monarchy party), the National Front, and the National Block began to arrive and helped strengthen the anticommunist movement. At the same time, the first large wave of Kosovars followed and soon afterward created Lidhje Prizreni (League of Prizren), which concentrated its efforts on the Kosova question.

Still relatively small in number, the various political parties in exile and the political organizations united under the idea that Albania must first be freed from communism — and that the Kosova question would be addressed later. This remained the political platform until the early part of the 1970s, when a third wave of Albanian émigrés arrived in the U.S. Many of the new arrivals were from Kosova and can be divided into two groups: Kosovars, native Albanians from Kosova; and the "Immigranta," the smaller of the two groups, Albanians from Albania proper who had fled Hoxha's regime to Kosova. The majority of the new arrivals stayed clear of the various political parties and organizations. Those who opted to participate strengthened the anticommunist movement and slowly began to strengthen the Kosova movement.

The 1981 Kosova student demonstrations brought the Kosova issue to the forefront of the American public's attention for the first time. A *New York Times* article on the demonstrations, combined with the Kosova-based activists' protest writings that appeared in western European newspapers, shifted the political focus from anticommunist to anti-Yugoslavian. Anti-Yugoslav demonstrations were organized in Washington, D.C., and the other major cities with large ethnic Albanian communities. The demonstrations were followed by meetings with congressional leaders and U.S. State Department officials. During the 1980s the deteriorating political situation in Kosova forced many young and educated Kosovars to leave for western Europe and the U.S. Those who came to the U.S. found work and support mostly in the New York City and Detroit-based Albanian communities. By the early 1980s, New York and Detroit became the centers for a stronger Kosova autonomy movement. Kosova-based academics/activists spurred on ad hoc Albanian-American groups that were formed to address the suppression of the Kosovars by Belgrade.

By 1985 several ad hoc lobby groups were established in Detroit, New York, and Chicago. In New York the Civic League, led by former Congressman Joseph DioGardi, gave U.S. congressional leaders a glimpse of the enormous financial wealth of the Albanian-American community. With the financial backing of the Albanian-American community, the Civic League opened offices in other U.S. cities. Detroit and Chicago followed suit by creating their own groups. In 1986, Belgrade's imprisonment of a young Albanian-American from Detroit, Pjeter Ivezaj, coincided with Secretary of State George Schultz's visit to Europe. The Detroit ad hoc lobbyist contacted U.S. Congressman Broomfield of Michigan, who in turn notified Schultz that an American citizen was being held in a Yugoslav prison for participating in a 1981 anti-Yugoslav demonstration in Washington, D.C. This sent alarms ringing through Washington and a call by the State Department for the removal of most-favored-nation status from Yugoslavia if Ivezaj was not immediately released. U.S. media picked up on the Ivezaj case and helped bring the Kosova issue to the forefront. Led by Detroit and supported by the other Albanian-American organizations, Ivezaj's case was driven to the highest levels of the State Department and the White House. At the same time, the issues surrounding Kosova, specifically Belgrade's suppression of the Kosovars, began to find some support in Congress and some interest in the State Department and the White House. Separately but collectively, the various Albanian-American groups managed to persuade Congress to pass a number of resolutions condemning Yugoslavia. But not one of these resolutions had any teeth, and the Albanian-American community was beginning to learn about the intricacies of Washington.

However, discovering the Albanian-American community's wealth, some individual congressional leaders quickly turned their attention to them. Having received promises to bring the Kosova issue to the forefront of State Department foreign policy, the Albanian community began to donate large sums of money to Senator Robert Dole of Kansas and Senator Larry Pressler of South Dakota. As the situation in Kosova deteriorated and the Democratic League of Kosova (LDK) was established in Kosova, the Albanian-American community began to play a more active role. Albanian-Americans were essential in establishing meetings between the Kosovar-based activists and U.S. congressional leaders, State Department representatives, and the American media. By the latter part of 1989, Pristina was beginning to dictate the marching orders, and LDK chapters were soon replacing the Civic League and other such Albanian-American-founded organizations.

By early 1991, the fall of Communism in Albania had led to the closing of the Albanian Free Committee and the return of the Albanian political parties in exile bases from the U.S. to Tirana. The original plan that Albania must first be freed, and then Kosova, appeared on course. LDK chapters in the U.S. had by this time established themselves as the sole representatives of the Kosova issue and the center for distribution of information in the Albanian language. With Albania free from communism, LDK received almost exclusive support from the Albanian-American community. A centralized funding program was established whereby donations to the LDK chapters would be used for lobbying Washington, D.C.; for hiring public-relations firms to influence the U.S. media; and for providing direct support to the LDK leadership and its underground government. This remained the status quo until March 1998, when Albanian-Americans shifted their financial and political support from the LDK to the KLA. Whatever the future direction of Albanian-American political movements, one thing is clear: Pristina, Tirana, and Tetove in Macedonia will dictate the marching orders.

Balkan Diaspora II: The History and Future of the Serbian Community in America

NICK VUCINICH

Introduction

The twentieth century has been a costly one for Serbs. Serbs suffered much death and destruction during World War I and World War II. During the breakup of the former Yugoslavia and the wars in the region in the 1990s, including the recent NATO "humanitarian intervention" over Kosovo, Serbs have had to flee from Croatia, from the Muslim- and Croat-controlled parts of Bosnia-Herzegovina, and from Kosovo.

At the end of the century, the Serbian people find themselves in a difficult and tragic situation. Serbia is impoverished; unemployment is rampant. The country's economy and infrastructure have been ruined by NATO bombing, and its society is facing civil and political strife. There are serious tensions between Serbia and Montenegro. Serbs in Bosnia-Herzegovina enjoy some autonomy, but they live in a Western-policed enclave and thus are denied true self-determination. Many Serbs who hold dear the values of liberalism, free speech, democracy, and respect for individual rights, and who have looked toward the U.S. as a beacon of these values and their ally in two World Wars, have been disillusioned by the use of military means to supposedly defend these values on the territory of former Yugo-slavia. While not having to suffer the depredations that Serbs in the homeland have experienced, Serbs in the U.S. now find themselves in a position that many of them would have never believed possible: they are having to reconcile 150 years of history in America with the recent action of U.S. foreign policy.

It is the U.S., the nation with the largest contingent of Serbs of any country outside of Yugoslavia,[1] that took the leading role in the war over Kosovo. Whether

---

1. Although Serbs living in Germany, France, and Sweden still tend to regard themselves as Serbs, in Australia and Canada the situation is analogous to that in the U.S., with one important difference: only the U.S. has such a high proportion of Serb descendants of pre–World War I immi-grants. The current Serbian population in the U.S. can only be estimated; it is at least in the hun-

the Serbs in America are recent immigrants or third- and fourth-generation Americans, the experience of having their country, which they have served[2] and in which they have flourished,[3] go to war with their country of origin has been an extremely demoralizing one.[4]

---

dreds of thousands. The 1990 U.S. Census lists 116,795 Serbs, but also lists 257,994 Yugoslavs, many of whom are no doubt Serbs. However, the U.S. Census has been traditionally unreliable in determining numbers of Serbs in America. The early censuses did not even list South Slavs, and many Serbs were labeled Austrians or Hungarians, coming mostly from the Habsburg Empire. The census has also not been very good at picking up third- and fourth-generation descendants of Serb immigrants. The Illinois Ethnic Coalition, for example, estimates that there are between 30,000 and 50,000 Serbs in the Chicago area, making it the largest Serbian community in America. But Serb community leaders contend that the number is far higher, as many as 100,000 to 200,000. While Serbs are undeniably a relatively small ethnic group in America, it is not unreasonable to estimate the population of Americans of Serbian ancestry at 500,000 to 750,000. The best overview of the Serbs in America was published in the *Harvard Encyclopedia of American Ethnic Groups* by Michael B. Petrovich and Joel Halpern in 1980 ("Serbs," in *Harvard Encyclopedia of American Ethnic Groups,* ed. Stephan Thernstrom [Cambridge and London, 1980], pp. 916-26). Obviously, today it is somewhat dated, because it is unable to take into account the events that would lead to the breakup of Yugoslavia and consequently a new wave of Serbian immigrants to America as a result of the wars there. An excellent resource for research on Serbs in America is Milan Radovich and Robert Gakovich, eds., *Serbs in the U.S. and Canada: A Comprehensive Bibliography* (2nd ed. Minnesota Immigration Research Center, 1992).

2. Serbs have served in all of America's wars since at least the Spanish-American War, and among them are a number of Congressional Medal of Honor recipients. Serbs also served on both sides during the American Civil War.

3. Many have distinguished themselves in American life. Two American Serbs worthy of mention were heads of major American companies: William Jovanovich, president of Harcourt, Brace and Jovanovich Publishing Company; and William Salatich, president of Gillette. Numerous Serbs have played professional sports, perhaps the best known being basketball great Pete Maravich. Currently Vlade Divac and Peja Stojakovic play for the Sacramento Kings. Many Serbs work in Hollywood, most notably Academy Award–winner Karl Malden (Mladen Sekulovich), but also younger stars such as Lolita Davidovich, Mila Jovovich, and Natalija Nogulich. George Voinovich, who is half-Serb and half-Slovene, is a Republican member of the U.S. Senate from Ohio. Congressman Rod Blagojevich (D-Illinois) was a member of Jesse Jackson's delegation that freed the American prisoners of war in Yugoslavia. Helen Delich Bentley served in Congress as a Republican from Maryland. Two Americans of Serbian ancestry served simultaneously in the California State Senate, George Zenovich (D-Fresno) and Rose Ann Vuich (D-Dinuba). Rose Ann Vuich was the first woman to serve in the State Senate of California. Nor can we forget the famous Serbian-American scientists Nikola Tesla and Michael Pupin. But this only touches the surface of successful American Serbs. During the years of the recent wars in Yugoslavia, Americans have encountered other Serbian-Americans in the news and on the talk shows, among them Milan Panich, a California industrialist who served briefly as prime minister in Serbia; Alex Dragnich, a retired professor from Vanderbilt University; and, most notably during the war over Kosovo, Daniele Sremac, who works with the Serbian Unity Congress in Washington, DC, and was often seen on CNN, the Fox News Network, and other talk shows representing a Serbian point of view on the crisis in Kosovo.

4. Serbs in the U.S. have also been disturbed by what they see as a "demonization" of the

Serb Migration to America:
The Creation of a Long-standing Community

Three broad yet distinct waves of Serbian immigration to America can be identified: (1) *old settlers* (1880-1924); (2) *newcomers* (1925-1964); and (3) *recent arrivals* (post-1965).[5]

1. *The old settler wave* can be divided into three distinct parts. The first sig-
nificant groups of Serbs to immigrate to the U.S. came from the Bay of Kotor
(Boka Kotorska), which is today part of Montenegro, and, to some extent, from
the parts of Herzegovina and Montenegro that border on this part of the southern
Adriatic coast. They started settling in and around New Orleans in the 1830s, and
then in greater numbers in California after gold was discovered in 1848. The San
Francisco Bay Area became the most important early Serbian community in
America.[6] In addition to mining for gold, these early Serbian pioneers became
prominent fruit and liquor merchants. Many worked in and owned restaurants
and saloons. Others eventually owned ranches and tended orchards in the fertile
San Joaquin and Santa Clara valleys.[7]

The second part of the old settler wave (1880-1914) made up the largest influx of Serb immigrants the U.S. has received. Serbs from the Bay of Kotor,
Herzegovina, and Montenegro arrived in greater numbers than ever, and many
Serbs began to immigrate from the northwestern regions of the Balkans that were
part of the Austro-Hungarian Empire — Croatia, Slavonia, and Vojvodina — to
escape economic hardship and conscription into the Austro-Hungarian Army.
Serbs from the military frontier of Croatia (Krajina) and from Vojvodina, particularly, poured into the coal mines, steel mills, and industrial cities of Pennsylvania,
the Ohio Valley, and the Great Lakes region. Serbs from Lika, Bosnia, and
Montenegro worked on the Minnesota Iron Range; and Serbs from Herzegovina,

---

Serbian people and double standards in both news coverage and the Administration's policy in
the Balkans. Few Serbs in the U.S. support Slobodan Milosevic, although some may have initially
responded positively to his overtures toward Serbian nationalism.

5. A good study of the differences between the three waves is Deborah Padgett's *Settlers
and Sojourners: A Study of Serbian Adaptation in Milwaukee, Wisconsin* (New York: AMS Press,
Inc., 1989).

6. A few Serbs could also be found in Chicago in the 1870s, which would later become the
leading Serbian center in the United States. Some of these early immigrants from the southern
Adriatic also moved from California into Nevada and Arizona.

7. In time, California became the birthplace of the first Serbian-American newspaper, the
first mutual-aid society, and the nation's first Serbian Orthodox Church, St. Sava, established in
Jackson in 1894. In an American television interview during the war in Kosovo, then Serbian
Deputy Foreign Minister and sometime opposition leader Vuk Draskovic would speak of his
love for America and his pride in his ancestors having worked in the goldmines of Jackson, California.

the Bay of Kotor, Montenegro, and Lika went to the mines of the Far West, where one of the largest concentrations of Serbs at one time was in Montana.

The third part of the old settler wave (the interwar years)[8] was small in number due to the onset of World War II, the restrictive American immigration policies passed by Congress in 1921 and 1924, and the Great Depression. Because the old settlers were conservative and largely of the working class, they tended to align themselves with Franklin D. Roosevelt's New Deal coalition. Only a minority of them supported the Socialist or Communist parties, and the vast majority supported Draza Mihailovic and his Chetniks (the Serbian nationalist resistance forces) over Josip Broz (Tito) and the Communist Partisans during World War II.[9]

The old setters organized the first mutual-aid societies, ethnic newspapers. and churches. The oldest Serbian organization in America is the First Serbian Benevolent Society of San Francisco (1880), which is still in existence. The largest fraternal organization is the Serb National Federation, which is headquartered in Pittsburgh and publishes the oldest existing Serbian-language newspaper in America, *The American Srbobran*. The Serbian National Defense took its name from a patriotic organization that was first established after the crisis over the Austro-Hungarian annexation of Bosnia and Herzegovina in 1908. An American central committee of the Serbian National Defense was organized in New York City in 1914, with Columbia University professor Michael Pupin as its president. It was later reestablished during World War I and supported the Mihailovic movement. After World War II, its activities were largely taken over by the postwar wave of Serbian political immigrants.

2. *The newcomers* often came from urban origins and were more educated than the largely village-born old settlers. Most settled in already well-established Serbian communities where jobs were available, namely Chicago, Milwaukee, Gary, and Cleveland; some later relocated to the sunbelt states of California, Arizona, and Florida.

This wave of Serbs was comprised of thousands of refugees, former Royal Yugoslav Army officers and soldiers who were prisoners of war or attached to Allied forces, and veterans of armed units that fled the victorious communist Yugoslav Partisans at the end of World War II.[10] While all were anticommunist, there were many

---

8. Thousands of Serbs left America as volunteers for the Serbian and Montenegrin armies during the Balkan Wars and World War I. Some returned to America, but others remained in their homeland. Some of the Serbian and Montenegrin volunteers from Lika, Bosnia-Herzegovina, and Montenegro were given land in the more fertile regions of Kosovo and Vojvodina by the royalist government.

9. Following World War II, the new Communist government resettled Serbian Partisans from these Dinaric regions in Vojvodina, but would not let Serbs who had fled Kosovo return there.

10. These included members of the Chetniks, members of the Serbian State Guard of

divisions among these immigrants and internal divisions among the Chetniks, including regional and personal loyalties. These divisions, and the differences in backgrounds between many of the newcomers and the old settlers, were a contributing factor to the split in the Serbian Orthodox Church in America in 1963.

The split was over the issue of the relationship between the Serbian Church in America and the mother church in communist-dominated Yugoslavia. Though both sides opposed the communist government, the refugee political organizations took different sides in this controversy: followers of Dimitrije Ljotic and Chetnik leader Momcilo Djujic were on the side of the mother church; followers of Chetnik leader Dobrosav Jevdjevic and Slobodan Draskovic, the leader of the Serbian Cultural Club ("St. Sava"), supported American Bishop Dionisije, who broke allegiance to the mother church. The Orthodox clergy, many of them refugee priests, tended to follow their political leaders. The majority of old settlers aligned with the mother church, but this varied somewhat from community to community. Unity between the two sides was finally achieved in 1992.

Many new Serbian Orthodox churches were built in America after the arrival of the newcomers, and it is undeniable that the Serbian Orthodox Church has become the single most important institution in Serbian-American community life. The church parishes are the centers of most social, cultural, and political — as well as religious — activities among American Serbs. The newcomers also formed their own political organizations, clubs, veterans organizations, newspapers, and journals. The focus of most of these groups was anti-communism and particularly opposition to the Titoist regime in Yugoslavia.

3. *Recent arrivals* to the U.S. are "economic immigrants" from Yugoslavia who began to arrive after 1965, when the U.S. lifted its quota system at the same time that Tito's Yugoslavia was encouraging migration to offset internal unemployment. Some of these immigrants were workers and some were professional people. In recent years many professionals and students have immigrated to escape the turmoil of the breakup of Yugoslavia and the wars that ensued.

What the waves of recent arrivals since 1965 have in common is that they were born, raised, and educated in Titoist Yugoslavia. Many of these Serbs think of themselves as Yugoslavs and take pride in the country's multiculturalism, ethnic mixing, and intermarriage with Bosnian Muslims, Catholic Croats, Jews, and other groups. However, among the refugee immigrants there are still no doubt many Serbian nationalists, and the recent wars and American media coverage have brought about a defensiveness among many Yugoslav-oriented, nonnationalist Serbs.

Many of these newer immigrants attend Serbian Orthodox Churches, but in general they have been less eager than the old settlers or newcomers to organize ethnic, cultural, or political organizations.

General Milan Nedic, and the Serbian volunteers from Dimitrije Ljotic's "Zbor" party, who were organized under the occupation forces in Serbia during the war.

Conclusion

Today, after the defeats and tragedies that the Serbs have suffered under Slobodan Milosevic's rule, most would probably like to see him exit the scene. The Serbian Unity Congress,[11] incorporated in 1990, has become the most influential Serbian public affairs group in America. It is an international organization that works for the democratization and reconstruction of the Serbian territories. Members of this group have testified before Congress and the Administration. This group has also worked with prominent Washington public affairs groups such as the Cato Institute. The Serbian Unity Congress has been critical of President Slobodan Milosevic and supportive of the opposition in Serbia. This organization has also attempted to play a central role among Serbs in the U.S. in opposing the Clinton Administration's intervention in Yugoslavia.

What of the future? A Cleveland-area Serbian Orthodox priest, Irinej Dobrijevic, who was a member of the Jesse Jackson delegation to Serbia, believes that in time Serbs will again be seen as America's best and staunchest ally in the Balkan region. He believes that the U.S. "missed the boat" by not supporting the Serbian opposition to Milosevic in 1996-97, and that once Milosevic is removed, peace, reconciliation, and reconstruction will be possible.[12]

---

11. Their web address is www.suc.org.
12. See the *Cleveland Plain Dealer,* June 9, 1999.

The Balkans: From Invention to Intervention

MARIA TODOROVA

In 1989 a joke was being recycled in some eastern European countries. Frustrated by the failure of communism (as a shortcut to modernity), two politicians were discussing strategies of how to bring their country into capitalism (as a shortcut to modernity):

> I think the best way is to become the 51st state of the U.S.
>> Excellent. But how do we do that?
> We declare war on the U.S.
>> And then?
> Then, they take us seriously; they invade us; they occupy us; they set us straight.
>> Brilliant. And what if we win?

Ten years later this does not appear to be a joke.

As a specialist in Balkan history, I have refrained from making brief pronouncements about present affairs in the Balkans (two to ten minutes long, depending on the news program; 600-800 words, depending on the paper or journal). After all, my profession is about arguing complex issues and avoiding simplified recipes, and I happen to believe in this professional ethos. However, what is happening now is not merely, and definitely not primarily, a Balkan problem: it is a global international problem. And since I am not a specialist in international relations and the new world order, I think I can summarize my views in a

---

The following essay was presented at a Forum on the Kosovo war at Columbia University in New York on May 11, 1999, at the height of the bombing campaign. It was not meant to be an elaborate scholarly meditation on the roots and character of the conflict but was rather an ad hoc critical human reaction to the simplistic righteousness of the political discourse and to the deplorable unanimity of conformist journalism. In order to preserve this primary function, and thus, the authenticity of the text, I have edited its main body minimally and almost exclusively stylistically. Any subsequent comments, refinements, and explanations aimed at updating the essay after the end of the war have been included in the footnotes.

comparatively short statement. Let me begin with a brief survey concerning the history and character of the conflict.

The situation of the Albanians in Kosovo represents a grave case of human rights abuses. An autonomous *region* of Serbia since 1946, Kosovo was elevated to the status of autonomous *province* like the Vojvodina in 1963, and both were given extensive rights in 1974, which de facto gave them privileges close to a republican status short of the name. A considerable number among the Kosovar Albanian elites since the late 1960s lobbied for republican status within the Yugoslav federation, culminating in the riots in 1981, a year after Tito's death. Repressed but not suppressed, the Kosovar leaders operated within a particularly unfavorable climate during the subsequent years. The demographic boom of the Albanian population resulted in a tremendous increase of their absolute numbers and a shift of the population ratio: from a majority of about 65 percent in 1948, the Albanian majority had reached close to 90 percent by the end of the 1990s.[1]

In the general economic crisis that swept Yugoslavia in the 1980s, this was coupled with an increase in the unemployment rate from an endemic 20 percent to over 70 percent in the last decade. While the two enlightened republics of Slovenia and Croatia were openly and justly sympathetic to the aspirations of the Kosovo Albanians and bemoaned the heavy-handed and intransigent treatment they suffered at the hands of the Serbs, they also consistently boycotted the traditional Yugoslavist policy of Belgrade to redistribute funds from the wealthier republics to the poorer regions of Yugoslavia: Bosnia, Macedonia, and especially Kosovo, whom they referred to as the "dirty southerners," the Timbuktu in the civilized space of Ljubljana and Zagreb.

By the second half of the 1980s, the situation became particularly tense as a consistent flow of Serb population left Kosovo. Most of this outflow was due to the dire economic situation, exacerbated by group claims along ethnic lines for control over limited resources. While there were undoubtedly cases of harassment on the part of the Albanians against the Serbian minority, they did not correspond to the horrendous stories that were circulating among Serbs of a systematic ethnic cleansing, rapes, and so forth at the hands of Albanians. Nonetheless, this was a strong and growing perception among the Serbs that was not allowed any official verbal outlet in the dominant Yugoslav policy of trying to harmonize, downplay, and control ethnic conflict. It was on the wave of this perception that Milosevic

1. This demographic shift, which to me constitutes the single most significant development and precluded the "loss" of Kosovo even before its political loss, was due primarily to an enormous natural population growth. The very high birthrate was commensurate with the one in Albania proper (the highest in Europe) and in Turkey (for both places: 23 per thousand). It was coupled with the falling mortality rate of the post-1945 period due to the modern medical system. This accounts for the drastic increase in absolute numbers of the Kosovo Albanian population. Additionally, but to a lesser extent, the shift of the ratio between Albanians and Serbs was due also to the outflow of the Serbian population.

made his career after 1987. One thing should be clear: Milosevic did not create Serbian nationalism. What he did do was legitimate its most extreme articulation and use it as a means to curb the Titoist (or Yugoslavist) faction in the Serbian/Yugoslav leadership, which was trying against all odds to oppose the growing centrifugal momentum in Croatia and Slovenia.

On March 8, 1989, the autonomy of Kosovo and Vojvodina was revoked; on July 5, 1990, Kosovo's regional parliament was dismissed and a state of emergency was introduced. In September of the same year, Albanian deputies proclaimed the constitution of the Kosovo phantom republic at a clandestine meeting at Kacanik; a year later, in September 1991, they organized a secret plebiscite in Kosovo that returned a vote of over 90 percent in favor of independence. This *intifada*-like, extremely precarious situation continued for nearly a decade and may have continued further had it not been for an unpredictable event: the collapse of the pyramid scheme in Albania, presided over by the great democrat and friend of the United States, Sali Berisha. The subsequent complete disintegration of the state institutions and the brief civil war that followed, with the disappearance of the army and the opening of the arms depots, created a free cheap market for Kalashnikovs ($10 apiece) and hand grenades. With funds from the diasporic Kosovo community in Germany, Switzerland, Britain, Belgium, the United States, and elsewhere, the increasingly radicalized youth in Kosovo were armed to form what was claimed last year to be a 40,000 strong force — but turned out to be a 15,000-man armed force — of the KLA (Kosovo Liberation Army).

These are facts that I think would generate a more or less broad consensus. What follows is a series of statements that summarize my views on the present conflict. I have arranged and balanced them so that by the end I will have offended almost everyone.

Statement 1. Serbian nationalism at the end of the twentieth century is a particularly extreme type of nationalism in the Balkans, rivaled and at times surpassed only by its twin brother, Croatian nationalism. What makes Serbian nationalism unique in the Balkan space is that since its inception at the end of the eighteenth and the beginning of the nineteenth century, this has been the only Balkan nationalism that has never been effectively humiliated or defeated.[2] It has

---

2. This does not mean that the nationalist elites have not perceived it as humiliated. This is particularly true of the World War II era, where one has to look for the roots of a Serb defensiveness that was further incensed with the passing of the virtually confederative constitution of 1974. It was this defensiveness that provided the feeding ground for the political mobilization of the 1990s. Yet, much as perception has been posited to be real and to create reality, it nonetheless stayed in the realm of perception. Only after the mass expulsion of the Serbs from the Krajina, Bosnia, and now from Kosovo, and thus the contraction of the Serbian demographic space, would I speak of *effective* humiliation and defeat. It remains to be seen how the next generation of Serbs is going to digest this defeat: turn it into victory like the Kosovo battle of old, or accept it as a sobering *fait accompli*. Very preliminary sounds of the latter can be heard in Dobrica Cosic's essay in this volume.

paid very heavy prices, as have all the others; but, psychologically, it has always been victorious. Had it not been for the Asia Minor catastrophe of 1922 (i.e., the defeat of the Greek invasion of Asia Minor of 1919 by the Turkish army of Atatürk and the subsequent flight and expulsion of over one million Greeks from their ancestral homelands), Greek nationalism would have vied for the dubious honor of being first in displaying its superiority complex. But as it is, defeat is always instructive and sobering and, in the long run, often beneficial. Serbian nationalism was particularly ugly in the mirror of the Albanian question. Until 1998, Serbian bravado was still precariously balanced on the side of the bearable as far as actions went, but it was increasingly speaking with hysterical and racist overtones. With a few extremely honorable individual exceptions (some of them friends over whose heads NATO bombs are raining), the Serb opposition never seriously dealt with the Albanian question as a national question in the past decade. In this light, the accusations of the Serbian opposition — that by boycotting the parliamentary elections in Yugoslavia, the Albanians did not give it a hand in overthrowing the Milosevic regime — ring hollow.

Statement 2. Serbian nationalism is an extreme nationalism but it is not a genocidal nationalism. Milosevic is no Hitler. This has been so apparent to me that I would not have even addressed it as a separate statement were it not for the fact that I encounter many respected intellectuals, even friends, who have genuinely bought into the Holocaust analogy.

No case can be made about Milosevic as a threat to world peace, to European peace, even to Balkan peace.[3]

The expansionism argument is quite lame even considering the previous cases framing him as an aggressor against "sovereign independent states," which were hastily and precipitously recognized by the European Union (EU) and the U.S. after the *fait accompli* German initiative for the recognition of Slovenia, Croatia, and other former Yugoslav applicants, without any explicit guarantees for the numerous Serb minorities, especially in Croatia. In the case of Kosovo, this clearly doesn't wash.

The more serious accusation and the one that needs to be addressed is that in the past decade there has been a Serb pattern of ethnic cleansing: there is the lesson of Bosnia, with the shadow of the Holocaust looming behind it. On Bosnia, the Serb record is dismal. But I would go only that far. I despise the exercise of comparing and measuring evil, but I am forced to resort to it because it has been imposed by the Hitler and Holocaust analogies. (Some intellectuals who judi-

---

3. The only case that could be made was that he proved to be a threat to the peaceful dissolution of Yugoslavia. After all, what makes the difference between the peaceful dissolution of the USSR compared to the bloody Yugoslav one is, among other factors, the fact that Milosevic is no Gorbachev. Yet the international community abundantly helped his intransigence by taking sides from the outset instead of trying to arbitrate patiently.

ciously, and I think correctly, did not endorse Goldhagen's thesis about Hitler's willing executioners are now willing to accept the thesis of Milosevic's willing executioners.)[4]

Ethnic cleansing — that is, the forceful displacement of populations from a given territory — though not under this name, has been the historical accompaniment of most wars, and it reached astronomical figures during World War II, at the end of which the ethnically cleansed Germans alone reached 13 million. The ethnic cleansing in Bosnia pales in comparison to that and to later world events of a similar nature. In Bosnia there was a severe case of ethnic cleansing, and its main perpetrators at the beginning were the Serbs. But let us also not forget that the Serbs, ironically, ended up being the greatest casualty of this policy, with 650,000 or 700,000 Serb refugees in today's Yugoslavia; and that the single biggest ethnic cleansing during the war, the expulsion of the Krajina Serbs from Croatia, happened with the tacit approval of the West.[5]

I do not think that the allegation of genocide is sustainable. Aside from the Holocaust, which stands as the indisputable metagenocide, the international community has not come to an agreement about genocidal events. It has not even recognized the 1915 Armenian massacres as genocide, splitting hairs over numbers and intentions. The extermination of millions of Poles, Belorussians, and Russians during World War II has not been officially termed genocide, nor has the extermination of the Serbs at the hands of the Ustasha, the fascist party of Independent Croatia during World War II. It is perfectly fine by me if Arkan or Karadzic or whoever is tried individually as a war criminal; but when we are analyzing phenomena that have (or ought to have) legal repercussions, we ought to be careful.[6]

---

4. *Hitler's Willing Executioners* by Daniel Jonah Goldhagen (New York: Knopf, 1996). [Ed.]

5. These were the pre-Kosovo war figures. The number of Serb refugees has swelled, and Kosovo is the last in line of ethnically cleansed monoethnic territories, a circumstance very clearly expected by all but the most naive of observers. It is symptomatic that today the mantra-like refrain of the multicultural nature of de facto partitioned Bosnia is not even repeated for Kosovo.

6. The defenders of the genocide hypothesis object on the basis that the reduction of all genocides to the Holocaust is harmful because, according to them, it means that there is no genocide without the recurrence of the Holocaust. Thus, they maintain, genocidal violence other than the Holocaust is trivialized and minimized. However, the much-flaunted definition of genocide in the 1948 Geneva Conventions — a systematic effort to destroy, in whole or in part, a people based on ethnic, religious, or racial identity, and involved in organized mass-killings, annihilation of cultural heritage, attack on procreative future potential, etc. — is so unspecific, unquantifiable, and elastic that it easily dissolves into a synonym for any great war violence and renders the notion of genocide simply metaphysical (and thus trivial). If genocide, conversely, is to bring about legal repercussions, it ought to have a very concrete definition. As far as the prosecution of war criminals goes, I have no objection to Milosevic's being held responsible before the war crimes tribunal in the Hague for the death of some 200,000 people

As far as Kosovo goes, the case is even flimsier. We hear about the satanic genocidal plan of Milosevic, but the record is that in the course of the past ten years there was a state within a state in Yugoslavia that was practicing internal exile, and there was no existential crackdown until 1998. The crackdown began last summer when the secessionist guerilla force came to control 40 percent of the territory of Kosovo. Belgrade responded in the way any central government (authoritarian or democratic) does — with an attempt to suppress it. Since then, in the course of a year, two thousand casualties on all sides have been reported by the Western press, among them many civilians.

In a guerilla war, where the fighters operate within a very tight familial network, these casualties were to be expected.[7]

To return to the Holocaust card: if Milosevic is Hitler, the reverse must also be true — then Hitler is Milosevic. If the plight of the Bosnian Muslims or the Kosovo Albanians is comparable to the Holocaust, then the Holocaust can be reduced to it. For those who do not care about the dangers of rhetorical excesses in whipping up public opinion, perhaps the dangers of normalizing and trivializing the Holocaust would sound more menacing.

Statement 3. What is the KLA?[8] There have been accusations (mostly hurled by the Serbs, but interestingly corroborated in the NATO rhetoric) that this is a terrorist organization — funded by drug money; resorting not only to murdering members of the Serb police force but also to assassinating moderate Albanians; practicing extortions and forced recruitment; and espousing a dubious mix of ideologies — from hard-nosed right-wing nationalism to Maoist tactics. All of this may be true (it is, in fact, true). But what national liberation movement has not resorted to dubious tactics from the point of view of the status quo powers, and has not been branded as terrorist at the beginning?

Let me make two other analogies here that, I think, are much more pertinent to the Kosovo case.

---

from Bosnia, and another 10,000 from Kosovo. But if legality is consistent (at least this is the claim it makes), the same measure ought to be applied to the leaders of the United States (several presidents) for the extermination of over three million Vietnamese (McNamara's estimates).

7. There are no final figures for the war casualties yet, although the most often cited ones are 10,000 in Kosovo and 1,600 in Serbia. Recently, the international commission confirmed 2,000 casualties in Kosovo. Tim Judah speaks cautiously that "the final total of innocent civilians murdered during the two and a half months of NATO's bombing campaign . . . will certainly be in the thousands" (*The New York Review of Books,* August 12, 1999, p. 24). This is horrendous, and the atrocities of the Serb paramilitaries are being slowly documented (just as, one expects, the retaliation against the Serbs), but what exactly makes them genocide? The cavalier use of the term "genocide" by Western politicians and the press matches only its equally cavalier use by the Serbian propaganda machine.

8. UCK is the acronym for *Ustria Clirimtare e Kosoves,* or Kosovo Liberation Army (KLA). [Ed.]

In doing so, I am adding to the list of offended sensitivities that I am consciously challenging today:

A. The first one is Palestine. This is how the Kosovo problem was increasingly referred to in Belgrade. Self-perception and historical emulation are important. As is well known, Hitler was inspired and accordingly instructed the governor of Poland to act toward the Slavs as the Americans had toward the "red-footed Indians." The Serbs have not been inspired by Hitler. But they see themselves in their relationship to Kosovo and the Albanians as they do Israel in its relationship to Jerusalem and the Palestinian problem. There is no need to go further into details and compare the number of casualties in each case. What would be more instructive would be to compare the reactions of the outside world, which has been incredibly patient and, because of that, constructive in the several-decades-old Israeli-Palestinian conflict, while it has displayed none of these attitudes toward the junior Albanian-Serb conflict. The mere comparison with Serbia, I know, alienates many Jewish intellectuals, who don't even acknowledge accusations of Hitlerite behavior made by Palestinian activists.

B. The second analogy is to the Kurdish problem in Turkey. Despite attempts to argue that one cannot compare the two cases based on a legal argument (and, to my disappointment, launched even by liberal Turkish intellectuals), I believe that there are only two basic differences: (1) Turkey is a NATO member and has not lost its geo-strategic significance for the United States; and (2) while the PKK has failed to sell its separatism to the West (conversely, the West — i.e., the CIA — sold Öcalan to the Turkish security forces), the KLA has succeeded in doing so. Again, I am not going into a detailed comparison of casualties (37,000 in the Kurdish case) or military operations on the territory of a sovereign state (Iraq) or a civil war in one's own territory. The analogy again has incensed many Turks, who would rather focus on the differences between the two cases.

But, of course, all cases are different. As Tolstoy pointed out long ago, only happy families look alike. The point I wish to make is a more general one. Historical analogies are rarely appropriate if their purpose is to facilitate the analytical understanding of an event or phenomenon. Most often the purpose of historical analogies is to evoke and manipulate predictable emotional responses.

Statement 4. What do we do about circumstances that, before March 24, could be described, I would say, as a severe case of human rights abuses but not a humanitarian crisis, and certainly not a genocide? The humanitarian disaster was provoked as a response and, at the same time, is the side effect of the actions of NATO.

There were three possible responses to the crisis in Kosovo. Two are based on the legitimate but incompatible principles of sovereignty and self-determination. Much can be said in favor of both, but I shall be extremely brief:

A. If one is to stay with the principle of sovereignty, one would have had to stand aside and not act for fear of upsetting an extremely precarious balance and

165

producing a destabilizing — and possibly a domino — effect. How can the sovereignty of Bosnia be upheld if the sovereignty of Yugoslavia is abused? If the principle of sovereignty is abused, this is a dangerous message for all secessionist movements, who can then hold governments hostage. On the other hand, this is a distinctly uncomfortable moral option that makes one feel helpless and guilty, an option that makes the appeasement argument easy to accept. It is offset only by the feeling that inaction often creates the lesser of two evils. The defense of this principle of sovereignty, as defined by the hitherto existing international system, has been the basis of the argumentation coming from critics of the NATO action, notably Moscow and Beijing.

B. However, one could argue equally convincingly that the principle of self-determination be embraced. After all, haven't most countries in the region, and in Europe as a whole, been created first by this principle in the past century and a half? But then, if one is to choose this principle, one has to see it through and prepare for the foreseeable repercussions.

C. The third option was to persist with diplomatic means, to exert pressure through coordinated international channels, to insist on negotiations, and, above all, to accord this case the same patience and tact that has been accorded for decades to equally serious cases all over the world: Tibet, Palestine, Kurdistan, to mention the obvious. This last option was not taken: Rambouillet was a nonstarter, not acceptable to either side. Its second version, signed by the Albanians, and the one that then served as the ultimatum against Serbia, actually provided for a referendum for independence within three years; created a NATO protectorate on Yugoslav territory; and provided for privileges for NATO that effectively abrogated any semblance of Yugoslav sovereignty. Should one make the inappropriate historical analogy to the 1914 ultimatum that sparked off World War I, when Austria-Hungary deliberately sent an unacceptable ultimatum to the Serbs?

Statement 5. The West effectively embraced the second of the three options (i.e., the principle of self-determination) despite protestations to the contrary. I personally have no problems with this, but the West (1) did not see it through, and (2) did not provide a safety net for the repercussions. Not only that, but at the time of the NATO summit, President Clinton constantly repeated that there would be no change of international borders. In fact, despite NATO's de facto choosing of version B, the pitfalls were so obvious that the bombing was formulated as an intervention on behalf of human rights. Let me add quickly that I do not for a moment question the sincerity of the disgust of Western leaders (Clinton, Blair, Solana, Chirac, Schroeder, and so forth) over the reprehensible behavior of Milosevic and the murderers on the ground, a disgust that was, of course, coupled with the hypocrisy of double standards. I will go even further and disappoint some analysts in the Balkans who are now devising and recycling the most intricate of conspiracy theories. (The wildest one circulating is that Kosovo is one of richest uranium and gold sites of the world, that there is an ongoing conflict between British and German firms over control of the region, and that there is a macabre plan to depopulate the territory in order to exploit it more efficiently. Another conspiracy theory links NATO's desire to be in the Balkans with the pipeline from Kazakhstan, and the need of NATO to control the Caspian and Black Sea regions.) Unfortunately, I don't believe in conspiracy theories, and I don't believe that the West has immediate, let alone territorial, geo-strategic interests in the Balkans. I could even buy the argument that at moments the normal human outrage that "something should be done" might have been the main motive in the behavior of the more ideological (or messianic, or crusading) leaders of the alliance, such as Albright, for example; but it could hardly be true for the majority of the less romantic ones, for whom "the credibility" of NATO and the West was the primary argument.

Finally, within this rubric I would add that I understand the logic behind it, and I would support a vision that reconsiders the philosophical basis of international relations and seeks to create a new international system in which human rights figure prominently.

But before this has been well thought through and has received international support, I refuse to agree that the populations of the Balkans be guinea pigs in an aborted experiment.[9]

Statement 6. Lest it seem that the West in this scheme of reasoning looks less like a villain and more like a simple ignoramus sucked into an impossible situation against its goodwill and despite its good intentions, I wish to be explicit: my strongest, unreserved, and unconditional wrath is directed against its leaders.

A. They severely and consistently mishandled the situation in Yugoslavia during the past decade, and instead of contributing to an accommodating and compromising spirit, they have in fact exacerbated (without creating) the process of the ugly disintegration of Yugoslavia.

B. In the concrete recent crisis, they came in unprepared to handle a humanitarian disaster that, according to their own protestations, they knew was going on or was inevitably coming. In fact, they actually created it. When the refugees began pouring in, Emma Bonino, EU Commissioner on Humanitarian Aid, suggested that Romania and Bulgaria should take the bulk of the refugees since this was a regional problem, that is, their problem. This is a division of labor in good faith: the rich bomb, the poor feed. Most have followed the undignified preliminary plans to herd in 20,000 refugees in Guantanamo Bay. Even with the change of strategy, it

---

9. In a self-congratulatory coda to her piece in the *International Herald Tribune,* July 3-4, 1999, p. 6, Tina Rosenberg concludes that "the last 50 years have seen the rise of universally endorsed principles of conduct. The extent to which the world chooses to respect them, even when they conflict with sovereignty, is a good measure of civilization's progress." There is a slight logical inconsistency here. If universal principles are not universally applied, what makes them universal? As long as they are only universally claimed, this makes them only universal rhetoric.

took a month and a half to fly in the first 400 people to the U.S. In the meantime, dozens and dozens of American journalists were flown in the opposite direction to photograph the plight of the Albanian refugees and explain to the American public the intricacies of Balkan history (Charlie Gibbson and Peter Jennings, for example, enlightened American viewers by saying that Macedonians hated and feared Albanians because they were, in fact, Serbs). Even with the 40,000 promised to be taken care of by Germany, 20,000 by Turkey, and 5,000 each by Bulgaria, Romania, Greece, and some other small countries, this was still one-sixth or one-seventh of this tragic human wave.

The West also came in unprepared (not physically but psychologically) to see through its mission. NATO members actually stated firmly their conviction up front, that they were not going to jeopardize the life of a single one of their civilized citizens for any Balkanite (implicitly in the line of Bismarck's nineteenth-century pronouncement about the bones of a single Pomeranian grenadier, but not explicitly articulated, true to late twentieth-century politically correct discourse). Let me remind you parenthetically that, for all its ulterior motives, Russia fought a war with the Ottoman Empire for Bulgaria's independence in which tens of thousands of Russian officers and soldiers died on Bulgarian territory alone (the overall toll on all fronts being 220,000). Are there 220 Americans or West Europeans who are ready to die for the cause of the Kosovar Albanians? There are surely more than 220 ready to play "arcade games" with B2 bombers and other billion-dollar toys.[10]

C. As a result, the West has severely destabilized the Balkans, achieving what it professed it wanted to avoid: Albania is on the verge of a civil war between north and south; Macedonia is in an extremely explosive situation; not to mention the long-term destabilizing effects on the immediate neighbors, Bulgaria and Romania — the severe economic crisis into which they are being plunged deeper and deeper. Greece and Hungary are also casualties but, as members of the club, with much less severe repercussions. All throughout, after 1989, the West has consistently refused to pay *any* attention to the Balkans as a region, and has been consistent only in its policy to lock the region out in a ghetto by erecting prohibitive economic and administrative barriers, not to mention the cultural abuse that has been heaped on the region in line with the Huntingtonian division along civilizational fault lines between Western (Catholic and Protestant) and Eastern (Orthodox) Christianity. It is caricatured as a region of ancient hatreds, organic antidemocratic and authoritarian spirit, primitivism, tribalism, barbarity,

---

10. The more sinister side of this equation is the ease with which the enemy side is being degraded and dehumanized, and there is no attempt to even remotely justify the death of thousands of civilian victims ("collateral damage"). We see this on an even larger scale in Iraq. As a friend put it, Tom Clancy's books and movies tell us more about the Kosovo intervention than volumes of scholarly analysis.

caesaropapism, Orthodoxy, and so on and so forth — plus, of course, the Cyrillic script.[11]

Statement 7. In the meantime, there was never a Balkan war in the 1990s. Neither Greece, nor Bulgaria, Albania, Romania, or Turkey has been at war despite the constant implications to that effect in the Western press. All of them have been careful to avoid any temptation to get involved. The war in the 1990s was a war for the Yugoslav succession. But now let us be very clear: it is no longer a Yugoslav war. There is now an undeclared European war, no, a world war, of nineteen nations against one Balkan country, and this has enormous, frightening implications not only for the region but for the world.

During the past decade, the United States has consistently and consciously undermined and effectively compromised international organizations such as the United Nations and the OSCE, and has instead promoted NATO as the only global arbiter and policeman.[12]

The latest Kosovo blunder is only the last in a chain of such policies. It was, of course, morally unacceptable, as Clinton pointed out, to enter the new millennium with the terrible twentieth-century legacy of ethnic cleansing. It is also frightening to enter the new millennium with a legacy of unchecked, erratic, and arbitrary behavior on the part of a power that claims to be the arbiter. It could be a short millennium.

Back to my opening joke: the ongoing war has created a situation in which whoever wins, everyone will lose. But isn't this the case with all wars?

---

11. This verdict is not significantly changed after the end of the bombings, except for the defusing of the immediate incendiary situation in Albania and Macedonia with the retreat of the refugee population. Yet Macedonia continues to be potentially explosive, especially after the precedent with Kosovo. In Kosovo itself, NATO effectively sanctioned a monoethnic protectorate. The much-trumpeted Pact for Stability in the Balkans is only words thus far. The U.S. refuses to contribute to it, based on the argument that it paid the largest part of the war bill. The Europeans are good at procrastination until the inevitable "Balkan war fatigue" sets in. By refusing to include Serbia in any reconstruction project with its present leadership, the West is dooming the rest of the region, given Serbia's central location. It is also creating fertile ground for revanchism, anti-Westernism, and the perpetuation of a victim mentality. If analogies are of any help, the difference between the treatment of Germany after World War I, and then after World War II, should give some food for thought.

12. For a harrowing indictment of U.S. policies, see the latest memoir by Boutros Boutros-Ghali, *Unvanquished: A US-UN Saga* (New York: Random House, 1999).

III. VOICES OF TODAY'S BALKAN PEOPLE

What Do People from the Region Think?

ALBANIANS

Portrait of a People

ISMAIL KADARE

They file mechanically across the television screen as if drugged by the tragedy they are living, without cries or gestures of protest, often dropping their eyes before the humiliation they have suffered. One sees clearly a whole people on the move, but notes quickly that an important element is missing in these pictures: the young men. They have been kept as hostages in Kosovo.

During a television interview, the brother of the Serbian dictator referred maliciously and not without salacious intent to the beauty of some young Albanian girls that he had seen in this human wave. After this remark, they became rare in the footage. Spectators were not long in learning the macabre truth: their appearance on film was being suppressed to avoid stirring up viewer sympathy for them. Surviving deportees affirmed that many young women were being killed or raped.

The image of the Albanian population of Kosovo was to become yet more profoundly mutilated: soon there were no more than the children, some of the mothers, and old people on film. In the Serb view of things, these were the last remnant of the population that would contribute the most to create in the minds of viewers a disfigured picture of the Albanian people — haggard creatures, blackened by suffering, some clothed like little old Muslim men.

The Serbian propaganda machine that prepared this slaughter, after having monstrously falsified history and deformed the truth about the Albanians' religion, proceeded to falsify the reality of their external physical appearance, as the Nazis had done before them to disparage the Jews. The sight of more than a quarter million of the children of Kosovo — blond, for the most part, like so many other little Europeans — was a surprise for a multitude of people deceived until then by Serbian propaganda. Albanian children and infants have become the best testimony about the image of the nation that engendered them. That explains why the hatred of the Serbs has so often targeted them. Notably, it is why not one of these children has been vaccinated, with the serious consequences anticipated by

---

This essay was translated from the French by Cathy Bodin.

their executioners. This omission alone suffices to prod the conscience of the world health organizations, which tolerated the situation. Add to that the case of the mass poisoning of Kosovar children in 1989. This act implicates the professional actions of certain doctors in Europe who, unlike their colleagues, alerted no one and who became, for reasons known to them alone, defenders of this crime.

Every evening, on little screens the world over, processes the Calvary of a people. Though the picture has been edited and is run incomplete, there are still in this human multitude, among these darkened elders and beaming children, a multitude of beings: Christian priests and Muslim clergy, university professors, scientists, artists, but no persons unidentifiable. They are struck dumb by the tragedy. Then when suddenly they are heard to speak German, French, or English, we have a hard time believing it.

This unending human chain carries with it one of the most solemn tragedies of the century. These people have left everything behind them, what's left of their houses, their near and dear killed in front of them, their raped daughters. They carry in their arms their only hope, their children. But often, instead of live little ones, they have carried for days and nights on end little cadavers in search of a tomb, because even that was denied them.

Hearing the echo of the horrors that sound across Kosovo, an age-old question, one to end the century, but one which as yet has received no solid response, surges spontaneously: Whence and how can such sinister and implacable hatreds arise between peoples? Opinions and explanations vary, but there is one point on which they converge: these hatreds are always fueled by centuries-old jealousies and complexes. In this case, unjustly attacked over the course of centuries and especially under the long Ottoman dominion — the object of humiliations, treated brutally as underlings, as "serfs" — the Serbs have apparently accumulated an ocean of avenging bile that, little by little, has reached their veins. Unable to spit it in the face of the bygone empire, which crushed them repeatedly, they have sought, as is frequent in such situations, to discharge their complex on another people. The Albanians were the most opportune victims for this transfer. Different in origin, culture, language, alphabet, and religion (which is nonetheless split among three faiths, including Orthodox as well as the Catholic and Muslim confessions), they were the best of targets for another reason especially: during five centuries of Serbian humiliation, the Albanians, according to the Serbs, had known a better fate.

Today, even the idea that the Albanians had ever been the object of jealousy brings a smile; but in a not-too-distant past, especially during the seventeenth through nineteenth centuries, things went differently in the Balkans. At that time the Albanians constituted one of the foremost populations of the Empire; their presence was felt everywhere. To understand their importance, one has only to remember that the greatest Turk conqueror, Sultan Mehmet II, having taken Constantinople in 1453 (or sixty-four years after the battle of Kosovo), had to march

174

twice on Albania to take it. Later, when the Balkans were definitively taken, the Ottoman Empire was anxious to turn to its own profit the immense energy of the Balkan peoples, and tried to win the support of some of them by offering high posts and privileges, though without excluding brutal measures if needed. In so doing, it won over some Albanians and also some Greeks, some Jews, rarely the Southern Slavs, but other peoples too, like the Kurds and the Armenians (before the massacre). To understand the particular attention that the Albanians attracted in this hierarchy, we have only to remember that in the seventeenth century they were offered the office of prime minister (grand vizir) of all the empire, the second-highest office, inferior only to the sultan, endowed with unlimited civil and military power. Astonishingly, this position long remained among the Albanians, in a quasi-dynastic form. One well imagines that, besides this almost hereditary office, Albanians accordingly occupied a mass of other prestigious offices, such as ministers, generals, and governors.

This is part of the crux of the Albanian tragedy: the gulf that opened up between them and their neighbors, principally the Serbs. The power of these generals and governors, ambitious and hard, typical products of their era, who were serving throughout the empire, undoubtedly gave rise over a long period to a serious problem in the Albanians' relationships with their neighbors. Albania itself drew no real profit from this, other than the jealousy of its neighbors and vainglory for itself. Later, to its misfortune, when the hour of vengeance came, its so-called privileged status was fruitfully exploited by the [ethnically] chauvinistic propaganda of its neighbors. Far from explaining that the Albanians were in no way responsible for Serbian misfortunes, that they too had suffered like all subjected peoples despite the prestigious offices that they had occupied, that they had not called the Serbs "serfs," the Serbs stated exactly the opposite — and the Ottoman oppression came to be considered an Albanian domination. So much so that when the Slavs of the South created their own state, Yugoslavia, and when Europe committed the fatal error of leaving half of the Albanians to the mercy of this state, thenceforth hostile to them, Serbian nationalism heard the awaited hour of vengeance strike. The byword of this nationalism became and remains "Now you pay for your past, yesterday's 'masters of the Balkans.'" This movement began one of the most savage persecutions that Europe has known, and its last act now plays before our eyes. Trying to avenge themselves on the Albanians for the Serbian humiliation of five centuries, the Serbs believe they are able to expunge the problem. In reality, they are burying themselves in the whirlpool of crime. And if they don't hurry to get out of it, they will certainly drown in it.

It is not excessive to say that the Balkans, Europe's backyard, has been attacked by the plague. Like every epidemic, this one risks spilling over into the whole continent. There is no time to lose in establishing peace in this yard; it must be done urgently and by all means.

Kosova: A Place Where the Dead Speak

BATON HAXHIU

Kosova is a place where the voices of the dead speak as loudly as the voices of the living, maybe more loudly. The dead are nowhere and everywhere. Some will never be found, others are scattered in endless graves, with bones piled in the ruins of what were once their beautiful village homes, and their last moments written in the memories and faces of those who survived. Everyone, it seems, is in a close relationship with the dead: almost every village, every neighborhood, every family has been touched in one way or the other by these brutal killings. The scale of the killings is just now becoming apparent as NATO peacekeepers are all over Kosova and the expelled Albanians are coming back. When they return home, the people of Kosova find nothing more than the ruins of a giant house. The number of the dead is still only an estimate; military officials and western humanitarians say that up to ten thousand people may have been killed in an orchestrated campaign of crimes committed by the Serb police and paramilitary troops. Sometimes they find the consequences of these crimes on their doorsteps: body parts fill family wells, and corpses still remain in the very places where they were slaughtered. They find these things while doing the most ordinary things, such as cooking lunch or watching TV.

"Killing is a popular art," writes Yugoslav-born writer Charles Simic in his book *Orphan Factory*, a collection of poems and essays published last year. "They continue to perfect it without ever being satisfied with the results," he says. On the other hand, a villager from Krusha thinks his eyes will always be turned toward the crime scene. "It is so difficult to only be here," he said several days ago. "Everyone is dead in a way, even those who were left to live. . . . There are children who are feelingless; they are not sad, they are just empty. There are the elderly who only cry. The young girls who were raped — I think they will never speak of this, but their lives have been destroyed. And it is just as terrible for the men. They had vowed to protect their families, and they were not able to." On almost all the walls there are graffiti saying "Die."

This essay was translated by Lindita Imami.

There must be an enraged Albanian who has killed too. We must say that that crime has the same face, because it is not quantity that makes it condemnable, but rather quality. Some have been hurt tremendously and cannot forgive. They might even kill the innocent. This is what Kosova has become today.

Many things have been shelled: [the city of] Vukovar [in Croatia] became a ruin, Sarajevo was destroyed, and Mostar is almost a rubble. All of this happened in a cycle of fighting, and I cannot say which was the most difficult to absorb. I felt terrible when Sarajevo was being shelled, when Vukovar and Srebrenica followed; but for me Kosova was really painful. And while all these terrible things were happening, Belgrade did not react. We must stress this. All these things were considered as taking place "beyond the mountains,"[1] and the people in Belgrade did not bother when Sarajevo was being shelled. It has always been said that all Albanians must go beyond the Cursed Mountains.[2] And I always considered this an idiot's verbalism. I never believed that this could really happen. I could not believe that crime would be equal to this verbalism so often stressed in the past years.

It has been weeks now since the bombing of Serb targets by NATO ended.[3] But we cannot say that the war has ended. And from the day the international troops marched into Kosova for the first time since World War II, into a land troubled by terror and nightmare, a new confrontation has begun — although not an open one. On the surface we have KFOR still uncompleted. Assassinations and counter-assassinations are taking place in a semilegal environment. As it seems, both sides are going toward the last battle. The international community seems somehow alone with its concept of a multiethnic, civil, and tolerant society. A group of Albanians, not a small group, who have lost their loved ones in a barbaric and violent campaign see the calls for "coexistence with the neighbors" as a repetition of the socialist past when there were calls for "brotherhood and unity."[4] Understandably, the international community thinks differently. But how can this message be understood by ordinary people who find dark holes instead of their wealthy possessions when returning from a forced exile? It is only natural that the feeling of revenge boils in everyone's chest. Therefore, the sporadic acts of revenge against "our neighbors" are not surprising. The same was echoed by the President of the United States and the German foreign minister.

We come to the question, which is greatly disputed, as to whether there is collective blame. If not, at least there must be collective responsibility. After World

1. The author uses an Albanian rendering of a popular and cynical Serbian expression meaning "far away"; an English paraphrase could be "out of sight, out of mind. . . ." [Ed.]

2. In the translator's notes to the Cosic essay in this volume, Bardos explains that this is a reference to the Prokletije Mountains (literally, "the Damned Mountains"), which are on the border between Kosovo and Albania. [Ed.]

3. The Albanian version of this essay was originally submitted on June 30, 1999. [Ed.]

4. Tito's conception of a multiethnic society was expressed in the slogan "brotherhood and unity." [Ed.]

War II, the Germans were frequently blamed collectively. The truth is that many writers (Thomas Mann, Bertolt Brecht, etc.), artists, and intellectuals — the brains of the society, so to speak — sought sanctuary in other countries. Therefore, today most voices in German public opinion oppose blaming Serbs collectively. It might be that the Germans, in whose name Hitler's gangs committed horrific crimes, know the issue of collective blame better.

Can Serbia learn from the German experience of the postwar period? Certainly. Last week the German Parliament adopted a project for commemorating a memorial for the victims of Nazism. The memorial will be located next to the Brandenburg Gate, a historic location of national significance for the Germans. A long debate preceded this decision. Intellectuals from different fields had discussed ideas, issues, and dilemmas. Can German pain for its victims be expressed with concrete? Some thought yes and others thought no. The debate about crimes committed by Germans had ended. And there are constant calls that the past should not be forgotten. Some can say that, fifty years later, the time has probably come to end the debate. But after an ethnic cleansing, after a true catastrophe, the German public is acutely aware of how facing the truth about crimes with pain and repentance helps to prevent the repetition of these crimes in the future.

How about Serbia? During NATO's bombing campaign, a Serb literary critic pioneered the opinion that necessary steps to supposedly clarify the crimes committed in the past had already begun in Serbia, because books on the truth of the wars in Bosnia and Croatia were being published. But it is strange how cleansing from such crimes can happen so easily. Four or five books on the truth, on the crimes, and that's it. Serbia can saunter toward Europe, where it will be welcomed wholeheartedly. On the other hand, we have the German experience as proof of an intensive fifty-year period of facing the crimes committed by Hitler. The debate in Germany about the Holocaust will not end, perhaps not for another two or three generations. But in Serbia this issue has been resolved with four or five books. There is no doubt that, no matter how intelligent the opinions of this Serb critic are, they are completely unrealistic.

It has been thirteen years since the publication of the infamous *Memorandum of the Serb Academy of Sciences and Arts*.[5] Last week the Serbian Orthodox Church was preparing to issue a statement in the name of its believers in which it would ask forgiveness from Albanians for their barbaric victimization at the hands of Serb paramilitary, military, and police forces. Serbian Archbishop Pavle is also quoted as having said after these vicious crimes, "We must ask for forgiveness if we want to save our souls." After thirteen years, this would only be the first step. Other, more convincing, steps must follow — because we must not forget that the Serbian Church has tolerated and been silent about these crimes for at least the past thirteen years. It has been silent about its shame.

5. See discussion by Tim Judah on the "History of Serbia" in this volume. [Ed.]

These days, the news has been that the Synod of the Serbian Orthodox Church has asked Milosevic to step down for the sake of the Serb population. I analyzed two things: these are the same people, the same clergy, who walked with the bones of Prince Lazar in Eastern Serbia; and wherever they arrived, the villages were burnt and there was war. Serbia has many sins in its soul for the wars in former Yugoslavia, and now the Serbs are being cleansed and are blaming it all on Milosevic. Milosevic, of course, bears the greatest blame, but such is the tale on the Kurban.[6] We must not doubt that Milosevic is the Kurban nor that he is guilty, but we must also not doubt that the Orthodox Church, the Academy of Sciences and Arts, and the intellectuals of Serbia are to blame as well. This tale on the Kurban and the cleansing of souls seems so ugly to me. Slobodan Milosevic did not torch every single house in Kosova. Serb individuals did. They did this of their own free will and often with pleasure, according to eyewitness accounts that are only now being gathered by journalists, criminal investigators, and NATO peacekeepers.

The majority of the Serbs who systematically destroyed their neighbors' houses are leaving now. Their houses are burning as fast as the first Albanian refugees are coming back home. As a result, the Serb population of Pec is going rapidly toward a new demographic: zero. Serbs leaving Kosova are not victims of a new ethnic cleansing, nor a result of the unjust call for collective blame, as many apologists are saying. They are victims of their supporting their community and agreeing with Milosevic's war. As individuals they may be innocent, but the attempt to kill Kosova was done willfully by the Serbs as a national act, institutionalized and implemented by their national leaders, who remain in power. The campaign to bring Albanians under the absolute rule of Serb political will has brought forth failure and its consequences for the Serbs.

Milosevic is a man who did things; he always listened to others [who thought them out]. He did what he was told to do by Mirjana or the Academy of Sciences, but also by the Serbian Orthodox Church. He did not have great ideas: even in the negative sense, he always acted as though he were under hypnosis. Milosevic was pushed by someone. He is a criminal, but he cannot alone be accountable for what a whole community has done in the last ten years. The same people are celebrating victory in Serbia. This is the strange part: some Serbs who returned to Pec came back triumphant, with three fingers held up high. They were proud of the crimes they had committed. I do not know how to live together with people who celebrate crime and killing, even in the presence of priests and Serb leaders — even side by side with the international community.

The historic battle of Kosova was a small battle and was not solved as other larger battles with the Turks were solved, such as the Marica battle.[7] No one knows

6. This refers to the tale of the sacrifice in the Qur'an. One might say, "Milosevic is being used as a scapegoat. . . ." [Ed.]

7. The battle between Serbs and Turks in 1371. [Ed.]

who won the battle, but initially it was thought that the Serbs had won. So a battle that was not a failure was celebrated as a failure by the Serbs for 500 years. And now that they've really lost, the failure cannot be more clear and obvious. This shows that we live in a crazy world — in a world of crazy categories and values. And now there is no doubt that after such an aggression of lies, people in Serbia have gone mad, because in Milosevic's long-time government there must be a factor of insanity. Serbia is not a product of Milosevic, but the other way around: Milosevic is a Serb product.

The Serb campaign of terror did not begin on March 24, 1999, the day NATO began bombing Serbia, nor in March 1998, when the massacres of Drenica happened, nor in 1988 or 1981. Rather, it has been an entire period of hatred and cultivating racism by Serbs pushing the idea that they are superior to the Albanians, a period that has lasted at least from 1912 to the present. Since the Albanians have been confronted with physical and psychological terror that is nearly a century old, it is only normal that they have retained a great hatred for the Serbs. But this is the hatred of the oppressed; it is a measure of how little the victim thinks of the bearer of arbitrariness, the Serb state. This is thus the main difference between the Serb and Albanian hatreds for each other: the hatred of the victim for the occupier is never the same as the hatred of the occupier for the victim.

Representatives of the international community who are settling in Kosova in large numbers to begin the difficult process of pacification must be aware that after all this we cannot go back to a normal everyday life as if nothing has happened. For now, coexistence is a beautiful illusion. The realization of this illusion is possible; however, it can be achieved only when Serbia produces a politician like the German chancellor of the 1970s, Willy Brandt, who in honor and in repentance knelt before the memorial for the victims of the Warsaw ghettos. And 99 percent of the Germans were with him, at least spiritually. Germany needed almost three decades for this to happen, not because of a lack of will but because during this time there was a good deal of mind cleansing. How long will it take Serbia to cleanse itself from its crimes? Will it ever happen that a Serb politician asks forgiveness for the crimes committed by his fellow countrymen? To speed up the process, at least the Serbian Church must ask for forgiveness as it has shown its intention to do so. It must do it now: ask for forgiveness before a mass grave or a crime scene, such as Krusha e Madhe, where more than 120 people, Albanian women, children, and men, were torched.

It goes without saying that horrific things happened in Kosova. For a long time the Serbs have committed crimes, ending with massive graves in Kosova. Thus there cannot be coexistence so soon. At best, there can only be life near (but not next to) each other. It is difficult to think that people who endured all this could accept life within the state of Serbia or the Federal Republic of Yugoslavia. If the world had the courage to divide Germany and the Germans as a single people and state with the objective of condemning and punishing crime, I do not see any reason why Kosova should join Serbia within Yugoslavia for the sake of crime and Serb collective silence. After all that has happened, Serbia now mourns the bridges but is silent about the crimes. I do not believe that Kosova can live with crime and with the people who keep a sword of death for Albanians under the pillow they sleep on. For 120 years the Serbs have had the opportunity to live with the Albanians; instead, they have committed massacres and deportations. The Albanians cannot erase their memory every twenty years. Therefore, the Albanians must again forgive but must not forget. Crime must be punished, and we can live as neighbors. Yet Serbia has no moral right to reign over Kosova.

For the outside world, present Serb efforts consist of doing nothing; this only delays the national assessment that Serbs must make of themselves and their society. War and a lack of internal Serbian opposition disclose how their political framework is not based on the terror of the police state but rather on voluntary Stalinism. Censorship and propaganda do not fully explain the general indifference to Kosova's Golgotha. With reference to Serb public reactions, there were no big differences between those who had access to Western sources and live broadcasts and those who did not. Individuals felt free to criticize Milosevic in front of Western journalists, but Serb political parties did not debate the sanity and morality of the war. Minds were closed and hearts were transformed into rock in ways that are frankly difficult to imagine at the end of the twentieth century.

Therefore, it is important for all nations to find a way to continue expressing moral condemnation because the actions of the Milosevic regime deserve this. Only such condemnation could pressure Belgrade to begin any change. The Serbs should not be left to suffer in isolation and become more enraged. The relations the West has with Belgrade now must be based on change and not merely reconstruction, which would only help them escape the painful consequences of their evil. They may have leaders drenched in blood; they may have Western aid for economic reconstruction and coexistence with others. But they may not have both.

Conflict and Empowerment

AFERDITA KELMENDI

Deportation — Empowerment Stripped

On April 14, 1999, only days after being forced from my home and my homeland, I was invited by the United States Senate Judiciary Committee to tell my story. It was one common to many Kosovars and indicative of how those in positions of authority can effectively strip every concept of empowerment from a suppressed population:

"I hope you will hear my story and ask yourselves, 'How could this have happened?' But more importantly, I hope you will ask, 'How can we stop it?' I wish it were over, but I know it is not over, especially for thousands of people still trapped inside Kosovo. They are starving, and they are afraid for their lives. I know this because I was starving, and I was afraid for *my* life, and my children's lives.

"I want to make one important point. . . . I am not a refugee. I did not leave Kosovo by choice. I was forced to leave, and my family was forced to leave. I am not running from a civil war. I am a deportee. I was forced to leave by men with black caps and guns, who came specifically to make me leave.

". . . When I came to the [Radio 21 station] on the morning of March 29, before I arrived I saw from a distance the police raiding the station. They broke down the door and destroyed the entire station and all of its equipment. I stayed back by the car, and then I drove quickly to where my family was hiding. Three families were hiding in one house — twenty-one people in two rooms.

"We were very afraid that they would come to find us, so we left in three cars, seven people in each car. We were going to hide in another flat; we did not want to leave Prishtina. But as soon as we were on the road, we were stopped by two armed men in a green Mercedes. They demanded that we pay them 200 Deutsche marks for each car, or they would burn our cars with us inside. So, of course, we paid. These men then forced us to follow them. When we asked where we were going, they told us to shut up and threatened to kill us. They led us to the edge of the city on the road to Macedonia, and they told the police at the checkpoint to let us pass, apparently because we had paid.

182

"About one and a half miles from the border, we reached the end of a long line of cars. We stopped there, and we waited. We waited there for three days. We had no food. There were seven in our car, and we were all starving. Everyone in all the cars around us was starving. You could hear children crying for lack of food. We had only a little bit of water, so we took small sips and stayed very still, to conserve energy.

"After three days, my son decided to walk to the border, to see what was happening. He came back after three hours, and he told us that the border was closed to cars. So we abandoned the car, and we all got out and walked one and a half miles. . . ."

At that point in my life, there could not have been a deeper sense of despair; I had lost any concept of empowerment that I had struggled to build in myself and the young women with whom I have worked for five years. And at that moment my dream of developing a radio station founded upon the principles of conflict resolution had been stripped at the end of many rifles.

Media and Empowerment

My dream, however, would somehow not only survive but thrive. On July 18, 1999 — only a few days after the conclusion of the NATO bombing campaign — Radio 21 became the first independent Albanian radio station in the history of Kosova to broadcast twenty-four hours per day, seven days per week. Since we have resumed our broadcasts, Radio 21's schedule has included news and information programs, interactive discussions with studio guests and the outside audience, sporting events, live broadcasts of speeches by United States Secretary of State Madeleine Albright and British Prime Minister Tony Blair, and an exclusive interview with KFOR mission commander General Sir Michael Jackson.

Radio 21 and its soon-to-be-operating partner station TV 21 are committed to the belief that a dedicated, fair-minded, and independent indigenous media must offer the entire population of Kosova access to all shades of opinion as a primary component of rebuilding a civil society. Our organization's staff is steadfast in maintaining a high standard of editorial professionalism, broadcasting news and highlighting issues in a balanced and unbiased manner. Central to this objective is the makeup of the Radio 21 staff: 70 percent are women. It has been our primary belief that Kosovar women have a tremendous amount of energy and expertise that must play a significant role in helping both the women and men of Kosova discuss the traumatic events that now dominate our group identity. Using Radio-TV 21 as a vehicle, these women can assist all members of the Kosovar population develop a new sense of self-confidence and a belief in the possibilities that are beginning to exist for the first time in Kosova — now as a free and democratic society is formed from burned-out houses and mass graves.

Opportunity and Empowerment — the Media Project

The utilization of a free press — by women — as a mechanism for constructing a Kosovar civil society, however, began long before the conflict in Kosova became front-page news in the *New York Times*. In November 1995, Xheraldina Vula and I established the Media Project in Prishtina, an initiative to train young women in a brand of professional, independent journalism with attention to conflict resolution and the inclusion of multiple points of view. Based out of our respective homes, we recruited participants from nearby neighborhoods, and later from farther afield by word of mouth. By the end of 1996, more than one hundred training courses had covered aspects of print, radio, and television journalism emphasizing the importance of conflict resolution skills. Well-known Kosovar and foreign journalists led the sessions.

In 1997 the Media Project, with contributions by a cadre of newly trained journalists, published two issues of the bulletin *Dea* and produced a television documentary (broadcast throughout homes in Kosova via direct-to-home satellite over the Tirana-based station TVSH) in conjunction with a public campaign entitled "Invest in Today's Girls, Tomorrow's Women." This was a response to the increasing number of female dropouts in urban and rural schools. In December 1997 the Media Project published the first edition of *Eritrea*, its monthly magazine for women. The magazine provided a forum for women's perspectives on politics, economics, health, and society until it was forced to cease publication in March 1999.

Testimonial from a Media Project graduate:

> Eli is a twenty-one-year old interpreter for the American Military in Kosova. In fatigues and boots, she accompanies the troops patrolling the troubled streets of Gjilane in southeastern Kosova. Last week, when a distraught Serbian woman, believing Eli to be Serbian, confided in her that all Albanians should be murdered, Eli responded that such an attitude only creates further terror, contributing nothing to the rebuilding of Kosova. "The conflict resolution training I had at sixteen allowed me to remain calm and emphasize the need for common ground between her people and mine."

Participation and Empowerment — "The Saturday Night Program"

Each Saturday night, Radio 21 broadcasts a program in which audience members phone in to discuss themes always present in Kosovar society, yet particularly important in the reestablishment of civil society after a brutal conflict. Core topics for any single program could be democracy, love, activism, or (as on August 28, 1999) leadership:

> "A good leader must have *supporters,* and *potential supporters;* the leader must not consider certain individuals as enemies simply because they do not follow his or her wishes — 'if you are not with me, you are not my enemy, but my potential supporter.'"

This weekly program serves to empower women and men throughout Kosova on a minimum of three levels. First, the studio presenters become both leaders and facilitators, encouraging dialogue for dialogue's sake, not to divide opinions but to develop an atmosphere emphasizing *inclusivity* of ideas. Second, the phone-in participants are allowed to express opinions in an open forum — an entirely new concept to multiple generations of Kosovars. Finally, and not least important, the listening audience enjoys access to a free exchange of ideas, a public exhibition of democratic activism. The "Saturday Night Program," which initiated broadcasts only three months after the forced deportation of hundreds of thousands of Kosovars, represents an astonishing, and yet tremendously positive, step toward the establishment of liberal democracy in Kosova.

Because Kosovars Are Western, There Can Be No Homeland without a State

BLERIM SHALA

What did the Albanians of Kosova learn from their great sufferings in the spring of 1999? What is the central and uppermost message from this tragedy of biblical proportions? Bearing in mind that this was also the last year of the second millennium of Christianity, a civilization that began with sacrifice and suffering but also with eternal hope, such a characterization is particularly apt. It seems that the main lesson learned by the Albanians, whose sufferings undoubtedly marked the year 1999 in Europe and the whole world, is really the idea that there can be no homeland without a state. It may have been the Jews who initially came to this conclusion in the spring of 1945, after they had survived the Holocaust. It is statehood that gives a homeland its true identity.

The principle of statehood for Kosova is a genuine Western value because it is based on the following components: the right of a people for self-determination; the will of the overwhelming majority of Kosova citizens; and the fact that Kosova's statehood would only contribute toward security and peace in the region and in Europe. The events of last spring made it clear that Kosova's violent occupation and submission under the Serb state is the greatest threat to peace and security in the region and in Europe, as well as the greatest enemy of Western values in this part of Europe.

It also became clear during this year that there is no place in Kosova for both the Albanians and the Serb regime. And it became apparent that Western civilization was siding with the Albanian position on the expulsion of the Serb regime from Kosova. War in and over Kosova became inevitable in order to expel the Serb regime from Kosova. This expulsion included the withdrawal of tens of thousands of Serb military, police, and paramilitary troops, tanks, artillery pieces, and other instruments of violence. Does anyone seriously believe that this withdrawal could have happened without the West?

This essay was translated by Lindita Imami.

From the very first day in the second decade of this century, the Serb presence in Kosova was a presence of violence, and Kosova was kept under Serbia with violence. Therefore, the withdrawal of the Serb military from Kosova meant freeing Kosova from the violence; in other words, it meant the withdrawal of Serbia itself from Kosova. The withdrawal of Serbia from Kosova was impossible without the West's involvement in the Kosova problem, that is, without the West getting closer to the Albanian side of the Kosova issue. We all know this very well now, based on our recent experience, as well as on the previous fruitless attempts of Albanians to be liberated from Serbia on their own. The West began to get closer to the correct side of the Kosova issue during the years of Yugoslavia's disintegration, when it was obvious that the Belgrade regime was only the last remaining vestige of a fifty-year "Cold War reign," and that this regime was the main perpetrator of the wars that engulfed half of this country's land. Western support for the Albanians in Kosova was initially expressed as a concern for human rights in the first half of the 1990s. Initially, it came as a result of the Albanian nonviolent political movement and eventually — after the Albanians' pursuit of freedom from Serbia was strengthened — by manifestations of their readiness to fight and die.

The West got involved to resolve the Kosova issue directly — politically and militarily. This repositioning of the West toward the Albanians was not possible without certain factors that were crucial. The readiness of Albanians to fight was very important. Another essential element drawing Western support was the political skill of the Albanians in understanding that the Kosova peace agreement, formulated at the conference in Rambouillet and in Paris, must be accepted. The signing of the agreement by the Albanian delegation in the French capital on March 18 opened the doors for a military intervention of the West and opened avenues for the expulsion of Serb troops from Kosova. This signing demonstrated that the Kosova leadership understood that Kosova's statehood cannot happen with one immediate step that once and forever redefines Albanian-Serb relations on the issue of Kosova by means of some final and conclusive Albanian-Serb war. On the contrary, this statehood is a midterm process that would be facilitated by the political, economic, and military presence of the West. In brief, the Albanian leadership of Kosova understood that Serbia cannot just get out, and the process of independence for Kosova cannot be initiated without the presence of NATO, the EU, and the OSCE. A Western protectorate, and later independence through a referendum, is the national strategy of the Albanians in Kosova. We believe that this is a realistic strategy that will bring to realization our national ideal, that is, independence for Kosova. The Western presence in Kosova is not the only fundamental element toward the realization of this ideal. It is the Albanian ability to embrace genuine Western values that is even more significant. With our actions and behavior, we Albanians must prove that from now on we deserve freedom and statehood for Kosova, not only because of our readiness to give our lives, but because we are Western in our political positions and actions.

Independence will be the final result of a transition period in Kosova only if the Kosova society is fully democratic. The democratization of the Kosovar society in the coming years will open the way for Kosova's independence and for it to gain state identity.

Kosova

HASHIM THAQI

With the withdrawal of the Slav peoples from former Yugoslavia, the Albanians of Kosova had no additional reason to remain in the new state creation of Serbia and Montenegro. Interethnic tensions between Albanians and Serbs in Kosova, which ran deep in the past, have become even deeper in the past several years. The Albanian people of Kosova had the least reason to worry about Yugoslavia's disintegration, especially because of the way it disintegrated and because of the way they were treated during the existence of that state.

The disintegration of Yugoslavia, as well as the new circumstances created in the world after the Cold War, made up the most convenient political moment for articulating and realizing the historic and legitimate aspirations of the people of Kosova. The actions of the Kosova people for a separate and independent life from former Yugoslavia were political actions, only natural for the concurring events, while other federal units were essentially changing their constitutional positions. All the judicial and political actions of Kosova since the beginning of Yugoslavia's disintegration were free of any ideological elements; yet they were directed against the reigning ideology of a one-party communist system.

Since Kosova was stripped of its autonomy by force, the Albanians refused to accept the legitimacy of the Serb system; they did this by declaring Kosova an independent republic and by attempting a peaceful strategy as the only means to solve the Albanian-Serb conflict. The question of time — when would the Republic of Kosova function freely in its territory? — was a question linked to the balance of powers. Nonetheless, outside of verbal support, the peaceful strategy employed by the Kosova Albanians for years lacked ample support for changing the situation. Under the circumstances of Serb occupation, the Albanians of Kosova — especially the youth — did not see a future.

The Kosova Albanians were subjected to Serb violence for a long time, always treated as second-class citizens and always living under the efficient control of the Serb police. Although the issue of Kosova had been addressed in the international arena for years, mainly because of human rights violations, there was no change or improvement in either human rights or any other issue in Kosova's overall situation. Human rights and civil rights were constantly being violated.

However, it was not merely an issue of a strict government violating the human rights and freedoms of its citizens; rather, the core problem was the repressing of the political will of a people — the will to freedom and independence. It was these primary rights that were violated in order to repress the collective being of the Albanian people.

Unfortunately, the Dayton Peace Agreement's exclusion of the Kosova issue from its agenda, and its recognition of the FRY (Serbia and Montenegro), gave a clear signal to the people of Kosova that peaceful policies are not the way to achieve political objectives in this part of the Balkans. Politics should achieve these goals as an "art of the possible," as Diverger said. "The primary task of politics is the elimination of violence so that bloody conflicts are replaced with other means, a milder way of war; so politics is war, but at the same time it is limiting war through force." These were some of the reasons for the creation of a new force [the KLA], which would choose a less political means for the realization of its aims, but would again use politics to meet its objectives.

Since the creation of the KLA in 1992, its political and command structures embraced the modern theory of international relations: that strength is not only in military force but also in other political, diplomatic, and economic means. The birth of the KLA was difficult; and the process of its perfection was even more difficult. It was born and tried to perfect itself in conditions of a tough and unequal war. The KLA was a creation that primarily came out of the military and political repression that was exercised for years in Kosova; but it was also the result of the long wait by the Kosova people for a solution to their problem to be the fruit of their peaceful policies. Above all, the KLA originated from the political will of the Kosova people for a free and independent life, regardless of the scale of sacrifice. Therefore, the KLA is part of the political will of the Kosova people: it was generated from the people and was then embraced by the people with no reservation. The KLA's coming onto the scene began to raise the hopes of Albanians for liberation from the Serb occupying forces. Since its creation, the KLA has been pro-Western, especially pro-American. It has been aware that the people of Kosova belong to that world, and that Western support would be of vital importance for the war effort and for victory.

Within the KLA there were people of different ages, opinions, and convictions, but all acted toward the same goal and under the same freedom-fighter uniform.

The KLA needed a political platform but not a political wing. So that is how we proceeded. The platform for a free and independent Kosova was supported with no party or ideological colorings. The only objective of the KLA was the withdrawal of Serb occupying forces from Kosova and the achievement of freedom and equality for all its citizens. After a long and difficult war, and with the help of our international allies and NATO, we achieved this objective.

As in war, now also in peace, the KLA is undergoing the process of improvement and reform. The KLA has always been cautious and acted in conformity with the actions and requests of the international community. After successfully achieving its objective, the KLA had to change its liberating character. It was out of respect for the positions of the international community that we accepted and achieved the demilitarization and transformation of the KLA. Today the KLA has become a new force: the Defense Troops of Kosova (TMK). Some KLA members have become members of this force. This force and these members will act within authorizations determined by bilateral agreements between us and the international community. The other members of the KLA will be incorporated into other mechanisms of the new society in Kosova; some of them will go back to their previous duties in civilian life. However, all former members of the KLA have a moral obligation to protect and advance the values they fought for.

KLA members are especially concerned that representatives of other ethnic communities in Kosova, such as Bosnians, Serbs, and Turks, experience the fruits of liberty, because the KLA's objective was not war against the Serbs but the creation of freedom for all. This means that the main force that led and supported the resistance is interested in these groups participating in the democratic building of the institutions and the government, in accordance with Kosova's needs. All of us together should build Kosova's future. It was and remains our permanent objective to build a democratic society, equal for all who live and act in Kosova. We see the affirmations of other ethnic groups in Kosova as an important issue for Kosova.

We are aware that the ramifications of the war in Kosova are great and cannot be overcome quickly. But the difficult economic situation strongly compels us to begin with the reconstruction and renewal process as soon as possible. Besides the readiness and already proven sacrifices of the people of Kosova, we also expect to get the assistance and cooperation of the international community. We are, however, aware that Kosova cannot be rebuilt to meet its objective needs with aid alone.

SERBS

Now That We Have Lost This Little World War: A Message for Slobodan Milosevic

DOBRICA COSIC

I assume you all know that I was among those academicians who did not agree with the current politicization of the academy. Even today I feel the same way. However, the "today" in which we find ourselves is perhaps unlike any other "today" in the last decade for the Serb people. With that belief I am standing at this podium, for the first time in six years, in solidarity with those who think that today, from this house, an opinion must be heard about the political situation in Serbia. I am certain that the people of this country want to hear that message.

In the institution in which we are members and associates, politics should be the essential understanding of the human and national situation, and the intellectual responsibility for the fate of the people and its culture. For the Serbian Academy of Sciences and Arts, slandered by ill-intentioned and amoral interpretations of the *Draft Memorandum* of 1986, even politics as meta-politics, which would be appropriate for academicians and for the Academy to engage in, has become a boogyman that people who have dedicated themselves to science and art avoid.[1]

The trauma of the *Memorandum* left too strong a stamp on the public face of the Academy; it might have darkened it for those who believe in our competence and authority. But exactly at that time, history stampeded by us and we were speechless as Serbia plunged [into a chasm]. Disintegrating Titoism and the destruction of Yugoslavia, aided by anti-Serb elements from abroad, provoked an existential crisis within the Serb people — the deepest since 1813[2] — a crisis for which we lacked competent people and thus lacked adequate, delivering answers

---

1. The *Memorandum* to which Cosic refers is a controversial document drawn up by a group of Serb academicians in 1986. It is essentially a social, political, and economic critique of the Titoist system from the Serb perspective. [Ed.]

2. A reference to the collapse of the First Serbian Revolution (1804-1813) against the Ottoman Empire.

This article was originally given as an address to the Serbian Academy of Sciences and Arts in July 1999.

from 1991 to the Kosovo collapse today. Some of the Serb defeats and misfortunes of these times were unavoidable, but, it seems to me, there were more that could have been avoided with reasonable, flexible, and imaginative policies. The catastrophic results of our national and state policies in this Serb twilight distilled politics into the question of the very fate of the Serb people, and thus into the essential question of the sciences and arts that we serve.

Where are we, what are we, and where do we go?

In the last decade epochal changes have occurred in the world and in the existence of the Serb people. In those changes within Europe, the Serb nation has suffered the greatest losses and today is in the worst position. Politically, wars waged for the liberation and unification of the Serb people have been lost. The state we mistakenly considered our fatherland (former Yugoslavia) has been destroyed. With the exodus from Croatia, Bosnia-Herzegovina, Kosovo, and Metohija, Serbs have lost territories where they had dwelled for centuries. The remainder of the Serbs in Bosnia-Herzegovina live under the occupation of the Western Alliance. The rift between Serbia and Montenegro threatens the disintegration of the provisional state [called] the Federal Republic of Yugoslavia. Serbia, constitutionally and legally constructed along the lines of a centralist state model, with a nondemocratic regime of retarded Titoism, is permeated with dangerous dissatisfaction in Vojvodina, Belgrade, and other areas demanding more self-government, while elements from abroad are instigating its disintegration. With injustices and sanctions, lies and hate manufactured in the media, the world has humiliated us, assigning to us the role of a scapegoat for its goals, and we helped it in that.

Serbia is in limbo, regressing economically, politically, and culturally, isolated from the world under burdensome sanctions, which America and the European Union have recently made even harsher. Throughout all that, the economy was ruined and society was impoverished, corrupted, and criminalized. A caste of "robber-barons," with a lumpen-bourgeoisie and mafia-like clans, was created, while all of the features of the welfare state and the elements binding society together have imploded. We are entering into a state of societal poverty and existential uncertainty of a type we have not had in the twentieth century.

After the collapse of Bolshevik socialism in Russia and the Eastern countries, in the so-called postcommunist period, Serbia was the one country in which the political order did not fundamentally change, in which a property-rights transition was not carried out, and in which an autocratic regime now rules over the party-state structure. Yet among the socialist states, Serbia was the country with the deepest democratic traditions and, in Tito's Yugoslavia, had the strongest democratic opposition to Titoism.

We have experienced the greatest tragedy, which was avoidable, in this Little World War, waged by America and the European Union against Serbia and Montenegro. The tragic consequences of this war will not end with the capitulation and the current expulsion of Serbs from Kosovo and Metohija;[3] they will only emerge and wound the Serb national being in decades to come. I doubt that the glory earned through the heroic resistance of our army to that most technologically advanced aggression, and the dignified endurance of the people for the seventy-eight days of killing and destruction committed by American and European aviation, will be adequate compensation for all the victims and the suffering that await us. We lost Kosovo and Metohija. Milosevic's unreasonable policy toward Kosovo — if it can be called a policy — merely completed what Tito and his Serb vassals initiated and almost brought to a conclusion during the period of so-called socialist self-management. And to think that the protagonist of that policy calls its outcome a victory and claims that the territorial integrity and state sovereignty of Yugoslavia have been defended!

What we have lived through in the past decade is probably not the end of the Serb misfortunes. The continuation of the present policies will endanger even this remnant of a state we are left with, will spell further loss of freedom and the loss of the right to determine our own destiny and future.

These days, from the political capitals of Europe, we hear about projects for the postwar reconstruction of the Balkans and the conditions for associated membership in the European Union. Both the European Union and the heads of the G-8 group premise all investment in Serbia and the removal of sanctions on changes in the political order and the removal of President Milosevic from power. Noting that this is just another in a long line of policies pressuring and blackmailing Serbia, we should not forget that the powerful usually carry out their threats against the Serb people. Such conditions for the removal of sanctions or for entry into the European Union are by no means democratic. However, if because of its president Serbia is the only European country left in a ghetto and the only Balkan country outside the European Union — with no foreign investments to increase economic development and modernize the country — then the salvation of the Serb people demands that we all bow down, particularly the president of Yugoslavia himself. All the more so because, by the acceptance of the ultimatum that Ahtisaari and Chernomyrdin delivered, our state sovereignty has been seriously violated: our state borders have been moved from the Prokletije mountains to Kopaonik, and a protectorate is being established in Kosovo and Metohija.[4]

3. The appellation "Kosovo and Metohija" is the formal name used by Serbs for the Yugoslav province of Kosovo. Metohija, literally "land of the monasteries," refers to the western part of the province. [Ed.]

4. The reference is to the conditions for an end to the NATO bombardment delivered to Yugoslav President Slobodan Milosevic by Maarti Ahtisaari, the President of Finland and the U.N.'s designated mediator for the Kosovo conflict, and Viktor Chernomyrdin, Russia's mediator for the conflict, on June 2, 1999. The Prokletije Mountains (literally, the Damned Mountains) to which Cosic refers are on the border between Kosovo and Albania. Kopaonik is a mountain in southern Serbia proper bordering Kosovo. [Ed.]

The time that history allowed us to transform Titoist society has been squandered. In this country President Slobodan Milosevic can no longer be allowed to obstinately determine state and national policy according to American and EU ultimatums. We can only hope that the calamity we have lived through over the past decade has made us, as a people, more mature as to our self-perception and our understanding of the world around us. To save ourselves from the abyss that we are staring at, we must leave behind present national and state policy and change the political order in the country. That change has to come about through a legitimate, democratic procedure.

With whom to begin the democratic renewal of Serbia is a crucial question. The Serb political scene is presently dominated by parties and politicians with the retarded ideologies of the civil war,[5] ideologies that have been defeated by world developments. Those ideologies and parties, nominally "left" and "right," which today demagogically employ democratic rhetoric, have been morally compromised in government and are historically conservative and without personal authority. With them in power, Serbia will continue to lag behind and face ruin. Serbia needs competent people with new ideas and visions of new policies for an enlightened, civilized, and democratic society. But such people are mostly outside of today's political parties; they are people for whom power is not the goal but only the instrument of national renewal. Political changes in the country should begin with the resignation of the President of the Federal Republic of Yugoslavia, Slobodan Milosevic.

I call upon the patriotic consciousness and the human and civic responsibility of Slobodan Milosevic to allow for the beginning of the necessary changes in Serbia and the Federal Republic by resigning.

---

5. A reference to the civil war that took place in Serbia (and Yugoslavia as a whole) during World War II, primarily between Tito's Communist Movement and forces loyal to the Yugoslav Royal Government. [Ed.]

Not Exactly New Hampshire:
A Short Survey of Contemporary Serbian Politics

DEJAN ANASTASIJEVIC

Compared with any other Eastern European country, Serbia has set many precedents. It is the only former communist state that has so far failed to go through a transition toward democracy and a free-market economy; defying the trend of globalization, Serbia walked out — or was kicked out — of almost every international organization, including the United Nations and the Organization for Security and Cooperation in Europe; and finally, it is not only the sole European country that was ever bombed by NATO, but the only country in the world with a McDonald's franchise that was ever bombed by U.S. planes.

It would be easy to visualize Serbia as a lonely and dark fortress, or as some sort of Mordor of the Balkans. The reality is quite different: among the peoples of Eastern Europe, Serbs have been — and still are — among the most pro-Western and least xenophobic. Moreover, during the reign of the late Yugoslav leader Josip Broz Tito (1945-1980) Serbia was, as are all other former Yugoslav republics, quite open to Western influence. However, Serbs have had the historical misfortune of being endowed with a uniquely destructive, resilient, and clever kind of autocrat who has led them through the stormy seas of recent Balkan history. It was Slobodan Milosevic's deadly mixture of brilliant tactics and idiotic strategy that finally pushed the country into the abyss and made it an international pariah.

Nominally, Serbia is a parliamentary democracy; in real life, it is a thinly masked autocracy ruled not so much by political parties but by a small circle of Milosevic's friends and cronies, who are not necessarily in leadership positions that are publicly seen. To explain this paradox, let us scroll down the list of main political parties and their leaders:

Socialist Party of Serbia: Socijalisticka Partija Srbije (SPS)

The largest and best organized party in Serbia is, naturally, Milosevic's own. It was created in 1989, at a time when it became apparent that the one-party communist system could no longer be sustained. Succumbing to pressure to legalize pluralism, Milosevic reluctantly allowed others to compete, but only after picking the best horse and securing his control of the rules of the race. The Socialist party was forged by the joining of the political and financial resources of the two most powerful political organizations at the time: the Alliance of Communists of Serbia (the official title for the Communist party), and the Socialist Alliance of Working People, a crypto-communist organization that in Tito's time served as a vehicle to ensure control over institutions the party did not control directly. After the fusion, the newly formed SPS inherited not only enormous funds from its predecessors but also their political infrastructure: a branch in every district, every factory, and every administrative institution in the country. Opposition parties were much slower to organize grassroots support; even now, ten years later, they are well behind SPS in terms of organization and finance. The fact that there is still no legal regulation of how political parties are financed helps Milosevic maintain SPS's dominant role: he uses government resources to fund his party, and vice versa. Couple that with Milosevic's control over the national media and, more importantly, secret police files accumulated over fifty years of communist rule, and it is not difficult to understand why SPS always emerges victorious at the polls. Although its majority in the parliament is gradually decreasing after every election, SPS — and its smaller coalition partner JUL — still controls a comfortable majority in the parliament.

Just as in the country itself SPS is a one-man show, and Milosevic rules it with an iron hand, consolidating his leadership by periodic purges and reshufflings. The latest party official to be purged was Zoran Lilic, SPS vice president and former chief of the Yugoslav federation, who was dismissed in August 1999 amid rumors that he was flirting with some opposition figures.

United Yugoslav Left: Jugoslovenska Ujedinjena Levica (JUL)

After the transformation of communists into SPS in 1989, a small piece of the original Communist party was still left to linger under a slightly altered name, the Communist Alliance Movement for Serbia (SKPJ), and under the leadership of Milosevic's wife, Mira Markovic. The party had played a marginal role in Serbian political life until 1996, when it teamed up with several other fringe groups and acquired its present name. Though she was openly Stalinist and one of the least popular political figures in Serbia, Ms. Markovic's influence over her husband — as well as her party's coalition with the SPS — secured her a fair number of cabinet seats in both the Serbian and the federal [Yugoslavian] parliaments. However, the question remains whether JUL should be seen as a separate political entity or — as I tend to believe — merely as a far-left faction of the ruling party. According to the latest polls from the Markplan Agency in June 1999, the SPS-JUL faction enjoys the support of some 21.9 percent of the voters (all over eighteen years of age).

Serbian Radical Party: Srpska Radikalna Stranka (SRS)

The SRS borrowed its name from a centrist party that dominated Serbian political life from the late nineteenth century until World War II. Unlike their respectable predecessors, contemporary radicals fully deserve their name: founded and led by former Marxist Vojislav Seselj, the SRS is a far-right party verging on Nazism, openly promoting territorial expansion and ethnic discrimination. Once described by Milosevic as "the only opposition leader with a degree of respectability," Seselj has always been openly or covertly allied with the Serbian strongman. During the war in Croatia and Bosnia (1991-1995) the SRS was deeply involved in recruiting and dispatching paramilitary "volunteer" units and maintaining close links with the military and police. During peacetime Seselj's thugs are often engaged in intimidation and harassment of the opposition. In the theater of Serbian politics, Seselj's role as mock antagonist is to make Milosevic look almost decent by comparison, though the two are practically two sides of the same coin. Since he enjoys considerable support among the less-educated and pauperized layers of Serbian society, Seselj may continue to be a threat to democracy even after Milosevic's eventual departure. The SRS has the support of 10.5 percent of the population.

Serbian Renewal Movement: Srpski Pokret Obnove (SPO)

Led by the charismatic Vuk Draskovic, the SPO is probably the strongest party within the democratic opposition in Serbia. Draskovic's political program is a mixture of ideas ranging from conservatism to liberalism and back. A popular novelist during the eighties, Draskovic started as an ardent nationalist, then gradually evolved toward the center, with occasional lapses toward either side of the political spectrum. He led violent anti-Milosevic riots in March 1991 that ended in his arrest; he was arrested again in 1994, along with his wife, and severely beaten by Milosevic's police. In November 1996, Draskovic was one of three leaders of the "Zajedno" ("Together") coalition, which won the municipal elections and then staged massive protests after Milosevic failed to recognize the results. After three months of protests, Milosevic eventually recognized the "Zajedno" victory; but the coalition immediately fell apart amid internal squabbles, and the SPS eventually regained power in most districts.

Since that time, Draskovic has rebuffed every effort to forge a unified front against Milosevic, and has generally spent more time blasting other opposition leaders than fighting Milosevic. During the NATO intervention against Serbia in the spring of 1999, SPO briefly entered Milosevic's cabinet; but the party was kicked out after Draskovic publicly expressed some doubts about Serbia's capacity to win the war. All in all, Draskovic's egotism and inconsistency are his own worst enemies and are likely to haunt him in the future. Numbers move up and down, but in June his party enjoyed the support of 14.7 percent of the population.

Democratic Party: Demokratska Stranka (DS)

Founded in 1990, the DS occupies the center right of the political spectrum. Its leader, Zoran Djindjic, is a 54-year-old professor of philosophy who obtained his doctorate in Germany under the mentorship of Juergen Habermas. He is also the only one of the original twelve founders of the party who is still in the leadership. After Milosevic's split with Bosnian Serb leader Radovan Karadzic in August 1994, Djindjic flirted with Karadzic but failed to score many political points within Serbia proper. During the November 1996 protests, Djindjic secretly met with Milosevic, and that meeting later became a cause for the breakdown of the "Zajedno" coalition. During the NATO bombing campaign, Djindjic fled to neighboring Montenegro, which led many to write him off as a coward. He is now one of the leaders of the "Alliance for Change," a loose coalition of about a dozen parties and groups, with DS being the largest of them. Djindjic's fluent German and English make him a favorite of Western powers, but he enjoys much less support at home, where people tend to see him as a somewhat Machiavellian figure. In June his party commanded about 3.2 percent support.

Civic Alliance: Gradjanski Savez (GS)

Founded by Vesna Pesic, a prominent dissident figure from Tito's era, the GS is a classic liberal party that promotes ethnic tolerance and the welfare state, and was consistently antiwar during the breakup of former Yugoslavia. Unfortunately, the party has almost negligible support among the people, and it earned its two seats in the federal parliament only because of its membership in the "Zajedno" coalition. After the breakup of "Zajedno," the future of the GS is uncertain. The party's new leader, Goran Svilanovic, may bring some fresh ideas and improve a poor organizational structure. The GS is also a member of the "Alliance for Change."

Conclusion

There are about a hundred other smaller parties in Serbia, some regional, some created to represent the interests of Serbia's ethnic minorities (Hungarians, Slovaks, Bosniaks, Romanians, Roma, etc.). However, their overall impact in Serbia is negligible: together, these parties command no greater than 15.7 percent support. Kosovo, having effectively become a NATO protectorate, is now a different country, and its politics are separate. The same is true of Montenegro, which has gradually dropped out of federal institutions and is slowly moving toward secession. The parties described above are going to play a significant role in Serbia's future, whatever that future brings. Despite overwhelming ideological and structural differences, they all have one thing in common: with the exception of the Civic Alliance, all are led by egocentric, autocratic figures who do not tolerate dissent and do not respond well to criticism. In addition, none of these parties is immune to the nationalism that has brought so much misery to the Balkans. No party has developed a mechanism of internal elections and control; each is internally run as a little autocracy, replicating Milosevic's system on a smaller scale. Those opposition parties that still have some rule at the municipal level — such as SPO — exert their power in exactly the same corrupted way as does Milosevic's SPS. In fact, in the June poll, about one out of five voters reported that they will not vote. It is no wonder, then, that the Serbian electorate seems more and more reluctant to take part in the election process, effectively ensuring Milosevic's rule in the years to come.

Kosovo and Us

VUK DRASKOVIC

In the coming year, the last one of the twentieth century, our nation and state are faced not with wishes but obligations that are subordinated to the only goal — to defend Kosovo: to defend the foundation of the national and state home, the source and symbol of everything that makes us Serbs and Christians. Our first obligation is to understand that this is a crucial fight for the Serbian people and that we have dangerously little time. The clock is about to start ticking, and the enemy has enough time to waste. This means that what we have to do needs to be done immediately. Every delay we take to stick our head into the sand is baleful, irreparably baleful.

Swift moves must be coordinated with reality, not with dreams or a belief in sudden world storms and miracles. We should calm our feelings: the battle for Kosovo cannot be won with anger and heart but with cooperation between resoluteness and reason.

Baleful Stretching of the Rope

Reason requires us to estimate the world in which we live, brutally and calmly, as well as the world position, our power, and the power of our enemies; and we must act in accordance with that. With the collapse of the Soviet Union, and at the same time of the Warsaw Pact, the balance of fear and power in the world was dramatically disturbed. The United States of America is the only big power on our planet. That colossus commands NATO and has crucial influence on the streams in Europe, as well as on the behavior of the United Nations.

Russia is in trouble greater than ours. In Moscow there is a danger of a rebellion of tens of millions of people, before whose eyes an enormous empire has

Vuk Draskovic's essay, which was adopted by the main body of the Serbian Renewal Movement, was presented to President Milosevic on January 27, 1998. Some of its sentiments appear more concisely in a spring 1999 essay in *Koha Ditore,* available at www.kohaditore.com. The editor would like to thank Pedrag Simic for his assistance.

fallen apart and who, in return, do not believe any better, but even worse. Some other people want to follow the example of Chechnya, so that Russia itself is threatened with the tragedy of possibly coming apart. That great country is aware of its great troubles and is not resolving them with a cold war against America and NATO, but is trying to stand on its feet with the support of America and Europe, regardless of how bitter the financial and economic help of the West can often be.

Nor does China want conflicts with America and NATO. Patiently and persistently, the Chinese are building their dream to become a big power in the world some day. United Germany, too, is more openly showing ambitions to become a big power. Its goal is to achieve economic and technological supremacy in Europe and to become connected to Russian strategic resources and its market before the Americans. By moving the capital to Berlin, to the heart of Prussia, from whence the great German wishes have always started, the current moderate German politics and strategy will acquire acceleration and impatience.

Whether we like it or not, this is the reality of the world in which we live today. At least three states and the European Union, as a union of states, are trying to deny the world domination of America and to become its equal partner in all world businesses. None of them, however, spoils its relationship with Washington because they have estimated that the damage would be greater than the benefit. And what about us? For an entire decade we have been stretching the rope with the U.S., NATO, and the European Union. We want to prove to them that they are wrong and make them change their attitude toward the Serbs, the Serbian state, and the national question. That stretching of the rope has caused our hands to feel tired; it has made our palms sore, and our great state has fallen apart. So many graves have been dug, so many people have lost their homes, many parts of where Serbs had lived for centuries have been lost, and a sea of misfortune and suffering has been created.

And on the other side? They did not even feel that stretching of the rope between us. We must immediately stop competing with those stronger than we are. It is clear that they are not going to let the rope slacken and change their attitude toward Serbia; they are going to make it even tighter. Let us not fool ourselves. In our world, at the beginning of the twenty-first century, there is less power of law and justice and more law and justice of power. It is always the weaker ones who suffer when they do not want to accept such an order, and when they act in spite of their powerlessness.

Wisdom, Not the Sword

These times are not for Karadjordje's sword.[1] When Austria-Hungary sent us the ultimatum in 1914, we knew that the Russian empire would get into war for Serbia

1. Karadjordje ("Black George") was the leader of the first Serbian uprising in 1804. [Ed.]

and that France and Britain would be on our side.[2] Even in 1941 we were not alone. Today we are alone, more than ever. These are the times for Milos Obrenovic's wisdom.[3] We are not the ones to correct the mistakes of the world and establish the international order according to justice and our wishes. In the current conditions, our obligation is to do what is best for our state and nation. We need the resoluteness to change what we can change, the courage to stand what we cannot change, and the wisdom to distinguish the difference between those two things.

With the Milosevic-Holbrooke agreement the U.S., NATO, and the European Union are included in the resolution of the Kosovo drama.[4] Those are the powers that rule this world and time. We cannot defend Kosovo if we are in conflict with those powers. Cooperating with them, we are going to definitely defend Kosovo and secure it in a strengthened Serbia. How? By coordinating our interior politics with the Milosevic-Holbrooke agreement; by starting, without delay, fundamental democratic changes of both the political and economic systems in order to straighten out the conflicts and misunderstandings with America and Europe; and by joining all international organizations and institutions — to attract foreign capital, to get credits for the recovery of a collapsed economy, and, as soon as possible, [to make sure] that our state becomes a full member of the European Union.

None of these obligations means losing dignity. On the contrary, they are in our state and nation's highest interest. In order to get small concessions and benefits for Serbia and his people, Prince Milos used to kiss the coattails, sleeves, and shoes of pashas and sultans.

Saharov and Rugova

The one who leads the state and nation must behave as a grand master at the chessboard. All the moves and chess pieces serve only one purpose: to win the game. In defending Kosovo, all moves, all party programs, all ideological passions, and all personal vanities and envies of our leaders must be subordinated to victory

---

2. The First World War began after Serbia gave qualified (instead of what was regarded as complete) consent to an ultimatum issued to them by Austria on July 23, 1914, following the assassination of Archduke Ferdinand. See Tim Judah, *The Serbs: History, Myth, and the Destruction of Yugoslavia* (New Haven: Yale University Press, 1997), as well as Fred Singleton, *A Short History of the Yugoslav Peoples* (Cambridge: Cambridge University Press, 1989), p. 118. [Ed.]

3. Milos Obrenovic was leader of the second Serbian uprising in 1815. In an act of politically shrewd deference to Ottoman rule, in 1817 Obrenovic had Karadjordje murdered and his head presented to the sultan, who in 1830 recognized Obrovenic's claim to found a hereditary princeship. See Tim Judah's essay in this volume, "A Brief History of Serbia," as well as his book *The Serbs;* also see Singleton, pp. 82ff. [Ed.]

4. This is a reference to the Dayton Accords, signed on November 21, 1995. [Ed.]

in the fight for Kosovo. Are we behaving like that? Unfortunately, no. Many make moves whose goal seems to be to lose the fight. Many find neither Serbia nor Kosovo their primary values, but for them the primary values are their ideologies, leadership vanities, personal greed for power, and arrogance at the cost of the nation.

While Albanian terrorists are killing our children and people in Kosovo, the entire powerful West is pointing the finger at us because of the repressive and hazardous laws about university and information. Local unreasonable individuals are making terrible efforts to prove that those laws are good laws. They cannot get into their heads the thought that anything that harms Serbia is not good for Serbia, neither here nor in the world.

The ink on the Milosevic-Holbrooke Agreement had not yet dried when the official state delegation went to Moscow to preach about the renewal of the Soviet Union and our country's joining that empire. As a beginning, they offered a state union with Russia and Belarus. Advocating and offering the impossible, those irresponsible people have put an additional thorn in the side of the powers on whose decisions the outcome of our fight for Kosovo pretty much depends. And what is the result? While our arrogant and inexperienced politicians are deceiving our people, preaching about creating an Orthodox empire, Hill's document about Kosovo is being altered in Washington at our expense, and in Strasbourg, Ibrahim Rugova is being awarded as a fighter for human rights and democracy, an award — to make the irony greater — that bears the name of a Russian, Andrei Saharov, whose roots are, on his mother's side, Serbian and in Kosovo.

The Mountain and Muhammad

Doubly hazardous and unreasonable moves are being made. On one hand, Serbia is disunited and weakened from the inside, and on the other, new disagreements and conflicts with America and Europe are provoked. Our enemies in Kosovo are not feeding on their successes and wisdom but on our failures and stupidity. Let us go toward Europe, without litigation and without stipulations. Let us change, so that they might change. If the mountain will not come to Muhammad, Muhammad must go to the mountain.

European reforms in the state will strengthen the state and become our ally in the fight for Kosovo. Albanian terrorists and separatists will lose support for their claims that they are forced to fight for independence because Kosovo in Serbia and Yugoslavia will never become a part of democratic and rich Europe. As soon as we start going toward Europe and America, our enemies will take the masks off their faces and admit that they do not care for democratic rights but only for Nazi principles. At that moment, they will turn both Europe and America against themselves.

Let us learn something from what is happening in Macedonia. There the Albanians make up one-third of the population; but neither Europe nor America is thinking about forming an Albanian republic, not even an autonomy. Why? Because Skoplje is not in conflict but cooperates with the West. Because they understand the reality in Macedonia, and the trees do not prevent them from seeing the woods and from finding their national and state interest in that woods. As long as we do what is useful to us, we will not expect others to do it for us.

Gambling with the State's Head

Let us not teach Americans about patriotism. On the same day that the Republicans voted for the impeachment of the Democrat Clinton, they strongly supported his order of air strikes against Iraq, with the explanation that they were in opposition to the president of the state but not in opposition to the state. Let us learn to look at things that way. If we do so, we will not be in the situation that party or any other particularities cloud our vision concerning Kosovo, Serbia, and the values that we always have to serve and defend. It is not the Americans' fault that some people here, who are nothing, want to sell Kosovo in order to become something — to surrender it, to divide it, or say that they would like to see foreign missiles and aircraft carriers in the harbors of our sea.

It is not the Americans' fault for our disgrace that certain self-centered people, if something does not suit them, immediately threaten the collapse of the state. "Either Montenegro gets this or that chair, or we are not together." "I will either be a deputy, or I am going to make Vojvodina secede from Serbia." "I will either be the master in the county, or my county will proclaim autonomy." They foolishly put at risk what is most sacred and most valuable, the head of the state and of the nation.

Kosovo Orders Us

Kosovo orders us all that it is above all and everyone. Kosovo orders us not to make new enemies, but friends. It tells us that no enmity is ended by enmity, but only by friendship. Kosovo begs us not to run away from the Christian West, because Kosovo is not only the greatest Serbian church but the greatest European church. Even six centuries ago, when Milos beheaded Murat, Serbian messengers of good news rode off to Paris. Kosovo orders us, even during its current suffering and Golgotha, not to leave the foundations of Christ's faith. Let us offer every highest and human right to those whose program is to take Kosovo away from us and blind the Serbian nation, so that the world may see if we are throwing pearls to humans or nonhumans.

There is no Kosovo without Serbia, nor Serbia and the Serbs without Kosovo. We should always repeat this to ourselves, to our friends, and to our enemies. We should immediately give up everything that is an obstacle to the defense of Kosovo and accept everything that contributes to its defense and victory. Let us hope for an agreement and a triumph of life over death, and let us do everything to make it so.

How to Solve the Kosovo Problem

ZORAN DJINDJIC

Let me start with two remarks. The question we should be asking ourselves is not how to solve the Kosovo problem, but how to go about resolving it. This is not a linguistic matter only. We have a chance to start moving forward only if we are realistic. And since a final resolution to the problem of Kosovo does not appear realistic, all participants in the process of its resolution should be psychologically prepared for a strategy of small steps.

The other remark concerns the framework of the Kosovo problem's resolution. In my view, this framework should be the legal and political system of modern Europe. In modern Europe's legal and political system, all major problems are dealt with by establishing and guaranteeing rights. Such an approach excludes violence, intolerance, endangering human rights, and similar nonlegal mechanisms. How, then, should we go about resolving the problem of Kosovo by way of law instead of violence?

The first consequence of what is, in my view, the only right decision — dealing with the problem of Kosovo within the framework of the legal and political system of modern Europe — is that the Kosovo Albanians have no right to an independent state. There are no legal grounds for founding such a state. The right to self-determination, quoted by ethnic Albanian politicians and intellectuals in support of their demands, from a legal point of view, does not imply independence or secession. The right to self-determination is a basic democratic right to freely shape one's own life within an existing state. The right to create a state does not stem from the democratic right to self-determination, but many other rights are indeed its consequence. They include human, personal, political, collective, and other rights. And — what is even more important — all these rights require institutions to guarantee that these can and will indeed be implemented. Without an

This essay was written for a series of exchanges between chiefly Kosovar Albanians and Serbian authors that appeared in *Koha Ditore* (Spring 1999). The editor would like to thank Marijana Pavlovic for her assistance with this essay.

independent judiciary, unbiased media, and free elections, of what use would a person's human, civic, or political right be?

If, for an instant, we reduce the problem of Kosovo to a dispute between the Serbian authorities and the ethnic Albanians, we have but to criticize both sides. The Serbian authorities have failed to secure institutions that convincingly guarantee basic human rights. Not only in Kosovo, but in the entire country, there is no independent judiciary, objective public informing, or free elections. The Albanians, on the other hand, should be criticized for inferring their right to secession from the fact that, in Serbia, there are insufficient guarantees for exercising democratic rights. Such a conclusion is in opposition to the modern European legal system. Namely, the fact that a state lacks institutionalized guarantees for citizens' rights results in the right to create political, union, and other organizations aimed at democratizing such a country. This is the only proper course when our country is in question as well. Of course, this holds true only if the intent of the parties involved is to deal with problems in the manner of modern Europe, instead of in the ways of the Stone Age.

The problem of the Albanians in Serbia, beyond doubt, is not only the problem of personal rights, but of collective rights as well, even of political status. We have inherited this issue from the times of Tito's Yugoslavia in the form of the autonomy problem. Whatever the contents of this autonomy, it is clear that it involves a set of specific rights. Autonomy can be achieved only within a lawful state. Tito's Yugoslavia was not a lawful state, and in it autonomy was only a means of political manipulation. One of the aspects of such manipulation lies in the fact that the issue of territorial autonomy was confused with the issue of collective ethnic rights. The territorial autonomy of Kosovo and Vojvodina is one matter, while specific rights for national minorities and ethnic groups is something entirely different. That knot, so skillfully entangled by Tito, we have now to disentangle with much patience and with the assistance of the proper legal instruments.

We may choose between two paths. One is short and radical: it is the path of force, pressure, attempts to rearrange the facts (create a new state), for which subsequent international approval would be requested, and the path of suspending all rights by violence, under the excuse that they endanger the survival of the state. This is a path traveled by political extremists. I do not know what is at its end, but I am certain that it does not lead into modern Europe. The other path is long and winding. It involves a painful process of establishing and guaranteeing rights. Its stages are clear: institutional guarantees of basic rights must be created. These are the guarantees without which no democratic solution is stable. Whatever form of autonomy is agreed on for Kosovo during the political process, it would be but words on paper without democratic institutions to support the functioning of that autonomy on a daily basis.

My message and my conclusion is the following: the problem of Kosovo cannot be dealt with in the ways of modern Europe without an enhanced democratization of Serbia. If we wish to deal with it as a legal problem, and not as an issue necessitating force, we need legal institutions that deserve and enjoy our respect. It is an enormous task for the future, both for the Serbs and the Albanians living in Serbia. The reader may well view this conclusion as excessively theoretical and lacking practical answers. He or she may well add that the time of thinking is behind us and that now the time has come to act. I agree that a lot of time has passed and that very few issues have been properly addressed or solved. But this does not mean that speedy solutions would resolve anything. I believe that it is better to try to put out a fire with buckets of water, however small, than with a tankful of gasoline. Speed and radicalism solve nothing. It is much better to make a small step in the right direction than ten huge paces leading the other way.

Fascism, Feminist Resistance, and the Kosovo Crisis

ZARANA PAPIC

With the crisis in Kosovo, the circle of crime has returned to its starting point.

Today the symbolic sign of the scope of the immensely shallow (mis)understanding of a dead country's destiny is (for those of us who still remember) painfully visible in CNN headlines: "War in Yugoslavia."[1] The Kosovo crisis is not at all the war of the self-proclaimed Federal Republic of Yugoslavia,[2] but is exclusively the war of Milosevic's Serbia.[3]

The Kosovo crisis is at the heart of a decade-long war drama of the country formerly known as Yugoslavia. The wars in former Yugoslavia during the last decade were a series of ill fated, revengeful, and deadly "broken brotherhoods."[4] The wars practically started when Milosevic, in his Stalinist style of taking over state-power by taking over the Serbian Communist Party in 1987, decided to build his fascist hatred power engine on a Machiavellian mutation of the communist totalitarian principle of "class struggle." Class struggle became the even more lethal principle of "ethnic struggle." Milosevic fed an endless series of cultural, historical,

---

1. What "Yugoslavia" is the world now talking about? The trick with people's memory and amnesia may be unintentional, but it is no less misleading. The "Yugoslavia" CNN describes is the "phantom Yugoslavia" Milosevic would like us to take for granted as being still alive and kicking. "Yugoslavia" does not exist any more.

2. Serbia and Montenegro proclaimed themselves as the Federal Republic of Yugoslavia in 1992, but have never been recognized by the UN. Montenegro is, in an ironic sense, a double collateral civilian victim: by Milosevic's power-system that persists in keeping her puppet-republic status, and by NATO that is bombing Milosevic-controlled military forces in Montenegro.

3. Milosevic's Serbo-centric claim to be the only rightful "inheritor" of the former Yugoslavia is yet unfulfilled, as its seat in the UN remains empty.

4. Tito's conception of a vital multinational, multiethnic and multiconfessional federation was expressed in the exclusive identity/difference male-dominated slogan, "Brotherhood and Unity."

ethnic, national, and racist antagonisms among Serbs, Croats, Slovenes, and Bosnians while shamelessly claiming to be the only "true" defender of the "Yugoslavian Idea." He (ab)used the Serbs' "trauma" under Tito and their tragic destiny during World War II to plant and nourish the notion that Serbian hatred of Albanians is "legitimate" and is even a "basic" element of Serbian national identity. His generation of ethnic hatred and demand for totalitarian ethnic exclusionary politics led to war, displacement, destruction, and annihilation of the Other.

Why were so many Serbs influenced by this hatred power engine? The long process of solidifying pro-fascist nationalism in Serbia required Milosevic to produce multiple structural mutations that would reinforce his symbolic and psychological manipulation of Serbian identity. Self-identity, civic-identity, gender-identity, and the identity of the Other were systematically refashioned as his regime evolved from state socialism to state nationalism; from state nationalism to mafia etatism [socialism]; from mafia etatism to oriental despotism; from oriental despotism to the tyranny of fascism. The social realm in Serbia was systematically constructed by a series of all-too-familiar steps: first, exclusivist political discourse was aimed at representing the Other as an intrusive outsider, then an erasure of empathy was followed by the denial of tolerance; in short, these steps induced social amnesia of our shared history of living together. This social amnesia facilitated the development of the fascist "culture of normality" and simultaneously enabled "inevitable barbarity."

To encourage pro-fascist Serbian nationalism, the Milosevic regime used the media to radically invert "civilized" norms into "civilized" taboos. Living with Others was deemed "impossible," and thoughts and emotions of interethnic peace, tolerance, friendship, and understanding became suspect. Social life was depersonalized, and Serbs were subjected to the violent propagation of collective ideas of nation, tradition, and culture. Men became "warriors." Women became identified with a nation to be protected; likewise, women became one of the targets of violence by the enemy nation.

Instead of a slow disillusionment of the "Brotherhood and Unity" Shangri-La, the Serbs' fascist/nationalist awakening was like waking to an "uncontrolled" cultural *delirium tremens*. They awoke to the mutation of the "Yugoslavian Idea" — the irredentist dream of regaining their historical hegemonic position and achieving the reversal of the widely dispersed Serb population — and the unleashing of Milosevic's cultural, political, and military hatred power engine that had manipulated the Serbian population and now made the wars in Slovenia, Croatia and Bosnia and Herzegovina possible.[5]

5. Even in the most recent Kosovo campaign, a Yugoslavian general commended soldiers who died and those who returned as heroic "knights" — an image disclosing the secularized retrospective utopian ideology of Serbia as a glorified medieval kingdom, engaged in a holy war against the Other. [Ed.]

After more than a decade of "brotherly killings and dis-unifications," it is more than obvious that former Yugoslav "brothers" were the easiest decoy and the most effective tool of the destructive politics of "ethnic struggle." That is the reason why, among other things, there have never been significant democratic alternatives to Milosevic's war-politics. Even the "men-leaders" of the so-called opposition could not help themselves and took part, each to his abilities, in the "I-don't-mind-if-you-are-cleansed" game. The only political subjects in Serbia who dared to challenge this deadly game when it first started to be played were some women politicians (now very much marginalized) and some feminist and pacifist groups.

Against the fascist culture of exclusion and the chauvinist hate-politics of former "brothers," Belgrade's *Women in Black* raised their voice and said, "Bosnian, Albanian, and Roma [Gypsy] women are our sisters!" Against the cold lack of empathy that characterized the "culture of normality" in Serbia, these "women-citizens" showed compassion to all suffering women and children, and men who were subject to the draft. The extent to which the cultural, political and *etat d'esprit* has been dominant in the political life of Serbia is revealed in the "discursive loneliness" of the following statement, entitled "I Confess," issued by *Women in Black* on the seventh anniversary of the group's anti-fascist activity.[6]

WOMEN IN BLACK AGAINST WAR, Belgrade

7 Years of Women in Black: 9 October 1991–9 October 1998

I CONFESS:
— To my longtime anti-war activity;
— That I did not agree with the severe beating of people of other ethnicities and nationalities, faiths, race, sexual orientation;
— That I was not present at the ceremonial act of throwing flowers on the tanks headed for Vukovar, 1991, and Prishtina, 1998;
— That I opposed the politics of repression, apartheid, massacres and war of the Serbian regime against the Albanian population on Kosovo;
— That I fed women and children in refugee camps, schools, churches, mosques;
— That for the entire war I crossed the walls of Balkan ethno-states, because solidarity is the politics that interests me;
— That I understood democracy as support to anti-war activists/friends/ sisters: Albanian women, Croat women, Roma women, stateless women;

6. Since October 1991, Women in Black have organized nonviolent protests in the streets of Belgrade and international meetings of their women's solidarity network. They have engaged in the publishing of women's voices against war (in several languages) and have supported men in their quest to give conscientious objection to military service the status of a basic human right in Serbia. The group also tries to help women refugees regain their self-respect.

— That I first challenged the murderers from the state where I live and then those from other states, because I consider this to be responsible political behavior of a woman-citizen;

— Throughout all the seasons of the year I insisted that there be an end to the slaughter, destruction, ethnic cleansing, forced evacuation of people, rape;

— I took care of others while the patriots took care of themselves.

The expression "I Confess" marks the fundamental inversion of dominant pro-fascist sensibilities and denial; it also articulates a political sensibility that demands individual responsibility and public counter-action. The making of such a statement is evidence of a coherent feminist political opposition with powerful symbolic potential, however marginalized the women might be.

Another Belgrade women's group that exemplifies feminist resistance to the internal fascist processes is the Autonomous Women's Center Against Sexual Violence.[7] During the first two weeks of the NATO bombing of Serbia, four counselors from the Center called some 400 women in Belgrade, Vojvodina, Sandzak, Kosovo, and Montenegro to offer support and counseling. After two weeks of documenting women's feelings of fear and mechanisms of survival, the Center issued a report that was not only a testimony to the political and psychological effects of NATO bombing, but also a testimony to the effects of fascist martial law that was promptly introduced the day the bombing started. *(Fear became the fact of life overnight. Every woman became a possible client. . . .)*[8]

During the 77 days of NATO bombing in Serbia we witnessed and experienced a new type of "state of war." We experienced state-organized oppression in which violence and fear were so strongly intertwined that we were affected at every level of our realities. We experienced an atmosphere of terror aimed at forcing us toward one very precise goal — fixation on "our" victimization through NATO bombing. The "happy-to-persecute-traitors" martial law in Serbia had as its primary aims the paralyzing of the political resistance, the making of "ordinary" people into fascists, and the cleansing of Albanians from Kosovo. The national media insisted that denial of ethnic cleansing in Kosovo was legitimate, while silent remembering, not to mention speaking out loud, that Albanians, rightful citizens of the FRY, were being brutally cleansed from Kosovo, was strictly "taboo."

The two months of the state of war in Serbia could be defined more accurately as the state of fascism. Fascism is, in fact, a very active process, a cooperation

---

7. The Center was founded in 1993. Its psychological methods are modeled after the experiences that therapists gained from the Women's Therapy Center, "Medica Zenica," that worked with women in Bosnia and Herzegovina.

8. "Active Support of Women in Overcoming Fear," Activity Report during the War Time (25 March–24 April 1999), Autonomous Women's Center against Sexual Violence, Belgrade.

constantly invoked for the normalization of its codes; it is a nontransparent but powerful demand for every individual to share its norms up to the point of no return when consensus/silence about the annihilation of the Other is reached. At this point collaboration becomes "forcefully voluntary." The denial of ethnic cleansing and the seductive Serbian narcissism over being (finally) a victim of NATO bombings show ever so clearly the real face of all previous wars, of the Kosovo crisis, and of what politically and historically has become of Serbia today.

IV. VOICES OF WORLD LEADERS

What Do Authorities Say?

Fresh Cause for Hope at the Opening
of the New Century

JAVIER SOLANA
Secretary-General of NATO

The crisis in Kosovo was perhaps the greatest challenge the international community has faced since the end of the Cold War. Never before has responding to a crisis raised so many dilemmas — moral as well as political, military as well as legal. That NATO took action, that it achieved its aims,[1] and that it is now playing a major role in creating long-term stability for the wider region of southeastern Europe is proof that Europe may finally mature into a common space — a space where "ethnic cleansing," mass deportations, and the systematic abuse of human rights have no place.

To take military action against Belgrade was a decision we did not enter into lightly. We knew, before beginning the air campaign, how difficult it would be. We knew that Yugoslavia would use our efforts as an excuse to step up its repression of the Kosovar Albanians. We knew the air campaign would take time. Civilian casualties would inevitably occur. Our important relationship with Russia was likely to

---

1. A North Atlantic Council statement of April 12, 1999, stated that NATO had five goals: air strikes would be pursued until President Milosevic (1) ensures a verifiable stop to all military action and the immediate ending of violence and repression; (2) ensures the withdrawal from Kosovo of the military, police, and paramilitary forces; (3) agrees to the stationing in Kosovo of an international military presence; (4) agrees to the unconditional and safe return of all refugees and displaced persons and unhindered access to them by humanitarian aid organizations; (5) provides credible assurance of his willingness to work on the basis of the Rambouillet Accords in the establishment of a political framework agreement for Kosovo in conformity with international law and the Charter of the United Nations. In a statement to the U.S. Senate Armed Services committee on April 15, 1999, Secretary of Defense William S. Cohen said: "Our military objective is to degrade and damage the military and security structure that President Milosevic has used to depopulate and destroy the Albanian majority in Kosovo." Further details are contained in NATO websites and U.S. Defense Department websites. As discussed throughout this volume, while not officially stated as *objectives*, NATO military *tactics* also seemed to include efforts to pressure Yugoslavians to depose the regime (e.g., disrupting electrical power grids, dual-use targeting, etc.). [Ed.]

suffer. And, last but not least, NATO would be charged by some with taking international law into its own hands.

Yet, despite these potential risks and drawbacks, we went ahead. We did so for three reasons:

First and foremost, we acted to stop the humanitarian tragedy. This is an argument usually scoffed at by hard-nosed proponents of "Realpolitik," who argue that humanitarian grounds are not sufficient for justifying intervention. But to stand idly by while a brutal campaign of forced deportation, torture, and murder is going on in the heart of Europe would have meant declaring moral bankruptcy. The entire logic of turning Europe into a common political, economic, and security space would have been invalidated if we had tolerated the barbaric ethnic cleansing at our doorstep. One of the lessons of Bosnia was that acting earlier might have been less costly in the end. We learned this lesson. We would not repeat that mistake.

Second, we acted to break the impasse on the search for a political solution. All other means — political and economic — had been exhausted before we reverted to military action. President Milosevic's refusal to sign the Rambouillet agreement made it clear that he had no interest in a political solution. He tried instead to create a new ethnic reality on the ground. Any honest observer realized that only through military force could he be made to reconsider. This required that the Allies stand firm, leaving Milosevic with no alternative but to accept a just peace.

Finally, we acted to prevent a further destabilization in the Balkans. As the U.N. Security Council had already confirmed months earlier, the destabilization caused by Milosevic's security forces constituted a threat to the entire region. We knew it would not be the first time that a regional crisis in the Balkans turned into something far bigger and nastier. With several hundreds of thousands of refugees streaming into neighboring countries, the entire region faced a serious threat of general conflict. Those neighboring countries, which themselves faced serious political and economic problems, had long reached the limits of their ability to cope with this exceptional burden. In short, if Belgrade's policy of deliberate displacement of the Kosovo-Albanians would not have been energetically opposed, even more instability and bloodshed would have been the result.

What was key to the air campaign — above even the superb professionalism shown by Allied military forces — was the firmness and resolve of Allied governments in the face of sometimes strong domestic opposition. Such resolve was demonstrated by others as well. Witness the courage and steadfastness shown by countries neighboring the FRY [Federal Republic of Yugoslavia] — most of them new and still fragile democracies in a historically turbulent region. All suffered economically from the effects of Belgrade's policies and from the damage inflicted by the air attacks on the FRY. Albania and the former Yugoslav Republic of Macedonia were filled with teeming numbers of refugees. Bulgaria and Romania had transportation and commercial routes along the Danube destroyed. Yet not one of them wavered in their support of NATO's action. They saw all too clearly that the use of force was the only language that President Milosevic would understand and heed.

Now we are tackling the next phase: to start the process of building a Kosovo where all its residents share security, democracy, economic opportunity, and justice. Getting this phase off to the right start is vital. In particular, three objectives must be achieved before we can begin to address stability over the longer term in the Balkans:

First, a secure environment must be established. Under NATO leadership, KFOR will have, by September, 50,000 soldiers deployed to keep the peace in Kosovo, in accordance with U.N. Security Council Resolution 1244. This is much more than just a NATO operation. Many other partner and third countries have indicated their desire to participate in KFOR, as a contribution to peace and stability in southeastern Europe. Russia, too, is part of this endeavor.

Second, the U.N., the EU[European Union], the OSCE [Organization for Security and Cooperation in Europe],[2] and other international bodies must be ready and able to begin their work in assisting the reconstruction of the province and thus laying the groundwork for political stability and economic prosperity. Here we are seeing good progress. The U.N. is already implementing its plan to assume interim civilian authority in Kosovo now, before slowly delegating authority back in time to a local, multiethnic civilian administration. International organizations and financial institutions are well into their planning for Kosovo's reconstruction.

Third, we must continue our efforts to support justice for all Kosovo citizens. This society cannot regain its health until those who have perpetrated war crimes against innocent civilians are identified and brought to justice. Careful gathering of evidence by teams of experts is vital so that the U.N. International Criminal Tribunal for the Former Yugoslavia, which has already indicted Mr. Milosevic and several members of his government for war crimes, will be able to prosecute the perpetrators of such atrocities.

Taken together, these steps are the key to a successful start to building long-term peace and stability in Kosovo. But to ensure success, we cannot look at Kosovo in isolation. The entire Balkan region has suffered too long from instabil-

---

2. The OSCE was founded in 1995, has headquarters in Vienna, and includes 54 members (since Yugoslavia was suspended) as well as seven "partners for cooperation." It includes non-European countries (U.S.), neutral countries (Switzerland, Malta), and tiny states (Andorra, Liechtenstein). Although it includes nations unaffiliated with NATO (Ireland) or the former Soviet bloc, the OSCE has been the only regional security organization that includes *both* the NATO nations and the countries of the former Soviet bloc. Until 1994 this organization was known as the Conference on Security and Cooperation in Europe (CSCE). For one account of its roles in the Dayton Accords, see Richard Holbrooke's *To End a War* (New York: Random House, 1998), pp. 290-91, 319, 321, 322, 341, 365. [Ed.]

ity and violence. If the international community is to help stabilize this region, then we must both broaden and lengthen our perspective. We must broaden it to include other countries of southeastern Europe. And we must lengthen our perspective to include longer-term goals — such as greater economic prosperity, greater political and security cooperation, and greater integration among the countries of this region.

This is a common project, with the United Nations and the European Union in the lead. The EU-led Stability Pact for South-Eastern Europe will provide coordination for the efforts of other international organizations, agencies, and nongovernmental actors. NATO will certainly play a role in supporting the Pact. In this region, security is at the heart of all endeavors. The Alliance contributes through its presence in Kosovo as well as in the stabilization force in neighboring Bosnia. But that is not the only means of offering support. We have already created a consultative forum on security matters with seven nations of southeastern Europe as a means of promoting regional security cooperation and building confidence.

I firmly believe that a new era is dawning for southeastern Europe — an era of lasting peace, economic opportunity, and deeper integration into the European family. We in the international community must persevere in making this a reality. We cannot do it, though, without the political will and determination of the democratic forces in the region and the support of the peoples of southeastern Europe. But at least we can promise that, if they shoulder their part of the burden of political and social reconstruction and reconciliation, they will have the support, assistance, and encouragement of the rest of Europe. Such a bargain is possible; it is doable; and it would bring fresh cause for hope at the opening of a new century.

The Effectiveness of the International Rule of Law in Maintaining International Peace and Security

KOFI ANNAN
Secretary-General of the United Nations

With the founding of the United Nations, a legal regime of international peace and security was institutionalized through the Charter of the United Nations, obligating signatory states to a wide range of limitations on the use of force. Respect for international legal obligations remains the indispensable core of the international security system we seek. The renewal of the effectiveness and relevance of the Security Council will be the cornerstone of the United Nations' efforts to promote international peace and security in the next century.

Since the end of the Cold War, the world has witnessed important instances in which the Council rose to the challenge and legitimated both peacekeeping operations and the use of force when they were just and necessary. Central America and the reversal of the Iraqi aggression against Kuwait are prime examples of the Security Council's playing the role envisioned for it by its founders.

However, more recently, there has been a regrettable tendency for the Security Council not to be involved in efforts to maintain international peace and security. The case of Kosovo has cast into sharp relief the fact that member states and regional organizations sometimes take enforcement action without Security Council authorization.

A parallel trend has been the flouting of international sanctions imposed by the Security Council by individual member states, and even regional organizations. In addition, states have failed to cooperate with the Security Council in a variety of

---

Secretary-General Annan wrote this essay on August 13, 1999, in partial response to the essay in this volume by NATO Secretary-General Javier Solana, particularly to the latter's claims about responsibility for collective security and assumptions about the effectiveness of the United Nations. Secretary-General Annan also responds to claims made by Henry Kissinger and Zbigniew Brzezinski in essays that appear in this volume (with the exception of Brzezinski's final essay, "The Failed Double Cross"). [Ed.]

areas, from disarmament and nonproliferation to cooperation with the International Tribunal for the Former Yugoslavia and with United Nations investigative human rights missions.

Of course, national interest has a great and permanent role to play in the occasional choice of states to choose alternatives to collective security. What has been most worrying, in my view, has been the inability of states to reconcile national interests when skillful and visionary diplomacy would make unity possible. As the world has changed in profound ways since the end of the Cold War, I believe our conceptions of national interest have failed to follow suit. A new, more broadly defined, more widely conceived definition of national interest in this new century would, I am convinced, induce states to find far greater unity in the pursuit of such basic Charter values as democracy, pluralism, human rights and the rule of law.

I say this not least because I believe we were presented with just such a case in Kosovo. At the time of NATO's decision to take enforcement action without seeking explicit Security Council authorization, my response was twofold: I identified the Security Council as having the primary responsibility for maintaining international peace and security. With equal emphasis, I also stated that it was the rejection of a political settlement by the Yugoslav authorities that made this action necessary, and that, indeed, there "are times when the use of force may be legitimate in the pursuit of peace."

My regret then — and now — is that the Council was unable to unify these two equally compelling interests of the international community. For this much is clear: unless the Security Council is restored to its preeminent position as the sole source of legitimacy on the use of force, we are on a dangerous path to anarchy. But equally important, unless the Security Council can unite around the aim of confronting massive human rights violations and crimes against humanity on the scale of Kosovo, then we will betray the very ideals that inspired the founding of the United Nations.

This is the core challenge of the Security Council and the United Nations as a whole in the next century: to unite behind the principle that massive and systematic violations of human rights conducted against an entire people cannot be allowed to stand. For in a world where globalization has limited the ability of states to control their economies, regulate their financial policies, and isolate themselves from environmental damage and human migration, the last right of states cannot and must not be the right to enslave, persecute, or torture their own citizens.

The choice, in other words, must not be between Council unity and inaction in the face of genocide — as in the case of Rwanda, on the one hand, *or* Council division and regional action, as in the case of Kosovo, on the other. In both cases, the member states of the United Nations should have been able to find common ground in upholding the principles of the Charter, and to find unity in defense of our common humanity.

On the eve of a new millennium, it is this United Nations we seek: responsive to a dynamic and changing world, respectful of the sovereignty of states, and resilient in its determination to advance the rights and freedoms of the peoples of the world.

Winning the Peace:
America's Goals in Kosovo

MORTON H. HALPERIN
Director, Policy Planning Staff, U.S. Department of State

Rationale for Action

The Balkans is the crossroads where the Western and Orthodox branches of Christianity and the Islamic world meet. World War I began there, and major battles of World War II were fought in the region. Over the past decade the worst fighting in Europe since the Nazis' surrender has raged throughout the former Yugoslavia.

Instability in the Balkans directly affects the security of our Greek and Turkish allies to the south, our new NATO allies Hungary, Poland, and the Czech Republic to the north, and the region's own small struggling democracies. This region is the critical missing piece in the puzzle of a Europe whole and free. That vision of a united and democratic Europe is critical to our own security. And it cannot be fulfilled if this part of the continent remains wracked by conflict.[1] By

1. These first three paragraphs are drawn, almost verbatim, from the April 20, 1999, testimony of Secretary of State Albright to the Senate Foreign Relations Committee (p. 2). The only slight change is the deletion in Halperin's text of the following clause that was originally in-

A number of persons in the U.S. State Department were invited to contribute individual essays about various aspects of American policies with respect to the Kosovo crisis. The State Department decided that Policy Planning Staff Director Dr. Morton Halperin would contribute this single essay (following wide consultation) on behalf of all, in response to included essays by Solana, Annan, Kissinger, and Brzezinski in order to detail (1) why America acted, (2) what needs to be done to win the peace in Kosovo, and (3) what the implications are for U.S. Foreign Policy. It was submitted on 8/21/99. Although it contains some important modifications discussed below, this essay derives in part from two separate speeches made by Secretary of State Madeleine K. Albright. One is entitled "U.S. and NATO Policy Toward the Crisis in Kosovo" for the Senate Foreign Relations Committee in Washington on April 20, 1999. The other is entitled "After Kosovo: Building a Lasting Peace" for the Council on Foreign Relations in New York on June 28, 1999. Statements about Kosovo have been made by various other government officials and are available online at www.state.gov (under "outreach," see speeches listed by date), www.secretary.state.gov, and www.whitehouse.gov. [Ed.]

acting with unity and resolve, NATO reaffirmed its standing as an effective defender of stability and freedom in Europe. It validated the strategy for modernizing the Alliance approved at the Washington Summit in April 1999. It underscored the importance of the leading nations on both sides of the Atlantic acting together in defense of shared interests and values. Our action in Kosovo was a fulfillment of our nation's and the Atlantic Alliance's highest ideals: the protection of democracy, human rights, and fundamental freedoms.

If we are as resolute in building peace as we were persistent in conflict, the crisis in Kosovo may come to be viewed as a turning point in European history.[2]

Western planners had long recognized the potential for violence in Kosovo.[3] The NATO air campaign against Yugoslavia was the culmination of years of American and European efforts to prevent Serbian repression against the province's Albanian majority. In the end, Serbian strongman Slobodan Milosevic chose to ignore the West's warnings and many opportunities for constructive engagement by turning his formidable military and internal security apparatus against Kosovo's civilian population.

---

cluded after the above words "struggling democracies . . .": ". . . that are being overwhelmed by the flood of refugees Milosevic's ruthless policies are creating." [Ed.]

2. For example, of the preceding five sentences, the first three and the last are from Secretary Albright's June 28 speech (p. 3 [from "By acting . . . in European history"]). Albright concludes those June 28 remarks with two sentences (not used in Halperin's essay) that claim that American interests and values are linked, universal, and timeless: "From that time [of the Berlin airlift] to this, the United States has defended its own interests, while promoting values of tolerance and free expression that are not 'made in America' or confined to the West, but rather fundamental to world progress and peace. It is in this spirit of melding present interests with timeless values — a spirit fully in keeping with the highest traditions of U.S. foreign policy — that we have acted in Kosovo, and that we strive now for a lasting peace throughout Southeast Europe." [Ed.]

3. Now Halperin's discussion shifts to retrieve elements from Albright's April 20, 1999, statement (pp. 1, 2) about how Westerners/NATO (the two are virtually equated in Halperin's account) have responded to what Milosevic has done, rather than using Albright's 6/28/99 salute to Russian help. Although Russian cooperation was cited by Albright as one important diplomatic goal on April 20, the situation surrounding the June 11 surprise arrival of Russians at Pristina's airport seems to have influenced a decision to praise Russian assistance on June 28. Albright's June 28 remarks add one of the most succinct presentations (not included in Halperin's essay) of what has been termed "aggressive multilateralism": ". . . the time-tested marriage of diplomacy and force played a central role from the beginning of the crisis. At Rambouillet, we sought an interim political settlement that would have protected the rights of all Kosovars. To the vast detriment of Serb interests, Milosevic rejected that agreement. But the talks helped bring the Kosovar Albanian leadership together in an unprecedented way. After NATO launched its campaign, we shifted from diplomacy backed by the threat of force to diplomacy in support of force. We worked hard to assist the front-line states in coping with the flood of refugees. We received help from countries on every continent, including those in the Muslim world. We consulted constantly with our allies, who stayed together every step of the way. And we made full use of public diplomacy to explain NATO's objectives." (Compare Albright, April 20, pp. 4-5, with June 28, p. 4.) [Ed.]

Milosevic vaulted to prominence and power a decade ago by exploiting the fears of ethnic Serbs in the province,[4] where they comprised about 10 percent of a population of two million. In 1989, after assuming power in Belgrade, he catered to those fears by robbing Kosovo's Albanian majority of the autonomy it had enjoyed under Tito and his immediate successors. For years the Kosovo Albanians sought to recover their rights by peaceful means.[5] Meanwhile, as the Yugoslav Federation broke apart, President Milosevic was the primary instigator of three wars, attacking first Slovenia, then Croatia, and finally triggering a devastating and prolonged conflict in Bosnia. In 1992, as fighting raged on in other parts of the former Yugoslavia, President George Bush warned Belgrade not to institute a policy of military repression in Kosovo.

In early 1998, the Belgrade government initiated a more extensive and violent campaign of repression against ethnic Albanians in Kosovo. One result was a humanitarian crisis, as tens of thousands of people fled their homes. A second consequence — unforeseen by Milosevic — was the strengthening of the Kosova Liberation Army (KLA), which contributed to the unrest by committing provocative acts of its own.

With our NATO allies and partners, including Russia, the United States sought to end this cycle of violence by diplomatic means. Last October, President Milosevic agreed to a cease-fire, to the withdrawal of most of his security forces, and to the entry of a verification mission from the OSCE. It soon became clear, however, that Milosevic had never intended to live up to this agreement. Instead of withdrawing, his security forces positioned themselves for a new offensive. Early this year, they perpetrated a massacre in the village of Racak. Following this event, the Contact Group, including Russia, agreed to summon the parties to a meeting to agree on the withdrawal of Serb forces, the introduction of an effective international military force, and autonomy for Kosovo.[6]

At the peace talks in Rambouillet and then Paris in February and March, Belgrade rejected a plan for peace that was accepted by the Kosovar Albanians. The Rambouillet plan included provisions for disarming the KLA and safeguarding the rights of all Kosovars, including ethnic Serbs. As he blocked our plan for peace,

---

4. The use of the term "province" is deliberate. Because Croatia, Slovenia, and Bosnia-Herzegovina were republics, they were constitutionally permitted to become independent. However, as a province that was officially autonomous from 1974 to 1989, Kosovo is not constitutionally permitted to secede. [Ed.]

5. Perhaps reflecting the postwar status of the KLA, the word "thereafter" is dropped from Albright's April 20 statement: "For years thereafter, the Kosovo Albanians sought to recover their rights by peaceful means." [Ed.]

6. This sentence has been added by Halperin to Albright's April 20 statement; the following sentence contains a phrase about meetings in Paris in February and March that has also been added to Albright's sentence. One effect of these additions is to emphasize Milosevic's intransigence. [Ed.]

Milosevic was preparing a plan for the ethnic cleansing of the entire Kosovar Albanian community. First, his security forces threatened and then forced the withdrawal of the OSCE mission; then they began a new rampage of terror.

They expelled roughly one and a half million civilians from their homes. Families were torn apart as Serb security forces herded as many Kosovar Albanians across the border as they could. Thousands were killed and many more violently abused. There are still several thousand missing Kosovar Albanians, some of whom are presumed to be held as prisoners in Serbia proper.[7] A massive buildup of Serbian military forces was underway even as Milosevic "negotiated" at Rambouillet. These preparations and the speed and thoroughness of the ethnic cleansing in Kosovo point to an undeniable conclusion: this campaign of terror was planned well ahead of time. It was the cause, not the result, of NATO action.

On March 24, 1999, following repeated attempts to negotiate a peaceful solution to the crisis, NATO launched Operation Allied Force. The goals of the aerial campaign against Milosevic were:

1. A verifiable stop to Serb military action against the people of Kosovo;
2. The withdrawal of Belgrade's military, police, and paramilitary forces from Kosovo;
3. The return of refugees to Kosovo;
4. The entry into Kosovo of an international military presence with NATO at its core;
5. Self-government and autonomy for the people of Kosovo.[8]

7. This new paragraph by Halperin updates events subsequent to April 20 and displaces a paragraph about refugees. In both Albright's April 20 statement and this essay by Halperin, the language is deliberate: these civilians are not really war refugees (i.e., fleeing from NATO bombing as claimed by Belgrade) but Milosevic's deportees, forcibly evacuated. This description sets the stage for the causal claim in the next paragraph: Milosevic is to blame for the campaign of terror that was the cause, not the result, of NATO action. [Ed.]

8. Although the entire previous section has been drawn from Albright's April 20 statement, two revisions are especially noteworthy. In her April 20 statement she states this fifth NATO objective as: "And the people of Kosovo must be given the democratic self-government they have long deserved." One plausible explanation for why this sentence is not used again is that it could be construed as supporting Kosovar independence, whereas Halperin's essay links self-government to autonomy. Another of Albright's April 20 statements is not repeated on June 28 or retrieved in this essay: "Behind these images [of deportees] is a reality of people no different in their fundamental rights or humanity than you or me — of children no different than yours or mine — cut off from their homes, deprived of their families, robbed of their dreams." Why does this sentence evaporate? Arguably, because it could be construed as a basis for supporting the "rights of Kosovars" to independence. After being briefly mentioned at the beginning of this essay, the language of values and principles that is so prominent in Albright's April and June statements recedes from view here. This reflects a new effort to reconcile aspirations for independence with "the politics of interest" (as discussed in the editorial essay that follows this text). [Ed.]

Winning the Peace

After seventy-eight days of air attacks, Operation Allied Force ended in accordance with the conditions the Alliance set. Now we face the even harder task of building a lasting peace there and throughout southeastern Europe. Assembling the nuts and bolts of a durable peace in Kosovo is a daunting challenge.[9] Our expectations should be realistic. The mission will take time; there will be setbacks; and despite KFOR's presence, the danger of violence will persist. Success will require an extraordinary team effort. Notwithstanding all this, there are three reasons for optimism.

First, for most of the past decade, Kosovar Albanians coped with Serb repression by maintaining parallel political, educational, and social structures. They have experience managing institutions.

Second, while we will support the efforts of the international community in Kosovo, the countries of Europe recognize that this is primarily a European responsibility, and they are determined to succeed. Failure is not an option.

Third, the international community has learned some hard lessons in recent years about how to succeed at building peace in post-conflict situations.

It is essential that these lessons be heeded in Kosovo. The military and civilian components must work toward a unified effort. Both must make effective use of their mandates and focus on results. Donors must back them not just with promises but with resources of sufficient quantity and timeliness to make a difference.

Now there are some who see an insurmountable obstacle in the desire of many Kosovars for immediate independence — a position that neither NATO nor governments in the region support. The yearning for independence is powerful among Kosovars, but Belgrade's withdrawal has altered the reality within which the people of Kosovo will formulate their aspirations. Until now, independence has seemed to be the only alternative to repression.[10]

In the near future Kosovars will have something they've never had: genuine self-government. They will be out from under Milosevic's boot, with the freedom to choose their own leaders and shape the laws by which they are governed. Milosevic and his henchmen won't have the capacity to intimidate Kosovars or deny them their rights. That's why the Kosovar Albanian leadership signed on to

---

9. With only slight modifications, the rest of this section is taken almost verbatim from Secretary Albright's June 28 remarks (". . . assembling the nuts . . . [to] . . . continent whole and free"). [Ed.]

10. These carefully phrased three sentences are taken verbatim from Albright's June 28 statement, but she nowhere else elaborates on their meaning. The clarification that the editor received is as follows: "Prior to recent events, for Kosovars, the only alternative to repression was independence; now that KFOR is there, this new reality reiterates autonomy as possible within the Federation of Yugoslavia. While short of independence, notions of self-government and autonomy are not mutually exclusive." For commentary on this issue, see "The Evolving Question of Kosovar Independence" in the editorial essay following this text. [Ed.]

the Rambouillet Accords — despite the absence of an independence guarantee — and why KFOR is receiving strong cooperation from most Kosovars.[11]

Another key issue is whether the new Kosovo will include its ethnic Serb, Roma, and other minorities, and whether they will be able to live safely now that Belgrade's forces have been withdrawn. Given the extent of destruction inflicted by Serbs, the risk is obvious that some ethnic Albanians will take the law into their own hands. Many unacceptable incidents have already occurred. KFOR, however, takes seriously its mandate to protect all Kosovars, including Serbs, and its effectiveness will increase as demilitarization gains steam. Moreover, hundreds of United Nations International Police (UNIP) are arriving each week. The UNIP will work together with a local police service that will be selected, trained, and supervised by the international community to help build a Kosovo that is safe for all of its inhabitants.

Kosovo will be a better place if Serbs who did not commit crimes stay and help rebuild; but that is their decision to make. We will measure our success by whether the rights of all those who choose to live in Kosovo are respected. The same principle, incidentally, should apply elsewhere in the region. The international community must continue to press for the safe return of other refugees, including ethnic Serbs to the Krajina region of Croatia. This is crucial, for there could be few greater gifts to the twenty-first century than to exorcise the ghosts of Balkans past and consign Milosevic's tactics of hate to the trash bin of history.

Even as we work to help Kosovo regain its feet, we are acting to secure the future of the region. With our partners in the European Union playing a leading role, we have launched a pact to stabilize, transform, and eventually integrate all of southeastern Europe into the continent's democratic mainstream. We undertake this effort because it accords with our principles, but also because it is sound policy. For we know that America cannot be secure unless Europe is secure. Our strategy with our partners is to apply the model of help and self-help reflected in the Marshall Plan half a century ago, as well as in efforts to aid democratization in central Europe this decade. In this spirit President Clinton met with his counterparts in the region this summer. Together they discussed ways to mobilize the resources of a wide range of governments and organizations, while coordinating with the European Community and the World Bank. Our intention is to work urgently and effectively with leaders in southeastern Europe as they strive to attract capital, raise living standards, reconcile ethnic and religious tensions, and promote the rule of law.

In this way we hope to enable countries throughout the region, over time, to participate fully in the major economic and political institutions of the Trans-

---

11. This leadership was in fact pressured to sign on — and offered unpublicized assurances for doing so. See the essays in this volume by Blerim Shala, Veton Surroi, Hashim Thaqi, and Fatos Lubonja. [Ed.]

Atlantic community. This would greatly serve America's interest in expanding the area within Europe where wars simply do not happen. And it would mark another giant step toward the creation of a continent whole and free.

Implications [for Foreign Policy]

By confronting massive ethnic cleansing in the Balkans, we have made it less likely that NATO will be called upon to use force in the future. And by supporting democracy and promoting human rights, we contribute to a future of stability and peace throughout Europe. This is fully consistent both with American interests and with NATO's purpose, which is to prevent war while defending freedom.

Some hope — and others fear — that Kosovo will be a precedent for similar interventions around the globe. Such sweeping conclusions are misleading. Every circumstance is unique. The response to Milosevic, for instance, would not have been possible without NATO, and NATO is a European and Atlantic — not a global — institution. Whether a crisis is in Europe or elsewhere, any president will make decisions on the use of force on a case-by-case basis after weighing a host of factors. Military force is always a last resort: we exhaust other options before making the decision to deploy it. We will continue to act, however, where we can and where our interests are at stake to protect against and stop gross abuses.[12]

12. The final two sentences in the third paragraph of this important section are *the first time* the U.S. Administration has offered a public policy rationale for humanitarian intervention that can be linked to some of those considerations articulated in just-war criteria. For analysis, see my response to Halperin's essay. [Ed.]

Not Losing Sight of Justice:
A Response to Halperin's Statement

WILLIAM JOSEPH BUCKLEY

Whether or not military evaluations are "always learning to fight the last war better," many public resources have been used to evaluate military aspects of the Kosovo intervention. Wider public policy analysis is still emerging. Nonetheless, the ethical significance of two of the claims in Mr. Halperin's essay call for concise comment: (1) the ethical implications of a "humanitarian" foreign policy, and (2) the political status of those territories in which there is an intervention (in this case, the evolving question of Kosovo independence).

I. Ethics and the Justice of Humanitarian Interventions

Whether a crisis is in Europe or elsewhere, any president will make decisions on the use of force on a case-by-case basis after weighing a host of factors. Military force is always a last resort; we exhaust other options before making the decision to deploy it. We will continue to act, however, where we can and where our interests are at stake to protect against and stop gross abuses.

These final sentences of Halperin's essay are the first time the American administration has offered a public-policy rationale for humanitarian intervention that can be linked to some of the considerations enshrined in just-war reasoning. How might we ethically assess this rationale? There has been a great deal of media speculation and commentary concerning oblique Administration references about humanitarian interventions, as well as the more general "humanitarian foreign policy," also known as "combining force with diplomacy," "coercive diplomacy," and "aggressive multilateralism" — and there are important distinctions among these terms. My remarks

---

I want to thank Richard Miller and Kate McCann for their helpful comments on an earlier draft of this response.

I want to thank Richard Miller and Kate McCann for their helpful comments on an earlier draft of this response.

restrict themselves to the Kosovo intervention, but they do have wider implications. Some of the questions raised were indirectly discussed by Samuel R. Berger, Assistant to the President for National Security Affairs, on at least two separate occasions (March 24, 1999, and April 25, 1999).[1] Without specifically stating criteria for intervention, Berger invoked examples from the Kosovo situation (e.g., last resort, military and diplomatic abilities, American/NATO interests, gross abuses). With the exception of its final two sentences, which are new and important, the rest of the final three paragraphs of Halperin's essay are taken almost verbatim from Secretary Albright's June 28 speech (p. 4). Thus, as a whole, these final paragraphs can be interpreted as an effort to address a series of questions about humanitarian intervention raised by, among others, Zbigniew Brzezinski, Henry Kissinger, Edward Luttwak, and U.N. Secretary-General Kofi Annan (in essays in this volume).

Because of the extraordinary importance of this issue for foreign-policy debates, I received some clarifications from the Administration to questions I raised about Halperin's final paragraphs. While the following remarks obviously cannot adequately evaluate this embryonic public formulation of a "doctrine" of humani-

---

1. For Berger's interviews, see CNN's *Larry King Live,* March 24, 1999 (pp. 3-6 of printed text), and CNN's *Late Edition* with Wolf Blitzer, April 25, 1999 (pp. 5-9). In addition, claims about "humanitarian intervention" have been widely reported in the press (e.g., "The Three Ifs of a Clinton Doctrine," by Douglas Waller, *Time* (6/28/99): 35; "Redefining the National Interest," by Joseph S. Nye Jr. in *Foreign Affairs* (July/August 1999); "A Perfect Failure: NATO's War against Yugoslavia," by Michael Mandelbaum, *Foreign Affairs* (September/October 1999): 2-8. Though many in Belgrade characterize this "humanitarian intervention" as an act of "NATO aggression" or an illustration of the historically recurrent imperial hegemony exercised by the powerful over Serbia (Tanaskovic), the U.S. Administration has used the language of case, example, exception, and precedent to describe (and justify) the Kosovo intervention. For domestic general audiences prior to and during the conflict, the language of "example as warning/punishment" predominates, not least of all because of the tendency to point to Milosevic as the culprit (although Berger does not make typical comparisons to Saddam Hussein in the cited interviews). The language of precedent predominates for American foreign policy elites (as in Albright's 6/28 speech); on the other hand, some critics of Administration foreign policy (including some in this book) deny or marginalize the language of precedent. For the general public both during and after the war, the State Department emphasized multilateralism (as in Albright's 4/20/99 statement and Berger's 4/25/99 remarks about Russian participation in an international security presence). For non-NATO nations, the U.N., and especially the Russians and Chinese, the Administration combined the language of highly unusual, virtually unprecedented exceptionalism with this multilateralism (e.g., see Under Secretary of State Thomas Pickering's 6/17/99 "Oral Presentation to the Chinese Government regarding the Accidental Bombing of the PRC Embassy in Belgrade," on the web at www.state.gov). For the contraction of justifications from universal values to state interest, compare Albright's May and June speeches with Halperin's (August) and Clinton's U.N. address (September, on the web at www.whitehouse .gov). For General Wesley Clark's view, see his essay in this volume and my commentary on it. For Richard Miller's view, see his essay in this volume. For Zbigniew Brzezinski's view on this subject, see his essay in this volume entitled "The Failed Double Cross."

tarian intervention, they do raise a set of concerns that should be important for further public discussion:

1. Any decision to employ lethal force requires widespread public knowledge and discussion, even though the discourse of international politics and diplomacy is not lavish in self-disclosure. Political leaders of democracies must display high canons of publicity.
2. Because normative justifications for such "humanitarian interventions" mimic the well-known Babel of moral languages prevalent in the postmodern culture of the West, cultural leaders (in the academy, media, religious traditions, etc.) should publicly scrutinize and debate such matters.
3. Humanitarian catastrophes are rarely surprises; nonetheless, the invaluable experience and research of nongovernmental and intergovernmental organizations (NGO's and IGO's) are largely at the margins of public discussions. Why?
4. Some of the Clinton Administration's public claims about what was done in the Kosovo intervention, and why, present problems demanding more scrutiny. I will explore three: (a) The U.S. Administration's brief articulation of criteria for humanitarian intervention touches "just-war reasoning" but provokes numerous questions. (b) There are conflicting assumptions behind various public characterizations of the humanitarian intervention as a case, an exception, an example, and a precedent. (c) For example, Administration language displays a tension in viewing the outcome of conflict as a "success" in either military or wider political terms. At least part of this issue is related to a necessary wider public conversation about the responsibilities and limits of being a superpower after the Cold War.
5. My questions appear below in italics; the clarifications **in bold print** are my summary and interpretation of the answers I received in consultation with the Clinton Administration. (They are not direct quotations from the author[s] of the Halperin essay.)

(1) *What are specific criteria for humanitarian intervention?* As set out by Mr. Halperin, the Adminstration's criteria for humanitarian intervention seem to function in some sort of equilibrium. With caveats about interpretation, several of the criteria echo elements contained in classic just-war criteria as articulated by Richard Miller's essay in this volume (just cause, competent authority, right intention, last resort, reasonable hope for success, relative justice, and proportionality describe *whether* force is justified; discrimination [noncombatant immunity], proportionality, and right intention survey *how* force must be used). Despite their historically Christian development of pre-Christian Western thought, these criteria are not the exclusive domain of one particular cultural (or religious) tradition; nor do they completely exclude the use of force in any and all circumstances.

Rather, just-war criteria can be viewed as one (not the only) common moral language derived from the experience of differing communities that aims to enable and constrain force as a means to secure justice.

Halperin's criteria for humanitarian intervention include **military force as last resort . . . where our interests are at stake** — as hedged by — **to protect against and stop gross abuses** (each relevant to classic just-war criteria of just cause, right intention, last resort, and proportionality) and **where we can**, related to "reasonable hope for success." These criteria raise many questions. What are the threshold implications of "to protect and stop gross abuses"? Whereas the *jus in bello* criteria (of discrimination and proportionality) are consigned to the military in a division of labor, why are criteria of competent authority and relative justice missing? Aside from the KFOR and UNIP, why is the United Nations not even mentioned in Halperin's text? Some Administration personnel who are not in the State Department concede that a deliberate decision was made to ignore the U.N.; but the truth is more complex. A close comparison of President Clinton's September 16, 1999, U.N. address and Kofi Annan's subsequent defense on September 16 and 20, 1999, of humanitarian intervention shows close agreement: regional interventions can serve U.N. interests.

Although such convergence is neither accidental nor implausible, it does call for further discussion. Despite other differences, Kofi Annan and Henry Kissinger concur that we live in an era needing greater international consensus about how to regulate our interconnectedness and sovereignty. Those who see the Kosovo intervention as a "just war" must concede the many differing kinds of failures that led to it; those who consider it unjust must constructively respond to the injustices that gave rise to it — and will follow in its wake. America and the West must learn from the "successes" and "failures" of the Kosovo intervention. If "coercive diplomacy," "blending diplomacy with force," "aggressive multilateralism," and a "humanitarian foreign policy" are to be anything other than veneer for power, they must be persuasive and not merely coercive.

(2) *Is the so-called Clinton doctrine of humanitarian intervention now American foreign policy?* No, "every circumstance is unique"; hence, Kosovo is not a precedent, contrary to the beliefs of those who would either endorse or criticize it as such. This is directed at two divergent groups: those who favor aggressive interventionism in many places (e.g., in the name of human rights) as well as those who oppose interventionism, either on *Realpolitik* grounds (e.g., Kissinger) or on the grounds that it eclipses the Westphalian state-centered system (the view of some overseas opponents of American unilateralism).

As with the question of criteria, the assessment and interpretation of circumstances will be contextual and shaped by diverging interests. Despite State Department denials, Henry Kissinger's essay "As the Cheers Fade" argues that there is, in fact, an effort to construct a new humanitarian foreign policy.

(3) *Does the so-called Clinton doctrine of humanitarian intervention represent*

a doctrinal shift in foreign policy? **No, our foreign policy retains its historic commitments, but this does not foreclose future possibilities (i.e., of humanitarian intervention on a "case-by-case basis" according to the criteria mentioned).**

In an effort to preserve diplomatic discretion in humanitarian interventions, Halperin invokes the moral language of cases. Discretion exists in tension with public consensus. As I show in note 1 on p. 232, the Administration's language has led many to question whether the Kosovo intervention should be interpreted as a *case* (of virtually "unique circumstances," understandable only to the President), an *exception* (to the rule against nonintervention), an *example* (for potential abusers of human rights), or a *precedent* for future policies (aggressive multilateralism). These four publicly given and ostensibly similar descriptions of humanitarian intervention rely on significantly different assumptions. For example, the first invokes an epistemological privilege difficult to reconcile with democratic public debates about such weighty matters. The second assumes international consensus about a set of rules and exceptions (e.g., doesn't Article 7 of the U.N. Charter permit intervention if refugee flows threaten neighbors?). The third presupposes that potential abusers of human rights can be influenced. And the last suggests a future action guide with troublesome implications (e.g., Russia interceding for ethnic Russians in the Ukraine? China in Indonesia?). None of these assumptions requires inaction in the face of injustice; but each demands a more finely grained analysis because of its tentative presuppositions and different audiences.

Three trends in this language of discretion as applied to Kosovo are noteworthy: (1) a contraction of public reasons for humanitarian interventions from "universal timeless values" (of "freedom and security") to narrower foreign policy language about "state interests"; (2) an undefended expansion of the scope of potential interventions (**whether a crisis is in Europe or elsewhere . . .**), raising reasonable questions about just controls and the use of existing international agencies. Even when used to correct injustice, discretion can mask interests that create other injustices. (3) A widespread dissatisfaction with *Realpolitik* as it is variously understood as a *prescription* for international relations. Only rarely, as in Talbott's August essay, do we see the rudiments of an alternative set of assumptions about intergroup relations (derived from systems theory). Like Kofi Annan, I find newer systems models more *descriptively* compelling; but the case-based reasoning of the Administration offers few details and can, understandably, appear as a mere veneer for the politics of power (Tanaskovic).

Strategic Opportunity for Public Discussion?

Could these ethical reflections be a strategic opportunity for a public conversation about the moral responsibilities (and limits) of multilateral interventionism in the world? As a test case, let us examine some of the moral tensions between military and political notions of "success" in the Kosovo intervention. To the extent that it simply describes American ability to do *something,* Halperin's criterion **where we can** indicates the ability to achieve some goal or objective. In a limited way, this criterion *formally* coheres with the traditional just-war criterion "reasonable hope for success." However, whether this "ability" criterion *substantively* coheres with the traditional "success" criterion requires two further clarifications:

1. Is this resort to force prohibited because it is rash, futile, or irrational, given certain specific goals and objectives?
2. Are the objectives that define "success" themselves moral?

The political and military commentary essays in this volume display the tension between viewing the moral criterion of "success" in military or wider political terms. As illustrated by the contrast between the Halperin and Wesley Clark essays in this volume, a linguistic division of labor seems to function: the State Department articulates goals and purposes in political terms (relevant to the *jus ad bellum* criteria of *whether* and under what conditions it is permissible to use force). In contrast, the military describes "objectives" in military terms pertinent to the *jus in bello* criteria (*how* a just war must be fought). Claims about "success" illustrate how interconnected these two forms of reasoning are. Despite the five goals of NATO's Kosovo campaign, which Halperin states above, it is reasonable to ask: (a) For what political reasons did objectives for the use of force (military criteria for "success") themselves shift: preventing or stopping Serbian repression/aggression, degrading Serbian assets (military and dual-use) so as to reverse ethnic cleansing, demoralizing a population in order to motivate it to remove a regime? (b) Shouldn't these shifts be open to further moral scrutiny according to other just-war criteria? For example, did the air campaign stop the gross abuse of human rights? Generals Clark and Shelton agree: No, it did not, but ethnic cleansing was reversed. Was this reversal due to the air campaign? Should we modify our expectations of what an air campaign alone can do to protect human rights? Should NATO's military "competence" have overridden the U.N.'s political "authority" (Walzer, Solana, Annan)? The estimation of "reasonable hope for success" in just-war reasoning involves considerations that are political, military, and prudential. State and Defense Department officials have recurrently spoken of "objectives" that are military, diplomatic, and humanitarian (Albright, April 20, 1999).

An analysis of the responses from General Clark and his office makes it clear that NATO's objectives were wide-ranging and shifting in two ways. The first shift was diplomatic: maintaining alliance cohesion, isolating Yugoslavia, humanitarian relief, monitoring implications for the Dayton Accords. The second shift was military: strategic attacks and Kosovo tactical, or ground, operations. In short, military aims disclosed evolving political commitments: deterring, interdicting, and eventually reversing ethnic cleansing; forcing a Serb withdrawal; aiding the KLA

— and ultimately a strategic campaign designed to diminish popular support for a regime (which does not rely on popular support for its power base!).

Not only must we assess the "justice" of these objectives; we must be more careful and discriminating when the criterion of "success" refers to the language of political goals, military objectives, or eventual outcomes. Why? So that we avoid the myopic congratulations for "maintaining alliance unity" that have been granted by Albright, Clark, Kissinger, and Brzezinski, which overlook *why* such unity cannot be assessed merely instrumentally in terms of the outcome of the conflict and *how* such "alliance unity" was purchased by shifting the risks to civilian populations in an air campaign of combatant immunity (Elshtain, Walzer, Miller, Cook). This is not to deny that the outcome has had important benefits for the Kosovars; it is merely to remind us that just-war criteria require that we morally appraise all of the relevant considerations — not just a "favorable outcome" that "preserved alliance unity."

Then there is the matter of comparative justice. Has the demonization of Milosevic led to such a demonization of all Serbians that none of their claims is just? Nothing justifies the injustices, the human rights abuses, the atrocities, or the simplistic criminalization of Kosovar secession movements by the Serbs. But politically motivated media stereotypes do not help Westerners accurately discern claims and counterclaims for just intervention. It is morally nearsighted to simply point to "alliance unity" and "Kosovar autonomy" as achievements without factoring in other costs. It is likewise factually narrow-minded to assert that one factor that was arguably important in ending the hostilities (alliance unity, bombing, the threat of invasion, the Russian effort) was in itself decisive — prior to the disclosure of more information.[2]

---

2. For discussions of the role that the threat of a ground invasion played in concluding the war, see *Washington Post* (9/17/99): A22, reporting on the 9/16/99 NATO study released from Brussels prior to the Pentagon study; see also the series in the *Washington Post* (9/18/99 and 9/19/99): 1ff. for General Wesley Clark's answers to questions at his presentation at the American Enterprise Institute on 8/31/99 (available online at www.aei.org/nai/naiclark.htm); see also his remarks at the initial survey of the findings from a review of attacks on mobile targets made under the auspices of the U.S. European Command on 9/16/99, entitled "Press Conference on the Kosovo Strike Assessment" (available online at http://www.nato.int/kosovo/press/p990916a .htm). On 10/14/99, Secretary of Defense William S. Cohen and Chairman of the Joint Chiefs of Staff General Henry H. Shelton both gave an "in-progress update" on the Pentagon assessment before the Senate Armed Services Committee, entitled "Joint Statement on the Kosovo after Action Review," which also mentions the role of the threat of a ground invasion (available online at http://www.defenselink.mil/news/Oct1999/b10141999_bt478-99.html). For discussions of the use of precision munitions, see General Clark's essay in this volume; Michael Ignatieff's essay "The Virtual Commander," *The New Yorker* (8/2/99): 30-36, as well as the aforementioned *Washington Post* essays and the Pentagon report. For R. Jeffery Smith's comment, see "Specter of Independent Kosovo Divides US, European Allies," *The Washington Post* (9/28/99): A19. See Deputy Secretary of State Strobe Talbott's address at the Aspen Institute on 8/24/99 entitled "The Balkan Question and the European Answer" (available at www.state.gov).

Now is the time for public discussion at national and international levels of the merits and liabilities of nonviolent and violent "humanitarian interventions." Because these criteria and "clarifications" raise as many questions as they answer, the public-policy conversation will continue.

II. The Evolving Question of Kosovo's Independence

The larger question of what will become of the political status of territories after an intervention is neither novel nor merely theoretical. Complex questions of internal legitimacy and external relations arise. At least ten considerations are pertinent to this evolving question in the case of Kosovo.

(1) The current position of the United States government presents a *theoretical conundrum,* even though it can endorse some practical measures to go forward. The U.S. government does not officially recognize the "rump state" of Yugoslavia, composed of Serbia and Montenegro. "[T]he US view is that the Socialist Federal Republic of Yugoslavia (SFRY) has dissolved and that none of the successor republics represents its continuation" (CIA *World Factbook,* 1999). In short, on what grounds can we oppose independence yet require an autonomous affiliation with a rump state that is not recognized? Despite differences, other precedents are telling (e.g., Palestine).

(2) Predictable *negative justifications* for opposing international boundary changes (e.g., to discourage coerced boundary changes, secessionism, "Greater" Albanias, Serbias, or Croatias) are typically given to sustain the stability of an alliance (NATO, the U.N.), not to persuade belligerents in a dispute over sovereignty, even though such justifications sometimes function to ratify preexisting territorial boundaries that subsequently have been ethnically cleansed (Vatican).

(3) As articulated in the *positive language* of Wilsonian idealism by Deputy Secretary of State Strobe Talbott, opposition to Kosovar independence is an effort to forestall the violent dismemberment of states in an era and a Europe that features two trends: federated statehoods in which minorities and majorities prosper, and the convergence of liberal democracies as a European Union. In other words, national sovereignty has evolved into pooled sovereignty among nations in some fields (e.g., economics) and greater devolved governance for autonomous regions in other fields (language and education). In short, according to Talbott, Kosovar independence would "buck the trend" in those innovations in national identity and international relations that Western Europe is putting in place. R. Jeffery Smith has articulately posed the dilemma between this and the preceding consideration: "instead of European nations serving as a model for Kosovo, there is increasing concern on the continent that Kosovo's troubles might somehow serve as a prototype of Europe's future." In short, these positive arguments about the European marriage of pooled sovereignty and devolved

autonomy do not dissuade Kosovar aspirations for independence. (See Veton Surroi's essay in this volume.)

(4) As Talbot's presentation hints (p. 6), in the case of Kosovo and Yugoslavia, it is also reasonable to assume that NATO (including especially the U.S.) has interests in *not alienating* or further fragmenting (a) Yugoslavian domestic political opposition to Milosevic by openly advocating independence for Kosovo or (b) Greeks, Macedonians, and Montenegrins nervous about their own ethnic Albanian populations.

(5) Likewise, in the hopes of restabilizing an externally attacked and internally fragmented system of political affiliations, numerous Kosovar political leaders and parties have been periodically meeting, with Western guidance, since the end of the conflict. The essays by Kosovars in this volume (two of whom were at Rambouillet: Surroi and Shala), suggest that the *Allies have promised them more than autonomy* within Yugoslavia; they also signal that no less will be acceptable (e.g., Maliqi, Thaqi).

(6) Despite official opposition to independence for Kosovo, there is a widespread sense in the U.S. State Department of the *inevitability* of some form of political bifurcation between Kosovo and Yugoslavia, whether that is parsed in terms of "independence" or "partition."

(7) Despite private efforts at Rambouillet to coerce Kosovar unanimity on gradual, not immediate, independence, subsequent State Department language returns to "autonomy": *early unguarded language about Kosovar self-governance becomes hedged by claims about other European policitical interests.*

(8) The *mutual displacement and (in)voluntary segregation* of Albanians and Serbs from Kosovo have left a virtually partitioned territory that provides an obstacle to claims about unity between Kosovo and Serbia/Yugoslavia.

(9) Because we have a cessation of hostilities rather than a peace agreement or surrender, the UNMIK and KFOR administration of the protectorate leave ongoing *political and constitutional questions* either (a) in the same status as before the war (so the Serbs base the future on the Military Technical Agreement); (b) in an entirely new framework (so many Albanian Kosovars, formerly with the KLA, base the future on their interpretation of U.N. Resolution 1244 via Rambouillet); (c) or ambiguous on important issues (Kissinger). Hence it is reasonable to forecast *ongoing contentiousness about practical issues.*

(10) In addition to many differing contemporary locales where *practical and local work* on sovereignty issues is undertaken by various multinational agencies, a *sophisticated commentary literature* that draws on historical examples has emerged, for example, in the ongoing working group meetings of the International Law and Ethics Conference Series on "Secession, Transitional Justice, and Reconciliation" between some Western and Balkan scholars. Many in this group engage neo-Marxian and post-Marxian thought with liberal political theories (Rawls). Whether and when this more theoretical work will have practical implications remains to be seen.

Address to the Senate and the House of Commons of the Parliament of Canada

VÁCLAV HAVEL

I certainly do not need to emphasize how honored I am to address you. With your permission, I shall use this opportunity for a few remarks concerning the state and its probable position in the future.

There is every indication that the glory of the nation-state as a climax of the history of every national community and the highest earthly value — in fact, the only one in whose name it is permissible to kill or which is worth dying for — is already past its culminating point.

It seems that the enlightened endeavors of generations of democrats, the horrible experience of two World Wars, which contributed so substantially to the adoption of the Universal Declaration of Human Rights, as well as the overall development of our civilization, are gradually bringing the human race to the realization that a human being is more important than a state.

The idol of state sovereignty must inevitably dissolve in a world that connects people, regardless of borders, through millions of links of integration, ranging from trade, finance, and property, up to information — links that impart a variety of universal notions and cultural patterns. Furthermore, it is a world in which danger to some has an immediate bearing on all; in which — for many reasons, especially because of the massive advancement of science and technology — our fates are merged together into a single destiny; and a world in which we all, whether we like it or not, suffer responsibility for everything that occurs.

It is obvious that in such a world, blind love for one's own state — a love that does not recognize anything above itself, finds excuses for any action of the state simply because it is one's own state, and rejects anything else simply because it is different — inevitably turns into a dangerous anachronism, a hotbed of conflicts, and, eventually, a source of immeasurable human suffering.

I believe that in the coming century most states will begin to transform from cult-like objects charged with emotional contents into much simpler and more civil administrative units that will be less powerful and, especially, more rational, and will constitute merely one of the levels in a complex and stratified planetary societal self-organization. This change, among other things, should gradually antiquate the idea of noninterference, that is, the concept of saying that what happens in another state, or the measure of respect for human rights there, is none of our business.

Who will take over the various functions that are now performed by the state?

Let us first speak about the emotional functions: these, I believe, will begin to be distributed more equally among all the various spheres that make up human identity, or in which human beings exercise their existence. By this I mean the various layers of what we perceive as our home or our natural world: our family, our company, our village or town, our region, our profession, our church or our association, as well as our continent and, finally, our earth — the planet we inhabit. All this constitutes the various environments of our self-identification; and if the bond to one's own state, hypertrophied until now, is to be weakened, it must necessarily be to the benefit of all these other environments.

As for the practical responsibilities and the jurisdictions of the state, these can go in only two directions: downward or upward. Downward applies to the various organs and structures of civil society to which the state should gradually transfer many of the tasks it now performs itself. Upward applies to various regional, transnational, or global communities or organizations. This transfer of functions has already begun. In some areas, it has progressed quite far; in others, less so. However, it is obvious that the trend of development must — for many different reasons — go along this path.

If modern democratic states are usually defined by such characteristics as respect for human rights and liberties, equality of citizens, the rule of law and civil society, then the manner of existence toward which humankind will move from here, or toward which humankind should move in the interest of its own preservation, will probably be characterized as an existence founded on a universal, or global, respect for human rights, a universal equality of citizens, a universal rule of law, and a global civil society.

One of the greatest problems that accompanied the formation of nation-states was their geographical delimitation, that is, the definition of their boundaries. Innumerable factors — ethnic, historical, and cultural considerations, geological elements, power interests, as well as the overall state of civilization — have played a role here. The creation of larger regional or transnational communities will sometimes be afflicted with the same problem; to some extent, this burden will possibly be inherited from the very nation-states that enter into such entities. We should do everything in our power to ensure that this self-definition process will not be as painful as was the case when nation-states were formed.

Allow me to give you one example. Canada and the Czech Republic are now allies as members of the same defense association — the North Atlantic alliance. This is a result of a process of historic importance, that is, NATO's being enlarged by states from central and eastern Europe. This process is significant because it is the first truly serious and historically irreversible step to break down the Iron Curtain and to abolish, in real terms and not just verbally, what was called the Yalta arrangement.

This enlargement, as we all know, was far from easy and has become a reality only ten years after the bipolar division of the world came to an end. One of the reasons that progress was so difficult was the opposition on the part of the Russian Federation; they asked, uncomprehendingly and worriedly, why the West was enlarging and moving closer to Russia without taking Russia itself into its embrace. This attitude — if I disregard all other motives for the moment — reveals one very interesting element: an uncertainty about where the beginning is, and where the end is, of what might be called the world of Russia, or the East. When NATO offers Russia its hand in partnership, it does so on the assumption that there are two large and equal entities: a Euro-Atlantic world and a vast Euro-Asian power. These two entities can, and must, extend their hands to each other and cooperate; this is in the interest of the whole world. But they can do this only when they are conscious of their own identities; in other words, when they know where each of them begins and ends. Russia has had some difficulty with that in its entire history, and it is obviously carrying this problem with it into the present world in which the question of delimitation is no longer about nation-states but about regions or spheres of culture and civilization. Yes, Russia has a thousand things that link it with the Euro-Atlantic world or the so-called West; but it also has a thousand things that differ from the West, just as Latin America, Africa, the Far East, and other regions or continents of today's world do.

The fact that these worlds, or parts of the world, differ from one another does not mean that some are more worthy than others. They are all equal. They are only different in certain ways. But being different is not a disgrace! Russia, on the one hand, deems it very important to be seen as an entity of moment, an entity that deserves special treatment, that is, as a global power. At the same time, it is uncomfortable with being perceived as an independent entity that can hardly be part of another entity.

Russia is becoming accustomed to the enlargement of the Alliance; one day it will become acclimated to it completely. Let us just hope that this will not be merely an expression of Engels's "recognized necessity" but an expression of a new, more profound self-understanding. Just as others must learn to redefine themselves in the new multicultural and multipolar environment, Russia must learn it also. This means not only that it cannot forever substitute megalomania, or simply self-love, for natural self-confidence, but also that it must recognize where it begins and where it ends. For example, huge Siberia, with its vast natural resources, is Russia, but tiny Estonia is not Russia — and never will be. And if Estonia feels that it belongs to the world represented by the North Atlantic alliance or the European Union, Russia must understand and respect this and not see it as an expression of enmity.

With this example, I would like to illustrate the following: the world of the twenty-first century — provided humankind withstands all the dangers that it is preparing for itself — will be a world of ever-closer cooperation, on a footing of equality, among larger and mostly transnational bodies that will sometimes cover whole continents. In order for the world to be like this, individual entities, cultures, or spheres of civilization must clearly recognize their own identities, understand what makes them different from others, and accept the fact that such "otherness" is not a handicap but a singular contribution to the global wealth of the human race. Of course, the same must also be recognized by those who, on the contrary, have the inclination to regard their "otherness" as a reason for feeling superior.

One of the most important organizations in which all states, as well as major transnational entities, meet as equals for debate and make many important decisions that affect the whole world is the United Nations. I believe that, if the United Nations is to successfully perform the tasks to be imposed on it by the next century, it must undergo a substantial reform.

The Security Council, the most important organ of the United Nations, can no longer maintain conditions from the time when the organization first came into being. Instead, it must equitably mirror the multipolar world of today. We must reflect on whether it is indispensable that one state — even if only theoretically — could outvote the rest of the world. We must consider the question of which great, strong, and populous nations do not have permanent representation in that body. We must think out the pattern of rotation of the nonpermanent members and a number of other things.

We must make the entire vast structure of the United Nations less bureaucratic and more effective.

We must deliberate on how to achieve real flexibility in the decision-making of U.N. bodies, particularly of its plenary.

Most importantly, I believe we should ensure that all the inhabitants of our earth regard the United Nations as an organization that is truly theirs, not just as a club of governments. The crucial point is what the U.N. can accomplish for the people of this planet, not what it does for individual states as states. Therefore, changes should probably also be made in the procedures for the financing of the organization, for the application of its documents, and for the scrutiny of their application. This is not a matter of abolishing the powers of states and establishing some kind of giant global state instead. The matter is that everything should not always flow, forever, solely through the hands of states or their governments. It is in the interest of humanity — of human rights and liberties as well as of life in general — that there be more than one channel through which the decisions of planetary leadership flow to the citizens, and through which the citizens' will reaches the planetary leaders. More channels mean more balance and a wider mutual scrutiny.

I hope it is evident that I am not fighting here against the institution of the state as such. It would, for that matter, be rather absurd if the head of a state addressing the representative bodies of another state pleaded that states should be abolished. I am talking about something else. I am talking about the fact that there is a value that ranks higher than the state. This value is humanity. The state, as is well known, is here to serve the people, not the other way around. If a person serves his or her state, such service should go only as far as is necessary for the state to do a good service to all its citizens. Human rights rank above the rights of states. Human liberties constitute a higher value than state sovereignty. In terms of international law, the provisions that protect the unique human being should take precedence over the provisions that protect the state.

If in the world of today our fates are merged into a single destiny, and if every one of us is responsible for the future of all, nobody — not even the state — should be allowed to restrict the right of the people to exercise this responsibility. I think that the foreign policies of individual states should gradually sever the category that has, until now, most often constituted their axis, that is, the category of "interests" — "our national interests" or "the foreign policy interests of our state." The category of "interests" tends to divide us rather than bring us together. It is true that each of us has some specific interests; this is entirely natural and there is no reason why we should abandon our legitimate concerns. But there is something that ranks higher than our interests: it is the principles that we espouse. Principles unite us rather than divide us. Moreover, they are the yardstick for measuring the legitimacy or illegitimacy of our interests. I do not think it is valid when various state doctrines say that it is in the interest of the state to uphold such and such a principle. Principles must be respected and upheld for their own sake — as a matter of principle, so to speak — and interests should be derived from them.

For example, it would not be right if I said that it is in the interest of the Czech Republic that there is an equitable peace in the world. I have to say something else: there must be an equitable peace in the world, and the interests of the Czech Republic must be subordinated to that.

The alliance of which both Canada and the Czech Republic are now members is waging a struggle against the genocidal regime of Slobodan Milosevic. It is neither an easy struggle nor a popular one, and there can be different opinions on its strategy and tactics. But no person of sound judgment can deny one thing: this is probably the first war ever fought that is not being fought in the name of interests but in the name of certain principles and values. If it is possible to say about a war that it is ethical, or that it is fought for ethical reasons, it is true of this war. Kosovo has no oil fields whose output might perhaps attract somebody's interest; no member country of NATO has any territorial claims there; and Milosevic is not threatening either the territorial integrity or any other integrity of any NATO member. Nevertheless, NATO is fighting: it is fighting in the name of human interest for the fate of other human beings. It is fighting because decent people cannot sit back and watch systematic, state-directed massacres of other people. Decent people simply cannot tolerate this, and they cannot fail to come to the rescue if a rescue action is within their power.

This war gives human rights precedence over the rights of states. The Federal Republic of Yugoslavia has been attacked without a direct United Nations mandate for NATO's action; but NATO has not acted out of license, aggressiveness, or disrespect for international law. On the contrary, it has acted out of respect for the law — for the law that ranks higher than the protection of the sovereignty of states. It has acted out of respect for the rights of humanity as they are articulated by our conscience as well as by other instruments of international law.

I see this as an important precedent for the future. It has now been clearly stated that it is not permissible to slaughter people, to evict them from their homes, to maltreat them, and to deprive them of their property. It has been demonstrated that human rights are indivisible and that if injustice is done to some, it is done to all. . . .

I am well aware that Canadian politics has long and systematically advanced the principle of the security of the human being, which you deem equally important as that of the security of the state, if not even more important. Let me assure you that this Canadian ethic enjoys a profound respect in my country. I would wish that we are not merely allies in a formal or institutional sense as members of the same defense alliance but also as partners in promoting this worthy principle. . . .

Many times in the past I have pondered the question of why humanity has the prerogative to any rights at all. Inevitably, I have always come to the conclusion that human rights, human liberties, and human dignity have their deepest roots outside this earthly world. They become what they are only because, under certain circumstances, they can mean for humanity a value that people — without being forced to — place even higher than their own lives. Thus these notions have meaning only against the background of the infinite and of eternity. It is my profound conviction that the true worth of all our actions — whether or not they are in harmony with our conscience, the ambassador of eternity in our soul — is finally tested somewhere beyond our sight. If we did not sense this, or subconsciously surmise it, certain things could never get done.

Let me conclude my remarks on the state and on the role it will probably play in the future with the following statement: While the state is a human creation, humanity is a creation of God.

Winning Peace: The Vatican on Kosovo — An Interview with Archbishop Jean-Louis Tauran, the Vatican's Secretary for Relations with States

Rome, June 9, 1999

Your Excellency, in your opinion, what are the specific aspects characterizing the war in Kosovo, and what are the connecting points to the previous clashes that have taken place in the former Yugoslavia?

The armed conflicts in that part of Europe originated from the collapse of communism and from the decision of some federated republics to secede from Belgrade and set up a democratic process. However, while there existed a constitutional basis for secession for Croatia, Macedonia, Slovenia, Bosnia, and Herzegovina [as republics], no such basis existed for Kosovo, which, until 1989, had enjoyed the status of being an autonomous province of the Yugoslavian Federation. The Albanians of Kosovo were supposed to enjoy all the rights and the duties [*di tutti i diritti e doveri*] enjoyed by all the minorities within the confines of the Federation. Unfortunately, from 1989 on, these rights have been denied, and that was one of the causes of the tragic Yugoslavian crisis [in Kosovo]. If one were to compare this conflict to that in Bosnia and Herzegovina, one couldn't help but notice that this conflict has been much more complex. [In Bosnia and Herzegovina] three principal ethnic components (40 percent Muslim, 30 percent Serb, 20 percent Croatian) faced the Serbs' design of territo-

---

In his response of 7/24/99 to the invitation to contribute an essay that details the position of the Holy See, Vatican Secretary for Relations with States and Special Balkan Envoy Archbishop Tauran wrote to the editor: "I trust to be of some assistance to you, if I conclose a copy of an interview I gave recently to the Italian magazine 'Il Regno' *which illustrates well the position of the Holy See*" (emphasis added by editor). Thanks to Tauran, we now have a highly nuanced articulation of the Holy See's interpretation of the conflict and an application of Just War criteria to it. This interview was translated by Sally VanderHoof and Roberto Severino, Georgetown University, revised by the editor, and approved by Archbishop Tauran.

rial expansion for the benefit of their own ethnic group. War in Bosnia and Herzegovina was practically fought between three armies, and although some of the armies were regarded as very rudimentary, it still caused the exodus of many refugees. The conflict, however, remained circumscribed within the region.

In the present Kosovo crisis, we are witnessing a conflict between the Albanian majority and a Serbian minority that was, nevertheless, determined to consolidate its power with the adoption of discriminatory measures against the Albanian population. It is a well-known fact that the Serb minority in Kosovo is backed by the military and paramilitary forces of Belgrade. As far as the war is concerned, one can readily note that military confrontations have become a daily reality after the formation, two years ago, of the KLA (Kosovo Liberation Army). Finally, unlike what happened in Bosnia and Herzegovina, the conflict in Kosovo has immediately spread over the whole region with the problem of refugees pouring into Albania, Macedonia, and even into Italy.

No to Ethnic Territories

Can the solution reached with the Dayton Accord (See Regno-attualità, 6, 1996, 141) and the partitioning of Bosnia be considered a stable peace and a feasible model for the solution of the Kosovo conflict?

We must remember that the 1995 Dayton Accord was the result of a compromise that enabled an end to military confrontation and ethnic cleansing. On the other hand, we cannot deny that these agreements also sanctioned in large measure the establishment of ethnic enclaves and the territorial conquests that were at the very root of the conflict. And this is exactly the paradoxical aspect of the Dayton Accord.

We should also add that this Accord has not yet allowed the return of the refugees, and this despite the presence of the 30,000 SFOR men, whose mission is to prevent the recurrence of hostilities between the opposing factions; to ensure the normalization of the activities in Bosnia and Herzegovina; and to establish a stable military situation.

Considering the particular nature of the Kosovo crisis that I mentioned earlier, certainly we cannot think of reissuing a kind of carbon copy of the Dayton Accord, also because the KLA's presence in the region is a specific element to be taken into account. The presence of a security force that is being readied for Kosovo, on the model of the SFOR, will be a much more complicated affair: it will have to be larger, made up of soldiers whose nationalities can be acceptable to the populations directly at risk as well as to the federal government [of Yugoslavia], and it will have to protect not only the Albanian people but also the Serb population living in Kosovo. We can thus expect that the working out of the plan will be very complicated and not without risks.

The interventions of the Holy See have been persistent and at times critical vis-à-vis all participants in the conflict. Can you elaborate on this statement?

The Holy See did not condemn per se NATO's operations [*non ha condannato in se l'operazione della NATO*], which began on March 24, because it shared the opinion that such an initiative could be interpreted as an intervention for a humanitarian purpose [*un interveto a scopo umanitario*] having the goal of stopping the intolerable violation of the most basic human rights [*al fine di mettere termine alle insopportabili violazioni dei deritti umani piu elementari*] endured by the Kosovo population once all possibilities of a diplomatic solution were exhausted. But, yes, the Holy See has had some perplexities about the means chosen [*ha nutrito perplessita sui mezzi scelti*] to stop the violation of human rights that has been perpetrated in Kosovo. Just like many other observers, the Holy See has asked: Is it possible to protect a threatened population from an altitude of 5,000 meters? Does protecting the Kosovars' legitimate aspirations justify the destruction of the whole of Serbia?[1] Can the U.N. be kept out of the peace process?

Already on March 26, the Cardinal Secretary of State presented to the ambassadors of the member nations of NATO and the permanent member nations of the Security Council of the U.N. a proposal that later, and in large part, was included in the peace plan recently presented to the Belgrade government:[2]

- an immediate stop to the operations led by the army and the Serbian police against the people of Kosovo;
- the cessation of NATO's intervention to allow a return to the negotiating ta-

---

1. In numerous statements North American Bishop Joseph A. Fiorenza of Galveston-Houston, who is President of the National Conference of Catholic Bishops and the United States Catholic Conference, raised "serious questions about the means chosen to confront aggression." More specifically, he stated, "Concerns that strategic bombing risked violating relevant moral norms of discrimination [noncombatant immunity], proportionality and likelihood of success." See his statements on March 24, March 31, May 7, June 22, as well as the April 1 reprinted excerpt of a 1994 USCC text entitled *The Harvest of Justice Is Sown in Peace* (written to commemorate the tenth anniversary of the Bishops' landmark pastoral letter on nuclear war entitled *The Challenge of Peace: God's Promise and Our Response*). *The Harvest of Justice* sought to shape public discourse about how the just-war tradition (especially in light of the Gulf War) should be seen as a system of effective moral constraints on the uses of force; more particularly, this text called for further reflection on the ethical restraints pertinent to the use of air forces. These documents are available on the NCCB website: www.nccbuscc.org. What is officially known in the summer of 2000 as the United States Conference of Catholic Bishops (USCCB), is the organization which combines the offices of two former organizations (NCCB and USCC). The National Conference of Catholic Bishops (NCCB) handled issues within the life and discipline of the episcopal conference of the United States. The United States Catholic Conference (USCC) handled all issues external to the episcopal conference in relation to society. [Ed.]

2. A reference to the agreement reached by NATO and Russia on June 3, 1999. [Ed.]

ble, and with the goal of guaranteeing the autonomy of the peoples in Kosovo with respect to history and law;[3]

- sending immediate humanitarian aid to the region;
- the convening of a Peace Conference that would include neighboring countries;
- the involvement of the United Nations and of other specialized agencies in the peace process;
- the recourse, in the peace process, to a political role for the Organization for Security and Cooperation in Europe.[4]

Returning to the Rationale for the U.N.

In the position taken by the Holy See and the comments expressed by the Orthodox hierarchy in Belgrade, Bucharest, and Moscow, one can notice certain similarities and parallels.

Yes, I think so, because the first duty of a Christian conscience confronted with such a tragedy is to go toward the brother who has been victimized; therefore, it is normal that all Christians are united in the duty of "humanitarian intervention," which is none other than the contemporary application of the Good Samaritan parable [*l'attualizzazione della parabola del buon samaritano*]. However, this solidarity must not make us forget that the only lasting solution to the war is a peace based on justice [*la pace fondata sulla giustizia*], which, in this concrete case, means restoring to the Kosovars their rights, the first of which is the right to return to their land.

Moreover, the religious leaders of the communities of believers present in Serbia could not but be in agreement in emphasizing[5] the primacy that must be given to a dialogue that takes into account history and law [*della storia e del*

3. The important phrase "with respect to history and law" (*nel ripetto della storia e del diritto*) occurs three times in this interview and several times in statements by the Holy See. See the final footnote below. [Ed.]

4. Although the specific details of Vatican Secretary of State Cardinal Angelo Sodano's proposal to which this phrase refers are unknown to us, both the context and the Italian text indicate that the "Organization" to which this phrase refers is the Organization for Security and Cooperation in Europe (OSCE) rather than the U.N. (as in the previous phrase), the initiative for a common European security, the Organization for Economic Cooperation and Development (OECD), or some branch of NATO. The OSCE was founded in 1995, has headquarters in Vienna, and includes 54 members (since Yugoslavia was suspended), as well as seven non-European "partners for cooperation." [Ed.]

5. To avoid misinterpreting the Italian phrase *non potevano non essere d'accordo nel sottolineare* as a putative description of a factual consensus (i.e., "the religious leaders . . . in fact, could not agree more in emphasizing . . ."), the translation emphasizes how the actual meaning is a more nuanced normative claim (i.e., "the religious leaders . . . could not be otherwise than in agreement . . ." or "the religious leaders could not disagree in emphasizing . . ."). [Ed.]

diritto][6] as the only means of creating the conditions for a just and lasting peace that would permit the return of the refugees, shorten the suffering of all those who live in the Federal Republic of Yugoslavia, and provide the basis for a new peaceful coexistence of all the peoples in the [Yugoslavian] Federation. This was the thrust of the mission entrusted to me by the Holy Father last April 1, when I went to Belgrade to meet with the leaders of the Federation and Patriarch Pavle.

One specific aspect of the present conflict is the absence of the U.N. and NATO's total responsibility. What is your opinion of NATO's transformation from a defensive alliance to an interventionist alliance?

Certainly we have recently witnessed an erosion of the U.N.'s mission. The Dayton Accord, for example, which we were just discussing, took place under the aegis of the United States. The same was true of the Wye Plantation Agreements for the Middle East (see *Regno-attualità*, 20, 1998, 661), and the same can be said regarding the recent bombing of Iraq. At stake is the credibility of the U.N., the only supranational institution, as it were, that remains for everybody a firm point of reference for the prevention and solution of conflicts. That is the reason why the Holy See, from the very beginning of the present crisis in the Federal Republic of Yugoslavia, has always requested the return of the U.N. to the scene. The meeting of the Pope with Secretary-General Kofi Annan last June 3 was, in this respect, very eloquent. We should return, without delay, to a rigorous respect for the rules agreed upon, which are, after all, the result of the tragic experience of World War II.

In regard to the transformation of NATO into an interventionist alliance, as you have pointed out, one perceives in such a change the predicament in which today's Europe has found itself, facing a situation that puts its [Europe's] own stability and credibility at stake. Today's Europe will still have to learn how to better anticipate and more effectively deal with the crises that take place in its own territory, and to better adapt its own institutions.

Exactly how do you see the time period before us in the aftermath of the agreement reached by NATO and Russia on Thursday, June 3?

I see it as particularly complex because there remain ambiguities and problems. One of these is the fate of the refugees. They will have to be convinced to return by being guaranteed an international military presence and credible peacekeeping forces that can foster mutual trust between Kosovars and Serbs. After the atrocities that have been committed, one cannot underestimate the desire for vengeance nor the dream that many refugees have for a greater Albania that forever would shield

6. The important phrase "with respect to history and law" (*nel ripetto della storia e del diritto*) occurs three times in this interview and several times in recent statements by the Holy See. See the final footnote below. [Ed.]

them from Serbia. Moreover, we are seeing in these days how difficult it may be to ensure that all the parties will respect what was agreed upon in the NATO-Russian peace settlement concerning Kosovo this past June 3.

The KLA factor is also an element that will be weighty in the peacemaking process in the region. In addition, one should also prevent, on the one hand, a destabilizing withdrawal of the Serbs [from Kosovo] and, on the other hand, an anarchical return of the refugees. There are, moreover, some who would like to make financial aid for the reconstruction of Serbia dependent on the exit of Slobodan Milosevic from the political scene.

These are some of the many questions that come to mind and give a glimpse of the complexity that needs to be dealt with in the peace process. The great challenge now is that peace be the victor. And as the Holy Father has repeated so many times, such a victory can only rest upon respect for history and law by and for all the people concerned.[7]

7. The important phrase "with respect to history and law" *(nel ripetto della storia e del diritto)* entails four kinds of issues: grammatical, methodological, substantive, and procedural. (1) *Grammatical:* In Italian usage, *diritto* in the singular means "law"; *diritti* in the plural means "rights" (e.g., as in the second paragraph of the translation: ". . . all the rights and duties . . ."). (2) *Methodological:* Used in recent statements about Kosovo and Yugoslavia (e.g., Archbishop Tauran's April 1, 1999, Mission to Belgrade), the phrase "with respect to history and law" is meant to convey that history, law, and human rights (in that order) must be balanced together. In methodological terms, all are to be given (equal?) consideration in interpreting and justifying claims (e.g., with regard to Kosovo's self-determination). (3) *Substantive:* In other words, appeals to law (e.g., majority consensus, international law) and human rights (e.g., minority rights) as the basis for political arrangements must also take history into account. How these elements must be balanced and what criteria exist for those circumstances in which historical claims may be said to trump the claims of law and human rights (and vice versa) are not stated; however, the interview of June 9, 1999, concurs with the notion of Kosovo's "autonomy" rather than independence. The implications for the situation in Kosovo are obvious. With a majority of ethnic Albanian Kosovars, who live in a land that is legally, politically, and historically tied to Yugoslavia, the adjudication of these conflicting claims is, on this interpretation, not to be made on the basis of simple appeals to majority rule, international law, human rights, or demographic realities that are the result of forced deportations, even though Archbishop Tauran recognizes that many refugees have a "dream . . . for a greater Albania that forever would shield them from Serbia." Indeed, he admits that one of the "paradoxes" of the Dayton Accords is that they seem to ratify ethnic enclaves and territorial conquests made on the basis of force. On the other side, the fact that there are historical ties is not in itself decisive, especially if law and human rights are not also (equal?) factors. Although deliberately ambiguous language can serve many diplomatic purposes, reductionistic explanations are insufficient. This delicate balancing act — or juggling of the terms "history," "law," and "rights" — is not merely an effort to protect the rights of minority Serbs in Kosovo, or some indication of a strategic concession based on the Holy See's well-known efforts to achieve better relations with the Orthodox Churches generally. Nor is it simply a predictably conservative diplomatic posture of *prima facie* opposition to border changes or just an act of Slavic solidarity from a Polish Pope — or only a default tactic of evenhandedness following a conflict. It represents an effort to show (a) how presumptively universal claims must take into account temporal realities; and (b) how a past heritage

need not constrain but should not be ignored by future possibilities which can accord with law and human rights. In addition, it represents (c) an aversion to coerced border changes; and (d) a resistance to the notion that current demographic realities caused by forced deportations (ethnic cleansing) should be the decisive basis for future political agreements. (4) *Procedural:* Notwithstanding the fact that individual American bishops have held a whole range of opinions about Kosovo and the Yugoslavian war, this specific language of an equilibrium among history, law, and human rights in separate public statements by the Vatican and NCCB is hardly coincidental or accidental. Such texts are always carefully constructed following widespread consultation. This can be seen, for example, in the 3/31/99 statement by Bishop Fiorenza, especially his call for "a political settlement that respects the wishes of the inhabitants of Kosovo, while also respecting history, international law, and minority rights." It is also contained in the 4/1/99 letter of eight U.S. Cardinals to Presidents Milosevic and Clinton urging negotiation, "to guarantee the populations of Kosovo a degree of autonomy which respects their legitimate aspirations, according to history and law." The most concise statement reflecting this balancing of history, law, and rights occurs in the June 22, 1999, USCC Policy Response to UN Resolution 1244 (ending the conflict): *With the Holy See, the USCC supports a negotiated political settlement that respects the wishes of the inhabitants of Kosovo, while also respecting* history, international law, and minority rights (emphasis added by editor). *Current USCC and Vatican policy opposes forcible changes in international borders, which would occur in the event of Kosovar independence without Yugoslav consent. The same objection would apply in the case of partition without the consent of both sides.*

Whether or not this USCC quote reflects the intentions of the phrase "history, law, and rights," the USCC statement contains two crucially unresolved ambiguities. The *form* of such consent is not addressed (i.e., *how* such consent should be achieved: by internal popular referendum, some internally enacted laws by elected officials, the decisions of multiparty coalitions, externally imposed international consensus with broad internal support, etc.). In addition, the *content* of such consent is unclear; that is to say, precisely *whose* consent is to be sought and how such consent is to be interpreted are not addressed. More specifically, there are two contending construals of majority consent at work in this statement (constituent and proportional). Presumably, when considered *separately* as coequal regions and constituencies, Kosovars would seek independence, whereas most of the rest of Yugoslavia (especially Serbia) would seek some form of affiliation if not unity (assimilation, autonomy, or perhaps even partition). However, when considered *together* as a single demographic entity (including Kosovo and the rest of Yugoslavia together), an absolute majority (proportionally) probably would favor one or another of the types of aforementioned unity. How will consensus be established among antagonists — by dual consent (between equal regions), absolute majority (within one entire demographic territory), or some kind of plurality? While the bicameral model of regional (constituent) and demographic (proportional) legislative representation already exists in Yugoslavia, with its respective Chamber of Republics and Chamber of Citizens, what is currently being proposed is "autonomy" for Kosovo within Yugoslavia. Of course, these are some of the very issues being worked out. In contrast to these claims about how "history, law, and rights" should be a part of any final settlement, the Pope made many statements prior to and during the war that reflected a series of four common elements: (1) solidarity with the victims of war (especially those in Kosovo but also victims of bombing throughout Yugoslavia); (2) various proposed initiatives (e.g., a peace corridor for humanitarian purposes, a ceasefire between commemorations of Easter in the West and East, April 4-11); (3) repeated calls for dialogue; and (4) cautions against war. See, e.g., Pope John Paul II's Easter *Urbi et Orbi* message, April 4, 1999, available on the Vatican website (www.vatican.va). For American episcopal statements about Kosovo/Yugoslavia, see the website of the National Conference of Catholic Bishops (www. nccbuscc.org). [Ed.]

The Strength of an Alliance

GENERAL WESLEY K. CLARK
Supreme Allied Commander, Europe

The Kosovo air campaign is over. With an international security presence (KFOR) in place to protect Serb and Albanian Kosovars alike, Kosovo begins the recovery process — though a peace agreement has yet to be reached. The air campaign creates a new legacy that will extend beyond the mountainous borders of Kosovo. It validates NATO's strength as an alliance and attests to its enduring properties, which will persist long after the limited vision of dictatorships. Also in its wake follow more questions and more controversy as the campaign's successes and its lessons are examined and reexamined. Its departure from doctrinal views of air power and the use of overwhelming force continues to stimulate spirited debate. Yet the most subtle and difficult lesson of the air campaign is that it always had a political rather than a military center of gravity. It was the cohesion of NATO that finally pressured President Slobodan Milosevic into accepting the alliance's conditions.

Allied Command Europe's mission was to halt, disrupt, and ultimately reverse a systematic campaign of ethnic cleansing. Almost from the onset we developed four measures of merit to assure that NATO's military actions would meet its political will. The first — avoidance of Allied losses — enabled the campaign to persist as long as it was needed. The second — impact on Serb forces in Kosovo — focused NATO's efforts on those who were committing the atrocities. The third — minimal collateral damage — required detailed risk analyses and use of precision munitions to avoid injury to innocent civilians. The last measure of merit was the maintenance of Alliance cohesion; no single target was more important than this.

The foundation of NATO is built on democracy, and each of its members has a voice and a vote in its decisions. Once a decision is made to employ force,

---

General Clark's essay, submitted on September 17, 1999, reflects his views concerning the success of the NATO intervention in Kosovo, and it engages issues raised by other contributors to this volume, such as the limits of air power and military objectives. General Clark's remarks followed NATO's assessment of the Allied intervention and preceded an evaluation by the Pentagon. Thus they represent a crucial contribution to that ongoing conversation.

NATO relies on national governments to fulfill their obligations and to support the Alliance's effort. Maintaining NATO's cohesion meant understanding and working through each nation's political processes to deploy and employ military forces. Governments had varying needs for consultation and influence; sensitivity to these needs was essential for maintaining their publics' support. For example, the political oversight of the more sensitive targets ensured that governments would support these decisions and rally public opinion.

Cohesion also required understanding European sensitivities in the Balkans. Many NATO countries had historic ties with Serbia and were reluctant to join a bombing campaign. Neighboring states feared retaliation by Milosevic. However, as the buildup of Serb forces became clear and Milosevic's designs became more obvious, the resolution of NATO hardened. Initially, NATO members agreed to a bombing campaign of a short duration, two or three nights, drawing on a select list of fifty-one targets. Some thought that Milosevic was merely looking for a way to save face and would negotiate a peaceful alternative; but that did not materialize. Instead, fuller media reporting on the scope of Milosevic's atrocities against his own people fueled public resolve as well as NATO's. As the NATO consensus grew, the campaign intensified and escalated. Although criticized as an incremental application of force, it was precisely this pattern of steadily intensifying NATO bombing that brought irresistible pressure to bear on Milosevic.

With his attachment to nineteenth-century Serb nationalism, Milosevic believed Serb interests in Kosovo would prevail over the interests of countries like Germany, Britain, the United Kingdom, and even the United States, who were farther away and had fewer connections. Not only did he believe his manipulations would outlast the Alliance's willingness to use force, but he also thought that the Alliance would fracture. After all, he had been successful on so many other occasions in resisting international pressures.

This is where Milosevic made his most serious miscalculation. Although Kosovo was not "vital" to most of the European countries in terms of conventional "Realpolitik," the resolution of the Kosovo problem was vital to Europe and the U.S. The international community determined that it had an obligation to intervene to stop Milosevic's policies of ethnic cleansing and repression and that NATO's success was also vital. We recognized that Milosevic had systematically stymied the efforts of every individual nation in Europe and every international agency. He had humiliated the United Nations in Bosnia, and he had driven the Organization for Security and Cooperation in Europe (OSCE) out of Kosovo. Only NATO stood in front of Milosevic and his designs. It had become the institution of last resort.

So NATO's cohesion strengthened and NATO's bombing continued. It received support from partner nations, such as Albania, Bulgaria, the former Yugoslavian Republic of Macedonia, Romania, and Slovenia, who granted NATO use of their airspace and allowed bases within their borders. These nations sought and won their publics' support to join NATO's efforts. This support from partner nations added to NATO's strength and further unsettled Milosevic. And then the withdrawal of Russia's support closed off the one last hope that he may have had. The growing isolation of the Federal Republic of Yugoslavia and Milosevic's loss of every option for ending the air campaign on his terms at last convinced him to agree to NATO's conditions.

Maintaining the cohesion of the Alliance was a continuous process. There were some who argued for a halt or a pause to the campaign at its various stages, while others sought a tougher, more punishing effort. Various options were proposed, considered, adapted, or discarded. But the process itself worked, and it harnessed the power of nineteen nations to end Milosevic's rampage of ethnic cleansing. The Serbs are out, NATO is in, and most of the refugees are back.

I continue to be optimistic about NATO's future and its resolve to be significant. It is the organization that can provide the foundation for security in the Euro-Atlantic region and promote that security beyond its members' borders. In working with its partners, including Russia, NATO is making an essential contribution to the creation of an even broader security environment for the Euro-Atlantic region.

The Strength of an Argument:
A Response to General Clark's Essay

WILLIAM JOSEPH BUCKLEY

General Clark makes a number of very important claims. How persuasive are they? The stakes are high: what does a leader of the world's most powerful military alliance understand and argue about the most significant military engagement in Europe since the end of World War II? I submitted questions and comments to him and his staff for further clarification, and I received extraordinarily generous assistance in answer to many of my inquiries.[1] This separate essay surveys those clarifications. It aims to (1) situate General Clark's claims in a historical context, and (2) compare and analyze Clark's essay in light of public claims he has made elsewhere. I alone am responsible for its contents.[2]

I. Historical Context

Contending evaluations of the objectives, aims, methods, and achievements of the NATO intervention exist among various parties: NATO itself, participating governments (including a U.S. Pentagon Report), Yugoslavia, NGO's, etc.[3] None of

---

1. I was also directed to extensive declassified documentation on the NATO website. See www.NATO.int for daily briefings, but especially those of March 25, April 1, and September 16, as well as others given by General Clark.

2. I would like to thank Kate McCann, William Lawbaugh, and Mary Elizabeth Kaslick for their editorial suggestions.

3. The title of the NATO assessment is the *Allied Force Munitions Effectiveness Assessment*, or "AF-MEA" report, which addressed both fixed and mobile targets. An initial survey of the findings from a review of attacks on mobile targets was made by General Clark under the auspices of the U.S. European Command on September 16, 1999, entitled "Press Conference on the Kosovo Strike Assessment," available on-line at http://www.nato.int/kosovo/press/p990916a.htm. On October 14, 1999, Secretary of Defense William S. Cohen and Chairman of the Joint Chiefs of Staff General Henry H. Shelton both gave an "in-progress update" on the Pentagon assessment before the Senate Armed Services Committee, entitled "Joint Statement on the Kosovo After Action Review," available on-line at http://www.defenselink.mil/news/Oct1999/b10141999_bt478-99.html. This latter

256

these evaluations is neutral; many interpret "data" in contradictory ways. As illustrated by the historiography of the American Civil War, evaluations of conflict occur for different audiences and evolve over time.[4] The rhetorical (or audience-specific) dimensions of evaluations of the Kosovo intervention are apparent in their language and timing.[5] For example, the prompt release of the NATO study in September was arguably an effort to make public "its version" of events prior to October's initial discussion of a Pentagon study.[6] In answer to (mainly) European media criticisms of the effectiveness of the air campaign, General Clark presented an extensive "Press Conference on the Kosovo Strike Assessment" in Brussels on September 16. His evocation of "Alliance cohesion" as crucial also conforms to a pivotal dimension of the New Strategic Concept of NATO, which, among other goals, seeks to avoid the renationalization of defense policies.[7] In short, Clark's essay is part of an ongoing and multilateral debate within many military and foreign policy circles about the NATO intervention. Without negating their value, and despite claims about the "objectivity" of such assessments, the elusiveness of discovering precisely why Milosevic ended the conflict makes their final adjudication an ever-receding goal. In fact, emerging assessments of the Kosovo intervention arguably have less to do with what actually happened than what key parties see as relevant to future cooperation in the region. Historical revisionism serves the interests of ongoing crisis management.

---

report claims to incorporate findings of the earlier one, although the differences are illuminating (discussed below). Given the influence of the Senate Committee on Military Spending, this report surveys the usefulness and problems of various weapons systems.

4. One must distinguish claims about how and why a conflict ended from what is said to have caused it. Nonetheless, as a case study of causal judgments in history, historian William Dray offers a fascinating overview of some of the "main lines of development in the causal historiography of the American Civil War" in *Philosophy of History* (Englewood Cliffs, NJ: Prentice-Hall, 1964), pp. 47-58.

5. What NATO and the American Administration refer to as a case of humanitarian intervention, Yugoslavian authorities call "NATO aggression."

6. Although authors of the Pentagon report are known to have disagreed with one another and General Clark about the intervention, it would be reductionist to assume that such versions are sheer propaganda or merely reflect the career interests of their proponents; each argues its case on the basis of some evidence. Most evaluations are committee documents that aim to reconcile differences.

7. For NATO's New Strategic concept, see www.NATO.int: *Talking Points — 11th NATO Review of Future Tasks of the Alliance* (Ebenhausen, 6-8 March 1998) at http://www.nato.int/docu/speech/1998/s980306a.htm; *NATO Handbook: The Alliance's Strategic Concept, Part I: The Transformation of the Alliance* at http://www.nato.int/docu/handbook/hb10300e.htm.

II. Analysis and Comparisons

Published interviews and public presentations by General Clark provide valuable additional resources for understanding his claims.[8] Questions *(in italics)* and comments were mine to General Clark and his staff; clarifications (**in bold print**) are the editor's summary and interpretation of answers received; citations from the essay are in ***bold and italicized.***

1. *What is the principal military discussion this intervention has provoked?* ***[T]he campaign's . . . departure from doctrinal views of air power and the use of overwhelming force continues to stimulate spirited debate.*** The use of incremental rather than overwhelming force continues to be widely debated (Miller, Cook).

2. *What is the thesis of your essay?* ***[T]he most subtle and difficult lesson of the air campaign is that it always had a political rather than a military center of gravity. It was the cohesion of the Alliance that finally pressured President Slobodan Milosevic into accepting NATO's conditions.*** Using orientational and substantive metaphors to describe this alliance cohesion, Clark claims NATO unity caused the outcome of the conflict.[9] The maintenance of such unity was clearly an ongoing process with a complicated interaction between political and military considerations. Corollary to this thesis: ***As NATO consensus grew, the campaign intensified and escalated. Although criticized as an incremental application of force, it was precisely this pattern of steadily intensifying NATO bombing that brought irresistible pressure to bear on Milosevic.*** In the language of just-war theory, this refers to the criterion of proportionality (defended values outweighed by damages and foreseen dangers; see the Miller essay in this volume).

Clark's text also makes claims about what Milosevic *believed,* his *miscalculation,* what *unsettled* him, and how ***the growing isolation of the Federal Republic of Yugoslavia and Milosevic's <u>loss of every option</u> for ending the air campaign on his terms at last <u>convinced</u> Milosevic to agree to NATO's conditions*** (editor's emphasis). To qualify assertions about Milosevic's past motives, Clark uses the language of "option reduction," which assumes a familiarity with and ability to influence Milosevic's future intentions. How persuasive are these assertions? Let us first answer other questions.

3. *Did Milosevic accept or agree to NATO conditions?* **Yes.** Clark's affirmation is actually an oversimplification. No one seriously argues that Yugoslavia "won,"

---

8. For example, see his August 31, 1999, presentation to the American Enterprise Institute (Washington, DC) as part of their New Atlantic Initiative (for the full text, see www.aei.org/nai/naiclark.htm). Additional sources are cited below.

9. For Clark's metaphors for the Alliance, see his descriptions of it as a "political center of gravity," "target," "ongoing process," that which "pressured" Milosevic, Milosevic's misplaced belief that it would "fracture," a cohesion "strengthened and supported" by NATO bombing and partner nations, etc. For the importance of orientational and substantive metaphors in argument, see the works of Lakoff and Johnson.

but there are important differences reflecting vital postwar issues among the original NATO stipulations stated at Rambouillet on February 23, 1999, as pretext for bombing and four subsequent tentative agreements: for example, NATO forces are in Kosovo under a U.N. mandate, not a Belgrade-NATO agreement; the sovereignty of Yugoslavia with Kosovar autonomy is affirmed; language of a referendum on Kosovo self-determination proposed by Rambouillet is absent from the Military-Technical Agreement.[10]

4. *How effective was the air campaign?* **Effective enough. It achieved NATO's goals.**[11] *The Serbs are out, NATO is in, and most of the refugees are back.* However, initial military objectives were not achieved by airpower alone: ethnic cleansing was neither deterred, stopped, nor effectively interdicted, whether or not airpower or alliance cohesion caused its "reversal." Evidently there are empirical limits to the ability of airpower alone to prevent or stop the abuse of human rights.

5. *Why did Milosevic capitulate?* **Alliance cohesion.** This crucial question is not merely academic, if military forms of humanitarian interventions are to have any future. Clark's plausible answer is only one among many that have evolved to meet new management challenges as groups renegotiate social relations in the fluid situation of Yugoslavia. Consider other candidates: (1) airpower, alliance cohesion, the threat of a ground invasion, Russian cooperation (this from Cohen and Shelton, arguing for resources to fight two major wars simultaneously); (2) a failed attempted double-cross by Russians through an unsuccessfully engineered Belgrade-Moscow agreement for Kosovo's partition and independent Russian occupation of a section of Kosovo (Brzezinski); (3) the effectiveness of a KLA ground campaign that brought NATO in for support (KLA and Kosovar leader Thaqi); (4) a threatened ground invasion that would have enforced onerous aspects of Rambouillet, such as the deployment of foreign troops in Yugoslavia who would have arrested Milosevic (Ahtisaari, Daalder, senior Yugoslavian officials); (5) one or more brain strokes (suffered by Milosevic) and/or emotional breakdowns (by his wife) following his indictment (senior Yugoslavian officials, Serbian opposition parties vying for succession). The list could go on to include Milosevic's concerns about domestic repercussions, economic sanctions, and so forth.

10. Compare Rambouillet with the principles of the G8 talks accepted by Belgrade on May 31, the language and terms accepted by Belgrade on June 3, the Military-Technical Agreement signed on June 9, and U.N. Security Council Resolution 1244 on June 10. The U.N. resolution uses the language of autonomy within Yugoslavia and self-governing institutions; the language of a referendum on self-determination in Kosovo proposed by Rambouillet on 2/23/99 is not present in the Military-Technical Agreement. Many of the agreements are available on-line at www.usip.org via "links" in the Peace Agreement Digital Collection.

11. Such a claim requires a strong causal connection, i.e., that tactical and strategic military actions motivated Milosevic to conclude the conflict when and how he did. See General Clark's September 16, 1999, presentation and answers to questions. Arguments continue over *how much* significance it had, not whether it had *any* role.

Elsewhere, Clark and others acknowledge that many variables influenced what most regard as Milosevic's surprisingly abrupt decision to end the conflict.[12] Critics contend that neither tactical military battlefield losses in Kosovo (however significant) nor strategic damage in the rest of Yugoslavia were likely very important considerations for Milosevic (Kissinger, Brzezinski). General Clark himself has publicly expressed skepticism about knowing Milosevic's reasons for ending the conflict, which qualifies if not undermines his assertion that alliance cohesion was crucial and bedevils efforts to rank variables as significant.[13]

Why do General Clark's confident assertions about alliance cohesion now eschew the very caution he publicly recommends to others? As noted, well-documented disputes over intervention strategy and tactics, as well as future interests, are at stake in asserting the priority of factors.[14] Who can reasonably deny

---

12. In answer to a question during his September 16 Press Conference, General Clark stated, "But in essence what we've said is that there were many, many factors [including damage inflicted on ground mobile targets] that ultimately resulted in President Milosevic's decision to accept NATO conditions. He'd exhausted all his options. But what was decisive was the effort of the air campaign. NATO's resolve did not falter. The air campaign continued. It became more and more intense and inflicted more and more damage on those assets, both strategic and tactical, that he valued most." At the same press conference, General Clark also pointed to the threat of a ground invasion as an important factor. The Cohen-Shelton "Joint Statement on the Kosovo After Action Review" of October 14 mentions the air campaign first (prior to alliance solidarity) but concedes, "Because many pressures were brought to bear, we can never be certain about what caused Milosevic to accept NATO conditions. . . ." Following this reversal of Clark's order, other factors are mentioned: Alliance-Russian diplomacy, the buildup of ground forces, "the persistent military efforts of the Kosovar Albanians," and other economic and political means (sanctions, war crimes indictment, etc.). By contrast, General Clark only mentioned "withdrawal of Russian support" as a factor closing off Milosevic's options.

13. For example, on June 26, General Clark responded to interviewer Michael Ignatieff's question about why Milosevic decided to withdraw by saying: "You'll have to ask Milosevic, and he'll never tell you." For Clark's later similar remarks about Milosevic, see the *Washington Post* series on 9/17/99, 9/18/99, and 9/19/99; Michael Ignatieff's essay in *The New Yorker*, "The Virtual Commander" (August 2, 1999): 30-36, as well as General Clark's observations following his September address to the American Enterprise Institute, which suggest that the threat of a ground invasion was a crucial factor. General Clark (and many others) make similar claims about Milosevic's elusiveness in Richard Holbrooke's book *To End a War* (New York: Random House, 1998).

14. During the conflict, members of the National Security Administration eventually favored a ground invasion, whereas many at the Pentagon (including Secretary of Defense Cohen) did not (see the interviews described in the *Washington Post* on September 19, 1999: A1, A30; *New York Times*, November 7, 1999: 1, 4). By October 14, Cohen and Shelton acknowledged the key role the threat of a ground invasion might have played. Why? Two reasons are plausible: assertions about its importance (1) correlate with requests for increased military funding so as to support a doctrinal capability to fight "two major wars" (as a deterrent to aggression); (2) help undergird a kind of rationale for the ongoing commitment of troops needed for the protectorate of Kosovo. If public support for a ground invasion was seen as too fragile earlier, the "threat of a ground inva-

that alliance cohesion was an *important* factor in Milosevic's reasoning? Clark's claim about the *decisiveness* of the alliance cohesion he skillfully managed isn't shown to be false — just premature. The lesson: assertions about why the conflict ended reflect prewar and postwar interests that deserve scrutiny themselves. In summary, the linchpin of Clark's thesis relies on a highly qualified — if not rebuttable — assumption about Milosevic's reasons for ending the conflict. We just don't know (yet).

6. *How did you assess the accomplishment of NATO's mission? What political considerations played a role? Allied Command Europe's mission was to halt, disrupt, and ultimately reverse a systematic campaign of ethnic cleansing.*[15] *Almost from the onset we developed four measures of merit to assure NATO's military actions met its political will. The first — avoidance of Allied losses — enabled the campaign to persist as long as it was needed. The second — impact on Serb forces in Kosovo — focused NATO's efforts on those who were committing the atrocities. The third — minimal collateral damage — required detailed risk analyses and use of precision munitions to avoid injury to innocent civilians.*[16] *The last measure was maintenance of alliance cohesion; no single target was more important than this.*

The content of these military "measures of merit" reflect highly controversial political and moral commitments (see the commentary on Halperin's essay in this volume). Together they address some of the traditional just-war criteria about *how* a war must be fought to be morally justifiable (*jus in bello* criteria), but they also bespeak what political leaders sensed as the vulnerability of popular support for (or passivity about) the campaign. The first and second refer to just-war claims about "proportionality"; the third speaks to "discrimination" or noncombatant immunity. The "statement of mission," as well as the fourth measure of merit, relates to "right intention." Among the controversies are that combatant risk aversion appears to be a higher priority than noncombatant immunity (arguably because alliance cohesion demanded no or few alliance military

---

sion" now can be retrieved as a plausible reason to persuade a public to support troops in the protectorate (e.g., "As we now know . . . only this threat will inhibit Serb aggression . . .").

15. I do not know how to reconcile the "halt, disrupt, and reverse" of this mission statement with the October 14, 1999, claim of the "Joint Statement on the Kosovo After Action Review": "Diplomacy and deterrence having failed, we knew that the use of military force could not stop Milosevic's attack on Kosovar civilians, which had been planned in advance and was in the process of being carried out. The specific military objectives we set were to attack his ability to wage combat operations in the future against either Kosovo or Serbia's neighbors." Some of the difference is between foresight and hindsight; but the latter statement sounds like a rationalization for the air campaign's limited ability to prevent or stop what was happening on the ground, as well as its extensive efforts to damage Serbian assets. This provokes serious questions about the ability of airpower alone to achieve humanitarian objectives.

16. For example, the NATO press conference of 4/13/99 listed three elements of collateral damage: attack only militarily significant targets; extraordinary measures to minimize collateral damage; highest percentage of precision weapon employment in history.

casualties).[17] However, my consultations with NATO revealed that the given order of these measures of merit does *not* reflect a hierarchy or rank. I was told:

a. There is no hierarchy in the measures of merit. Attempting to evaluate them by place order (sic) is incorrect. By the way, within Army training doctrine, mission essential tasks are not listed in order of importance either. Each is essential to successful completion of the mission. This was not a risk-free environment for pilots; there was damage to some planes.

b. The political nature of NATO did influence military planning; however, it was not only risk reduction of combat casualties that was an important factor. Aggressive protection of NATO assets was required to sustain public support because of the extremely high economic costs of those assets (both human and material). For example, unlike World War II, during which some 10 percent of invaluable pilots and relatively inexpensive aircraft were lost, resource usage in the Kosovo conflict had to be maximized and heavy losses could not be tolerated because of the contemporary expense of investments in personnel and material.[18]

c. Risk reduction for noncombatants and protection of the innocent were put on a par with risk assessment for training scenarios for military personnel. The complicated political and military process of targeting decisions involved detailed assessment of collateral damage from various types of munitions, the weather, and so forth. In other words, the ceiling for noncombatant risks was never higher than that for those in military training. Although meant to convey what extraordinary care was employed in bombing decisions, this claim morally equates risks to noncombatants with those to professional military in training. Despite detailed accounting of missions, munitions used, and targets destroyed, nowhere is there even an estimate of the number of military or civilians killed or injured. Let us be clear: (1) no one argues that military (or civilian) casualties should deliberately be high; at issue is how an asymmetric air campaign routinely gave more weight to the protection of Allied military than to that of Yugoslavian civilians; (2) lower-altitude (higher pilot risk) bombing is morally compelling to the de-

17. The final sentence of the October 14 Cohen-Shelton "Joint Statement on the Kosovo After Action Review" states: "The paramount lesson learned from Operation Allied Force is that the well-being of our [military] people must remain our first priority." Brzezinski refers to technological racism, and Richard Falk has argued that one-sided capabilities to inflict such violence in zero-casualty warfare is a lot like torture.

18. These sentiments are echoed in the Cohen-Shelton claim that "rather than expend air sorties to attack these threats [Serbian integrated air defense capabilities], commanders chose to operate at altitudes beyond which most Serbian antiaircraft systems could be effectively employed." Their statement goes on to claim that even these Serbian systems were not state of the art, hence the need for future preparation.

gree it can be more accurate (more proportionate and discriminate); (3) a rebuttable presumption is that high-altitude "dumb bombing" can be neither as proportionate nor as discriminate as lower-altitude bombing or the use of precision munitions (without equating the two); (4) data about precision munitions are variable, but the mere intention to be discriminate does not suffice for adequate moral scrutiny (so-called "indirect civilian casualties"). These maxims remind us of some of the moral limits of an air campaign.

d.   Reports that "no Allied losses" were stipulated to General Clark by government officials are untrue and oversimplify the complicated interaction between political and military decisions in NATO, especially its political decision-making body called the North Atlantic Council. General Clark's mandate is to execute the collective political decisions of NATO, which he did by developing **"Strategic Axes" or guidance for subordinates that are reflected in the described "military measures of merit"** (e.g., **an air campaign, isolating Yugoslavia, humanitarian relief, monitoring the impact on Dayton Accords, strategic attacks in greater Yugoslavia — especially Serbia), and Kosovo tactical or ground operations** (see Halperin commentary).

Whether and to what extent some portion of the strategic campaign aimed to diminish popular Serbian support for the war or the regime were not addressed by NATO.[19] In summary, the military "measures of merit" are deliberately tied to political commitments — what Clark calls NATO's "political will" but also arguable moral assumptions

8. *What political oversight shaped military decisions? For example, the political oversight of the more sensitive targets ensured that governments would support these decisions and rally public opinion.* Although the target approval process was different from political decisions, the ways in which tactical and strategic judgments were influenced by political considerations has been detailed elsewhere.[20] In brief, decisions to bomb some targets were sometimes negotiated with Allies in a complex and time-consuming process that General Clark and his staff streamlined near the end of the war.[21] Despite Clark's repeated insistence on the importance of public support, not one of the nineteen NATO democracies submitted the

---

19. Whether or not American predominance in the air war shaped targeting decisions aimed at undermining the regime, subsequent Administration approval of overt and covert operations against it suggests a punitive approach to the post-conflict period.

20. See the *Washington Post* and Ignatieff essays noted above.

21. Some operations did not involve NATO assets or its chain of command. In fact, General Clark managed all operations that used sensitive American assets (Stealth technology, cruise missiles) through EUCOM, not NATO. As reported by Ignatieff, "Clark would sign off on targets and pass them on to the Joint Chiefs, in Washington, who would send the particularly sensitive targets to the White House for clearance."

intervention to any kind of legislative vote, even though many nations have some form of legislative oversight.

9. *What political considerations shaped the bombing campaign? Initially, NATO members agreed to a bombing campaign of a short duration, two or three nights, drawing on a select list of 51 targets.* Consultation with NATO has revealed that air campaign planning involved some sixteen to eighteen plans involving varying conditions, parameters, and measures for success. Changes in Allied strategy were regarded as a continuous evolution of flexible responses in which options were kept open and feasibilities were not eliminated. Clark favored an initially "heavy" campaign of "going downtown" to Belgrade on the very first night. Other European sources confirm reports from the media that a preliminary proposal for a major air campaign involving five major targets and cyberwarfare from day one was vetoed, first by the French, then subsequently by the Germans, Belgians, and Greeks. This may well be part of the background to Clark's claim that *many NATO countries had historic ties with Serbia and were reluctant to join a bombing campaign.*[22] NATO discovered that Yugoslavia was given the first ten days of targets in advance.

10. *Why was the NATO defensive alliance chosen to engage in an offensive operation against a non-NATO nation with whom some countries had signed previous peace accords regarding Yugoslavian civil wars (e.g. the Dayton Accords)? Why not other multinational organizations? Only NATO stood in front of Milosevic and his designs. It had become the institution of last resort.* Also noted in Clark's August 31, 1999, presentation to the American Enterprise Institute (AEI), the "institution of last resort" alludes to the *jus ad bellum* criteria of "Possibility for Success," "Last Resort," and "Competent Authority." In other words, General Clark is claiming that (1) resort to NATO came only after the failure of the efforts of other institutions (the U.N., the OSCE); (2) only NATO could effectively carry out those operations deemed just; (3) NATO was "competent," even though the U.N. had "authority."

12. *After the end of the Cold War, what is the future of NATO? I continue to be optimistic about NATO's future and its resolve to be significant. It is the organization that can provide the foundation for security in the Euro-Atlantic region and promote that security beyond its members' borders. In working with its Partners, including Russia, NATO is making an essential contribution to the creation of an even broader security environment for the Euro-Atlantic region.*

Echoing themes used in his August AEI presentation, General Clark's claims converge with various American foreign policies described as "aggressive multilateralism," "blending diplomacy and force," "coercive diplomacy," and "a humani-

---

22. According to Ignatieff, "After the war was over, President Chirac, of France, boasted to a French reporter that if there were bridges still standing in Belgrade it was because of him" (p. 34).

tarian foreign policy." However, Clark's understanding is guided by NATO's new strategic concept regarding justification for its "out-of-area" operations, in which the meaning of security is widened (e.g., economic issues) and the range of its authority to intervene beyond strict definitions of one's own border is asserted (i.e., beyond NATO's adjoining countries).[23] Here, just as in the discussion of the Administration's language of "humanitarian intervention," questions about criteria naturally arise and concerns about control emerge. For further comments about the Administration's language about this foreign policy, see my commentary on Morton Halperin's essay.

23. For further information, see the NATO website cited above and in the Appendix below.

Two Roads Diverged, and We Took the One Less Traveled: Just Recourse to War and the Kosovo Intervention

MARTIN L. COOK

From 24 October 1945, the day the [United Nations] Charter entered into effect, it has had competition. Alongside it, and prefigured in the Charter itself, there ran a parallel legislative stream of humanitarian and human rights rules and standards which States undertook at least to take note of and which, if words mean anything, they should in some last resort be required to observe.... Members of the UN insist that they retain full sovereign rights, and nominally indeed they do so, yet they stand committed at the same time to a variety of human rights observances which in principle entitle their neighbours to complain in case of neglect.[1]

The decision to intervene in Kosovo is fraught with ironies. The most ardent advocates of the decision are, virtually without exception, civilian leaders inexperienced in military realities and with a history of opposition to the Vietnam War. Whether one thinks of President Clinton himself, of Secretary of State Albright, or Strobe Talbot or Sandy Berger, the senior civilian leadership of the administration to a person fits that profile.

In contrast, the military leadership of the nation, while officially supportive at the highest levels, has in fact been lukewarm at best in its enthusiasm for this use of military force. One military expert after another has questioned the reliance on airpower alone as a strategy likely to succeed in Kosovo. Yet they show an equal lack of enthusiasm when the use of ground forces is suggested as an alternative. As I write, it appears that, contrary to much expert military opinion, the airpower-only strategy *may* have succeeded. At least it has caused the Serbian leadership to say they are willing to withdraw from Kosovo. But even if it turns out to be true and the agreement does not collapse as the details are negotiated, it would be premature and dangerous to conclude that this intervention marks a success. At the

---

1. Geoffrey Best, *War and Law since 1945* (Oxford: Clarendon Press, 1994), p. 79.

level of military strategy, in terms of clear thinking about policy issues regarding the use of military force, and in terms of the ethical issues involved in extended strategic bombing campaigns, we need to examine the Kosovo intervention closely before we can be sure what "lessons" we can learn from it.

I will argue that there is a deeper issue underlying the disagreements between the current group of civilian leaders and the military leadership, which point to profound and abiding questions about the purposes of the use of military force, the relationship of national militaries to sovereign states, and, indeed, the meaningfulness of the idea of international community itself. I will argue that it is precisely this disagreement that the opening quotation from Geoffrey Best's magisterial *War and Law since 1945* captures — between international order conceived on the paradigm of sovereign, independent states, and international order imagined as a defender of universal human rights and values.

The objections to the Kosovo intervention — both from the perspective of the United States and that of Serbia, Russia, China, and many other states — rest on a view of international order and the use of military force as old as the Peace of Westphalia (1648). On that model, sovereign states possess territorial integrity and political sovereignty. This understanding generates what Michael Walzer has called a "legalist paradigm" as the standard case for thinking about military intervention, and it rules out initiation of military conflict except in response to aggression.[2]

From the standard military perspective as well, military force exists to serve the interests of sovereign states. The decision to use military power should be made only after careful and critical reflection about whether vital, or at least very important, national interests require action, and in particular the use of the blunt and costly instrument of military power. To this way of framing the problem, the wishes, desires, and even important values of the "international community" do not connect with an appropriate use of sovereign state power unless an analysis of vital interests makes that connection clear. It is universally agreed that Kosovo is a province of a sovereign state, and it is the stated policy of the United States (and others) to oppose any bid for the independence of Kosovo. To this way of thinking, no matter how tyrannical and oppressive the sovereign state of Yugoslavia may be toward its province Kosovo, it is an internal, domestic matter for that state to deal with.

From the military standpoint of the United States, in particular, there should be an additional stage of analysis before we make the decision to commit military forces. The gradual and ultimately ineffectual escalation of military force in Vietnam caused a deep and soul-searching reconsideration of principles guiding the use of force on the part of the United States. The reconsideration

---

2. Michael Walzer, *Just and Unjust Wars: A Moral Argument with Historical Illustrations,* 2nd ed. (New York: Basic Books, 1992), pp. 58-63.

culminated in the "Powell-Weinberger" doctrine — a virtual "creed" of United States military thinking. The central tenets of the creed are well known and include the following: the military forces of the United States should not be committed unless there is a clearly defined national interest, achievable by use of military force and specifiable in terms of a desired end; the cause to which military forces are to be committed must be unquestionably vital to national political interest and must have the expectation of the continuing support of the American people; finally, the forces committed to the operation must possess overwhelming capability in comparison to their opposition. Only such overwhelming force guarantees that the United States can avoid the long and painful war of attrition that Vietnam became.

Clearly, the Kosovo intervention is extremely difficult, if not impossible, to justify if one approaches it from either of these traditional moral and political perspectives. From the angle of the Westphalian "legalist paradigm," it is unquestionably an intervention inside the territory of an internationally recognized sovereign state. As such, it falls far short of being a response to international aggression, the sole legitimate cause for the use of military force on the legalist paradigm model. The Westphalian need not reject entirely a concern for the massive human rights violations in Kosovo in order to continue to reject intervention. In Best's words above, other states "take note of" the violations, complain about them, cajole about them. But since the line between verbal interferences in Yugoslav internal affairs and military intervention is quite salient in international relations, such concerns do not add up to a *causa belli*, a cause for war. Similarly, the military strategist need not be callous or unmoved by the scenes of suffering in Kosovo, nor unwilling to join in the wish that "someone" would do "something" about it. Where the practical military strategist hesitates is in moving from those moral sensibilities to operational military reality. The questions here are focused and practical: given all the demands on a downsized force, is the interest in Kosovo "vital" enough to expend limited resources, to stretch still further the deployment of soldiers, sailors, and airmen, and to risk loss of American life? Is the desired end clearly defined and achievable? Are the military strategy and forces committed up to the standard of "overwhelming force" to assure success?

The Kosovo operation as presently conceived and executed fails to meet the tests of either the Westphalian legalist model of international law or the hardnosed practical standard of real-world military planning. In that light, it is not difficult to see why many non-NATO states fail to see the legal and moral justification of the operation, or why many leaders and members of the military deeply question the wisdom and prudence of the intervention. Further, it is vitally important to note, this judgment obtains even if it happens that the present appearance of Yugoslav cooperation in withdrawing forces from Kosovo works out. One judges strategic decision-making not by whether it merely happens to turn out as one wished but by the quality of the thinking that went into the decision to intervene in the first place. And in this case, whether one views the decision through the lens of the Westphalian international system or of the Powell-Weinberger doctrine of the proper application of military force, the decision to initiate hostilities over Kosovo was unjustified and unwise.

It is not, however, this older and better-established body of law to which advocates of the Kosovo intervention appeal. They are correctly aware that the Westphalian international system was itself a compromise between the perceived ideal and the politically possible. It arose in Europe in the aftermath of the Reformation and the wars of religion that raged there; it brought those conflicts to a close with the realization that no side would be able to impose its own, supposedly universal, values on all the others. In place of a universal "Christendom" of the older Europe, peace would only be possible if each state were free to choose its own form of Christianity, no matter how odious that might be to its neighbors. In other words, the principles of territorial integrity and political sovereignty, the lynchpins of the Westphalian system, were accepted only when all sides came to terms with the fact that their own preferred and "universal" values could not successfully be imposed on the others. In this sense, Westphalia was a reluctant compromise between universalizing principle and recalcitrant reality.

The reformulated world system in the years following World War II and the founding of the United Nations saw the birth of a new kind of universalism that, in principle at least, challenged the absolute state sovereignty of Westphalia. The Holocaust made graphically clear that the principle of state sovereignty must be limited to a degree, and that human beings must be able to assert individual rights — even in the face of their governments. Without, perhaps, fully thinking through the consequences of their words, governments reacted to the horrors of genocide by committing themselves (on paper anyway) to intervene in internal affairs of states when abuses of their citizens rise to the level of "universally unacceptable." This reaction began a process that has evolved a newer body of international law and moral thought (and with it spawned a proliferation of nongovernmental organizations concerned with them) that exists in imperfect harmony with the older system of state sovereignty. This newer system speaks of the universal humanitarian responsibility of the international community and of universal human rights. As Best writes, "The wartime rhetoric which rushed them into commitment to post-war protection of human rights was tacked on to their political theory, not integrated into it."[3]

But, of course, universal human rights law and thought have the purpose of "averting or restricting the uses of violence by governments toward their own subjects," "a field of conflict for which international law by definition brought no remedies."[4]

3. Best, *War and Law,* p. 68.
4. Best, *War and Law,* p. 69.

Unfortunately, the ringing language of humanitarian law left a glaring and unresolved contradiction with existing Westphalian sovereignty law: ". . . [T]he concept of [humanitarian] intervention would still imply violating sovereign authority without having identified a higher authority on which the supremacy of human rights rests."[5]

It is this declaration of moral and legal principle in the absence of a clear delineation of authority that lies at the root of the ambiguity of the Kosovo intervention's justification. The principles are clearly stated, but the authority and military means to implement them are unclear. The United Nations Security Council, while ostensibly the nearest thing to universally valid legal authority, is rarely likely to find the political unanimity to enforce the principles (and certainly could not do so in Kosovo). NATO, possessing the military means of enforcement and (just barely) the united political will to do it, lacks even the appearance of universal legal authority.

Post–World War II humanitarian law drives the Kosovo intervention and, in the minds of its advocates, justifies it legally and morally. Appealing to the morally compelling post-Holocaust proclamation "never again," the NATO allies attempt to make real their commitment that, at least in Europe itself, mass deportation and ethnically driven killing and persecution will not be permitted.

The use of NATO in service of this newer body of ostensibly universal law is a "road less taken" by major powers since World War II. Obviously, the fact that the intervention is NATO-authorized rather than U.N.-sponsored raises questions about the "universality" of its motives. While non-NATO powers may view this rationale with cynicism or with alarm, it is in the minds of its advocates an affirmation of the use of military power for "idealistic" reasons. But the alarm is also understandable in light of the precedent being set by this action and the license it appears to give for future interventions in the name of humanitarian concerns.

Although national interest arguments for the Kosovo intervention are offered, they fail to ring true, at least for the United States.[6]

The central motive is clearly humanitarian idealism that is prepared to pursue ideals apart from clear or narrowly conceived national interest. It is, to borrow a phrase, a "humanitarian war"[7] — a concept poorly developed in theory and rarely seen in practice. It is a war genuinely fought for principles of humanity. Unfortunately, "humanity . . . is not a category for which we have prepared political

5. Jarat Chopra and Thomas G. Weiss, "Sovereignty Is No Longer Sacrosanct: Codifying Humanitarian Intervention," *Ethics and International Affairs* 6 (1992): 111.

6. The situation is, perhaps, quite different from a European perspective. And clearly what the whole course of the Balkans conflict has painfully revealed is the lack of an indigenous European military and political capability to deal with European problems without direct U.S. participation and leadership.

7. The phrase is from Adam Roberts, "Humanitarian War: Military Intervention and Human Rights," *International Affairs* 69 (1993): 429-49.

concepts, despite the seeming internationalization of human rights and humanitarian discourse."[8]

The Kosovo intervention points clearly to the divergence in two fundamentally different streams of international law and moral thought. It is a tension pointedly illuminated in the following question:

Are human rights exclusively within the domestic jurisdiction of states or are they an international concern with community jurisdiction? . . . Which authority is superior, state jurisdiction over individuals within its boundaries, or international jurisdiction over inalienable human rights?[9]

Conclusions

I'll conclude by pointing to two areas where the Kosovo intervention raises important issues and questions for reflection and future precedent. One concerns the *jus ad bellum* justification for the intervention, and the other the *jus in bello* considerations raised by the extended strategic bombing campaign against Serbia. On the *ad bellum* side, it is important to note the serious misfit between moral ideals (which surely press for a defense of the innocent victims of ethnic cleansing) and the limits of the presently possible in terms of international law and military power. As I've indicated above, no person of goodwill can resist the "something should be done about this" reaction to scenes of ethnic cleansing and murder in Kosovo. But as I've also argued, the body of law that warrants intervention is recent, and it is not well integrated into the older system of state sovereignty.

If there is an "international community" that is serious about intervening in Kosovo-like situations in the future, this intervention makes painfully clear that there is simply no effective international authority to provide legitimacy to such interventions. Except in the rare situation where the permanent members of the Security Council concur, humanitarian war will be conducted unilaterally by single powers or by coalitions. Kosovo points clearly to the need to continue the work on structures of international political authority that can prevent, assess, or even authorize appropriate interventions. The situation is similar on the military side. Only rarely can one imagine circumstances in which the military power of sovereign states will be provided to fight a truly humanitarian war. As the "no ground war" announcements in Kosovo made very clear, leaders of states are loath and unlikely to risk significant lives of their nationals in the humanitarian cause — even if such costs would be required to be militarily effective. We need to begin to come to terms with the moral limits of an air war, just as we have rethought the World War II tactics

8. Amir Pasic and Thomas G. Weiss, "The Politics of Rescue: Yugoslavia's Wars and the Humanitarian Impulse," *Ethics and International Affairs* 11 (1997): 126.

9. Chopra and Weiss, "Sovereignty Is No Longer Sacrosanct," p. 109.

of area-bombing and the fire-bombing of cities. Escalation of the target list in the determination to win a war from the air can lead to civilian death and destruction on a massive scale. Such civilian losses can occur even if civilians are not directly bombed but if they are deprived of the means to live — clean water, heat, medical-care facilities, and food distribution. If we are going to fight humanitarian wars, surely they must not be won over the bodies of innocent civilians. If wars fought to protect innocent civilians are to be won by destroying the lives of other innocent civilians, the moral calculus is too unclear to for us to analyze.

We Are Neither Angels Nor Devils:
An Interview with Slobodan Milosevic
by United Press International CEO
Arnaud de Borchgrave

BELGRADE, April 30, 1999

Q: What do you hope to get out of this?

Milosevic: I find it hard to believe what is happening. America is a great country and Americans great people. But your leaders are not strategic thinkers. Short-term quick fixes, yes. They said, "Let's bomb Yugoslavia and then figure out what to do next." Some said that Milosevic would give up Kosovo after a few days of aggression from the air. To set out to destroy a country for a pretext no one can buy is simply unbelievable. I don't expect to get anything out of this because I did not start it. You may recall there were no refugees before March 24, when the NATO aggression started. But the Clinton administration did expect to get something out of this terrible decision. I understand you had two general goals. One dealing with Europe, the other with the Balkans. First is to prove U.S. leadership in Europe, and the second is to reestablish U.S. leadership in NATO in the post–Cold War era. Regretfully, we were targeted as a guinea pig to achieve those goals. Simply because of our weaknesses and because of the internal problems we faced. But, as you know, you will find in at least 100 countries around the world different ethnic separatist movements. If you decide to support separatist movements, it is very hard to believe any country can survive. There are 4,000 ethnic groups in the world and only 185 members of the United Nations. In Yugoslavia, we have 26 different ethnic groups. Any one of them could cause trouble if agitated from the outside. Which is what happened in Kosovo. In Belgrade, we have 100,000 Yugoslav Albanians — and never a problem with them. Walk from our Parliament building and you will see many shops with their Albanian names. Not one window smashed here in all those years of violence in Kosovo. Our people never considered them responsible for the behavior of the so-called Kosovo Liberation Army terrorists. In Kosovo, Albanian Kosovars were bigger victims of the KLA than of Kosovar Serbs. When we looked at the figures, the number of Albanians killed by them was twice as large as Serbs dead. They simply terrorized Albanians to join their underground and to impose their idea of an ethnically pure state. That movement is Nazi in its character because of their publicly declared goals of a racially pure state. Where can you find such a state in the world today? It is precisely the opposite of what is happening in the world. Ethnically mixed states is the trend in the new global village. The Kosovar terrorists were trying to reverse a global phenomenon.

Q: Which you then attempted to do in Kosovo after March 24?

Milosevic: Absolutely not. That is the big lie, which, repeated often enough, becomes conventional wisdom.

Q: You are denying that your armed forces drove people out of their homes and torched entire villages?

Milosevic: We are not angels. Nor are we the devils you have made us out to be. Our regular forces are highly disciplined. The paramilitary irregular forces are a different story. Bad things happened, as they did with both sides during the Vietnam war, or any war for that matter. We have arrested those irregular self-appointed leaders. Some have already been tried and sentenced to twenty years in prison. We reinforced our forces after Rambouillet for a major offensive against KLA terrorists, not to ethnically cleanse Kosovo, as was done with the expulsion of 500,000 Serbs from Croatia, which was ignored by the world media. And the refugees were fleeing in panic because of the war against the terrorists and because of disinformation horror stories being spread by the terrorists, which then became word of mouth and forced ever more people to join the exodus.

Q: Satellite recon shows entire villages torched.

Milosevic: Individual houses, yes. But not whole villages as we saw on TV in Vietnam, when American forces torched villages suspected of hiding Viet Cong.

Q: Just in the past ten years, the Soviet Union has become fifteeen independent republics. Four former republics of Yugoslavia have declared their independence. Scotland and Wales are moving toward self-rule. It is becoming increasingly obvious that the nation-state is too big for small problems — and too small for big problems. Devolution is going on everywhere. Why not in Kosovo? What is so important there?

Milosevic: To us Kosovo is critically important because it is the heart of our country and an integral part of our long history. It is also home to a quarter of million

Serbs whose forebears have lived there for centuries. It is also home to some 5,000 Christian churches. A Swiss expert categorized 1,800 of them as historical monuments that are the heritage of world civilization, and that list was sent to President Clinton.

Q: After thousands of NATO strikes against Yugoslavia, most of your country's communications and transportation networks, as well as your petroleum production and storage capacity, have been largely destroyed, along with your principal bridges — or about $100 billion worth of damage and about 1,000 killed. Now NATO is raising the total number of warplanes in action against you from 700 to 1,000. Are you prepared to see Yugoslavia's entire infrastructure destroyed?

Milosevic: We never thought we could defeat NATO, an alliance of some 700 million people armed with the most advanced and sophisticated weaponry in the world. But NATO believes it can pick on a small nation and force us to surrender our independence. And that is where NATO miscalculated. You are not willing to sacrifice lives to achieve our surrender. But we are willing to die to defend our rights as an independent sovereign nation. The U.S. Congress is beginning to understand that bombing a country into compliance is not a viable policy or strategy. I think your strategic thinkers are also beginning to understand that missiles and other sophisticated weapons will not always be the monopoly of high-tech societies. And with the example it is now setting, we can see the day when lesser nations will be able to retaliate. The development of these weapons is taking place so fast that there is not a single spot on the planet that cannot be reached. America can be reached from this part of the world. We have no quarrel with America. We all know NATO is the strongest military machine in the world. We simply want them to stop being so busy with our country and worry about their own problems. NATO was formed to defend the Western democratic nations from totalitarian aggression, not to commit aggression. We just want to be left alone and free.

Q: At the cost of another month of bombing?

Milosevic: Tell me, what choice do we have?

Q: It seems to be that "left alone" is not an option in what you called a global village. Doesn't your future lie with the European Union in an increasingly integrated Europe? This will require compromise to end this war. Surely the rest of Europe has a stake in what happens in Yugoslavia. Doesn't EU have a role to play in this impasse? Isolation is not an answer.

Milosevic: Just the opposite. In fact, our policy has been consistent on this front. We launched a series of initiatives with a view to increasing integration in the Balkans.

We had a highly successful conference in Crete a year ago. I met with the Albanian prime minister in an attempt to normalize relations completely, with open borders and freedom of movement, free trade, and so forth. My point to him was that borders in Europe were becoming irrelevant and that we could not be holdouts against these trends. European countries have no other choice than to cooperate and integrate. We had a follow-up conference of all the southeastern European nations in Istanbul. I suggested to Bulgaria that we do the same thing we had already done with Macedonia, namely abolish customs duties and open borders for free trade. The same was offered to Bosnia and all other states in the region — with a very simple idea in mind: we are all market economies now. In fact, Yugoslavia is a little bit ahead in this respect, having started before the collapse of the Soviet Union and communism. I told all my neighbors that we could not afford to wait to enter the EU one by one in the years ahead. We had to do something together as a region that would then facilitate joining the wider European enterprise later but earlier than would otherwise be the case. Parallel with this was the process of privatization that we started long before our former communist neighbors. We privatized our telecommunications eighteen months ago with Italian and Greek companies. Telecom Serbia is now 50 percent owned by foreign entities. Up and down the line, our policy has been one of integration, not isolation. Your policy has been to isolate us and demonize us and get NATO to treat us as a pariah state.

Q: After you walked away from the Rambouillet Accords on Kosovo, did you really expect more than a month of sustained bombing?

Milosevic: Rambouillet was not a negotiation. It was a Clinton Administration diktat. It wasn't take it or leave it — just take it or else. We did not expect bombing. It was unbelievable to us that, even as an excuse that we didn't want to sign something that we weren't even negotiating, it would be used to bomb us as the Nazis did in World War II. Rambouillet was a recipe for the independence of Kosovo that clearly we could not accept, especially given the fact that we never contemplated depriving Kosovar Albanians of their legitimate rights. The proof is what happened when half a million Serbs were forced out of Croatia. We never retaliated by expelling a single Croat from Serbia. When Serbs were expelled from Bosnia, we protected all our Muslims from retaliation. We never considered Muslims in Yugoslavia to be responsible for what happened in Bosnia. Of course, there were irresponsible Serb politicians in Bosnia making all kinds of demagogic threats. But this was heated rhetoric. Foreign visitors are invariably impressed at how we handle our unique minorities problems. Go to Vojvodina in the north and see how the Hungarian minority of 360,000 is treated — even after Hungary became a member of NATO and has now offered its bases to American warplanes to attack us. They have schooling in their own language, their own newspapers and radio and TV programs. Twenty-six such communities enjoy the same rights.

There is no other way in such a diversified society. It has been our philosophy from the very beginning — and in Kosovo as well. Equality was the basic principle in Kosovo. Without equality between the two communities, there would be no basis for durable peace. That was our approach for Rambouillet. But the American approach was to favor the Albanian community. This could only lead to ethnic cleansing of anyone who was not of Albanian origin. Serbs clearly could not have stayed under the overlordship of Albanians. There are 250,000 Serbs in Kosovo and 200,000 Muslim Serbs who are not of Albanian origin but whose families converted to Islam under the Ottoman Empire. Then you have 150,000 Gypsies and 50,000 Turks. Even this last community has its own newspaper and TV program. U.S. diplomats knowledgeable about Kosovo have confirmed that we were indeed respecting those principles. So I said to them, "Okay, gentlemen, now please put those principles into the Rambouillet agreement." Equality means nothing unless incorporated into the institutions.

Q: And how did you propose to do this in practice?

Milosevic: Very simple. It takes only one minute to explain. The parliament in Kosovo has to be composed of two houses. The lower house is elected on the basis of one-citizen, one-vote, and the other house is made up of national communities, with each community entitled to five representatives. That way everyone is guaranteed against majority domination. That way, too, Serbs could not impose anything on Albanians and vice versa. When I talked to Ibrahim Rugova [the moderate Kosovar Albanian leader], we agreed that it was in our common interest to have real peace, welfare for all citizens, clean towns and villages, and development of industry. But at the back of the minds of Kosovar Albanians is how to become the masters of the rest of the population. Several decades ago, when the Albanians had complete power in their hands, they started a process of Albanianization of the rest of the population. Gypsies, for example, could not register a newly born child unless they were willing to give it one of the officially recognized Albanian first names. In Rambouillet, regardless of the fact that the delegations never met, never exchanged so much as a single word, we had a delegation in which Serbs were a minority. We had three Albanians, Serb Muslims, Turks, and four Serb Christians. Our delegation represented a real cross section of Kosovo. The Albanian Kosovars were all representatives of the Albanian separatist movement. The EU's dilemma at the end of the twentieth century is whether they are going to support a multiethnic and multicultural society and multireligious approach to society or a kind of Nazi-like approach, with one racially pure ethnic group ruling a diverse society like Kosovo. Henry Kissinger has said Rambouillet was a mechanism for the permanent creation of problems and confrontation. President Clinton should have listened to this wise geopolitical expert rather than some of his own less knowledgeable advisers.

Q: So how do we get out of this mess?

Milosevic: A political process, not by more bombing.

Q: But you must be prepared to compromise.

Milosevic: From the beginning of April, I have had five meetings with Rugova. He was not a prisoner or under duress. This week the President of Serbia went to Pristina [the capital of Kosovo], and he and Rugova signed a statement of agreed joint principles that called for respect for the equality of national communities, respect for the equality of all citizens, direct negotiations — because U.S. shuttle diplomacy was completely useless, as Rambouillet demonstrated. So we have ourselves begun a real political process. This first joint statement with the Albanian Kosovar leader is the first joint victory in our struggle for peace. At the same time, we have been talking about the formation of a temporary joint executive board for Kosovo composed of representatives of all the national communities in Kosovo. Its first task will be to help refugees return home. The problem for returning refugees will be bombing. So, clearly, this insanity will have to stop. Before bombing, regardless of what you hear from NATO and Pentagon briefings, there were no refugees. It wasn't only the Albanians who fled, but also the Serbs, Turks — everyone.

Q: Are you saying that the idea of a U.N. trusteeship or protectorate is a non-starter in your mind?

Milosevic: Please tell me why a U.N. protectorate is needed. That is not to say we are against a U.N. mission. Before the war, we accepted 2,000 verifiers from OSCE. It was OSCE's biggest-ever mission. We also had in Kosovo the International Red Cross and the United Nations High Commission for Refugees, both with huge missions. Plus 1,000 journalists from all over the world, with no restrictions. Plus Kosovo Observation Diplomatic Mission, run by embassies from Belgrade. All this in Kosovo. So who could say we were not open to the international community? They were all free to verify what was happening in this small territory. But this was abused.

Q: How?

Milosevic: Foreign diplomatic missions were to all intents and purposes supporting KLA terrorists — instructing them how to organize and what to do to achieve their objectives. Also to create something that would look more like a regular army. That way they were told to create the kind of situation that would make it look to the rest of the world that there was a war between the regular Yugoslav army and the KLA. The KLA was then composed of different terrorist groups. Just judge them by their acts. They were never able to attack any military or police unit. Instead they were taking hostages and killing civilians. One hundred and fifty hostages were never seen again. They were planting car bombs and dynamiting supermarkets. Classic terrorism.

Q: Are you suggesting that since the U.N. and other international organizations couldn't do anything before, you see no point in bringing them back now?

Milosevic: No, not at all. The U.N. can have a huge mission in Kosovo if it wishes. They can bear witness to the legal behavior of our law enforcement agencies and to the fact that everything is now peaceful, that the KLA has ceased to exist except for scattered small groups that can still stage ambushes.

Q: Is it possible to have a U.N. presence without a U.N. peacekeeping force?

Milosevic: We cannot accept an occupation force, whether it flies under a NATO or U.N. flag.

Q: So you accept a U.N. peacekeeping force?

Milosevic: Yes, but no army.

Q: Without weapons?

Milosevic: Self-defense weapons is normal, but no offensive weapons. We cannot accept anything that looks like an occupation. The idea behind Rambouillet was 28,000 troops, including 4,000 Americans, who would be occupying Kosovo with tanks, APCs, and heavy weaponry. Kosovo has social and economic problems that an army of occupation cannot alleviate. Aid, not arms, is what Kosovo needs.

Q: So, in your judgment, what is the nature of a compromise between NATO and Yugoslavia?

Milosevic: I will tell you. Several points. First of all, cessation of all military activities. Second, simultaneity between the withdrawal of NATO troops now concentrated on our borders in Albania and Macedonia, on the one hand, and the decrease of our own troops in Kosovo from their present level of 100,000 to the normal garrison strength of between 11,000 and 12,000, which was the regular Pristina Corps.

Q: You went from 40,000 to 100,000 troops in Kosovo since the bombing started?

Milosevic: Yes, because of the danger of aggression across our borders by NATO forces. Every day we heard NATO voices urging political leaders to order ground forces into action. But if the danger of NATO aggression is over, we can send our troops back to Serbia. Some are mobilized reservists, and they are anxious to get back to their regular jobs.

Q: How long would such a simultaneous withdrawal take in your judgment?

Milosevic: We can do it in one week.

Q: And the third point?

Milosevic: The return of all refugees, regardless of their ethnic or religious affiliation.

Q: And when would the U.N. peacekeeping force go in? Before the refugees can return presumably.

Milosevic: I don't like the word "force." We would welcome a U.N. mission, not what "force" implies. There is no job for forces. What would such forces do? Just ruin our roads with their tracked vehicles. We would welcome anyone, any mission, that accepts to be our guests. Their mission would be to observe that all is peaceful and not to act as an occupation force. They can see that we are not terrorizing anybody. Even now we are not terrorizing anybody. When the U.N. is here, they can bear witness that what we are saying is the truth.

Q: I assume you know that NATO will not accept your idea of a compromise.

Milosevic: Well, I don't know what NATO will accept. If NATO insists on the occupation of our country, we have no choice but to defend ourselves against this further act of aggression.

Q: If you wouldn't quibble about the word "force" for U.N. peacekeepers, the end of hostilities could be speeded up.

Milosevic: But I told you we are willing to accept a U.N. presence and are ready to negotiate its composition. But please understand that after all those crimes against our nation and its people, we cannot accept representatives of the countries that committed aggression against us. We would like to see representatives of neutral countries.

Q: Any further points?

Milosevic: My fourth point is the political process. We will continue direct negotiations with Mr. Rugova in the presence of the international community. They can listen to every single word that is spoken, but they cannot act as mediators. We want to achieve the widest possible autonomy for Kosovo within Serbia. So we must negotiate the composition of new institutions and the local police. Before the war, there were 120 villages with elected Albanian local police. Some were killed by KLA terrorists. My fifth point is free access for UNHCR and the International Red Cross. Sixth, an economic recovery plan for the three Yugoslav federation states that have been heavily damaged by NATO aggression.

Q: *Back to the composition of U.N. peacekeepers, which you don't like to call a force. Since NATO members are not acceptable, what would you say to European participation such as the EU, not as individual NATO countries.?*

Milosevic: There are European countries that are not members of NATO, like Ireland, that would be acceptable.

Q: *Contingents from Russia, Ukraine, and Belarus have also been mentioned.*

Milosevic: They, too, would be acceptable.

Q: *Surely you are not prepared to face several more weeks of NATO bombing as the diplomatic haggling continues.*

Milosevic: One more day is too much. But what choice do we have if NATO insists on occupying Yugoslavia? To that we will never surrender. We Serbs are as one on this life-and-death issue of national honor and sovereignty.

The KLA Brought NATO to Kosova:
An Interview with Hashim Thaqi

September 29, 1999

Q: A few days ago you and General Ceku signed an agreement with General Jackson, General Clark, and Mr. Kouchner, according to which the KLA will be transformed into the defense troops of Kosova. How do you envision this process? What do you think about this transformation — can this be considered a future army of Kosova?

Thaqi: The agreement signed between General Ceku, General Clark, and myself is a continuation of the Rambouillet Agreement. This is also a continuation of the agreement signed in June of this year on the transformation and demilitarization of the KLA. The latest agreement is the crowning work, so to say, of these efforts to fully transform the KLA. It is understood that the demilitarization was both a success and an assurance, but also an expression of respect for the political and military structures of the KLA, which gained and enjoyed the respect of international political and military mechanisms. As a result, the KLA was transformed into the Defense Troops of Kosova. As you know, there were last-minute questions that had not been resolved and postponed the signing of the agreement for twenty-four hours. After continuous consultations and talks with General Clark, who had come to Prishtina, talks about questions that were still unresolved, we reached the conclusions that are in the agreement. Thus the Defense Troops of Kosova will be the troops who will ensure Kosova's security, a force that will not only be an assurance for the citizens of Kosova but will also protect every inch of Kosova's land. From now on, Kosova's territory will have its own protection force for its citizens, which will also be the future army of Kosova.

Q: Who appointed Ceku? There is a question among journalists and diplomats on the appointment of General Ceku, the chief of this protection force of Kosova. Who has appointed him — you or the KFOR (NATO)? Because there are opinions and voices that General Ceku was appointed by structures in Brussels and not the government that you head.

Thaqi: There were open issues that were discussed during those ten days. We did discuss these issues and came to clear conclusions — such as the issue of the size of the Defense Force: it is to be five thousand; three thousand to be a regular force, and two thousand to be reservists. The weapons became General Ceku's issue. For the sake of informing the domestic and international public more accurately, General Ceku was appointed two weeks earlier as the leader of the Kosova Defense Troops. The decree on his appointment was issued based on Article 6, Point F of the law governing the operation of the Kosova Interim Government and the proposal of the Joint Chiefs. This was then approved by the Ministry of Defense, of course, under the special circumstances of KLA transformation. As a result of this special decree, General Ceku was also appointed chief of the Joint Chiefs. We have a fully structured Joint Chiefs, but also a fully structured Department of Defense, as well as other departments that will fall under the Defense Troops of Kosova. With a special decree, General Kernel Sylejman Selimi was appointed commander of the Kosova Guard. We have also appointed the commanders in all six of the regional zones.

Q: *According to what you are saying, Mr. Thaqi, this decision was made by the Kosova Interim Government? Then why were General Clark, General Jackson, and Mr. Kouchner present in these meetings? Were they also in agreement with General Ceku's appointment? You said that this decision was made two weeks ago, yet two weeks ago there was no Defense Troops of Kosova but rather Kosova Corps.*

Thaqi: Kosova Corps was a proposal by UNMIK and KFOR, whereas the naming Kosova Defense Force, or Kosova Defense Troops, was our suggestion. I feel good that our proposal was approved, as was the appointment of General Ceku as chief of the Kosova Defense Troops. His appointment was made by QPK, with a decree, but was approved by KFOR and UNMIK.

Q: *I would like to jump now from this question, which is so current and deals with political events in Kosova today, to explore your own political past. I would be interested to know, as would our viewers, if it is true that you have been a member of the People's Movement of Kosova. And why?*

Thaqi: I was one of the activists of the student movement, and I tried within my and our capabilities to counter Milosevic's regime in the period of 1988-89. And later, seeing that neither the political will of the people nor the politics of the future of Kosova was being respected, and recognizing that it was the time for armed resistance — we decided to begin establishing the KLA during the summer of 1992. We began its concrete actions in the fall of 1992.

Q: Who is the founder of the KLA? Wouldn't it be the right moment for you to say who founded the KLA? Are you one of its founders?

Thaqi: It is true that I contributed toward the founding of the KLA.

Q: Did you have a clear strategy? Today there is talk about how much the KLA could have done to defeat the Serb military and police with its capacity. Did you have this in mind or was it more important to begin the resistance at any cost? Your critics here say that the KLA was determined to set the fire in Kosova at any cost?

Thaqi: We are convinced that the strategy and tactics of the KLA were the most genuine of any military and political organization we have ever had in the past. . . . And the KLA was the highest level of organized resistance against Serbia. Based on this, our organization got even stronger: by working on military principles as well as political principles, we attracted many good people, honest people, people who were well prepared. . . .

Q: At that point did you make any effort to contact the Kosova political parties and inform them that the KLA was being created for the purpose of countering Milosevic's regime and dictatorship, which had lasted for years?

Thaqi: The legal and political mechanisms of Kosova knew very well what the KLA was, whom it was led by, who were its joint chiefs, and what the vision of the KLA was. However, the readiness was not there, nor the courage to cooperate, to help strengthen the KLA resistance. Regardless of these dilemmas or obstacles created by the so-called political parties of Kosova at that time, or the so-called institutions of Kosova, we continued to work within the capabilities, potential, and the mechanisms we had. And I believe that the support for the beginning and continuance of the resistance was at an adequate level, and precisely this is what enabled and strengthened the resistance.

Q: Did anyone help the KLA besides the fund "Homeland Calling"?

Thaqi: "Homeland Calling" was a fund that helped carry the biggest burden of the resistance in Kosova — equipping the KLA with technical and material means. The fund was the strongest pillar of support for the KLA. In addition, we received other help from various individuals and associations, but in particular from the citizens of Kosova.

Q: Does this mean that Bujar Bukoshi and his government did not help the KLA?

Thaqi: I think that you have read all our statements and communiques in regard to Bujar Bukoshi and other mechanisms.

Q: Do you think that during the KLA's fighting and actions in Kosova mistakes were made? Can you name at least three concrete ones?

Thaqi: Each organization has its weaknesses, makes its mistakes. However, I do not believe the KLA did anything fundamentally wrong. Even if there were mistakes, they were a result of our inability to implement our objectives due to the different obstacles created by the domestic and international factor. The greatest merit of the KLA was that it had a very clear political vision. This made it possible to quickly gain the support of the international community, especially the decisive powers. . . .

Q: Don't you think it was a mistake to prolong the mystique and the mask covering the KLA? An American journalist, Michael Ignatieff, says that only after direct contacts with the diplomat Burns did you decide to go public. Don't you think that this went too far and was a mistake?

Thaqi: The mysteriousness was not the problem. The issue was the deep illegality in which we found ourselves at that point; but exactly that illegality made it possible for us to strengthen and to avoid being attacked by the Serb authorities. That helped us carry out our activites undiscovered for a long time and helped us get better organized; and it helped us extend our net not only in Prishtina but in all cities of Kosova. With regard to our meeting with Mr. Burns, it is true that we spoke about different political and security issues for Kosova in relation to the international factor; but this was not a turning point for us, because we have had so many more meetings with the United States. Who decided at Rambouillet?

Q: Before going to the Rambouillet conference, did you ever think that you would be the leader of the delegation? Also, was the massacre at Recak the reason for this conference in European diplomatic circles?

Thaqi: Regarding the Rambouillet conference, much discussed earlier: the massacre at Recak did speed up the process of putting together the conference. But there was much prior talk about this conference, even open talks about it. So the conference was being planned. With regard to my leading the Kosova delegation, that was decided at Rambouillet, and it was the unanimous position of all political factions.

Q: Why did you hesitate to sign the agreement at Rambouillet?

Thaqi: It was an issue we talked about for a long time. There were undefined issues, unclear issues, and we discussed them. This was the position of the Kosova delegation and not just Mr. Thaqi's position.

Q: You were strongly criticized by Ismail Kadare, a writer of international fame, who said that he who was against Rambouillet and against signing it was in fact against the Albanians. As a member and head of the delegation, did you have all this criticism in mind?

Thaqi: Kadare did not direct this criticism toward me personally. We were in close contact with Kadare at Rambouillet and in Paris. This was the unanimous position of the Kosova delegation, as was our unified position to go back to Kosova and talk to the people and let them agree with everything. And then we would sign, because all of us represented someone at Rambouillet, though the weight of representation differed. So we came back to Kosova and convinced the people that this agreement had to be signed. We fulfilled our promise for doing principled work at Rambouillet.

Q: As a military organization of Kosovars, were you aware of the scale of violence that the Serbian regime would later exercise against the Albanian population — and that one million people would be deported? Were you aware that the KLA might not have the power to counter all this military violence that had been systematically prepared? What did you have in mind when signing an agreement on the protection of the population when you were being criticized by the media and the people for not being able to protect the people from massacres and deportation?

Thaqi: As far as Serb operations in Kosova are concerned, we had all their plans and details of the operations they were preparing. We presented these details at the international Kosova Conference at Rambouillet, and we asked from the very first day for a cease-fire between the Serb and Albanian parties, with the assurance of the international community as the third party. Our request was ignored, as were the Serb objectives for massive operations. All those plans had been written at Serb military academies; we had those plans, had studied them, and we took our measures according to the circumstances and our abilities. . . .

Q: During the Serb bombings, Albanian leader Ibrahim Rugova met with Slobodan Milosevic. In your interviews for the foreign media, you criticized this and called it an act of surrender. Today in Kosova this no longer seems to be an issue. Why doesn't Hashim Thaqi, as head of the QPK, speak out about Rugova's actions?

Thaqi: I have spoken, even during NATO's bombings in Kosova, when Mr. Rugova met with Milosevic in Belgrade. I do not have anything to add to the comments I made at that time. . . . I believe that the people of Kosova will be the ones to judge every meeting that each of us has.

Q: Who liberated Kosova? The KLA or NATO?

Thaqi: Kosova was liberated by the KLA with the help of NATO.

Q: *Some think that NATO was the liberator and that the KLA helped; some even say that NATO alone liberated Kosova.*

Thaqi: The KLA brought NATO into Kosova.

Q: *What are your relations with Bardhyl Mahmuti?*

Thaqi: My relations with Mr. Mahmuti are good. Mr. Mahmuti is the Foreign Minister at QPK, which I head, and our relations are constructive.

Q: *Why did you not join his party?*

Thaqi: There will be a party created from the political structures of the KLA. It has already created the Council, as you know.

Q: *However, many of your friends and collaborators of the KLA structures have joined Mr. Mahmuti's party.*

Thaqi: I do not believe that many friends of KLA political structures have joined. As you know, that party was created or transformed from the National Movement of Kosova. Everyone has the right to respect the democratic and pluralist spectrum in Kosova, and Mr. Mahmuti has the right to establish a party. I wish him success.

Q: *Does this mean that Hashim Thaqi will establish a political party?*

Thaqi: Hashim Thaqi has already established a party.

Q: *What is this political party called?*

Thaqi: This is an issue being discussed, and I believe that you will know soon about its name and structures.

Q: *It is better if we don't go too far so we are not misconstrued as being promoters of one side or the other. Mr. Kouchner says that there are three governments in Kosova: Mr. Kouchner's government; that of Mr. Bujar Bukoshi, who considers himself the prime minister of Kosova; and Mr. Thaqi's government, resulting from the Rambouillet Agreement.*

Thaqi: The Provisional Kosova Government (QPK), as you know, is an outcome of the agreement signed by LDK, LBD, and the KLA at Rambouillet. We have respected and created the QPK. How much the LDK has boycotted this government is another issue. Concerning Bukoshi's government, the public has had its say, and Bukoshi himself has spoken publicly on how much and in what way he has helped the issue before, during, and after the war. As far as Mr. Kouchner is concerned, I am not aware that he has a government, but . . .

Q: There is a Transition Council, and he says he is the so-called prime minister of Kosova.

Thaqi: We are not Mr. Kouchner's competitors; we are helping. As far as the Transition Council is concerned, that council is not functional and has failed.

Q: Do you call it a failure because the Serbs have left the Transition Council or because there is insufficient cooperation?

Thaqi: The problem is not the Serbs but the nonfunctioning of the council.

Q: What is your view — or your government's view — about what should happen in Kosova? Do you mean that Mr. Kouchner should go?

Thaqi: Mr. Kouchner would not have to leave, but he needs help; so we can find the way that works and have a true executive structure.

Q: After meeting Mr. Annan in New York, you stated that Mr. Kouchner should not behave like a king. What do you mean by this?

Thazqi: We meant that Mr. Kouchner has no right to make Serb laws nor to make decisions on Kosova's property. We have also asked that Mr. Kouchner be more active in the case of Mitrovica and not allow the division of that part of Kosova. We have called for an honoring of Security Council Resolution 1244, which states that Kosova's territory is respected and determines the withdrawal of Serb military troops up to five kilometers away from the border between Kosova and Serbia. These issues were not and are not respected by Mr. Kouchner. Our criticism against him was respectful criticism and not aimed at having him leave.

Q: Mr. Thaqi, lately there have been articles and reports in the Western media saying that members of the KLA are involved in Mafia-like activities in Kosova, that they are grabbing apartments and shops, are persecuting old Serb women, and so forth — this while you have stated that you support a multiethnic Kosova. What is your position on these accusations, which are on the increase in the West?

Thaqi: We have often made our position known on these issues, which are really of great concern to us. . . . But after the war in Kosova there have been so many negative phenomena, especially trafficking, crime, mafia activities — and drugs have found their way into Kosova, too. We have discussed all these issues with UNMIK and the international community and have informed them very expeditiously. Since KFOR was first established in Kosova, we have said that there are armed people in Kosova who are not overseen by the KLA, and who will destabilize Kosova. Of course, there are also those serving the Serb Secret Service who are working toward the destabilization of Kosova; but it depends on how many and what kind of measures were taken by KFOR and UNMIK. As far as the KLA is concerned, we trust the law and legal procedures. There are no confirmed cases that a KLA soldier or commander has been captured in illegal activities or with contraband materials, engaged in Mafia-type actions or other issues that have raised tensions in Kosova, or committed any act of violence.

Q: The offices of the QPK are on the main street in Prishtina. Many people complain about the loud music; you say that you represent the QPK and are not bothered by the music. What is the government undertaking to stop the loud music or clean the streets of Prishtina?

Thaqi: We have taken actions and measures within our abilities and authority but also according to our responsibilities concerning many current issues, things that must be improved in Prishtina now, as well as in other cities. For us there were more important issues to deal with than the music.

Q: That's clear. But if you represent the Kosova government, then your ministry and your departments must begin dealing with the true problems of citizens. Because we are in a phase that is called freedom in Kosova, and now we must deal with the problems of the people, the truly essential problems.

Thaqi: We have worked in this direction, and we are still working so that we will have true discipline in Kosova. But we also need to have citizen awareness, so that they respect this freedom and build it. We have worked and are working on these issues, and I think we have reached the people, so that anarchy and chaos do not dominate in Kosova, but rather the democratic rule of law.

Q: In the foreign press, in the beginning of the KLA's becoming public, many publicists and journalists portrayed you as an extremist. You have undergone a political transformation: you have given interviews to the Belgrade media, the NIN newspaper, and to local Serb television programs. How do you feel when you talk to the Serb media?

Thaqi: With respect to extremism, I am the same person I was before the war, during the war, and after the war. Regarding my communicating with the Serb media, I will make the effort (within my abilities) to help Serbia's democratization, even if it amounts to statements in the press and on television.

Q: A poll taken by a Kosova weekly revealed that Mr. Rugova would win by a convincing vote if the elections for the president of Kosova were to be held tomorrow. You are far behind. Do you have any comments?

Thaqi: I have not read the results of this poll, and I do not know which paper took the poll. Nevertheless, it is important that I work hard on organizing and establishing the political parties, and that they all enter the election race. . . . The citizens themselves will determine who will win the free elections. But it is important for us not to follow the path of boycotts in Kosova that is being practiced right now; and I believe that free elections will be organized quickly and will determine who will lead Kosova in the next two or four years.

Q: Does Hashim Thaqi think that he will be one of the future leaders of Kosova?

Thaqi: I will work diligently, as I have, and within the political party that has been established.

V. VOICES OF POLITICAL COMMENTATORS

How Is the Intervention Debated?

Kosovo and the Vicissitudes
of American Foreign Policy

HENRY A. KISSINGER

Doing Injury to History

Newsweek (April 5, 1999)

The war in Kosovo is the product of a conflict going back over centuries. It takes place at the dividing line between the Ottoman and Austrian empires, between Islam and Christianity, and between Serbian and Albanian nationalism. The ethnic groups have lived together peacefully only when that coexistence was imposed — as under foreign empires or the Tito dictatorship. President Clinton has asserted that, after a brief period of NATO occupation, the ethnic groups will reconcile. There is no realistic basis for that assumption. Ethnic groups in Bosnia have not reconciled after three years of NATO peacekeeping.

When American forces are engaged in combat, victory is the only exit strategy. And that requires a definition of issues that can survive scrutiny. The Administration, in pursuit of symbols that resonate with the public, has put for-

Given the collective title by the editor, not the author, these essays were originally published separately at the beginning, near the end, and subsequent to the NATO intervention in Kosovo. Dr. Kissinger declined the invitation to respond to authors in this volume who disagree with what they regard as his views about *Realpolitik* (Javier Solana, Kofi Annan, Jürgen Habermas, Mort Halperin, Wesley Clark). As one of the several models for understanding international relations, this "Realism" is interpreted in many (even contradictory) ways but gained historical prominence as a framework for negotiating and preserving international stability during the later cold war period (détente) by using concepts such as "balance of power politics" and "national power and interest politics." While not its originator, Kissinger is perceived as one of its chief proponents, especially in his work with several American Administrations (Nixon, Ford and Reagan), and as a subsequent public commentator. Even critics concede its (and Kissinger's) influential legacy for American foreign policy. For example, the final section of Mort Halperin's essay ("Implications [for Foreign Policy]") surveys the issues of humanitarian intervention, in part as a reply to Kissinger's claims (compare the interview with Slobodan Milosovec). [Ed.]

ward three categories of argument. The most convincing is that suffering in Kosovo is so offensive to our moral sensibilities that we will use force to end it even absent traditional considerations of national interest. But since this leaves open the question of why we do not intervene in East Africa, Sri Lanka, Kurdistan, Kashmir, and Afghanistan — to name just a few of the places where infinitely more casualties have been incurred than in Kosovo — the President has invoked historical analogies or current threats that are extremely dubious. Where he does injury to history:

Slobodan Milosevic is not Hitler but a Balkan thug, and the crisis in Kosovo has no analogy to the events preceding World War I. Neither Milosevic nor any other Balkan leader is in a position to threaten the global equilibrium, as the President constantly asserts. Milosevic bears a major responsibility for the brutalities in Bosnia, and I strongly supported the American deployment there. But unlike Bosnia, Kosovo is a war for territory considered by the Serbs as a national shrine. This is why there have been few, if any, signs of opposition in Belgrade to Milosevic's Kosovo policy.

World War I started in the Balkans not as a result of ethnic conflicts but for precisely the opposite reason: because outside powers intervened in a local conflict. The assassination of the Crown Prince of Austria — an imperial power — by a Serbian nationalist led to a world war because Russia backed Serbia, and France backed Russia, while Germany supported Austria. World War II did not start in the Balkans, much less as a result of its ethnic conflicts.

It is absurd to allege that the economic well-being of the European Union, with a GNP exceeding America's, depends on the outcome in impoverished Kosovo. This is even more true of Atlantic prosperity. The cohesion of NATO is threatened primarily because it was staked on the unsustainable Rambouillet agreement. It remains to be seen how long it can be maintained when public reaction to the scale and duration of the bombardment sets in, and when it becomes apparent that the long-term consequences of the present campaign have to be policed by NATO ground forces.

I respect the humanitarian motive for intervention. But this does not absolve the democracies from the necessity of coming up with a sustainable solution. The Rambouillet agreement does not meet that test. Conducting a negotiation based on an agreement drafted entirely in foreign chancelleries and seeking to impose it by the threat of air bombardment have only exacerbated the crisis in Kosovo. The Rambouillet text was sold to the Kosovo Liberation Army — which initially rejected it — as a device to bring the full force of NATO to bear on Serbia, and it may have tempted Milosevic into accelerating the repression of the KLA before the bombs fell. Now it risks involving NATO and U.S. ground forces in policing an agreement neither side really wants. It was a grave error to abandon any effort to strengthen the observers already in Kosovo in favor of NATO peacekeepers, who will find no peace to keep.

President Clinton, in a speech to the Serbian people, has declared: "The NATO allies support the Serbian people to maintain Kosovo as part of your country." He added that the agreement would "guarantee the rights of all people in Kosovo — ethnic Serbs and Albanians alike within Serbia." This is why the Rambouillet agreement provides for the KLA to surrender its arms to a NATO force. Some ten thousand Serbian policemen are to maintain security; some fifteen hundred Serbian soldiers are to safeguard the frontiers. None of this is achievable by agreement, only by imposition. The Serbs have rejected the Rambouillet agreement because they see in it a prelude to independence for Kosovo. They also see the presence of NATO troops as the sort of foreign occupation Serbia has historically resisted against the Ottoman and Austrian empires, Hitler, and Stalin. Even if they are bombed into capitulation, they can hardly be expected to be willing supporters of the outcome.

As for the KLA, its goal is independence, not autonomy; it acceded to Rambouillet as a tactical device to unleash NATO air power against the hated Serbs. The KLA is even less likely to agree to autonomy under Serbian rule now that Serbia has been so weakened by the NATO air campaign. The KLA will not turn in its weapons to NATO forces. And NATO forces will have no domestic support if they fight the KLA to impose disarmament. Nor will the KLA acquiesce to Serbian forces policing its frontiers. The role of Serbian police and military forces in the proposed agreement is both unclear and incapable of being implemented.

The ironic outcome of the Rambouillet agreement, in the name of which the NATO air campaign is being conducted, is that the NATO peacekeepers will replace the Serbs as obstacles to the national aspirations of the Albanians — especially if Serbia is too weak to provide a counterweight. Moreover, as Kosovo moves toward independence, the pressures on Macedonia, a third of whose population is Albanian, will increase. Why should they not be granted the same self-determination as their brethren inside Serbia? And that will risk expansion of the conflict as Bulgaria claims its own ethnic nationals in Macedonia, comprising at least a third of that population, and Greece perceives an opportunity to curtail — or to eliminate — a state whose very name it has rejected.

As the war continues, the Administration must redefine its objectives. NATO cannot survive if it now abandons the campaign without achieving its objective of ending the massacres. The Rambouillet agreement should therefore be stripped of its more esoteric components. The terms for ending the air war should be: an immediate ceasefire; the withdrawal of Serbian forces introduced after the beginning of the negotiations at Rambouillet; and the immediate opening of negotiations over autonomy for Kosovo. These negotiations are likely to be prolonged and bitter. But, at their end, Kosovar independence in some form is inevitable unless NATO insists by force on the kind of Serbian suzerainty that the President has promised — a course neither the alliance nor the American public will support.

If a ceasefire on such terms is rejected by Milosevic, there will be no alternative to continuing and intensifying the war, if necessary introducing NATO combat ground forces — a solution that I have heretofore passionately rejected but which will have to be considered to maintain NATO credibility. Whatever the outcome, the stationing of some NATO ground forces in either Macedonia or Kosovo will be necessary — to serve not so much as peacekeepers as to prevent the Balkan conflict from widening. I have consistently warned against such an outcome. But, as a result of hesitations and confusions, NATO now has little choice if it wants to avoid a larger war.

For someone who has supported every military action of the Clinton Administration — or who has criticized it for acting too inconclusively, as in Iraq — the war on Yugoslavia inspires profound ambivalence. Serbia fought at our side in two world wars and stood up to Stalin at the height of his powers. We cannot ignore Milosevic's brutality; yet the disappearance of Serbia from the Balkans' equilibrium may tempt eruptions in other neighboring countries containing ethnic minorities. Even more importantly, the problem of Macedonia's integrity will be upon us, threatening a wider Balkan war. Let us hope that it will be handled with greater foresight than the prelude to the current crisis.

New World Disorder

Newsweek (May 31, 1999)

A war at the far edge of the Balkans has had political consequences extending far beyond Kosovo. In Russia, an outraged sense of humiliation over NATO's actions has spread from the elites to the population at large and threatens to blight U.S.-Russian relations for years to come. In Beijing, the virulent reaction to the bombing of the Chinese Embassy in Belgrade has vented frustrations with the rollercoaster nature of Sino-American relations that have accumulated for many months. And in Europe, the seeming unity of the Atlantic Alliance has grown brittle: key allies are eyeing the exits; domestic opposition is mounting; the newly admitted members in Central Europe are uncomfortable that their first allied activity is as part of a NATO-initiated war.

The causes in Russia and China are plain enough. Their leaders are products of societies that interpret decisions about war and peace according to whether they enhance a nation's security or other vital interests. If they can discern no such traditional rationale to U.S. behavior, they ascribe our motives not to altruism but to a hidden agenda for domination. In Europe, the situation is more complex. The allies share our motives but are beginning to question our judgment. And they find themselves under increasing domestic pressure as the damage from the bombing of Serbia compounds the devastation of Kosovo.

A generation gap has exacerbated the crisis. The formative experiences of the Clinton Administration's key personnel were either in the trenches of the Vietnam protest movement or in presidential campaigns — or both. Suspicious of the role of power in foreign policy, they use it ineffectively and without conviction. They emphasize the so-called "soft" issues, like the environment, and have little concern with notions of the international equilibrium or of traditional U.S. interests, which they scorn as outdated. Obsessively driven by public-opinion polls, they are ever tempted to treat foreign policy as an extension of domestic politics. Their diplomacy is quite skillful in dealing with short-term tactical issues but obtuse with respect to strategy; adept at "spinning" public opinion but oblivious to a generation's worth of lessons about the limitations of air power and the futility of notions of "graduated escalation."

The rejection of long-range strategy explains how it was possible to slide into the Kosovo conflict without adequate consideration of all its implications — especially the visceral reaction of almost all nations of the world against the new NATO doctrine of humanitarian intervention. Before the start of the bombing, it was conventional wisdom in Washington that Serbia's historic attachment to Kosovo was exaggerated and that Slobodan Milosevic was looking for a pretext to get rid of the incubus it represented — which a few days of bombing was supposed to supply. But what if Serbia, the country that fought the Turkish and Austrian empires and defied Hitler and Stalin at the height of their powers, did not yield? How far were we willing to go? Not to ground war, it was announced at the very beginning, tempting Milosevic to test his endurance to sustained bombing. No provision was made for a war of attrition or the flood of refugees it was bound to create — not to speak of the ethnic cleansing that the war has accelerated and intensified.

From the start, there has been a vast gap between the rhetoric and the means with which to back it up. Allied pronouncements have ritually compared Milosevic to Hitler. But the transparent reluctance to accept casualties signaled that the Alliance would not make the commitment necessary to overthrow the accused tyrant. Now if the outcome is to be some kind of compromise, Milosevic will inevitably be legitimated and emerge as a valid interlocutor. By justifying the war in terms requiring total victory while conducting a strategy impelling compromise, NATO has maneuvered itself into a trap.

Several fateful decisions were taken in those now seemingly far-off days in February, when other options were still open. The first was the demand that 30,000 NATO troops enter Yugoslavia, a country with which NATO was not at war, and administer a province that had emotional significance as the origin of Serbia's independence. The second was to use the foreseeable Serb refusal as justification for starting the bombing. Rambouillet was not a negotiation — as is often claimed — but an ultimatum. This marked an astounding departure for an administration that had entered office proclaiming its devotion to the U.N. Charter and multilateral procedures. The transformation of the Alliance from a defensive military grouping into an institution prepared to impose its values by force occurred in the same months that three former Soviet satellites joined NATO. It undercut repeated American and allied assurances that Russia had nothing to fear from NATO expansion, since the Alliance's own treaty proclaimed it to be a purely defensive institution.

Kosovo has thereby become a symbol of Russia's post–Cold War frustrations. The tribulations of Yugoslavia, Moscow's traditional friend (leaving aside the interruption of the Tito years), emphasized Russia's decline and have generated a hostility toward America and the West that may produce a nationalist and socialist Russia — akin to the European Fascism of the 1930s. This would be a sorry end for the administration's policy of supporting Russian reform and coaxing Russia closer to the West.

This is why the expectations attached to the Russian mediation in Kosovo seem excessive. Russian leaders would hardly be brokenhearted if the outcome in Kosovo weakens NATO. A Russian intermediary faces a double dilemma: if he is seen as supporting the NATO program, he will lose standing at home; if he induces us to reduce our demands, he will become a scapegoat in the American domestic debate over compromising our war aims. Russia's most constructive role in my view would be as full participant at a conference for political arrangements in the Balkans following a ceasefire.

To its credit, the Administration from the beginning has recognized the importance of bringing Russia into the international community. But it has identified this effort primarily with democratic reform and market economics inside Russia and nonproliferation abroad. All this accentuates the Russian sense of having come under a kind of colonial tutelage. Russia, in turn, has clung to many aspects of its traditional diplomacy: seeking to reduce our influence, especially in the Middle East. Russia's image of itself as a historic player on the world stage must be taken seriously. This requires less lecturing and more dialogue; less sentimentality and more recognition that Russia's national interests are not always congruent with ours; less sociology and more foreign policy.

Before the attack on its Belgrade embassy, China's reaction to the air war was more muted than Russia's — but equally negative. Every nation views international events through the prism of its history. And to China, the new NATO doctrine of humanitarian intervention evokes Europe's unilaterally proclaimed civilizing mission in the nineteenth century, which led to the fragmentation of China and a series of Western interventions. These humiliations were followed in the twentieth century by the so-called Brezhnev doctrine, which proclaimed the Kremlin's right to punish by force of arms communist regimes that strayed from its ideological line. Indeed, it was to resist the Brezhnev doctrine that China moved to restore its relations with the United States in 1971.

That policy of close ties between the United States and China is now questioned in both capitals. President Clinton's policy has built on the conviction of all his predecessors since Richard Nixon that both China and the United States have much to gain from cooperation and risk exhausting themselves by confrontation. For China, a breakdown in relations would deal a severe blow to its economic program and modernization. For America, it would ensure turmoil throughout Asia, leaving China's neighbors torn by the need to choose between the world's most populous country, whose 5,000 years of history give it a special place in Asia, and America, the world's only superpower.

That cooperative policy is losing momentum on our side largely because of a stalemate between the Administration and opponents who see China as our principal strategic threat. The stalemate arises from the Administration's tendency to present its policy of engagement with China less in terms of common objectives than as a better method of achieving its critics' objectives. A "strategic partnership" has been proclaimed, but real strategic discussions on the highest level have been rare amid disputes over issues ranging from Taiwan to human rights to nonproliferation. And the administration has felt obliged to balance its China policy with periodic bows to its critics.

A good example was the visit to Washington in early April of Chinese Prime Minister Zhu Rongji — generally considered among the most reformist and market-oriented of the Chinese leaders. That visit was bracketed by the announcement — just before Zhu's arrival — that the United States would support a U.N. resolution condemning China's human-rights practices, and immediately afterward by the sale of long-range radars to Taiwan. And during the visit, the administration declined to sign an agreement on China's entry into the World Trade Organization, for which the Chinese had made major concessions and which they had reason to believe would be the centerpiece of Zhu's visit. (To compound Zhu's embarrassment, the administration published all the concessions he had made.) Whatever one's view of the substance of these decisions, their timing conveyed an impression of a government driven by its critics into subordinating to domestic politics a policy that should be based on mutual national interests.

The bombing of the Belgrade embassy was the match that set off the explosion. Mutual suspicions fed on each other. The Chinese viewed the President's original apology — made as a response to a question at a press conference during a visit to Oklahoma and linked to a justification of NATO bombing — as inadequate. Americans considered the Chinese violence against the American Embassy in Beijing unacceptable. But if the Sino-American relationship is not to spiral toward a confrontation, it is essential to call a halt to mutual recrimination and seek to restore a dialogue. The leaders of both countries seem aware that a confrontation would be catastrophic for both sides, as well as for the peace of the world. But both are under pressure from ideological opponents at home. However, there is no way to dodge this debate. In the United States the critics are serious, and so must be the Administration.

The critics of a cooperative China policy fall into two camps. The first group holds that the emergence of China as a major power automatically threatens American vital interests, especially under communist leadership. A second group is concerned about specific Chinese policies from human rights to proliferation. To be sure, China's actions on many fronts reflect the unsentimental policy of an emerging power. Nevertheless, Sino-American disagreements can be kept short of confrontation by patient and firm diplomacy. And there are many areas of congruent interests. If, in the absence of a direct challenge, the emergence of China as a major power and its political system are turned into the occasion for American hostility, we will be embarked on a lonely course without support from any major nation in either Europe or Asia. I would warn against such an adventure, which will distort our Asian policy for decades. There is no more important task for American foreign policy than to design a strategy recognizing and managing adversarial elements in our relations with China, yet drawing Beijing further into the international system. We must not repeat in Asia the emotional and un-thought-out policies that brought us such grief in the Balkans. The law of unintended consequences still operates.

Despite the seeming unity of the NATO summit, Kosovo has made a debate about the Alliance's future inevitable. It is being delayed by horror at Milosevic's barbarities and by the paradox that Europe's new left-wing governments — especially in Germany and Italy — are afraid of being accused of undermining their conservative predecessors' legacy of pro-American and pro-NATO foreign policy. But these new governments are likely to consider that they have now paid enough homage to the traditions of allied solidarity. They can be expected to be influenced by the mounting indignation of their rank and file, who would be protesting in the streets of Germany in the tens of thousands had former chancellor Helmut Kohl won the election and carried out a similar policy. Once the Kosovo crisis is over — or if the war drags on — these constituencies will become more dominant. And their influence has already been shown in the unprecedentedly abrupt refusal of the German chancellor to consider ground troops for Kosovo.

The issues ducked at the NATO summit brook no further delay. Specifically, what is the proper mission of NATO in so-called out-of-area conflicts? What are the relative roles of Europe and America? Does the Alliance have a serious political or military strategy for stabilizing parts of Europe or adjacent strategic regions? Europe (the U.K. included) has already begun to draw the conclusion from Kosovo that it needs to accelerate the elaboration of its own institutions in order to enhance its autonomy from the United States — hardly a vote of confidence in the middle of a war. But if Europe will not supply the resources for this task — as is likely — the Alliance will be left with the worst of all scenarios: a Europe asserting greater freedom of action from the United States but with little actual ability to act alone; and an America estranged from Europe.

No issue is more in need of rethinking than the concept of humanitarian intervention put forward as the Administration's contribution to a new approach to foreign policy. The air war in Kosovo is justified as establishing the principle that the international community — or at least NATO — will henceforth punish the transgressions of governments against their own people. But we did not do so in Algeria, Sudan, Sierra Leone, Croatia, Rwanda, the Caucasus, the Kurdish areas, and many other regions. And what will be our attitude to emerging ethnic conflicts in Asia, for example, in Indonesia and the Philippines? The answer often given is that we act where we are able to without undue risk, not elsewhere. But what are the criteria for this distinction? And what kind of humanism expresses its reluctance to suffer military casualties by devastating the civilian economy of its adversary for decades to come?

Moral principles are expressed in absolutes. But foreign policy must forever be concerned with reconciling ends and means. The fact that ethnic cleansing is repugnant does not obviate the need to devise the most appropriate response. At every stage of the Kosovo tragedy, other mixes of diplomacy and force were available, though it is not clear they were ever seriously considered. A strategy that vindicates its moral convictions only from altitudes above 15,000 feet — and in the process devastates Serbia and makes Kosovo unlivable — has already produced more refugees and casualties than any conceivable alternative mix of force and diplomacy would have. It deserves to be questioned on both political and moral grounds.

The United States can take pride in elevating human rights to an integral part of foreign policy. But when one observes the progression from the call for moral pressure of the 1970s, to economic sanctions in the 1980s, to military intervention in the 1990s, the time has come to call for a definition of purposes and a dialogue on the relationship between objectives and methods. But this is for the future. Now that the credibility of the Atlantic Alliance has been staked, we must persist — with ground troops if necessary — until Serb military forces leave Kosovo and the refugees are allowed to return.

The paradox is that a country that thinks of itself as acting in the name of universal values is seen by too many others as acting arbitrarily, or inexplicably, or arrogantly. A reexamination of the prevailing premises of our foreign policy is overdue. This is a tall order for the last eighteen months of an administration heretofore more given to tactics than strategy, more to Band-Aids than to healing. The agenda will not be completed in the time left. But if the President encourages a debate on a new agenda before the end of his term, he will have left an important legacy.

As the Cheers Fade

Newsweek (June 21, 1999)

Those of us who questioned the wisdom of the diplomacy preceding the war over Kosovo owe it to the Clinton Administration to express our respect for the fortitude with which it persevered and the skill with which it buttressed Allied unity and achieved Russian acquiescence. But victory leaves us with just as severe a challenge: to avoid being permanently mired in a corner of the Balkans as the modern equivalent of the Ottoman and Austrian empires. The so-called Petersberg Plan risks turning into an open-ended commitment toward ever-deeper involvement, casting us in the role of gendarme of a region where there are passionate hatreds and where we have few strategic interests.

Many commentators emphasize the differences between the plan put forward by the Finnish president and ratified by the Yugoslav parliament, and the Rambouillet proposals in the name of which the bombing was initiated. And there are nuances of some consequence. The NATO forces are entering Kosovo on the basis of a U.N. mandate rather than an agreement between Belgrade and the Atlantic Alliance. Kosovo is explicitly described as a part of Yugoslavia, albeit an autonomous one (Point 5); the territorial integrity and sovereignty of Yugloslavia are affirmed (Point 8). The provision for a referendum at the end of three years has been abandoned, and the initial insistence on complete NATO control has been watered down to some extent by a series of U.N. mandates and the presence of Russian forces.

But even where the peace plan still parallels the Rambouillet Accords, it threatens near-permanent American involvement in an endless set of predictable conflicts and possible guerrilla war. The turgid language of the accord was designed to be impenetrable, so that each party could interpret the inevitable ambiguities as favorable to itself. This diplomatic device is not without precedent, but it is a special problem when it involves parties that have refined their volatile passions for centuries in the crucible of mutual slaughter. The Petersberg Plan provides for four stages of political evolution: (1) an interim reign over Kosovo by a designated administrator; (2) an international civil presence; (3) substantial autonomy for the people of Kosovo within Yugoslavia, under the aegis of the U.N. Security Council; (4) the development of provisional democratic self-governing institutions.

Every aspect of this scheme is a potential land mine. According to Point 8, the political framework is supposed to take full account of the Rambouillet Accords and the principles of sovereignty and territorial integrity of the Federal Republic of Yugoslavia. How can those objectives possibly be reconciled? Rambouillet provided for the occupation of Kosovo by NATO and the referendum on the future of Kosovo at the end of three years. The peace plan stops at autonomy and repeatedly affirms Yugoslav sovereignty. But the KLA fought and suffered for independence, not autonomy. After what its members and the population of Kosovo endured during the ethnic-cleansing campaign, remaining within Serbia will be inconceivable to them. The additional provision of Point 8, for the "demilitarization of the KLA" by NATO, is even more difficult to imagine happening.

If any of these provisions are to be realized, they must be imposed by American and other Allied military forces. We will be in the ironic position that, having fought on the side of the Albanians for their autonomy, we may find ourselves resisting them (or perhaps even fighting against them) over the issue of their independence. And having gone to war to defend the Albanian population against Serbian ethnic cleansing, we may now be obliged to protect the Serbian population against the rage of their Albanian neighbors. Unless we are willing to sustain a near-permanent military occupation, ethnic cleansing of the Serbian population could well be the outcome.

The confusion is magnified by another provision of Point 8 that envisions "negotiations between the parties." But who are these parties? Presumably they are the Serbs and the Albanians. It adds that deadlock "should not delay or disrupt the establishment of self-governing institutions" — a provision that could paradoxically guarantee deadlock. The agreement is silent as to who should shoulder the task of imposing such self-governing institutions — implicitly leaving that responsibility with the United States. Not only are we imperceptibly on the road to replacing the Ottoman and Austrian empires in the Balkans; in time, we may face the same hostility from the native populations that they did.

The projected command arrangements compound the ambiguity. The military forces, in the words of the U.N. resolution, will be substantially NATO's. Additional troops from Russia will be assigned under uncertain command arrangements. To prevent the partition of Kosovo, the plan will not give Russian troops a separate area — unless they preempt the decision by occupying a part of Kosovo unilaterally, as they seemed to be doing last week. Moreover, the role of all these forces is vague, and their rules of engagement are defined by the Security Council.

Analogies to Bosnia are misleading. The Dayton agreement ending the Bosnian conflict was negotiated and approved by all the parties. In Kosovo, NATO has imposed an agreement on both sides. In Bosnia, the three armies ended up on homogeneous territories specifically assigned to them by the Dayton Accords. In Kosovo there is no such equivalent solution. Nor are there armies to separate, since Serb forces will presumably have left. NATO's task — to confirm the departure of Serb forces, to disarm the KLA, and to protect Kosovo's borders — is likely to bring them into conflict with Albanians seeking to influence events in Kosovo or Macedonia. All this may place our troops squarely in the middle of a civil guerrilla war, posing the same dilemma we encountered in Somalia.

Arrangements for civil administration contain comparable potential conflicts. The enormous tasks of reconstruction will fall to the civil administrator appointed by the U.N. Secretary-General — "in consultation with the Security Council" and operating under a mandate established by a U.N. resolution. The administrator will need to organize a police force and oversee the restoration of essential services in a totally devastated country. As indigenous Kosovar institutions come to life, they are likely to challenge the civil administrator's authority in the name of independence. What if the KLA emerges as the police force of autonomous authority? And, as Serbia recovers, it may challenge — possibly with Russia's backing — the civil administrator in the name of Yugoslav sovereignty.

The situation in Kosovo differs from Bosnia in yet another important respect. Bosnia was, in a way, sui generis. The evolution of Kosovo is bound to have a profound impact on its neighbors. The immediate impact is likely to be on the Albanians in Macedonia, who comprise about a quarter of the Macedonian population. They are likely to demand, at a minimum, the same status for themselves that the Kosovars are given. And the disintegration of Macedonia could ignite another Balkan explosion. Comparable pressures can be expected from the smaller Albanian minority in Montenegro. In addition, there exists a drive toward a greater Albania, encouraged both from Tirana and by émigré Albanians supplying much of the financial muscle. Aware of these tendencies — and as a sop to Russia and Yugloslav self-respect — the West has conceded Belgrade's sovereignty over Kosovo in order to keep it from emerging as an independent international presence. But the plan cannot possibly work smoothly. Russia and Yugoslavia will have every incentive to affirm Yugoslav sovereignty, while America and NATO cannot indefinitely stand in the way of Albanian self-determination.

In short, if we try to implement the U.N. resolution for any length of time, we will emerge as the permanent party to arcane and bitter Balkan quarrels. It would be far wiser to cut the Gordian knot and concede Kosovar independence as part of an overall Balkan settlement — perhaps including self-determination for each of the three ethnic groups of Bosnia. In such an arrangement, the borders of Kosovo and its neighbors should be guaranteed by NATO or the Organization for Security and Cooperation in Europe. As in Bosnia, the international forces would then patrol both sides of these borders for at least a substantial interim period.

Moving the issue to a definite resolution as quickly as possible is all the more important because of the hostility of the international environment. Most nations either supported or tolerated the Dayton Accords. This is not the case in Kosovo. Russia may have thrown in the towel on seeking to shape the immediate outcome significantly; but it feels deeply humiliated. Kosovo has become a public symbol of Russia's loss of influence and its public degradation by the West. It has no incentive to facilitate the arrangement once it is in place. Rather, Moscow is likely to seek occasions to obstruct it or to oppose elsewhere what it perceives as America's hegemonic tendencies. From the U.S. point of view, the more quickly the Kosovo issue is removed from the Russo-American agenda, the better for our long-term relations. And Russia should have no interest in perpetuating a state of affairs in which it can embarrass us but cannot prevail.

The same is true, to a lesser extent, of China, which rejects the unilateral manner in which NATO intervened in what Beijing perceives as the internal matters of Yugoslavia. Indeed, most of the nations of the world will have an incentive to create obstacles to the application of the Rambouillet principles enshrined in the Kosovo agreement. Countries concerned that they may be the subject of unilateral NATO action may distance themselves from us after the dust settles. They may have an incentive to acquire weapons of mass destruction as the surest deterrent to America's conventional superiority. How ironically history repeats its patterns. During the Cold War the democracies relied on nuclear weapons to balance an assumed Soviet conventional superiority. In the post-Kosovo period, it is the smaller countries that may turn to weapons of mass destruction in response to America's overwhelming technological edge in conventional weaponry. For all these reasons, it is imperative to undertake a major assessment of how to relate the new foreign policy to an international consensus.

Even the Atlantic Alliance will never be the same after Kosovo. The Clinton Administration skillfully held the Alliance together through more than ten weeks of bombing. But the decision of the European Union's heads of state at Cologne to accelerate a unified European defense and foreign policy reflects deep uneasiness about Europe's relative impotence in face of the imperious American tactics. A serious European effort to build autonomous centers of decision would be far from undesirable provided Europe backs up its new organization with appropriate resources. But it also requires a new thoughtfulness on both sides of the Atlantic if the vital American interest in close transatlantic cooperation is to survive.

For the foreseeable future, America will have a division and a half of our soldiers on near-permanent sentry duty at the fringes of the Balkans. We should, therefore, temper triumphalism with some reflection on the need to establish geopolitical priorities. Before we treat Kosovo as the model for a new era of humanitarian diplomacy, we should examine where else either the diplomacy or the strategy might apply. There are some 22 million refugees around the world and scores of ethnic conflicts. To which of them would a comparable mix of force and diplomacy be relevant? Where else could we bomb for ten weeks without U.S. military casualties, a prohibitive risk of escalation or creating untenable precedents? The demonstration of what democracies can accomplish when aroused will stand us in good stead in the years ahead. But the ultimate legacy of Kosovo will depend on whether our diplomatic endgame matches the display of our power.

Bestiality and Humanity: A War on the Border between Law and Morality

JÜRGEN HABERMAS

With the *Bundeswehr's* [German Armed Forces'] first combat activity [since World War II], there came to an end that long period of restraint which had strongly marked the civilian aspects of the German postwar mentality. A war is on. To be sure, the "air strikes" of the alliance are supposed to be something other than a traditional war. The "surgical precision" of the aerial attacks and the programmatic sparing of civilians do, in fact, have a high value with respect to legitimating these actions. All this points to a retreat from the kind of "total war" that has determined the physiognomy of the century now coming to an end. But even those of us who are only half-participants, who are served up the Kosovo conflict each night with the television news, know full well that the Yugoslavian population cowering under the bombardments is experiencing nothing but war.

Happily, the clunky noises are absent from the public discussion in Germany. No anguished longing for "fate," no intellectual beating of drums for the "good comrade."[1] During the Gulf War, the rhetoric of the worst-case scenario, the invocation of the pathos of the state, of honor, tragedy, and manly maturity were

---

1. This may be an allusion to the literary products of, for example, Ernst Juenger, who wrote rhapsodically about the *Kampferlebnis* of World War I as a source of great joy and camaraderie (John Torpey). [Ed.]

This essay, translated by John Torpey with some revisions by the editor, originally appeared in the weekly *Die Zeit* 18 (29 April 1999). It appeared in the context of an intense — if reassuringly "normal" — German public controversy over the justifiability of the NATO war against Yugoslavia, which testified to one of the main themes of Habermas's writings for a wider public: that, in the aftermath of the Nazis' catastrophic abandonment of the liberal tradition, Germany and the Germans have become firmly tied to the political institutions and philosophical traditions of the West. For more of Habermas's reflections on the broader themes addressed in the essay, see his "Human Rights and Popular Sovereignty," *Ratio Juris* 7, no. 1 (1994): 1-13. [The editor wishes to thank Jürgen Habermas for his translation suggestions and his approval of the essay's final form; Thomas McCarthy and John Joseph Buckley Jr. for their assistance; and Katrina Vanden Heuvel of *The Nation* for her suggestions.]

still being wheeled out against a noisy peace movement. Not much remains of either. Here and there one still finds a bit of sneering at a pacifism grown quiescent or the harsh phrase "we are descending from the heights of morality." But not even this kind of bark has much bite, because both advocates and opponents of the intervention are using a crystal-clear normative language.

The pacifist opponents of the intervention remind us of the moral distinction between action and forbearance, and direct our attention to the suffering of the civilian victims, who must "take in stride" even the most accurate application of military force. This time, however, the appeal is directed not at the good conscience of hard-bitten realists flying the banner of *raison d'Etat* but against the legal pacifism of a "Red-Green" government. Side by side with the old democracies, which have been more strongly shaped by theories of modern natural law[2] than have we, Ministers Fischer and Scharping appeal to the idea of domesticating the "state of nature" between nations for the sake of human rights.[3] The transformation of the "law of nations" into a law of world-citizens is thus on the agenda.

Legal pacifism seeks not merely to damp down the latent state of war between sovereign states via international law, but to transform it into a cosmopolitan order that is thoroughly governed by law. We Germans have also had exponents of this tradition, from Kant to Kelsen.[4] But only now has a German government taken it seriously for the first time. Direct membership in an association of world-citizens would protect the national citizen even from the arbitrariness of his or her own government. The most important consequence of a legal order that pierces the sovereignty of states — as the Pinochet case already suggests — is the personal liability of functionaries for crimes they commit in the service of the state or in war.

The public debate in the Federal Republic [of Germany] is dominated by the pacifists-by-conviction, on the one hand, and the legal pacifists, on the other. Yet even the "realists" slip on the cloak of normative rhetoric. The different positions, pro and con, bring together people with contradictory motives. Those who think in terms of power politics, who distrust in principle any normative constraints on the use of force by sovereign states, find themselves arm in arm with pacifists, while the committed "Atlanticists" must suppress their irritation with those in the government who enthusiastically defend human rights — with people, in other words, who not so long ago took to the streets to oppose the stationing of Pershing II missiles in Germany. [Christian Democratic Union (CDU) leader Alfred] Dregger and [long-time Social Democratic Party (SPD) foreign affairs expert

2. Although the German text can be rendered "legal-rational traditions," Professor Habermas has told the editor that "theories of modern natural law" are actually what he means. [Ed.]

3. Scharping is Minister of Defense, and Fischer is Foreign Minister. [Ed.]

4. Hans Kelsen was a leading German legal theorist. [Ed.]

Egon] Bahr stand with [Green pacifist/fundi Hans-Christian] Stroebele, [CDU leader Wolfgang] Schauble and [CDU former Defense Minister Volker] Ruhe with [left-wing Social Democrat Erhard] Eppler. In short, the twin facts of the left in government and the predominance of normative arguments explain not just the peculiar political alignments, but the reassuring situation that the public discussion and mood in Germany are no different than those in other west European countries. No *Sonderweg,* no peculiar sensibilities. Indeed, divisions are more apparent between continental Europeans and Anglo-Saxons, at least between those who invite the General Secretary of the U.N. to consult with them and who seek an understanding with Russia, and those who trust mainly in the efficacy of their own weapons.

Of course, the U.S. and the member states of the European Union, who carry the political responsibility, proceed from a common position. After the failure of the negotiations at Rambouillet, they are conducting the previously threatened military action against Yugoslavia with the declared aim of achieving liberal arrangements for the autonomy of Kosovo within Serbia. Within the classical framework of international law, that would have constituted interference in the internal affairs of a sovereign state — that is, as a violation of the prohibition on intervention. Under the premises of human rights politics, however, this intervention is supposed to be understood as an armed mission to establish peace that has the tacit authorization of the international community (despite the lack of a U.N. mandate). According to this Western interpretation, the war in Kosovo could signify a big step on the path from the classical international law of states to the cosmopolitan law of a society of world-citizens.

This process had begun with the founding of the United Nations and was, after its stagnation during the Cold War, accelerated by the Gulf War and other interventions. Admittedly, humanitarian interventions since 1945 have taken place only in the name of the U.N. and with the formal assent of the government involved (to the extent that a functioning state existed). During the Gulf War, of course, the Security Council intervened de facto in the "internal affairs" of a sovereign state by creating "no-fly zones" in Iraqi airspace and "protected areas" for Kurdish refugees in northern Iraq. Yet this was not justified on the grounds of protecting a persecuted minority from its own government. In Resolution 688 of April 1991, the U.N. appealed to its right of intervention in cases of "threats to international security." The situation is different today. The North Atlantic military alliance is acting without the mandate of the Security Council but justifies the intervention as emergency assistance to a persecuted ethnic (and religious) minority.

Already in the months before the beginning of the air attacks, some 300,000 persons were subjected to murder, terror, and expulsion. In the meantime, the disturbing images of the deportee columns on the routes to Macedonia, Montenegro, and Albania provided the evidence of a systematically planned process of ethnic cleansing. That those fleeing are on occasion also held back as hostages hardly improves the situation. Although Milosevic has used the air war to pursue his nefarious designs to the bitter end, the depressing scenes from the refugee camps do not permit us to confuse the chain of causation. Putting a stop to a murderous ethnonationalism was, after all, the aim of the negotiations. It is a matter of controversy whether the clauses of the Genocide Convention of 1948 can be applied to what is now taking place on the ground under the cover of the air war. More relevant, however, are the criteria concerning "crimes against humanity" that entered into international law as a result of the war crimes tribunals of Nuremberg and Tokyo. The Security Council has recently begun to treat acts meeting these criteria as "threats to peace" that may justify coercive measures under certain circumstances. But without a mandate from the Security Council, the intervening states in this case can only derive an authorization for emergency assistance from the *erga omnes* binding principles, which are international.[5]

However things may stand in legal terms, the claim of the Kosovars to coexistence on an equal footing and the outrage about the injustice of their brutal expulsion have garnered for the military intervention a broad, if nuanced, approbation in the West. CDU foreign policy spokesman Karl Lamers has elegantly expressed the ambivalence that has accompanied this approval from the outset: "Our consciences can be clear. That, at least, is what our reason tells us; but our hearts won't quite listen. We are uncertain and troubled. . . ."

There are several sources of disquiet. In the course of the last few weeks, doubts have grown about the wisdom of a negotiating strategy that left no other alternative but an armed assault. Doubts exist, too, about the suitability of the military strikes for achieving NATO's ends. While support for Milosevic's truculent, inflexible policy grows among the Yugoslav population, even deep into the ranks of the opposition, the frightening side effects of the war accumulate on all sides. The adjacent states of Macedonia and Albania, as well as the Yugoslav Republic of Montenegro, have for a variety of reasons slid into instability; in a Russia with considerable atomic weaponry, the solidarity of broad segments of the population with a "fraternal people" has put the government under intensified pressure. Doubts pile up, above all, about the proportionality of the military means. With each case of "collateral damage" — with each train unintentionally plunged into the drink along with a bombed Danube bridge, with each tractor carrying fleeing Albanians, each Serbian neighborhood, each civilian target that mistakenly falls victim to a rocket blast — there arises not just some unfortunate contingency of war, but suffering that "our" intervention has on its conscience.

Questions of proportionality are difficult to decide. Shouldn't NATO have announced the destruction of the state radio station half an hour earlier? The sense of disquiet increases also with the destruction that is intentional — the

5. This is the English translation of Professor Habermas. The Latin term *erga omnes* literally means "toward all." [Ed.]

burning tobacco factory, the towering inferno of the gas works, the bombed office buildings, streets, and bridges, the ruination of the economic infrastructure of a country already squeezed by a U.N. embargo. Every fleeing child who dies takes its toll on our nerves. For despite the clear chain of causation, the skeins of responsibility grow increasingly tangled. Amid the miseries of the expulsion, it is difficult to disentangle the consequences of the cruel policies of a state-terrorist from the side effects of military strikes that provide him with a pretext instead of putting a stop to his bloody operations.

And finally there are doubts about the political objective, which has become diffuse. To be sure, the five demands on Milosevic follow the same flawless principles according to which the Dayton Agreement for a liberal, multiethnic Bosnia was constructed. The Kosovo Albanians would not have had a right to secession if only their claim to autonomy within Serbia were fulfilled. The nationalism of a Greater Albania, which would receive a boost from a secession [of Kosovo from Serbia], is not the least bit better than the Greater Serbian variety, which the intervention was intended to thwart. In the meantime, each passing day's wounds from the ethnic cleansing make a revision of the objective of national coexistence on an equal footing ever more unavoidable. But a partition of Kosovo would surely constitute a secession that no one can wish to see take place. For its part, the creation of a protectorate would require a change of strategy, namely a ground war and the decades-long presence of peacekeeping forces. If these unanticipated consequences were to emerge, the question of the legitimacy of the undertaking would retrospectively arise again in a quite different form.

In the pronouncements of our government one finds a certain shrill tone, an overkill of questionable historical parallels — as if Fischer and Scharping needed the jackhammer rhetoric in order to drown out another voice in their own heads. Is it the fear that the political failure of the military action might place the intervention in a completely different light, perhaps setting back by decades the project of creating a comprehensive legal framework for the relations among states? Would the "police action" that NATO has magnanimously undertaken on behalf of the international community then not turn out to be an ordinary war, even a dirty war that has driven the Balkans into even greater catastrophes? And wouldn't that be water on the mill of a Carl Schmitt, who always knew better: "He who says 'humanity' wants to deceive."[6] Schmitt reduced his anti-humanism to the famous formula "Humanity, bestiality." The persistent doubt about whether or not legal pacifism is, in the end, the right project — that is the deepest of all the sources of disquiet.

---

6. Carl Schmitt (1888-1985) was one of the most influential German legal and political theorists of the twentieth century, known for his attacks on Weimar and his involvement with the Nazis (Tom McCarthy). [Ed.]

The Contradictions of *Realpolitik*

The war in Kosovo touches on a fundamental question, one much debated in political science and philosophy. To the democratic constitutional state belongs the great achievement for civilization of legally constraining political violence on the basis of the sovereignty of state subjects recognized in international law; while a "cosmopolitan" condition calls into question this independence of the national state. Does the universalism of the Enlightenment here come up against the stubborn persistence of a political violence inexorably inscribed in the drive to collective self-preservation of particular communities? That is the "realist" thorn in the side of human rights politics.

Of course, the realist school, too, recognizes the structural transformation of that system of independent states which came into being in 1648 with the Peace of Westphalia: the interdependencies of an increasingly complex world-society; the magnitude of problems that states can only solve cooperatively; the burgeoning authority and density of supranational institutions, regimes, and procedures — and not only in the realm of collective security; the "economization" of foreign policy and, indeed, the blurring of the classical boundary between domestic and foreign policy. But a pessimistic view of human nature and a peculiarly opaque concept of "the" political provide the background for a doctrine that wishes to stick more or less without exception to the principle of nonintervention adumbrated in classical international law. In the free-fire zone of international relations, independent national states should be free to move about in accordance with their own assessment of their interests — because the security and survival of the collective are nonnegotiable values from the perspective of the members, and because, viewed from the perspective of an observer, the imperatives of the rational pursuit of self-preservation are best adapted to regulating the relations among collective actors.

From this standpoint, interventionist human rights politics is guilty of a categorical mistake. It underestimates and discriminates against the more or less "natural" tendency to self-preservation. It wants to impose normative standards on a potential for violence that eludes normative regulation. Carl Schmitt had further sharpened this argument with his peculiarly stylized "essentializing" of the political. The very attempt to "moralize" an intrinsically neutral *raison d'Etat*, he claimed, is what lets the politics of human rights deform the natural struggle of nations into a bitter "struggle against evil."

Compelling objections can be raised against this view of things. It is not as if, in the postnational constellation, power-strutting national states are being brought to heel by the rules of the international community. On the contrary, it is the erosion of state authority, the civil wars and ethnic conflicts within collapsing states or in those being held together in authoritarian fashion, that call forth interventions — not just in Somalia and Rwanda, but also in Bosnia and now in

Kosovo. The critique rooted in ideological suspicion finds just as little nourishment. The present case demonstrates that universalistic justifications do not always mask the particularity of concealed interests. What the "hermeneutics of suspicion" claims to find behind the attack on Yugoslavia is rather meager. For politicians to whom the global economy leaves little room to maneuver domestically, foreign adventures may offer some opportunities for muscle flexing. But neither the motive ascribed to the U.S. of securing and expanding its spheres of influence, nor the motive ascribed to NATO of trying to clarify its future role, nor even the motive ascribed to "Fortress Europe" of an anticipatory defense against a wave of immigrants explains the decision to undertake so momentous, risky, and costly an intervention.

Testifying against the "realist" interpretation is above all the fact that the bloodstains left behind by the state subjects of international law in the catastrophic course of twentieth-century history have made an absurdity of the presumption of innocence in classical international law. The foundation of the U.N. and its *Universal Declaration of Human Rights,* as well as the threat of punishment for wars of aggression and for crimes against humanity — leading to at least a half-hearted revision of the principle of nonintervention — were necessary and proper answers to the morally significant experiences of the century: that is, to a totalitarian politics unbound and to the Holocaust.

Finally, the charge of a "moralization" of politics rests on a lack of conceptual clarity. For the attempt to establish a cosmopolitan condition would mean that violations of human rights would not be treated under moral precepts and battled as such, but rather would be prosecuted in the same way as are criminal actions within the legal order of a state today.[7] The creation of a comprehensive legal framework for international relations is impossible without established procedures for conflict resolution. The very process of institutionalizing these procedures will protect the juridically codified approach to human rights violations from blurring law and morality and will help to prevent any legally unmediated moral discrimination between "enemies."[8]

Such a condition can be attained even without the monopoly on violence of a world-state and without a world-government. What is necessary, however, is a functioning Security Council, the binding jurisdiction of an international criminal court, and the supplementation of the General Assembly of government representatives by a "second level" of representation of world-citizens. Given that this reform of the United Nations is not in the immediate offing, pointing to the difference between the creation of an international legal framework and the moraliza-

7. Professor Habermas has specifically formulated the English translation of this sentence. [Ed.]

8. Professor Habermas has specifically formulated the English translation of this sentence. [Ed.]

tion of politics is correct but of ambiguous significance. So long as human rights are relatively weakly institutionalized on the global level, the boundary between law and morality may blur, as in the present case. Because the Security Council is blocked, NATO can only appeal to the moral validity of international law — to norms, in other words, for which there are not yet effective mechanisms for applying and enforcing law that are recognized by the international community.[9]

The under-institutionalization of cosmopolitan law expresses itself, for example, in the gap between the legitimacy and the effectiveness of peacekeeping and peacemaking interventions. The U.N. had declared Srebrenica a "safe haven," but the troops legitimately stationed there were unable to prevent a grisly massacre after the Serbs marched in. In contrast, NATO can only move effectively against the Yugoslav government because it undertook the operation without the legitimation that would have been denied it by the Security Council.

. . . and the Dilemma of Human Rights Politics

Human rights politics aims to close the gap between these mirror-image situations. Often, however, in view of the underinstitutionalized cosmopolitan law, it is forced into a mere anticipation of a future cosmopolitan condition that it simultaneously tries to promote. Under these paradoxical circumstances, how can one pursue a politics intended to ensure respect for human rights, if necessary with military force? The question also poses itself even if one cannot intervene everywhere — not on behalf of the Kurds, not on behalf of the Chechens or Tibetans, but at least on one's own doorstep in the war-torn Balkans. An interesting difference is emerging in the understanding of human rights politics between the Americans and the Europeans. The U.S. pursues the global enforcement of human rights as the national mission of a world power that presses this aim under the premises of power politics. Most of the EU governments, in contrast, understand by "a politics of human rights" a project for the creation of a comprehensive legal framework for international relations that has changed the present parameters of power politics already.

The U.S. has assumed the tasks of keeping order that are incumbent upon a superpower in a world of states that is only weakly regulated by the U.N. Against that background, human rights function as moral orientations for the evaluation of national goals. Of course, there have always been isolationist countertendencies, and, like other countries, the U.S. pursues its own interests first and foremost — and they don't always square with the declared normative objectives. The Vietnam War demonstrated this; and the United States's approach to problems in its own "backyard" demonstrates it over and over again. But the "new hybrid of humani-

---

9. Professor Habermas has added the word *yet*. [Ed.]

tarian selflessness and the logic of imperial power" (Ulrich Beck) has a long pedigree in the United States.[10] In Wilson's motives for entering World War I and Roosevelt's for entering World War II, one also finds the orientation to ideals that are deeply rooted in the tradition of pragmatism. It is to this orientation that we — the country that was defeated in 1945 — owe the fact that we were also liberated at the same time. From this very American (i.e., national) perspective of a normatively oriented power politics, it must seem plausible to continue the struggle against Yugoslavia, full speed ahead and without compromise, without regard for all the complications, even to the point of introducing ground troops if necessary. That, at least, has the advantage of consistency. But what shall we say if one day the military alliance of another region — let's say Asia — pursues an armed human rights politics based on a very different (i.e., their) interpretation of international law or the U.N. Charter?

Things look different if human rights come into play not just as the moral orientation of one's own political action but rather as rights that must be implemented in such a legal sense. Irrespective of their purely moral *content*, human rights bear the *form* and characteristics of subjective rights that are intrinsically dependent on achieving positive validity in an order of enforceable law. Only when human rights have found their "seat" in a worldwide democratic legal order, with a status similar to that of basic rights in our constitutions, will we be able to take for granted that the addressees of these rights can simultaneously understand themselves as their authors.

The institutions of the U.N. are on the road to closing the gap in the application of enforceable law and democratic lawmaking. Where that is not the case, norms — however moral their content — remain coercively imposed constraints. To be sure, in Kosovo the intervening states are attempting to vindicate the claims of those whose human rights are being trampled by their own government. But the Serbs who are dancing in the streets of Belgrade are, as Slavoj Zizek puts it, "not disguised Americans waiting to be liberated from the curse of nationalism."[11] A political order guaranteeing equal rights for all citizens is being imposed on them with force of arms. That is also true from a normative standpoint, at least so long as the U.N. fails to adopt coercive measures against its member state Yugoslavia. Even nineteen undoubtedly democratic states remain "interested parties" if they authorize themselves to intervene. They exercise a power of interpretation and decision that, if things today were as they should be, would only be due to in-

10. Ulrich Beck is a well-known German sociologist who writes frequently for *Der Spiegel.* [Ed.]

11. Slavoj Zizek is a senior researcher at the Institute for Social Sciences, University of Ljubljana, Slovenia, and the author of many books, including *The Sublime Object of Ideology* (London: Verso, 1991), *Enjoy Your Symptom* (New York: Routledge, 1992), *Tarrying with the Negative: Kant, Hegel and the Critique of Ideology* (Durham: Duke University Press, 1993), and *The Ticklish Subject: The Absent Center of Political Ideology* (New York: Verso, 1999). [Ed.]

dependent institutions; to that extent, they act paternalistically. There are good moral reasons for them to do so. Those aware that they are acting on the basis of an unavoidable temporary paternalism, however, know that the violence they mete out does not yet have the character of a legal compulsion legitimated through the framework of a democratic society of world-citizens. Moral norms that appeal to our better insight may not be enforced *in the same manner* as are established legal norms.

From Power Politics to the Society of World-Citizens

Out of the dilemma of having to act as if a completely institutionalized cosmopolitan condition already existed, the achievement of which is supposed to be promoted, it does not, however, follow that the victims should be given over to their tormentors. The terroristic misuse of state violence transforms the classic civil war into a mass crime. If there is simply no other way, democratic neighbors must be permitted to come to assistance with the authorization of international law. Just at that point, however, the incompleteness of the cosmopolitan condition requires a special sensitivity. The existing institutions and procedures are the only available controls on the fallible judgment of one party who claims to act on behalf of the whole.

One source of misunderstanding, for example, is the historical noncontemporaneity of the political mentalities that confront one another. *Pace* Enzenberger, there is no temporal difference of 400 years between the NATO air war and the war of the Serbs on the ground.[12] When I think about Greater Serbian nationalism, I think more of [early nineteenth-century German nationalist] Ernst-Moritz Arndt than of Hans-Jakob Grimmelshausen [seventeenth-century author of the picaresque novel *Simplicius Simplicissimus*]. But political scientists have noted the development of a new kind of split between the "first" and "second" worlds. Only the peaceful, prosperous societies of the OECD [Organization for Economic Cooperation and Development] can afford to bring their national interests more or less into line with the halfway cosmopolitan standards of the United Nations.[13] In contrast, the "Second World" (according to the new interpretation) has taken up the power-political inheritance of European nationalism. States such as Libya, Iraq, and Serbia make up for their unstable internal conditions with authoritarian rule and identity politics, while they behave expansionistically toward other states,

12. Hans Magnus Enzenberger is a major literary figure, cultural critic, and political commentator. [Ed.]

13. The Organization for Economic Cooperation and Development (OECD) was effectively established in 1961 and currently includes 29 members, as well as one special member (European Union). [Ed.]

are touchy about border issues, and insist neurotically on their sovereignty. These kinds of observations raise the thresholds of restraint in dealing with one another. Today they justify the demand for intensified diplomatic efforts.

It is one thing for the U.S., in the tracks of however remarkable a political tradition, to play the role of a hegemonic guarantor of an order oriented to human rights. But it is another thing altogether if we come to understand the precarious transition from classical power politics to a cosmopolitan condition as a common learning process to be managed, somehow bridging the trenches of hot, armed conflict. The broader perspective urges greater caution. NATO's self-authorization cannot be permitted to become a matter of routine.

Get Serious about Kosovo

ZBIGNIEW BRZEZINSKI

In Kosovo, U.S. Cannot Avoid Grim Choices

The Wall Street Journal (March 24, 1999)

Congress should heed President Clinton's appeal for bipartisan endorsement of NATO's efforts to compel Serbian compliance regarding Kosovo. With Russian Prime Minister Yevgeny Primakov abruptly canceling his trip to the U.S. yesterday, NATO action appears imminent; indeed, the bombing may already have started by the time you read this. The stakes are enormous in their humanitarian as well as political dimensions. Failure to act is likely to generate savage ethnic cleansing and even to undermine NATO. A wider Balkan war might also erupt. Belgrade must either accept autonomy for Kosovo, retaining only nominal Yugoslav sovereignty, or be made to face the prospect of an independent Kosovo.

Such support for the administration's current policy does not obviate the need for a serious public discussion of the grave strategic dilemmas that the U.S. is now likely to confront. Nor does it absolve the administration of blame for the way it has handled the crisis thus far. American negotiators have persistently relied on Mr. Milosevic's word even after he has repeatedly broken it. Worse, U.S. policymakers have issued a series of unfulfilled ultimatums that have only convinced the Serbs that the world's only superpower has developed a penchant for theatrical posturing and that U.S. threats are idle.

The policy of threatening loudly but waving a wet noodle has also made it more difficult for Mr. Milosevic seriously to consider making any concessions. Faced by the near unanimous opposition of the Serbian people to any compromise regarding Kosovo, Mr. Milosevic has been unable to argue credibly that yielding is necessary to save Serbia from a pending disaster. The resulting paradox is that to "help" Mr. Milosevic make the right decision, NATO will have to act far more aggressively now than may have been necessary as recently as six months ago.

In the earlier conflict in Bosnia, NATO's air power was able to disrupt much weaker and partially irregular Serb forces, and the bombing campaign also exploited the concurrent successes on the ground won by the reasonably well-equipped and mobile Croatian military. Before long, confronted with the prospect of a massive political defeat, Mr. Milosevic conceded. That earned him official U.S. favor as a "realist," which later led to the administration's misguided expectations regarding his willingness to abide by last October's limited agreement on Kosovo.

Yet with the moment of truth finally upon us, it will be much more difficult to replicate in Kosovo what the use of force accomplished in Bosnia. For one thing, the Serbian forces there are stronger, with the regular Serbian army directly involved. For another, there is no equivalent on the ground to the Croatian military. The Kosovo Liberation Army is not as well equipped, and the Serbs are likely to wipe it out in any head-to-head conflict. Moreover, NATO's ability to hit the Serb forces hard in Kosovo is likely to be inhibited by a deliberate Serbian policy to deploy its heavy equipment within Kosovar villages and small towns, thus compelling any NATO air attacks to inflict considerable collateral damage — with all the concomitant political costs.

At some point, then, NATO will be faced with a painful choice: it can either commit its ground forces against the Serbs, or it can engage in a campaign of massive attrition not only of Serbia's military but also of its economic assets.

The first option could become necessary in the face of a swift and brutally successful Serbian military campaign against the Kosovars. Yet it is quite obvious that at present the NATO countries have no stomach for any serious ground combat. The absence of a viable ground option puts a heavy onus on the bombing campaign. It must destroy the Serb capacity to wage war, and it must induce Belgrade to concede politically. In effect, it must accomplish what normally would be attained by a combined air and ground operation.

Accordingly, the only strategic alternative available in the face of protracted Serb defiance is a massive air campaign that can only become increasingly violent in its social and economic effects. We can only hope that that prospect will not materialize, with Mr. Milosevic yielding at the last minute. Yet the manner in which the crisis has so far been handled both by the U.S. and its European allies may tempt the Serbs to engage in a test of wills for which the administration had better be fully prepared. And that, alas, means that the air assault, to be politically credible to the regime in Belgrade, will have to be very heavy from day one.

It also means that it will be essential for NATO leaders to make a special effort to sustain political support for a potentially messy and prolonged bombing campaign. Mr. Milosevic may believe that he can prevail on the ground even while not in control of the skies. Russia may calculate that the failure of the air assault, or rising domestic opposition to it in the West, will discredit both American global leadership and the recently enlarged NATO. All of that increases the international stakes involved and makes it essential that the air campaign be massive in order "to win" both militarily and politically.

To Stop the Serbs

The Washington Post (March 30, 1999)

NATO is currently engaged in primarily a strategic bombing campaign against Serbian command centers and air defenses. The problem with such a campaign is that it gives the Serbs time to engage in mini-genocide and in mass ethnic cleansing in Kosovo. Moreover, a strategic air campaign mobilizes not only Serbian but international public opinion against a perceived attack on civilians. Last but not least, it conditions the Serbs to dig in their heels and wait for a break in Western resolve.

To overcome this condition, NATO must take three major steps, each entailing risks but each contributing to a higher probability of eventual success. The first involves an immediate shift to a combined strategic as well as tactical air campaign. Presumably this is happening already, but the point is that the tactical air campaign has to be extensive, intensive, and persistent. Its object has to be to inflict maximum casualties on Serbian military formations, and especially on heavy tank and artillery concentrations. To the extent that Serbian forces are deprived of such assets, the remaining Serb units will gradually lose their mobility, and their firepower will be drastically decreased. The asymmetry between them and the Kosovo Liberation Army will thus be significantly reduced.

A tactical air campaign cannot be conducted without some loss of aircraft. Here, too, an adjustment in the prevailing Western outlook is needed. One cannot expect to wage war (and mostly with professionals — i.e., volunteers) without suffering casualties. The more intensive the tactical air campaign and the earlier it comes, the higher will be the allied losses. Yet, not to undertake such a campaign means a much more massive number of Albanians killed by the Serbs and a higher level of Serbian confidence that Serb forces on the ground will be able to achieve Slobodan Milosevic's fundamental political objective: the "cleansing" of Kosovo of its Albanian population. The tradeoff, however painful for the West, is thus clearly in favor of undertaking the tactical air campaign at the earliest possible moment, and doing it to the maximum tactical military benefit possible.

The second major step that is necessary is to deprive the Serbs of any illusion that they may be able to retain Kosovo by force of arms, even while absorbing Western air bombardment. That means, in the first instance, a deliberate decision by the West to arm the KLA. Such a decision is both politically and morally justifiable, for the Albanians in Kosovo are currently facing the prospect of social extinction.

The KLA is not a force capable of matching the Serbs on the ground, and it is currently woefully underarmed, particularly in anti-tank weaponry. Anti-tank weapons presumably could even be airdropped to some KLA units. A prompt injection of Western arms would boost Albanian morale and send an unmistakable signal to Belgrade that there is no prospect of a Serbian victory on the ground, either politically or militarily.

Should the efforts to arm the KLA and to engage in sustained tactical air attacks prove inadequate, at some point Western public opinion may reach the conclusion that NATO ground forces have to be injected. A decision to that effect can only be made with strong public support, but the political case for such intervention should begin to be made now, especially in view of the atrocities being committed.

The third needed step is to face the fact that Milosevic's dictatorship has now forfeited any moral or political right to continued sovereignty over Kosovo. The original proposed "compromise" formula involved retention of nominal Serbian sovereignty over Kosovo. The barbaric conduct of Milosevic's military and police has terminated such rights. It is therefore timely for NATO to make it clear that the alliance will not consider any solution that entails the retention of Milosevic's authority of Kosovo. The purpose of the continuing military operation now has to be political self-determination for the Kosovars, and only a democratic government in Belgrade can be a party to any transitional arrangements that might involve less than that.

Whether one likes it or not, the events of the past week have transformed both the military and political dimensions of the Kosovo problem. A failure to prevail would precipitate a fundamental crisis of unity within NATO and a more anarchic global state of affairs. That fact should be faced squarely. Whatever one may think of Western diplomacy and of American leadership over the past few months, the issue now has been joined. If the words "never again" are to have any meaning, a civilized Euro-Atlantic community cannot tolerate genocidal barbarity in its own midst.

Get Serious: Steps to Victory in Kosovo

National Review (May 3, 1999)

On April 23, NATO is scheduled to hold in Washington a huge celebration of its fiftieth anniversary. If by then the conflict over Kosovo is still on, the meeting will provide an opportunity for a council of war — yes, it is a war — and for a reaffirmation of NATO's commitment to prevail. If by then NATO has won, the event will be a true celebration. If, however, NATO has embraced a negotiated settlement that yields to Slobodan Milosevic some concession over what NATO demanded just prior to the bombing, it will be a wake.

The stakes now involve far more than the fate of Kosovo. They were altered dramatically the day the bombing began. It is no exaggeration to say that NATO's failure to prevail would mean both the end of NATO as a credible alliance and the undermining of America's global leadership. And the consequences of either would be devastating to global stability.

It is instructive to pause here and ask, Who endorses the use of force to stop the ethnic killing and cleansing in Kosovo, and who opposes it? All of NATO's nineteen democracies stand united (even if a couple are wobbly), and all of Europe's other democracies are generally supportive. Violently opposed are the erratic admirer of Hitler in Belarus and the current Russian regime, which failed in Chechnya in what Milosevic is attempting to do in Kosovo. Two visions of the European future are thus colliding: one that views Europe as a community genuinely bound by a shared respect for human rights, and one that believes ruling national elites have the sovereign right to engage even in a type of genocide against their minorities.

Ill-wishers of America and Europe understand this well. A leading Moscow newspaper (*Nezavisimaya Gazeta,* on March 25) gloated openly — while also informing the Clinton administration where the Kremlin really stands — that the crisis initiates "the epoch of the collapse of the U.S. global empire and, evidently, the epoch of Europe's final eclipse." It went on to urge Russia "to just sit on the fence, saying all the necessary things and watching NATO destroy itself."

So far, the administration has done very well in keeping NATO together. But it has not done as well on the military level, and its political fortitude is questionable. During the first three weeks, NATO's air campaign against Serbia was timid and morally irresponsible. Sadly, there has been a failure to react in a timely fashion to the bestial treatment inflicted on the defenseless Kosovars. Though the ethnic cleansing undeniably predated the bombing, it was accelerated after the bombing started. The White House team cannot escape responsibility for the failure to do at least the minimum possible to impede the victimization of the Kosovars.

It is simply incomprehensible why the needed attack helicopters were not assembled before the air operation was launched. Did it not occur to any senior official that Serbian forces would move against the Kosovars? Why were the helicopters denied to NATO commanders for some ten days after the operation started, with the entire world watching the mass expulsions and learning also of large-scale executions? A strong tactical air assault against Milosevic's ground forces should have been launched from day one, even at the risk of losses. It is painful to imagine young Albanians desperately scanning the skies before being either raped or shot.

Moreover, the bombing has been conducted in a manner that defies even the most elementary notions of human psychology under conditions of war. Instead of shocking and intimidating the opponent, the air campaign has striven to avoid casualties not only to allied airmen but even to Milosevic's officials, thereby inoculating the Serbs against fear of bombing while mobilizing Serbian nationalist passions in support of the Belgrade dictator.

Also noteworthy is that, paradoxically, the strategic bombardment of Serbian assets has been conducted as if its goal were the attrition of the Serbian army in preparation for a NATO ground campaign. But President Clinton ruled out the latter, and even into the third week of the bombing he continued to reassure Milosevic that the U.S. had no intention of engaging in ground combat. One cannot avoid the suspicion that political expediency was at work here, at a time when genuine leadership was needed. This self-denying posture has given Milosevic every incentive to hunker down and absorb the punishment from the skies, while completing his cleansing of Kosovo.

Admittedly, a ground campaign cannot be launched instantly. It requires careful and deliberate deployment of forces and (in democracies) a strong base of public support. But if the air campaign does not produce the required political success, ground combat will become necessary. So why not prepare for it now? And why, in the present circumstances, give Milosevic a greater sense of confidence that he need not worry about it? It just makes no sense for the president and his advisors to be proclaiming that NATO forces will enter Kosovo only with Milosevic's permission.

Guidelines for Action

What then must be done? Given the stakes involved, the United States, as the recognized leader of the alliance, must pursue a no-holds-barred approach to winning. The American leadership must project principled courage and not be guided by a political compass. Belgrade's ruling elite must be convinced — by NATO's military actions as well as its political posture — that Milosevic's crimes and obduracy portend for it a collective ruin. To that end, the following guidelines should shape policy:

1. The Rambouillet formula for Kosovo's autonomy within Serbia is dead. It was killed by Milosevic's crimes against humanity. For several years to come, Kosovo's formal status will have to remain indeterminate, under NATO's direct protection.
2. It follows that there cannot be any negotiations with Milosevic himself, except in order to implement the modalities of Serbian withdrawal following the imposition of NATO's terms. The alliance should reject the temptation to accept any deal contrived by Russia that would grant Milosevic an easing of NATO's original terms. To do so would mark the bombing as a tragically pointless failure, would reward Milosevic for his ethnic cleansing, and would represent a great political success for the Kremlin's anti-NATO posture. That has to be made crystal clear.
3. The air campaign should be intensified if it is either to destroy Milosevic's military power or to compel him to accept NATO's terms. The current tar-

geting restrictions have seriously limited the bombing's military as well as political impact.

4. Major deployments should now be initiated in preparation for a possible NATO ground operation, presumably out of Albania and Macedonia. Once the bombing has effectively isolated the Serbian forces currently in Kosovo from Serbia proper, they will become vulnerable — especially when out of fuel and ammunition — to a sweep by NATO ground forces. In any case, a mopping-up operation will become necessary if Milosevic refuses to capitulate even with his army seriously weakened by systematic attrition from the air.

5. The victims of Kosovo have a moral right to self-defense. Hence weapons should be provided to those who resist. And such aid would further signal to Belgrade that its strategy of ethnic cleansing in Kosovo will fail.

6. Yugoslavia's foreign assets should be subject to seizure in all NATO countries, both to exert pressure on Belgrade and as a prelude to eventual reparations for the damage inflicted on Kosovo by Milosevic's forces.

7. Without waiting for the hostilities to end, the United States and the European Union should jointly announce their intention to formulate a comprehensive plan for the resettlement, reconstruction, and rehabilitation of Kosovo. A strong commitment to that end, buttressed by a stated determination to return all refugees to Kosovo, would greatly enhance the credibility of the ongoing bombing campaign, stripping Belgrade of any residual hopes for the retention of Kosovo or some part of it.

8. The program suggested in (7) should also contain a provision holding out the hope that a democratic, post-Milosevic Serbia will be included in a wider Balkan-reconstruction effort, involving Macedonia, Albania, and Montenegro as well. That could encourage the more realistic Serbs to reconsider their current support for Milosevic's suicidal policies. In any case, both America and its NATO allies will now have to be engaged in a longer-term effort to ensure stability in the Balkans. Once the Kremlin sobers up, Russian peacekeeping involvement would also be desirable, as it has already proven in Bosnia.

9. Congress should pass a joint resolution endorsing the political aims of NATO's campaign and pledge U.S. resolve to attain them by all the necessary means. Given the stakes involved, America's commitment must be unambiguous and enduring.

Such a strategy would require much more determination and ethical motivation from the Oval Office and from the top Republican congressional leadership than we have seen so far. In these circumstances, it is up to those legislators who had the instinctive courage to take a stand — notably Senators McCain, Lugar, Hagel, Biden, Lieberman — to fill the strategic void.

Compromise over Kosovo Means Defeat

The Wall Street Journal (May 24, 1999)

President Clinton's conduct of the war over Kosovo has been feckless. His over-eager diplomacy has undercut the credibility of his military campaign, while his timid military tactics are depriving his diplomacy of serious clout. His vague talk of 50,000 "peacekeepers" does not answer the simple but also central question: How are they to enter Kosovo?

No wonder Serbian strongman Slobodan Milosevic has not yielded. NATO's morally callous failure to take any military risks in order to impede the ethnic cleansing has given Mr. Milosevic's thugs a completely free hand to destroy Kosovar society. At the same time Russia, which has vociferously denounced NATO's bombing as a "barbaric atrocity" while maintaining silence about the mass murders and communal deportations in Kosovo, has been courted by Mr. Clinton's State Department to serve as a mediator. Thus Mr. Milosevic is obviously waiting for a "diplomatic" outcome that — with Moscow's help — will soften the conditions NATO originally set out to impose on him by force.

*   *   *

Of NATO's five original conditions, two are of paramount importance; how they are implemented will determine the outcome of the conflict. Make no mistake about it: despite likely efforts to fuzz the issues in the usual Clintonesque fashion, NATO's Kosovo operation will be a failure if *any* armed Serbian personnel are al-lowed to remain in Kosovo; and unless the occupying force for *all* of unpartitioned Kosovo is predominantly (even if not exclusively) NATO-composed and NATO-commanded and includes a significant U.S. combat presence.

Everything else will flow from how these two issues are resolved. The Kosovar deportees will not return to their homes if the outcome is less than that. Legalistic quibbles pertaining to Kosovo's future status and its relationship to Belgrade are less important than the question of who will exercise de facto control on the ground. To accept any Serb military or police presence in Kosovo would guarantee continued conflict with the Kosovo Liberation Army, which would not only refuse to disarm but would seek to exact vengeance on the Serbs.

Moreover, the moral dimension of the conflict cannot be ignored in any eventual outcome. Only a Kosovo free of armed Serbs might partially redeem NATO's failure to make any effort whatever to save Kosovar lives. The painful reality is that the bombing campaign has been conducted as if the human lives at stake should be priced at three different levels: the most precious lives are those of the NATO pilots, with military tactics explicitly designed to minimize their loss; next are those of Mr. Milosevic's officials, whose headquarters have been targeted only when empty; least valuable are the lives of the Kosovars themselves, on whose behalf no risks have been taken.

Such seeming indifference has already hurt America's global standing. Any democratic government is understandably loath to lose the lives of its servicemen. But to conduct a war in which no effort is made — even at some risk to one's own professional warriors — to protect the most defenseless is to deprive the undertaking itself of its higher moral purpose.

To end the Kosovo campaign in a manner that not only redeems its original purpose but also safeguards the vitality of NATO, the alliance will have to take some risks. It is necessary to face the fact that at some point Kosovo will have to be entered forcibly. There is no reason to expect Mr. Milosevic to yield to the bombing alone — even if the Serb army is "degraded" by 90% — as long as Mr. Clinton keeps reassuring him that there will be no ground action. Serb control over Kosovo is simply too important, not only to him but to most Serbs. Under such circumstances, the Serbian dictator has every incentive to hold out in the hopes that the alliance will split under conflicting public pressures and that those in Washington who put great stock in Russian diplomacy will have their way.

It is striking in this regard that Moscow's role in the Kosovo crisis is officially interpreted by Washington as motivated by good intentions and not seen in the context of Russia's overall foreign policy. Moscow's policy is not driven by the desire to help the U.S. or strengthen NATO. In fact, a setback for NATO that also discredits America's global standing (while avoiding an outright collision between Russia and the West) is what Moscow really wants. It takes an extraordinary amount of naivete to think otherwise.

*   *   *

In these circumstances, the only acceptable solution is the imposition of de facto physical control of Kosovo by NATO forces, accompanied by the de facto disappearance of Serb armed personnel. Whether Mr. Milosevic is then eventually toppled by disaffected Serbs is a secondary issue.

The present bombing campaign will make retroactive strategic sense only if the degradation of the Serbian army's capacity to resist is then exploited by a NATO leapfrogging operation in Kosovo that takes full advantage of the alliance's control of the air, utilizing large airborne units and massive airlift capability, as well as its enormous superiority in firepower and ground mobility. Even if NATO as a whole chooses not to engage in a ground campaign, there is still good reason for the U.S., Britain, and France to do so on their own. Such an operation, however, will require a degree of political and military boldness that so far the Clinton administration has conspicuously failed to demonstrate.

ZBIGNIEW BRZEZINSKI

NATO Must Stop Russia's Power Play

The Wall Street Journal (June 14, 1999)

Slobodan Milosevic's somewhat conditional but hardly face-saving surrender is undeniably a success for NATO and for the U.S. Failure to prevail would have been a disaster, disrupting the alliance and globally discrediting America. But victory has already had an unwelcome complication: Russian troops occupying the airport in the Kosovar capital of Pristina. What's more, the way NATO conducted this war raises serious concerns about future conflicts.

The Clinton administration deserves credit for having done several things right. It recognized that force had to be used to compel Mr. Milosevic to terms. It persevered in the effort, and was very successful in keeping the NATO coalition together. It did not succumb to Russian entreaties to stop the bombing.

Writing on this page on May 24, I argued that the two issues defining either success or failure were whether *all* armed Serbs would have to leave Kosovo, and whether *all* of Kosovo would be placed under de facto NATO control. That now seems likely, unless the administration caves in to Russian-Serbian collusion in establishing a separate zone for the Russians.

It is also important to note that there are strong hints in the United Nations mandate that Serbia's sovereignty over Kosovo may be not only nominal but eventually terminal. The document refers more than once not only to "autonomy" but also to "self-government" for the Kosovars, noting that KFOR (the U.N.'s name for the predominantly NATO force) would be responsible for "facilitating a political process designed to determine Kosovo's future status, taking into account the Rambouillet accords."

At the same time, the militarily indecisive and morally compromising manner in which the 80-day bombing campaign was conducted leaves a residue of longer-term concerns, beyond Kosovo itself, that will have to be seriously addressed. Foremost among them are Russia's role in the crisis, the world's perception of the American way of war, and NATO's combat command procedures. The Kosovo crisis raises concerns regarding each.

Russia's conduct does not deserve the high praise that the Clinton administration has showered on the Yeltsin leadership. Perhaps some of the praise was tactical, designed to isolate Mr. Milosevic. The fact remains, however, that Russia's conduct was malicious and much of it involved deliberate collusion with the Belgrade sponsor of ethnic cleansing. The sudden deployment of Russian troops into Serbia had to be coordinated by Moscow and Belgrade, and its obvious aim was to force a partition of Kosovo, on Mr. Milosevic's behalf. That means that Russia's role in the Group of Eight discussions regarding Kosovo has been duplicitous. To obscure all of that and to reward Russia with a major role in Kosovo is to fuel further Russian ambitions. The bottom line is that Russia's good behavior should be rewarded; its hostile conduct should neither be propitiated nor be cost-free.

Boris Yeltsin's power play in Pristina, therefore, must not be allowed to stand. There are many nonviolent ways of isolating the Russian troop contingent at the airport and of preventing their resupply by air — such as simply floating balloons around the airport so that no unilaterally arriving Russian air transports can land. Failure to apply pressure decisively will mean that Mr. Milosevic and Mr. Yeltsin will have succeeded in de facto partition.

The second major issue growing out of Kosovo is that the American way of war smacks to much of the world as a new technological racism. The high-tech standoff war was waged as if its underlying premise was that the life of even one American serviceman was not worth risking in order to save the lives of thousands of Kosovars. Just consider how the public would feel if some policemen, reacting to thugs throwing children into a swift river, confined themselves to merely arresting the thugs, on the grounds that any attempt at rescue might risk a policeman's life. Gloating over the ultimate "score" of 5,000 Serbs killed to zero Americans simply reinforces the global perception of a troubling moral standard.

This new way of war may also set a dubious and even dangerous standard for the future. The definition of success in warfare should not be determined by the avoidance of any casualties. If the stakes, both political and moral, are imperative enough to warrant the use of force, then necessary force should be used to achieve the ends. A war fought at no political risk and at no human cost may prove to have set a paralyzing precedent for any future American president.

Finally, some serious thought will have to be given to whether NATO's governing mechanisms, which require political unanimity in setting war aims, are conducive to a truly effective war-fighting command. The awkward experience of the unnecessarily prolonged bombing campaign underlines the urgent need to review and revise NATO's decision-making procedures. A clearer distinction will have to be drawn between the requirements for basic unanimity in committing NATO to action and the need for a military command authority endowed with the discretion to execute that commitment by military means. The Normandy landings never could have been carried out under the procedures NATO followed in Kosovo.

The outcome of the conflict demonstrates that NATO is Europe's only effective security system and that the American-European connection remains central to Europe's stability. That makes it all the more important that the Kosovo experience be assessed in a constructively critical fashion.

The Failed Double-Cross

The Wall Street Journal (August 30, 1999)

The unresolved mystery of the Kosovo crisis is why Milosevic capitulated. Though several interpretations have been advanced, none by itself seems convincing — and, even when combined, they still fail to explain why the 79-day-long air campaign suddenly produced the white flag in Belgrade. The principal explanations can be summarized as follows:

Version 1, initially favored by NATO spokesmen: NATO, the Military Victor

Milosevic gave in because NATO bombing of his troops finally became more effective, especially after the KLA drew the Serbian military out of their camouflaged and reinforced positions. The problem with this version is that it is now manifest that the Serbian army withdrew from Kosovo in relatively good condition, having suffered not very many of the highly exaggerated NATO-claimed personnel and material losses. From a battlefield perspective, the bombing campaign was a bust.

Version 2, the fallback position of NATO spokesmen: NATO, the Strategic Victor

Milosevic gave in because NATO bombing of the Serbian economic infrastructure finally became more painful. The problem with this version is that, while painful, the bombing had not cracked the Serb civilian nor military morale, and the Serb army seemed quite willing to wait until NATO gathered enough courage to engage in ground combat, at which point the Serbs were hoping to inflict politically damaging casualties. Since Milosevic is not a sentimentalist, it is doubtful that the limited economic discomfort of his people was decisive.

Version 3, favored by White House boosters: NATO, the Relentless Warrior

Milosevic gave in because he realized that NATO was quietly gearing up for a decisive ground campaign, with the U.S. President gradually accepting its strategic necessity. The problem with this version is that any NATO preparations for ground warfare were in fact minimal at the time of Milosevic's capitulation. Moreover, given President Clinton's continuing assurances to the contrary, it is far from clear that the U.S. leadership would have mustered the necessary courage to undertake a potentially bloody ground operation.

Version 4, favored by the State Department: NATO, the Political Success

Milosevic gave in because he finally realized, despite his initial calculations, that NATO — thanks to constant diplomatic consultations — will stick together and will persist in the bombing, no matter what. There is doubtless an element of truth in that view, but it still does not explain why Milosevic gave in so one-sidedly and suddenly, especially given the military ineffectiveness of the bombing, the relatively still limited economic scope of the strategic air assault, and U.S. reluctance to fight on the ground. Public passivity and the good condition of his army were still his assets.

Version 5, favored by those who always see Russia as helpful, even when it is manifestly not: Russia as NATO's Savior

Milosevic gave in because Russia on June 3 — after having strongly supported him — suddenly opted for the West, leaving Belgrade isolated and thus without any choice. That explanation, explicitly endorsed among others by Sir Michael Jackson (the British KFOR commander), seems to have some plausibility, especially when combined with some of the other "explanations." But it still does not explain satisfactorily what Russia was trying to achieve when it seemed to embrace the Western demand for Milosevic's full withdrawal from Kosovo (even beyond the formula previously demanded by NATO) nor why Milosevic suddenly became so accommodating.

The answer to the conundrum is to be found in a careful chronological analysis of Moscow's reactions to the crisis and particularly in the Kremlin's seemingly bizarre conduct during the crucial ten days from June 2 to June 12. Russia's policy toward the Kosovo crisis can best be understood as having involved three phases. The *first* was largely visceral and vitriolic. It involved an emotional and almost instinctive solidarity with Milosevic, violent denunciations of NATO's bombing, and promises of support for Milosevic. The Duma, even prior to the bombing, went on record on February 3 in calling for aid to Yugoslavia if NATO struck. When the strikes began, Russia sought a U.N. condemnation, and then Prime Minister Primokov attempted to split off the Germans with a peace proposal much more in Milosevic's favor.

There were persistent rumors that during this initial phase a "volunteer"

Russian contingent went to Serbia in order to fight on the Serb side. Western intelligence sources also reported that some Russian military equipment was delivered to the Serbs and that Russian military advice was provided. The overall Russian approach was well summarized by a leading Moscow paper (*Nezavisimaya gazeta*, March 25), which hopefully concluded that the Kosovo action was initiating "the collapse of the U.S. global empire" and that it was in Russia's interest to let "the United States and NATO with its demented West and East European members bog down as deep as possible in a Balkan War."

The *second* phase came into play once it dawned on the Kremlin that the NATO alliance would not split and would not quit. Russia then somewhat shifted its stand, seeking to be instead part of the Western decision-making process. The chosen avenue was the G-8 foreign ministers' consultations, with former Prime Minister Chernomyrdin assuming a highly visible role in seeking to convince NATO that it should soften its demands if it wished to reach a "political" solution.[1] By late May this process assumed the form of a two-headed effort, with Chernomyrdin and Finnish President Martti Ahtisaari taking the lead on behalf of the G-8 in discussions with Milosevic. However, Chernomyrdin would at times also meet alone with Milosevic, while the Russian's public pronouncements became increasingly strident and one-sided.

On May 26, Chernomyrdin published an altogether hysterical piece in the *Washington Post*. In it he asserted that "the United States lost its moral right to be regarded as a leader of the free democratic world when its bombs shattered the ideals of liberty and democracy in Yugoslavia," he demanded the payment of reparations to Yugoslavia, and he warned that he would urge President Yeltsin to freeze all American-Russian relations unless the bombing stopped. The next day he met alone with Milosevic.

Within days the *third* and critical phase in Russian policy was set in motion. Two days after his extraordinary outburst, Chernomyrdin suddenly let it be known that he was pleased with his discussions with Milosevic. On June 2 Russian TV reported that Ahtisaari and Chernomyrdin "have brought not one but two different plans to Belgrade," and then added that "Moscow is . . . talking about a virtual partition of Kosovo," with "a Russian contingent" under separate Russian command in control of northeast Kosovo. The very next day, June 3, Milosevic accepted NATO's demand for the withdrawal of all Serb forces, while Chernomyrdin in an interview with Russian TV stated that "at Yugoslavia's special request, Russia will also be represented" in the occupying peacekeeping force.

1. The G-8 refers to "the heads of state or government of the major industrial democracies who have been meeting annually to deal with the major economic and political issues facing their domestic societies and the international community as a whole." It includes France, the United States, Britain, Germany, Japan, Italy (since 1975), Canada (1976), the European Community (1977), and Russia (full participation since 1998). (Source: The University of Toronto G-7 Information Center.) [Ed.]

Events then unfolded quite rapidly. On June 4 the Russian Foreign and Defense ministers held a closed meeting with the Duma, to reassure it that Yugoslavia had not been betrayed. On June 5 Russian officers did not show up at the first scheduled encounter between NATO and Serb officers, held to coordinate the Serb withdrawal that was to take place promptly within a week. Between June 5 and 7 Serb officers continued stalling in the negotiations, and on June 10 NATO agreed to a delay in the Serb withdrawal.

On the same day, June 10, a Russian military contingent left its positions in Bosnia and — benefiting from full Serbian cooperation — moved swiftly through Serbia toward Kosovo. As this was happening, the Russian government reassured the U.S. Vice-President that the Russian contingent would not enter Kosovo. The White House, always trustful, then disallowed the NATO commander's plan to execute a preemptive seizure of Pristina. On June 11 at 1:30 A.M. the Russian forces entered Pristina and, with Serbian military cooperation, took up defensive positions at the airport, barring the later-arriving NATO forces. (According to some intelligence reports, the Russians secured there some military equipment previously provided by Russia to the Serbs.)

A detailed account in the *Moskovskiy Komsomolets* (June 14) tells the rest of the story, both of what happened and what did not happen. Crowing over the Russian military coup and over Serbian crowds in Pristina burning U.S. and British flags, it reported that as of June 12 a contingent of 2,500 Russian paratroopers was ready to be flown into Pristina and that "it has already been decided that Russia will have its own sector" in Kosovo. It noted that Hungary had denied Russia its airspace, "but this is not a problem — Bulgaria, for example, gave the go-ahead. Our planes could make a detour — from the Russian coast over the Black Sea and Bulgaria then straight to Kosovo." Kosovo would thus be partitioned by a unilateral fiat, NATO like it or not.

Alas for the Kremlin, it did not turn out so. Not only Hungary but Bulgaria and Romania refused access to their airspace, and the Kremlin prudently decided that it could not run the risk of having its air transports forced down. As a result, the Russian contingent in Pristina was left stranded. In the meantime, the Serbian forces, already in full retreat on exposed roads, could not reverse course without facing enormous vulnerability to resumed air attacks. Even though for a week the Kremlin continued to insist on a separate sector, on June 18 Russia reluctantly agreed to have its troops dispersed within the French, U.S., and German zones.

It thus appears that Milosevic's sudden acquiescence was part of a desperate double-cross maneuver engineered jointly by Belgrade and Moscow. When Moscow realized that it could not sway the West, it used its role as the West's co-mediator to fashion secretly with Milosevic a preemptive maneuver masked as accommodation. The collusion was contrived to outwit NATO by salvaging for Serbia — under Russia's protection — the northeastern part of partitioned Kosovo while gaining for frustrated Russia a significant boost in international prestige. The attempt faltered because three small European countries had the gumption to defy Moscow, while NATO remained firm in not agreeing to a separate sector to Russia. Under these circumstances, the double-cross did not work. At the end of the conflict, President Clinton effusively praised the Kremlin for its helpful role.

Kosovo

MICHAEL WALZER
[May 1999]

At this writing the NATO bombing of Yugoslavia continues, and the Serbian destruction of Kosovar society also continues. Yes, the Serbian campaign must have been planned before the bombing began; the logistics of moving forty thousand soldiers are immensely complex. In some parts of Kosovo the harsh realities of ethnic cleansing were already visible before the decision to hit the Serbs with missiles and smart bombs was made. And given the Serbian record in Bosnia, the mobilization of soldiers on the borders of Kosovo, and the refugees already on the move, military intervention seems to me entirely justified, even obligatory. But the brutal emptying of Kosovo in the ensuing weeks is still in some sense a response to NATO's air campaign, and the speed with which it has been carried out is obviously a response — an effort to create facts on the ground before (as Milosevic apparently believes) the bombing stops and negotiations resume. Ethnic cleansing is perfectly consistent with the air campaign, and is partly its consequence.

I don't know what the expectations of NATO commanders were last March; ordinary citizens in the United States and Europe were certainly led to expect that the bombing would solve the problem fairly quickly. Once again, our faith in airpower is revealed as a kind of idolatry — we glorify the power of our own inventions. The truth remains, however, what it was before the inventions: soldiers with guns, going from house to house in a mountain village, can't be stopped by smart bombs. They can only be stopped by soldiers with guns.

But the countries involved in the NATO intervention are committed, for now at least, not to send in soldiers with guns. The promise wasn't made to Milosevic, obviously, but to the citizens of all the NATO countries: we won't send your children into battle. This promise was probably a political prerequisite of the intervention, and it is only after a month and more of bombing has failed to move the Serbs that political leaders are trying to crawl out from under it. We engaged ourselves, morally and politically, to provide the Kosovars with a technological fix,

---

Walzer's discussion of the moral and practical aspects of international rescue develops some of the themes in his early essay, cited by a number of authors in this volume, "The Politics of Rescue," *Dissent* (Winter 1995): 35-41. [Ed.]

and if the fix didn't work, or didn't work quickly enough, we were ready (actually, as it turned out, not quite ready) to provide them with bread, blankets, and bandages. More than that, we said, we can't do. But there is something wrong here, for neither of these ways of helping is helpful enough. They don't meet the requirements of either politics or morality.

Maybe the bombing will eventually bring Milosevic down; maybe NATO will eventually decide to send in troops. But the initial form of the intervention raises a hard question. Are countries with armies whose soldiers cannot be put at risk morally or politically qualified to intervene? Even with a just cause and the best of intentions, how can we use military force in someone else's country unless we are prepared to deal with the unintended consequences of our actions? I suppose that, had we been visibly ready in February or March to go into Kosovo on the ground, full-scale ethnic cleansing might have been forestalled. But that is too easy. Deterrence isn't effective unless the threat is plausible, and it's not clear at this moment that any of the Western democracies can pose a plausible threat.

We have armies that can't, or can't easily, be used. There are good democratic and even egalitarian reasons for this. Obviously, U.S. national security is not at stake in Kosovo (nor is the security of any of the European nations, but I will focus now on the United States), and so it isn't possible to mobilize citizens to defend their homes and families. In other countries, in earlier times, wars in faraway places were fought by the lower orders or by mercenaries, people without political clout. But though the United States is still, even increasingly, an inegalitarian society, no soldier's mother or father is without political clout. This is an advance for Americans, since our political leaders cannot send soldiers into battle without convincing the country that the war is morally or politically necessary and that victory requires, and is worth, American lives. But there is an easier path for these same leaders. They can fight a war without using armies at all and do so without convincing the country of the war's necessity. It is an easier path that leads, however, to a moral anomaly: a new and dangerous inequality makes its appearance.

We are ready, apparently, to kill Serbian soldiers; we are ready to risk what is euphemistically called "collateral damage" to Serbian, and also Kosovar, civilians. But we are not ready to send American soldiers into battle. Well, I have no love of battles, and I fully accept the obligation of democratically elected leaders to safeguard the lives of their own people, all of them. But this is not a possible moral position. *You can't kill unless you are prepared to die.* No doubt that's a hard sentence — especially so because its two pronouns don't have the same reference (as they did when Albert Camus first made this argument, writing about assassination): the first "you" refers to the leaders of NATO, the second to the children of ordinary citizens. Still, these political leaders cannot launch a campaign aimed to kill Serbian soldiers, and sure to kill others too, unless they are prepared to risk the lives of their own soldiers. They can try, they ought to try, to reduce those risks as much as they can. But they cannot claim — we cannot accept — that those lives are expendable, and these not.

If the building is burning, and there are people inside, firefighters must risk their lives to get them out. That's what firefighters are for. But that isn't our building; those aren't our people. Why should we send in our firefighters? Americans can't be the world's firefighters.

This is a familiar argument, and not implausible, even though it often comes from people who don't seem to believe in putting out fires at all. I have heard it especially from people on the left (not only in America), and it is to them, especially, that I want to respond. Indeed, Milosevic should have been stopped years ago, when the first reports of ethnic cleansing came out of Bosnia. And he should have been stopped by the European powers. The Balkans is a European mess. Austo-Hungary carved out an empire there; Germany fought a war in Yugoslavia; the Italians invaded Albania; the British armed Tito's partisans. There is a long history of military intervention and diplomatic intrigue. But today Europe as a military force exists only in alliance with the United States. That's not an eternal truth, and people who believe in international pluralism and a balance of power can hope for the emergence of an independent European Union with an army that it can put into action on its own. But it is true for now that no Kosovo intervention is possible without strong American involvement. If you want to stop Milosevic, you can argue about how to do it; but there is no argument about who can do it.

That doesn't make us the world's firefighters. It was the Vietnamese who stopped Pol Pot in Cambodia, the Tanzanians who stopped Idi Amin in Uganda, the Indians who ended the killing in East Pakistan, the Nigerians who went into Liberia. Some of these were unilateral military acts, some (the Nigerian intervention, for example, and now the campaign in Kosovo) were authorized by regional alliances. Many people on the left yearn for a world where the U.N., and only the U.N., would act in all such cases. But given the oligarchic structure of the Security Council, it's not possible to count on this kind of action: in most cases on my list, U.N. intervention would have been vetoed by one of the oligarchs. Nor am I convinced that the world would be improved by having only one agent of international rescue. The men and women in the burning building are probably better served if they can appeal to more than a single set of firefighters.

But what is most important for the future of the left is that our people, our activists and supporters around the world, see the fires for what they are: deliberately set, the work of arsonists, aimed to kill, terribly dangerous. Of course, every fire has a complicated social, political, and economic background. It would be nice to understand it all. But once the burning begins, something less than full understanding is necessary: a will to put out the fire — to find firefighters, close by if possible, and give them the support they need. From a moral/political perspective, I don't think it matters much if this particular fire isn't dangerous to me and mine. I can't just sit and watch. Or rather, the price of sitting and watching is a kind of moral corruption that leftists (and others too) must always resist.

Debating Kosovo: An Exchange

ROBERT SKIDELSKY AND MICHAEL IGNATIEFF

Dear Michael,   *3 May 1999*

I have been instinctively against NATO's bombing of Serbia from the day it started. I am amazed that NATO seemed to have no military strategy except to bomb Serbia to smithereens. Above all, I was alarmed that a new doctrine of international relations was being forged which would make the world a much more dangerous place.

The U.N. was founded on the principle of national sovereignty. States could and should be sanctioned for acts of aggression against other states, but within their borders they were free (with one large caveat) to do what they liked. The U.N. was founded on prudential, not ethical, rules, and it was a great advance to get states to sign up to them.

Now to the caveat. Chapter 7 of the U.N. Charter says that states can be sanctioned for actions which are a "threat to peace." This allows the U.N. to take into account the spillover effects of domestic policies — if, for example, they produce floods of refugees or destabilise other states. But human rights abuse per se is not a ground for intervention. This is because there is no international agreement on the standards to be upheld and the means to uphold them.

The old imperialism had its own way of overcoming this problem. Advanced states conquered "barbarous" ones and imposed "civilised standards" on them. But as Churchill conceded, this process became "contrary to the ethics of the 20th century." Not, apparently, to the ethics of Tony Blair. In his Chicago speech on 22 April, he said, "Globalisation means we cannot turn our backs on the violation of human rights in other countries if we want to be secure." This fact required an "important qualification" to the principle of noninterference.

Blair wants international cooperation on the basis of agreed values and rules. But NATO did not agree on the values or rules with Russia, China, or anyone

---

This exchange has been abridged slightly by David Goodhart, editor of the London journal *Prospect*, in which it first appeared.

else before it began bombing Serbia. Nor did it seek U.N. authorisation. Russia tried to find a compromise, but its official line was that the bombing of Serbia was an "act of aggression" that flouted the U.N. Charter and international law.

We stand at a fork in international affairs. Does the West have *carte blanche* to make its values prevail whenever it chooses? Or will it confine its ethical ambitions to limits acceptable to other great powers with different values and interests?

Let me end with four assertions and one question. First, there is no international consensus on the standards expected of states in dealing with their own subjects or on the sanctions appropriate to breaches of agreed standards. Second, NATO did not seek U.N. authorisation because it knew it would not get it. Third, NATO's by-passing of the U.N. sends a clear message that force, not law, governs international affairs. Fourth, if membership in the U.N. no longer protects states from invasion, all governments that can will acquire weapons of mass destruction to deter or repel foreign invasion. Now the question: do you really think that the West has the guts to fight its way into other countries and occupy them indefinitely?

> *Yours,*
> *Robert Skidelsky*

Dear Robert,   *4 May 1999*

I couldn't disagree with you more, but we need to clear away the common ground to figure out where our disagreement lies. I agree that there should be a general presumption in favour of state sovereignty in international affairs. Such a presumption provides alibis for dictators, but it also protects weak but democratic states from more powerful neighbours. I also accept that human rights abuses, by themselves, do not legitimise military intervention. Other kinds of "soft" intervention — formal protests, boycotts, and sanctions — are preferable. Military intervention should always be the instrument of absolute last resort. So the question is to define when human rights abuses justify that last resort. Armed intervention can only be justified in two instances: first, when human rights abuses rise to the level of a systematic attempt to expel or exterminate large numbers of defenceless people; second, where these abuses threaten the peace and security of neighbouring states. Two further conditions: first, all diplomatic alternatives must have been exhausted; second, force can only be justified when it stands a real chance of stopping abuses and restoring peace.[1]

---

1. Consciously or not, the four criteria draw upon some of the distinctions made in classic just-war discussions. For a sketch of that doctrine, see Richard Miller's essay in this volume. Not-

Before we consider whether Kosovo meets these criteria, we must clear away another matter. You maintain that there is "no international consensus on the standards expected of states in dealing with their own subjects." Not so. Since Nuremberg, since the Universal Declaration of Human Rights, there has been a set of international norms on the internal conduct of states which those who sign these conventions — and Yugoslavia did — are supposed to abide by. Serbia's violation of these norms in Kosovo is not a matter of serious dispute.

In my view Kosovo meets the strict criteria for a justified intervention. A defenceless people have been driven from their homes and their arrival in Albania and Macedonia is destabilising the region. Your position — to stay out and do nothing — is sustainable only assuming that Milosevic is telling the truth, and that the deportees were driven out by NATO bombing. Having spent a week in the camps in Macedonia, talking to families evicted from Pristina, I am in no doubt that the ethnic cleansing was systematically planned and under way before the NATO bombing, and Western intelligence confirms this.

You make a crucial concession: that the U.N. Charter mandates interventions where domestic policies "produce floods of refugees or destabilise other states." But this is precisely the case in Kosovo: Milosevic decided to solve an "internal" human rights problem by exporting an entire nation to his impoverished neighbours. His actions bequeathed chaos to a whole region and guaranteed that there will be armed conflict until Kosovo can rule themselves free of Serb repression.

We also need to understand Milosevic's consistent attempt to deny the right of self-determination to anyone except his own Serbian people. In 1991, he chose war when Slovenia and Croatia exercised their rights of self-determination. In 1992, he armed an insurrection against a UN recognised state, Bosnia, and since 1989 he has systematically withdrawn the limited rights of self-government enjoyed by the Kosovars. At any point, he could have chosen to peacefully negotiate minority rights guarantees for the Serbian minority within the new republics. Instead he chose war, and the result has been the death of up to 250,000 people and the displacement of two million people. It is difficult to respect the territorial integrity and sovereignty of a state that has shown such disregard for the integrity and sovereignty of its neighbours. His regime has been a clear and present danger to the stability of the Balkans for nine years.

---

withstanding some differences, Ignatieff's criteria also have an affinity with the criteria for "humanitarian intervention" as set forth in the United States State Department document authored by Morton Halperin, included in this volume, which have generated a great deal of discussion. Both cite last resort and gross abuses; Ignatieff stresses the possibility of success, and the essay by Morton Halperin of the State Department merely states, "where we can [succeed?]." What Ignatieff interprets positively as a threshold of "when abuses rise to the level of a systematic attempt to expel or exterminate large numbers of defenceless people" or negatively as "dangers to others," the State Department simply claims "where our interests are at stake to protect against and stop gross abuses." [Ed.]

Our second disagreement is whether military intervention can be justified without U.N. sanction and approval. In principle, member states should seek approval of the use of force from the Security Council. The veto system in the council can provide a useful break on imperialist misadventure. But the system has also prevented the U.N. from intervening when it should have, in Rwanda and Bosnia. Where a veto threatens to make the international community complicit in evil, coalitions of member states should be able to act on their own. This entails risks, but coalitions can exert restraints on their more excitable members. It is precisely because each of NATO's 19 member states must be persuaded before undertaking military action that such action has not become indiscriminate or disproportionate.

You say, finally, that NATO action will send a message that force, rather than law, governs international affairs. There are occasions, on the contrary, when if force is not used there is no future for law. Failure to reverse the most meticulous deportation of a civilian population since the Second World War would have set a fatal precedent.

Yours,
Michael Ignatieff

Dear Michael,   *6 May 1999*

You define several areas of disagreement between us. The first concerns the principle of noninterference in the domestic affairs of states. You admit that there is a "general presumption" in favour of noninterference, but you qualify this so heavily as almost to turn it into its opposite. That is, you believe that intervention is justified whenever human rights are violated, but must be proportional to the offence. Military force is reserved for two cases: genocide or mass expulsion; and when human rights' abuses threaten the peace and security of neighbouring states. Since many regimes are engaged in barbarous acts, the scope for intervention is in principle huge. Moreover, since NATO (or, rather, the U.S.) has overwhelming air superiority almost everywhere, your qualification, "only when force has a real chance of working," is less than it seems.

You also weaken the presumption of noninterference unduly by omitting that it offers the only secure basis for peaceful interstate relations in a world where values differ. This has been the conclusion of three centuries of European statecraft, first enunciated at the Treaty of Westphalia. Perhaps you, unlike me, rate justice higher than peace.

This brings me to your contention that all U.N. members accept the same norms of domestic behaviour. You cite Nuremberg verdicts and the Universal Declaration of Human Rights. Nuremberg only gave legal force to two universally accepted norms: that genocide and the planning and waging of aggressive war are wicked, and should always be prevented or punished. I doubt if there is genuine consensus on much else. You believe that when states sign up to lists of rights they all think that they mean the same thing. This is a familiar Western (particularly American) delusion, and I'm surprised you fall for it. I'm talking about substantive agreement, not legal decoration.

Practical problems nearly always arise when norms conflict. The classic case is when two ethnic or religious groups have claims on the same territory and cannot work out a modus vivendi. In such a case, separation (which always involves some ethnic cleansing) may be the best solution. Yet this was never on the table at Rambouillet, despite the fact that there have been many relatively successful postwar examples, such as the separation of Jews and Arabs in Palestine. Our inability to accept that large parts of the world do not work according to Western rules has brought enormous troubles on us and those we succour.

You say that force should only be used when it "has a chance of stopping abuses and restoring peace." But do you seriously believe that NATO bombing is a credible method of achieving these goals? There is nothing more immoral than making promises to endangered people and then leaving them to their fate.

Finally, you discard the objection that NATO is making war on a U.N. member without U.N. authorisation. The veto is not an inconvenient obstacle to humanitarian designs. It ensures international consensus for U.N. intervention. Such a consensus does not exist in the Security Council — and most members of the U.N. are opposed to the NATO bombing.

This does not mean we should "stay out and do nothing"; nor do I believe Milosevic's propaganda. Had NATO accepted from 1998 that force was ruled out without clear evidence of genocide or mass expulsion, the diplomacy would have been different. A joint approach would have been hammered out between the U.S., the EU, and Russia as the basis of any demands on Serbia. It was NATO's willingness to use force without achieving a Great Power consensus that is directly responsible for this tragic turn of events.

Yours,
Robert

Dear Robert, 7 May 1999

Our disagreement is wider than the issue of Kosovo. We have different views of the international system itself. You are a Westphalian. Thus for you the only relevant actors in the international system are states; their inviolability is all but absolute; and there are no agreed norms to regulate their conduct other than the obligation not to commit genocide or wage aggressive war. I am an internationalist: states have rights and immunities, but so do individuals. When these rights are violated, individuals have recourse in law to the U.N. system. When persecuted individuals or national groups have exhausted all remedies and stand defenceless before aggression, they have the right to receive humanitarian and even military assistance. Contrary to what you say, I construe the grounds for military interventions narrowly: they should always be a last resort, when every other means of assisting a vulnerable population has been exhausted.

Unlike you, I believe there is a widening range of internationally agreed norms for the conduct of both international and domestic policy. All nations formally accept that torture, rape, massacre, and forcible expulsion are violations of international humanitarian law. There is no substantive dispute as to whether such abuses have occurred in Kosovo.

You dismiss this structure of international law as nothing more than the homage that vice pays to virtue. It is incontrovertible that international rights norms do operate as a real constraint on the domestic behaviour of a growing number of states. If the conduct of states were as you describe, Serbia's behaviour in Kosovo would not be the exception that it is. There is simply no other state in Europe that commits such violations of internationally agreed norms.

You construe attempts to monitor human rights as a meddlesome post-imperial moralism, attempting to apply "Western rules where these do not apply." But our military intervention in the Balkans is not imposing moral standards on a people who do not accept their validity. Kosovar Albanians have been begging for our help in the face of more than 12 years of increasing Serbian repression.

You suggest that the West should have negotiated with Milosevic on the basis of a joint approach hammered out between the U.S., EU, and Russia. This is exactly what happened: such an approach was agreed upon by the Contact Group, which included the Russians.[2] It respected the territorial integrity of Yugoslavia, insisted that the KLA insurgents be disarmed, and provided for explicit guarantees of Serb minority rights and protection of their holy places. Milosevic turned down the deal.

You maintain that the tragedy has occurred because the West resorted to force without securing a Great Power consensus. On the contrary, the tragedy occurred because Milosevic thought that he could divide Russia and the West, and get away with a final solution of the Kosovo problem.

Your suggestion that the ethnic groups be separated, logically implies partition — which in turn implies a substantial erosion of the sovereignty of Yugoslavia. If this is your position, it contradicts your support for noninterference. In any

2. The Contact Group refers to six nations who have been meeting with one another and outsiders to coordinate international policies on the Balkans. It includes France, Germany, Italy, the Russian Federation, the United Kingdom, and the United States. [Ed.]

event, partition is impractical, because both communities are distributed throughout the province, as are their cultural and religious sites.

As for the U.N., your objections are focused on the failure to secure their approval. The Western countries did not bypass the U.N.: the Russians were eventually prepared to approve a resolution in the Security Council that would have returned the whole operation under a U.N. umbrella where it belonged (with NATO troops as its core). The real obstacle to a settlement remains Milosevic himself. It is disingenuous to claim that only one side has failed to abide by the U.N. Charter: the list of U.N. resolutions that Milosevic has ignored or violated is exceedingly long.

As for the bombing, I framed my conditions for the use of military force in the belief that force can only be justified if it achieves precise military objectives. If Milosevic agrees to negotiate a settlement that allows for the refugees to return under international protection, then the bombing should cease. If he refuses to negotiate, the bombing should continue until Serb forces are sufficiently weakened to permit a ground invasion of Kosovo, whose aim would be to disarm Serb forces, return the refugees, rebuild the province, place it under U.N. administration, and then exit as soon as a permanent ceasefire could be negotiated. The bombing must be directed at military targets with the aim of introducing ground troops as soon as possible.

Yours,
Michael

Dear Michael,   *8 May 1999*

Evidently we disagree both about the nature of the international system and about the facts of the case. What you see as the actually existing international order, I see as a project to refashion it according to Western norms. I believe strongly in these norms. But the attempt to conduct international relations as though all these states accepted them can only serve to make the world more war-prone. This is why I am, as you say, a Westphalian.

As for the facts, I am amazed that you continue to believe that Russia at any time supported the NATO solution. The bombing united all Russians, from liberals to communists, in opposition to NATO action. Historians will argue about when or whether Milosevic's savage reprisals against the KLA turned into a deliberate programme of ethnic cleansing. What is undeniable is that the exodus from Yugoslavia started after the bombing. But above all, the NATO action has made the world a more dangerous place.

Yours,
Robert

Dear Robert,   *10 May 1999*

You can only maintain your position by misrepresenting the facts. Ethnic cleansing was under way in Kosovo ten months before the bombing began. The departure of the Kosovars was not an "exodus," but systematic deportation, using military units. You argue as if these facts are still in dispute; but the facts are plain. They constitute the worst political crime in Europe since 1945.

You cling to the fiction that diplomacy might have averted war, and argue that we didn't do enough to line up the Russians behind diplomatic pressure. What do you suppose was going on between May 1998 and March 1999? The Russians were at Rambouillet, and they did everything they could to get the Serbs to sign on to the deal. The fact that you do not wish to face is that every peaceful diplomatic alternative to war was tried and failed. Why? Because Milosevic gambled that we would fold. And you seem to wish that we had. The word for this is appeasement.

> *Yours,*
> *Michael*

Why the Balkans Demand Amorality

ROBERT D. KAPLAN

The following essay is in two parts: the first part was published originally in the *Washington Post* following the failure of the Rambouillet peace talks and before the bombing campaign. The second part identifies what I got right in the *Post* article and what I may have got wrong.

Several years ago, I was at a conference where intellectuals held forth about the moral responsibility of the United States in the Balkans. The Holocaust and humanist philosophers were mentioned in the course of the discussion. It was all very impressive. Then I took a cab back to the airport and the driver asked me, "If there's no oil there, what's in it for us?"

It was a question that none of the intellectuals had answered. Nor, sufficently, has the Clinton administration, even though it has been trying (and so far failing) to negotiate a Kosovo agreement that would put more American troops on the ground in ex-Yugoslavia. The irony is that there is a good answer to why we are in the Balkans — a reasonable, albeit complex, one that has nothing to do with either the Holocaust or morality.

For years now, there have been two different views on the former Yugoslavia: a high-minded intellectual one and a pragmatic one that knows the limits of what the American public will tolerate. The Clinton White House, with its typical Democratic weakness for wanting to impress intellectuals, has been torn between these two outlooks. The result in the case of Kosovo has been moralistic bluster followed by hesitancy and inaction.

The intellectual point of view on the Balkans goes something like this: The war in Bosnia was brought about not by ethnic hatreds as much as it was by evil men, and it could have been stopped at any point along the way. Indeed, Muslims and Christians in Sarajevo have a long history of peaceful communal relations. There were Serbs fighting on the Bosnian side, and Bosnians fighting on the Serb side. Contradictions and ironies abound, and thus to categorize the fighting in ex-Yugoslavia as a tribal war is to dehumanize individuals. Moreover, given the legacy of the Holocaust, the West has a particular responsibility to prevent another genocide in Europe. Otherwise, what were World War II and the Cold War really about?

344

Such a viewpoint is partly motivated by the fact that many in the baby-boomer generation have grown up with the false notion that World War II was fought to save the Jews — or should have been fought for that reason. But saving the Jews as a reason to justify the death of American GIs would not have sustained the Roosevelt Administration for even one week of the war. What happened was that the Japanese bombed Pearl Harbor, and the Nazis declared war on us — and only then did we decide to fight. To pursue the line of thought that our mission in the Balkans is a moral one, however emotionally satisfying, is partially wrong and much beside the point. Tens of thousands of words and a shelf of books in recent years about our moral interest in the region do not add up to one sentence of national interest.

Obviously, if you look closely at Bosnia — as well as the Caucasus, Rwanda, and other places — you will find that there is a lot more going on than just ethnic disputes. But that does not mean that the ethnic nature of those wars should be minimized. Every war is full of myth-breaking details. Nevertheless, generalizations are necessary or else discussion would be immobilized. It is only from bottom-line summaries that clear-cut policy emerges, not from academic deconstruction.

The fact is that there has been a great war in this decade in the former Yugoslavia, and it has been fought overwhelmingly along ethnic lines — lines that have a long and rich history. Of course, the war could have been short-circuited more quickly had the United States acted more decisively. But one of the reasons it didn't — and still doesn't in Kosovo — is that neither the Clinton Administration nor the intellectual community has articulated well a crystalline and naked national interest that the millions of ordinary Americans can immediately grasp — people, like my cab driver, who don't concern themselves with hair-splitting foreign-policy discussions.

The media once made fun of James Baker when, as Secretary of State, he said that the Gulf War was "about jobs." But Baker was far more successful in communicating a reason for sending American troops into harm's way than the Clinton Administration has been regarding the Balkans. Had more of our troops died in the Gulf, the public would have stuck it out with the Bush Administration. If twenty soldiers were killed tomorrow in a terrorist bombing in Bosnia, the Clinton Administration would have to invent, generally from scratch, a national-interest reason for being there.

The history of U.S. foreign policy on this point is undeniable: moral arguments will sometimes be enough to get troops abroad, but as soon as they start taking casualties, an amoral reason of self-interest is required to keep them in place. Look at Somalia: most of the public supported the U.S. intervention to feed starving people there, but they wanted the troops home as soon as soldiers started to lose their lives, because no clear national interest had been established.

We have had troops on the ground in Bosnia for three years now, and it is likely that we will continue to have troops in the region for years to come, so it is reasonable to assume that the U.S. military will eventually suffer casualties there. The American public has to be able to tolerate those casualties. Otherwise, our troops will be constrained to a point at which they will lose all credibility — if not in Bosnia then surely in Kosovo. With its inability to fully spell out an amoral self-interest — one that would make sense as a reason for putting American soldiers in harm's way — the administration is gambling on the hope that there never will be any casualties.

Right now there are two choices in the Balkans: imperialism or anarchy. To stop the violence, we essentially have to act in the way the great powers in the region have always acted — as pacifying conquerors. The kind of moral solution that many yearn for is one the Romans and the Austrian Hapsburgs knew well how to provide, one motivated by territorial aggrandizement for their own economic enrichment, strategic position, and glory. Instead, in the Western Alliance we basically have a bunch of people acting like labor lawyers arbitrating a dispute between two sides so that everything will be perfectly clear on the ground, so that nobody will ever want to kill an American soldier. Because if that happens, our confidence-game-of-a-policy unravels.

A moral solution to Balkan violence, like most moral solutions throughout world history, can only be provided by amoral interest. And that, I believe, exists.

World Wars I and II both could have been stopped sooner, saving us countless lives and millions of dollars. The same is true in Bosnia, saving us the risk and expense of putting troops on the ground there. But Kosovo's violence could lead to something far more costly in terms of money and the lives of our soldiers: you see, Kosovo is smack in the middle of a very unstable and important region where Europe joins the Middle East. In fact, Europe is redividing along historical and cultural lines. Dangerous new alliances are forming, as they were before World War I. Preventing their growth means pacifying Kosovo.

Following the admission of Poland, Hungary, and the Czech Republic into NATO, there are now two Europes. There is a Western, Catholic-Protestant Europe and an Eastern Orthodox Europe; the latter is poorer, more politically unsettled, and more ridden with organized crime. That Orthodox realm has been shut out of NATO and is angrier by the day, and it is fiercely anti-Muslim. Greece and Turkey stare at each other through the eyes of missile guidance systems, each part of a dynamic and dangerous new cultural alliance. Theater war that fuses Balkan and Middle Eastern hatreds is not out of the question. Russia, which is pro-Greek, pro-Serb, and anti-Turkish, bristles with irrationality and loose nuclear weapons. It could be drawn into any conflict. Greece is still a member of NATO, yes, but if the security situation in the Balkans deteriorates, it could be pulled further into this unacknowledged — yet psychologically real — Orthodox alliance.

Such dangers are, of course, hypothetical — just as were many of those before the two world wars. Let's keep them that way by stanching the flow of blood in

Kosovo. If fighting continues there, it will probably destabilize neighboring Macedonia, which is ground zero for the age-old battle between Greek Orthodoxy and Turkish Islam. But Kosovo is crucial for a bigger reason. Healing the emerging divide in Europe — one that is potentially worse than the division of the Cold War because it is based on religion and culture — means taking at least one more Orthodox country (such as Romania or Bulgaria) into NATO. But that is impossible as long as Kosovo remains violent. In fact, fighting in Kosovo has geographically stranded Bulgaria because so much of Bulgaria's trade travels overland through southern Yugoslavia. Worse, both Romania and Bulgaria are fighting incursions of Russian-backed criminal groups: the Red Army of the post–Cold War world. Romanian and Bulgarian elites are deciding whether to pitch their tents with the Americans or the Russians, depending on which one seems to have more staying power in the region.

With the Middle East increasingly fragile, we will need bases and flyover rights in the Balkans to protect Caspian Sea oil. But we will not have those bases in the future if the Russians reconquer southeast Europe by criminal stealth. Finally, if we tell our European allies to go it alone in Kosovo, we can kiss the Western Alliance goodbye.

It could be said, too, that occasional small wars and occupations are good for us. They allow our military and NATO to improve by experience, honing their skills for any truly major catastrophes ahead. (Eisenhower honed his analytical skills for World War II by helping to reorganize the Philippine army in the 1930s during our occupation there.) Without the Red Army in Europe, the various national contingents of NATO must now acquire common memories of serving together, or the alliance will dissolve. And NATO is still important because Europe and beyond are less secure than many believe. Besides, we are not bearing the burden of Bosnia and Kosovo; we are sharing it with our allies. The post–Cold War is about multilateral operations precisely because there will be reasons to intervene that are not quite persuasive enough for any one power.

President Clinton, Secretary of State Madeleine Albright, and U.N. Representative-designate Richard Holbrooke are all such good communicators that I am sure they can condense a lot of this into folksy shorthand. But speaking and writing for an elite audience is not enough. They will have to speak again and again to average Americans via the mass media. Because when troops take casualties, the whole country suddenly becomes involved, not just the policy elite. This is far more complex than the reasons for the Gulf War. But in foreign affairs, moral reasons rarely suffice to achieve moral ends.

For the most part, the above seems more relevant now than before. For example, however much the moral angle was emphasized publicly by both the Clinton Administration and the media-intellectuals, the fact remains that had Kosovo not been in Europe — threatened by refugee influxes and other fallout from an unchecked Milosevic — and had NATO's very existence and credibility not been directly challenged on its fiftieth anniversary, I doubt whether the Alliance would have been willing to bomb for over two months. After all, how many Western governments, and publics, would support the same effort to prevent ethnic cleansing in Abkhazia and Nagorno Karabakh (whose similarities to Bosnia in the early 1990s are striking), and also sub-Saharan Africa?

The moral argument worked because there were no significant American casualties. Indeed, a reason why Clinton was so loath to consider ground troops in a hostile environment is that he knew that, after a certain number of body bags, support for the war might well collapse without a strategic argument, which he had not sufficiently articulated. True, military technology may well be able to offer the opportunity of a war with few casualties. However, to assume that in advance is an irresponsible way to proceed with a war.

But there is another "however": if it turns out to be true in the future that technology will be able to provide us the means to fight wars with few casualties, and to know that in advance, then perhaps we will be able to fight wars based on moral arguments alone. For my argument in favor of amorality is a reluctant one, one that bows to necessity and the lessons of the past. But if technology will allow us to escape that bind, I would be only too happy to admit that my argument is flawed.

Give War a Chance

EDWARD N. LUTTWAK

Premature Peacemaking

An unpleasant truth often overlooked is that although war is a great evil, it does have a great virtue: it can resolve political conflicts and lead to peace. This can happen when all belligerents become exhausted or when one wins decisively. Either way, the key is that the fighting must continue until a resolution is reached. War brings peace only after passing a culminating phase of violence. Hopes of military success must fade for accommodation to become more attractive than further combat.

Since the establishment of the United Nations and the enshrinement of great-power politics in its Security Council, however, wars among lesser powers have rarely been allowed to run their natural course. Instead, they have typically been interrupted early on, before they could burn themselves out and establish the preconditions for a lasting settlement. Ceasefires and armistices have frequently been imposed under the aegis of the Security Council in order to halt fighting. NATO's intervention in the Kosovo crisis follows this pattern.

But a ceasefire tends to arrest war-induced exhaustion and lets belligerents reconstitute and rearm their forces. It intensifies and prolongs the struggle once the ceasefire ends — and it does usually end. This was true of the Arab-Israeli war of 1948-49, which might have come to closure in a matter of weeks if two ceasefires ordained by the Security Council had not let the combatants recuperate. It has recently been true in the Balkans. Imposed ceasefires frequently interrupted the fighting between Serbs and Croats in Krajina, between the forces of the rump Yugoslav federation and the Croat army, and between the Serbs, Croats, and Muslims in Bosnia. Each time, the opponents used the pause to recruit, train, and equip additional forces for further combat, prolonging the war and widening the scope of its killing and destruction. Imposed armistices, meanwhile — again, unless followed by negotiated peace accords — artificially freeze conflict and perpetuate a state of war indefinitely by shielding the weaker side from the consequences of refusing to make concessions for peace.

The Cold War provided compelling justification for such behavior by the two superpowers, which sometimes collaborated in coercing less powerful belligerents to avoid being drawn into their conflicts and clashing directly. Although imposed ceasefires ultimately did increase the total quantity of warfare among the lesser powers, and armistices did perpetuate states of war, both outcomes were clearly lesser evils (from a global point of view) than the possibility of nuclear war. But today neither Americans nor Russians are inclined to intervene *competitively* in the wars of lesser powers, so the unfortunate consequences of interrupting war persist, while no greater danger is averted. It might be best for all parties to let minor wars burn themselves out.

The Problems of Peacekeepers

Today ceasefires and armistices are imposed on lesser powers by multilateral agreement — not to avoid great-power competition but for essentially disinterested and indeed frivolous motives, such as television audiences' revulsion at harrowing scenes of war. But this, perversely, can *systematically* prevent the transformation of war into peace. The Dayton Accords are typical of the genre: they have condemned Bosnia to remain divided into three rival armed camps, with combat suspended momentarily but a state of hostility prolonged indefinitely. Since no side is threatened by defeat and loss, none has sufficient incentive to negotiate a lasting settlement; because no path to peace is even visible, the dominant priority is to prepare for future war rather than to reconstruct devastated economies and ravaged societies. Uninterrupted war would certainly have caused further suffering and led to an unjust outcome from one perspective or another, but it would also have led to a more stable situation that would have let the postwar era truly begin. Peace takes hold only when war is truly over.

A variety of multilateral organizations now make it their business to intervene in other people's wars. The defining characteristic of these entities is that they insert themselves in war situations while refusing to engage in combat. In the long run this only adds to the damage. If the United Nations helped the strong defeat the weak faster and more decisively, it would actually enhance the peacemaking potential of war. But the first priority of U.N. peacekeeping contingents is to avoid casualties among their own personnel. Unit commanders therefore habitually appease the *locally* stronger force, accepting its dictates and tolerating its abuses. This appeasement is not strategically purposeful, as siding with the stronger power overall would be; rather, it merely reflects the determination of each U.N. unit to avoid confrontation. The final result is to prevent the emergence of a coherent outcome, which requires an imbalance of strength sufficient to end the fighting.

Peacekeepers chary of violence are also unable to effectively protect civilians who are caught up in the fighting or deliberately attacked. At best, U.N. peacekeeping forces have been passive spectators to outrages and massacres, as in

Bosnia and Rwanda; at worst, they collaborate with it, as Dutch U.N. troops did in the fall of Srebenica by helping the Bosnian Serbs separate the men of military age from the rest of the population.

The very presence of U.N. forces, meanwhile, inhibits the normal remedy of endangered civilians, which is to escape from the combat zone. Deluded into thinking that they will be protected, civilians in danger remain in place until it is too late to flee. During the 1992-1994 siege of Sarajevo, appeasement interacted with the pretense of protection in an especially perverse manner: U.N. personnel inspected outgoing flights to prevent the escape of Sarajevo civilians in obedience to a ceasefire agreement negotiated with the locally dominant Bosnian Serbs — who habitually violated that deal. The more sensible, realistic response to a raging war would have been for the Muslims to either flee the city or drive the Serbs out.

Institutions such as the European Union, the Western European Union, and the Organization for Security and Cooperation in Europe lack even the U.N.'s rudimentary command structure and personnel, yet they too now seek to intervene in warlike situations, with predictable consequences. Bereft of forces even theoretically capable of combat, they satisfy the interventionist urges of member states (or their own institutional ambitions) by sending unarmed or lightly armed "observer" missions, which have the same problems as U.N. peacekeeping missions, only more so.[1]

Military organizations such as NATO or the West African Peacekeeping Force (ECOMOG, recently at work in Sierra Leone) are capable of stopping warfare. Their interventions still have the destructive consequence of prolonging the state of war, but they can at least protect civilians from its consequences. Even that often fails to happen, however, because multinational military commands engaged in disinterested interventions tend to avoid any risk of combat, thereby limiting their effectiveness. U.S. troops in Bosnia, for example, repeatedly failed to arrest known war criminals passing through their checkpoints lest this provoke confrontation.

Multinational commands, moreover, find it difficult to control the quality and conduct of member states' troops, which can reduce the performance of all forces involved to the lowest common denominator. This was true of otherwise fine British troops in Bosnia and of the Nigerian marines in Sierra Leone. The phenomenon of troop degradation can rarely be detected by external observers, although its consequences are abundantly visible in the litter of dead, mutilated, raped, and tortured victims that attends such interventions. The true state of affairs is illuminated by the rare exception, such as the vigorous Danish tank battalion in Bosnia that replied to any attack on it by firing back in full force, quickly stopping the fighting.

---

1. This may be a subtle reference to the OSCE's Kosovo Verification Mission (KVM), verifiers who were among those on the ground in Kosovo but who were evacuated prior to NATO air strikes. [Ed.]

EDWARD N. LUTTWAK

The First "Post-Heroic" War

All prior examples of disinterested warfare and its crippling limitations, however, have been cast into shadow by NATO's current intervention against Serbia for the sake of Kosovo. The alliance has relied on airpower alone to minimize the risk of NATO casualties, bombing targets in Serbia, Montenegro, and Kosovo for weeks without losing a single pilot. This seemingly miraculous immunity from Yugoslav anti-aircraft guns and missiles was achieved by multiple layers of precautions. First, for all the noise and imagery suggestive of a massive operation, very few strike sorties were actually flown during the first few weeks. That reduced the risks to pilots and aircraft but of course also limited the scope of the bombing to a mere fraction of NATO's potential. Second, the air campaign targeted air-defense systems first and foremost, minimizing present and future allied casualties, though at the price of very limited destruction and the loss of any shock effect. Third, NATO avoided most anti-aircraft weapons by releasing munitions not from optimal altitudes but from an ultra-safe 15,000 feet or more. Fourth, the alliance greatly restricted its operations in less-than-perfect weather conditions. NATO officials complained that dense clouds were impeding the bombing campaign, often limiting nightly operations to a few cruise-missile strikes against fixed targets of known location. In truth, what the cloud ceiling prohibited was not all bombing — low-altitude attacks could easily have taken place — but rather perfectly safe bombing.

On the ground, far beneath the high-flying planes, small groups of Serb soldiers and police in armored vehicles were terrorizing hundreds of thousands of Albanian Kosovars. NATO has a panoply of aircraft designed for finding and destroying such vehicles. All its major powers have anti-tank helicopters, some equipped to operate without base support. But no country offered to send them into Kosovo when the ethnic cleansing began. After all, they might have been shot down. When U.S. Apache helicopters based in Germany were finally ordered to Albania, in spite of the vast expenditure devoted to their instantaneous "readiness" over the years, they required more than three weeks of "predeployment preparations" to make the journey. Six weeks into the war, the Apaches had yet to fly their first mission, although two had already crashed during training. More than mere bureaucratic foot-dragging was responsible for this inordinate delay: the U.S. Army insisted that the Apaches could not operate on their own; they would need the support of heavy rocket barrages to suppress Serb anti-aircraft weapons. This created a much larger logistical load than the Apaches alone, and an additional, evidently welcome, delay.

Even before the Apache saga began, NATO already had aircraft deployed on Italian bases that could have done the job just was well: U.S. A-10 "Warthogs," built around their powerful 30-millimeter antitank guns, and British Royal Air Force Harriers, ideal for low-altitude bombing at close range. Neither was used, again because it could not be done in perfect safety. In the calculus of the NATO

352

democracies, the immediate possibility of saving thousands of Albanians from massacre and hundreds of thousands from deportation was obviously not worth the lives of a few pilots. That may reflect unavoidable political reality, but it demonstrates how even a large-scale disinterested intervention can fail to achieve its ostensibly humanitarian aim. It is worth wondering whether the Kosovars would have been better off had NATO simply done nothing.

Refugee Nations

The most disinterested of all interventions in war — and the most destructive — are humanitarian relief activities. The largest and most protracted is the United Nations Relief and Works Agency (UNRWA): it was built on the model of its predecessor, the United Nations Relief and Rehabilitation Agency (UNRRA), which operated camps for displaced persons in Europe immediately after World War II. The UNRWA was established immediately after the 1948-1949 Arab-Israeli war to feed, shelter, educate, and provide health services for Arab refugees who had fled Israeli zones in the former territory of Palestine.

By keeping refugees alive in spartan conditions that encouraged their rapid emigration or local resettlement, the UNRRA's camps in Europe had assuaged postwar resentments and helped disperse revanchist concentrations of national groups. But UNRWA camps in Lebanon, Syria, Jordan, the West Bank, and the Gaza Strip provided a higher standard of living on the whole than most Arab villagers had previously enjoyed, with a more varied diet, organized schooling, superior medical care, and no back-breaking labor in stony fields. They had, therefore, the opposite effect: they became desirable homes rather than transit camps that the Arabs would eagerly abandon. With the encouragement of several Arab countries, the UNRWA turned escaping civilians into lifelong refugees who gave birth to refugee children, who have in turn had refugee children of their own.

During its half-century of operation, the UNRWA has thus perpetuated a Palestinian refugee nation, preserving its resentments in as fresh a condition as they were in 1948 and keeping the first bloom of revanchist emotion intact. By its very existence, the UNRWA dissuades integration into local society and inhibits emigration. The concentration of Palestinians in the camps, moreover, has facilitated the voluntary or forced enlistment of refugee youths by armed organizations that fight both Israel and each other. The UNRWA has contributed to a half-century of Arab-Israeli violence and still retards the advent of peace.

If each European war had been attended by its own postwar UNRWA, today's Europe would be filled with giant camps for millions of descendants of uprooted Gallo-Romans, abandoned Vandals, defeated Burgundians, and misplaced Visigoths — not to mention more recent refugee nations such as post-1945 Sudeten Germans (three million of whom were expelled from Czechoslovakia in

1945). Such a Europe would have remained a mosaic of warring tribes, undigested and unreconciled in their separate feeding camps. It might have assuaged consciences to help each one at each remove, but it would have led to permanent instability and violence.

The UNRWA has counterparts elsewhere, such as the Cambodian camps along the Thai border, which incidentally provided safe havens for the mass-murdering Khmer Rouge. But because the United Nations is limited by stingy national contributions, these camps' sabotage of peace is at least localized.

That is not true of the proliferating, feverishly competitive nongovernmental organizations (NGOs) that now aid war refugees. Like any other institution, these NGOs are interested in perpetuating themselves, which means that their first priority is to attract charitable contributions by being seen to be active in high-visibility situations. Only the most dramatic natural disasters attract any significant mass-media attention, and then only briefly; soon after an earthquake or flood, the cameras depart. War refugees, by contrast, can win sustained press coverage if kept concentrated in reasonably accessible camps. Regular warfare among well-developed countries is rare and offers few opportunities for such NGOs, so they focus their efforts on aiding refugees in the poorest parts of the world. This ensures that the food, shelter, and health care offered — although abysmal by Western standards — exceed what is locally available to nonrefugees. The consequences are entirely predictable. Among many examples, the huge refugee camps along the Democratic Republic of Congo's border with Rwanda stand out. They sustain a Hutu nation that would otherwise have been dispersed, making the consolidation of Rwanda impossible and providing a base from which radicals can launch more Tutsi-killing raids across the border. Humanitarian intervention has worsened the chances of a stable, long-term resolution of the tensions in Rwanda.

To keep refugee nations intact and preserve their resentments forever is bad enough, but inserting material aid into ongoing conflicts is even worse. Many NGOs that operate in an odor of sanctity routinely supply active combatants. Defenseless, they cannot exclude armed warriors from their feeding stations, clinics, and shelters. Since refugees are presumptively on the losing side, the warriors among them are usually in retreat; by intervening to help, NGOs systematically impede the progress of their enemies toward a decisive victory that could end the war. Sometimes NGOs, impartial to a fault, even help both sides, thus preventing mutual exhaustion and a resulting settlement. And in some extreme cases, such as Somalia, NGOs even pay protection money to local war bands, which use those funds to buy arms. Those NGOs are therefore helping prolong the warfare whose consequences they ostensibly seek to mitigate.

Make War to Make Peace

Too many wars nowadays become endemic conflicts that never end because the transforming effects of both decisive victory and exhaustion are blocked by outside intervention. Unlike the ancient problem of war, however, the compounding of its evils by disinterested interventions is a new malpractice that could be curtailed. Policy elites should actively resist the emotional impulse to intervene in other people's wars — not because they are indifferent to human suffering but precisely because they care about it and want to facilitate the advent of peace. The United States should dissuade multilateral interventions instead of leading them. New rules should be established for U.N. refugee relief activities to ensure that immediate succor is swiftly followed by repatriation, local absorption, or emigration, ruling out the establishment of permanent refugee camps. And although it may not be possible to constrain interventionist NGOs, at the very least they should be neither officially encouraged nor funded. Underlying these seemingly perverse measures would be a true appreciation of war's paradoxical logic and a commitment to let it serve its sole useful function: to bring peace.

Force and Humanitarian Intervention:
The Case of Kosovo

DAVID LITTLE

The recent policy on the part of the North Atlantic Treaty Organization of using force to protect the ethnic Albanians in Kosovo against massacre, ethnic cleansing, rape, and other forms of gross and systematic human rights abuse by Serbian military forces raises deep legal and moral questions in regard both to the case of Kosovo itself and to a general doctrine of force and humanitarian intervention. Though the subject is complex, we may here single out and deal briefly with three major problems attending the recent use of force in Kosovo: its authorization, effects, and conduct.

Authorization

The NATO bombing campaign, carried out between March 24 and June 10, 1999, was undertaken without specific authorization by the U.N. Security Council. Thus NATO on this occasion effectively ignored the very body that is invested by the United Nations Charter with final responsibility for certifying a use of force among states, because two member states, Russia and China, would surely have vetoed any resolution directly supporting such military action as was undertaken.

In addition, there is, as things stand, no explicit provision in the Charter for using force in the name of "humanitarian" causes, such as thwarting extensive human rights violations. Article 2.7 is taken to summarize the "status quo" character of the Charter: that article prohibits the United Nations from intervening "in matters that are essentially within the domestic jurisdiction of any state." While the Charter does enunciate other objectives, such as advancing human rights, self-determination, and social and economic development, its overriding concern is clearly international peace and stability. The understanding has been that pursuing these additional objectives "could not justify the use of force between states;

they would have to be pursued by other means. Peace was more important than progress and more important than justice."[1]

The "status quo bias" of the Charter has of late been sharply challenged, in part in response to situations such as those in Kosovo. No less an authority than U.N. Secretary-General Kofi Annan has referred to the prevailing interpretation of the Charter as "old orthodoxy," something that, to his mind, calls for immediate amendment. The idea that the international community should have to stand by while governments are left free to do whatever they like to their citizens is, he says, unacceptable. While he believes that preserving international peace is vitally important, protecting the rights of "peoples" and of individual human beings is equally fundamental to the aims of the Charter. The document "was never meant as a license for governments to trample on human rights and human dignity. Sovereignty implies responsibility, not just power." Getting specific, the Secretary-General goes so far as to endorse "the clear determination expressed by NATO" on the basis of a policy of "diplomacy backed by force," "to prevent a further escalation of the fighting [in Kosovo]," and to "encourage all steps that may deter the further use of ethnically driven repression and the resort to force in Kosovo."[2]

Though caution is called for in talking of revising or reinterpreting the U.N. Charter, there is, as it happens, strong warrant in "just-war teaching" — the tradition of commonly accepted moral limits taken to govern armed combat — in favor of using force to restrain or discourage wrongdoing *inside* a given state. Hugo Grotius, one of the founders of modern just-war thinking, explicitly justifies armed intervention in the name of curtailing the violation of human rights by a government against its citizens.[3] In contrast, the U.N. Charter, as currently understood, has disregarded that appeal and has enshrined only one of the standard "just-war" reasons for resorting to force, namely, self-defense. Article 51 is the *locus classicus:* "Nothing in the present Charter shall impair the inherent right of individual or collective self-defense if an armed attack occurs against a Member of the United Nations." The problem is that the reference to self-defense on the part of a U.N. member state under armed attack in no way covers the humanitarian crisis *within* the Federal Republic of Yugoslavia prior to March 24.

As Kofi Annan's comments imply, the self-evident enormity of the Serbian government's offenses against its citizens, the Kosovar Albanians, provides strong reason to consider reinterpreting and possibly revising the Charter so as to allow for a doctrine of armed humanitarian intervention. Such modifications would, in effect, make room for the traditional just-war appeal of discouraging wrongdoing

---

1. Louis Henkin et al., *Right versus Might: International Law and the Use of Force,* 2nd ed. (New York: Council on Foreign Relations, 1991), p. 38.

2. Secretary-General Kofi Annan, Ditchley Lecture, June 26, 1998, p. 2.

3. Hugo Grotius, *Prolegomena to the Law of War and Peace,* trans. Francis W. Kelsey (New York: Liber Arts Press, 1957), p. 18.

inside sovereign states as a justification for using force. Moreover, such an argument would appear to lend moral, if not legal, weight to the decision by NATO to initiate force against the Serbian government in apparent disregard of Article 53 of the Charter, which permits "regional arrangements" to engage in "enforcement action" but only so long as it is undertaken (as the NATO action was not) with "the authorization of the Security Council." We seem to have here a case in which moral considerations both certify extralegal action and urgently compel international legal reform.

To be sure, this is a highly precarious line of argument. The potential for abuse is manifest. Along with the evidence of severe wrongdoing, the specific intentions and objectives of using force, as just-war teaching also requires, must be practical and effective in overcoming the conditions of wrongdoing and in creating greater justice and peace in the area in question. That brings us to the second and third of our concerns.

Effects

The practicality and effectiveness of NATO military policy in Kosovo remain highly controversial. There are allegations that by intensifying Milosevic's policy of ethnic cleansing and expulsion in Kosovo, the NATO campaign actually made matters worse, both for the ethnic Albanians and for the Serbs living in Kosovo, and did very little to weaken Milosevic's overall capacity for further mischief both inside and outside the Federal Republic of Yugoslavia.

While any assessment is at this stage provisional, the allegations appear to be overstated. The policy of massive ethnic cleansing has been terminated, and though hundreds of thousands of Kosovar Albanians were displaced as the result of NATO action, huge numbers of refugees have already returned or soon will return, and they are doing so under a comparatively improved prospect of justice and peace. At present, the fortunes of Kosovo Serbs are admittedly not bright, and the chances for creating an equitable multiethnic society are doubtful; but the odds of ethnic balance and fair treatment are surely better under NATO and U.N. supervision than under a system controlled exclusively by the Serbs or the ethnic Albanians.

It is difficult to argue that Milosevic has been strengthened by the NATO action. He has by no means lost all domestic support, but his legitimacy is now widely challenged, even by prominent members of the army; and though reports of damage to the Yugoslav military were perhaps exaggerated, morale is clearly down. Moreover, the revanchist resurgence, either in the Serbian army or outside it, that was predicted as a likely consequence of the loss of Kosovo has certainly not materialized. Finally, the autonomy movement within Montenegro is inconceivable apart from the results of the NATO action. Events have undoubtedly strengthened the hand of President Djukanovic, outspoken opponent of Milosevic and strong advocate of democratic reform, thus adding to, rather than detracting from, the democratic cause within Serbia.

Significantly, leaders of the neighboring Balkan countries have regarded the defeat of Milosevic's Kosovo policy as indispensable to their security and development. "Milosevic must not win the war in Kosovo" was the unanimous message of a conference of Balkan leaders held at the United States Institute of Peace on April 23, 1999. According to a report of the conference, "[f]ront-line states urged NATO to use the necessary means to defeat Milosevic; as they see it, their future as members of Europe depends on a NATO victory in the region."[4]

Conduct

There remains the controversy surrounding the military strategy and tactics used by NATO to restrain Milosevic's wrongdoing in Kosovo. There is space here for only a cursory assessment. There seems little doubt that the policy of high-altitude bombing undertaken in order to protect NATO pilots is, in just-war terms, highly questionable. The principle of noncombatant immunity is not served by effectively shifting the burden of risk from combatants to noncombatants, as happened as a matter of consistent practice in the bombing of Serbia, and on occasion in the bombing of Kosovo. There are, of course, the familiar political arguments in favor of giving priority to the protection of allied forces. However, protection of combatants is not a convincing basis for compromising the principle of noncombatant immunity. If armed humanitarian intervention is licitly to be undertaken in the future, greater provision will have to be made for the welfare of noncombatants than occurred in the Kosovo operation.

As I have said, the NATO operation in Kosovo raises a host of legal and moral problems, of which I have have identified and touched on only three. Regarding the first two problems — legal authority and overall effectiveness — I incline to find the operation justified, though the question of legal authority for humanitarian intervention leaves much unfinished business on the international agenda. The third problem — the conduct of the war, and particularly the bombing policy — was on balance not justified in my opinion.

Above all, what is now called for is a vigorous review and debate of the Kosovo operation so as to shape a doctrine regarding force and humanitarian intervention that is legally and morally acceptable.

4. "Balkan Leaders Speak Out: 'Don't Allow Milosovic to Divide Us from Europe,'" *Newsbyte,* United States Institute of Peace (April 29, 1999). Representatives of Bulgaria, Albania, Bosnia and Herzegovina, Croatia, and Romania were present.

VI. ETHICAL AND RELIGIOUS VOICES

How Is the Crisis Ethically and Religiously Evaluated?

Kosovo and the Just-War Tradition

JEAN BETHKE ELSHTAIN

Why are we in the Balkans? The answer voiced most frequently is couched in the language of justice, specifically the just-war tradition. That tradition aims simultaneously to limit resort to arms and to respond to urgent requirements of justice. There are times when claims of justice may override the reluctance to take up arms. For there are grievances and horrors to which we are called to respond — if we can do so in a manner that avoids, to the extent that it is humanly possible, either deepening the injustice already present or creating new instances of injustice. This is a tall order, no doubt, but it is one that humans beings in the Western tradition of warmaking have placed on themselves as one way to chasten collective violence, to stanch the rivers of blood, to reduce the mountains of corpses. The just-war tradition also makes contact with ancient notions of the honor of warriors that turned on strict rules of engagement and some notion of fair fighting between armed combatants.

The just-war tradition is not only demanding, it is inherently complex. One part of the just-war tradition speaks to whether or not a resort to war is justified. War must be fought only for a just cause of substantial importance. The primary "just cause" is a nation's response to direct aggression, a central dictum that has solidified over the years. Yet that dictum is problematic if one starts with St. Augustine, who insisted that it was better to suffer harm oneself than to do harm to another. That said, statesmen did have the responsibility of protecting the people under their charge, and it scarcely counts as protection if one makes no response when one's own citizens are being slaughtered, hounded, routed from their homes, and the like. Aggression need not be directed against one's own to trigger the *jus ad bellum* argument. The offense of aggression may be committed against a nation or people incapable of defending themselves against a determined adversary. If one can intervene to assist the injured party, one is justified in doing so. From St. Augustine in the fourth century on, saving "the innocent from certain harm" has

---

This essay includes portions from two previously published op-ed pieces that appeared in *Newsday* (May 16, 1999, p. B5) and *The Washington Post* (May 16, 1999, p. B3).

been recognized as a justified cause. In the twentieth century this is usually referred to as "humanitarian intervention."

This is where the plight of the Albanian Kosovars comes in. Their ill treatment — the killings, rapes, torture, displacement — adds up to a humanitarian catastrophe by any measure. In this situation, they are the innocent, not in a metaphysical or ontological sense, of course, but in the sense that they are those being tormented by a superior force. Thus it was that we proclaimed ourselves the Kosovars' defenders, if not their saviors. We would "stop" ethnic cleansing. If World War II taught us anything, it was that genocide is a crime that must not go unpunished. Other avenues — or so a plausible case can be made — had been exhausted. Slobodan Milosevic seemed immune to diplomatic overtures. NATO makes up a legitimately constituted concert of states and, therefore, has authority to act, if need be, for humanitarian reasons and in a collective self-defense, protecting the whole idea of a European comity of nations.

None of this implies that any one nation or even a group of nations can or should respond to every instance of ethnic cleansing. The just-war tradition adds a cautionary note about overreach: Be certain before you intervene, even in a just cause, that you have a reasonable chance of success; don't blunder in and make a bad situation worse. But isn't that what we have thus far managed to do in the prolonged bombing of Serbia proper and of Kosovo, part of what promises to become a drawn-out conflict or, alternatively, to end with a face-saving deal that did not save those it set out to save — Albanian Kosovars? They have not been spared ethnic cleansing. The possibility that they might safely return to their homes absent armed protection, despite all the sunny rhetoric from the President of the United States and NATO spokesmen, is remote. What went wrong?

For starters, the means deployed to halt and to punish ethnic cleansing only sped up the process. The opening sorties in the bombing campaign gave Mr. Milosevic the occasion he needed to kick out all international observers and organizations who had played some role in trying to mitigate the damage and to declare martial law, thereby giving himself a free hand. He moved rapidly to complete what he had already started, entrenching his forces in Kosovo before NATO might change its mind about introducing ground troops into the conflict. It seems we hadn't given a moment's thought to the likely reaction to our bombs, namely, a deepening of the terror and expulsion. If we did think this was likely but went ahead nonetheless, we are guilty of egregious irresponsibility. There was no decent preparation for the influx of desperate humanity, their plight made ever more desperate by lack of food, water, medicine, and shelter at their points of terrified egress.

Considerations such as these take us to the heart of the second part of the just-war tradition, the so-called *jus in bello* rules. These are restraints on the means to be deployed even in a just cause. Means are supposed to be proportionate to ends. The damage must not be greater than the offenses one aims to halt. Above all, noncombatant immunity must be protected insofar as it is humanly possible.

Noncombatants historically have been women, children, the aged and infirm, all unarmed persons going about their daily lives, and prisoners of war who have been disarmed by definition. Knowingly placing noncombatants in jeopardy, knowingly putting in place strategies that bring greatest suffering and harm to noncombatants rather than to combatants, is unacceptable on just-war grounds. Better by far to risk the lives of one's own combatants than the lives of "enemy" infants. This is a strenuous demand. But we haven't even attempted to meet it. We are engaged in a war in which not only our combatants but the army of the other side is more or less immunized from the conflict. This turns the traditional just-war concern for civilian lives on its head. In the war against Serbia, it is noncombatants who face much of the greatest danger — from "collateral damage," such as folks in marketplaces shredded to death by cluster bombs as they carry home a dozen eggs or a bunch of carrots.

With our determination to keep NATO soldiers out of harm's way, we have embraced *combatant* immunity, both ours and, by indirection, theirs. We can do lots of damage from the air, of course, reducing buildings to rubble and tearing up bridges. It is far more difficult to face determined combatants on the ground, to use the only means that might have allowed us to achieve just ends: the old-fashioned way, yard by yard, hill by hill, valley by valley, until Kosovo becomes once more a safe environment for all who want to live there. It is a terrible thing to kill or to be killed. But that is the occupational risk of men and women in arms. The restraints of the just-war tradition are always difficult to implement in what Clausewitz called the "fog of battle." But if combatant immunity is to become our new organizing principle, we shall face many more situations in the future in which we refuse to do what is necessary to meet our stated objectives and resort instead to means that undermine not only those objectives but the centuries-old effort to limit war, as much as possible, to combatants.

What a strange turn of events! The Serbian army remains dug in in Kosovo. They can operate without any worry about facing their opponents on the ground. But Chinese nationals in their country's embassy in Belgrade, women, children, and old men in markets — these are the people in harm's way. "Collateral damage," to be sure. But it's getting hard to tell what's collateral anymore. Having pretty much exhausted obvious military targets, we are busy degrading the entire infrastructure on which civilian life depends, this despite the disclaimer by the President of the United States that we have no quarrel with the Serbian people because they, too, are victims of the Milosevic regime. In this regard, what we have thus far done is solidify support for Milosevic. It is always difficult to criticize a government in wartime, even in a democratic society. Consider some of the demagogic rhetoric on the floor of the House and the Senate when those raising questions about the bombing and criticizing the President's judgment in this matter were accused of weakening our will to fight, in fact, of near-treason. Much more difficult, then, to expect even those thousands of Serbs who have little but contempt for Milosevic to rally against him as the bombs drop relentlessly night after night.

Just-war thinking insists that a war's aims must be made clear, that criteria for what is to count as success must be publicly available, and that negotiation must never be ruled out of court. But our war aims at this point have been sucked into the White House fog machine. We've already lost the aim that took us into this fight — stopping the flow of refugees. Now our aim is to degrade Milosevic's ability to make war. When will we know if that has happened? We aren't actually fighting his military in a direct confrontation. Here there is no substitute for a test on the ground. Putting soldiers on the ground is the only way to guarantee a permanent rollback of Serbian forces; it is the only way to protect Albanian Kosovars who remain and to provide safe passage for those who hope to return. But that we are not prepared to do. You cannot stop atrocities on the ground by dropping cluster bombs on marketplaces, whether by mistake or not. The means deployed by NATO (pretty much a 90 percent American force, of course) and the ends sought are ships passing one another in the night. The overall incoherence of this operation becomes painfully clear with each passing day. If one adds reports of destabilization in the entire region, who would now predict with any confidence that the Dayton Accords will hold, that Montenegro will not fall?

These realizations make the remarks of the President of the United States seem terribly out of touch with reality. He has, for example, voiced the most extraordinary domestic analogies in an attempt to put a distinctively American stamp on the Balkans tragedy, events that can only be shoehorned within our reigning political categories and preoccupations through the most tortuous rhetoric. Thus President Clinton has likened the signing of a federal hate-crime statute to the good works to be brought about by bombing Belgrade. He has spun out a "vision" for a new postwar Kosovo that sounds like a multiculturalist pipe dream, unrealistic even for a pluralist democracy let alone a fractured, destabilized region in the Balkans that will be reeling from these events for the next half-century and beyond. In a May 23, 1999, op-ed piece in the *New York Times*, the President not only proclaimed restoration of the status quo ante as the number-one priority, but with Kosovo now under a kind of protectorship and more or less run by the KLA (Kosovo Liberation Army), who want a separatist, all-ethnic Albanian micro-state, not a Balkans version of New York City politics. Clinton claimed that there were no signs of strain in the NATO alliance; yet the same paper that contained his op-ed piece prominently featured an article making precisely the opposite case. The President spoke, astonishingly, of strengthening our relationship with Russia as a result of all this, when that relationship, along with our dealings with the Chinese, has soured horribly. And he insisted that Serbians were fracturing in their loyalty to the regime, though every article by journalists on the scene reports a dogged determination to see the thing through and to support, however grudgingly, the Serb government — not because of their Kosovo policy, but because it is their government and it is defying those who are flying hundreds of sorties every single day using the world's most sophisticated aircraft and weaponry against a people that has little chance at all of fighting back.

Through it all, President Clinton avoids the tough questions every statesman who sends his nation into war must face, plus additional questions every statesman who evokes the just-war tradition should face: Are we prepared to commit men, women, and material to Kosovo for the next twenty or thirty years in order to rebuild the region and guarantee a fragile peace through force of arms? Are we prepared to launch a "mini Marshall Plan" to spur civic development and growth? Having turned the war against Serbia into a crusade of sorts, the President discusses the situation in the language of a campaign rather than the language of strategy, diplomacy, rueful recognition of unintended consequences, and limits to what our power can accomplish.

There was one way to intervene in order to slow down if not halt ethnic cleansing: it was to put our own men and women at risk. That we were unprepared to do. So we have not saved the innocent from certain harm. The events that have unfolded since the bombing campaign started have deepened the harm. Are Milosevic and his henchmen feeling the sting? Are they being punished? That is none too clear. But it is overwhelmingly clear that ordinary Serbs, many of them no lovers of Milosevic, are suffering. Will this suffering prepare them for that wondrous multicultural festival the President envisions as the ultimate endgame? Not likely. So we blunder on. Every day the message resounds: the bombing campaign is effective. We are seeing the light at the end of the tunnel. It's probably a bit difficult for hungry, sick, grief-stricken Kosovars, who are crammed into tents within the borders of countries that do not want them, to see that light. Beyond admitting a token number to the U.S. with great fanfare, what are we going to do?

Is there no one in Washington prepared to talk straight to the American people? With the President's popularity waning and support for the bombing ebbing, as more and more reports and terrible photographs of errant bombs on retirement homes and hospitals hit us, the justness of it all seems terribly remote. Admitting a small number of refugees into the United States with a huge amount of media hoopla does nothing for the hundreds of thousands who are malnourished, without decent shelter, languishing in refugee camps with no prospects ahead save quasi-permanent exile or a return to a fragmented ruin of the place they once called home. The environment in Kosovo is hostile; it will take months of concerted efforts just to clear land mines. This might have gone differently, and, just perhaps, we could have used the word "just" or "justified" in a strong ethical sense to describe the war and our part in it. That moment died aborning when we decided we would buy safety for ourselves and sacrifice not only "enemy" noncombatants but the very people we said we were rescuing, when we were unwilling to risk anything ourselves save many millions of dollars in ordnance and aircraft. We may come up with a face-saving strategy. But saving lives? That is a different and very sad story indeed.

367

The Ethno-Religious Challenge
to Global Order

MARK JUERGENSMEYER

The Kosovo crisis is something of a paradigm of recent global trends. It exemplifies the weakening of old secular state frameworks, the rise of potent new ethno-religious nationalisms, and the difficulty of dealing with these new dynamics on a global level — especially when the peacemakers are themselves perceived as ideological foes.

The Vulnerability of the Secular Nation-State

Yugoslavia from its inception as a political entity has been something of a fragile artifice. Yet this is to some extent true of all nations in the modern world, especially those created by retreating colonial powers, such as Britain, France, and the Soviet Union. These imagined nations were not accepted by everyone within their boundaries, and the global triumph of nationalism celebrated by many Western policymakers and scholars in the 1940s turned out to be a short-lived victory. The newly created nations had only brief histories of prior colonial control to unite them, and after independence they had only the most modest of economic, administrative, and cultural infrastructures to hold their disparate regions together.

By the 1990s these ties had begun to fray. The global economic market undercut national economies, and the awesome military technology of the U.S. and NATO reduced national armies to border patrols. More significantly, the rationale for the nation-state came into question. With the collapse of the Soviet Union and the post-colonial, post-Vietnam critique of Western democracy, the secular basis for the nation-state seemed increasingly open to criticism. In some instances, such as in Yugoslavia, when the ideological glue of secular nationalism began to dissolve, the state fell apart.

The Rise of Violent Forms of Ethnic and Religious Nationalism

The weakening of the nation-state around the world has not, however, caused the sentiment of nationalism to become less intense. Quite the contrary: the fading of the nation-state has produced both the opportunity for new nationalisms and the need for them. As post-Soviet and post-colonial secular ties began to unravel, people in regions such as those of the former Yugoslavia searched for new anchors to ground their social identities and political loyalties. Many turned to ethnicity and religion.

What is ideologically significant about ethno-religious movements such as those associated with the Serbs and Kosovars is their creativity. They have invented the elements of new nationalisms. Although it is true that they have reached back in history to find ancient images and concepts that offer them credibility, these are not simply efforts to resuscitate old ideas from the past. They also meet present-day needs.

In the modern context this is a revolutionary notion: that indigenous culture provides the basis for the nation-state. Movements that support ethno-religious nationalism are, therefore, often confrontational and sometimes violent. They reject the intervention of international agencies and, at the risk of being intolerant, pander to their cultural bases and enforce social boundaries. It is no surprise, then, that they get into trouble with each other and with defenders of the secular state.

The Demonization of America

Such conflicts with secular modernity serve a purpose for those who wage them. It helps them define who they are as a people and who they are not. They are not, for instance, transnational secularists. And they are not Americans.

Why is America often targeted as the enemy? One reason is that America has had a vested economic and political interest in shoring up the stability of regimes around the world. This has often put the United States in the position of being a defender of secular governments. A second reason is that the United States supports a globalized economy and a modern culture. In a world where villagers in remote corners of the world increasingly have access to MTV, Hollywood movies, and the Internet, the images and values that have been projected globally have often been American.

So it is understandable that America would be disdained. What is perplexing to many Americans is why their country would be so severely hated, even caricatured. I believe that the demonization of America by many ethno-religious groups fits into a process of delegitimating secular authority that involves the appropriation of traditional religious images of cosmic war. In such scenarios, competing ethnic and religious groups become foes and scapegoats, and the secular state becomes religion's enemy. Such satanization is aimed at reducing the power of one's opponents and discrediting them. By humiliating them — by making them sub-human — ethno-religious groups assert the superiority of their own moral power.

The Difficulty of Responding to Ethno-Religious Conflict

When America is demonized, it is difficult for it to be seen as a neutral observer and peacemaker. Even when its actions are allegedly humanitarian, they are suspect. After all, recent history has ample examples of superpowers covering with altruism their acts of political and economic self-interest. Moreover, when military force is brought into the picture, the distrust can deepen into images of cosmic war: America becomes the evil foe, indiscriminately using its power to destroy. Military intervention for even the most benign reasons can make America look like a sinister bully rather than an agent of peace. Alas, however, in an unstable world there are instances when social unrest — even ethnic cleansing and genocide — cry out for external intervention.

In such instances it is tempting for America to play a policeman's role. But it is one that America should not accept easily, since heavy-footed intervention can often exacerbate tensions rather than relieve them. On the other hand, America has a responsibility to use its power to alleviate suffering. Hence broad-based multilateral efforts — ideally sanctioned by the United Nations — offer the best opportunities for providing an effective and neutral position. The aim is to provide a shield of support without fanning the flames of tension between established secular states and newly emerging movements for ethno-religious nationalism.[1]

---

1. Sources for this essay include Benedict Anderson, *Imagined Communities: Reflections on the Origin and Spread of Nationalism* (London: Verso, 1983); Mark Juergensmeyer, *The New Cold War? Religious Nationalism Confronts the Secular State* (Berkeley: University of California Press, 1993); idem, *Terror in the Mind of God: The Global Rise of Religious Violence* (Berkeley: University of California Press, 2000); Michael A. Sells, *The Bridge Betrayed: Religion and Genocide in Bosnia* (Berkeley: University of California Press, 1996); Stanley Tambiah, *Leveling Crowds: Ethnonationalist Conflicts and Collective Violence in South Asia* (Berkeley: University of California Press, 1996); and David Westerlund, ed., *Questioning the Secular State: The Worldwide Resurgence of Religion in Politics* (London: Hurst and Co., 1996).

The Former Yugoslavia:
A Warning Example for World Peace,
a Challenge for World Churches

HANS KÜNG

Only when it was too late did it become clear to politicians and diplomats that the complexity of the problems in Yugoslavia can only be understood when one takes seriously the fact that for a thousand years — grounded in the separation of West Rome and East Rome — two completely different civilizations developed and two different paradigms of Christianity met in the middle of Yugoslavia. For more than a millennium, in matters of religion Serbs have looked toward East Rome, Byzantium, or Moscow, while the Croats and Slovenes have looked to Latin West Rome. Accordingly, different liturgies, theologies, hierarchies, church constitutions, mentalities, and political histories developed. Every ethnic group in former Yugoslavia has its own myths, legends, justifications, excuses, and prejudices handed down for centuries — in short, its history of suffering and guilt.[1]

In the former Yugoslavia, Serbs, Croats, and Bosnians (including the only indigenous and originally very tolerant Muslims in Europe) are all "southern Slavs" ("Yugo-Slavs"). They speak the same language and, despite different religions, have lived together peacefully for a very long time and have often intermarried — a living argument against the allegedly unavoidable "clash of civilizations."[2] Despite the fact that Yugoslavia was an example of overlapping and interpenetrating

---

1. For example, the 600-year history of Turk occupation of Serb territory (since the Serb defeat at the battle of Kosovo, "The Field of the Blackbirds," in 1389) has produced, for Serbs, a nationalist ideology of a lasting suffering and endurance that very often does not correspond (or no longer corresponds) to reality.

2. Samuel Huntington puts forth this thesis in "The Class of Civilizations?" *Foreign Affairs* 72, no. 3 (1993): 22-49. See also the critical comments on Huntington by F. Ajami, R. L. Bartley, L. Binyan, J. Kirkpatrick, and K. Mahbubani in *Foreign Affairs* 72, no. 4 (September/October 1993) and Huntington's response in no. 5 (November/December): 186-94.

This essay was abridged, adapted, and edited chiefly by Kate McCann from *A Global Ethic for Global Politics and Economics* (Oxford: Oxford University Press, 1998), pp. 121-38.

civilizations, political actors and the churches failed to develop policies and take actions that would protect the interconfessional and intercultural civilization of Yugoslavia. The failure of politics and the failure of the churches to address the crises of the Balkans appropriately enables us to use the case of Yugoslavia as a warning example for world politics and a challenge for world churches.

The Failure of Politics

When I studied in Rome with Slovenes and Croats and, as early as 1984, lectured in Belgrade, Zagreb, and Dubrovnik, which were then peaceful, I followed events with passionate concern. I know from direct information that neither in the Foreign Office in Bonn nor on the Quai d'Orsay in Paris was a serious analysis made of ethnic and religious perspectives at the beginning of the conflict; and it was no different in Washington and London. Had such analyses been made in the foreign ministries of the great Western powers, and had the ethno-religious antagonisms not been dismissed as the long-outdated quirks of a few surviving fanatics and lunatics, the governments could easily have avoided many of the disastrous mistakes in the various phases of the Balkans conflict after 1989. Instead of striving for some uniform centralistic or antagonistic and separatist solution, the world political community should have been able to find a "federal solution"[3] and impose it unconditionally, with support from the great powers. But what happened?

The following short survey of the three phases of this conflict is not meant to pass reproachful verdicts on the past but to draw lessons from it for the future.

Phase One

The first mistake was the attempt to establish a uniform Yugoslavian state. At that time, the European Union (E.U.), the United Nations (U.N.), and especially the United States (U.S.) engaged in a "do nothing policy."[4] The consequence was a lack of any ethical will to resist the blatant Serbian aggression (the bombardment of the civilian population of Vukovar, Dubrovnik, Sarajevo, and other Bosnian cities) on

---

3. "Federal" here means: The greatest possible autonomy of the different ethnic and religious groups in respect of language, education, business, administration, academic research, media, folklore, traditions, culture, and religion generally; but also one government, one army, one currency, one foreign policy.

4. Badly advised (as was honestly conceded by the U.S. ambassador in Belgrade, Warren Zimmermann) and led by a president, George Bush, who was uninterested in the Serbian invasion of Croatia in 1991 and tied the U.S. superpower to a "do-nothing policy" that President Clinton continued until 1995 instead of forging an alliance against the aggressor, as the U.S. did in the Gulf War (Huntington totally overlooks phase 1, in which Islam plays no role).

the part of the European great powers and, with them, on the part of the American President, George Bush, without whose leadership nothing in a disunited Europe went. A timely and well-considered threat of economic sanctions and military force[5] could have stopped the aggression at that time. U.S. Ambassador Zimmerman would later say that "not only would damage to the city [of Dubrovnik] have been averted, but the Serbs would have been given a lesson in Western resolve which would at least have prevented something of their aggression against Bosnia."[6] As it was, the Serbs learned another lesson: that there was no Western resolve and that they could advance as far as their power would take them. So the lack of an ethical will to resist made possible and encouraged the aggression of the "Yugoslavian" — but in fact Serbian — army against Croatia, Slovenia, and then also Bosnia.[7]

Phase Two

The second fatal mistake was to give immediate diplomatic recognition to Croatia and Slovenia as sovereign states — in the face of massive Serbian aggression. Recognition came first of all from the Vatican, which regarded Croatia as a "bulwark of (Western) Christianity" and also had an interest in seeing two more "Catholic states" in the alliance of European powers. Under massive pressure from the Vatican, recognition came from the government of the Federal Republic of Germany (so far its most serious diplomatic mistake); then, under pressure from Germany, recognition came from the E.U. without any concern to give serious protection to the minorities in Croatia (the Krajina Serbs), which was urgently necessary due to the policy of Croatian President Franjo Tudjman.[8]

The diplomatic recognition of Croatia (and Slovenia) had highly negative consequences for the unity of multiethnic and multireligious Bosnia-Herzegovina and for the common foreign policy of the E.U. Bosnia-Herzegovina was delivered over to the criminal games of Milosevic, Karadzic, and Mladic. To restore the balance of power in the Balkans, in the wake of German and Vatican support of Croatia and Slovenia, England and France (supported by the Netherlands) placated Serbia. Offi-

5. No ground troops but massive NATO air attacks on air bases, military camps, munitions factories, and strategically important bridges.

6. Quoted in Rosenfeld, "How America Might Have Helped Avert the Slaughter," in *Washington Post/International Herald Tribune,* 13 March 1995.

7. It is already significant that American Secretary of State Warren Christopher hardly traveled in the Balkans, but instead went to Syria twenty-four times and to Israel thirty-five times, though even there without exerting the necessary political and financial pressure at the right time, so that at the end of his period in office he had to watch the Israeli-Palestinian peace process collapse because of the obstruction of the new Likud government.

8. Like the Serb Slobodan Milosevic, an ex-communist (and authoritarian nationalist) who suppressed all opposition within Croatia and engaged in aggression.

cially "neutral," U.N. troops were sent to Bosnia-Herzegovina as "observers" and thus prevented any serious military intervention against Serbian aggression.

Phase Three

The third fatal mistake was to draw arbitrary frontiers in Bosnia-Herzegovina, in the style of colonial powers, which meant de facto recognition of "ethnic cleansings" and thus a promise to the aggressors, contrary to all existing international law, of territories that had been occupied by force. The result of this unparalleled political drama will probably be abiding hostility, revenge at the first opportunity, and, if the prospects seem good, a new war.

Many people from all over the world felt that it was allegedly "realist" diplomacy that in fact led to the greatest political hypocrisy since the glorious European year of 1989. It is scandalous that Croatia was accepted into the Council of Europe in 1995 in spite of the fact that President Tudjman, rejected by the majority of his people and contrary to the demand of the Council, did not cooperate in the arrest of war criminals, did not allow the elected opposition leader to take up his post as mayor of Zagreb, and did not enable Serbian refugees to return. It is equally scandalous that Milosevic, the chief author of the Yugoslavian war and a war criminal, discreetly protected by English and French diplomacy, could have held on to power so long despite the peaceful protests of the Serbian democratic movement, which went on every day for many weeks. The Serbian democratic movement was not to be empowered by either the European community or NATO.

I remember a remark by the Englishman Brian Beetham: "Hypocrisy [is] the ultimate sin in the making of foreign policy." Due to the political or diplomatic hypocrisy present in the international community's response to the war in Bosnia-Herzegovina, no one knows whether the present artificial product of diplomacy will or will not fall apart after the departure of NATO troops. The demographic separation of the three ethnic groups continues, despite the 1995 Dayton Agreement; the newly created national institutions (tripartite presidency, interethnic judiciary) exist only on paper; countless refugees are prevented from returning to their homeland; and the principal war criminals remain free. In short, a military conflict could break out again at any time if the hitherto undemocratic authorities in Serbia and Croatia are not replaced by truly democratic and tolerant regimes.

Lessons Learned?

What can be learned from this history of calamities for world politics? How can a new political fiasco such as the one in the Balkans be avoided? Here are just a few brief remarks:

- A diplomacy without any ethical will, a politics of interests beyond any morality, a global politics without a global ethic — these always produce new injustices and thus new crises, new conflicts, and new wars.
- When secession is striven for, there is no call for uniform solutions, as has been the aim of the U.S. and E.U. in Yugoslavia and by Russia in response to ethnic violence in Chechnya.
- The automatic recognition of ethnic groups as sovereign states is uncalled for. The solution in complex cases of conflict is not the "sovereign" nation-state but, rather, the widest possible cultural and political autonomy.[9]
- Instead of uniform or antagonistic solutions, the goal should be a federal model, of the kind achieved in the face of similar difficulties in the past century by the United States, the Swiss Confederation, and Canada, and today by Belgium, Spain, South Africa, and others. This is even more urgent in cases of even stronger ethnic mixes — as an alternative to ethnic "cleansings."

The Failure of Challenge to the Churches

In such a region, will there ever be peace unless the religious dimension of the conflict is taken seriously? Initially the sympathies of many people in Europe were with Croatia (not because it was Catholic but because it had been attacked), and then above all with the Muslims. However, it has not been forgotten that it was the Catholic Croatian Ustashi, under the protectorate of the German Nazis, who killed tens of thousands (some claim hundreds of thousands) of Serbs. Neither then Catholic Archbishop Aloisius Stepinac of Zagreb nor then Pope Pius XII protested, though they were very well briefed on what was happening.

Both Catholic Croats and Orthodox Serbs have their own long list of offenses. There are no innocent nations anywhere, far less in the Balkans. For almost fifty years, since the end of World War II, both churches had time to sort out the situation, to acknowledge guilt, and to ask for forgiveness. Observers of the war ask, in retrospect, whether it was really "worthwhile." The challenge for the churches is to reflect on the relationship between peace and justice and between a Christian ethic and a global ethic that applies to all.

The withdrawal of the Dutch U.N. troops from the greatest massacre in Europe since World War II in Srebrenica, for policy reasons, has caused people to search their consciences, even in the Netherlands.[10] However, an absolute pacifism

9. This must lead to the independence of ever smaller units (one need think only of the Basques, Catalonia, Northern Italy, Scotland, Corsica). If this went on, I was told at a U.N. headquarters, there would soon be about 450 "sovereign" states instead of the 185 U.N. members there were in 1996 (as compared with the 51 founder states in 1945).

10. With 8,000 to 10,000 civilians dead. The scene of their commander drinking champagne with General Mladic, the butcher of Srebrenica, remains stamped on the memory.

for which peace is the supreme good to which all must be sacrificed is irresponsible. The legitimate right to self-defense according to Article 51 of the U.N. Charter is not abrogated even by the Sermon on the Mount. The requirement of nonviolence may not be put into practice in a literal, fundamentalist way. Pacifism is not enough to keep the peace. What is called for is not a hollow peace but peace as the work of justice (as Augustine said, *Opus iustitiae pax*), which in some circumstances means defending those who are attacked and disarming the attackers. What is appropriate here is not an "ethics of conviction," which is heedless of the consequences. Some "peace fighters" must be told that mere moral conviction without reason has had, and can again have, catastrophic effects.

With regard to justice, mass murderers and megalomaniacal dictators cannot be allowed the decisive power over a region that is important for the life of the whole world. War criminals should be brought before an international tribunal. The fact that the U.N. and NATO troops have so far not arrested the Serb leader Karadzic and General Mladic, both accused of crimes against humanity, must not be blamed on the soldiers but on those governments who do not want an arrest to occur. It is vital for the credibility and success of the international tribunal that these people in high places are called to account. It is the responsibility of Washington, London, Paris, Rome, and Bonn that the U.N. troops, contrary to the Dayton Agreement, were not instructed to arrest Karadzic and Mladic. To quote Richard Goldstone, the chief prosecutor of the International Criminal Tribunal for Yugoslavia (ICTY), "The whole court — the judge, the prosecutors, the administration — feels extremely frustrated by the restrictive policy of these states"; and "people rightly feel it unjust that the main culprits escape justice and those far below them in the hierarchy are caught and punished."[11] Recognizing that there are too many perpetrators in the former Yugoslavia to prosecute, Goldstone has called for the trial of the chief culprits before the ICTY and the bringing of the others before a truth commission.

The challenge for the churches is to remember and espouse that injustice remains injustice even if it is in the garb of state legislation — that injustice does not become justice by being ordained by law, but becomes simply "legal injustice." The "convictions about the value and dignity of human beings common to all nations" and "the elementary demands of justice" have priority over "positive law." Ethical values like human dignity and justice apply independent of any legal recognition, so that in grave cases a legal norm "is to be disobeyed *a priori* if it is in manifest, intolerable contradiction with justice." Thus state legislation presupposes an ethic common to all human beings, a worldwide ethic of humanity. The "convictions about the value and dignity of human beings common to all nations" of the

11. See Richard Goldstone's interview "Über Frustration und Glaubwürdigkeit in Den Haag. Der Chefankläger des Uno-Kriegsverbrechertribunals zieht Bilanz," *Neue Zürche Zeitung* 20/21 July, 1996.

"worldwide community of law" are "normative, and indispensable for human life together; they are part of the unassailable nucleus of the law" (1996 German Federal Constitutional Court).

But, of course, laws and judgments are not enough to preserve a country from war and crime nor enough to hold a society together. We must go deeper here and ask about a matter of principle. What holds modern society together? "The free secular lives by presuppositions which it cannot itself guarantee without putting its freedom in question." Modern society needs social and political guidelines. These emerge from common convictions, attitudes, and traditions that precede freedom and make use of it as a medium. These resources are not there by nature, but they need to be cultivated, activated, and handed down by upbringing. There is no disputing this, but it raises the question: What is to be done when it appears that these common convictions, attitudes, and traditions that precede freedom have largely gotten lost? One can hardly cultivate what no longer exists, and who is to "activate" what seems to have gone to sleep?

The modern liberal social order has for a long time been able to rely on "habits of the heart," on a thick "cushion" of premodern systems of meaning and obligation that today are "threadbare." Respect for the authority of the state, obedience toward the laws, and a work ethic have long been able to rely on this traditional cushion. But in the meantime the traditional resources of meaning and the ingredients of traditional public-spiritedness have come to be exhausted. This raises a question: Can citizens themselves "generate" such resources of meaning? That is asking far too much of them. The human beings of today cannot invent everything all over again. So from where is present-day humankind to draw the "moral resources" and prelegal conditions of cohesion? What is the role of religion?

Like secular philosophy (i.e., the human-rights tradition), religion has made undoubted contributions to tolerance and democracy — and human rights. Those who banish or ignore religion create a vacuum. In any case, they must declare what they have to offer in its place.

Kosovo Crisis Contexts: Nationalism, Milosevic, and the Serbian Orthodox Church

STANLEY SAMUEL HARAKAS

The recent tragic events in Kosovo are the sad and almost inevitable consequence of a long line of conflicts predestined by the very formation of the nation of the "Land of the South Slavs" — Yugoslavia. In this brief essay I will discuss the issues of nationalism in Yugoslavia, the role of Slobodan Milosevic, and the relationship of the Serbian Orthodox Church to the policies and methods of the Milosevic regime — with the major focus on that last point. From the beginning of the modern nation of Yugoslavia the seeds were sown that almost guaranteed its eventual dissolution.

There have been three manifestations of Yugoslavia. The first Yugoslavia was created by the Paris Peace Conference following World War I. A "kingdom of Serbs, Croats and Slovenes" was formed with a constitution in 1921 in what was, significantly, an effort to craft a "multinational state." Thus, from its very beginning, rival and conflicting ethnic interests were bound together in a political structure that would be held together only with difficulty. Also from the beginning, demographic facts would control the policy interests of the various parties. The ethnic groups were not evenly scattered throughout the country. Rather, each ethnicity was fairly well centralized. Thus the areas of Serbia, Croatia, Bosnia and Herzegovina, Dalmatia, Slovenia, and Montenegro had clear ethnic identity. This ethnic identity sometimes transcended religious loyalties and sometimes served to enhance their differences. The controlling factor was not religion but tribe-like ethnicity.

But an important demographic reality was that peoples of varying ethnic groups with distinct identities were scattered about in ethnic clumps and cultural clusters within regions of a different ethnic unity. In most cases these were small or tiny minorities. The only group that had significantly large minority populations in most of the constituent ethnic regions was the Serbs.

This reality governed the different approaches to the way the nation should be governed. While the Serbs considered it important to have a strong and centralized state for the sake of the interests of its scattered Serbian ethnic enclaves, the other ethnic groups, led by Croatia, preferred to emphasize a federal approach that would give greater power to the ethnic republics. In 1929, King Alexander declared a royal dictatorship and recrafted the boundaries of the unified state's nine prefectures so as to break up national unities. In 1939, however, this solution weakened with the formation of a unified prefecture that brought together the divided Croatian regions. This "First Yugoslavia" ended with the victory of the Axis powers in April 1941.

The "Second Yugoslavia" appeared at the end of World War II — under the influence of communism. In 1946 a new constitution established the Federal People's Republic of Yugoslavia, which was constituted of six ethnically determined republics: Bosnia-Herzegovina, Croatia, Macedonia, Montenegro, Serbia, and Slovenia. The predominantly Albanian population of Kosovo and the predominantly Hungarian population of Vojvodina were given a certain autonomous status within Serbia. Again, a centralized approach to the economy, with the strong communist dictatorial government of Joseph Broz Tito, held together the ethnic diversity of the land for a good part of his rule. When Yugoslavia was expelled from the Comintern in 1948, the liberalizing tendencies fostered by the "market socialism" of the "Yugoslav road to socialism" also brought with it demands for more regional independence in the federation. Though Tito was able to suppress much of this centrifugal impetus, he was forced, six years before his death, to grant greater authority to the republics. When he died in 1980, the hitherto "President for Life" was replaced by a collective presidency according to which each republic was to exercise the presidency in rotation. It was the beginning of the end for the Second Yugoslavia.

The "Third Yugoslavia" (composed only of Serbia and Montenegro), together with the independent nations of Slovenia, Croatia, Bosnia-Herzegovina, and Macedonia of the former republic of Yugoslavia, was the fruit of the nationalist interests of the republics overwhelming the meaningful interests of a central administration. A key player in bringing about this consequence was Slobodan Milosevic, who had been a communist from the age of eighteen. Upon his graduation from the University of Belgrade, he had held a number of business-oriented jobs. In 1984, four years after Tito's death, he took control of the Communist party in Belgrade, and two years later he became the leader of the Serbian Communist party. In 1989, Milosevic became president of Serbia and began instituting policies favorable once again to central control. In 1990, becoming aware of the rise of Albanian nationalist interests in Kosovo, he engineered the practical curtailment of the region's autonomous status and returned full authority to Serbian control.

In 1991, Milosevic provoked the final step leading to the dissolution of the "Second Yugoslavia." The Croats were due to assume the revolving presidency of Yugoslavia in May of 1991. Milosevic blocked that accession, and it became clear that a federalist Yugoslavia could not survive. Slovenia, closely followed by Croatia and the former Yugoslav republic of Macedonia, withdrew from the federation. Early in 1992, Bosnia's Muslims and Croatians also voted to leave the federation. Milosevic gave some military assistance to Serb populations in Croatia and

Bosnia, but eventually he became the de facto leader of what remained — Serbia and Montenegro, the "Third Yugoslavia."

Milosevic endorsed the tradition of a strong federalist Yugoslavia, but the policy was flawed by his tactic of asserting superior ethnic privilege to the Serbs. His rule was perceived in the other ethnic republics as supporting Serbian nationalist hegemony rather than fostering a true federalist spirit and administration. Historically speaking, this was a counterpoint to the Croatian hegemony fostered by Tito at the expense of the Serbs during the "Second Yugoslavia." There was little in Milosevic's policy that would foster tolerance and accommodation among Yugoslavia's ethnic groups or would allow for a successful multiethnic federalist Yugoslavia. Thus Milosevic's extreme ethnic policies were perceived in Yugoslavia, following the Serbian defeat in the Bosnian war, as failures.

In municipal elections in 1992, Milosevic's party was soundly defeated. But Milosevic annulled the elections, provoking weeks of public demonstrations that sought to overturn the decree. Significantly, elections were also held in 1992 among Kosovo's Albanians, and a shadow government headed by Ibrahim Rugova was established. The Albanians withdrew their children from Serb schools and taught them only Albanian. The Kosovo Serbs, with their fourteenth-century roots there, found themselves increasingly a minority in Kosovo. Milosevic's policies sought to reverse the statistics. Just as the 200,000 Serbian minority in Croatia's Krajina region were ethnically cleansed in a week's time in August 1995 by the Croatian army — with U.S. and NATO tolerance, if not approval — Milosevic's army and police assumed that they could change the population ratios in Kosovo with a similar offensive. And until the beginning of the NATO air war on March 24, 1999, Milosevic seemed to be succeeding. With the NATO occupation and the effective removal of the Serb population, the eventual independence of Kosovo as an exclusive Albanian entity seems inevitable. Only partition will preserve some of the historic Serbian sites for the "Third Yugoslavia."[1]

The main dynamic force in this recounting is nationalism. Failed efforts to form a nation that is capable of uniting disparate ethnic interests in a single political unity has bedeviled the three-stage history of Yugoslavia since its founding. Each of the national groups exploits the religious distinctiveness of its people to heighten its nationalist identity. But the motivation is not religious; it is nationalistic. As a communist, Milosevic has no personal interest in religion, though he has used the Serbian Orthodox Church to further his nationalist interests.

What role has the Serbian Orthodox Church played in these conflicts? The

---

1. The concept of three Yugoslavias as a function of the inherent federalist-republics tension is developed succinctly in the *Encyclopedia Britannica 1997 CD-Rom* under the heading "The Balkan States: Yugoslavia." Only pertinent elements of that account are included here. The information regarding Slobodan Milosevic comes also from an entry titled "Slobodan Milosevic," in the *Encyclopedia Britannica 1997 CD-Rom.*

assumption by many in the West is that the war in Kosovo has been a religious war between "Orthodox Serbs" and "Muslim Kosovars." This was baldly expressed in an editorial in a small Florida newspaper in April 1999.[2] The editor wrote an editorial regarding the civilized world's abhorrence of the ethnic cleansing in Kosovo. But the editorial also opined that "Muslims justify killing in the name of Allah and call it a holy war or jihad. Orthodox white Christians in Yugoslavia may not have such a doctrine, but make no mistake about it: they believe they are helping God by ridding the nations of Muslim Kosovars."

This view is simply incorrect, both for the Albanian Muslim Kosovars and for the Orthodox Christians in Kosovo, and, more broadly, for the Serbian Orthodox Church. The truth is that during the Bosnian war religious leaders of all persuasions supported the struggles of their people to gain religious and territorial integrity. Orthodox clergy, Roman Catholic bishops, and Muslim imams were equally involved.

But as long ago as mid-May 1992, the Holy Synod of the Serbian Orthodox Church, under its octogenarian leader, Patriarch Pavle, expressed in writing severe condemnation of the national government in Belgrade. In that letter the Serbian Orthodox religious leaders highlighted the many human rights violations by the government and countered with appeals for peaceful solutions to resolve ethnic differences. The Synod of the Serbian Orthodox Church condemned President Milosevic's war policies and human rights crimes against Serbians, Croatians, and Muslims. It no longer considered the Bosnian war a righteous expression of legitimate national goals but a pogrom. It called for Serbian President Slobodan Milosevic's resignation. In light of that position, Patriarch Pavle did something without precedent: on June 14, 1992, he led a public demonstration in Belgrade for peace — in opposition to the Milosevic government.[3]

In January 1994, Patriarch Pavle issued a statement directed to the Central Committee of the World Council of Churches meeting in Johannesburg that called for an end to the violence in the former Yugoslavia and decried the suffering caused by ethnic violence, "of whatever kind and by whomever it is used, regardless of religion or nation."[4]

In the same spirit, and in support of the patriarch, "the WCC Central Committee, meeting between January 20 and 28, 1994, issued a strongly worded statement condemning the violence in the former Yugoslavia and calling for resistance against 'every attempt to use religious sentiment and loyalty in the service of aggressive nationalism.'"[5] Shortly afterward, Patriarch Pavle denied Serbian Church blessing on the Serbian government's military action. In response, Milosevic's gov-

---

2. *Hernando Today* (Florida), Thursday, April 1, p. 5.

3. Stanley S. Harakas, entry on "Eastern Orthodox Church," in *1993 Britannica Book of the Year* (Chicago: Encyclopedia Britannica, Inc., 1993).

4. "Patriarch Pavle of Serbia Calls for End of Violence," *Ecumenical News Service*, February 4, 1994, no. 41.

5. Ibid.

ernment withdrew the permission of the patriarch and the Serbian Orthodox Church to appear on the state-controlled television network.[6]

On January 2, 1997, a communique from an "Emergency Session of Serbian Orthodox Bishops" was released, in which the Synod condemned Milosevic's regime on behalf of the Serb people as "putting us at odds with the whole world and now trying to mislead and bloody us just in order to hold onto power." The message continued: "For this, the Holy Synod of the Serbian Orthodox Church, as the centuries-old guardian of the things people hold sacred, energetically and openly brands and condemns such conduct by the ruling regime. The Holy Synod is convinced that only respect for democratic principles and human rights and recognition of the results of the November 17 elections can bring hope in a better future and a peaceful life to the entire Serbian people and the other citizens of Serbia."[7]

Thus, long before the ethnic cleansing of the Albanian population of Kosovo, the Orthodox Church was officially opposed to the Milosevic government's antidemocratic and increasingly extremist nationalist policies. When Milosevic instigated the ethnic cleansing of the Albanian population in Kosovo by recalling their autonomous status, his extremist nationalist policies resurrected extremist Albanian nationalist sentiments. While Rugova followed moderate and democratic policies, extremist wings of Albanian nationalism in the form of the Kosovo Liberation Army were fueled by Milosevic's policies and the sudden availability of a large number of weapons following the looting of military supplies in Albania. Armed insurrection followed, and the worst of nationalist extremism appeared on the scene.

Where was the Orthodox Church in this? Since only 10 percent of the Kosovo population was Orthodox, the monasteries in Kosovo were islands of good sense for both Orthodox Serbs and Muslims in Kosovo.[8] In January 1998, Pavle protested a government crackdown on Albanian students in Kosovo. One independent news agency reported that Patriarch Pavle "said the police not only 'broke the rules [regulating peaceful protest] but besmirched the honor of the country where we live.' He called for an Albanian-Serbian dialogue and for compromise. Pavle said the Albanians, for their part, should recognize that Serbia is their country and not equate Serbia with the current regime."[9]

Finally, early in June 1999, in a Holy Synod document, "Patriarch Pavle called for Milosevic's resignation 'for the good and salvation of the Serbian peo-

---

6. *Ecumenical Press Service*, May 30, 1994, no. 43.

7. "Text of Statement of Serbian Orthodox Bishops." This text was submitted to Orthodox World News by Monastery Decani and was issued January 2, 1997, on the internet by ACCESS_Administrator@omaccess.com (ACCESS Administrator), owner-orthodoxnews@goarch.org, a site of the Greek Orthodox Archdiocese of America.

8. Full information has been available on the Decani Monastery internet sites: http://www.decani.yunet.com; http://www.egroups.com/list/decani/).

9. "Serbian Patriarch Condemns Kosovo Crackdown," *RFE/RL Newsline*, vol. 1, no. 188, January 5, 1998.

ple.' Milosevic's response was hard and inconsistent: he labeled the Patriarch 'a NATO puppet' and attacked the Church in the government newspaper, *Borba*, accusing the ecclesiastical hierarchy of treason."[10]

The Western media still labor, however, under the illusion that the Serbian Orthodox Church has been an ally of Milosevic and his extreme nationalist policies. A Reuters story issued on June 15, 1999, declared: "But in a surprise breaking of ranks, Serbia's influential Orthodox Church called on Milosevic to resign."[11] Yet the record shows that the Serbian Orthodox Church's anti-government and pro-democracy stance against the extremist Milosevic policies continued throughout the Kosovo conflict and following the NATO victory.

Extreme ethnic nationalisms are the sources of the Kosovo tragedy. Neither have Muslim leaders proclaimed the Albanian insurgency a jihad, nor has the Orthodox Church backed Milosevic. The war in Kosovo was not a religious war. It was the fruit of extreme nationalism on both sides, largely provoked by Milosevic's communist/socialist, antidemocratic, and misdirected efforts toward a failed Serbian hegemony in an ill-advised effort to maintain the federalist ideal for Yugoslavia. Extreme nationalist policies have been the downfall of the "Third Yugoslavia." The "Fourth Yugoslavia" may soon consist only of Serbia, marking the complete dissolution of what once was an experiment in the creation of a "multinational state."

10. Quoted under the heading "Two Zenit (RC) Articles on the Suffering Orthodox Church in Kosovo," June 20, 1999, internet communication, BELGRADE, JUN 18 (ZENIT).

11. Douglas Hamilton, "Kosovo Refugees Ignore Dangers, Head Home." Reuters, June 15, 1999, 12:40 PM ET.

Legitimation, Justification, and the Politics of Rescue

RICHARD B. MILLER

Civic Virtue and the Ethics of Calibration

States engaged in military interventions often seek to describe (and justify) their actions as defending humanitarian principles and purposes, enforcing international and order, or preventing the spread of conflict. All of these goals are relevant to NATO's effort to remove Serbian troops from Kosovo and enable ethnic Albanian refugees to return to their homeland. NATO's intervention in Yugoslavia was an example of what Michael Walzer calls "the politics of rescue,"[1] in which a nation, or a group of nations, moves military troops into another region for purposes that are, in part, philanthropic: to stop the oppression of a defenseless group, protect humanitarian relief efforts, help refugees escape from or return to their country, or support a fledgling independence movement. Those who inter- humanitarian ends resemble good Samaritans, assuming great risks to others in need. Citizens who endorse such ventures appear to exhibit civic the disposition to support political decisions and institutions that aim to social justice.

However laudable such interventions appear to be, they nonetheless involve complicated matters of political leadership, for rescue operations endanger sol- dier-citizens' lives for reasons that have little immediate connection to an inter- vening state's interests. Interventions carry a heavier burden of political proof than self-defensive wars, requiring political authorities to work harder to secure support from citizens when deciding to use military force. That is to say, interven- tions can put a strain on citizen loyalty and pose a special test of civic virtue. As Stanley Hoffmann puts the point, "The peaceful citizens of democratic countries, even when they are stirred by compassion and shocked by atrocities, are reluctant to wage wars 'for others' — self-defense is another matter."[2]

---

1. Michael Walzer, "The Politics of Rescue," *Dissent* (Winter 1995): 35-41.
2. Stanley Hoffmann, "What Is to Be Done?" *New York Review of Books*, 20 May 1999,

In his first speech to the American public on using force in Kosovo, President Clinton directly addressed this concern about intervention and national interest. Clinton asked: "Do our interests in Kosovo justify the dangers to our armed forces? I thought long and hard about that question. I am convinced that the dangers of acting are far outweighed by the dangers of not acting — dangers to defenseless people and to our national interests." At the core of his argument is the claim that an intervention would prevent the conflict from spreading further into Europe. Foremost in Clinton's mind was the prospect of escalation in the geopolitical tinderbox of the Balkans. Albania, Turkey, Greece, and Macedonia, each having minority ethnic and religious groups with a history of animosity, all stood at risk of being drawn into war. Noting those facts, Clinton remarked: "Eventually, key U.S. allies could be drawn into a wider conflict, or we would be forced to confront [problems] later . . . at a far greater risk and greater cost." The rationale was to establish a firewall: "We have an interest in avoiding an even crueler and costlier war, and because our children need and deserve a peaceful, stable, free Europe."[3]

The *weight* of such interests and the risks they justify are, however, other matters. Throughout the conflict, NATO officials pledged to restrict their use of force to bombing and missile strikes. "I do not intend to put our troops in Kosovo to fight a war," Clinton promised the American people.[4] Even if he had sought to break that pledge, Congress had voted to bar any decision to commit U.S. ground troops without its approval.[5] That decision was not premised on judgments that ground troops would be militarily ineffective; rather, it was designed to render the war politically palatable by limiting risks to allied forces.[6] Political leaders could secure popular support for a war that was not carried out in the nation's immediate interest by calibrating the means of war to an acceptable level of risk. Writing for the *New York Times* in May, Jane Perlez put the point well: "The White House has repeatedly tried to avoid public discussion of

---

17. Joseph S. Nye, Jr., argues differently. Viewing moral values as "intangible interests," Nye argues that "a democractic definition of the national interest does not accept the distinction between a morality-based and an interest-based foreign policy." In his view, "the American people clearly think that their interests include certain values and their promotion abroad." If that is true, however, then it is unclear why Americans were generally uninterested in intervening to protect human rights in Rwanda, Sudan, and East Timor in the 1990s. See Joseph S. Nye, Jr., "Redefining the National Interest," *Foreign Affairs* 78 (July/August 1999): 22-35, at 22-24.

3. "In the President's Words: 'We Act to Prevent a Wider War,'" *New York Times*, 25 March 1999, p. A15.

4. Ibid.

5. Alison Mitchell, "House Votes to Bar Clinton from Sending Ground Troops to Yugoslavia without Congressional Approval," *New York Times*, 29 April 1999, p. A1.

6. Clinton defends NATO's exclusive use of airpower in William Jefferson Clinton, "A Just and Necessary War," *New York Times*, 23 May 1999, p. 17.

combat forces, fearful of public opinion polls that show there is little appetite for such a venture and of a likely backlash against American casualties that would inevitably occur."[7]

In this essay I want to focus on the ethics of this calibration, for it rested on a tension between the popular support for the war in Kosovo — or at least its alleged support — and the morality of its means. We will eventually examine (the argument takes several steps) the distinction between the *legitimation* and the *justification* of a public policy. These two values are by no means the same, and the tension between them was palpable in U.S. officials' statements regarding the NATO cause. Legitimation turns on democratic support and the presence of consent (tacit or explicit) to acts authorized by public officials. Its value lies in the democratic commitment to hold authorities accountable to citizens and to provide a firm basis for political representation. Justification focuses less on the procedures according to which a policy is endorsed than on whether it is morally sound. It turns on the good of having policy that is morally commendable, not on the value of accountability in political representation.

In the war in Yugoslavia, a tension existed between these values of legitimation and justification insofar as politically acceptable methods in that war were not the morally preferable ones, and vice versa.[8] In making the case for rescuing Kosovo, public officials restricted the use of force to an air campaign, reducing risks to NATO forces by keeping ground troops out of harm's way.[9] From Clinton's perspective, the democratic base of support for NATO's intervention may have appeared a mile wide but an inch deep. Hence the need to calibrate risks. We should note an irony here: an intervention described in terms that include an important national interest is not one that officials would risk their ground troops to defend.[10]

However that irony is sorted out, I want to focus our attention on the fact that, in seeking to decrease risks to NATO soldiers, policymakers resorted to methods that increased risks to Serbian and Kosovar civilians and the conditions of ci-

7. Jane Perlez, "Clinton and the Joint Chiefs to Discuss Ground Invasion," *New York Times*, 2 June 1999, p. A12.

8. This is but one broad issue that has been put into sharp relief by cases of war in the aftermath of the Cold War. For a more general discussion, see my "Casuistry, Pacifism, and the Just-War Tradition in the Post–Cold War Era," in *Peacemaking: Moral and Policy Challenges for a New World*, ed. Gerard F. Powers, Drew Christiansen, and Robert T. Hennemeyer (Washington, DC: United States Catholic Conference, 1994), pp. 199-213.

9. Wars with widespread legitimation do not necessarily employ means that are morally commendable. Indeed, popular wars may allow leaders to violate moral restraints on the conduct of war, as we see in the decision to use atomic weapons on Japan. That morally lamentable decision was nonetheless wildly popular among Americans, at least initially. For a discussion, see Paul Boyer, *By the Bomb's Early Light: American Thought and Culture at the Dawn of the Atomic Age* (New York: Pantheon Books, 1985).

10. I am grateful to Lisa Sideris for calling attention to this irony.

vilian life in Serbia.[11] Whether that policy was justified is a critical question for us to consider; I will argue that it was not. The challenge to NATO leadership was whether to continue a policy that was not unpopular, even if morally dubious, or whether to take political risks to embark upon a more morally acceptable use of force and secure support for an intervention on terms that both reflect and strengthen civic virtue. Such were the issues lying behind the option of expanding NATO's intervention to include the use of ground forces.

In order to see that political challenge and the background issues that shaped it, we need briefly to rehearse just-war criteria at the outset. Among other things, the tension between the legitimation of an intervention and the justification of its methods reflects a tension internal to just-war criteria themselves. After noting that, I will argue that NATO should have adopted another resolution to this tension. I will conclude by discussing a more general problem regarding the ethics of calibrating risks in interventions and how such calibrations affect the moral quality of civic virtue in a democratic society.

Just-War Criteria

In moral discourse about war today, the chief reasons adduced for using lethal force are to protect and promote human rights, defend state sovereignty, or enforce international law.[12] Various essays in this volume testify to the historical and moral importance of just-war ideas in assessing the use of force for such ends. Just-war criteria provide a framework for nonpacifists (and perhaps some pacifists) to evaluate the resort to war as a means of settling disputes between groups. Generally, the just-war tradition evaluates the use of force by asking *whether* force is justified and, if so, *how* it may be carried out. These questions, the "whether" and the "how" questions, are assessed in light of two sets of moral criteria, the *jus ad bellum* and the *jus in bello*, respectively.

Stated briefly, *jus ad bellum* criteria include the following:

Just Cause: A just war is occasioned by the need to defend international law, innocent victims of aggression, or sovereign territory.
Competent Authority: The representative(s) of the community must declare war and marshal a defense.

---

11. I do not mean to suggest that no ground war occurred. For a firsthand account, based on three weeks with the Kosovo Liberation Army, see Janine di Giovanni, "The Ground War That Was," *New York Times Magazine,* 13 June 1999, pp. 35-41.

12. For discussions, see U.S. Catholic Bishops, *The Challenge of Peace: God's Promise and Our Response* (Washington, DC: U.S. Catholic Conference, 1983); Michael Walzer, *Just and Unjust Wars: A Moral Argument with Historical Illustrations,* 2nd ed. (New York: Basic Books, 1992).

Right Intention: The aim of war should be to reestablish relationships of
   peace and fairness among the relevant parties.
Last Resort: Diplomatic efforts must be reasonably tried and found wanting
   before authorities resort to lethal force.
Reasonable Hope for Success: Rash, futile, or irrational resort to force is prohibited.
Relative Justice: Neither side in war has a monopoly on absolute justice in defense of its cause.
Proportionality: The foreseen risks of war must not outweigh the foreseen
   values. War must be "worth it," morally speaking, given the stakes and
   values involved.

Whether resort to force is justified depends on the manner and extent to
which these *ad bellum* criteria can be satisfied.

The "how" question, *jus in bello,* focuses on the morality of means: which
methods are permissible in pursuit of a justified action? Raising the "how" question implies that not all actions are appropriate in pursuit of one's goals, that the
ends do not justify every available means. We are thus required to enter into a
morality of limits, or limited means. Two criteria, enshrined in the *jus in bello,*
shape the assessment of how war is waged: discrimination and proportionality.
Consider an abbreviated version of each, soon to be amended in a way that
sharpens the tension between the legitimation of war in Yugoslavia and the morality of its methods.

1. Discrimination

This criterion prohibits the intentional attacking of civilians; the shorthand is the
phrase "noncombatant immunity." It is premised on two distinctions. The first
distinction is between combatants and noncombatants: *combatant* denotes those
who are materially cooperating with the war effort (e.g., soldiers and those working for war-related industries, such as bomb factories); *noncombatant* refers to
persons who are not contributing materially to the war, including children, the
disabled, the sick, farmers, teachers, and health-care professionals, to name a few.
The second distinction calls attention to the difference between *intentional* (i.e.,
purposeful) and *foreseen, but unintentional* effects of an act. *Ceteris paribus,* individuals or groups are more responsible for the effects of purposeful acts than for
effects that are unwanted and unintended.

Combining these two sets of distinctions, we get the following directive: intentional attacks against noncombatants are not permissible because those attacks
are inflicted on people against whom defense is unnecessary; such persons are "innocent" in the sense that they are not contributing materially to the war, however

much they might otherwise endorse the war effort. In effect, the principle of discrimination introduces into just-war criteria features of disinterested morality, for it imposes limits on how one's citizens and neighbors are to be protected.[13] That is to say, the principle of noncombatant immunity implies that the rights of strangers or distant neighbors may not be compromised in the effort to protect near neighbors and preferential relations.

Foreseen, unintentional loss of innocent life passes the test of discrimination but is subject to moral scrutiny required by the second *jus in bello* criterion, proportionality.

2. Proportionality

As a *jus in bello* criterion, proportionality requires us to balance foreseen, unintended dangers against the values that are defended in a particular act of war. Here we must think about the morality of specific tactics: is the good that is being pursued or defended balanced by the regrettable, unintended risks that may reasonably be expected? Tactics are immoral when the foreseen, unintended loss of life outweighs the defended values, even if those tactics are discriminate. At a minimum, this condition prohibits risking lives for trivial purposes.

Taken together, these *jus in bello* conditions impose a nuanced set of restrictions on the use of force in war. They prohibit the intentional taking of civilian life and the disproportionate imposition of foreseeable risks on civilians. According to *in bello* considerations, however, not all loss of innocent life is immoral. Rather, it is the intentional killing of innocent people, excessive collateral damage, or culpable negligence in military strategy that is immoral.

We need to propose an important amendment to these *jus in bello* restraints, one that involves the distinction between "thin" and "thick" renditions of an appropriate intention to avoid civilian casualties in war. According to the standard account of *in bello* criteria, risks to civilians are acceptable when they are unintended and proportionate to the ends of a particular use of force. That account, involving what I call a "thin" view of moral intention, would excuse civilian casualties that occur as unintended collateral damage if such casualties are proportionate to the overall goal of a military mission. A "thick" or robust account of intention, by contrast, would require strategists and/or soldiers to exercise caution to avoid such casualties, even if such caution increases risks to one's own troops. Such an account is premised on a core feature of noncombatant immunity and the disinterested morality on which it relies: civilians have a right not to have war waged upon them, a right not to be terrorized by the use of force. Soldiers enter a profession in which they (tacitly or expressly) agree to assume risks to themselves

13. I am grateful to Jennifer Girod for requesting clarification on this and related points.

in order to provide for the common defense and/or protect others; but civilians enter into no such agreement. War is fought between armies to save civilians' lives and to restore justice to the conditions of social life, and only combatants have the right intentionally to kill each other for such ends. A robust account of intention would include a soldier's duty to reduce, as far as reasonably possible, foreseeable risks to civilian life. That is to say, a thick account of moral intention requires combatants to decrease civilians' risks to the extent that such caution would not subvert a legitimate act of war. Walzer puts the point well: "What we look for . . . is some sign of a positive commitment to save civilian lives. Not merely to apply the proportionality rule and kill no more civilians than is militarily necessary — that rule applies to soldiers as well; no one can be killed for trivial purposes. Civilians have a right to something more. And if saving civilian lives means risking soldiers' lives, the risk must be accepted." The goal of a thick intention as it shapes *in bello* restrictions is for combatants to exercise "due care" in the use of force, hoping to "minimize the dangers they impose."[14]

Self-Defense and Rescue

I will return to just-war criteria, especially the *jus ad bellum* criterion of proportionality and *jus in bello* limits on the use of force (duly amended) when I consider the politics and ethics of NATO's war against the Serbs. But first I want to note that, however important just-war criteria may be, they do not enable us to track some important differences between two kinds of wars, self-defensive wars and interventions, between wars that readily join value and interest and those for which it is harder to do so. Just-war criteria provide little help in marking the different challenges of legitimation as they arise in different kinds of conflicts. That is because the value of human rights can justify both self-defensive wars and interventions and thus provide an affirmative answer to the question of whether either kind of conflict has a just cause.[15]

To date, little work has been done in just-war theory to help us refine the *motivational stakes* involved in different uses of force.[16] Although both rescue operations and wars of self-defense can be justified in light of human rights, the sacrifices required by the latter are more intelligible to a citizenry that is (understand-

14. Walzer, *Just and Unjust Wars*, pp. 155-56. Walzer uses the language of "double" rather than "thick" intention, but the meaning is the same.

15. See, e.g., U.S. Catholic Bishops, *The Challenge of Peace*, par. 86; "The Harvest of Justice Is Sown in Peace," in Powers et al., eds., *Peacemaking: Moral and Policy Challenges for a New World*, pp. 320, 336-37. That is not to say that wars of self-defense or wars in defense of state sovereignty are no different from humanitarian intervention. For a discussion, see Walzer, ch. 6.

16. For a fuller theoretical discussion, see my "Humanitarian Intervention, Altruism, and the Limits of Casuistry," *Journal of Religious Ethics* 28 (Spring 2000): 3-35.

ably) interested in protecting and transmitting its heritage and way of life. Insofar as self-defense is viewed as protecting human rights *and* a state's interest in preserving its heritage, it provides the sort of rationale that allows for a marriage of justification and legitimation. Stated differently, there is little reason to think that a democratic state that is under attack will face a "legitimation crisis" owing to the decision to marshal forces on behalf of self-defense.

Rescue operations cannot promise an easy alliance between legitimation and justification, even in situations — and I consider Kosovo to be one of those — where the protection of human rights is unambiguously urgent and allows for the use of force. While the decision to use force to protect vulnerable populations may be sound, it is not clear why any particular country should assume such risks. Stated abstractly, it is not clear why the *general* duty to care for others falls on any *specific* groups or political communities.[17] The politics of rescue, unlike self-defensive war, can involve situations in which moral principle and self-interest are precariously alloyed. As a result, the moral motivation for socially responsible action remains less determinate in a rescue operation than in a self-defensive action.

This difference between wars of self-defense and rescue operations can go unnoticed in ethics and international affairs. But it calls to mind a cluster of issues that bear on matters of political and moral motivation. Self-defensive wars appear to join the right and the good more easily than do rescue operations and thus are likelier to secure civic support. For that reason, wars of self-defense can more readily satisfy realist concerns that war be carried out in the national interest. Interventions, in contrast, can appear idealistic and philanthropic. However justified its cause may be, a rescue operation nonetheless possesses fewer resources in all but altruistic countries (and I know of none of these) when it comes to rallying national support.

Calibrating Risks

In noting that the criterion of just cause fails to track the different kinds of risks and motivations in self-defensive wars as opposed to interventions, I am not suggesting that just-war criteria have become obsolete or useless in the ethics of international affairs. But when thinking about what I am calling NATO's ethic of calibration and the tension between the legitimation of war and the justification of its means, we need to invoke just-war criteria less as a framework for the casuistry of war and more as a set of concepts that bear upon broad matters of practical reasoning in political leadership. Several just-war criteria provide a vocabulary for

---

17. For an instructive account of general and specific duties, see Onora O'Neill, *Towards Justice and Virtue: A Constructive Account of Practical Reasoning* (Cambridge: Cambridge University Press, 1996), ch. 5.

understanding the tension between legitimation and justification as that tension materializes in crises like that in the Balkans. As I noted above, the tension between legitimation and justification amplifies a tension internal to the criteria themselves. Perhaps a better way to state the point is that just-war criteria provide terms for understanding a basic challenge to political leadership, a challenge that goes beyond the casuistry of war toward more general issues of weighing risks to one's own soldiers against risks to an enemy nation's civilians in a war that is, first and foremost, a rescue operation. In the case of Kosovo, consider such risks as they bear on matters of legitimation and justification by recalling the *ad bellum* criterion of proportionality and the *in bello* limits on the use of force.

Judgments about legitimation turn on weighing the costs of war that a democratic society, or an alliance of democratic societies, is willing to shoulder. Such estimations involve imprecise, rough-and-ready "readings" of the popular will. At stake are the risks that a society seems willing to bear in light of the values that are protected by the use of force. In restricting the methods of war to an air campaign, NATO concluded that the values involved in protecting Kosovo were not sufficient to risk ground troops and engage in a potentially protracted land battle.

In just-war terms, that is a judgment regarding the war's proportionality. Proportionality as an *ad bellum* criterion bids citizens and policymakers to ask, "Is the war, in moral terms, worth risking?" In part, that question requires us to consider the level of risk appropriate to the moral stakes involved in war. During the Vietnam War, for example, the U.S. Catholic bishops (and many others) came to the eventual conclusion that, on grounds of proportionality, the war was immoral.[18] In their judgment, that war's risks and sacrifices outweighed the good that was sought. In more general terms, proportionality is a device by which nations can weigh duties to themselves. It enables them to ask what kinds of sacrifices they can demand of themselves in light of a war's importance to them. In cases of self-defense, as I noted above, the connection between value and interest usually enables citizens and policymakers to conclude that a nation's duty to itself justifies the use of force. In rescue operations, however, matters of proportionate reasoning are considerably less determinate.

One way to interpret the decision to restrict the use of force to bombing missions, then, is to see it as an *ad bellum* judgment of proportionality: NATO would assume a level of risk that, on balance, seemed appropriate to its overall interests and values. Increasing risks would have required a commensurate adjustment of NATO's account of the war's stakes and would have jeopardized whatever legitimation the intervention enjoyed.

But were such methods justified? Here the decision to confine risks to air

18. U.S. Catholic Bishops, "Human Life in Our Day," in *Renewing the Earth: Catholic Documents on Peace, Justice, and Liberation,* ed. David J. O'Brien and Thomas A. Shannon (Garden City, NJ: Doubleday, 1977), pars. 135-45.

forces finds less support in just-war criteria. Although early raids in March 1999 appeared to abide by the principles of discrimination and proportionality, subsequent events raise serious questions about the morality of NATO's air campaign. Equally important is the question of whether limiting the war to the use of air power abided by *in bello* criteria, understood according to a robust account of moral restraint and responsibility in war. Let us take this second question first.

The decision to rely exclusively on air power was premised on the judgment that increasing risks to civilian life in Yugoslavia is an acceptable trade-off for decreasing risks to NATO soldiers. Air raids during April, May, and June 1999 also killed many Kosovars and jeopardized the lives of ethnic Albanians seeking refuge in Albania and Montenegro.[19] A robust understanding of intention as it shapes *in bello* criteria suggests that those outcomes were wrong — that dangers to civilians' lives should have been reduced. Deploying soldiers to fight a land war would likely have resulted in less accidental or collateral damage to civilian life in Serbia and Kosovo, yet would have increased risks to NATO troops. If noncombatant immunity had any role in NATO's strategy, it was premised on a thin account of intention.

Walzer puts the point well: "The structure of rights stands independently of political allegiance; it establishes obligations that are owed, so to speak, to humanity itself and to particular human beings and not merely to one's fellow citizens."[20] Noncombatants, whatever their political affiliation, have the right not to have war waged on them, generating the duty for soldiers to avoid civilian casualties when they can do so without subverting their own legitimate goals.

That idea should have informed NATO's policy, which jeopardized Serbian and Kosovar life in order to reduce risks to NATO soldiers.[21] Serb and Kosovar noncombatants, regardless of political allegiance, have the right not to have war indirectly waged on them when realistic alternatives are available. In seeking to render the war against Serbia palatable to the citizens of NATO countries, NATO officials traded off the rights of Serbs and Kosovars.

When would it have been appropriate for NATO to consider using ground troops? In April, only a few weeks after the bombing started, NATO decided to widen its targets to include public utilities, water and oil supplies, and communications

---

19. Ian Fisher, "Bombs Hit Albania Town near Kosovo Border," *New York Times*, 2 June 1999, p. A13.

20. Walzer, *Just and Unjust Wars*, p. 158.

21. Problems surrounding NATO's exclusive reliance on airpower are exacerbated by the fact that the air campaign prompted Milosevic to intensify the ethnic cleansing of Kosovo. Lacking forces on the ground, NATO was unprepared to respond effectively to that contingency. Nigel Biggar puts the point precisely: "NATO's decision to rely solely on airpower meant that it was powerless to stop the 'ethnic cleansing' when, in the event, it not only continued but intensified." See Nigel Biggar, "So Was It Just? Taking Moral Stock of the Kosovo War," *The Church Times*, 18 June 1999, p. 14.

and transportation networks. At that point it would have been more moral, and perhaps more effective, to maintain a bombing policy restricted to military targets and to introduce land forces along the borders of Kosovo. Having ground troops in the region in April would have provided greater time to secure a footing well before winter arrived, and would have shown Milosevic that NATO was prepared to support its negotiating position with a credible use of force. Yet, in view of the time needed to marshal and coordinate troops from several countries, arranging for a land battle would have been necessary in early March and perhaps February.[22] Unfortunately, nothing in the public record indicates that such an option was seriously considered prior to the decision to deploy warplanes in the Balkans.

Beyond the issue of relying exclusively on air power is the problem of *how* the air raids proceeded. Here even a thin account of *in bello* criteria would raise questions about NATO's air campaign. Although the earliest sorties (in March) appear to have been accurately targeted, precision soon faltered. During the war's eleven weeks, the following grisly events in Serbia and Kosovo were reported:

- April 6: NATO bombs struck two residential areas in the Serbian town of Aleksinac, killing seven civilians and wounding at least fifty others.[23]
- April 12: Targeting a railway bridge in Grdelica, Serbia, NATO missiles hit a train, killing at least ten passengers and wounding sixteen others.[24]
- April 14: NATO planes, flying at high altitude to reduce danger to themselves, bombed two convoys of refugees on a road southeast of Djakovica in Kosovo, killing more than seventy-four Kosovar civilians.[25]
- April 28: One of NATO's laser-guided bombs missed its target and exploded in a neighborhood of Surdulica in southern Serbia, killing twenty persons and destroying several homes.[26]
- May 3: A NATO warplane strafed a bus and some cars at a police checkpoint in the mountains near Pec in eastern Kosovo, killing at least seventeen and wounding forty people.[27]

22. For a discussion of using ground troops, see William Pfaff, "Land War in Kosovo?" *New York Review of Books,* 6 May, 1999, p. 20.

23. Steven Erlanger, "Small Serbian Town Is Stricken by a Deadly 'Accident of War,'" *New York Times,* 7 April 1999, p. A1.

24. Steven Erlanger, "At Sites of NATO Accidents, Scent of Death, Sound of Fury, " *New York Times,* 13 April 1999, p. A1.

25. Michael R. Gordon, "Civilians Are Slain in Military Attack on a Kosovo Road," *New York Times,* 15 April 1999, p. A1; Michael R. Gordon, "NATO Admits It Hit 2d Convoy on Road That Refugees Used," *New York Times,* 20 April 1999, p. A1.

26. Craig R. Whitney, "Laser Bomb Missed Target and Hit Houses, NATO Says," *New York Times,* 29 April 1999, p. A15.

27. Steven Erlanger, "Fleeing Kosovars Dread Dangers of NATO Above and Serbs Below," *New York Times,* 4 May 1999, p. A1.

- May 8: The Chinese Embassy in Belgrade was hit by a NATO aircraft, killing three civilians and wounding more than twenty others. That attack came shortly after the bombing of a marketplace and medical facility in Nis.[28]
- May 14: More than sixty ethnic Albanians were killed and scores were badly wounded after NATO bombs blasted Korisa, a village in southwest Kosovo.[29]
- May 21: NATO hit what Yugoslav sources called a prison in the Kosovo town of Istok, killing nineteen persons.[30]
- May 31: NATO air attacks killed at least sixteen civilians and injured forty-three more when four missiles hit a hospital in Surdulica. Later that day, missiles aimed at a local television station in Novi Pazar, close to Kosovo, hit an apartment building, reportedly killing at least ten people and wounding twenty more.[31]

Perhaps these events can be excused as accidents of war, as unintended and regrettable uses of force. They seem small in number, given the fact that NATO pilots flew over 31,000 sorties. Still, we should note that only two NATO planes were shot down, and no pilots died or were captured behind enemy lines. Hence the phrase "combatant immunity" to mock the priorities of the air campaign.

More problematic is the fact that the reported accidents were part of a wider strategy of weakening Serbia's forces and crippling the infrastructure that supported both the military's efforts and civilian life. Starting in late March, NATO forces relentlessly bombed Serbia and Kosovo, impeded by little more than inclement weather. During March, April, and early May, those missions were carried out at high elevations, typically above 15,000 feet, to reduce risks to pilots.[32] By the end of April, the air campaign had cut Yugoslavia's economic output in half, throwing more than 100,000 people out of work.[33] Targets included electrical grids, fuel depots, oil refineries, rail and communication networks, factories, fertilizer and chemical plants, and heating plants. Widespread devastation and degradation of the environment were reported. Toxic fumes spewed into the air, civilians went without water, there were no electric lights in Belgrade and other Serbian cities at night, and gasoline rations were cut from ten to five gallons a

28. Michael R. Gordon, "NATO Says It Thought Embassy Was Weapons Depot," *New York Times,* 9 May 1999, p. A1.

29. Steven Erlanger, "Albanians Killed As Kosovo Village Is Blasted Apart," *New York Times,* 15 May 1999, p. A1.

30. Steven Lee Myers, "NATO Jets Hit Prison, Killing 19, Serbs Report," *New York Times,* 22 May 1999, p. A7.

31. Steven Erlanger, "Dozens of Civilians Are Killed as NATO Strikes Go Awry," *New York Times,* 1 June 1999, p. A12.

32. Eric Schmitt and Steven Lee Myers, "NATO Planes Flying Lower, Increasing Risk of Being Hit," *New York Times,* 4 May 1999, p. A13.

33. Steven Erlanger, "Production Cut in Half, Experts Say," *New York Times,* 30 April 1999, p. A1.

month. Cities without power had no means to activate air-raid sirens when NATO jets attacked, leaving civilians no time to seek shelter. In late May it was reported that Belgrade was down to ten percent of its water reserves and that hospitals were relying on water trucks to bathe patients and sterilize instruments.[34] Serbia's five main transmitting plants were hit by NATO bombs, and each time Serbia's power was restored by the national electricity grid, NATO attacked again.[35]

Such events raise the *in bello* question of proportionality: did the military benefits of attacking Yugoslavia's infrastructure outweigh the harm to civilians? NATO's rationale was that electrical grids, factories, oil refineries, bridges, and fuel depots were vital to Serbia's military, and that the attack on these targets hampered Milosevic's capacity to wage war. Yet the damage also affected civilians' ability to keep food, bathe, fertilize their crops, seek shelter during air raids, communicate with relatives and friends, and attend to the needs of the sick. Public health in Serbia was (and remains) seriously at risk, generating grave questions about the morality of NATO's use of air power and targeting strategy.

These problems produced little outcry from citizens in NATO countries, which would seem to confirm that Clinton and other NATO leaders made the correct political gamble: intervention in Kosovo would be less controversial so long as it jeopardized Yugoslavian noncombatants rather than NATO personnel. By seeking legitimation, NATO officials put innocent Serbian and Kosovar lives in the balance. One wishes that this imbalance had been redressed and that public officials had found ways to decrease dangers to noncombatants in Serbia and Kosovo, even if that meant increasing risks to NATO pilots and soldiers. Herein lies a fundamental question of civic virtue, because citizens were asked to dispose themselves favorably to a war that traded off risks in the wrong way.

The decision to decrease dangers to civilians in Yugoslavia would have doubtless required the politically risky use of ground troops. To be sure, a ground war does not ensure the discriminate and proportionate use of force. But it could have decreased the chances that trains would be accidentally bombed from afar, that neighborhoods and villages would be inadvertently destroyed, that buses and convoys would fall victim to bombs from high above. Civilians in Yugoslavia do not deserve Slobodan Milosevic, but they did not deserve a NATO intervention that could have been more morally commendable, and perhaps more effective, in its effort to deliver Kosovo from Serbia's nationalism, tyrannical leadership, and ethnic hatred.

---

34. Steven Erlanger, "Reduced to a 'Caveman' Life, Serbs Don't Blame Milosevic," *New York Times*, 25 May 1999, p. A1.

35. Ibid., p. A16.

Another Sliding Scale

NATO's ethics of calibration in Kosovo points to a more general issue in the morality of war, one that we do well to note as a lesson from the Balkans crisis: interventions are likely to involve a *sliding scale* of means in relation to political needs and values. Given that a rescue operation shoulders a heavier burden of political proof than a self-defensive war, public officials who follow the precedent of Kosovo will be inclined to adjust war's means in ways that trade off risks to relevant parties in the wrong way. That has untoward implications for citizens' dispositions and loyalty to the commonweal since it nurtures civic habits that have little to commend themselves, morally speaking.

In its familiar guise, the "sliding scale" refers to the relationship between the justice of a war's cause and the weight of restrictions on a war's means. That is to say, the phrase refers to the stringency of *in bello* limits given the weight of *ad bellum* considerations. The greater a country's justice upon entering a war, the more right it has to pursue that justice. "More right" implies fewer restrictions on the war's means, although some limits or rules may remain inviolable. Conversely, the weaker a country's justice, the more it should abide by moral means. Either way, the sliding scale calibrates means to ends.

Exactly what attitude just-war theorists take toward a sliding scale of *ad bellum* prerogatives and *in bello* responsibilities can range from setting aside the latter whenever it inhibits the former to never allowing the violation of the latter, regardless of the merits of the former. The application of just-war criteria to specific cases can thus be framed by second-order commitments to utilitarianism or deontology, respectively.

In the Balkans crisis we see a new version of the sliding scale, what might be called a "political-moral sliding scale": *the fewer the combatant casualties, the stronger a war's legitimation.* The standard sliding scale allows a nation or alliance to trade off means for ends in order to win the war. In that way it calibrates means to ends that are internal to just-war considerations: *in bello* limits may be set aside, if necessary, so that *ad bellum* justice may be effectively defended. A political-moral sliding scale is different: it allows a nation or alliance to trade off noncombatant lives for combatant lives in order to win support at home for the war. It thereby compromises moral values for political ones.

Behind this scale is a morally controversial decision, since the bargain trades off noncombatants' lives in order to limit risks to one's own combatants. That bargain urges citizens to support interventions that distribute the burdens of war wrongly. Political leaders who solicit citizens' support for such wars cultivate democratic habits that enjoin civic loyalty on morally unacceptable terms. That is to say, a political-moral sliding scale enjoins little by way of morally commendable civic virtue from members of the wider political community. Civic virtue rightly ordered would have dispositions that are more disinterested, recognizing the rights of strangers and the duty to reduce risks to them in decisions about recourse to lethal force.

A political-moral sliding scale is likely to materialize in conflicts like rescue operations that shoulder a greater burden of political proof than wars of national defense. Such a scale works as follows: the stronger the need for legitimation, the stronger the need to protect one's combatants, regardless of the effect on noncombatants. I have argued that this trade-off is generally unwarranted on just-war grounds for policymakers and social critics committed to protecting noncombatants, even when it is necessary to take special, sometimes risky, efforts to do so. Political officials in democratic societies who cultivate support from citizens on such terms are nurturing civic habits that are vices rather than virtues.[36]

36. I wish to thank Nigel Biggar, Jennifer Girod, Judith Granbois, John Kelsay, Barbara Klinger, and Lisa Sideris for comments on an earlier draft of this paper, and William J. Buckley for correspondence regarding the Balkans crisis.

Kosovo: A War of Values
and the Values of War

J. BRYAN HEHIR

In his *New York Times* column commenting on religious issues (4/17/99) Peter Steinfels makes a measured criticism of religious leaders and moralists who fail to provide either clear foundations or clear conclusions for their assessments of the war in Kosovo: "What is distressing is how often the moral pronouncements offer only the surface of a position without following that line of thought through to its logical conclusions or its rock-bottom principles." This critique is characteristically precise and deserves a response. What follows is one person's response to it — an effort toward clarity and specificity on Kosovo.

My "rock-bottom principles" are entirely unoriginal: in this case, as in multiple other instances of conflict and war, I find the traditional categories of the "Just-War Ethic" (developed with the combined resources of religious conviction and philosophical analysis) still the most adequate instrument of moral analysis. The strength of the ethic lies in its complexity, its multidimensional method of analyzing the use of force. The same complexity often makes it difficult to produce unanimity on conclusions. But Steinfels is right: solid principles should yield specific choices, even in the dense web of moral issues that constitutes the puzzle of Kosovo.

Kosovo requires a multidimensional ethic because morality does not lie in one place in this conflict, which George Will has called "a war of values." The moral challenge for policy arises from the intersection of competing moral demands. The first question of the traditional ethic is determining "just cause": are the values at stake in a particular conflict of such a character that the conscious, systematic taking of life (and risking of lives) may be required to preserve them? At one level, the story of Kosovo yields a decisive yes to this question: over one million people driven from their homes by brutal methods of killing, rape, and the burning and looting of their villages. As Mark Danner points out in *The New York Review of Books* (5/6/99), this purge of the Kosovars was not the result of the fog of war but the product of "planned rationality." In Kosovo, prefigured by the ethnic cleansing of Bosnia, the world (both individual citizens and their states) knows exactly what is happening, and we know who is responsible. If the product of this planned rationality does not

399

constitute "just cause," it is difficult to know what the category means. While that is my first conclusion, it is useful to note that "just cause" has been a much debated issue in the United States over the last two months. Its critics have relied on at least three arguments. First, an issue that is at the heart of Kosovo but extends well beyond it: the claims of sovereignty are weighed more heavily by some than the horrors of ethnic cleansing. The argument is that Serbian tactics and strategy are reprehensible but that Kosovo is an *internal issue,* a struggle for self-determination *within* a sovereign state, and it is folly to open the road for external actors to get engaged in the innumerable conflicts of self-determination across the globe. In brief, Kosovo is not Hitler's Germany in 1939 or Hussein's Iraq of 1991. The *causa belli* must be strictly defined, and "humanitarian intervention" does not qualify as a reason to resort to war. Henry Kissinger exemplifies this position: "'Humanitarian intervention' asserts that moral and humane concerns are so much a part of American life that not only treasure but lives must be risked to vindicate them. . . . No other nation has ever put forward such a set of propositions." Second, NATO is the wrong agency to respond to Kosovo; it is a defensive alliance that was never contemplated to be catalyzed to action by internal conflict. Third, from the perspective of U.S. foreign policy, this kind of war is a diversion from the necessary tasks in which the "one superpower" of the world should engage. As Charles Krauthammer puts the case, humanitarian conflicts are for middle-size powers, not for the United States. These are large arguments, each of which I oppose.

The first one is the most important, because Kosovo, like Somalia, Rwanda, and Haiti before it, does challenge a fundamental conviction of realist statecraft that draws a radical distinction between the external behavior of states and their internal policies. In brief, we must oppose aggression (e.g., the Gulf War) but not repression. My support of Kosovo as "just cause" is part of a larger argument, which calls for recasting the moral-legal-political calculus of policy in the direction of justifying *some* interventions for humanitarian reasons. Recasting NATO's purposes, therefore, is for me a subordinate corollary of a prior premise: I believe that the number of interventions should be tightly contained (by political and moral criteria), but the offensive/defensive argument is not a conclusive reason to oppose NATO policy in Kosovo. For similar reasons, the Krauthammer arguments about the sole superpower, while decisive in some cases, are not determinative of an entire policy. Again, in my view, "just cause" is established beyond doubt in Kosovo.

The complexity of the Just War ethic builds into moral analysis a continuing tension between "just cause" and "just means": compelling moral causes must be pursued with limited means because in war not all are implicated in evils, so only some are to be targeted, restrained, captured, or killed. In what Raymond Aron called "the century of total war," the issue of what constitutes limited means has been at the heart of the war and morality arguments. I should note in passing that the learning curve on this question shows progress. Fr. John Ford's 1944 article in *Theological Studies,* "The Morality of Obliteration Bombing," stands as a singular critique of World War II, where the policy was pursued by both sides and opposed by very few. The postwar debates, the nuclear arguments over thirty years, and the Gulf War analysis all served to restore the principles of "just means" to a central place in the public policy arguments. Civilians have already been hit in the NATO air campaign, not because they were targeted but in spite of precautions taken to protect them. Unlike war in the 1940s, war in the 1990s requires both apologies for such actions and an extended defense of why the policy is designed to exclude civilian targets. Such arguments were not considered necessary in World War II.

Favorable comparisons with the past are not sufficient, however, to address NATO policy in Kosovo. Maintaining "limited means" faces two different kinds of challenges. The first arises, paradoxically, from the realist voices who have doubted or opposed the decision to engage NATO in Kosovo. Kissinger, Krauthammer, and others argue that, however mistaken the policy is, the only objective now is "to win." Senator John McCain, whose life experience and strategic judgments give him unique credentials to be heard on questions of war and peace, also makes this argument: "What shall we do now? Win, by all means necessary." In one sense the objective is uncontested: to defend the "just cause," one must defeat the adversary. The problem with this statement is that it implies that the objectives of "just cause" might ultimately require that limits be set aside as an encumbrance.

Here, too, lies a realist principle: the realm of war is not hospitable to moral limits; once initiated, the moral objective is to end the war with victory and then return to life within the moral universe where normal restraints on behavior can be observed. It is reasonable to infer that because this argument in some form always lurks beneath the surface of any war policy, Pope John Paul II — a participating observer of a war without limits in the 1940s — has consistently placed himself in opposition to initiating the use of force. He has done this in spite of crucial statements where he has defended the Just War ethic. While not pacifist in principle, John Paul II has been consistently nonviolent in policy prescription — resisting "just revolution" claims of theologians, the "just war case" made by President Bush for the Gulf War, and by word and deed distancing himself from NATO policy in Kosovo. Peter Steinfels understands the logic of the position but questions its adequacy.

There is, I believe, good reason to do so. My judgment would be that the Holy Father's position is informed not only by the nonviolent convictions that have marked his pontificate but also by his intellectual and experiential understanding of the Balkans. These are powerful resources in assessing the problem of Kosovo. But the record of Milosevic in the 1990s provides a compelling case in which there is a personality and a policy of the kind the Just War ethic was designed to confront. Anyone invoking the systematic taking of life (war) for moral reasons should do so with hesitation. But the logic of the argument from Augustine through Michael Walzer and Paul Ramsey has been the same: some facts propel hesitant individuals and states to the ultimate means of politics because failure to use them threatens the very foundations of political community.

Mark Danner's article ("Endgame in Kosovo") traces the "planned rationality" of Milosevic's policy in Bosnia and Kosovo through five steps: (1) concentration of the target population; (2) decapitation of its leaders; (3) separation of men and women; (4) evacuation of women, children, and elderly; and (5) liquidation of those whom Milosevic opposes. These facts lead me to a second conclusion, that the Holy See's invocation of Pius XII's statement, "Nothing is lost by peace, all can be lost by war," does not capture the problem of Kosovo. Milosevic wants peace as time to evacuate and/or liquidate. Neither NATO nor the United States, nor the European Union nor the United Nations should allow this explicit strategy to proceed unchallenged.

Then, it would seem, those opposing Milosevic "must win." Yes, but they must win rightly. A multidimensional ethic is bound by limits, which cannot be transgressed lest just causes become crusades. So those who say nonviolent resistance is not sufficient (the position of this article) must oppose the version of realism that is reducible to winning at all costs.

How does NATO policy stand up under the "just means" tests? Two broad questions emerge: How has the air war been conducted? Will air power be adequate as a means? Both strategic convictions (Milosevic will fold if hit) and political judgment (NATO publics won't support a ground war) yielded the NATO strategy of exclusive reliance on air power. If we accept that strategy for the moment, how should we judge it? There are three historical reference points (the 1940s, the 1960s, and the 1990s) and two criteria (noncombatant immunity and proportionality). The three prior uses of air power involve World War II, Vietnam, and the Gulf War. The aforementioned obliteration bombing of World War II failed every aspect of the moral calculus, from Dresden through Tokyo to Hiroshima; moreover, postwar studies of its strategic effectiveness in Germany complemented the moral judgment that it should not be imitated or repeated.

Vietnam, in retrospect, is a classic case of the gap between intention and consequences: the *Pentagon Papers* contain a picture of Secretary McNamara seeking a policy of force within limits but producing a policy of massive destruction carried out with a logic and rationale that made it both devastating *and* ineffective. It produced a reaction against restraints that echoes through the Kosovo debate as John McCain criticizes the Clinton administration policy as "McNamara-esque" in its restraints. The Gulf War strategy sought to silence the moral critics *and* provide a free hand for the generals. The result was a policy that could not be fairly indicted as obliteration bombing (because civilians were not *targeted*) but left gaping questions and documented doubts about the proportionality of depriving a civilian society of water, electricity, and minimal health-care facilities — while still in the secure control of the dictator who provoked the conflict. In brief, World War II failed the moral test because of its intentions and methods; Vietnam failed because of its consequences; and the Gulf War was defensible in intention but left doubt about both means and effectiveness. The Kosovo campaign is being planned and analyzed in light of these analogies and "lessons." Where does it fit?

As in the Gulf War, there are quite convincing characteristics of the policy that convey a determination not to target or strike civilians. The primary moral criterion of "just means" appears to be an intrinsically important guide to policy. This conclusion (my third) can be challenged on at least two grounds. First, civilians have been hit by NATO attacks on at least two occasions — a Serbian train and a convoy of Albanian refugees. Both were horrific, but neither was intentional and neither contradicts the conclusion drawn above about the policy. Second, a more complicated assessment: what risks of civilian casualties ("unintended" or "collateral" casualties) is the NATO policy willing to run? The dilemma is exemplified in the NATO cruise missile attack on the Serbian Interior Ministry in the center of Belgrade. The strike successfully demolished the ministry building (a component element in Milosevic's repressive policies) and *did not hit* a hospital in the same city block. But was it worth the risk? More precisely, if the target comes up again for a strike (which it could), should NATO take the risk? I would acknowledge the first success, but I would vote against another strike as prudentially too great a risk of civilian casualties.

In my judgment, NATO strategy thus far passes the "just means" test of noncombatant immunity, but it will not sustain that record if it pursues the "must win" dictum without qualification. A more complicated challenge to limited means arises from within the ethic itself. One criterion of the doctrine is "reasonable hope of success": in other words, one should not undertake war if there is no reasonable hope of achieving one's objectives. The norm seeks to connect ends and means in something more than a purely mechanistic or utilitarian fashion. There should be some moral fit between objectives and contemplated strategies: war should not be initiated or continued if the use of force seems without definable purpose. Policy can fail the moral test either because it exceeds moral limits or because it is ineffective in achieving legitimate objectives.

The tension inherent in this norm lies between the possibility of success and proportionality. If strategic advocates propose that success can only be attained by violating noncombatant immunity, the moral judgment is simple: there is no justifiable war that is pursued by murderous conduct. A more complex decision arises when it is proposed that standards of proportionality must be loosened to achieve success. The nature of the proportionality criterion is that it is inherently open to revision. A claim that it is too tightly drawn and should be revised in the name of a competing norm cannot be instantly rejected. But continuous, incremental relaxation of standards of proportionality can yield simply another version of "must win."

NATO air strategy is being escalated steadily in the face of Serbian atrocities and resistance, and at some point, sooner rather than later, those who support the basic strategy must be willing to resist proposals for continual escalation. For example, Senator McCain has been quoted as advocating dropping the bridges around Belgrade and turning out the lights. Both Vietnam and Gulf War images play into this recommendation. The Senator's deep frustration with Vietnam makes him oppose incrementalist strategies that fail to take the war to its perpe-trators. The Gulf War legacy of strategies to turn off lights, water, and sanitation on civilians gives one reason to pause. I would drop some bridges (those carrying military supplies) at night and not turn off the lights.

This casuistry of the air-war strategy inevitably raises questions of whether air power alone can ever promise reasonable hope of success. The public debate is often about the politics of using ground troops, but the question of air-war strategy is per-tinent to the moral calculus of Kosovo. It can be argued that continual reliance on air power alone will not stop the ethnic cleansing (it has not yet) and will systematically increase the risk to civilians, precisely because of the tensions between success and the risks to proportionality of incessant escalation of the bombing in or near Bel-grade. The use of ground troops will directly confront Milosevic's scorched-earth policy; it will certainly mean combatant casualties; and it may reduce the drive to bring ever-increasing pressure on the population of Belgrade. To some degree (and *only* to a degree) the focus of the war would shift to Yugoslav troops in Kosovo.

How, then, should the decision about ground troops be evaluated? Fred Kaplan, a seasoned military analyst and journalist, echoes the dominant strategic view outside the NATO policy process when he says that there is no record of an em-battled state changing its objectives or policy solely because of air attacks upon it. On both strategic and moral grounds, therefore, it is necessary to conclude that ground troops should not be ruled out absolutely in a plan that seeks to be strategically effi-cient and ethically acceptable. Ground troops will inevitably widen the war (for NATO, the U.S., and Serbia) and will bring new issues of proportionality to the fore-front of the policy and public debate. I would not rule out ground troops as present NATO policy does (my fourth conclusion), but I would acknowledge that propor-tionality is a category that must be used *before* one acts, continuously reviewed *dur-ing* a war, and assessed retrospectively *after* a war. Hence, if ground troops are used and the war widens, the debate between the possibility of success and the cost of pro-portionality has to continue. In Vietnam a point was reached where neither success nor the limits of proportionality were being realized.

The memory of Vietnam must come to bear as we assess the decision to make Kosovo an "air-land battle." William Pfaff highlights the complexity of this decision (*New York Review of Books*, 5/6/99) when he advocates a ground assault on Yugoslav forces in Kosovo. He makes a convincing case that a quick assault from north and south could put NATO in control of Kosovo. But his argument that the KLA could then successfully dispose of Serbian forces in the mountains is less convincing, and his prediction that Kosovo could be sustained independently without NATO forces is not persuasive at all.

In my judgment, a ground war will widen the conflict, will change the fac-tors involved in assessing the proportionality of the conflict, and will ultimately make the success of the policy more likely. Ultimately is a wiggle word because it envisions the possibility of a long and bitter conflict. Peter Steinfels wants clarity from religious and moral voices on how many casualties are too many and how many months are too long for this war. I have argued that proportionality is a judgment that must be made over time, and I do not think it reduces to the specific numbers he seeks, at least in an *a priori* judgment. Proportionality will depend, in part, on the objectives sought and the skill with which it is pursued. This brings me to a final set of comments on the NATO strategy.

To affirm that NATO has a "just cause" is not necessarily to be enthusiastic about the policy it has pursued. I noted above that support for the specific decision to engage Kosovo is a piece of a broader argument that seeks to revise accepted norms about humanitarian intervention. In other places I have argued that the status of sovereignty should be relativized and a broader range of justifications for intervention legitimated (cf. Johnathan Moore, ed., *Hard Choices* [Lanham, MD: Rowman and Littlefield, 1999]). In the face of multiple internal conflicts, the phenomenon of failed states, and the human rights obligations incumbent on sovereign states, the virtually absolute status given to the nonintervention principles in law and U.N. practice does not serve individuals in the international community well. The status of both sovereignty and nonintervention should be relativized. Hence the NATO decision to intervene was and is, in my judgment, a justifiable and necessary action.

The definition of objectives of NATO policy has been surpassed by events. The idea of restoring the autonomy of Kosovo within Serbia may have been possible before the purge of the Kosovars, but it is hardly feasible now. On this point Henry Kissinger and others are correct in calling now for the objective of an independent Kosovo removed from any Serbian control. This goal will require an international force to be in place for some time to deter the irredentist inclinations of the Serbs, who have shown us that they do not forget defeat easily. While a non-U.S. or non-NATO force may make a diplomatic agreement easier, there should be no illusions about the reality that such a force must implicitly be understood to be supported politically and militarily by NATO. Equally important to planning for the postwar security status of Kosovo should be planning for the reconstruction of both Kosovo and a post-Milosevic Serbia. The latter may not coincide with the end of the war, but NATO policy should sustain the argument that this war has not been fought against Serbs as such, but against a Serbian policy in the 1990s that, to use the traditional terms, violated the conscience of humanity.

To return to the Steinfels questions: the "bedrock principles" used here have been traditionally addressed to interstate warfare. Intervention is a harder case, but for this student of the ethic, those principles do provide some clarity. In summary, the cause is just; force is necessary; it must be kept limited; it is desirable but not likely that a ground war be avoided; it is crucial to win but only within limits; the future of Serbia and Kosovo will not be a return to the past. The design for the future will ultimately be delegated to the diplomats, for war is not an end in itself. But Kosovo is a case where war must play its role so diplomacy can follow.

A Pacifist Response to Ethnic Cleansing

JAMES W. DOUGLASS

In March 1994, I stood in Republic Square in Belgrade in support of a courageous group of Serbian peacemakers, Women in Black. The women were holding their weekly vigil in resistance to Slobodon Milosevic's policies of ethnic cleansing that were then decimating Bosnia and Croatia and increasingly threatening Kosovo.

Dressed in black for the victims of war, the Serbian women were regularly attacked by their fellow citizens. Yet every Wednesday afternoon they publicly stood their ground with smiles and banners. They then organized for peace the rest of the week out of an unidentified office that was often moved for security reasons. But even such limited spaces for peacemaking in Belgrade have been politically demolished by our bombs.

Stasha Zajovic, one of those Women in Black, summed up the plight of Serb and Kosovar peacemakers for me at the beginning of NATO's bombing: "This conspiracy of militarism — global and local — dangerously reduces our space. Soon there won't be this space. With the horror the people of Kosovo are experiencing in this NATO intervention, they are paying a price even greater than before: NATO in the sky; Milosevic on the ground."

Veran Maric, leader of Radio B92, another dissident Belgrade group I visited in 1994, wrote at the same time that the grassroots movement that struggled against Milosevic for years felt betrayed by the NATO bombs: "These people now feel compelled to take up arms and join their sons serving in the army. With bombs falling all around, nobody can persuade them — though some have tried — that this is only an attack on their government and not on their country."

Kosovo's own massive nonviolent resistance to Milosevic was driven into political oblivion by the West even before our planes started bombing. For most of the 1990s, the Albanian Kosovars waged a remarkable nonviolent struggle against Serbian oppression with strikes, marches, widespread noncooperation, and even their own parallel government, schools, and medical clinics. For a while Milosevic seemed stymied by the Kosovar popular movement. But it received little support from Western governments and was demoralized by the Dayton peace agreement.

With the November 1995 Dayton Accords, the United States made a deal with Milosevic on Bosnia that failed to secure autonomy for Kosovo, yet recognized Bosnian borders that were created by ethnic cleansing. Thus, Dayton's lesson was that violence pays. It encouraged Milosevic to intensify the ethnic cleansing of Kosovo, while spurring the rise of the Kosovo Liberation Army, which then provided a convenient military rationale for Milosevic's razing all of Kosovo. But what alternative international response might there have been to the policies of Milosevic? How could the struggling peace movements of Serbia and Kosovo have been effectively supported by the West, rather than ignored, driven to violence, and bombed into oblivion?

Let us consider the following proposal for a nonviolent intervention in Kosovo that was issued by Nashville peace activists Karl Meyer, Pam Beziar, and Angela Schindler:

1. As the conflict began to develop, the United Nations Security Council would define the principles for UN intervention and a just settlement.
2. The secretary-general would begin to assemble a "nonviolent army" to be led by influential world figures such as (a) religious leaders, including bishops delegated by the pope, Orthodox patriarchs, and Islamic and Jewish leaders; (b) Nobel Peace Prize winners such as former Costa Rican president Oscar Arias, the Dalai Lama, Mairead Corrigan Maguire of Northern Ireland, President Nelson Mandela and Archbishop Desmond Tutu of South Africa; (c) retired world leaders such as Jimmy Carter and Mikhail Gorbachev; (d) diplomats from Russia and all the other European neighbors of Yugoslavia; (e) experienced activists trained in nonviolent tactics, such as veterans of the civil rights movement and Christian Peacemaker Teams that have worked in the West Bank and Haiti.
3. In the case of Kosovo, this nonviolent brigade would have been divided into two units: one would have gone to Serbia to engage in dialogue with all sectors of civil society; the other would have gone to Kosovo to interpose itself between Serbian forces and the KLA and to begin dialogue and mediation between them.

The realistic assumption behind the Nashville proposal is that the power of a government is dependent on the support and cooperation of its people. For that reason nonviolent resistance based on truth and supported by the world community can dislodge any unjust government's popular support. Milosevic's hold on power was in fact shaky before the Dayton agreement and the NATO bombing. The Serbian and Kosovar nonviolent movements were threatening his power.

Can nonviolent intervention, as envisioned in this proposal, begin to replace our reliance on vastly destructive weapons when we face an intolerable evil such as ethnic cleansing? Martin Luther King put all such questions in the context of a post-Hiroshima prophecy: nonviolence or nonexistence. King saw profoundly that Jesus' principle, "Those who take the sword will perish by the sword," had been heightened by the advent of nuclear weapons to the threat of humanity's extinction. In the nuclear age we are playing games with human survival when we uphold the anachronism of war. Nonviolence or nonexistence is more than a contingent prophecy; it is the fundamental law of our time.

At the same time, thanks to the exemplary campaigns of Gandhi, King, and others, we can now make the life-sustaining choice of nonviolent action in visibly transforming ways. Serb and Kosovar peacemakers were developing such campaigns until Western policies and bombs blew them away. But when nonviolent initiatives are at last given the support, sacrifices, and resources we have previously devoted to war, they will be able to stop ethnic cleansing in its tracks.

Is the primary obstacle to nonviolent alternatives in Kosovo and elsewhere our own attitude that only violence can respond to violence?

On Giving the Devil
the Benefit of Law in Kosovo

NIGEL BIGGAR

There are times when the pursuit of justice should yield to the constraints of law for the sake of general order and peace. The case for this is made with forceful eloquence in *A Man for All Seasons,* Robert Bolt's play about Sir Thomas More. In one scene, More is urged by his daughter Alice and his future son-in-law, Nicholas Roper, to arrest Richard Rich, an informer. The subsequent argument rises to this climax:

> *Alice (exasperated, pointing after Rich):* While you talk, he's gone!
>
> *More:* And go he should if he was the Devil himself until he broke the law!
>
> *Roper:* So now you'd give the Devil benefit of law!
>
> *More:* Yes. What would you do? Cut a great road through the law to get after the Devil?
>
> *Roper:* I'd cut down every law in England to do that!
>
> *More:* Oh? And when the last law was down, and the Devil turned round on you — where would you hide, Roper, the laws all being flat? This country's planted thick with laws from coast to coast — Man's laws, not God's — and if you cut them down — and you're just the man to do it — d'you really think you could stand upright in the winds that would blow then? Yes, I'd give the Devil benefit of law, for my own safety's sake.[1]

The power of law (as distinct from force) to order a society, national or international, and so to safeguard the rights of its members, depends on its authority; and this authority, in turn, depends on the willingness of those whom it commands to obey it. But such voluntary obedience will only be forthcoming so long as those who remain subject to the law are confident that those who break it will not be able to keep the unfair advantages they have thereby seized; that is, that the law will be enforced against lawbreakers. If the law is not so enforced, and if law-

---

1. Robert Bolt, *A Man for all Seasons* (London: Heinemann, 1960), pp. 38-39.

breakers are seen to secure unfair advantage relative to the law-abiding, then the respect of the latter for the law will be shaken and its authority will diminish. If this diminution proceeds far enough, then the rule of law will disintegrate and society will dissolve into anarchy; and here those who have taken advantage of others' law-abidingness will find themselves reduced to an equality of defenselessness — the laws all being flat.

Usually, of course, those who disobey the law do so in order to gain some private advantage — material goods, say, or an increase in political power. But sometimes, paradoxically, people are moved to break the law in the pursuit of justice. This is because there are occasions when those with the power to enforce the law cannot do so, typically because they do not have sufficient evidence to make an arrest or secure a conviction. And in these cases private bodies might be moved to take the law into their own hands in order to administer rough justice to those whom they know — or presume to know — are criminals. As a rule, however, they should not. Why? Because the laws governing law enforcement are in place to protect the innocent against wrongful arrest and excessive punishment on mistaken or fraudulent grounds. This is a protection that would-be vigilantes expect for themselves, so they cannot consistently deny it to others. Further, if they do so without penalty, their action will diminish the law's authority and discourage its observance by suggesting that it serves only to disadvantage the weak in relation to the strong. So, for the sake of the general order and peace that ensues from prevalent respect for the law, particular pursuits of justice must be legally constrained — even at the expense of letting the Devil himself escape.

Or, as some have recently argued, Slobodan Milosevic and his forces. One of the most basic objections raised by critics of NATO's military intervention in Kosovo is that, lacking authorization by the Security Council, it has presumed to run roughshod over international law, thereby weakening the law's authority and setting a precedent for any sufficiently powerful state to invade another's sovereign territory on moral grounds of its own choosing. As a result, the security of states everywhere is now weakened, and relations between them more distrustful. NATO's high-handed action has made the world a considerably more dangerous place.

Although I fully embrace the importance of the rule of international law, and therefore the importance of maintaining that law's authority, I do not agree with this line of argument. I shall spend the rest of this essay explaining why.

First of all, the illegality of NATO's action is a moot point — even among eminent experts in international law.[2] There is no doubt that the U.N. Charter for-

---

2. For example, at the International Court of Justice in the Hague on 10 May 1999, the Professor of Public International Law at Oxford University, Ian Brownlie, argued on behalf of the Government of the Federal Republic of Yugoslavia that NATO's action was illegal, while his counterpart at the London School of Economics, Christopher Greenwood, argued the opposite on behalf of the Government of the United Kingdom.

bids the unilateral use of force, except in self-defense; and that it restricts all other use of force to what is specifically mandated by the U.N.'s Security Council for the maintenance of international security and peace. Controversy arises, however, over whether or not this is the last word on the matter of armed intervention for humanitarian purposes. On the one hand, Ian Brownlie, Professor of Public International Law at Oxford University, thinks that it is. He has argued that the Charter's position is clear and that it remains unqualified. In support of his argument, he makes the following points: that the preparatory work of the Charter indicates unequivocally that intervention for special motives was ruled out; that the Charter's position was confirmed in 1970 by the Declaration on Principles of International Law concerning Friendly Relations and Cooperation in its restatement of "the principle concerning the duty not to intervene in matters within the domestic jurisdiction of any State"; and that there is no evidence of the development of a doctrine of humanitarian intervention in customary international law. To demonstrate this last point, he cites statements made between 1971 and 1999 by seven legal authorities of various nationalities, including (most powerfully) a British Foreign Office document that contains this passage:

> In fact, the best case that can be made in support of humanitarian intervention is that it cannot be said to be unambiguously illegal. . . . But the overwhelming majority of contemporary legal opinion comes down against the existence of a right of humanitarian intervention, for three main reasons: first, the UN Charter and the corpus of modern international law do not seem specifically to incorporate such a right; secondly, state practice in the past two centuries, and especially since 1945, at best provides only a handful of genuine cases of humanitarian intervention, and, on most assessments, none at all; and finally, on prudential grounds, that the scope for abusing such a right argues strongly against its creation. . . . In essence, therefore, the case against making humanitarian intervention an exception to the principle of non-intervention is that its doubtful benefits would be heavily outweighed by its worth in terms of international law.[3]

On the other hand, against this position it can be argued that the U.N. Universal Declaration of Human Rights (1948) and subsequent treaties on the maintenance of human rights have subjected the internal conduct of sovereign states to international norms: "From their inception these texts were regarded as a significant crack in the shell of state sovereignty."[4] It is doubtful, however, that they es-

---

3. Foreign Policy Document No. 148, *The British Year Book of International Law*, vol. 57 (1986), p. 619. Brownlie's argument as a whole may be found in the Record of the public session of the International Court of Justice, 10 May 1999, to hear the Case of Yugoslavia v. Belgium et al. concerning the legality of the use of force.

4. J. Bryan Hehir, "Just War Theory in a Post–Cold War World," *Journal of Religious Ethics* 20, no. 2 (Fall 1992): 244.

tablish a right of unilateral intervention in defense of the rights they affirm.[5] Such a right might be inferred from Article 1 of the Genocide Convention (1948), where the signatories "undertake to prevent and punish" genocide; but, arguably, this is then qualified by Article 8, according to which contracting parties "may call upon" the U.N. to take action under its Charter. Certainly, it is generally taken for granted that all subsequent treaties are to be read as subordinate to the Charter.

Nevertheless, there is good reason to doubt whether the Charter's rule of nonintervention should be understood as absolute, applying always and everywhere. As with any other human document, the Charter's inception had an historical context — one in which particular concern about certain kinds of intervention was predominant. Like any others, its rules draw their specific meaning from certain typical cases. In 1945 the typical cases of intervention were probably expansionist and (neo-)colonialist. This is borne out in the aforementioned 1970 Declaration on Principles of International Law, whose commentary on the principle of nonintervention specifies its meaning in these terms:

> No State may . . . coerce another State in order to obtain from it the subordination of the exercise of its sovereign rights and to secure advantage of any kind. . . . Every State has an inalienable right to choose its political, economic, social and cultural systems, without interference in any form by another State.[6]

So far, as Brownlie claims, this confirms the U.N. Charter's position. But it also develops it by making specific mention of a case that is unlikely to have been in the minds of the Charter's authors in 1945:

> . . . no State shall organise, assist, foment, finance, incite or tolerate subversive, terrorist or armed activities directed toward the violent overthrow of the regime of another State. . . .[7]

If the meaning of the Charter can be developed in the light of a new case, surely it can also be revised by one. Is it not highly improbable that its signatories envisioned a case where a state is perpetrating genocide against a minority within its own borders, and thereby posing a threat to international peace and security, but where the U.N. is powerless either to act itself or to authorize another body to act instead, because a single member of the Security Council would veto it for reasons of regional politics? And is it not highly probable that

---

5. As Hehir might be suggesting when he writes: ". . . the UN texts affirm an obligation on the part of states to defend human rights in states found guilty of persistent and gross violations of rights" (ibid.).

6. Quoted by Brownlie before the International Court of Justice, 10 May 1999. See Section III of his speech.

7. Ibid.

they agreed to outlaw unilateral intervention on the (idealistic) assumption that the U.N. would be able both to recognize genocide when it saw it, and to decide to act against it — by force of arms, if need be? If this is not so, then the signatories to the Charter must be deemed to have agreed that, the next time a Hitler decides upon a Final Solution for a minority group within the borders of his own state, and is not dissuadable from this policy by diplomatic or economic pressure, and restrains himself from invading a neighbor, should the politics of the Security Council preclude sufficient unanimity to enable armed intervention either directly by the U.N. or by an authorized body, then international law will forbid any state to intervene instead. Those who do not find this supposition credible (and I am among them) have good reason, therefore, to regard the case of NATO's military action in Kosovo as an exception to the U.N. Charter's rule prohibiting unilateral intervention.

Whatever the intentions of the original signatories to the U.N. Charter, it is clear that many of their successors recognize that, under present circumstances (that is, where the power of the U.N. to enforce international law is so weak and trammeled), an unconditional ban on unilateral intervention is intolerable. Evidence for this is furnished by the wide acceptance in recent decades of interventions for humanitarian purposes that have not been explicitly authorized by the Security Council — this "wide acceptance" being expressed in the form of supportive Security Council resolutions. Two recent examples of this are the Anglo-American intervention in northern Iraq in 1991 to save the Kurds, and the imposition of a no-fly zone in southern Iraq to save the Shiite Muslims.[8] Insofar as this improvisation has met with widespread acceptance, it may be deemed to constitute "customary" international law. The crucial question then arises as to whether this unwritten law should be allowed to interpret and qualify what is inscribed in treaties such as the U.N. Charter.[9] I believe that it should, because otherwise international law would become so rigid as to be incapable of learning from situations its original authors never envisioned, and of revising it-

---

8. Stanley Hoffman wonders whether the protection of the Kurds might have been "a simple extension of the classical security operation against Iraq, that would never have occurred if Iraq had not invaded Kuwait," rather than the application of a new principle of humanitarian intervention on behalf of oppressed minorities (*The Ethics and Politics of Humanitarian Intervention* [Notre Dame: University of Notre Dame Press, 1996], p. 28). While it was, no doubt, diplomatically convenient to have the intervention ride on the coat-tails of the Security Council's authorization of the Allies' defense of Kuwait against Iraq, it is hard to see how it could plausibly be described as an "extension" of that defense.

9. This is the basic point of disagreement between Ian Brownlie (who denies it) and Christopher Greenwood (who affirms it). For Brownlie's position, see his speech before the International Court of Justice. For Greenwood's, see his article in *The Observer*, 28 March 1999, p. 22 ("Yes, but Is the War Legal?"); and the report on "Law and Right" in *The Economist*, 3 April 1999, pp. 19-20.

self accordingly — and that would certainly detract from its authority. If customary law is permitted to play this qualifying role, then NATO's intervention in Kosovo has some claim to legality. For it is indicative of considerable international acceptance that, two days after the bombing campaign began, the U.N. Security Council rejected Russia's proposal of a condemnatory resolution by twelve votes to three.[10]

But even if we were to judge that customary law cannot be allowed to qualify the U.N. Charter, and that NATO's unauthorized intervention was therefore illegal, there still remains the question of whether it was nevertheless morally right. I believe that it was. To begin with, if NATO was taking the law into its own hands, it was doing so in a context other than that of the typical case presupposed by the rule prohibiting vigilante justice. The typical case comprises the following features: the crime has already been committed; the criminal is arrested and punished by the victim or his relatives; and these have decided to substitute their own rough justice for the publicly authorized kind because they are unwilling to let the apprehension of the one whom they presume to judge guilty be hindered by proper judicial procedure, or to let his punishment be limited by it. The case of NATO's intervention in Kosovo is different on all three counts. The crime of "ethnic cleansing" was still in progress.[11] NATO intervened, not primarily to arrest and punish the perpetrator, but to stop the crime and (as far as possible) to restore to the victims what had been taken from them. Only one of NATO's nineteen member states (Turkey) had any ties of ethnic or cultural kinship to the victims of the crime; and this was balanced by the ties of another state (Greece) to their oppressor. NATO was motivated, then, not by partisan vengeance but by humanitarian concern.

Some, of course, doubt this — but more out of prejudice than reason. One ground for doubt is the apparent hypocrisy of NATO's action: if the West didn't intervene in Rwanda or Kurdish Turkey or the Krajina (where 600,000 Serbs were "ethnically cleansed" by the Croats in 1995), why should it have intervened in Kosovo? The implication here is either simply that Western powers were being inconsistent or that the reason for their unusual solicitude in the case of Kosovo was that they had some selfish material or political interest in it.

There are two ways of responding to the charge of inconsistency. One is that even if the West should have intervened in these other places, that still would not

10. In their highly tendentious article, "Has US Power Destroyed the UN?", Simon Chesterman and Michael Byers say that Russia's proposal was defeated "in large part" by the votes of the five NATO countries currently on the Council (*London Review of Books,* 29 April 1999, p. 29). They discreetly omit to mention the role of the other seven votes cast against Russia by non-NATO states.

11. Although the "ethnic cleansing" in Kosovo was accelerated after NATO's bombing campaign began, an estimated 400,000 people had already been driven from their homes and left to die on the hills from cold, malnutrition, and disease in the twelve months before.

amount to a reason not to have intervened in Kosovo — unless there were some virtue in maintaining, as one journalist nicely put it, "a level apathy field."[12] Surely it is better to be responsibly inconsistent than consistently irresponsible?

Another response to the charge is to deny it altogether. The reason for the West's intervening in Kosovo rather than, say, Rwanda is that, given the demonstrable impotence of the U.N., there was to hand another international body that had an interest in the stability of the Balkans, and that also had the political cohesion and military power to maintain it — NATO. The problem with Rwanda was that once the U.N. had abandoned its responsibility there, it was not clear which alternative body was both obliged to fill its shoes and capable of doing so.

Distinct from the issue of inconsistency is that of motivation. Some doubt that NATO's motives were genuinely humanitarian. But I have yet to hear a plausible account of the alternatives. No one, to my knowledge, has suggested that NATO was really covetous of physical resources or territory. Ian Brownlie speaks knowingly of "a geopolitical agenda unrelated to human rights," but declines to elaborate.[13] The playwright Harold Pinter, representing the unthinking British Left, has proposed the motive of American domination:

> The truth is that neither Clinton nor Blair gives a damn about the Kosovar Albanians. This action has been yet another blatant and brutal assertion of U.S. power using NATO as its missile. It sets out to consolidate one thing — American domination of Europe.[14]

Never mind that in recent years European nations have proven perfectly capable of distancing themselves from American foreign policy when they have seen fit to do so, for example, over Iraq. Never mind that in the forefront of NATO's military intervention stands France, which has made an international career out of *not* doing whatever America wants. Never mind that America's military involvement in Kosovo was patently reluctant — to the frustration of at least one European leader, Tony Blair. And never mind that America's reluctance is intelligible precisely because its national interest in the outcome of the Kosovo conflict, as distinct from the interest of its European allies, was so weak.

In a piece similarly riven with anti-Americanism, Simon Chesterman and Michael Byers identify NATO simply with the United States and assert that its military interventions throughout the 1990s — including that in Kosovo — have been simply self-interested. They close with this:

---

12. Steve Crawshaw, "A Journey into the Unknown," *The Independent on Sunday,* 28 March 1999, p. 15.

13. See his speech before the International Court of Justice, Section V.

14. As reported in *The Guardian,* 7 June 1999.

One might well conclude that the greatest long-term threat to peace is neither Slobodan Milosevic nor Saddam Hussein, but the impulsive (if well-meaning) sole remaining superpower — undeterred by rules and procedures, driven only by the inconstant winds of its own self-interest.[15]

Before reaching this conclusion, however, the authors themselves mention two occasions when American action has been impelled by humanitarian motives: Somalia in 1992 ("Driven by images of starvation in Somalia, the US once again led the good fight . . ."); and Bosnia in 1995 ("Frustrated at the Serbian massacre of Bosnians in U.N. "safe havens" and at Europe's powerlessness to stop the madness, NATO found a cathartic release in air-strikes . . .").[16] And in the conclusion itself, does not the parenthetical qualification "if well meaning" rather subvert the claim that the U.S. is "driven only by . . . self-interest"? By Chesterman and Byer's own inadvertent admission, then, recent U.S. foreign policy has shown evidence of humanitarian motivation. So if in Somalia and Bosnia, why not also in Kosovo?

Edward Said, too, prefers to collapse NATO into the U.S.,[17] and asserts that the Kosovo intervention was basically "a display of [American] military might" to "show the world who is boss."[18] This account also depends on the fiction that NATO is simply an American tool. It passes over the reluctance with which the U.S. became involved. It raises the question of why America chose to show off its military might by way of such a half-hearted and precarious strategy. And it gains plausibility at the expense of fairness to the alternatives.[19]

It is certainly true that NATO — but much less its North American than its European members — had an "interest" in the stability of the Balkans and there-

15. Chesterman and Byers, "Has US Power Destroyed the UN?", p. 30.

16. Ibid. Note, in the second quotation, that NATO is distinguished from Europe, and that no mention is made of the fact that the Dutch (i.e., European) troops, who had to stand by helplessly in Srebrenica and watch "the madness" of Bosnian men being taken out for slaughter by the Serbs, were under UN command. The point is this: that Chesterman and Byer's account obscures the fact that NATO was frustrated at the powerlessness, not of Europe, but of the UN.

17. "In its arrogance, the US has forced NATO to go along with it" ("It's Time the World Stood up to the American Bully," *The Observer*, 11 April 1999, p. 19).

18. Harold Pinter took a similar tack in a BBC2 television program, broadcast on 4 May 1999, when he described NATO's intervention as "an act of deplorable machismo" (as reported by Timothy Garton Ash in his sharp critique, "Vivid, Dark, Powerful and Magnificent—but Wrong," *The Independent*, 6 May 1999).

19. Said tells us that "not even the Kosovo Albanians believe that the air campaign is about independence for Kosovo or saving Albanian lives: this is a total illusion" ("It's Time," p. 19). But NATO did not claim that its campaign was for Kosovan independence—that certainly would have been unacceptable to Russia and China; and there is ample evidence that the Albanian Kosovars welcomed NATO's action wholeheartedly as a means of saving their life as a people—even after NATO airstrikes had killed some of them by accident.

fore in curbing the activity of the main source of recent disturbance, Milosevic and his regime. But this interest was not private to NATO; it was shared, presumably, by the Balkan peoples themselves. Indeed, it was shared by the U.N., whose Security Council had adopted resolutions (1160, 1199, and 1203) in 1998 that legally bound the Federal Republic of Yugoslavia to cease all action by its security forces affecting the civilian population of Kosovo, to withdraw all security units used for civilian repression, and to implement, in full, all agreements with NATO and the OSCE. These, together with more recent statements following the Racak massacre in January 1999, judged that the government in Belgrade had created a humanitarian emergency in Kosovo that constituted a threat to peace and security in the Balkans.[20]

NATO's intervention in Kosovo, then, does not fit the paradigmatic case that informs the rule against taking the law into one's own hands. It was not about bypassing judicial procedure to wreak punitive vengeance on the presumed criminal. Rather, it was about intervening to stop an internationally recognized crime in progress, and to restore to the victims the basic conditions of civilized life, in a situation where authorized police protection was not available. In such circumstances it would be contrary to natural justice for positive law to forbid private bodies from coming to the rescue. All the more so when the crime was of an atrocious kind and was being perpetrated on a massive, arguably genocidal, scale.[21] And all the more so still, when the reason for the absence of any authorized police protection was that one member (Russia) of the quasi-global government that is the Security Council would have vetoed it, perhaps because of ties of ethnic and cultural kinship with the perpetrator, and certainly because of its resentment toward NATO's role.

In conclusion, then, I judge that NATO's action was arguably legal and certainly morally right. Whether it does damage to the authority of international law depends on how successful NATO's diplomats are in persuading other states of their case. As I see it, that case is a strong one and ought to be persuasive. It would, of course, be stronger had NATO managed to secure authorization from the Security Council. But since this would very probably have been impossible, and since

20. Resolutions 1199 and 1203 both speak of "impending humanitarian catastrophe" and assert that the situation in Kosovo "constitutes a threat to peace and security in the region."

21. The Genocide Convention, adopted by the General Assembly of the U.N. on 9 December 1948, defines the crime of genocide as consisting of "acts committed with intent to destroy, in whole or in part, a national, ethnic, racial or religious group"—such as "(a) killing members of the group" and "(c) deliberately inflicting on the group conditions of life calculated to bring about its physical destruction in whole or in part." Therefore, the fact that Belgrade was not attempting to eliminate every last living Albanian Kosovar, and sought instead only to expel them from their homes, rob them of their livelihoods, and kill those males capable of military service or political leadership, does not mean that Milosevic's regime was not guilty of attempting to commit genocide.

the humanitarian need was both grave and urgent, and since nothing but armed force would have been effective,[22] NATO was right to refuse the Devil in Kosovo benefit of dubious law, and to intervene unilaterally.[23]

22. I have heard from a Serbian source the claim that the talks at Rambouillet collapsed because of the West's intolerable demand (in the Military Annexe to the proposed agreement) that its troops should have right of access to the whole of Serbia. However, it has also been told me that a senior member of the diplomatic corps of Austria—neither a member of NATO, nor hawkish about Kosovo—has reported that the Serbian delegation did not even begin to negotiate the Annexe, and that they showed little sign of being seriously interested in the talks at all. This corroborates the account given by Christopher Hill, the American Ambassador to Macedonia, to Michael Ignatieff ("Balkan Physics," *The New Yorker,* 10 May 1999, pp. 73-74).

23. I would like to thank Richard Miller of Indiana University and Jeremy Hill of the Foreign Office, London, for their help as I wrote this essay. The responsibility for what I have written is, of course, mine, not theirs.

Islamist Response to the War in Kosovo/a:
Materials for an Ironic Narrative

JOHN KELSAY

Muslim responses to the war in Kosovo/a are mixed, as are those of Europeans and North Americans. Small wonder, given the nature of the case. When President Clinton spoke of NATO's action as just and necessary in order to protect the rights of ethnic Albanians living in Kosovo/a (i.e., Kosovars), Muslims listened. They also watched as massive numbers of Kosovars became refugees during NATO's bombing campaign and wondered, "Whose rights are these bombs protecting?" Muslims stood, hopeful that the Kosovars would not suffer in the same degree as their co-religionists in Bosnia had done. They also wondered, sometimes in very quiet voices, why the governments of Muslim states were relegated to the sidelines in discussions of policy for Kosovo/a.

A general survey of Muslim opinion around the world would, it seems fair to say, reflect considerable relief that the United States and its allies did not delay intervention for quite so long as in the case of Bosnia. Nevertheless, the mix of rhetoric, strategy, and suffering that made up the war in Kosovo/a did give rise to a different, more suspicious interpretation among certain Muslim groups. Islamists viewed the war in what we might call "ironic" terms — terms that stress the paradoxical, even dark side of war. For ironists, war becomes an endeavor in which close analyses tend to blur distinctions between good and evil, justice and injustice. As one prominent (non-Muslim) proponent of ironic interpretations of war puts it: Woodrow Wilson said that World War I was fought to make the world safe for democracy; an ironist wonders whether the war really made the world safe for Hitler. Or again: In response to those who interpret World War II as a fight against totalitarianism in Europe, an ironist notes that, however much the war accomplished by defeating Hitler, the postwar settlement left most of Europe under the domination of the Soviet Union.[1]

---

1. See Paul Fussell, "Introduction: On Modern War," in *The Norton Book of Modern War,* ed. Paul Fussell (New York and London: W. W. Norton & Company, 1991), pp. 17-26. More generally, see the outline Fussell offers of the development of his ironist approach to war in Paul Fussell, *Doing Battle: The Making of a Skeptic* (Boston: Little, Brown, and Company, 1996).

The ironist, then, views the rhetoric of high morality with great suspicion. Among Muslims, Islamists represent a point of view much disposed to think in ironic terms.[2] For Islamists, the promise of U.S. dominance in world affairs ought to give one pause — especially if one is a Muslim. The United States, after all, led the coalition of forces that placed (and now keeps) the people of Iraq in a condition of great suffering. Even if resistance to Saddam Hussein's invasion of Kuwait was necessary, how could (and can) one justify economic and military policies that seem calculated to strike at the Iraqi government *through* the Iraqi people? How could a great power, ostensibly committed to the protection of human rights, be so quick to strike at the Muslim people of Iraq, yet so slow to intervene to protect the Muslims of Bosnia?

Islamist suspicion of the United States and its allies runs deep. And so it is not strange that one could follow the pages of Islamist journals of opinion during this recent conflict and find ample material there for an ironist point of view. Consider, for example, the following reflections, developed from a reading of one such journal's articles regarding Kosovo/a during 1998 and 1999.[3]

(1) President Clinton claimed on more than one occasion that NATO's action was a form of opposition to religious (and specifically anti-Muslim) bigotry. Wasn't it odd, then, that so many people undertaking a defense of the Muslims spoke primarily of the province by its Serbian designation (Kosovo) rather than that preferred by the Muslims (Kosova)? As the war progressed, awareness of the distinction increased, and Clinton among others attempted to alternate pronunciations. As Islamists put it, this still left room for confusion. Whose rights was NATO protecting? Whose possessions would be restored?

(2) Given that the Serbs' refusal to follow the directives of NATO and of the U.N. by curbing violence against the Muslims of Kosovo/a was often framed in the language of national sovereignty ("No one has the right to tell us how to treat people within our own borders . . ."), wasn't it odd that NATO's stipulation of terms of peace left the province (and, thus, the Kosovars) under the control of the Serbs? Wouldn't protection of the rights of the Kosovars be better achieved by accepting, and facilitating, their clear wish — that is, for territorial auton-

---

2. Islamists arc often called "revivalists," "fundamentalists," or "militants," or their position is indicated by the label "political Islam." I discuss some aspects of the movement, with special relevance to the justification and conduct of war, in *Islam and War: A Study in Comparative Ethics* (Louisville: Westminster/John Knox, 1993). For a recent, journalistic survey of the various movements and parties covered by the Islamist label, see Mark Huband, *Warriors of the Prophet: The Struggle for Islam* (Boulder: Westview Press, 1999).

3. Here I am following *Crescent International*, a Toronto-based publication styling itself "the newsmagazine of the Islamic movement." *CI* publishes news analyses and editorials of particular interest to those following Islamist views of international affairs. The journal's website, found at http://muslimedia.com, contains current issues, archives, and a rich set of links to other sites of interest, for example, of the Muslim Student Association (http://msanews.mynet.net).

omy? In addition, one might think that wishes for autonomy from Kosovars, who constitute somewhere between 80 and 90 percent of the provincial population, would come under the often expressed, though less often honored, right of a people to self-determination.

(3) Leaving aside such "quibbles," Muslims found further — and more profound — material for irony in the results of the NATO bombing campaign. Indeed, on this point, "irony" seems an overly artful characterization. One is, after all, speaking about a military campaign that took hundreds of lives, inflicted even more injuries, and, arguably, provided cover for the expansion of the Serbian campaign against the Kosovars. Prior to the March 24, 1999, beginnings of NATO's bombing campaign, one could speak about discrimination, even persecution of Muslims. With the bombing came full-scale ethnic cleansing. As one analysis put it, following March 24

> The Serbs' campaign against the Kosovars, which had been running for over a year at low-medium level, was immediately intensified, particularly in northern and western Kosova, and in the capital Pristina. The Serbs unleashed a savage drive of genocide and ethnic cleansing for which preparations had obviously been carefully laid in advance. While the area's few Serb residents placed markers on their doors to show that they should not be attacked, Serbian troops and police drove tens of thousands of Kosovars from their homes, killing, looting and pillaging as they went. Many of the worst features of the Serbs' campaign in Bosnia have been repeated: the separation and murder of the menfolk; the targeting of professionals and intellectuals; and the razing and torching of entire villages to make any resettlement unlikely.[4]

At the least, such consequences raised questions about the effectiveness of NATO's strategy. When coupled with observations like the following, however, one could find Muslims expressing the deepest suspicions of the ironist — that is, that NATO's policy was "secretly" led, or at least limited, by the desire to avoid a strong Muslim presence in Europe. Thus,

> The breadth of NATO's strikes surprised observers because it amounted to all-out war on Yugoslavia. . . . The resultant war atmosphere inside Serbia has led to Milosevic's position being consolidated, and total opposition to the west and the Kosovars. . . . By making the whole country a war zone, Milosevic has been strengthened, not weakened. . . . As the attacks started, western leaders insisted that their only objective was to force Milosevic to accept the Rambouillet agreement which the Kosovars had signed a week earlier . . . the west's bombing strat-

4. "NATO's Bombing Strategy Raises Questions about Their True Intentions," *Crescent International,* April 1-15, 1999.

egy is inconsistent with this objective. For force to be effective in this way, it should have been limited to Serb targets in Kosova rather than taking the form of all-out war on Yugoslavia as a whole. All-out war makes any concession on Milosevic's part a surrender, and much harder to swallow. . . . How can we explain the west's wholly illogical position here? It must be seen in the overall context of their strategy towards Kosova from the outset. This has been to insist that the Kosovars relinquish all claims to independence, and to support the Serbs' position that Kosova is an integral part of Serbia. The fear of the emergence of a strong Muslim state in Europe remains paramount in western thinking.[5]

(4) Now an analyst speaking from a NATO, and particularly a U.S., standpoint will likely respond that such rhetoric goes beyond the ironic and verges on the paranoid style. But consider the following. In the case of Bosnia-Herzegovina, where a prominent Muslim elite held considerable power, President Alija Izetbegovic, among others, long held to a strategy of cooperation with, not to say dependence on, European and North American power to deal with the Serbian irregulars. Such irregulars, with assistance from Belgrade, carried out a brutal campaign of ethnic cleansing beginning in 1991. That Izetbegovic did so was in part a response to U.S. pressure; U.S. policy was to urge Izetbegovic not to arm his people, but rather to rely on the international community for protection. Indeed, when the Bosnian Muslims finally did secure arms to defend themselves, most of their support came from Iran, rather than from NATO, and such military training as could be had came not from U.S. or European advisors but from the so-called Afghani Arabs — people like the now infamous Osama bin Laden, who learned to fight with the *mujahiddin* in Afghanistan during the 1980s.[6]

In addition to U.S. pressure, however, Izetbegovic had other motives for cooperating with the West. In his book *Islam between East and West,* the Bosnian leader expressed the hope that the Muslim community of Bosnia might lead the way in a spiritual-moral revival of European culture.[7] Presenting an interpretation of Islam that allied it with democratic values, Izetbegovic argued that Islam offered a vision of human nature that could overcome the split between facts and values, science and religion, and instrumental and value-oriented rationality, which he saw as a threat to the continued flourishing of modern industrial societies. Islam, for Izetbegovic, was fully at home in the Western world. Unfortunately, as more than one observer commented regarding the Western delay in dealing

5. Ibid.

6. Huband, *Warriors of the Prophet,* is particularly useful in pointing out the exemplary status attributed by Islamists to the Afghani Arabs.

7. Alija 'Ali Izetbegovic, *Islam between East and West,* 3rd ed. (Plainfield, IN: American Trust Publications, 1993). For a discussion of this book, and the way Izetbegovic's proposals look to a post-Bosnia Muslim audience, see John Kelsay, "Bosnia and the Muslim Critique of Modernity," in *Religion and Justice in the War over Bosnia,* ed. G. Scott Davis (Routledge, 1996).

with violence in Bosnia-Herzegovina, Europeans did not seem to be fully at home with Islam. As Serbians carried out the cleansing of Bosnia relatively untrammeled by outside military, many of NATO's member nations were dealing with their own Muslim populations — the French, with the problems of assimilating immigrants from Northern Africa; the Germans, with Turkish guestworkers; the Scandinavians, with South Asians seeking expanded economic opportunities; the British, with the conflict occasioned by the Salman Rushdie affair.

In all this, the question for Muslims was, Why did the West take so long in responding to the plight of the Bosnian Muslims? And the answer, as many came to see it, lay in the resistance of Western societies to the presence of Muslims. Even when the U.S. finally turned its full attention to the problems of Bosnia, the resulting peace outlined in the Dayton Accords actually left the Serbs in control of most of the areas won by irregular forces during the fighting, and failed to address the problem of Muslims' return to their homes.

(5) Given this background, the tendency toward deep suspicion of Western motives is perhaps less mysterious. And it also helps to explain the way Muslims viewed yet another aspect of the war of Kosovo/a in ironic terms. Why, given the failure of Izetbegovic's policies to protect Muslims in Bosnia, would the NATO powers expect a group of Muslims, again victims of Serb aggression, to support Ibrahim Rugova's program of peace through negotiation with Belgrade and of dependence on Western military power? After Bosnia, why wouldn't — why shouldn't — Muslims view the KLA — that is, Kosovars armed and ready to fight for their own — as preferable to Rugova? In some quarters, the latter was explicitly compared with Izetbegovic:

> The Democratic League of Kosova [Rugova's party] . . . which has been effectively ruling Kosova through an unofficial "parallel government" since 1989, and which is firmly committed to a pacifist path, has always maintained that the KLA is a figment of the Serbs' imagination, deliberately dreamt up to discredit the Kosovars and justify their oppression. . . . In this case, too, the contemporary Kosovar situation is similar to that in Bosnia at the beginning of the war there. Prior to the Serb invasion of Bosnia, the government of Alija Izetbegovic had been reluctant to organize any defenses against Serb aggression for fear of provoking and justifying precisely such an aggression. When it came, therefore, independent of any provocation or reason, the Bosnians were hopelessly unprepared. The Kosovars' position now is depressingly similar, except that it is even more disadvantaged.[8]

And,

8. Iqbal Siddiqui, "Muslim Kosovars Fear Action Replay of Serbian Assault on Bosnia-Herzegovina," *Crescent International*, March 16-31, 1998.

Like Alija Izetbegovic then, Rugova has gambled that reason and good sense will head Milosevic off. . . . Rugova must be aware that Serb nationalism remains an unpredictable, brutal and ruthless force with the potential to do immeasurable damage should Milosevic choose.[9]

Obviously, Milosevic did so choose, and Rugova's credibility seems to have suffered, at least in the short run.

(6) With this in mind, perhaps the most significant factor in the development of an ironic narrative of the war of Kosovo, at least among Muslims, is found in NATO's insistence on the postwar disarmament of the KLA. According to the June 21, 1999, demilitarization agreement, the KLA agrees to give up its arms and, in effect, to turn over protection of the Kosovars to an international peacekeeping force.[10] As a Muslim ironist might put it: Why would a war fought to protect Muslims from Serbian aggression end with the victims unable to defend themselves?

Not a bad question, that.

9. "Kosovar Aspirations, Serb Nationalism Clash in the Balkans," *Crescent International*, May 1-15, 1998.

10. Full text in *The New York Times*, June 23, 1999. Iqbal Siddiqui, in "NATO Looking for a Compromise instead of Arming the KLA to Fight," *Crescent International*, May 1-15, 1999, makes the interesting point that the KLA, often with little training and equipment, did important work during NATO's aerial bombardment, particularly by way of protecting Kosovar refugees who remained in Kosova — displaced, but without fleeing the country. Siddiqui's comments fit well with the ironist frame suggested above: "More disappointing [than the unwillingness of NATO to send in ground troops to rescue the Kosovars] — though perhaps not surprising — has been the west's steadfast refusal to help the Kosovars to defend their own people."

Kosovo: The Ethics of
Heaven, Earth, and Hell

GABRIEL FACKRE

Kosovo posed, and continues to pose, perennial questions about the place of violence in Christian ethics. No place at all — the bombs of NATO being as bad as the Serbian slaughter of Kosovars? Some place — as in the restraint of evil by a peacekeeping military? The only place when all else fails — as in both the air war's falling bombs and the ground war's marching feet?

The long Christian debate about violence can be characterized as the difference between the ethics of "heaven," "earth," and "hell."[1] These varied perspectives were reflected in alternative proposals for action in Kosovo. Each gives pride of place to either the uncompromising absolutes of the Sermon on the Mount, the earthly approximations of "law and order," or the hellish ambiguities of sword and gun.

In the ethics of heaven, human attitudes and behavior must conform to the ways of the final reign of God, a self-giving and vulnerable neighbor love. Conduct is to be judged by the standard of what the world *will be* when the kingdom comes, by what Jesus *was* — cheek-turning, crucified agape — and who God *is*, the triune Life Together of perfect mutuality.

In the ethics of earth, two kingdoms are discerned and their norms distinguished. The heavenly standards are for the Not Yet. They cannot be imported into the fallen Now, especially so in matters of public ethics, where sin abounds and vulnerability is exploited. In that realm government is charged to maintain law and order and given police powers of latent violence to carry out its purposes. Further, the wider society requires for its survival minimum standards of justice and civility, seeking such by the deployment of structures of political, economic, and social force.

Hell is terrain on which we confront "both horns and all the forked feet of the devil" (Reinhold Niebuhr). Because Satan does not play by the rules of the earth, we must resist with commensurate means. The ethics of hell, therefore, le-

---

1. Explored in the author's *The Christian Story: A Narrative Interpretation of Christian Doctrine*, vol. 1, 3rd ed. (Grand Rapids: Eerdmans, 1996), pp. 199-203.

gitimates *patent* violence. While "war is hell," there may be worse inhabitants of the lower region, as with the perpetrators of holocausts of hate. Which nightmare scenario must we pursue in dealing with the devil?

Out of such a dilemma has come the search for a little light from tiers above. The *justice* norm of earth suggests a "just-war" theory. But where all options are those of the damned, war is only arguable as the lesser evil, earth's "just" better translated into hell's "justifiable." Such war is carried out with an eye cast on heaven's care for the neighbor in need, but in penitence for the death and destruction inflicted to achieve that end. By the standards of heaven, the bloodshed is that of the Savior himself, forgiveness made possible alone by the same wounds.

Ethical Options in the Kosovo Crises

Major alternative policies align with the three foregoing perspectives. Heavenly ethics bewailed, and bewails, the terrors inflicted on the Kosovars by Milosevic, and also the counterhorrors of NATO bombing. All fall short of the glory of God. What, then, is to be done? Neighbor love demands Samaritan/humanitarian outreach on the refugees' Jericho roads. But let it be for all victims — Kosovars in flight to Macedonia and Albania, but also Serbs killed by NATO's bombs and in the war's aftermath leaving Kosovo in droves for fear of reprisal. And because Satan has been cast out of heaven, let no one be demonized, especially not our enemies. We are called to love the villain, forgive those who trespass against us, pray for those who despitefully use us. Even pray *with* them as occasions arise. Thus the bowed heads and held hands of Jesse Jackson and Slobodan Milosevic.[2]

Heavenly ethics requires nonviolent strategies. In absolute terms, that means no recourse to violence, latent or patent. Given the NATO policy, pacifists demanded the end to bombing and rejected a ground war out of hand. They insisted that moral suasion must be the method in international affairs. With other war protesters they engaged in campus teach-ins, street demonstrations, and on occasion civil disobedience. Because heaven is what the world is made for, anything short of it is self-destructive, a devil's brew that poisons all subsequent relations. The ethics of heaven, it is argued, over time will prove to be the only viable way, as well as the only responsible Christian norm. NATO's policies of violence, as well as Serbian ethnic cleansing, will bring history's judgment on its executors. The way to that goal is, of course, marked by suffering, as the peace of heaven collides with a hellish earth.

2. The picture of Jackson and Milosevic in prayer was shown around the world; we should not forget that the delegation included a broad range of religious leaders. See Joan Brown Campbell and Leonard Kishkovsky, "Journey to Belgrade," *The Christian Century* 116, no. 16 (May 19-26, 1999): 550-52.

Earthly ethics acknowledges the self-destructive nature of war and will avoid it where possible. But while striving to speak softly, it also carries a big stick. The realities of earth mean that heaven's soft answer alone will not turn away the wrath of an aggressor. Given our fallen nature, the tyrant will exploit vulnerability, smash the turned cheek, and slaughter the innocents. The police stick must be visible to both the street criminal and rogue nation. Here is the place for *latent* violence, the threat of force. In terms of international affairs, a police club means the deployment of armed forces assigned, such as a patrol officer, to keep the peace. These armed forces establish visible boundaries that preclude the outbreak of aggression. The peacekeeping troops in Bosnia play that role. In Kosovo it must be soldiery in sufficient numbers and with adequate credibility (a NATO command structure) to assure the return of the Kosovars.

Allied to the threat of physical violence is the active deployment of economic, political, and social force. This presupposes the intransigence of hostile powers but represents an alternative method of restraining sin, the checkmating of tyranny and accountability to earth's minimal standards of justice. Here the economic boycott, the vote of reproof in the United Nations, and the mustering of world outrage through mass means of communication are critical pressure points.

Since earth is not without rays of light from heaven, all forms of force will reflect some of heaven's purer purposes. They will give support of, and protection to, humanitarian efforts to feed, house, and resettle refugees. And their agents will be from the broadest possible spectrum of nations, thus organized under U.N. auspices. Befitting its reluctance to activate instruments of violence that stand at the ready means the preference for negotiating rather than bombing, though the threat of the latter is an incentive to the former. They would have sought an alternative to war from the beginning by pressing for much more protracted Rambouillet negotiations, noting that their cessation coincided with the assault on and removal of Kosovar Albanians. And, of course, humanitarian efforts should be a constant refrain, with emphasis on justice for the refugee population as victims of a campaign of patent violence rather than the both-ands of heavenly ethics.

Proponents of the ethics of hell hold the advocates of heaven to be hopelessly naive and the earthly moderates to have compromised their pretensions of realism. In the abysses of hell, *patent* violence must be met with patent violence. Here none of earth's conventional restraints work, so tyranny must be confronted by armed opposition, not just the threat of it. Hell is the place where war must be made, not peace kept. For all that, an ethics of hell cannot ignore the little light visible even here, for Christ has already made the descent into hell (Apostles' Creed). The church's struggle for discernment in the inferno has led to its judgment that war, always wrong, may be the only option when:

> undertaken by the lawful authority . . . for the vindication of an undoubted and proportionate right that has been certainly infringed . . . a last resort . . . the good

to be achieved shall outweigh the evils that war will involve . . . a reasonable hope of victory . . . a right intention . . . the methods of warfare . . . legitimate.[3]

While war is hell, there is a difference between the ethically doable and not doable, the justifiable and unjustifiable war. Was NATO's war against Yugoslavia just? Brian Hehir argues for a qualified "Yes" in the pages of *America* and does so elsewhere in this volume.[4]

Multi-tiered Ethics in the Kosovo Crises

In the Kosovo events, and in similar crises yet to come, the foregoing single-tier approaches do insufficient justice to both the profundities of Christian faith and the complexities of political fact. Recent commentary on matters of war and peace by two figures from very different Christian traditions presses toward a more encompassing framework. The broad outlines of Pope John Paul II's approach and the midwar Kosovo specifics of President Jimmy Carter are part of a quest for a more inclusive view.

Drew Christiansen, tracking recent papal teaching on violence, finds evidence of "a growing presumption against the use of force and an increased appeal to strategies of nonviolence and negotiation. . . . The tradition of just-war theory is playing a decreased role in official Catholic teaching. . . ."[5] Qualifying the standard recourse to the just-war tradition has been John Paul's linkage of "sufferings for the sake of truth and freedom to the sufferings of Christ on the cross," his awareness of twentieth-century achievements of nonviolent protest and agony over the "culture of death" that warmaking spreads. In our framework, these represent an effort to associate aspects of the ethics of heaven (the norm of the cross) and the ethics of earth (a prudential argument for negotiation and persuasion based on raised public awareness of war's consequences) with a just-war version of the ethics of hell (the pope's "I am no pacifist"), albeit now applied in a "stringent" way by the tightening of its standards.

President Carter shocked the political establishment on May 27, 1999, by writing an op-ed piece in the *New York Times* on Kosovo policy that took issue with administration policy. Carter called for an end to NATO bombing, a policy he

3. "War," *A Catholic Dictionary,* ed. Donald Attwater, 3rd ed. (New York: Macmillan, 1961), p. 522. For a slightly different listing, see Jacques Ellul, *Violence: Reflections from a Christian Perspective,* trans. Cecelia Gaul Kings (New York: Seabury, 1969), p. 6.

4. J. Bryan Hehir, "Kosovo: A War of Values and the Values of War," *America* 180, no. 17 (May 15, 1999). John Kavanaugh disagrees in "Outcasts and the In Crowd," *America* 180, no. 16 (May 8, 1999).

5. Drew Christiansen, S.J., "Peacemaking and the Use of Force: Behind the Pope's Stringent Just-War Teaching," *America* 180, no. 17 (May 15, 1999).

viewed as unjust since it had moved to targets affecting the civilian population and entailed increasing collateral damage. Carter would have used ground forces from the beginning to secure both the Albania-Kosovo border and carve out a section of Kosovo as a safe haven for refugees, with the stated intention of resettling them after the war, along with those troops and more as Kosovo peacekeepers. Regardless of whether ground troops were to be used, Carter urged negotiation as an alternative policy even with Milosevic as a declared war criminal. Carter's proposals, therefore, included elements of "heaven" (nondemonizing of Milosevic, bombing cessation), "earth" (negotiation with the big stick of a potential warmaking army at that time and peacekeeping force later), and "hell" (NATO warmaking ground troops from the beginning, but just-war theory used to disqualify bombing).

A Triple Approach Continued

Building on the efforts at a full-orbed ethics by the pope and the former president, I present another alternative to the truncation of heaven, earth, and hell in the Kosovo crisis and future comparable circumstances — with the inclusion and integration of elements of each.

Heaven

Witness to the nonviolence of heaven is needed and did take place in:

1. Imaginative initiatives of the sort taken by the Reverend Jesse Jackson and his company of religious leaders. Given an unusual opening — with both American and Serbian pragmatists supporting ethics in their mutual desire to make the release of the three American soldiers possible — Jackson and his entourage used the occasion to make a public case for both ending the NATO bombing and the Serbian ethnic cleansing, and they did so with a visual demonstration of the New Testament injunction to pray for one's enemy.[6]
2. The plea to "not demonize the perpetrator." An acknowledgment of our complicity in sin and the mandate to let God, not our partisan interests, be the final judge must temper our self-righteous fury. That Serbian Orthodox leaders during the war called for compassion toward Albanians and in June, 1999, urged the ouster of Milosevic is refutation of any Manichean reading

---

6. The incapacity of advocates of an ethics of hell alone to understand, much less honor, the intention of Jackson and his entourage is illustrated by the caustic dismissal of their visit by the editorial writer of *The New Republic*, "Sympathy for the Demon: The Foreign Policy Mischief-making of Jessie Jackson," *The New Republic*, May 24, 1999, 11-12.

of events. And is not Milosevic himself a test of whether we can pray for the soul of a perpetrator?

While no tier is devoid of the desire for humanitarian aid, the ethics of heaven has the clearest eye for the neighbor in need. Especially important is its view of the enemy as well as the innocent. Its advocates will be our conscience in the rebuilding of Kosovo and also the Serbian lands we despoiled, a new Marshall plan with no political strings attached.

Earth

Standing alone, an absolutist ethics of heaven that expects gestures of self-abnegating love to evoke a response in kind, or trusts persuasion to change the lust for power, does not gauge human sin deeply enough. Given sin's imperial tendencies, limits must be set by an ethics of earth. As in domestic matters so in international affairs, this means a place for police presence. The "thin blue line," for all of its own internal problems and corruptibility in a fallen world, is constitutive of civil society, and in the following specific ways in the current crisis:

1. Policing Kosovo and thus providing a peacekeeping force, one of sufficient strength and credibility to assure the return of those refugees who choose to do so. The threat of violence is necessary given the history of Serbian-induced evacuation and extermination. By the same token, the Serbs who continue to live in Kosovo, and the religious sites treasured by the Serbian Orthodox, must also be protected from Albanian reprisals or KLA incursions. The makeup of the force should be guided by principles in accord with an ethics of earth: realism about Albanian fears and possible Serb intentions, and thus a NATO core together with a vision that reflects the higher norm of an international force (U.N. sponsorship and leadership).
2. The foregoing backed up by a second expression of latent violence — the threat of continued NATO action in some form — along with the pursuit of negotiations using whatever effective intermediaries can be recruited. Russia's role continues to be crucial, given its contribution in negotiating the end of the bombing. Realism dictates, however, wariness of both Russia's internal instability and its imperial designs, as seen in Russian forces' unexpected entry into Pristina.
3. The cessation of bombing is an absolute necessity, because the "bully boy" image of NATO, and especially the United States, has planted the seeds of hate for decades to come. The move from patent to latent violence is the contribution of the ethics of earth in Kosovo. The thin blue line functions best when it stands by with big stick in hand, a symbol of law and order.

Hell

Did, and do, the Kosovo crises warrant an ethics of hell? While the ethnic cleansing of a million Albanians is not the inferno of six million Jews, the holocaust survivors and many in the Jewish community were among the first to see the continuities in "ethnic obliteration" and to call for radical response.[7] This was hell and, as such, war is *for* hell. The mounting evidence of mass executions and torture adds to the known uprooting and exile of a whole population, along with the destruction of homes and identity records, and qualifies as "just cause" for the necessary evil of warmaking. The return of the refugees is the commensurate good that "shall outweigh the evils that war will involve." The conditions of "last resort" and "hope for victory" were also met. And a case can be made that the consensus of eighteen nations in the Western community constitutes a version of "lawful authority," although the U.N. would have been closer to this criterion, one that is now in place as supportive of peacekeeping forces.

While war was justified in the Kosovo crisis by most of the classical criteria, the *way* this war was waged collided with a crucial standard of justifiable conflict: high-altitude bombing with its many civilian casualties, other collateral damage, and the devastation of Yugoslavia's infrastructure. Such tactics were of a piece with the "polls morality" to which Western, especially American, decision-making succumbed, a public mind that demanded casualty-free war, associated with refusal to make sacrifices of its own for its professed moral purposes.[8] Time will tell whether this departure has evoked a long-term bitterness that will undo the apparent achievements of the evils of warmaking. And eternity, too, will have its judgments.

Conclusion

Christian decision-making in the Kosovo crises, and any like circumstance, requires a multi-tiered framework. It must include elements of the ethics of heaven — some witness to the ultimate *good* in the being of God; the ethics of earth — the practice of the penultimate *right* in the peacekeeping restraint of evil; and the ethics of hell — the penitent *fit* of counterviolence in the context of radical evil. The first is the conscience that judges and lures beyond themselves lower actions, and reminds us that all swords not turned into plowshares invite the cycle of violence. The second acknowledges the state of our fallen world and translates the final norm of love into the feasible approximations of justice, law,

---

7. See the letter writer in *US News and World Report* 126, no. 24 (June 21, 1999): BC-38.

8. On the temptations of "servility before fact" (Dietrich Bonhoeffer), see Gabriel Fackre, ed., *Judgment Day at the White House* (Grand Rapids: Eerdmans, 1999), pp. 104-5.

and order. The third is an interim ethics, necessary in the worst of circumstances and justified only as a route through the valley of shadows on the way to higher plains.[9]

---

9. A case for a three-tiered ethics can be made on general grounds as well as in the Christian-specific terms used throughout this essay (based on a doctrine of "common grace"). For example, its configuration is paralleled by the coalition of "innovators," "early adopters," and "early majoritarians" that sociologist Robert Hoover's research found necessary for effective institutional change. However, the burden of this essay is to argue for a mind of its own for the Christian community, one that will not succumb to the pragmatics of the moment or the polls of the day.

VII. VOICES FOR THE FUTURE

What Issues Must Be Faced?

The Protectorate

TIMOTHY GARTON ASH

In the village of Velika Hoca — now a Serbian ghetto guarded by Dutch tanks — a woman called Snezana jabbed an angry finger at me. "I don't know where I live any more," she said. "Is it Serbia? Is it Yugoslavia? Is it . . . whatever?"

The correct answer is: whatever. In Kosovo the so-called "international community" has embarked on an extraordinary adventure. We are setting out to build a whole new state, while pretending not to. Even in Somalia or Cambodia, the U.N. never had a job as ambitious and complex as this. Every aspect of a state has to be built literally from ruins. Yet at the same time, because of the ambiguity of the peace deal with Milosevic and the subsequent U.N. Security Council resolution, attention has to be paid to the continued formal sovereignty of the Federal Republic of Yugoslavia over the devastated province.

It's a test case for post–Cold War liberal internationalism. A war justified as a humanitarian intervention leads to an international protectorate, which in turn is supposed to end with a viable, self-governing — um, er — something. How can it possibly work? The job starts with the most elementary necessities of life: water, shelter, food, electricity for heat and light. Crops are destroyed. You see the severed heads of dead cattle along the roads. Rubbish lies all over the place, stinking. It is not cleared, unless the local NATO troops do the job. The troops are also getting the hospitals working again. But the soldiers can't go on doing these jobs. Civilians have to take over. Here, in the essentials of life, we have one major ally: the hardiness and resourcefulness of the Kosovar Albanians. It's incredible — and moving — to see people who have lost their houses, their life savings (usually taken from them by Serb paramilitaries), the equipment, cattle, everything, just starting over with a wry shrug of the shoulders. They're used to adversity. They'll survive — and rebuild.

But some of them are stealing what they need to rebuild; and a few are killing Serbs in revenge. When I was there in early July, there were still virtually no civilian police, although in the northern town of Kosovska Mitrovica, I did meet a spruce colonel of the French Gendarmerie, fresh from Versailles. If you occasionally wonder why we need a state at all, you should visit a place, like Kosovo, that has none. This has advantages, of course. For example, you don't need to worry about speeding fines. But you can also get robbed or killed at night, and no one will take any notice.

Everyone agrees that the top priority at the moment is law and order, which means bringing in international civilian police and appointing judges to support them. Then local police are to be trained: the gendarme from Versailles or the bobby from Liverpool is to patrol the streets side by side with a local cadet. But what laws will they enforce? At the moment, the answer given is: the criminal code of the Federal Republic of Yugoslavia, modified by international human rights conventions when Yugoslaw law violates them.

Then there is the matter of schools for the children who currently line the roadside, selling cigarettes and giving the V-for-Victory sign to any passing Westerner. And what about work for their parents? The economy is central to the prospects of recovery. Here the problems deriving from the ambiguity of status are acute. Cafés, restaurants, and shops may reopen easily enough, but most of the larger companies still have Yugoslav owners. Then, who will set and collect the taxes? And what about border controls and customs duties? And a currency? The D-Mark is the universal unofficial tender. A restaurant owner turns up his nose when my companion offers Yugoslav dinars. A formal currency reform, such as in Bosnia, where the official currency is now the *konvertibilna marka* (exchange rate fixed at one KM to one D-Mark), would be the best thing for the economy. But wouldn't that tear away even the pretense of Yugoslav sovereignty?

Meanwhile, the newly reopened cafés of Pristina are filled with handsome, idealistic, suntanned foreigners — earnest Danes, charming Chileans, quiet Americans. They hardly knew where Kosovo was six months ago; now they are running it. "Hello, we met in Rwanda," they greet each other, or "Weren't you with the OSCE in Kazakhstan?" Their byzantine, polyacronymic structures of international administration are to be superimposed on a "transitional council" of Kosovar Albanians and Serbs, with local consultative commissions for various practical aspects of reconstruction.

Beyond this formal, polit-bureaucratic pattern there is the informal, sometimes inspiring, often corrupting reality of interaction. The names of the military occupation force, KFOR, and the skeleton civilian administration, UNMIK (United Nations Mission in Kosovo), have already become Albanian and Serbian words: UNMIK is pronounced with a short *u*, as in "unpick," and KFOR is pronounced "kufaw," as in "guffaw." Prices of any decent apartments soar. A whole local industry grows up servicing the internationals: restaurants, drivers, interpreters. Blerim Shala, editor of the leading Kosovar Albanian weekly *Zeri*, tells me he is having difficulty getting his journalists to come back to work for him, since they can all earn three times as much working as interpreters for international organizations. Some of the pretty girls among them will get married and start new lives in Stockholm, Paris, or a small town in Texas.

In the longer term, Kosovo simply can't work as a colony. The international architecture alone is far too complicated. There are endless disagreements and turf wars between the international organizations involved, starting with intense rivalries among the U.N.'s own different agencies. There are even greater differences between the participating nation-states, including all those absurd matters of prestige. Thus Britain has the military commander, so France has to get the civilian governor — and poor old Kosovo is lumbered with a Bernard Kouchner. Meanwhile, the Americans are taking a whole street of houses for a 50-strong embassy (sorry, non-embassy) to run the show from behind the scenes. Then, having all stuck their fingers in the pie, the major powers will all lose interest before the job is done, as domestic political priorities turn elsewhere.

The key to making this unprecedented experiment work, therefore, lies in enabling the Kosovars to govern themselves — as much as possible, as soon as possible. Full, formal independence is not the most urgent thing. That must and can wait until Serbia itself becomes more democratic and cooperative, and perhaps even longer. What matters is giving substance to those "democratic self-rule institutions" to which even Milosevic has already agreed. One great advantage here, as against Bosnia, is that the vast majority of the population is of one nationality. Even special minority privileges for the few remaining Serbs — and there is, ironically enough, a case for such privileges — will not change that.

The great problem is the fissiparous nature of Albanian politics. Already this small territory with fewer than two million people has one unofficial president, two unofficial prime ministers, and at least five political parties or proto-parties. (Another one was founded, or relaunched, while I was there.) For the Kosovars themselves, this is an historic test. There is a real danger that they will prove incapable of taking over to govern themselves in a halfway organized, civilized fashion. And, as we all know, long-term dependency breeds irresponsibility.

So I find myself, over an evening drink with a sophisticated British official, discussing whether old Rugova can still pull the votes; whether something can be made of young Thaci; or if Kosumi might be a "player" after all. Almost as my grandfather, who was an imperial civil servant in India, must have sat on a verandah in Delhi in 1929, wondering what old Gandhi was up to, and if young Nehru could be brought on.

It's a rum way to begin the twenty-first century.

"Peacekeeping" in Kosovo: Mission Impossible?

JULIE MERTUS

NATO, welcome to Kosovo. Kosovars have been waiting for you and the entire international community for a long time. Now the hard work can begin.

Bombing Milosevic into agreeing to pull out of Kosovo was nothing compared to what has to come next. Dropping bombs from the air did not require the kind of ingenuity that creating a peaceful and just society will. The creators of the Kosovo peace plan have not made the task easy for the incoming peacekeepers. On the contrary, the latter are asked to accomplish the impossible: to maintain the illusion that the two sides have agreed to a peace. Both Albanians and Serbs claim victory in Kosovo. This can only be so because both sides have diametrically opposed views as to the future.

Serbs think that they have won because Kosovo will remain part of Yugoslavia. In their view, the international peacekeepers will ensure that Kosovo Albanians do not break away. In the past, Serbs could only keep control over Kosovo through gross and systemic human rights abuses directed against Albanians. They think that international peacekeepers will permit them to maintain control over Kosovo Albanians by law.

Albanians think they have won because they will be able to return to their homes. In their view, international peacekeepers will ensure that they have human rights, including the right to decide their own political destiny. In the past they established illegal, "parallel" Albanian institutions in order to exercise some semblance of control over their political destiny. When they grew tired of enduring Serbian oppression, some Albanians took up arms. They think that international peacekeepers will permit them to create their own institutions to govern their lives.

These two viewpoints cannot be reconciled. Serbs living in Kosovo know this; that is why many of them are leaving the territory as fast as they possibly can. Kosovo Albanians know this as well; that is why many of them are already planning for either a referendum on the independence of Kosovo or a future war. Many international relief agencies also understand that they have been asked to help construct an unlikely peace. Relief agencies think in practical terms about two things: assistance and protection. Neither can be satisfactorily achieved under the present scenario. Postwar assistance efforts will include the provision of emergency food and housing within Kosovo, de-mining of roads and fields, purification of wells, and a massive reconstruction of roads, homes, and offices. None of this can be achieved, however, without Belgrade's permission.

Belgrade will still effectively control Yugoslavia's (and thus Kosovo's) borders, imports of goods, and international bank transfers. It will regulate the activities of local and foreign companies and nongovernmental organizations. As anyone who has worked in Kosovo in the past knows, this means that Belgrade can use its control over these factors to meddle in the work of any outsider, from the World Bank to the small, grassroots conflict-resolution group. Doing humanitarian work in Kosovo has always meant "giving in a little to Belgrade," for example, by building the hospital in a Serbian village rather than an Albanian village (even though under 10 percent of the people of Kosovo are Serbian). There is no reason to suspect Belgrade will suddenly permit international organizations to work freely in Kosovo.

Postwar protection efforts will require the establishment of institutions and mechanisms to ensure the legal rights and physical security of all people. This will entail the creation of human rights monitoring groups, the protection of minority rights, and the formation of a well-trained and just police force. Democracy requires citizen participation, transparency, and accountability in government operations. Again, however, Belgrade holds the reins to the accomplishment of these objectives through its control over the conduct of local and international organizations. The main deficit of the peace proposal accepted by Serbs is that Kosovar Albanians will be returned to a land still overseen by Belgrade. Perhaps this could have been acceptable before, but not after all of the deportations and killings. Kosovars can tell you what autonomy within Serbia or Yugoslavia means. For them, it means a future of continued oppression.

I am thinking of the many families who lost children in Serbian shelling campaigns — not this year but last year, when NATO was not involved in the war. I am thinking about the old man who was released from a prison camp less than two weeks ago who stutters when he talks about his own brutal torture and the killing of his sons. I am thinking about the boy who sobs uncontrollably at the sight of any military uniform. I am thinking of the mothers who talk about their children watching their fathers and uncles and brothers being pulled out of a line and gunned down in ditches. Try telling them that it is perfectly acceptable to go home and live under the people who destroyed their lives. And then, lest we forget, most people's homes no longer exist. Telling people to "go home" is not so simple. I challenge people who support the quick return of refugees to explain how people will live in Kosovo after their homes, livestock, shops, and markets have all been ravaged. Not only has property been devastated, but fields and roads have been heavily mined, wells poisoned and water systems destroyed, and the infrastructure gutted. I challenge the international community to continue their level of support and concern through an extensive regional reconstruction period.

Kosovar children had a hard time going to school before the war. Today their schools no longer exist and the fields in which they played are littered with explosives. Women faced overwhelming obstacles in taking care of themselves and their families before the war; now many of them are widows, survivors of sexual torture and other violence, and in great need of medical and psychological support. Before the war, unemployed young men were fed up with the old Kosovar strategy of "passive resistance," and some began to take up arms. When they return, there will be even fewer jobs and greater reasons for them to exact revenge.

The international peacekeepers have one thing on their side: force. But force cannot create a just society. Only people working together can create a just society. For any peace to work, at a minimum both sides must share a common understanding of what comes next. Serbs and Albanians have never been farther apart, especially in light of the events in the last eleven weeks.

The international community needs to level with itself and with the people of the Balkans. It is in fact creating a protectorate that paves the way for Kosovar self-determination. What is needed is sober analysis that contributes to a fuller understanding of the problems that lie ahead as the protectorate unfolds. For reconstruction to work, internationals must coordinate all stages of humanitarian intervention — from registration of humanitarian groups to imports of goods to transfers of finances. And for any peace to have a chance, Kosovar women and men should be involved in all stages of peacemaking, peacekeeping, and reconstruction. If this entire effort is to be done on behalf of Kosovar Albanians for humanitarian reasons, the least we can do is respect their right to participate actively in the rebuilding of their lives, as well as their right to refuse to return to an unsafe land.

Baltimore, June 1999

Montenegro Pushes for Statehood

JANUSZ BUGAJSKI

July 27, 1999

In the shadow of the Kosova conflict, a new crisis has been brewing in the remnants of Yugoslavia that could complete the dissolution of this failing state. With renewed vigor, the republic of Montenegro is pushing for self-determination and economic independence. Meanwhile, internationally isolated Serbia has been fast descending toward political chaos and a possible civil war.

For the Montenegrin government of President Milo Djukanovic, sovereignty from Belgrade has become a question of political and economic survival. The proposals lodged by Podgorica in its negotiations with Belgrade, calling for a restructured "confederation," seemed like a last attempt at decentralizing power in post-Titoist Yugoslavia. A cross section of Montenegrin politicians and intellectuals concur that it is not possible to build a democratic Montenegro within an autocratic Yugoslavia run by indicted war criminals.

The confederation proposal lodged by the Djukanovic government appeared to be a political cover for an eventual referendum on national independence. In recent months, a team of leading Montenegrin academics, led by economist Veselin Vukotic, has drafted a blueprint for economic sovereignty. But its basic premises are likely to be unacceptable to Belgrade.

The program calls for fiscal independence through the introduction of a separate Montenegrin currency, the creation of an internationally monitored currency board to control state spending, full control by Montenegro over its own budget, accelerated privatization, and far-reaching legal reforms to encourage foreign investment.

This virtual declaration of economic independence also includes some crucial political and security demands that have outraged Belgrade. These involve constitutional reforms to balance power in all "confederal" institutions, Montenegrin control over any Yugoslav army units stationed on its territory, and full Montenegrin supervision of the country's borders.

The mood for independence has been rising in Montenegro in the wake of the Kosova war and the NATO victory over Serbia. Djukanovic and his previously

441

hesitant government were clearly testing the waters for public support. In recent opinion polls, some 70 percent of the population declared that they would back the administration if it opted for independence or manages to negotiate a confederation arrangement, and only 12 percent of Montenegrins were in favor of preserving the status quo.

For the political leadership in Podgorica, economic and political independence is now imperative. If Montenegro is unable to detach its economy from that of Serbia, it will be dragged into an economic tailspin, its chances of obtaining any substantial foreign assistance through the planned international South East European Stability Pact will remain slim, its goal of joining the process of European Union integration will be postponed, and foreign investors and tourists will stay clear of the country.

The alternative to independence may not be "confederation" but comprehensive absorption by the Serbian state. For Milosevic and for Serbia's political and military elites keeping Montenegro in a centrally controlled "federation" is much more important than controlling Kosova. Without Montenegro, Serbia becomes a medium-sized, landlocked country without a navy and with little room for maneuver in the region.

Even more ominously for President Milosevic, without Montenegro Yugoslavia ceases to exist, and so does the federal presidency. Indeed, by declaring independence Montenegro will actually remove Milosevic from office — something that the Serbian opposition and the international community are now committed to achieving. Hence, paradoxically, Montenegro could bring democracy to Serbia by detaching itself from Yugoslavia and allowing Serbia to focus on its own internal reforms.

To prevent such a scenario, Milosevic has kept several potential tricks up his sleeve. First, he could try to engineer a military coup in Podgorica. But this will meet with substantial armed resistance from Montenegro's specially trained and 15,000 strong police forces loyal to Djukanovic.

Second, Belgrade could provoke ethnic tensions with Albanian and Muslim minorities through provocations engineered by Serb paramilitaries relocated from Kosova. But this may also precipitate an armed conflict with the Montenegrin police and could actually provoke a civil war. Djukanovic remains dependent on Albanian and Muslim support to maintain his coalition government.

Third, Milosevic may offer Djukanovic a new political deal in which his party (the Democratic Party of Socialists) would nominate the next Yugoslav federal Prime Minister after the removal from that office of former Montenegrin president Momir Bulatovic, a bitter rival of Djukanovic. However, if Djukanovic were tempted to accept such an arrangement not only would he sever his close ties with Serbia's oppositionist Alliance for Change but Montenegro's coalition government could quickly dissolve. In the midst of the ensuing political paralysis, Milosevic could engineer some new "state of emergency" and implant his own loyalists in Podgorica.

An armed conflict in Montenegro, provoked by Belgrade, could rapidly spiral into an all-out civil war between "greens" (traditional pro-independence lobbies) and "whites" (pro-Serbian forces) as well as between diverse political factions. Such a conflict may not be containable inside Montenegro and could quickly spread to Serbia itself. Indeed, if the peaceful protests in Serbia fail to dislodge the current regime from power, then a bloody civil war may prove to be the only alternative and Montenegro could provide the spark in the coming conflagration.

Some observers believe that Podgorica may have missed its chance for statehood by failing to declare Montenegrin independence during the war over Kosova. This would have enabled the country to automatically gain NATO protection against Yugoslav military and Serbian paramilitary formations. It may prove exceedingly difficult for the Atlantic Alliance to restart a bombing campaign against Belgrade even though Montenegro obtained a non-specific pledge of protection from NATO Secretary-General Javier Solana.

However, the international community is not helpless in these circumstances. NATO's employment in both Bosnia and Kosova has set a precedent for protecting the Montenegrins who may face a new round of centrally planned "ethnic cleansing" if they decide on statehood. Above all, Milosevic should not receive another "green light" for aggression because NATO publicly discounts the use of force.

The regime in Belgrade, whose leaders have been indicted for war crimes, should not be permitted to obstruct the progress of either Montenegro or Kosova toward stability and European integration because of their own isolationist and anti-reformist policies. To forestall a Serbian attack and to put pressure on Belgrade, a Dayton or Rambouillet type conference may need to be arranged for Montenegro.

If the popularly elected Montenegrin government chooses independence because of Serb intransigence, then the international community must promptly recognize the legitimacy of the new state and the illegitimacy of Yugoslavia. This may be the only way to finally dislodge Milosevic from power.

Some Reflections beneath the Bombs in Belgrade

SVETOZAR STOJANOVIC

International Community or Selfish Empire?

Since the collapse of communism and the Soviet Union, an ideology has been dominating the West, primarily in the United States: it combines a triumphalist self-evaluation about the "end of history" with a vulgarized pragmatism toward the rest of the world. It is a "pragmatism" that is characterized by basically changing the approach "from case to case." In cases that are virtually identical, Western powers have employed opposite "principles" that they tacitly or even explicitly justify by invoking the interests of the state or group of states using them. If that does not constitute the double standards of nationalism in action, I do not know what does. Depending on whether the existence of a state suits dominant circles in the West or not, the West supports within that state either the civic principle of "one citizen, one vote" or the demand of cultural-ethnic groups for political-territorial autonomy, special status, and even full secession. Illustrations of the former are Turkey, with its persecuted Kurds, and Croatia, with its hundreds of thousands of local Serbs "ethnically cleansed" and forced to flee to Serbia in 1995; an example of the latter is the case of the Albanians in Serbia's Kosmet (the proper name of the combination of Kosovo and Metohija). While NATO, led by the United States, has turned a blind eye on the repressive policies of Turkey and Croatia, it has militarily attacked Serbia. Is the United States now going to give an ultimatum to Croatia to allow those Serbs to return and accept NATO troops as the guarantor of their safety — or else face the bombing?

In order to cover up its own nationalism of double standards, the U.S. administration has been promoting "postmodernist" asymmetries, contradictions, and simulations regarding some states' sovereignty and territorial integrity. Thus Bosnia-Herzegovina, through the Dayton agreement, became a big simulacrum of one state that in reality consists of three separate states "united" only by the NATO troops and protectorate. Another example is the Clinton administration's attempt to sell to the Serbs and the rest of the world a de facto separatist arrangement for

Kosmet under the *formal* disguise of its political-territorial autonomy within Serbia. The distinction between "national majority" and "national minority" has also become misleading in many instances. Namely, due to the external support of NATO, a minority may become more influential and powerful than a majority in a country. How about the rights of majorities?

I don't see any practical proofs of NATO's repeated proclamation that it is not attacking the Serbian people but only the ruling regime. And Western mass media have made a crucial "contribution" to NATO's collective demonization of the Serbian nation. Here is an illustration from a recent op-ed piece by Thomas L. Friedman in *The New York Times* (April 23, 1999): "Like it or not, we are at war with the Serbian nation (the Serbs certainly think so), and the stakes have to be very clear: Every week you ravage Kosovo is another decade we will set your country back by pulverizing you. You want 1950? We can do 1950. You want 1389? We can do 1389 too."

Many intellectuals use the category "international community" unreservedly. Any genuine community ought to be characterized by equality and solidarity instead of force and selfishness. When intellectuals follow the power structure closely, including its obvious contradictions, caprices, and hypocrisies, they lose their political, intellectual, and moral autonomy and credibility. Because there is currently no true counterweight to the power of the West — and especially to that of the United States — the West's own self-restraint should be of utmost importance. How realistic is it, however, to expect this at the West's power climax? After all, as Karl Deutsch stated, "Power is the ability to afford not to learn." As a rule, such power has historically led to moral decadence in the long run. Let us therefore slightly edit Lord Acton's famous dictum and say: Global power corrupts — and absolute global power corrupts absolutely.

Election competition for power and influence in nation-states unfortunately favors those who have a short-term and parochial perspective instead of a long-term and global one. They arrogantly impose Western views and interests on the whole world and are by no means prepared for self-criticism, empathy, and cooperation on equal footing with others. Instead of acting as checks and balances of sorts, the overwhelming majority of Western mass media "patriotically" support and encourage such leaders. The body of human, civil, and national rights has been playing a big part in the humanization and democratization of capitalism, and in the criticism and destruction of communism. However, those rights have also been applied by the West to justify its own domination in the world. Western mass media are the main hothouse for the pop ideology of such rights. Even more than their own governments, they suffer from a reckless superficiality in the name of those rights when dealing with other states.

In the West a sense of the present increasingly predominates as the basic disposition of prosperous capitalism and its mass culture. I am referring to the fixation on immediacy and a total disregard for the past, particularly that of other nations — thus the irresistible temptation to extrapolate the future merely from a here and now without history. For a true understanding of the present and an anticipation of the future, we need an in-depth (and not the prevailing shallow) cartography and cartoanalysis. What I mean is many-layered maps of states and their mutual borders that bring to the fore linguistic, religious, ethnic, and cultural sediments and faults — including war and genocide. The domination of electronic media over print, of images over words, both reflects and strengthens this present-oriented state of mind. The mass media even attempt to create what from their standpoint is desired reality by means of "informing" — let us call it "inform(cre)ation."

The West has no valid justification for behaving arrogantly since it is no exception to the rule of the contradictory character of civilizations' traditions and identities. The West means not only humanism, democracy, division of power, the rule of law, and respect for human, civil, and national rights; it also means genocide, colonialism, slave-owning, Nazism, aggression, and disrespect for those rights. Unfortunately, the West is continuously elated by the "realism" of its new-versus-old world order, comparing it with former Soviet leader Mikhail Gorbachev's naive "new thinking" and the expectation that he would be reciprocated by humanist globalism. Can we hope for a Western Mr. Gorbachev to appear, someone who would successfully resist mass egoism and triumphalism to help us all establish a new humanist world order based on the United Nations and not NATO? Rich democratic-capitalist countries are far more willing to dictate standards and methods of internal transformation to other countries than to commit any significant portion of their riches to help them. This is an attempt at social engineering from the outside, and at an extremely low cost to oneself. If things continue to unfold in this direction, neo-communist accusations of the future are likely to characterize the West as a vast "selfish empire" — an updated echo of Ronald Reagan's 1980s charge ("evil empire") against the Soviet Union.

A Long-term Solution for Kosmet

A somewhat overlooked potential long-term solution for the Kosmet problem, only occasionally mentioned and argued for in the West, involves some sort of partition. The idea was actually launched almost twenty years ago by Dobrica Cosic, arguably the most prominent living Serbian author and former president of Yugoslavia (between mid-1992 and mid-1993), who was removed by Milosevic. The partition idea envisions one part remaining within Serbia, with the other part allowed to *gradually* separate after several preconditions are met. First, the Serbian Orthodox Church would once again take possession of the tens of thousand of hectares of land confiscated by the communist state after World War II; second, tens of thousands of Serbs forced out of Kosmet by Albanian Nazis during that war (and forbidden by the communist government in 1945 to return there) would have to be compensated for their property and suffering. Unfortunately, the U.S. administration — in tacit cooperation with Mr. Milosevic — has prevented representatives of the Serbian Orthodox Church and those Serbian refugees to participate in the Kosmet negotiations. Representatives of both groups will have to be included if and when a new round of negotiations begins. Finally, some sort of compensation has to be worked out for the non-Albanian taxpayers for the several billions of dollars they have invested in Kosmet since 1945.

Serbs in Yugoslavia are generally unaware of the partition idea. They might receive it with some enthusiasm if it were part of a broader solution based on national self-determination. Namely, it is becoming increasingly clear that the redrawing of the internal administrative borders should not have been prevented when the Socialist Federal Republic of Yugoslavia (SFRY) started unraveling in 1991. The territorially concentrated populations should have been allowed to secede and join their mother countries. Thus the regions of Croatia and Bosnia-Herzegovina with majority Serb populations should have been allowed to join Serbia; Croats in Bosnia-Herzegovina should have been allowed to join Croatia (and consequently there would have been an independent Muslim state between greater Serbia and greater Croatia); Macedonia would have been smaller than it is today because the Albanian minority in its western part (where it is a majority), together with the two-thirds of Kosmet in Serbia, would have been allowed to join Albania (greater Albania). Naturally, none of those states could or should have been allowed to become "ethnically pure," but only states with overwhelming ethnic majorities.

Should Kosovo-Metohia Remain a Part of Serbia/Yugoslavia? A Plea for a Just Solution

SLOBODAN SAMARDZIC

The military intervention of NATO forces with disastrous human and material consequences to all citizens of the Federal Republic of Yugoslavia and deployment of international forces in Kosovo-Metohia has merely postponed resolution of the basic problem, which is the political status of this province. The formula to which the international community stuck, from the first version of the American proposal (known as the Hill proposal) in late September 1998 until the Resolution of the Security Council on the solution of the Kosovo crisis of 10 June 1999, reflects neither the essence nor the depth of the conflict. That formula contains two benign provisions — territorial integrity for the Federal Republic of Yugoslavia and wide autonomy for Kosovo — the reality of which is not trusted by anyone. Whereas the Serbs would be inclined to accept this formula even if they only believed that its second provision, wide autonomy for Kosovo, would not actually lead to secession of the province, it is refused by the Albanians because it does not guarantee to them exactly what the Serbs are most afraid of — the actual prospect of secession. Although it may seem strange to those unfamiliar with the problem, the awesome consequences of military operations have not changed one whit the strategic positions of the two parties in conflict. When the time comes for negotiations on the "interim political solution," as set forth in Annex 1 of the said SC Resolution, each party, no matter who represents them, will keep resolutely its original position. The decisive factor will be which party's strategic interests will be favored by the "international community" at the expense of the other party. Here the Serbs have many more reasons to be worried because the main mediator, the United States, has for a long time stayed on the Albanians' side.

If the negotiations on the interim political solution are kept within the terms of the Rambouillet document, which is unequivocally pointed out by the SC Resolution, Kosovo will be separated from Serbia's legal system and de facto divided from the Federal Republic of Yugoslavia. That would not be a just solution and therefore could not be accepted by the Serbs. As clearly stated by an American analyst having in mind the first two versions of the American plan: "Thus the American plan for Kosovo would foster the illusion of Kosovo's continuation within Yugoslavia, while ensuring that republican and federal authorities would be unable to exercise any authority in Kosovo."[1]

On the other hand, the Albanians are not ready to accept any arrangement that would imply high standards of minority protection, the status of regional autonomy for Kosovo, and the democratization of Serbia and the federation. In their determination, they have been guided not only by repression under Milosevic's regime in the last ten years but, much more than that, by the teleology of sovereignty they have been following for the last hundred and twenty years.[2] Their political goals in this long period have been characterized exactly by this constant: aspiration to state sovereignty on an ethnic basis in the region of Kosovo-Metohia. That constant can be traced from the First League of Prizren (1878) to the present day. Since the time when this region came under the sovereignty of Serbia in 1912, that is, from the war that Serbia waged against Turkey to the present day, the ethnic Albanians have been continuously disloyal to the state. In the period between the two world wars, all legal associations of ethnic Albanians in Yugoslavia served the cause of Albanian irredenta.[3] During the Italian fascist occupation of the Kosovo-Metohia region, the Albanians accepted en masse a satellite form of Greater Albania in order to attain their historical goals. When Italy capitulated in 1943, they founded the Second League of Prizren with the same objectives regarding Kosovo-Metohia, but this time under the auspices of the military intelligence service of the German Abwher. The comparatively slight participation of ethnic Albanians in the partisan guerrilla movement was exclusively politically motivated by an open prospect of union with the future communist Albania under Enver Hoxha. Their loyalty to communist Yugoslavia was stipulated with the autonomy of Kosovo-Metohia, including state attributes, which they have begun to achieve since 1968. Although this province, now renamed Kosovo, achieved constitutional status almost identical to that of federal republics, inclusively in 1974, they continued to fight for the "Kosovo Republic," as well as for constitutional status as a constitutive people. This has been done in two parallel ways — legal and illegal. The latter was rhetorically tied to Marxist-Leninist ideology, and politically to the Enver Hoxha regime in Albania. Both these fronts united in 1981, resulting in the late 1980s and 1990s in a completely new liberal rhetoric regarding human rights, democracy, and pro-Western orientation. Now, following destruction brought by the war,

1. See Robert M. Hayden, "The State as Legal Fiction," *East European Constitutional Review* 7, no 4 (1998): 47.

2. I have taken the expression "teleology of sovereignty," which precisely points to the continuity of several decades in political strategy of the Kosovo Albanians, from a paper by Milan Kovacevic published before Milosevic came to power in Serbia. See the article "Kosovski procentni racun" (The Kosovo Percentage Calculation), in *Theoria*, Belgrade, nos. 3-4, 1987, p. 87.

3. See Dimitrije Bogdanovic, *Knjiga o Kosovu* (A Book on Kosovo) (Beograd: SANU, 1986), p. 191

along with its mass victims and waves of refugees, Albanians are expecting from Western states, primarily from the United States, an award for their several decades-long struggles and suffering. Almost everything has changed; only their teleology of sovereignty has remained the same.

Under the present circumstances, the biggest problem for the Serbians is the undemocratic nature of the regime. This fact even now, as it was ten years ago, defines all disputes in the state, and to the highest degree the gravest one — the Serbo-Albanian dispute regarding the sovereignty of Kosovo-Metohia. The nature of such a regime is such that it will attempt to "resolve" all disputes with repressive mechanisms, thus deepening them even more. This is not to say that democratization of Serbia and Yugoslavia would solve the age-old Serbo-Albanian conflict. That is a comfortable illusion fostered by Western states when mediating in the resolution of foreign disputes. The Rambouillet document is a fancy illusion. Complying with its provisions, the Federal Republic of Yugoslavia would not function in Kosovo even with the least of its competencies. Thus a responsible analyst may conclude with the following question and the consequent responses to it: "Can a dysfunctional state provide an environment in which a democratic system can develop? It is difficult to imagine positive answers to such a question. Yet if they cannot be answered affirmatively, the whole policy of building fictive states in the Balkans is counterproductive, at least insofar as the goals really do include security, stability, and democracy for the peoples living there."[4]

But if democracy cannot solve this problem, it certainly can cultivate the manner in which it should be resolved. Here, too, the mediator in the form of international community is as responsible as the two sides in conflict. This at least means that the interests of both parties should be taken into account and that the solution should be looked for in a compromise. If the goal of this process is to arrive at a democratic solution, then such a goal is too abstract unless it is instrumental in arriving at other goals, because neither party would accept a democratic solution if it were not also just. And only that solution can be just which meets the interests of both parties even if they willingly give up their maximal, that is, ideal demands.

In the endeavor to arrive at a just solution, it is necessary to start with the nature of the conflict. It has been most aptly expressed by a Serbian analyst who argues that the essence of the matter is the conflict between historical (Serbian) and ethnic (Albanian) rights.[5] Kosovo-Metohia is the heart of the medieval Serbian state, the cradle of Serbian culture and national identity. It abounds in medieval cultural monuments (67 monuments of category 1 and 2 under UNESCO classification, as well as an enormous number of category 3 monuments, 80 percent of which were built before the sixteenth century), testifying to the historical continu-

4. Hayden, "The State as Legal Fiction," p. 50.
5. See Branislav Krstic, *Kosovo izmedu istorijskog i etnickog prava* (Kosovo between Historical and Ethnic Rights) (Belgrade: Kuca Vid, 1994).

ity of state and cultural life of the Serbian people in this region. On the other hand, according to the census of 1991 Kosovo-Metohia is populated with about 81 percent ethnic Albanians and only about 10 percent Serbs. While the ethnic Albanians claim their right to an independent Kosovo on the basis of this demographic fact, the Serbs claim Kosovo as part of Serbia on the basis of historical fact. During the whole of the twentieth century the conflict between these two peoples was based on the irreconcilability of these two facts.

The basic problem in the Western understanding of this conflict lies in its untranslatability into the lexicon of modern democracy and modern international law. Neither historical nor ethnic rights are easily translatable legally and politically. What arrangement of the solution, which necessarily must have its legal form, would be suitable to such a definition of this conflict? The internal protagonists (Serbians and ethnic Albanians) and the international community have been going in opposite directions. They have proceeded from familiar legal and political arrangements with the intention of applying the most appropriate as a solution to the case in point. Thus in the last few years there has emerged a whole spectrum of proposals for the solution of this problem: the creation of an autonomous province within Serbia, minority rights for ethnic Albanians complying with the highest international standards without a special territorial autonomy, regionalization of Serbia and Kosovo-Metohia as one or two regions within this framework, reinstatement of the status of the province from 1974, the secession of Kosovo, and the creation of an independent state of ethnic Albanians. In most recent times, giving special status to Kosovo within FRY without ties with Serbia or making Kosovo a third federal unit within FRY has been proposed.

However, it is certain that none of these solutions would satisfy both parties in the conflict, or, to be more precise, in any of the said solutions a clear advantage is granted to one party. Customary logic based on international and public law would require consistent implementation of the existing standards of minority protection, with possible recommendation for regionalization of Serbia, but the Albanians would feel that their "ethnic rights" were denied. Contrary to that, in recent years the dominant political logic in the international community, using as the point of departure the repression by the Serbian regime of ethnic Albanians, demands such a degree of political autonomy for Kosovo-Metohia, which would mean the freedom of this region from the legal system of Serbia, violation of its territorial integrity, and giving hopes to ethnic Albanians for a later secession from Yugoslavia too. Thus the Serbs would feel that their "historical rights" are denied.

If the great international arranger would then say that historical and ethnic rights are not operative categories in terms of international law, he would certainly be right, but the problem would not be solved, for behind these non-legal categories lies the essence of the dispute. This is a collision of two "non-legal rights," two collective existences that mutually exclude and deny each other.

What, then, would be the solution that would be closest to the nature (essence) of the conflict? The two aforementioned rights are in dispute not only in the specific territory, but also about the said territory. For the Albanians it involves living space in which they have demographically prevailed, but exactly on this account they need full political independence to arrange it according to their will and rules. For the Serbs it primarily concerns an area of concentrated repositories of national culture, threatened by Albanian demographic expansion. These are two fundamental reasons for the attachment of these two peoples to the same territory and for their feeling mutually threatened. The Serbs fear that they are going to lose this area in a possible aftermath to this decades-long dispute, while the more numerous ethnic Albanians, encountering at each step Serbian cultural monuments and Serbian toponyms, feel a collective embarrassment of living on other people's sacred land and therefore an uncertain existence as long as even the tiniest degree of Serbian authority encompasses this region.

Bearing this in mind, a just solution would be one implying simultaneously gain and sacrifice on both sides. As two rights are in dispute regarding the territory on which they would be sovereignly exercised, a just solution would include a partition of the territory.

This proposal entails many problems. Two of them, however, are major ones: first, how to redefine territorially the present-day province of Kosovo-Metohia and on the basis of what criteria; and, second, how thereby to comply with, that is, not to violate, the principles and norms of human rights and of international law as well.

1. Only a division that would meet the condition of relative territorial wholeness of the areas containing Serbian cultural monuments, on the one hand, and the condition of compactness of space of Albanian political autonomy, on the other hand, would be able to satisfy the interests of both parties to a sufficient degree. Two key criteria result therefrom: first, the territorial location of cultural monuments, not only the Serbians' but also the Albanians', and, second, the ethnic structure of the population, not only of the Albanians but also of the Serbs. The next two criteria would concern material values: first, the criterion of ownership of the land — individual, corporate (church-owned), and state-owned; and, second, the criterion of disposition of industrial facilities.[6]

What would be the epilogue if these criteria of territorial redefinition were to be implemented? Serbia would have to give up its sovereignty over a part of the Kosovo-Metohia territory. Thus a small portion of Serbian cultural monuments would cease to be under its direct care. In return, a considerable part of this area would be permanently secured from immediate Albanian environment. In that part of present-day Kosovo, Serbia would be able to exercise its cultural, spatial, and demographic policies without opposition from the Albanians. In order to in-

---

6. Branislav Krstic formulated the first three criteria in the said book and on this basis suggested four concrete steps in the redefinition of the Kosovo-Metohia territory, providing appropriate maps. See ibid., pp. 207-30.

tegrate its cultural and historical area of utmost importance, it would have to estrange part of its territory. On that part of Kosovo-Metohia the Albanians would achieve their right to self-determination without any conditions. In a word, they would be able to enjoy complete political autonomy there. Their compatriots on the part of the territory under Serbia's jurisdiction would be able to opt to move to the territory with full autonomy or to stay with guarantees of minority rights. The same right to option would be granted to the Serbs on the territory under Albanian autonomy. The Kosovo Albanians would not solve the problem of space, at least not as complete population, but in the given territory they would solve the problem of their political autonomy, within which they would search for an autonomous solution to their demographic problem. Someday it could be an independent state with the possibility of uniting with Albania.

2. With such territorial division of Kosovo-Metohia, it would be far easier to secure human and minority rights. In other words, that would be integral to the process of democratization. That process would be free from laborious state issues that have directly affected the state of human rights in Serbia, and particularly in Kosovo. The regime in Serbia would no longer have an ongoing alibi for its undemocratic policy, while the Albanian national movement would no longer be able to present their secessionist policy as a struggle for human rights.

International law would not be violated in the wake of possible and probable change of state boundaries. As is well known, state boundaries are inviolable but not unchangeable. They may be changed only through the mutual agreement of the parties in conflict. The representatives of the Kosovo Albanians do not in fact have the capacity based on international law to negotiate in this case. But then the international community, represented by some of its organizations (U.N., OSCE, and EU), would be the guarantor of such an agreement.

However, this would create an unfavorable precedent. Why should the problem of the political status of an ethnic community be resolved through territorial concessions? Could not then the Albanians in Macedonia, or the Turks in Bulgaria, or perhaps the Hungarians in Transylvania (Romania) pose the same demands? It should be stated here that Serbia and Yugoslavia do not need this precedent. Viewed in comparison, both legally and politically it would be most correct to grant the Albanians status after the model of the status of other minorities in the Balkans, in Europe, and in the world. And that status does not assume political and territorial autonomy as a special right. The Albanians in Serbia, however, tie their rights directly to the status of a particular territory, Kosovo-Metohia. This is the heritage of the former communist Yugoslavia, which they not only do not wish to be deprived of but want to raise to the level of independent statehood. And this is the fundamental precedent that is nowadays widely supported in international politics. Serbia and FRY have failed in their fight against this precedent. In time it has acquired an internal and an external validity. The whole construction with the partition of the Kosovo territory as a just solution proceeds from the experience of this precedent.

Why Kosova Should Be Independent

SHKËLZEN MALIQI

After NATO's intervention and the withdrawal of Serb troops from Kosova, new circumstances were created for the resolution of a long-lasting crisis. This is reflected not only in present and future relations between Albanians and Serbs but in overall regional security as well. It is understood that Kosova's status will be an interim status. For the moment, no one knows how long international military and civilian control will last in Kosova. The immediate objectives of NATO's intervention in Kosova are clear and consist of three major operations: the return of the expelled Albanians in Kosova; creating conditions for a normal life for all citizens; and establishing democratic institutions and self-rule in Kosova.

The first two objectives seem to be more technical and operational. The realization of both will be difficult in terms of the length of time and the maintenance of security, but not conceptually. On the other hand, the objective of establishing self-governing institutions, which at first seems clear and achievable, in reality deals with the same flashpoints that have characterized the Kosova crisis for years as an insoluble and dangerous conflict — not only for Serb-Albanian relations but for the security of the whole region. The building of self-governing institutions in Kosova is always tied to the status of Kosova. At first these institutions will be under the auspices of an interim international administration. During and after this interim period, the crucial issue will be the relations between the administrative unit of Kosova and Serbia/Yugoslavia. Will Kosova remain within the present Serb-Montenegro Federation, or will it be an independent entity?

According to the agreement reached at the peace conference in Rambouillet, Kosova must remain within Yugoslavia. Yet Rambouillet is neither the best nor the most preferred solution. After the full withdrawal of Serb forces from Kosova, reintegrating Kosova with Serbia/Yugoslavia recomplicates an issue that both sides consider resolved. The Serbs consider Kosova practically lost, while the Albanians think that they are triumphant and will do anything to prevent attempts to reintegrate it within Serbia/Yugoslavia. The Albanians, as the majority in Kosova, do not

---

This essay was translated from the Albanian by Lindita Imami.

insist on unconditional independence from Serbia/Yugoslavia. Their arguments, however, about why Kosova should be independent are more convincing than the arguments Belgrade might raise against independence.

Since 1912 and the Treaty of Versailles, the Serbs have had time and opportunity to ensure more effective control of Kosova but have not found the way to do so. In fact, they have demonstrated quite the opposite: the inability to integrate Kosova into their state. Their last attempt to reign over Kosova with violence, total repression, and finally ethnocide proved to be a failure. The Serbs were successful in expelling one million Albanians by applying the strategy of torching lands and destroying everything they had the opportunity to destroy. Now this has come back to them like a boomerang. With NATO's intervention in Kosova and the withdrawal of Serb military and paramilitary forces from Kosova, the majority of the Serb civilian population has left. The demographics that were once 9:1 in favor of the Albanians is now 19:1 (as of this writing in July 1999). What do the Serbs want in such a demographic ratio besides the full respect of their cultural rights and the protection of their historical and cultural monuments?

The Albanians, on the other hand, have a series of more convincing arguments in favor of independence. Allow me to mention a few:

1. Kosova is a unique land in all aspects, unique as a geographic entity (a valley surrounded by mountains) and culturally very different from Serbia. The way of life, the customs, the organization of life in cities and villages, the language, and the dominant culture have nothing to do with Serbia. When one crosses the border from Kosova into Serbia, the differences are immediately apparent. Serbia and Kosova are separate lands and belong to two different worlds.

2. The Albanians suffered a historic injustice when the occupation of Kosova was legalized in 1912. Almost half of the Albanian nation has lived and continues to live in Kosova (the other half was allowed to create its own independent state, Albania). On the other hand, the Serb population living in Kosova constitutes only 1 percent of the overall Serb population in the Balkans. If the redrawing of the map of former Yugoslavia is based on the principle of ethnic territory, dictated in the most militant terms by Belgrade, it would be an extraordinary anomaly for Kosova to be forced to be under Serb sovereignty.

3. The Serbs have never been able to develop a reasonable policy based on neighborly relations and equality with the Albanians. For the Albanians, the experience of living together under Serb sovereignty has been one of constant bitterness for the last eighty years. Finally, the Serbs have clearly demonstrated that they are only interested in a Kosova without Albanians. A people threatened by genocide has every right to seek independence.

4. Kosova's independence enables the creation of a regional equilibrium. With an end to Serbia's anomalous reign over Kosova, there will not be any more permanent flashpoints of crisis threatening the security and peace of the region. In fact, the creation of a Republic of Kosova would lead to the solution of the Alba-

nian issue in the Balkans, similar to the creation of Republika Srbska in the Bosnian Union, which was another solution of the Serb issue in the Balkans. Although the creation of these state entities was preceded by wars and crimes against humanity, they still created a necessary geostrategic equilibrium in the Balkan Peninsula. Milosevic's reign is guilty of devilish acts, and he and his collaborators merit trial for war crimes in the Hague; but as even cynical geostrategists such as Henry Kissinger admit, we must fight our battles on the ground.

5. Any solution that involves keeping Kosova within Serbia/Yugoslavia, be it advanced autonomy or federal unit, would still reignite the crisis and a Serb-Albanian war in the future. Federations that are politically imposed on states have not proven to be successful. The present Federation of Serbia and Montenegro seems to be going through its last days as well. It makes no sense to insist that Kosova integrate with a state that has begun to disintegrate. In fact, without full disintegration of former Yugoslavia, there cannot be a process of integration based on new principles. The regime and system in Serbia must change for us to be able to envisage a new future. There must also be a "denazification" of Serbia so that it can find a new and healthy path to follow with its neighbors. These processes cannot be completed easily and quickly. Therefore, Kosova cannot be imagined as an entity in waiting — waiting for its insane sovereign to be cured. It will be easier and quicker to use international control to gain Kosova's independence than to try to bring the two sides together.

6. Kosova's independence would create conditions for the complementary development of the Albanian nation as a whole. Kosova's independence would strongly encourage a definite end to Albania's tendencies toward isolationism. The Albanians would find their second pole of strength and the potential for development (thus far inhibited). This does not mean the unification of Albania and Kosova. A more open border between Albania and Kosova (than the current boundary, which was a tragedy of the twentieth century) will become a strong factor for the relativity of all other borders in the Balkans. The idea of having sovereign states with closed and rigorously controlled borders has vanished in all the Balkans. The Bosnian Union is an example of how necessary it is to have open borders. The same is true of the borders between the Albanian entities. When realized, Kosova's independence will not be based on the classic model of a closed state but rather on the principle of an open state with limited sovereignty, similar to today's most powerful states, which are more and more getting away from the idea of total sovereignty.

7. Kosova's independence will have a long-term stabilizing effect on Macedonia. FYROM is a fragile state with two dominant ethnic components, where neither component can realistically hope for the elimination of or long-term domination over the other. The intersection of many interests rules out the idea of a partitioning of Macedonia, absent some catastrophic scenarios. Macedonia can be developed according to the model of Belgium; the precondition must be intensive

economic development not only in Macedonia but for the whole peninsula. Forecasts that Albanians could use Kosova's independence to initiate a secession of the Albanian-populated areas in Macedonia are not serious. This does not mean that such ideas do not exist among the Albanians. But the two centers of Albanian settlements, Tirana and the future Pristina, cannot support the idea of Macedonia's partition for very long, not only because they lack the might to encourage Albanian secessionism in Macedonia but because this would create such a great regional and continental crisis — and the Albanians would inevitably be the losers. Albania and Kosova have their own problems, and they cannot be solved with the militarization of the Albanian issue. The Serb experience of trying to unify the Serbian lands through force should not be a motivating factor for the Albanians.

8. The most powerful argument for Kosova's independence will be the will of the Albanians, who for a long time to come will not want to remain under the rule of Belgrade and the Serbs, despite all formal assurances from institutions that eventually are to protect their interests. There is no Albanian movement, party, or serious organization that favors "political coexistence" with the Serbs. The determination of the Albanians on this issue cannot be changed soon and maybe not at all. In the end, the Albanians of Kosova and the majority of the minorities who support them (Turks, Muslims) prefer to be free first and have their own citizenship; later they will make ties and arrangements with their neighbors. They have every right to self-determination.

Religious Dynamics in Kosovo
and the Potential for Cooperation

WILLIAM F. VENDLEY AND JAMES L. CAIRNS

On June 15, 1999, the Holy Synod of the Serbian Orthodox Church issued a statement that in part demanded "the present President of the State and his Government to resign, so that new people, acceptable to the domestic and international public, could, as the Government of National Salvation, take over the responsibility for their people and its future."[1] This bold statement of opposition to the Milosevic regime came only a week after the end of hostilities between NATO and Yugoslavia, and it draws attention to the role religious communities have played in the Kosovo situation. By looking at this role during the last eighteen months of conflict in Kosovo in the context of their long historical presence, we can see that the efforts of the religious leaders offer a vision of the potentially vital contribution they can make to the process of reconstruction and reconciliation in Kosovo.

Religion has been inexorably entwined in the wars of dissolution of former Yugoslavia due to the broad overlap of national and religious identity in the region. In Kosovo, however, the stark ethnic, linguistic, and cultural differences between Serbs and Albanians have lessened the centrality of religion to the conflict. In addition, while the same three religions that dominate the region are present in Kosovo (Islam, Eastern Orthodoxy, Catholicism), they are split between only two main national groups, since the Muslims and Catholics are, for the most part, both ethnically Albanian, and the Orthodox are ethnically Serbian. All three communities have deep historical roots in the region. Christianity has been present since the late Roman era, with congregations following both eastern (Greek) and western (Latin) rites. After the Great Schism between Rome and Constantinople in 1054, these two strands became the Orthodox and Catholic churches respectively. The Serbian Orthodox Church became autocephalous in the early thirteenth century, and during the next 150 years it established numerous monasteries and its patriarchate in Kosovo, which was at that time a central part of the medieval Serbian kingdom. Albanian Christians identify their roots primarily in the Latin/Catholic tradition, but there does exist a

---

1. "Statement of the Holy Synod of Bishops," Serbian Orthodox Church, June 15, 1999.

small Albanian Orthodox Church in Albania. The Ottoman Empire took control of Kosovo in the mid-fifteenth century, and during its rule a great number of Albanians converted to Islam, so that today a large majority of Albanians are Muslim.[2]

This long-term presence gives the religious communities a particular legitimacy with the people, but it also means that they have each compiled a record of positive and negative actions during centuries past that shape how they are perceived, particularly by members of other communities. There is another dimension, however, that complicates the roles of the different religions in Kosovo. For the Serb community and for the Serbian Orthodox Church, Kosovo holds particular historical and spiritual importance, which has lent the struggle over its destiny a "holy" character. Unfortunately, political forces in Serbia have misused this aspect of Kosovo's history, most recently and most damagingly Mr. Milosevic, who rose to power on the "myth" of Kosovo and turned a tradition of noble suffering into a license for brutality and repression.

The long-simmering conflict in Kosovo exploded in early 1998, when Serbian police and special forces cracked down on an emboldened and armed militia known as the Kosovo Liberation Army (KLA). The fighting between March and October 1998 left thousands dead and tens of thousands displaced; it was brought to a halt only by the agreement struck by Richard Holbrooke and President Milosevic under the threat of NATO airstrikes. Throughout this period, Bishop Artemije of the Serbian Orthodox Diocese of Raska-Prizren (which includes Kosovo) was quite outspoken in condemning the violence perpetrated by "extreme elements" on both sides and calling for a peaceful settlement that would allow all people in Kosovo to live together in the future. Bishop Artemije, supported in particular by the monks of Visoki Decani Monastery, understood that the future of the Serbian community in Kosovo would be extremely insecure in the face of an Albanian majority that had been radicalized and traumatized by the heavy-handed policy of the Serbian and Yugoslavian regimes. This threat also jeopardized the continued presence of the Serbian Orthodox Church in a region it considers its birthplace and the site of its holiest shrines. With the consent and quiet support of the patriarch and Holy Synod of the Church, Artemije traveled to numerous Western capitals and spoke through the media, at conferences, and in meetings, appealing for a resolution of the Kosovo situation that would enable all people in the province — Serbs, Albanians, and others — to remain and to find ways of building a new life together. He often emphasized that the problem "is primarily an issue of human rights and absence of democracy, not a territorial problem which is to be resolved by territorial changes."[3] Such statements set the bishop

---

2. For a more detailed analysis, see James L. Cairns, "Interrupted Dialogue: Religious Leaders in Kosovo," *The Christian Century,* April 21-28, 1999, pp. 438-40.

3. Letter from Bishop Artemije to Ambassadors Hill, Petritsch, and Maiorsky, March 10, 1999.

increasingly at odds with the Yugoslav regime and created significant tensions between the church and the government.

These tensions were covered over during the NATO bombardment of Yugoslavia because the church condemned the destruction being caused and called for an end to the bombing. These statements, however, also appealed to the Yugoslav authorities to do all that they could to bring about peace. As the statement at the end of the hostilities revealed, the tensions had remained beneath the surface, and now the church leadership has become one of Milosevic's strongest critics. In Kosovo, Patriarch Pavle, Bishop Artemije, and other senior bishops have been striving to convince Serbs to stay and pressing the KFOR troops and other international organizations to protect Serbs and their property against revenge attacks being carried out by returning Albanians after they were expelled during the war.

Muslim and Catholic leaders in Kosovo have not been as directly involved in the conflict for several reasons. First, the religious dimension is not as important to the Albanian community as it is to the Serbs, so religious leaders have not been pressured to legitimate the struggle. Second, the massive dislocation and suffering of the Kosovo Albanians has forced the religious communities to use all their resources just to survive. Many religious officials were expelled and their mosques damaged, which has restricted their ability to be key voices in the political process. Finally, the religious leaders tend to share the aspirations of the Albanian community and have been under significant pressure from forces within the community not to do anything that could be seen as collaborating with "the enemy," despite the critical stance taken by the Orthodox Church against the regime.

Despite these problems, the Islamic leader in Kosovo, Mufti Rexhep Boja, courageously issued a statement in October 1998 that acknowledged the calls for peace from Artemije and others, and called for all people of goodwill to work together to promote a peaceful and just resolution of the crisis.[4] Mufti Boja and the Roman Catholic Bishop of Prizren, Msgr. Marko Sopi, also responded positively to Bishop Artemije's calls for dialogue among the religious leaders to promote a just and peaceful solution. Based on requests from all three religious leaders, the World Conference on Religion and Peace (WCRP) began working with them in September 1998 to develop a process of contact and dialogue. The first step was to form a working committee of representatives appointed by each leader. Despite the uncertainty surrounding the peace negotiations in France in February-March 1999, the members of this working committee met together for the first time on March 2, 1999, in Pristina. It marked the first such meeting in more than ten years. In a joint statement the participants agreed that the violence had to be stopped, that all people have a right to live in Kosovo, and that religion and religious symbols must not be used to promote violence and intol-

4. Statement by the Islamic Community of Kosova, October 23, 1998.

erance. They expressed their commitment and desire to continue to strengthen their dialogue and cooperation.[5]

The NATO operations began three weeks later and halted this process of dialogue. However, since the end of the hostilities, there are encouraging signs that all three leaders remain committed to this process. Reports from Prizren indicate that Bishop Sopi and other Catholic officials have been using sermons and other public statements to condemn the violence against Kosovo Serbs and to call for tolerance. In an interview with the *New York Times,* Mufti Boja expressed that while he was disappointed that the Orthodox Church leaders had not been stronger in condemning the anti-Albanian terror, he understood the constraints they faced and that the Milosevic regime must be held responsible. He expressed his conviction that despite all the suffering, "reconstruction and tolerance could overcome bitterness and revenge."[6] The Orthodox Church is seeking to use any means possible to try to convince Serbs to stay in Kosovo, and joint appeals for tolerance and calm from the religious leaders in the province might be a positive step.

Realistically, however, what role can religious institutions effectively play in promoting tolerance, rebuilding trust, and supporting the rights of all to live in Kosovo in the aftermath of the violence, trauma, and hatred that this conflict has spawned? Religions do possess moral and social assets that, if effectively mobilized, would uniquely equip them to be constructive forces for promoting the common good. Morally, religious communities can offer not only a code of ethics but also language and ritual that address human tragedy, suffering, and failure, as well as joy and transformation. Socially, religions have a ubiquitous presence at virtually every level of society. Their institutions provide a well-established and effective network for sharing information; they possess considerable historical legitimacy within the society; they have vast experience in providing social welfare, health, and educational programs; and they can mobilize members of the community around issues of social concern.

These assets too often remain blocked, underdeveloped, or, worse, misused. In Kosovo, two factors have contributed toward preventing the religious communities from effectively mobilizing their social assets. First, the correspondence of national and religious identity has left the religious communities at least partially captured by pernicious forms of nationalism that have dominated politics in the region for over ten years. Second, the experience of forty years of communism has drained considerable strength, resources, and capacity for social action from the religious communities. In this context, multireligious cooperation can be a real asset in releasing religion's tremendous potential to promote the common good. Together, the religious communities can better resist the trap of nationalism and can

5. Public Statement, issued March 4, 1999, from Working Committee meeting of March 2, 1999.

6. Peter Steinfels, "Beliefs," *New York Times,* June 12, 1999.

multiply their social assets through having religious leaders work together. Common statements and joint actions can have both substantive and great symbolic power in helping the people of Kosovo begin a process of reconstruction and reconciliation that is crucial for the future of the region.

In Kosovo, the efforts of the religious leaders over the past year to open a process of dialogue represent the only attempts of any institutions in the society to build bridges between the Serbian and Albanian communities. While their power may be limited, the religious leaders have already demonstrated courage and commitment in seeking a path of tolerance and peace. Their efforts do carry symbolic significance and will be essential for creating a climate in which other forces in the society can begin to work together with the religious communities to promote reconstruction and reconciliation.

Kosova and the Transition of the Century

VETON SURROI

When, on March 24, 1999, the bombs started falling over Prishtina and other cities in what was known as the FRY, a whole century of totalitarian ideologies was about to enter into transition toward an expected century of the building of democracy. Under attack that night was the fascism of the Serbian state that had promoted its ideology ten years earlier with the call to arms to "defend the holy Serbian soil" against 90 percent of its inhabitants who happen to be non-Serb. Under attack was the inherited communism of an untransformed Serb society that was ruled through the control of state levers in the economy and at every other significant level of societal life. Yet this is a new version of communism in which multiparty elections are held regularly. However, partly because the communists ultimately count the votes and partly because the nationalist agenda is held by consensus in the society, the electoral results didn't mean much in matters of war and peace, but rather in terms of who would benefit directly from delivering import/export licenses to privileged companies.

Also under attack was a system of apartheid, a new system that didn't differentiate people on the basis of the color of their skin but on the basis of their ethnicity. For ten years Mr. Milosevic and his followers had consistently built a system by which the Albanians would be excluded from any previous form of social life they had known (jobs, education, policing, decision-making) to the point of not even being allowed to enter the only swimming pool in Prishtina. And, one can arguably claim, under attack was the historic vacuum that the death of the Ottoman and Austro-Hungarian empires left at the beginning of the century, a vacuum within which Kosova was simply conquered by the then strong Serbia without having the benefit of the Wilsonian right to self-determination.

Today, if we have the benefit of historic hindsight, the likely answer to the question of why this happened when it did would be that the Northern world (the North Atlantic world and Russia) is in a phase of redefining itself after the end of the Cold War. Ten years after the fall of the Berlin Wall, the Atlantic world found itself watching a continuous war of the disintegration of former Yugoslavia, without much ability to change the course of history. It has been a bloody collapse. And when the West decided to intervene in the case of Kosova, the course of history led to the first mass expulsion of a people since the times of Hitler and Stalin.

If this is the case, the Western world has assumed a new role for itself in the post–Cold War era, that of stabilizing the eastern part of the European continent by means of an interventionist approach. Part of this approach is strongly visible in the numbers of soldiers that NATO has deployed in both Bosnia-Herzegovina and Kosova. Part of it is also evident in the more expedient integration policies for countries aspiring to EU membership; part is also apparent in the new thinking of massive EU-supported programs for the region of southeastern Europe, such as the stability pact promoted by the new and strong German pillar in the new Europe.

Within this context the Kosovar transition toward democracy will be a test case for the Western transition into a proactive role within the next century. Democratic institutions will have to be built from scratch in Kosova, and the Western role with its tradition is a *conditio sine qua non*. A viable economy will have to be built on the ruins of communism, and this has not proven to be an easy task elsewhere. And relations with neighboring people and states will have to be established — not a very nice task for an unhealthy neighborhood such as Kosova's.

These tasks will find themselves further complicated by the lack of an answer in the immediate years to come for the following questions: What kind of entity is the present protectorate of Kosova? What kind of region will southeastern Europe be, compared to the western part of the continent? I believe that the answer to these questions will be sought in our present century, both in Wilson, the father of self-determination for Europeans of this century, and in Monet, the father of self-determination on the Continent itself.

The figure of Wilson will be important because I have no doubt that by the time self-rule is established in Kosova, it will be more than obvious to the outside world that there is no way in which Kosova may form part of any kind of Yugoslavia or Serbia, and that self-determination is definitely a right for the Kosovars, a right that has not been granted. Ultimately, it will be the definitive test for democracy-building: how can a democracy be built if the people within that democracy are not allowed to vote about their future?

The figure of Monet will be important because, though the Kosovars will opt for their independence, Europe is becoming increasingly interdependent. Kosova will vote for independence, but independence is not autarchy. And Kosova can be viable only within a larger process of democratic integration. The only happening in Europe is the EU expansion and the integration of southeastern Europe into it. Wilson and Monet could perhaps meet each other at the beginning of the next century on the Kosova issue: the independence becomes relative to the interdependence. If that happens, we will have entered a transition to the next century with a new concept.

Why Try?

MARTHA MINOW

"[T]he Yugoslav tribunal[1] has served as little more than provocation — yet another threat that Milosevic can weave into his nationalist myth, lamenting yet another indignity visited upon the Serbian people by foreign imperialists. Ethnic cleansing in Kosovo may yet be halted by Western intervention, and perhaps even punished by the ICTY. But the cycle of vengeance concocted, implemented, and nursed by Serbian leaders will likely continue — as it has in Rwanda, Latin America, and elsewhere."[2]

This American commentator, like many others, argues that criminal prosecutions for violations of human rights and international conventions cannot hope to stem cycles of vengeance in the Balkans. Yet others — such as Aryeh Neier — treat such prosecutions as essential for establishing civil society, accountability, and justice after genocide.[3] Which view is the realistic one and which the naïve?

With a short-term time horizon, the answer is easy. The threat of prosecution has not deterred enough of those who foment and orchestrate mass violence

---

1. Unlike the International Court of Justice (ICJ), established in 1945 by the U.N. as its primary organ for states to bring charges against other states, the ICTY can prosecute only individuals. Justice Louise Arbour of the ICTY presided over the May 24, 1999, indictment of five men for war crimes: President Slobodan Milosevic; Milan Milutinovic, president of Serbia; Nikola Sainovic, deputy prime minister of the FRY; Dragoljub Ojdanic, chief of staff of the Yugoslav army; and Vlajko Stojiljkovic, minister of internal affairs of Serbia. As pointed out by Justice Arbour, "This indictment is the first in the history of this Tribunal to charge a Head of State during an on-going armed conflict with the commission of serious violations of international humanitarian law." The indictment alleges that, between 1 January and late May 1999, forces under the control of the five who are accused persecuted the Kosovo Albanian civilian population on political, racial, or religious grounds. The five stand accused of "murder, persecution and deportation in Kosovo." Complete details of the indictment can be found on the ICTY website, http://www.un.org.ICTY.

2. Nicholas Confessore, "Rwanda, Kosovo, and the Limits of Justice," *The American Prospect* (July-August 1999): 90, 96.

3. See Aryeh Neier, *War Crimes: Brutality, Genocide, Terror, and the Struggle for Justice* (New York: Times Books, 1998).

to eliminate it; the prosecutorial enterprise itself is often marred by insufficient resources, inadequate abilities to arrest those accused, and perceptions that the entire process is too politicized or improvised to establish respect for law and human rights. Three days after Justice Louise Arbour of the ICTY faxed a letter declaring her intention to investigate violations of international humanitarian law by Slobodan Milosevic and twelve other senior Yugoslav officials, Serbian troops pursued massive violence in Pristina and forced some 13,000 Kosovars out into Albania. Yet surely the time frame for assessing the work of the international tribunal should be longer than three days, and the geographic reach of its audience extends far beyond those immediately addressed by it.

Moreover, deterrence is at most one of many goals of prosecutions and trials following mass atrocities. In my mind, deterrence is the goal least likely to succeed. But other compelling goals can be reached. Trials seek to create official records of the scope of the violence, the participants, and the victims. Beyond this knowledge, they seek public acknowledgment of what happened and its utter wrongfulness. They pursue some accountability by individuals, not an entire people. It is important to know who is a war criminal and who is not. Otherwise, what festers is the only too familiar tendency of all of us to blame whole groups and nations for violence. Because of our vulnerability to this kind of sorting of people into groups that so often underlies intergroup violence — and the demagoguery that foments it — the trial's insistence on the individuality of wrongdoers and victims alike offers a vital alternative.

Yet it would be wrong to imagine that criminal prosecutions following mass atrocities exhaust what can and should be done. Truth commissions gather the testimony of victims without the interruptions of cross-examination and the focus on individual defendants' guilt. Fact-finding commissions can also produce reports examining the large and multiple contributing factors leading to mass violence. These reports can rebut claims that tribal hatreds simply erupt and can show exactly how economic privation, a manipulated and constrained press, malicious but charismatic figures, and the fear and passivity of bystanders come together. Educational programs to tell these truths can be crucial responses after genocide or mass violence. Reparations can provide symbolic as well as practical succor for survivors. Heroic efforts to build democratic institutions can provide living memorials for the dead and daily guards against oppression. In this mix, however, criminal trials offer the unique chance to enact a ritual devoted to truth, public acknowledgment, and individual accountability. The twentieth century, drenched in vicious bloodshed, also produced this remarkable practice. Not to use it, once we know how, would leave perpetrators as victors in their campaign to paralyze the instruments of justice. Not to try would turn the pretended sophistication of cynics into the final triumph of those who hate and violate human dignity.

APPENDICES

Balkan Spellings and Pronunciations

Spelling conventions in this region present complex and delicate issues for English readers because political identities and territorial claims are contested between two cultures with very different languages. In addition, Albanians, Serbs, and Croats have different names for some of the same places (e.g., Orahovac is the Serbian name for the city that ethnic Albanians call Rahovec) and different ways of spelling the same places and names. The territory whose ethnic Albanian inhabitants call "Kosova" is what Serbs call "Kosovo and Metohija," sometimes contracted to "Kosmet." Moreover, there is no generally accepted standardization for either Albanian or Serbo-Croatian when used in an English context. Furthermore, different alphabets have similarities permitting some transliteration in the Latin (i.e., English) script; but there are differences that can confuse an English reader (Đakovica = Djakovica = Gjakova). Albanian place names can be given with or without the definite article, which is indicated by a suffix: "Prizren" (indefinite) or "Prizreni" (definite). Some changes are minor, and for easy recognition we follow the standards accepted by Western news media (e.g., "Kosovo"). Other changes are slight and easily recognizable: Priština (Serbo-Croatian), Prishtina (Albanian), Pristina (Anglicized form). Obvious differences are noted in the text. Each essay used one or the other (or even a third) form of spelling for names and places, which presented an editorial dilemma: will readers be confused by these variant spellings (e.g., Haqim Thaci, Hashim Thaqi, etc.)?

Adapted from *Albanian-English Dictionary* by Ramazan Hysa (New York: Hippocrene Books, 1993), p. 9; *Colloquial Albanian* by Isa Zymberi (New York: Routledge, 1995); *Standard English-Serbo-Croatian: SerboCroatian-English Dictionary* by Morton Benson (Cambridge: Cambridge University Press, 1998, 1982); *The World's Major Languages,* ed. Bernard Comrie (Oxford, 1990), pp. 42-43, 391-409, *passim; Kosovo: A Short History* by Noel Malcolm (New York: New York University Press, 1998), pp. 11-14; *The Serbs* by Tim Judah (New Haven: Yale University Press, 1997), pp. xv-xvi.

We have thus tried to standardize some of the spellings for ease of reading, though these efforts do not represent a political endorsement. In deference to the integrity of authors, we encouraged them to consistently use their own spellings. However, readers of differing essays may still be confused by some terminology. For example, for some of the Western authors, a "Kosovar" = "Kosovo Albanian"; but for some of our Kosovar and Albanian authors, a "Kosovar" is simply an "Albanian." Although some distinguish between "Serb" as a general "ethnic-linguistic-cultural" category and "Serbian" in narrower reference to inhabitants of Serbia, usage is not consistent among these essays (nor among Western publications in general).

Albanian

Albanian is classified as one of the eleven major groups of Indo-European languages. It has two principal dialects: *Gheg*, spoken in the north and in Yugoslavia, and *Tosk*, spoken in southern Albania and various colonies in Greece and Italy (Comrie, p. 43). The Albanian alphabet has thirty-six letters: seven vowels and twenty-nine consonants, of which seven are letter combinations (dh, gj, nj, sh, th, xh, zh). For English speakers, the main pronunciation differences can be concisely shown as follows:

c is pronounced as **ts** in "Tsar" (Czar)

ç = **tch** in "match, cherry"

dh = **th** (always voiced as in "this, these, that")

e = **e** in "set"

ë = **e** in "term," "ugh" (like the u in "radium" or like the French "deux"; virtually silent if it comes at the end of a word)

gj = **g** in "legion"

ll = **ll** in "all"

nj = **ni** in "onion"

q = **ky** in "stockyard" (softened tch)

rr = **rr** in "burrow"

th = **th** in "thin" (always unvoiced; not like "this")

x = **dz** in "judge," "adz(e)"

xh = **j** in "jester," "jam"

y = **u** in French "tu," "une" (umlauted "u" as in German "über")

zh = **si** in "vision," "collision," "pleasure"

Serbo-Croatian or Serbian

Based on a language group completely different from Albanian, Serbo-Croatian ("Serbian") is classified as one of the South Slavic languages: South Slavic (Bulgarian, Macedonian, Serbo-Croat, Slovene); West Slavic (Czech, Slovak, Polish, Sorbian [in Germany]); East Slavic (Russian, Ukrainian, Belorussian). The term "Serbo-Croatian" denotes a South Slavic language in at least three tiers of numerous dialects and two forms of writing. Latin letters emerged in the west of the region after Cyrillic letters (first brought in the twelfth century) became widespread in the east, during separate early nineteenth-century language reforms. Named after the ninth-century "Apostle to the Slavs," St. Cyril (†869), the Cyrillic alphabet is modeled on the Greek alphabet but the current "Serbian Cyrillic" alphabet includes six characters not found in Russian; conversely, Russian has nine characters not used in Serbo-Croat (Corbett in Comrie, p. 391). However, in Serbo-Croatian there is an exact correspondence between the Latin and Cyrillic alphabets; thus transliteration is automatic (characters from one alphabet spell those of another). In the mid-nineteenth century, the *Štokavian* dialect of Serbo-Croatian was made regulative; other dialects survive, but the impacts on all of them of the upheavals of war and mass population movements have not yet been systematically studied. Before the recent civil war, *Cakavian* survived, for example, along the Dalmatian coastal fringe, and the *Kajkavian* dialect around Zagreb and in northern Croatia bordering on Slovenia. One *Old Štokavian* dialect *(Prizren-Timok)* existed in southeastern Serbia, bordering Bulgaria and Macedonia. *New Štokavian* includes the dialect of Serbia *(Ekavian)*, the *Ikavian* dialect in Dalmatia, the west of Bosnia-Herzegovina, and parts of Lika and Slavonia. The *Ijekavian* dialect was found in the western part of Serbia, Montenegro, the east of Bosnia-Herzegovina, and those parts of Croatia not mentioned above. Contemporary varieties of Serbo-Croatian are described by using political and territorial terms for areas that comprised the former Yugoslavia. People living in Bosnia-Herzegovina now usually call their language Bosnian *(bosanski)*. People living in Croatia now usually call their language Croatian *(hrvatski)* and write in the Latin alphabet. Croatia and western Bosnia-Herzegovina comprise the "western variant" of "Serbo-Croatian." People living in Serbia and Montenegro now usually call their language Serbian *(srpski)*, which is written in Cyrillic or Latin letters. Whereas people living in Serbia and eastern Bosnia-Herzegovina comprise the "eastern variant" of "Serbo-Croatian," the Serbo-Croatian spoken in Montenegro contains elements of both.

Once again, for English speakers, the main pronunciation differences can be concisely stated:

ae	is pronounced as the **a** in "sad"
aj	= **i** as in "five"
au	= **ou** as in "house"
c	= **ts** as in "hats"
č	= **tch** as in "match," "cheese"
ć	= like **tch** but a slightly thinner sound
dj	= **g** as in "adjourn," "jam"

dž = j as in June
ej = ay as in "pay"
ij = ea as in "eat"
j   = y as in "yellow"
oj = oy as in "boy"
r   = when rolled, can fill in between consonants like a vowel
š   = sh as in "shallow"
ž   = zh as in "regime," "Zhivago"

GEOGRAPHIC NAMES IN KOSOVO

Place names in Kosovo on our maps are given as the English forms of Serbian names in Latin letters (e.g., Pristina). For the corresponding English forms of Albanian names, see the names below in italics (e.g., *Prishtina*). As explained in this Appendix, Serbians can and Albanians do use the Latin script — as in English. However, despite a version proposed by the 1998 *U.S. Geographic Names Index*, there are no universally accepted conventions for rendering either the Serbian or Albanian language in English. Customs among Western media vary — hence adding fuel to the fire of debates over whether the proprietary naming of places is an effort to "Serbianize" or "de-Slavicize"/"Albanianize" them.

Anglicized forms of Serbian place names

Anglicized forms of Albanian place names in Kosova are italicized (words ending in "ë" are rendered with an "a"; e.g., *Prishtinë* = *Prishtina*)

KOSOVO   ## KOSOVA

Serbian	Albanian	Serbian	Albanian
Belacevac		Obilic	*Obiliq*
Decani	*Decan*	Ogoste	
Djakovica	*Gjakova*	Orahovac	*Rahovec*
Djurakovac	*Gurrakoc*	Pec	*Peja*
Dobrcane		Podujevo	*Podujeva*
Gnjilane	*Gjilan*	Pristina	*Prishtina* (*Prishtinë*)
Istok	*Istog*		
Izbica		Prizren	*Prizreni*
Klina	*Klina*	Racak	*Racak*
Kosovo Polje	*Fusha Kosova*	Restelica	
Kosovska Kamenica	*Kamenica*	Srbica	*Skanderaj*
Kosovska Mitrovica	*Mitrovica*	Urosevac	*Ferizaj*
Lipljan	*Lipjan*	Vitomirica	
Malisevo	*Malisheva*	Vucitrn	*Vushtrri*
Musutiste	*Mushtishta*	Vrela	
Novo Brdo	*Novobarda*	Zur	*Zhur*

Albania

The Republic of Albania (formerly the People's Socialist Republic of Albania), situated in southeastern Europe on the Balkan Peninsula, is bordered by Greece to the south, by the former Yugoslav republic of Macedonia to the east, Montenegro to the north, and Serbia (the province of Kosovo-Metohija) to the northeast. To the west is a 420-kilometer (260-mile) coastline along the Adriatic Sea and the Strait of Otranto (parts of the Mediterranean Sea). Albania's total land area is 28,750 square kilometers, of which more than three-quarters is mountainous or hilly; more than one-half of the country is covered by woodlands. It is slightly smaller than the North American state of Maryland. The official language is Albanian, the principal dialects being Gheg (spoken north of the River Shkumbin) and Tosk (in the south). The literary language is a fusion of the two dialects, with the phonetic and morphological structure of Tosk prevailing. Ethnic Greeks continue to use their own language.

According to a July 1999 estimate, the total population of Albania is 3,364,571, of which 95 percent is ethnic Albanian. The population growth rate is 1.05 percent, with a net migration rate of -2.93 migrants per thousand. A 1989 estimate revealed that Greeks, the majority of whom live in the south, constitute 3 percent of the population, with the other 2 percent consisting of Vlachs, Gypsies, Serbs, and Bulgarians. (Other 1989 estimates of the Greek population ranged from 1 percent [official Albanian figures] to 12 percent [by a Greek organization].) The official ban on religious worship, which was in effect between 1967 and 1990, makes it difficult to assess the religious affiliations of the population. According to

Data included here are taken from the 1999 CIA *World Factbook*, the World Bank (1999/2000 World Development Report), and the *Eastern Europe and the Commonwealth of Independent States* (London: Europa Publications, 4th ed. 1999). Official Albanian and Yugoslav government data are available on their respective websites (see the Internet Resources appendix in the back of this book). This information was compiled by Kate McCann and the editor.

the religious census of 1945, 73 percent of the population was Muslim, 17 percent Eastern Orthodox, and 10 percent Roman Catholic. Of the Muslim population, an estimated 75 percent were members of the liberal Bektashi sect, a Sufi dervish order. A half century later, the 1999 CIA *World Factbook* lists the religious percentages as follows: Muslim, 70 percent; Albanian Orthodox, 20 percent; Roman Catholic, 10 percent. In late 1990 and early 1991, the small community of 300 Albanian Jews emigrated in its entirety to Israel.

The majority of the Albanian people live on the coastal plains, and nearly half the population lives outside major cities and towns. Many ethnic Albanians live in other countries, including some 1.7 million in Yugoslavia — mainly in the Kosovo region of Serbia (Kosovar Albanians) — and another .4-.8 million in Macedonia; a small number of Albanians live in northern Greece (the Cam community). Albanian's capital, Tirana (Tirane), is situated in the center of the country and had a mid-1990 estimated population of 244,200. Other important towns include Durres (Durazzo), Albania's largest port (85,4000); Elbasan, a major industrial center (83,300); and Shkoder (Scutari, 81,900).

A 1996 estimate revealed that 19.6 percent of the population is living below the poverty line. The 1999/2000 World Development report lists the GNP at $2.7 billion, or $810 per capita (with the population at 3 million). The unemployment rate was officially estimated at 14 percent in October 1997, but now it is likely to be as high as 28 percent. Agriculture remains the principal sector of the Albanian economy (estimated at 54 percent of the GNP in 1998). Industry profit (food processing, textiles and clothing, lumber, oil, cement, chemicals, mining, basic metals, and hydropower) constitutes 25 percent of the GNP (1998). A 1994 estimate listed the Albanian labor force at 1,692,000 (including 352,000 emigrant workers and 261,000 domestically unemployed) with 50 percent of the domestically employed working in agriculture (nearly all private, but some state employed), 22 percent in the private sector, 28 percent in the state business sector (including state-owned industry, 7.8 percent).

An extremely poor country by European standards, Albania is making the difficult transition to a more open-market economy. The collapse of financial pyramid schemes in early 1997 — which had attracted deposits from a substantial portion of Albania's population — triggered severe social unrest, leading to more than 1,500 deaths, widespread destruction of property, and an 8 percent drop in the GDP. The new government installed in July 1997 has taken strong measures to restore public order and to revive economic activity and trade. The economy continues to be bolstered by remittances from the 20 percent of the labor force that works abroad, mostly in Greece and Italy. These remittances supplement the GDP and help offset the large foreign trade deficit. Most agricultural land was privatized in 1992, substantially improving peasant incomes. In 1998, Albania probably recovered most of the 8 percent drop in GDP of 1997.

Albania gained its independence from the Ottoman Empire on November 28,

1912. After many years under communist socialism, the Albanian government is now an emerging democracy. The administrative divisions consist of thirty-six districts *(rrethe)* and one municipality *(bashki)*. A new constitution was adopted by popular referendum on 28 November 1998, in a vote that was boycotted by the opposition Democratic Party. The government's executive branch consists of a chief of state (President of the Republic Rexhep Meidani), a head of government (Prime Minister Pandeli Majko), and a cabinet consisting of the Council of Ministers.

The legislative branch, the unicameral People's Assembly *(Kuvendi Popullor)*, consists of 155 seats. Elections held on June 29,1997 (next to be held in 2001) resulted in the following representation percentages (by party): Albanian Socialist Party (PS) (formerly the Albania Workers Party), chaired by Fatos Nano, 53.4 percent; Democratic Party (PD), chaired by Sali Berisha, 25.3 percent; Albanian Republican Party (PR), chaired by Fatmir Mehdiu, 2.3 percent; Social Democratic Party (PSD), chaired by Skender Gjinushi, 2.5 percent; Unity for Human Rights Party (PBDNJ), chaired by Vasil Melo, 2.8 percent; the National Front (PBK), chaired by Hysen Selfo, 2.4 percent; The Democratic Alliance (PAD), chaired by Neritan Ceka, 2.9 percent; Movement of Legality Party (PLL), chaired by Guri Durollari, 3.1 percent; the Christian Democratic Party (PDK), chaired by Zef Bushati, 1 percent; the PBSD, 0.8 percent. Seats by party: PS 101, PD 27, PSD 8, PBDNJ 4, PBK 3, PAD 2, PR 2, PLL 2, PDK 1, PBSD 1, PUK (Party of National Unity, chaired by Idajet Beqiri) 1, independents 3. Other parties are: the Democratic Party of the Right (PDD), chaired by Petrit Kalakula; the Social Democratic Union Party (USdS), chaired by Teodor Laco; and the Albanian United Right (DBSH).

The judicial branch consists of a supreme court, the chairman of which is elected by the People's Assembly for a four-year term. The military branches include an army, navy, air force and air defense force, interior ministry troops, and border guards. Albanian military expenditures constitute 2 percent of the nation's GDP ($60 million) in 1998.

Serbia and Montenegro

The Federal Republic of Yugoslavia (FRY), formerly known as the Socialist Federal Republic of Yugoslavia (SFRY), is the joint independent state or federation of two republics, Serbia and Montenegro.[1] The FRY has a rugged mountainous terrain, except in the north, where the Pannonian Plains begin. The fertile plains of Vojvodina and northern Serbia are watered by the River Danube (Dunav), as well as the Tisa (Tisza), Drava, and Sava rivers. The highlands of the southwest are known as the Black Mountains (Crna Gora), from which Montenegro takes its name.

The Republic's geographical position grants it strategic control of one of the major land routes from western Europe to Turkey and the Near East. The FRY is situated in the central Balkan Peninsula and is bordered by Hungary to the north, Romania and Bulgaria to the east, Macedonia to the southeast, and Albania to the south. In the extreme southwestern corner there is a short border with Croatia to the Adriatic coast; but the main border with that country is in the northwest, and the central western border is with Bosnia-Herzegovina. Yugoslavia has a total area of 102,173 square kilometers (39,449 square miles): Montenegro, with an area of 13,182 sq. km., is in the southwest, on the Adriatic coast; the land-locked territo-

---

1. The Federal Republic of Yugoslavia (FRY) declared itself the successor to the Socialist Federal Republic of Yugoslavia (SFRY) on April 11, 1992. The FRY constitution was accepted on April 27, 1992. This entity has not been formally recognized as a state by the United States. The U.S. view is that the SFRY has dissolved and that none of the successor republics represents its continuation.

Data included here are taken from the 1999 CIA *World Factbook*; the World Bank (1999/2000 World Development Report); *Eastern Europe and the Commonwealth of Independent States*, 4th ed. (London: Europa Publications, 1999); and the International Crisis Group August 1999 report on "Who's Who in Kosovo." Official Albanian/Yugoslav government data are available via the respective government websites (see the internet resources appendix).

ries of Serbia (with an area of 88,361 sq. km.) occupy the rest of the country. Serbian territory includes two formerly autonomous provinces: Kosovo-Metohija (formerly known as Kosovo),with an area of 10,887 sq. km., occupies the plateau lands in the southwest of Serbia; Vojvodina (21,506 sq. km.) is in the north of the republic.

A July 1999 estimate lists the total population of the FRY at 11,206,847 people (Serbia, 10,526,478; Montenegro, 680,369), with population growth rates of .02 percent for Serbia and .07 percent for Montenegro; net migration rates are 2.65 migrants per thousand for Serbia and 5.09 migrants per thousand for Montenegro. It should be noted that all data dealing with population are subject to considerable error because of the dislocations caused by military action and ethnic cleansing.

The principal language in the FRY is Serbo-Croat in its Serbian form, *Ekavian,* and is written in the Cyrillic script. The Montenegrins (6 percent of the total population at the 1991 consensus) also speak a Serbo-Croat dialect *(Ijekavian),* use the Cyrillic script, and many see themselves as ethnically distinct from the Serbs. The non-Slavic ethnic Albanians are actually the second largest group in the country (14 percent of the total population in 1991) and have their own language: Albanian is spoken by all; many live predominantly in the province of Kosovo-Metohija. The other main non-Slavic group in the country is the Hungarians (Magyars, 4 percent). The province of Vojvodina, in the north of the country, was formerly part of the Banat, a border territory of the Habsburg realm. Although it is an area of very mixed ethnic composition, it originally had a large Hungarian population. However, by the latter part of the twentieth century it was dominated by Serbs. Those, usually of mixed parentage, who choose to define themselves as ethnic "Yugoslavs" also make up some 3 percent of the country's total population. The Slavic Muslims (3 percent) live mainly in the Sandzak region (on the Serbian-Montenegrin border) and to the north of Kosovo-Metohija (the chief city of the region is Novi Pazar, historically known as Raska). Other minority communities in the FRY include Roma (Gypsies), Vlahs (Vlachs), Bulgarians, Czechs, Slovaks, and Ruthenians (Ukrainians).

The FRY capital and largest city is Belgrade, Serbia (also the capital of that republic), which had a population of 1,168,454 at the March 1991 census. The Montenegrin capital is Podgorica (formerly Titograd), which had a population of 117,875 in 1991. The Serbian province of Kosovo-Metohija had a population of 1,954,747 in 1991 (an increase of some 23 percent over 1981, the highest population growth rate of any region in the former SFRY). The provincial capital is Pristina (155,4999). Serbia's other province, Vojvodina, had a 1991 population of 2,031,889; its capital is Novi Sad, which had 179,626 inhabitants. Other important towns in the FRY include Nis (175,391 in 1991), Kragujevac (147,305), Subotica (100,386), and Zrenjanin (81,316).

About 65 percent of the Serbian people adhere to the Eastern Orthodox faith, as represented by the Serbian Orthodox Church. Islam is the religion of a significant minority (19 percent); it is concentrated in the south of the country among the Slavic Muslims and most of the Albanian population. Four percent of the population is Roman Catholic (in Vojvodina and among the Albanian minority), and 1 percent is Protestant. The remaining 11 percent of the population includes those practicing Judaism and non-believers.

Reliable economic statistics continue to be difficult to assess, and the GDP estimate is extremely rough (estimated at $25.4 billion — $2,300 per capita — in 1998). Industry profit constitutes the largest percentage of the GNP at 50 percent (1998 est.); profits from agriculture and services each constitute about 25 percent of the GNP. A 1994 estimate revealed that 41 percent of the FRY labor force works in the republic's various areas of industry: machine building (aircraft, trucks, and automobiles; tanks and weapons; electrical equipment; agricultural machinery); metallurgy (steel, aluminum, copper, lead, zinc, chromium, antimony, bismuth, cadmium); mining (coal, bauxite, nonferrous ore, iron ore, limestone); consumer goods (textiles, footwear, foodstuffs, appliances); electronics; petroleum products; chemicals; and pharmaceuticals. Thirty-five percent work in the services area; 12 percent work in trade and tourism; 7 percent in transportation and communication; and 5% in agriculture (cereals, fruits, vegetables, tobacco, olives, and livestock.

The troubled economy of the FRY resulted from the swift collapse of the Yugoslav federation in 1991, the highly destructive warfare that followed, and U.N. sanctions. The borders of the FRY were destabilized, and critical inter-republic trade flows were severed or interrupted (the disintegration of the SFRY created specific geographical problems for the FRY in terms of access to the Adriatic coast). The Kosovo crisis particularly affected trade with Macedonia (which has its own Albanian minority "problem"). More serious than any difficulties with the other successor states were the increasingly difficult relations between the two member states of the FRY. With Montenegro accounting for less than 5 percent of the GDP, difficulties of balance between the two members of the Republic were bound to emerge. In mid-1998, against a backdrop of increasing resentment in Montenegro at the price the FRY was paying for Serbia's quarrels with the outside world, relations deteriorated further.[2]

Between 1991 and 1996 there was a dramatic collapse in the federation's production, along with "hyperinflation," high and rising unemployment, and fall-

2. The Republic's government has disputes with Bosnia-Herzegovina over Serb-populated areas; with the Albanian majority in Kosovo that seeks independence from Serbian republic; with Croatia over Croatia's claim to the Prevlaka Peninsula in southern Croatia because it controls the entrance to Boka Kotorska in Montenegro. Prevlaka is currently under observation by the U.N. military observer mission in Prevlaka (UNMOP); the border commission formed by the Former Yugoslav Republic of Macedonia and Serbia and Montenegro in April 1996 to resolve differences in the delineation of their mutual border has made no progress so far.

ing consumption. The recovery of the Yugoslav economy from war and international sanctions began in mid-1996. But the economic boom anticipated by the government after the suspension of U.N. sanctions that lasted from May 1992 until November 1995 has failed to materialize. Government mismanagement of the economy is largely to blame. The legacy of the old Yugoslav market-socialist economy was preserved in the FRY and, it seemed, might provide the basis for a market economy. A "new" and flexible private sector had also emerged out of the imposition of sanctions; but this sector was deeply criminalized.

The FRY government's executive branch consists of a head of state (President Slobodan Milosevic), along with Milan Milutinovic as president of Serbia and Milo Djukanovic as president of Montenegro; a head of government (Prime Minister Momir Bulatovic), who is supported by deputy prime ministers — Nikola Sainovic, Vuk Draskovic, later dismissed, Jovan Zebic, Vladan Kutlesic, Zoran Lilic, and Danilo Vuksanovic); and a cabinet consisting of the Federal Executive Council. The legislative branch, the bicameral Federal Assembly (Savezna Skupstina), consists of the Chamber of Republics (Vece Republika), with 40 seats — 20 Serbian, 20 Montenegrin — and the Chamber of Citizens (Vece Gradjana), with 138 seats. Of the 138 seats in the Chamber of Citizens, 108 are Serbian, with half elected by constituency majorities and half by proportional representation; 30 seats are Montenegrin, with 6 elected by constituency and 24 proportionally. The judicial branch consists of a Federal Court (Savezni Sud) and a Constitutional Court; all the justices are elected by the Federal Assembly. The FRY army includes ground forces with border troops, naval forces, and air defense forces. The FRY's military expenditures amount to 6.5 percent of the GDP ($911 million), according to a 1999 estimate.

Elections for the Chamber of Republics, last held on December 24, 1996 (to be held next in 2000), and for the Chamber of Citizens, last held on November 3, 1996 (also to be held next in 2000), had the following results: the SPS/JUL/ND coalition won 64 seats; Zajedno (a coalition including SPO, DS, and GSS) won 22; DPSCG won 20; SRS won 16; NS won 8; and SVM won 3. The remaining 5 seats are registered as "other."

Slobodan Milosevic is chairman of the Serbian Socialist Party (SPS), formerly the Communist Party; Vojislav Seselj chairs the Serbian Radical Party (SRS); the Serbian Renewal Movement (SPO) is chaired by Vuk Draskovic. Zoran Djindjic is chairman of the Democratic Party (DS); Vojislav Kostunica chairs the Democratic Party of Serbia (DSS); the Democratic Party of Socialists of Montenegro (DPSCG) is chaired by Milo Djukanovic; Novak Kilibarda is chairman of the People's Party of Montenegro (NS); Momir Bulatovic chairs the Socialist People's Party of Montenegro (SNP); the Social Democratic Party of Montenegro (SDP) is chaired by Zarko Rakcevic; Slavko Perovic is chairman of the Liberal Alliance of Montenegro; Sandor Pall chairs the Democratic Community of Vojvodina Hungarians (DZVM); the League of Social Democrats of Vojvodina (LSV) is chaired by Nenad Canak;

Aleksandar Popov is chairman of the Reformist Democratic Party of Vojvodina (RDSV); Bela Tonkovic chairs the Democratic Alliance of Vojvodina Croats (DSHV); the League of Communists-Movement for Yugoslavia (SK-PJ) is chaired by Dragomir Draskovic; Dr. Ibrahim Rugova is chairman of the Democratic Alliance of Kosovo (LDK); Rexhep Qosja chairs the Democratic League of Albanians; the Parliamentary Party of Kosovo (PPK) is chaired by Bajram Kosumi; Dr. Sulejman Ugljanin is chairman of the Party of Democratic Action (SDA); Goran Svilanovic chairs the Civic Alliance of Serbia (GSS); the Yugoslav United Left (JUL) is chaired by Mirjana Markovic (wife of Slobodan Milosevic); Dusan Mihajlovic is chairman of the New Democracy (ND) Party; Jozsef Kasza is chairman of the Alliance of Vojvodina Hungarians (SVM); and the leader of the coalition party Zajedno (translated as "Together") is not specified.

Local government in the FRY is based on the municipality, or commune: Montenegro is divided into 21 municipalities; Serbia is divided into 29 administrative regions, including territories of the formerly autonomous provinces of Kosovo-Metohija and Vojvodina, both of which have held referendums for independence.[3] Following the enactment of the 1990 Serbian Constitution and, subsequently, of the Federal Constitution of 1992, Vojvodina retained its provincial assembly. In the mid-1990s there were signs of increasing opposition among Vojvodina's inhabitants to Serbia's domination. On May 13, 1996, a total of 17 political parties, associations, and organizations signed the Manifesto for Vojvodina Autonomy. This move was the beginning of a campaign to amend the Serbian Constitution of 1990 and the Federal Constitution of 1992 to restore the province's autonomous status — with full legislative, judicial, and executive powers. Currently, the president of Vojvodina's provincial assembly is Zivorad Smiljanic; the provincial president is Bosko Perosevic; and the premier is Koviljko Lovre.

Kosovo

The 1990/92 removal of Kosovo's autonomous status exacerbated decades of institutional, reactionary, and repressive upheavals and further fueled secessionist ambitions. In July 1990, Albanian delegates to a technically dissolved Kosovo Assembly declared sovereignty; in 1991 a local referendum overwhelmingly supported sovereignty. Presidential elections brought the provisional coalition government of Bujar Bukosi in 1991, and later Ibrahim Rugova, the leader of the Democratic Alliance of Kosovo (DAK) (1992, 1998).[4] The DAK, now the Democratic League

3. In October 1991 the Slav Muslims of the Sandzak area voted for autonomy in a banned referendum. Their leader was Sulejman Ugljanin.
4. Western governments did not formally recognize the "Republic of Kosovo" and maintained that the province was an integral part of the FRY.

of Kosovo (LDK), also organized elections for a shadow provincial assembly, which were held that same month, March 1998. The LDK still upholds the legitimacy of their leader, Ibrahim Rugova, as president of the new "Republic," since he was officially elected by Kosovar Albanians; thus they reject the legitimacy of the newer provisional government, even though Rugova himself agreed to its formation during the February 1999 Rambouillet peace talks.[5] The chairman of the provisional government of the "Republic of Kosovo" is Dr. Bujar Bukoshi; the chairman of the interim executive council of the "Autonomous Province of Kosovo-Metohija" is Zoran Andjelkovic.

The composition of the Kosovo Provisional Government, as listed by a recent report by the International Crisis Group, is as follows:[6] prime minister, Hashim Thaqi (Kosovo Liberation Army); deputy prime minister, Mehmet Hajrizi (Albanian Democratic Movement); secretary of the government, Ramadan Avdiu (Democratic Union Party); minister of defense, Azem Syla (PBD); deputy, Fatmir Limaj (UCK); foreign minister, Bardhyl Mahmuti (PBD); deputy, Hydajet Hyseni (LDSh).

Political parties with active representation in the provisional government are: the Kosovo Liberation Army (KLA or UCK), with Hashim Thaqi as political leader and Agim Ceku as military leader; the Democratic League of Kosovo (LDK), chaired by Ibrahim Rugova; the Albanian Christian Democratic Party of Kosova (SCDPK), led by Mark Krasniqi and Zef Morina; the Liberal Party, chaired by Gjergj Dedaj; the United Democratic Movement, a coalition of seven parties headed by Rexhep Qosja (Albanian Democratic Movement, Parliamentary Party of Kosovo, Albanian Unification Party, Albanian Liberal Party, Albanian National Party, Greens, Albanian Republican Party). Other parties active in Kosovo are: the People's Movement of Kosovo; the Democratic Union Party; and the National Movement for the Liberation of Kosovo. Serb organizations in Kosovo have not, for the most part, survived recent events. Serb interests are represented on the Transitional Council (see below) by Momcilo Trajkovic's Serb Resistance Movement (SPO) and the Serbian Orthodox Church (Bishop Artemije and Father Sava). The representative of the Belgrade government is Zoran Andjelkovic.

5. Three main Kosovar Albanian political groupings were recognized at the Rambouillet peace talks: the UCK/KLA led by Hashim Thaqi; the LBD coalition led by Rexhep Qosja; and Ibrahim Rugova's LDK. Rugova, Qosja, and Thaqi signed an agreement at Rambouillet on February 23, 1999, to form a provisional government that would represent the Kosovar Albanians until elections could be held.

6. "Who's Who in Kosovo," International Crisis Group (ICG), August 1999. According to the ICG, "the list of Provisional Government members should be treated with caution. It has been compiled from several sources within the Provisional Government which contradict each other, each claiming to be authoritative. Party affiliations in particular seem likely to be fluid for some time to come." Please note that not all of the government positions are listed in this appendix. To download this exceptional report on the complexity of the political organization of Kosovo, visit the ICG website: http://www.intl-crisis-group.org.

As of the beginning of August 1999, the following persons are members of the Kosovo Transitional Council, set up by the United Nations Mission in Kosovo:[7] Hashim Thaqi and Xhavit Haliti (UCK); Rexhep Qosja and Mehmet Hajrizi (DBD); Ibrahim Rugova and Edita Tahiri (LDK);[8] Blerim Shala and Veton Surroi (independents); Bishop Artemije and Momcilo Trajkovic (representing the Serbs). Representing other minorities in Kosovo are Numan Balic (a Bosniak member of the SDA, the Democratic Action Party in Bosnia) and Sezair Shaipi (Turkish People's Party).

7. The Transitional Council, under the direction of Special Representative for the U.N., Secretary-General Kouchner, brings together all the ethnic communities in Kosovo and will serve as an intermediary with U.N. officials.

8. Rugova and Tahiri boycotted this meeting but attended the third meeting on August 25.

On-line Resources for Further Inquiry

Comprehensive Sites • World Governments • Regional Political Parties • Military and Defense Agencies and Research Organizations • Intergovernmental Organizations • Human Rights and Humanitarian NGOs • Academic and Advocacy Groups • War Diaries • Media and News Agencies • Maps and Guides

Comprehensive Sites

Federation of American Scientists (Target Kosovo) provides a comprehensive set of links that covers security/intelligence issues and agencies, military analysis sources, news sources, international agencies, government organizations, and a discussion of U.S. congressional debate and background information on the conflict. *http://www.fas.org/man/dod-101/ops/kosovo.htm*

Information contained in the websites listed here is not a representation of the opinions of the editor or of Eerdmans Publishing Company. Because the World Wide Web is a very fluid environment, the websites listed here may no longer contain documents or links referred to in the site descriptions. Nonetheless, this list is comprehensive; it alerts users to the sources of information available. No information is completely free of all potentially distorting interests or biases; on-line data must be scrutinized carefully for accuracy, reputation, and currency of electronic sources because most Internet materials are not independently refereed and many are self-published. Jan Alexander and Marsha Tate, reference librarians at the Wolfgram Memorial Library of Widener University, have created a World Wide Web site collecting useful information and materials on the evaluation of electronic resources; see http://www.science.widener.edu/~withers/webeval.htm (Joseph Gibaldi, *MLA Style Manual and Guide to Scholarly Publishing* [New York: MLA, 1998], pp. 209-11). Special thanks to the staff of the United States Institute of Peace library for their guidance regarding the creation of this appendix and the use of annotation on USIP links included in this document. This information was largely compiled by Kate McCann, with help from the editor, and completed in December 1999.

Hellenic Resources Institute posts a collection of links covering news sources, agencies, organizations, political parties, and lists of links from commercial search engines such as Yahoo! and Alta Vista. *http://www.hri.org/nodes/ balkans.html1#Yugoslavia*

Initiative on Conflict Resolution and Ethnicity (University of Ulster) posts guides to Internet sources on conflict and ethnicity in Kosovo, Albania, and former Yugoslavia comprised of lists of annotated links to news sources and listservs, academic articles and documents, NGOs, maps, and discussion groups. *http:// www.incore.ulst.ac.uk/cds/countries/*

International Security Network (Switzerland) posts annotated links to statements, press releases, and documents from government agencies, organizations, and news sources. *http://www.isn.ethz.ch/linkslib/*

Kosovo Conflict 1999 — Special Study Section, compiled by Homework Central, features extensive resources on Kosovo for high school students, including links to sources for news, country and historical information, international organizations, languages, ethnic groups, religion, biographies, culture, and the arts. *http://www.homeworkcentral.com/knowledge/vs1_sectionsasp?=sectionid= 24460+tg=NA&st=GNR5*

Mario's Cyberspace Station (Croatia), produced by freelance journalist Mario Profaca, provides links to an array of regional and international news sources and organizations with information on and reactions to the background and current situation in Kosovo, plus links to full-text articles, information on the Kosovo Liberation Army (KLA), and a search engine. *http://mprofaca.cro.net/ kosovo.html*

United States Institute of Peace (USIP), an independent federal institution that promotes peaceful resolution to international conflicts and provides excellent regional sections on the Balkans, complete with links to general resource sites, government agencies, international organizations, humanitarian assistance and refugee sites, maps and guides, media and news sources, special reports issued by the Institute, and transcripts of USIP current issue briefings on Kosovo with U.S. Secretary of State Madeleine Albright and "Sandy" Berger (U.S. National Security Advisor). See the Peace Agreements Digital Collection for the full text of the Military Technical Agreement, the U.N. Security Council Resolution 1244, and the Rambouillet Agreement. *http://www.usip.org/library/regions.html*

World Governments[1]

Albania Ministry of Foreign Affairs: *http://www.tirana.al/minjash/*

Australia Department of Foreign Affairs: *http://www.dfat.gov.au/*

Belgium Ministry of Foreign Affairs: *http://www.angora.stm.it/*

Canada Department of Foreign Affairs: *http://www.dfaitmaeci.gc.ca*

Denmark Royal Ministry of Foreign Affairs: *http://www.um.dk/*

French Ministry of Diplomatic Affairs posts statements, analysis, and interviews concerning the crisis in Kosovo. *http://diplomatie.fr.actual.dossiers/kossovo/kossovo.gb.html*

Greece Ministry of Foreign Affairs: *http://www.mfa.gr/*

Italy Ministry of Foreign Affairs: *http://www.italyemb.org/*

Provisional Government of Kosova: *http://www.kosova.org*

Republic of Kosova: *http://www.kosova-gov.com.* This site is still under construction.

Temporary Executive Council of Autonomous Province Kosovo and Metohija (Republic of Serbia): *http://www.pivkim.org.yu/home_e.htm*

Macedonia Ministry of Foreign Affairs: *http://www.mnr.gov.mk/*

Republic of Montenegro: *http://www.vlada.cg.yu*

Republic of Serbia Ministry of Information includes official Serbian news reports, a profile of the president, foreign policy papers, and the Serbian position on Kosovo. *http://www.serbia-info.com.* The G17 (Stability Pact for Serbia), a group of Serbian economists and academics for the Transitional Government of Serbia, posts news on economic reform in Serbia, speeches by its members, and reports on the economic consequences of NATO bombardment, and includes the political agreement on the Transitional Government. *http://www.g17.org.yu/english/d.htm*

Russian Federation: *http://www.mid.ru/english/bod.html.*

Spain Ministry of Foreign Affairs: *http://www.mae.es/*

Sweden Ministry of Foreign Affairs: *http://www.ud.se*

Switzerland Department of Foreign Affairs: *http://wwwadmin.ch/site/g.html*

United Kingdom Foreign and Commonwealth Office provides Kosovo news, background information, and resources including speeches, statements, photographs, maps, and other information (via the Ministry of Defense site). *http://www.mod.uk/news/kosovo*

United States: The Department of State posts official statements, press briefings, fact sheets, special reports on "ethnic cleansing" and the situation in Kosovo, instructions on how to subscribe to a Department of State Kosovo listserv, updates from the Kosovo Diplomatic Observer Mission, and links to related web-

---

1. The ministries or departments of foreign affairs included here are those for the regional governments and, with the exception of Greece and China, those for the countries currently contributing military personnel to KFOR and/or are members of the Group of 8.

sites. Includes full text documents such as the Agreement on Russian Participation in KFOR. *http://www.state.gov/www/regions/euro/kosovo_hp.html*

See the United States Agency for International Development (USAID) for fact sheets on refugees and the humanitarian crisis in Kosovo. *http://kosovo.info.usaid.gov/*

See the United States Information Agency for regional information reports and to subscribe to the USIA Kosovo listserv. *http://www.usia.gov/regional/eur/balkans/kosovo/homepage.htm*

Federal Republic of Yugoslavia Ministry of Foreign Affairs features a Yugoslav Daily Survey, news, press statements, analysis, and full text of The White Book on NATO Crimes in the FRY. Official site: *http://www.mfa.gov.yu/*

See also *http://www.gov.yu/kosovo/index.html* for similar and other information. The Royal House of Serbia and Yugoslavia, the official site of the Karadjordjevic dynasty, which ruled from the early nineteenth century until being abolished by the post–World War II communist regime, posts statements on the Kosovo Crisis by Crown Prince Alexander. *http://RoyalFamily.org*

Regional Political Parties[2]

Civic Alliance of Serbia: *http://www.begrad.com/gss*
Congressional National Party: *http://www.geocities.com/CapitolHill/3563/*
Democratic League of Kosovo: *http://www.Idk.tip.nu/*
Democratic League of Vojvodina: *http://www.lsv.org.yu*
Democratic Party of Albania: *http://www.albania.co.uk/dp/*
Democratic Party of Montenegrin Socialists: *http://www.dps.cg.yu*
Democratic Party of Serbia: *http://www.dssrbije.org.yu*
New Communist Party of Yugoslavia: *http://members.tripod.com/nkpj/*
New Democracy Party for Serbia: *http://www.novademokratija.org.yu*
Progressive Party: *http://www.naprednas.org.yu*
Serbian Radical Party: *http://www.radicalparty.org*
Serbian Renewal Movement: *http://www.spo.org.yu/*
Social Democratic Party of Montenegro: *http://www.sdp.cg.yu*
Socialist Party of Serbia: *http://www.sps.org.yu*
Democratic Party of Yugoslavia: *http://www.demokratska.org.yu/*
Liberal Alliance of Montenegro: *http://www.lscg.crnagora.com/index.htm*
Montenegrin Association of America: *http://www.montenegro.org*
Vojvodina's Hungarian Union: *http://www.vmsz.org.yu*
Yugoslav League of Social Democrats (Vojvodina): *http://www.lsv.org.yu/*
Yugoslav Left: *http://www.beograd.com/jul/index.html*

2. The political parties included here are those with websites.

Military and Defense Agencies and Research Organizations

Allied Forces Southern Europe (NATO): Operation Joint Guardian (KFOR) includes background information, images, a list of participating forces, and related links. The Operation Allied Force site includes background information, images, maps, transcripts, multimedia documents, and a list of participating forces. The Operation Allied Harbor site includes information about the military humanitarian assistance alliance with UNHCR and Albanian civil and military authorities. The Operation Determined Falcon site has links to transcripts of press briefings, statements, photos, participating forces, and points of contact for the June 1998 operation. The Operation Determined Guarantor site includes information about its mission to extract OSCE Kosovo Verification Mission personnel and its later engagement in humanitarian assistance. *http:// www.afsouth.nato.int.*

Belgium Department of Defense: *http://www.mil.be/sid/perscom/1999/038.htm*

Canada Department of Defense: *http://www.dnd.ca/menu/Echo/index_e.htm*

Canadian Forces College posts media updates on the Canadian Forces Contribution to NATO operations in Kosovo, links to international military sights, and has a section entitled "Spotlight on Military News and International Affairs," where articles on Kosovo military issues are posted regularly. *http:// www.cfc.sc.dnd.ca*

Center for Defense Information (CDI), an independent, nonprofit research group monitoring the U.S. military and defense policy, posts a collection of military and political agreements, U.N. Security Council resolutions, the Rambouillet Agreement, and a number of resources on Kosovo (including the CDI Weekly Defense Monitor). *http://www.cdi.org*

Denmark Ministry of Defense: *http://www.fmn.dk/index_en.htm*

Federation of American Scientists Military Information includes detailed descriptions of the Serbian Council for Security, Ground Forces, General Staff Security Directorate, Counterintelligence Service (KOS), Military Police, Special Forces Corps (Red Berets), Navy, Air Force, State Security Service, Special Antiterrorist Force (SAJ), Special Police Unit (PJM), the Serb Volunteer Guard (SDG/SSSJ "Tigers"), the Gray Wolves (Sivi Vukovi), the White Eagles, and the Serbs' indigenous adversary, the Kosova Liberation Army (KLA). Links to the Belgrade "White Book" (on terrorism in Kosovo and Metohija and Albania) issued by the Yugoslav Federal Ministry of Foreign Affairs and an article on "Aspects of Contemporary Terrorism" by three Serb authors are also provided. *http:// www.fas.org/irp/world/serbia/index.html*

France Ministry of Defense: *http://www.defense.gouv.fr/actualites/event/kosovo/ index.html*

Germany Ministry of Defense: *http://www.bundeswehr.de/kosovo/index.htm*

Italy Ministry of Defense: *http://www.italyemb.org/*

Jane's Defense Weekly (Kosovo Special Feature) provides weekly postings on defense issues, foreign affairs, news, and articles on military action in Kosovo, an "Intelligence Review," maps, photographs, and "Missiles and Rockets" technology reports. *http://www.janes.com/defense/features/kosovo/kosovohome.html*

Kosova Liberation Army (KLA): *http://www.zik.com*

    See also the Federation of American Scientists site: *http://www.fas.org/irp/world/para/kla.htm*

    See also *http://www.kosovapress.com* for KLA perspectives and statements.

Netherlands Peacekeeping: *http://www.mindef.nl/english/index.htm*

North Atlantic Treaty Organization (NATO) homepage posts updates on the crisis in Kosovo, with links to documents and briefings on Operation Joint Guardian and a calendar of daily press briefings, statements, maps, and aerial views for Operation Allied Force. Also includes a historical overview of NATO's role in relation to the conflict and background information. *http://www.nato.int*

Norway Peacekeeping: *http://www.norway.org/index.html*

Spain Ministry of Defense: *http://www.mde.es/mde/index.html*

United Kingdom Royal Air Force: *http://www.mod.uk/news/kosovo/index.html*

    The Ministry of Defense homepage (*http://www.mod.uk*) posts a paper by Lord Robertson of Port Ellen (then Minister of Defense) entitled "Kosovo: An Account of the Crisis," with sections on historical background, the unfolding of the crisis, NATO air strikes, responding to the crisis, the politico-military interface, initial lessons learned, a chronology, statistics, objectives, and principles.

United States European Command links to country information for Kosovo, briefings from the U.S. Department of State, the U.S. White House, NATO, and other groups. Operation Joint Guardian, Operation Allied Force, and Operation Allied Harbor/Joint Task Force Shining Hope web pages describe the U.S. contribution to the NATO operations, links to daily reports and press briefings, maps, images, and other defense organizations and governmental organizations. Operation Joint Guardian links to the text of the Military Technical Agreement. *http://www.eucom.mil/europe/serbia_and_montenegro/kosovo*

    See also the U.S. Air Force Kosovo information via *http://www.usafe.af.mil/kosovo/kosovo.htm*

    See also *http://www.defenselink.mil* for the U.S. Department of Defense homepage.

Yugoslav Army Supreme Command Headquarters Information Center posts latest news, links to Yugoslav sites, magazine articles (Serbian and English), and the Yugoslav Commission for Damaged and Endangered Heritage of FRY), archived daily news posts during NATO air strikes, and a section on reactions from abroad to the NATO campaign ("Global Protest"). *http://www.gov.yu/presscvj/*

Intergovernmental Organizations

Contact Group for former Yugoslavia (France, Germany, Russia, United Kingdom, United States) statements on Bosnia and Kosovo (from 1995 to the present) are posted by the Office of the High Representative in Bosnia and Herzegovina. *http://www.ohr.int/contact.htm*

Council of Europe posts statements issued by the Council's Parliamentary Assembly on Kosovo's future political status. Search under "kosovo." *http://www.coe.fr*

European Union includes recent press releases, recent and archived statements, declarations, reports, and articles about Kosovo from EU officials and news sources available on EUROPA, the EU server. *http://europa.eu.int/geninfo/ keyissues/kosovo/index_en.htm*

ECHO, the European Community Humanitarian Office, provides humanitarian assistance in partnership with nongovernmental organizations, which the site details. *http://europa.eu.int/comm/echo/kosovo/index.html*

Economic Reconstruction and Development in South East Europe, joint site of the European Commission and the World Bank, created "as part of the international community's response to the Kosovo crisis," contains a calendar of events/conferences, news releases, speeches, and statements, including the Stability Pact for South Eastern Europe from June 10, 1999, and links to related sites. *http://www.seerecon.org/*

The World Bank site describes the launching of the joint web site and the scope and types of information that will be covered, including assessment of the economic impacts and costs of the Kosovo crisis, reconstruction needs, and donor assistance. *http://www.worldbank.org/html/extdr/extme/pr061299en.htm*

Group of 8 (Australia, Canada, European Union, Japan, Spain, Sweden, Switzerland, United States) information is posted by the University of Toronto's G8 Information Center, including documents of G8 meetings (e.g., the May 6, 1999, statement on the "general principles on the political situation to the Kosovo crisis," and proposals on the "civilian aspects of the implementation of an interim peace settlement in Kosovo," dated June 10, 1999). *http://www.library .utoronto.ca/g7/*

International Criminal Tribunal for the Former Yugoslavia (ICTY) includes press releases, information on the Tribunal, and the full text of the May 24, 1999, indictment of Slobodan Milosevic and four other FRY officials for "murder, persecution, and deportation in Kosovo." *http://www.un.org/icty*

Organization for Security and Cooperation in Europe Mission in Kosovo, established July 1, 1999, forms a distinct component within the U.N. Interim Administration Mission in Kosovo (UNMIK). OSCE posts latest updates (facts, figures, developments) with regard to the Mission's activities in the areas of police training, elections, democratization, and human rights/rule of law. *http:// www.osce.org/*

United Nations Interim Administration in Kosovo (UNMIK) groups U.N.-related news items, press releases, statements, declarations, reports, audio press conferences and briefings, images and documents concerning the U.N.'s involvement in Kosovo. It includes time lines, a fact sheet on the U.N. mission in Kosovo, and links to other U.N. organizations. The High Commissioner for Human Rights pages bring together press releases, statements, resolutions, and reports by the High Commissioner, the Secretary-General of the U.N., and the Special Rapporteur concerning the human rights situation in Kosovo and the Federal Republic of Yugoslavia. The U.N. High Commissioner for Refugees posts daily updates on the situation in Kosovo, press releases, statements, reports, articles, news, analysis, and statistics on refugees. *http://www.un.org/peace/kosovo/*

Human Rights and Humanitarian NGOs

Belgrade Academic Association for Equal Rights in the World has sections on "NATO Aggression on Yugoslavia," "NATO Losses," "NATO Destruction," and "Facts and Fiction," a picture gallery, and a selection of articles on "Kosovo History," including "Albanian Ethnic Cleansing of the Old Serbia." *http:// www.barw.org.yu*

British Helsinki Human Rights Group posts news, press releases from organizations, links to other Helsinki groups, maps, and articles. It also provides a news listserv. *http://www.bhhrg.org/*

CNN Humanitarian Organizations List links to the following humanitarian organizations not listed on the InterAction site: CCR Frontpage (Canada), International Committee of the Red Cross, Russian Committee for Helping Refugees, Norwegian Refugee Council, Caritas Italy, Peace Fund, World Health Organization (Europe). *http://www.cnn.com/SPECIALS.1998/10/kosovo/related sites/*

Center for the Development of the Non-Profit Sector in the FRY (Belgrade) posts an extensive directory of NGOs in Serbia and Montenegro, complete with contact information and web addresses where available. The 1999 directory lists civic organizations, women's groups, and an array of indigenous and international humanitarian organizations. *http://www.crnps.org.yu/docdir9.1/*

Common Dreams Humanitarian Organizations List links to the following humanitarian organizations not listed on the InterAction site: International Aid Inc. and Operation USA. *http://www.commondreams.org/kosovo/links/*

Greek Helsinki Monitor (Greek National Committee of the International Helsinki Federation) provides an updated archive of appeals, statements, and news releases on Kosovo by international organizations, and sections on "Voices from the Serbian Civil Society," "Articles about the NGOs in the Balkan Countries," and the "September 1999 OSCE Implementation Meeting." *http://www .greekhelsinki.gr*

Human Rights Archives features reports on human rights violations in Kosovo and copies of International Tribunal reports on war crimes in the Balkans, compiled by the chairman of Haverford College's religion department, Michael Sells. *http://www.haverford.edu/relg/sells/reports.html*

Human Rights Watch (Kosovo Human Rights Flash) offers a background briefing on Kosovo, several reports, and regular updates. *http://www.hrw.org*

InterAction Humanitarian Organizations List links to the following refugee and humanitarian organizations: American Friends Service Committee, Adventist Development and Relief Agency, American Joint Distribution Committee, American Jewish World Service, American Red Cross, American Refugee Committee, Baptist World Aid, The Brother's Brother Foundation, CARE, Catholic Relief Services, Christian Children's Fund, Christian Reformed World Relief Committee, Church World Service, Direct Relief International, Doctors without Borders/MSF, Doctors of the World, Episcopal Church Presiding Bishop's Fund for World Relief, Ethiopian Community Development Council, Food for the Hungry International, Heifer Project International, International Medical Corps, International Orthodox Christian Charities, International Rescue Committee, Islamic African Relief Agency USA, Jesuit Refugee Service, Lutheran World Relief, MAP International, Mercy Corps International, Operation USA, Oxfam America, Physicians for Human Rights, Presbyterian Disaster Assistance, Relief International, Save the Children Federation, United Methodist Committee on Relief, U.S. Association for UNHCR, U.S. Committee for UNICEF, World Concern, World Relief, and World Vision. *http://www. interaction.org./kosovo/index.html*

International Helsinki Federation for Human Rights in Albania includes a discussion on the protection of minorities in Albania. *http://www.ihf-hr.org/reports/ 9804gene.htm#Albania*

International Helsinki Federation for Human Rights — Kosovo Helsinki Committee posts background about its activities and current publications. *http:// www.ihf-hr.org/koshc.htm*

International Helsinki Federation for Human Rights in Serbia offers recent reports on the national minorities in Serbia. *http://helsinki.opennet.org*

Lawyers Committee for Human Rights "has worked since 1978 to protect and promote fundamental human rights." Its programs focus on building the legal institutions and structures that will guarantee human rights in the long term. LCHR also seeks to influence the U.S. government to promote the rule of law in both its foreign and domestic policy, and presses for greater integration of human rights into the work of the U.N. and other international bodies" (especially protecting refugees through the representation of asylum seekers). The LCHR examined conditions in Kosovo, including the operation of international institutions, as well as the absence of police and justice systems in two missions to the region, in July-August 1999 and September-October 1999. A full report, *A*

Fragile Peace: Laying the Foundations for Justice in Kosovo, is available on-line from the Lawyers Committee, as well as earlier documents: *Protection of Kosovar Refugees and Returnees: The Legal Principles* (June 1999), *Kosovo: Protection and Peace-Building,* and *Protection of Refugees, Returnees, Internally Displaced Persons, and Minorities* (August, 1999). *http://www.lchr.org*

The Council for the Defense of Human Rights and Freedoms, a Kosovo-based organization, provides information on their work as well as weekly, monthly, and annual reports on alleged human rights violations by the Serbian authorities in Kosovo. *http://www.albanian.com/kmdlnj*

Academic and Advocacy Groups

Advocacy Project, an association of professionals that records and disseminates information about the international debate on humanitarian issues, including "Civil Society in Kosovo," posts regular statements on Kosovo entitled "On the Record" and provides a news listserv. *http://www.advocacynet.org*

Amnesty International includes a special report on the refugee camps and regular news releases. *http://www.amnesty-usa.rog/kosocris.htm*

    Annual Reports are available via *http://www.amnesty.org/ailib/countries/index411.htm.*

Balkan Action Council, a U.S.-based advocacy group concerned with monitoring ultranationalist groups and developments, publishes *Balkan Watch,* a weekly review of events in the Balkans. *http://www.balkanaction.org/*

The Balkan Institute site, though last updated in July 1998, has archived a number of useful extensive reports, such as "Preventing Conflict in Kosovo" and "Kosovo and the Politics of Dismemberment." *http://www.balkaninstitute.org*

Balkania.Net, a volunteer effort of students and postgraduates of journalism and political sciences from Athens, Thessaoniki, Belgrade, Skopje, Sophia, and Timisoara, posts political, military, and legal analyses of the conflict, articles on NATO war crimes, and defenses of the Serbian historic claim to Kosovo, and offers access to a wide range of sources, including full-text books and academic articles. *http:/www.balkania.net*

Beograd.com posts news reports and other articles, links, and individual responses to various Serbian and international news reports, a timetable of the day's air raids, photos of the destruction in Kosovo, and a child's plea for peace. *http://www.beograd.com/NATO*

Citizen's Guide to Understanding the War in the Balkans, created by a former American aid worker in Bosnia, offers a small collection of mini-essays (including the historical and religious context and the rhetoric of nationalism) designed to help Americans understand the complexities of the war in Kosovo. *http://www.mikuliak.com/kosovo.html*

Committee against US Intervention includes bulletins, opinion, political cartoons, and an index of antiintervention sites and news stories. *http://www.antiwar.com*

Compendium of Materials regarding NATO Intervention against FRY, compiled by the Yugoslav Congressional National Party, includes news on legal instruments filed against NATO and ecological disaster in the Balkans, an in-depth historical analysis of the war, testimonies against "ethnic cleansing" allegations, maps, and pictures. *http://www.geocities.com/CapitolHill/3563/agresija.html*

Diaspora Net, "an independent, voluntary effort of academics and professionals from America to Europe, and from Japan to Australia [designed] to increase awareness on issues about Hellenic [Greek] interest," posts action alerts, a photo gallery, and background articles and political analysis of the crisis, including articles on collateral damage caused by NATO intervention. *http://diaspora-net.org*

European Movement in Serbia includes press clippings about NATO attacks against Yugoslavia, appeals for peace, the Europa Nostra resolution on Post-conflict Reconstruction in the Balkans, and links (in Serbian and English). *http://wmins.org/english*

International Women in Black Support Network passes on information from and works in solidarity with the Serbian group Women in Black against War in Belgrade and elsewhere in the FRY. E-mail jane@gn.apc.org (WiB London) or roal@nodo50.org (WiB Madrid) for information. *http://www.wib.matriz.net*

International Crisis Group (ICG), as part of its South Balkans Project, has compiled a series of excellent extensive reports and press releases on Kosovo, Albania, and Serbia such as "Who's Who in Kosovo" and "Transforming Serbia: The Key to Long Term Kosovo Stability." ICG also posts news and articles for its Kosovo War Crimes project, funded by ECHO. *http://www.intl-crisis-group.org*

JURIST: Law in Crisis (Kosovo and Yugoslavia), maintained by the international "JURIST: The Law Professors' Network," features an extensive collection of articles discussing the legal implications of the Kosovo Crisis, a variety of articles on reconstruction, human rights, refugees, a history of Kosovo and Yugoslavia, and the latest reports on the U.N. mission, KFOR, war crimes, the KLA, and NATO. *http://jurist.law.pitt.edu/*

Kosova Task Force USA, a grassroots organization, posts a select group of articles (anti-Yugoslavia/pro-Kosova independence), a short history of Kosova, links to Kosovar organizations and agencies, and a link-list of member organizations (including the Albanian Islamic Cultural Center and the American Muslim Council). *http://www.JusticeForAll.org*

Protest.Net attempts to keep track of the more than 2,500 "leftist and progressive" protests, meetings, and conferences around the world, including those against U.S. policy in the Balkans and Iraq. *http://www.protest.net*

Srpska Mreza posts a variety of opinion and analysis articles on the crisis and history of Kosovo (in Serbian and English) from a Serbian perspective, including one about the "Kosovo Heritage" complete with maps and photos of Serbian Orthodox churches, monasteries, and religious figures and artifacts. *http://www.srpska-mreza.com/mlad/*

Stop NATO Web Ring lists interlinked sites advocating the cessation of the NATO strikes. *http://www.webring.org/cgi*

Transnational Foundation for Peace and Future Research regularly issued press releases on Kosovo during the crisis. *http://www.transnational.org/*

United States Catholic Bishops Council (Migration and Refugee Services) posts statements on the refugee situation in Kosovo and the region and on NATO intervention, by the Most Rev. Theodore E. McCarrick and others. *http://www.nccbuscc.org*

War Resisters International, an organization with a long history of commitment to Kosovo and to the democratic opposition in Serbia, posts links to various resources (languages: English, Spanish, German, and French). *http://www.gn.apc.org/warresisters/xyu*

Women — East/West Network posts letters, statements, and journals of women from Pristina, Belgrade, and Zagreb; also links to media and gender references for war in Yugoslavia and hosts a listserv discussion/message board. *http://www.neww.org*

zNet, which describes itself as a "community of people concerned about social change," has generated some interesting debates about the NATO air strikes, with contributions from academics such as N. Chomsky and E. Said. *http://www.zmag.org/ZMag/kosovo.html*

War Diaries

Dispatches from Belgrade features e-mail reports from a U.S.-trained physicist living in Belgrade (from *Mother Jones*). *http://www.motherjones.com/total_coverage/kosovo/alex/*

KeepFaith.com is the family website of sisters Ivanka and Olga Besevic (Belgrade) and Ivanka's daughter Silvia (San Francisco). Detailed and extensive journal entries, e-mails, letters, and transcripts of phone conversations between Silvia and her mother and aunt during the NATO bombing campaign are posted. *http://www.keepfaith.com*

Kosovo Diary is a personal account of the Albanian conflict, as reported by photojournalist David Brauchli. *http://www.digitaljournalist.org/issue9806/kosovo01.htm*

The War Diaries is a video and written diary by Serbian independent filmmaker A.G. (name withheld), filmed between March 22 and April 3 in Belgrade. *http://www.webcinema.org/war_diaries/*

Media and News Agencies

Albanian Daily News is a mailing list dedicated to distributing news and information pertaining to Albania, Kosova, the Albanian population in Macedonia and Montenegro, the Albanian diaspora worldwide, and the Albanian people in general. Regular contributors include the Kosova Information Center, OMRI, Albanian Telegraph Agency (ATA), Council for the Defense of Human Rights and Freedoms (Kosova), KOHA Albanian weekly (Pristina), and other individuals, news agencies, and organizations. One can subscribe to ALBANEWS by sending an e-mail to listserv@listserv.acse.buffalo.edu and include this text in the body of the message: SUBSCRIBE ALBANEWS (first name) (last name). *http://www.albaniannews.com/*

Alternative Information Network (FRY), "a project of independent journalists from former Yugoslavia and the European Civic Forum," posts a weekly Balkan Press service that covers Kosovo (in Serbian and Albanian) and Bosnia daily news reports that mention Kosovo (selected daily reports in English). Subscription by e-mail is available. *http://aimpress.ch/*

Arta, an English daily news service on the situation in Kosovo, contains a series of Special Reports in addition to regular news bulletins. *http://www.kohaditore.com/ arta/*

BBC News features a collection of many BBC articles and summaries on Kosovo, recent news, analysis, profiles, and history, including a Kosovo Fact File, a Kosovo Crisis — Top Stories file, and Building the Peace — Week in Review. Some special sections include the Interactive Fact File, interactive maps, and databases providing information and positions on the NATO air strikes, military hardware, etc. It also analyzes how the conflict is being reported via the Internet. *http://news.bbc.co.uk/hi/english/special report/1998/kosovo/*

Balkan Media and Policy Monitor posts its digest, which culls articles from other publications. Issue 59/60, vol. 4 (April 1998), is devoted to events in Kosovo, with links to full text in cited publications. *http://MediaFilter.org/Monitor/ Mon.59-60/Mon.59-60.html*

Beta news agency offers daily news in the FRY and the region featuring articles on various topics and Kosovo history and political commentary (*http:// www.beta.co.yu/*) and hosts the "Kosovo On-Line" service (offered by Beta press agency), which features texts, articles, and reactions (Serbian and English), as well as a high-quality discussion group. *http://beta-press.com/index2.html*

Borba, a daily newspaper founded by the government of the Federal Republic of Yugoslavia in 1992, provides an on-line English-language service that provides news from a Serbian perspective. *http://www.borba.co.yu/daily.html*

CNN features news highlights and archives, commentary, details on the peace settlement and military campaign, background of the conflict, documents and transcripts, a discussion listserv, and related links. *http://www.cnn.com/ SPECIALS/1998/10/kosovo/*

Central Europe On-Line posts breaking news, special articles, news from regional agencies, book reviews, and links to humanitarian organizations, and hosts a message board for debate on issues in Kosovo. *http://www.centraleurope.com/ ceo/special/kosovo/intro.html*

Common Dreams News Center provides an excellent collection of links to international and regional news sources, opinion analysis, special reports on the Kosovo crisis, and human rights/activist/humanitarian organizations. *http:// www.commondreams.org/kosovo/kosovo.htm*

E.N.T.E.R., an independent Albanian news agency founded in 1997 by a group of independent journalists from Tirana, posts daily headlines and includes a section for archived news. *http://www.albania.co/uk/enter/*

Fairness and Accuracy in Reporting (Yugoslavia) posts "action alerts," articles, "CounterSpin" broadcasts (e.g., John Pilger on the Kosovo War and Seth Ackerman on Rambouillet), and "Media Beat" columns (e.g., "Spinning the Cycles of Grief and Retribution"). *http://www.fair.org/international/yugoslavia .html*

FreeSerbia — Other Voices from Serbia, a site maintained by the Students Union of Yugoslavia, includes daily news bulletins; a collection of statements by student groups, individuals, and NGOs; special feature articles on political parties; and a discussion forum. *http://www.freeserbia.org*

ITN — Kosovo Crisis posts news, analysis, a war diary complete with real audio and video and a section on "Virtual Conflict: The Net at War." *http:// www.itn.co.uk/Specials/Kosovo/index.htm*

Info@Kosovo.Nu provides articles and news from a Kosovar perspective and posts links to the KLA, Kosovar media sites, photos, and message boards. *http:// www.kosova.nu*

Institute for War and Peace Reporting, "an independent publishing and media group" based in London, posts several special reports on the conflict in the region, such as the Balkan Crisis Reports, the [ICTY] Tribunal Update, and Media Focus (analysis of media in the FRY). *http://www.iwpr.net/topstrap.html*

International Action Center, led by former U.S. Attorney General Ramsey Clark, posts selections from Western media and information collected on the ground in Yugoslavia for the Center's NATO war crimes indictment project. *http:// www.iacenter.org/*

International Justice Watch, a site maintained by Harvard University's Andras Riedlmayer and colleagues, contains archived discussions and news postings on Kosovo (and other countries) from a very active and high-quality listserv. *http:// listserv.acsu.buffalo.edu/archives/justwatch-1.html*

Kosova Discussion Forum is a discussion forum created to serve as a tool to discuss the current situation/crisis in Kosova. To subscribe, e-mail LISTSERV

@MAELSTROM.stjohns.edu, and include this text in the body of the message: SUB KOSOVA YourFirstNameHere YourLastNameHere.

Kosova Crisis Center, produced in support of Albanian students in Kosova, includes news, time lines, photos, maps, listservs, related links, information on Albanian cultural heritage, and background information on the struggle for Kosovar Albanians for independence. *http://www.alb-net.com/html/kcc.html*

Kosova Crisis News is a collection of news links compiled by the Eurasia Research Center, as well as search engines to Serbian, Albanian, and other organizations and government agencies. *http://eurasianews.com/erc/000kosova.htm*

Kosova Press Daily News, maintained by the Kosovo Liberation Army and Movement, posts daily news, political documents, KLA statements, a history of the KLA, and sections on "Kosova's Martyrs" and "Victims of Serb Terrors." *http:// www.kosovapress.com/english/index.htm*

Kosovo.Net posts coverage of the Kosovo conflict from a Serbian point of view. *http://www.kosovo.net*

Kosovo and Metohija, maintained by the Serbian Resistance Movement, Democratic Movement, and the Serbian Orthodox Church, includes political analysis, historical pieces, articles from the Serbian Orthodox Church, a section on "recent developments," and links to news and other agencies. *http:// www.kosovo.com*

Kosovo Information Page is maintained by the Serbian Orthodox Church in Kosovo and focuses on the Church's statements on the Kosovo Crisis. *http:// www.decani.yunet.com/kip.html*

MSNBC-TV (Flash Point Kosovo) posts current top stories, news and analysis, and interactive guides (maps of alleged atrocities, the peace deal, conflict background, peacekeeping operations, key facts, key actors, etc.). *http://www.msnbc.com/news/ KOSOVO_Front.asp*

Media Centar of Pristina posts general information, daily news, analysis and press conference information. *http://www.mediacentar.org/vesti_centra_e.htm*

New York Times (Kosovo in Transition) posts breaking news, archived coverage of NATO air strikes, the full text of various political agreements and U.N. resolutions, a map of the command structure for peacekeeping operations, proceedings from a "Kosovo Roundtable," information on the Albanian fight for self-determination and Serbian Nationalism/Christian Orthodox resistance, a photo essay, slide shows, and classroom resources. *http://www.nytimes.com/ library/world/kosovo-index.html*

Odraz B92 Daily News Service offers the latest news in real audio format and html format (available in English). *http://www.siicom.com/odrazb/*

OneWorld On-line features a special report on Kosovo, with extensive news coverage and analysis from OneWorld partner organizations, and an introduction that provides background to the conflict. *http://oneworld.org/news/europe/ serbia.html*

Orthodox Peace Fellowship has archived statements regarding the NATO attack issued by the Serbian Orthodox Patriarch Pavle and religious leaders in the U.S., Canada, and Europe. *http://www.incommunion.org/nato.htm*

Orthodoxia Listserv, run by the Democritus University of Thrace, posts articles and commentary on issues relating to the international Orthodox community. Articles on the Balkans are posted regularly. *http://www.durth.gr/maillist-archives/orthodoxia/current*

Press Now offers some of the latest news stories from the Balkans, including Kosovo, that are taken from a variety of news sources in the region. *http://www.dds.nl/~pressnow/*

Radio 21, "the first internet radio service in Albanian," founded by a journalist in Pristina, posts news stories and interviews (some in English) and hosts The Media Project, to promote progressive women's programs and to train prominent women in the region in peaceful methods of resolving conflicts and the use of media to build a civil and democratic society. *http://radio.21.net/english.htm*

Radio B92 On-line: Radio B92 was closed down and sealed off on April 2, 1999, by the Serbian authorities. The English-language service on the website has been suspended. The website links to the latest English bulletin before the ban and archives in Real Audio, HTML text, or PDF. It includes information in English and Serbian. The B92 Open Yugoslavia Archive has selected older news articles in English (html or pdf), but most are in Serbian. Free B92 "was established by the Help B92 coalition and is edited and published by the B92 team of journalists and associates, working from various parts of the world. Free B92 will focus on providing the international public with information on the status of independent media in Yugoslavia." *http://www2.opennet.org/*

Radio Free Europe/Radio Liberty — South Eastern Europe Newsline features a daily report of developments in the region and news from Kosovo, as does the REF/RL Balkan Report. Subscription through e-mail is also available. In addition, REF/RL has a special section on "NATO attacks Yugoslavia," with links to news broadcasts in four languages. *http://www.rferl.org/newsline/4-see.html*

ReliefWeb, a project of the U.N. Office for the Coordination of Humanitarian Affairs (OCHA), posts a database of the latest and archived news and reports on the humanitarian crisis in Kosovo. *http://wwwnotes.reliefweb.int/files/rwdomino.nsf/VComplexEmergenciesTheLatest/09493707*

Reuters News wire service site, as edited and prepared by Infoseek, posts news on Kosovo that is updated regularly. *http://www.reuters.com/news*

Russia Today posts English-language news articles and an archive that includes coverage of Primakov's diplomatic efforts regarding negotiating peace in Kosovo (beginning with March 29, 1999). *http://www.russiatoday.com*

Serbian Unity Congress (SUC), an organization "representing Serbs in the diaspora committed to ensuring the continuation of the Serbian heritage," hosts a number of press agencies that provide daily news on Serbia. Among those with news in English are: SRNA News Agency, Republika Srpska, and the SUC Bulletin. The SUC also posts an extensive link list of Serbian governmental and nongovernmental organizations. *http://www.suc.org/news/index.html*

Tanjug News Agency is the official news agency of Yugoslavia. *http://www.tanjug .co.yu/index.html*

The Nation magazine provides links to various organizations and includes articles such as Tom Hayden's Open Letter to President Clinton regarding U.S. Kosovo policy (see issue 990517). *http://www.thenation.com/*

Thrace Mailing List (News), run by the Democritus University of Thrace, posts articles and commentary on Kosovo (and other nations) by individual reporters and such organizations as the Greek Helsinki Monitor and Amnesty International. *http://platon.ee.duth.gr/data/maillist-archive/thrace/current*

The Washington Post offers a comprehensive report on Kosovo and the Balkans, background information, time lines, photos, maps, documents, and links. *http:// washingtonpost.com/wprv/inatl/longterm/balkans/balkans.htm*

Yahoo! Full Coverage — Kosovo links to numerous current articles from worldwide news sources on the Kosovo situation, including wire services (Reuters, Associated Press), major newspaper sites, audio and video sites (National Public Radio and the BBC), and several related sites from various organizations and governments. *http://headlines.yahoo.com/Full Coverage/World/Kosovo/I*

Yugoslav Media on Internet provides a comprehensive list of links to official Yugoslav media sources (including *Serbia Today, Serbia Bulletin,* YU Daily and Weekly Surveys). Some links have English versions. *http://www.mediacentar .org/medijiyue.htm*

Zoran.Net features a selection of articles from independent media around the world that gives background and opinions on the situation in Kosovo and posts reports on the environmental damage to Yugoslavia as a result of NATO air raids. *http://www.zoran.net.yu*

Maps and Guides

BBC NEWS/History File/Yugoslavia and the Balkans/1900-1998: Clicking on the dates of the time line gives a picture of the Balkan borders over time and a brief historical overview. *http://news.bbc.co.uk/hi/english/static/map/yugoslavia/*

Mario's Cyberspace Station — Road map of Kosovo: clicking on a particular section of Kosovo brings up a detailed road map of the area and zooms it to 1:500.000 in size. It also includes a new Albania-Yugoslav border map. *http:// mprofaca.cro.net/kosimgmap.html*

United Nations ReliefWeb links to maps of Kosovo produced by UNHCR, USAID, the U.N. Cartographic Section, the World Food Programme, and the U.S. Institute of Peace. *http://www.reliefweb.int/mapc/eur_bal/index.html*

United States Central Intelligence Agency posts maps detailing the political, ethnic, and economic terrain in Serbia (part of the larger Balkans Regional Atlas, which also covers Bosnia-Herzegovina, Croatia, and the Former Yugoslav Republic of Macedonia). *http://www.odci.gov/cia/publications/factbook/sr.html*

University of Texas (Austin) Perry-Castaneda Library posts a collection of maps created by the USCIA and the Army Corps of Engineers. *http://www.lib .utexas.edu/Libs/PCL/Map_collection/Kosovo.html*

Contributors

Sevdije Ahmeti is a journalist and the human rights director of the Center for the Protection of Women and Children in Pristina. Her interviews, testimonies, and chronicles of events are available on-line at www.neww.org/kosova.

Dejan Anastasijevic is a senior journalist for Belgrade's independent weekly *Vreme,* a correspondent for *Time* magazine, and a contributor to London's Institute for War and Peace Reporting. Because of his reporting of war crimes against Kosovo civilians, the Yugoslavian government charged him with war crimes and put him under state surveillance after the start of the NATO campaign. He currently lives in temporary exile in Vienna.

Kofi Annan is the seventh secretary-general of the United Nations (as of January 1, 1997), the first to be elected from the ranks of United Nations staff. From November 1995 to March 1996, following the Dayton Peace Accords that ended the war in Bosnia-Herzegovina, Mr. Annan served as special representative of the Secretary-General to former Yugoslavia, overseeing the transition in Bosnia-Herzegovina from the United Nations Protection Force (UNPROFOR) to the multinational Implementation Force (IFOR) led by NATO.

Timothy Garton Ash is a fellow of St. Anthony's College, Oxford.

Ivanka Besevic, after remaining with her sister Olga in Belgrade during the bombing, moved to San Francisco to live with her daughter.

Nigel Biggar is professor of theology and ethics at the University of Leeds; he also directs the Centre for the Advanced Study of Religion, Ethics, and Public Life.

Zbigniew Brzezinski, a former national security adviser in the Carter Administration (1977-1981), is currently counselor at the Center for Strategic and International Studies as well as professor of American foreign policy at the School of Advanced International Studies, Johns Hopkins University.

William Joseph Buckley is a visiting scholar at the Center for Clinical Bioethics and teaches ethics at the Medical School at Georgetown University.

Janusz Bugajski is a renowned expert on central and eastern Europe who has worked for many international organizations and the U.S. State Department, as well as contributing to newspapers, periodicals, and journals in the U.S. and eastern Europe.

James L. Cairns is the director of the Southeast Europe Project for the World Conference on Religion and Peace (WCRP), based in Sarajevo, Bosnia-Herzegovina.

General Wesley K. Clark became Supreme Allied Commander, Europe (SACEUR), on July 11, 1997, as well as being Commander-in-Chief, United States European Command. As director of Strategic Plans and Policy to the Joint Staff (April 1994 to June 1996), he was the staff officer responsible for worldwide politico-military affairs and U.S. military strategic planning; during that time he led the military negotiations for the Bosnian Peace Accords at Dayton (1995).

Martin L. Cook is professor of ethics in the Department of Command, Leadership, and Management (DCLM) of the United States Army War College (USAWC) in Carlisle, Pennsylvania.

Dobrica Cosic not only is the leading literary figure among Serbians but also has been very involved in Serbian politics. In 1992 he was elected the first president of the Federal Republic of Yugoslavia (Serbia and Montenegro) and was praised in the media as the "Father of the Nation." But following disputes with Milosevic and the ultranationalist Vojislav Seselj, Cosic was removed from office by Milosevic in May 1993.

Mark Danner, for ten years a staff writer at *The New Yorker*, is the author of *The Massacre at El Mozote: A Parable of the Cold War*, *Beyond the Mountains: The Legacy of Duvalier*, and *The Saddest Story: America, the Balkans, and the Post–Cold War World*.

Dr. Fokko de Vries left Amsterdam for Macedonia on behalf of Médicins sans Frontières (Doctors without Borders) to assist in the Brasda and Radusa camps for refugees from Kosovo. Dr. de Vries was trained as a psychologist and tropical doctor and is currently involved in reforming the health system of Lithuania and the Russian Federation.

Zoran Djindjic, a German-educated philosopher, is president of the Democratic party and leader of the Alliance for Change, a loose coalition of Serbian political parties in opposition to the Milosevic regime.

James W. Douglass is the author of *The Nonviolent Cross, Resistance and Contemplation, Lightning East to West,* and *The Nonviolent Coming of God.*

Vuk Draskovic is a journalist, dissident, and novelist, and the leader of the Serbian Renewal Movement, which remains the largest democratic political opposition group to President Milosevic (with 14.7 percent of the vote). In November 1996 he was one of three leaders of the coalition Zajedno ("Together"), which won municipal elections, then staged massive protests when Milosevic would not recognize the results. Draskovic has moved in and out of the government and the opposition: in April 1999, following the NATO intervention, he was appointed Deputy Prime Minister of Yugoslavia; but he was soon forced out after he criticized the regime's policies.

Jean Bethke Elshtain is the Laura Spelman Rockefeller Professor of Social and Political Ethics at the University of Chicago, is a contributing editor for *The New Republic,* and has written extensively on war in the Western tradition.

Gabriel Fackre is Samuel Abbott Professor of Christian Theology Emeritus at Andover Newton Theological School.

Jürgen Habermas, arguably postwar Germany's leading public intellectual, taught philosophy and sociology at Heidelberg and Frankfurt before becoming co-director of the Max Planck Institute in Starnberg. He returned to Frankfurt in 1983 as professor of philosophy until his retirement in 1994.

Morton H. Halperin is Policy Planning Staff Director at the U.S. State Department. He has taught at a number of universities and has served in the federal government with the Johnson, Nixon, and Clinton administrations.

Stanley Samuel Harakas, a priest of the Greek Orthodox Archdiocese of America, under the Ecumenical Patriarchate of Constantinople, is Archbishop Iakovos Professor of Orthodox Theology Emeritus, Holy Cross Greek Orthodox School of Theology, Brookline, Massachusetts, where he taught from 1966 until his retirement in 1995, and was dean from 1970 to 1980. He has been active in the ecumenical movement on local, state, and international levels.

Blaine Harden writes for *The New York Times.*

Václav Havel, Czech writer and politician, was elected president of Czechoslovakia in 1989 and president of the Czech Republic in 1992.

Baton Haxhiu is a political analyst and editor-in-chief of Pristina's main Albanian-language daily, *Koha Ditore.* Reported to have been killed by Serbs during the war, Haxhiu survived by hiding in Pristina basements before escaping to Tetovo in Macedonia. He resumed publication of *Koha Ditore* while in exile in Tetovo, distributing the newspaper free to refugees in the camps. He has now returned with other staff members to *Koha Ditore*'s offices in Pristina.

J. Bryan Hehir is professor of practice in religion and society at Harvard Divinity School, as well as dean of the Divinity School and faculty associate at Harvard University's Weatherhead Center for International Affairs. He also serves as counselor to Catholic Relief Services in Baltimore.

David Holdridge has worked with Catholic Relief Services (CRS) in Kosovo and Belgrade; he is CRS's regional director for Europe.

Michael Ignatieff has written, among other books, *Blood and Belonging: Journeys into the New Nationalism* and *The Warrior's Honor: Ethnic War and the Modern Conscience.* His recent book on the Kosovo conflict is entitled *The Virtual War.* Ignatieff also contributes to *The New Yorker.*

Tim Judah is the author of *The Serbs: History, Myth, and the Destruction of Yugoslavia* and *Kosovo: War and Revenge.*

Mark Juergensmeyer is director of Global and International Studies and professor of sociology at the University of California, Santa Barbara.

Ismail Kadare, the premier figure in contemporary Albanian literature, is a prolific author whose works have been translated into numerous languages. His literary accomplishments have won international acclaim and frequently place him among those short-listed for the Nobel Prize in literature.

Robert D. Kaplan is a correspondent for *The Atlantic Monthly* and the author of seven books, including *Balkan Ghosts: A Journey through History* and, most recently, *The Coming Anarchy: Shattering the Dreams of the Post–Cold War*, a collection of essays.

Aferdita Kelmendi is an award-winning Kosovar journalist. She served as editor of

504

cultural programs for Radio Prishtina (1981-1990), the station run by the autonomous government of Kosova, and she has been a Kosova correspondent for Radio France Internationale (1990-1992) and Voice of America (1993-1998). In 1998 she became editor-in-chief of *Eritrea,* the "first magazine dedicated to social, political, economic, and health issues affecting women in Kosova." While in exile in Skopje, Macedonia, during the NATO intervention, she established Radio TV 21, the first Internet station in Kosova, and reestablished it after the conflict with the first independent Albanian-language broadcasts in Prishtina since 1990. She is currently co-director of the Center for Training in Journalism and Conflict Resolution.

Flora Kelmendi, a 23-year-old student of English language and literature at the "illegal" University of Pristina before she fled Kosovo, is the daughter of a well-known human rights activist and lawyer. A few days after the NATO bombardments started, Flora fled with her brother and two sisters to Macedonia, arriving on the last train out of Pristina. (It was the second time Flora had fled Kosovo. In September 1998 she fled with her parents from their refuge in the mountains of Kosovo to Rozaje, Montenegro, after the approach of Serbian militia.) By December 1999, Flora had safely returned to a complete family and an intact home in Pristina. She now works there for the United Nations.

John Kelsay is professor of religion and chair of the department of religion at Florida State University. He is the author of *Islam and War: A Study in Comparative Ethics.*

Henry Kissinger served as secretary of state in the Nixon and Ford administrations (1973-1977) and as national security advisor to President Nixon (1969-1975). He was appointed by President Reagan to chair the National Bipartisan Commission on Central America (1983-1985) and served as a member of Reagan's Foreign Intelligence Advisory Board (1984-1990). Kissinger was a professor at Harvard University in both the Department of Government and the Center for International Affairs (1954-1969). He is currently chairman of Kissinger Associates, Inc., an international consulting firm.

Denisa Kostovicova holds a M.Phil. in International Relations from Cambridge University and is completing doctoral research there on segregation in the school system in Kosovo in the 1990s. She has published widely on Kosovo and Serbia for many Western publications and is co-editor of *Kosovo: Myths, Conflict and War.*

Hans Küng is professor of ecumenical theology and Director of the Institute for Ecumenical Research at the University of Tübingen (Germany). He is president of the Global Ethic Foundation.

David Little is the T. J. Dermot Dunphy Professor of the Practice of Religion, Ethnicity, and International Conflict at Harvard Divinity School and an associate at the Weatherhead Center for International Affairs.

Fatos Lubonja was imprisoned from 1974 to 1991 for being a member of a "counterrevolutionary organization." Following his release, Lubonja became involved in human rights as general secretary of the Albanian Helsinki Committee. In 1994 he founded the quarterly review *Përpjekja* ("Endeavor"), an "endeavor to introduce the critical spirit into Albanian culture." In January 1997 Lubonja became one of the three leaders of the Forum of Democracy, which called for peaceful dialogue in Albania's increasingly polarized political climate. Lubonja continues his work with the cultural journal *Përpjekja*.

Edward N. Luttwak is a senior fellow at the Center for Strategic and International Studies.

Shkëlzen Maliqi is a philosopher, journalist, political columnist, and independent publicist who has worked with the Open Society Institute, Kosovo. He publishes political analysis and essays in Kosovar and foreign periodicals and is editor-in-chief of the magazine *MM*.

Julie Mertus, a Fulbright scholar and human rights activist, teaches at Ohio Northeastern Law School and has been a visiting fellow at Harvard Law School.

Richard B. Miller is Finkelstein Fellow and professor in the Department of Religious Studies at Indiana University, where he has taught since 1985.

Slobodan Milosevic is president of the Federal Republic of Yugoslavia (since July 23, 1987). He became the Communist chief of Belgrade in 1984, and then of all of Yugoslavia in 1986, when Ivan Strambolic became president. Milosevic replaced Strambolic as president in 1987 by capitalizing on nationalist sentiments in response to the political unrest in Kosovo. Since 1990 his Socialist Party (formerly the Communist Party) has recurrently won elections by factionalizing the opposition. During this past decade of the disintegration of former Yugoslavia, Milosevic has played many parts in the civil wars and the peace proposals.

Martha Minow is a professor at Harvard Law School.

Fron Nazi is an Albanian-American writer currently living in Albania. His short stories and articles have been published in Europe and the U.S. in such periodicals as *New York Newsday, Le Monde, The Guardian,* and *The Independent.* He is senior editor at the Institute for War and Peace Reporting.

Zarana Papic was among the founders of the Women's Studies Center in Belgrade in 1992 as an alternative center of intellectual (and antiwar) women's activities; she is also a member of the editorial board of the Belgrade journal *Zenske studije* (Women's Studies) and editor-in-chief of the journal *Sociologija*.

Hugh Poulton is a consultant on the Balkans to the Minority Rights Group.

Michael A. Sells is the Emily Judson Baugh and John Marshall Gest Professor of Comparative Religions at Haverford College. He is a founder and director of the Community of Bosnia organization, which seeks to support a peaceful, multireligious Bosnia-Herzegovina and help retrieve the education of the Bosnian victims of "ethnic cleansing."

Slobodan Samardzic is a political scientist and senior research fellow in the Institute for European Studies, Belgrade.

Blerim Shala is editor-in-chief of *Zeri,* a political weekly published in Pristina, where he has worked since 1987. Shala was an independent representative and a member of the Albanian-Kosovar delegation at Rambouillet (the agreement was signed on February 23, 1999) and the Paris Peace Conference on Kosovo. Currently he serves as an independent representative (with Veton Surroi) on the Kosovo Transitional Council, which is the highest political Kosovar body under the United Nations Mission in Kosovo (UNMIK) operation. (For the complete text of the Rambouillet Agreement, see it as posted on June 23, 1999, by USIP Library at http://www.usip.org/library/regions/kosovo.html.)

Robert Skidelsky is a writer and British Conservative Treasury spokesman.

Javier Solana was a member of Spain's Parliament from 1977 to 1995 and held a variety of Spanish cabinet posts. He became NATO's ninth secretary-general in December 1995, and was succeeded by Lord Robertson in late 1999. As chairman of the North Atlantic Council (NATO's highest decision-making body), he coordinated the policymaking process and served as the main spokesman for the Alliance.

Svetozar Stojanovic is professor and director of the Institute for Philosophy and Social Theory at Belgrade University. He was the founder and first president of the Council for Democratic Transformation of Serbia, the founder and president of the Council for the Co-operation of Non-Governmental Organizations in Serbia, co-president of the International Humanist and Ethical Union in The Hague, and editor-in-chief of the journal *Praxis International,* published in Oxford.

Veton Surroi is the publisher of Kosovo's best-known Albanian-language newspaper, *Koha Ditore*. Under him the paper follows a politically independent line, equally critical of the LDK (Rugova's Democratic League of Kosovo) and the UCK (KLA). He is a long-time political activist, one of the founders of the PPK (Parliamentary Party of Kosovo), and one of the seven coalition members of the United Democratic Movement. A unifying figure in Kosovo's factionalized political scene, he played a crucial role in brokering the Rambouillet Agreement. While holding a seat in the U.N.-appointed Transitional Council, Surroi rejected offers by Thaqi's provisional government to serve as its "foreign minister." He stayed in hiding in Pristina during the war.

Darko Tanaskovic is a professor in the Department of Oriental Studies, Faculty of Philology, at the University of Belgrade and is Directeur d'etudes associe at the Ecole des Hautes Etudes en Sciences Sociales (EHESS) in Paris. In 1994 he was appointed to the rank of ambassador in the Federal Ministry of Foreign Affairs of the Federal Republic of Yugoslavia; he was the charge d'affaires at the embassy of the Federal Republic of Yugoslavia (1995-1996), and then served as its ambassador to the Republic of Turkey (1996-1999).

Archbishop Jean-Louis Tauran is the Vatican's Secretary for Relations with States and served as a special Balkan representative of the Holy See in meetings during the conflict.

Hashim Thaqi is currently the prime minister of the provisional government of Kosova (after an agreement reached by the three principal Kosovar Albanian delegates to the Rambouillet peace talks — Thaqi, Rugova, and Qosja), to be in that position until elections can be held. Thaqi was a university student movement leader who in the early 1990s joined forces with leaders of the LPK to found the armed movement that became the UCK (KLA) in about 1993. After being expelled from Prishtinë University by Serb forces, he went to Drenica to help agitate among Kosovar Albanians. He was sentenced (in absentia) to twenty-two years in prison for terrorist activities. But he fled to Switzerland, where he did postgraduate studies in political science at Lucerne and Zürich. He returned to Kosova in 1998 to fight with the UCK, and became the head of its political directorate.

Maria Todorova is a professor of history at the University of Florida and has published works on the Balkans, most notably, *Imagining the Balkans*.

William F. Vendley is secretary-general of the World Conference on Religion and Peace/International (WCRP/International), the largest worldwide coalition of representatives of religious communities, which works to address critical problems in areas such as conflict resolution, human rights, and development. Vendley coordinates the international activities of thirty-five WCRP national chapters and members in over 100 countries and has established the first representative multireligious task force in Kosovo dedicated to "common living."

Miranda Vickers is a political analyst for the International Crisis Group and the author of *Between Serb and Albanian: A History of Kosovo, The Albanians: A Modern History,* and (with James Pettifer) *Albania: From Anarchy to a Balkan Identity.*

Nick Vucinich is a regular contributor to *Serb World USA* magazine and has published several essays on Serbian immigration to America in *Serbian Studies,* the journal of the North American Society for Serbian Studies. He is a consultant to the California State Senate on such matters as international trade, economic development, local government, and budget issues.

Michael Walzer is co-editor of *Dissent* and professor of social science at the Institute for Advanced Study in Princeton.

Kallistos Ware, a world-renowned scholar of Eastern Christianity, is a Fellow of Pembroke College, Oxford; Spalding Lecturer in Eastern Orthodox Studies, Oxford University; Assistant Bishop, Orthodox Archdiocese of Thyateira and Great Britain; and Bishop Kallistos of Diokleia.

Permissions

The editor and publisher gratefully acknowledge permission to include material from the following sources:

Arnaud de Borchgrave, "Interview with Slobodan Milosevic," included by permission of the author and United Press International.

Zbigniew Brzezinski, "Compromise over Kosovo Means Defeat," *The Wall Street Journal*, 24 May 1999. Reprinted with permission of *The Wall Street Journal* © 1999 Dow Jones & Company, Inc. All rights reserved.

Zbigniew Brzezinski, "The Failed Double Cross," *The Wall Street Journal*, 30 August 1999. Reprinted with permission of *The Wall Street Journal* © 1999 Dow Jones & Company, Inc. All rights reserved.

Zbigniew Brzezinski, "Get Serious: Steps to Victory in Kosovo," *National Review*, 3 May 1999, pp. 27-28. © 1999 by National Review, Inc., 215 Lexington Avenue, New York, NY 10016. Reprinted by permission.

Zbigniew Brzezinski, "In Kosovo, U.S. Cannot Avoid Grim Choices," *The Wall Street Journal*, 24 March 1999. Reprinted with permission of *The Wall Street Journal* © 1999 Dow Jones & Company, Inc. All rights reserved.

Zbigniew Brzezinski, "NATO Must Stop Russia's Power Play," *The Wall Street Journal*, 14 June 1999. Reprinted with permission of *The Wall Street Journal* © 1999 Dow Jones & Company, Inc. All rights reserved.

Zbigniew Brzezinski, "To Stop the Serbs," *The Washington Post*, 30 March 1999, p. A17. © The Washington Post. Reprinted by permission.

Mark Danner, "Endgame in Kosovo," *New York Review of Books* 46, no. 8 (6 May 1999): 8-11. Reprinted with permission from *The New York Review of Books*. Copyright © 1999 NYREV, Inc.

Zoran Djindjic, "How to Solve the Kosovo Problem," originally written for a series of exchanges in *Koha Ditore* (Spring 1999). Reprinted by permission of Baton Haxhiu.

James Douglass, "The War in Kosovo" (adapted), *Commonweal*, 18 June 1999. © 1999 Commonweal Foundation, reprinted with permission. For subscriptions call toll-free: 1-888-495-6755.

Jean Bethke Elshtain, "What Makes a War Just; Whose Lives Are We Sparing?" *The Washington Post*, 16 May 1999, p. B3. © The Washington Post. Reprinted by permission.

Jean Bethke Elshtain, "When Means Defeat Ends," *Newsday*, 16 May 1999, p. B5. Reprinted by permission of the author.

Blaine Harden, "The Milosevic Generation," *The New York Times Magazine*, 29 August 1999. Reprinted by permission of the author.

Brian Hehir, "Kosovo: A War of Values and the Values of War," *America* 180, no. 17 (5 May 1999). Reprinted by permission.

Robert D. Kaplan, "Why the Balkans Demand Amorality" (revised), *The Washington Post*, 28 February 1999, p. B01. © The Washington Post. Reprinted by permission.

Henry Kissinger, "Doing Injury to History" (5 April 1999), "New World Disorder" (31 May 1999), and "As the Cheers Fade" (21 June 1999). Copyright 1999, Los Angeles Times Syndicate. Reprinted by permission.

"The KLA Brought NATO to Kosovo: Interview with Hashim Thaqi," was first published in *Koha Ditore*. Included by permission of Baton Haxhiu.

Hans Küng, "World Peace — A Challenge for the World Religions," chapter 5 in his book *A Global Ethic for Global Politics and Economics* (Oxford: Oxford University Press, 1998), pp. 121-37. Abridged and adapted by permission of the author.

Edward N. Luttwak, "Give War a Chance," *Foreign Affairs* 78, no. 4 (July-August 1999). Reprinted by permission of *Foreign Affairs*. Copyright 1999 by the Council on Foreign Relations, Inc.

Robert Skidelsky and Michael Ignatieff, "Is Military Intervention over Kosovo Justified?" A debate first published in *Prospect* Magazine (June 1999): 16-21. Reprinted by permission.

Archbishop Jean-Louis Tauran, "Vincere la pace," *Il Regno*, December 1999, pp. 369-71. English translation included by permission.

Michael Walzer, "Kosovo," *Dissent*, Summer 1999. Reprinted by permission.

Index